Complete Secretary's Handbook

sixth edition

Other professional books by Mary A. De Vries

The Complete Office Handbook
Guide to Better Business Writing
Legal Secretary's Complete Handbook
Legal Secretary's Encyclopedic Dictionary
The New American Handbook of Letter Writing
New Century Vest-Pocket Secretary's Handbook
The Practical Writer's Guide
The Prentice-Hall Complete Secretarial Letter Book
Professional Secretary's Encyclopedic Dictionary
Secretary's Almanac and Fact Book
Secretary's Standard Reference Manual and Guide

Complete
Secretary's
Handbook

sixth edition

Lillian Doris
and Besse May Miller

revised by
Mary A. De Vries

PRENTICE HALL
Englewood Cliffs, New Jersey 07632

Prentice-Hall International (UK) Limited, *London*
Prentice-Hall of Australia, Pty. Limited, *Sydney*
Prentice-Hall Canada, Inc., *Toronto*
Prentice-Hall Hispanoamericana, S.A., *Mexico*
Prentice-Hall of India Private Limited, *New Delhi*
Prentice-Hall of Japan, Inc., *Tokyo*
Simon & Schuster Asia Pte. Ltd., *Singapore*
Editora Prentice-Hall do Brasil Ltda., *Rio de Janeiro*

© 1988, 1983, 1977, 1970, 1960, 1951 *by*

PRENTICE-HALL, INC.
Englewood Cliffs, N.J.

10 9 8 7 6 5 4 3 2

Library of Congress Cataloging-in-Publication Data

Doris, Lillian.
  Complete secretary's handbook.

  Includes index.
  1. Office practice—Handbooks, manuals, etc.
2. Secretaries—Handbooks, manuals, etc. I. Miller,
Besse May. II. De Vries, Mary Ann. III. Title.
HF5547.5.D6   1988   651.3'741   87-25922
ISBN 0-13-163321-X
ISBN 0-13-162471-7 (slipcase)

ISBN 0-13-163321-X

ISBN 0-13-162471-7 (slipcase)

PRENTICE HALL
BUSINESS & PROFESSIONAL DIVISION
A division of Simon & Schuster
Englewood Cliffs, New Jersey 07632

PRINTED IN THE UNITED STATES OF AMERICA

An Important Message from the Reviser

The secretary's role in the modern office has not declined in the face of computer technology; it has expanded. Many tasks—ranging from correspondence to budgeting—formerly handled by management personnel are now often performed at the secretarial-administrative level. But even though the proliferation of electronic office equipment has widened professional horizons for the secretary and simplified many otherwise cumbersome, repetitive tasks, it has not eliminated the need for a capable professional secretary to have a full range of office skills. In many respects, it has increased the need for a solid background in basic secretarial functions and general office procedures. The changes and additions that you will find in this sixth edition of the *Complete Secretary's Handbook* reflect this philosophy—a currently popular view in the modern working world.

Two factors were ever present in our work on this edition and guided our selection of new material as well as the refinement of essential traditional information: First, we wanted to show the changing emphasis —and merging—of conventional mail, electronic and voice mail, conventional telegrams and cables, and various electronic message-transmission methods such as facsimile and telex. Second, we wanted to reflect the widespread view that a majority of companies want secretaries to upgrade their language (spelling, punctuation, and grammar) and written-communication (memos, letters, and so on) skills.

Most office handbooks are written for a diverse audience and are used by students, beginners, and experienced professionals. Readers are typically employed in companies of all sizes, from a one-room operation to a large international corporation. This handbook, therefore, contains a necessary blend of basic procedures and advanced technology. Since it is a *secretarial* handbook intended for office personnel, however, it also has another dual purpose—to provide discussions pertinent to workers in an automated, electronic office while still describing the conventional procedures followed by workers in offices that are not fully automated or electronically controlled.

A substantial amount of new information has been compiled for this sixth edition. These topics are examples of some of the important new material:

- Basic Filing Equipment (page 11)
- Filing Diskettes and Printouts (page 37)
- Basic Office Papers (page 75)
- Integrated Voice-Data Terminals (page 55)
- Telecommunications Interfaces (page 55)
- Keeping a Photocopy Log (page 67)
- How to Make Corrections with a Computer or Word Processor (page 73)
- Fair-Use [Copyright] Guidelines (page 116)
- Electronic-Mail Transmission (page 143)
- Facsimile Transmission (page 139)
- Following OCR Addressing Requirements (page 161)
- [Telephone] Operating Companies (page 169)
- Teleconference Calls (page 173)
- Videoconferences (page 174)
- Meeting with Assistants and Coworkers (page 189)
- Assisting with Seminars and Conferences (page 190)
- Travel Security (page 217)
- Handling Official Financing Statements (page 234)
- Filing Contracts and Other Legal Documents (page 235)
- Maintaining Securities and Property Records (page 238)
- Your Professional Image (page 259)
- Observing the Rules of Confidentiality (page 279)
- Flowchart Symbols (page 620)

In addition to having these new sections, this edition includes many more new examples and models to make all of the chapters more useful. Generally, every effort has been made to provide greatly expanded coverage with up-to-the-minute information while still retaining all of the traditional techniques that remain the foundation of the secretarial profession in all types and sizes of offices.

The contents of the sixth edition are organized in four parts:

I. ***Techniques for General Secretarial Duties***
Part One covers a broad range of practical information concerning general office practices and procedures: filing, word processing, report writing, conventional- and electronic-message transmission, postal information, telecommunications, meetings, travel, bookkeeping, human relations, and etiquette.

II. ***How to Write Effective Letters and Memos***
Part Two concentrates on the all-important area of correspondence: basic letter and memo formats, language aids, and model letters and memos.

III. ***How to Write Correctly***
Part Three focuses on guidelines for a contemporary writing style: correct word choice, spelling, word division, punctuation, and capitalization.

IV. ***The Secretary's Handy Information Guide***
Part Four provides a variety of essential reference material for daily use: lists, tables and charts, and a glossary of important business terms in law, accounting, and management.

While preparing this sixth edition, many individuals and businesses responded to my requests for suggestions and current information. I greatly appreciate the abundance of useful material they sent and the generous time and advice they gave. Some persons in particular contributed essential data, reviewed chapters, or generally provided ongoing professional assistance. My special thanks go to all of them for the material they supplied and their constructive comments and careful attention: Becky Arterbury, accountant, Sigafoos & Arterbury; Michael Cavanagh, director, Electronic Mail Association; SFC Daniel J. Donahue, U.S. Army Recruiting Station; Clifford Gallo, Associate Director of Public Relations, New Hampshire College; Clare Gorman, Advertising and Promotion, MCI International; Jerome Heitman, Executive Director, Professional Secretaries International; Brenda Hobbs, owner, Centralized Secretarial Services; Marsha Hollingsworth, Research Consultant; Robert Preston, travel agent, Kachina Travel Agency; Frederick Schultz, district representative, United

Parcel Service; and Sister Anne Vaccarest, director of communications, Sisters of Mercy of New Hampshire. In addition, I always appreciate the continuing efforts of Richard Balkin, The Balkin Agency, and Tom Power, Business and Professional Books Division, Prentice-Hall.

Mary A. De Vries

Contents

An Important Message from the Reviser   v

PART ONE
TECHNIQUES FOR GENERAL SECRETARIAL DUTIES

1. **Using Effective Filing and Follow-up Techniques**   3

Basic Filing Systems   3

Alphabetical Filing **3.** Numerical Filing **8.** Geographic Filing **9.** Decimal Filing **10.** Chronological Filing **10.**

Basic Filing Equipment   11

Standard Office Files **11.** Open Files **11.** Portable Files **11.** Safety Files **12.** Tray Files **12.** Rotary Files **12.** Cabinets and Containers **12.** Specialized Files **13.** Combination Files **13.** EDP Files **13.**

Indexing and Alphabetizing   13

Basic Indexing Rules **13.** Basic Alphabetizing Rules **14.**

Aids to Fast Filing and Finding   20

Using Timesaving Equipment and Techniques **20.** Typing Index Tabs and Labels **22.** Using Guides in the Files **24.** Using Cross-References **24.** Preparing Material for Filing **26.** Controlling Material Taken from the Files **27.** Retrieving Lost Papers **28.** Streamlining the Files **28.**

How to Order and Store Supplies   34

Purchasing and Distributing Supplies **34.** Organizing and Storing Supplies **35.**

Computers and Other Automated Procedures   *36*

Automated Information Storage and Retrieval **36.** Information Processing by Computer **37.** Filing Diskettes and Printouts **37.** Storing Material in Reduced Form **38.** Analyzing Time and Cost Benefits **39.**

Follow-up Filing Techniques   *39*

Material That Needs Follow-up **39.** Basic Follow-up Methods **39.** Operation of the Follow-up System **40.** Use of Computers and High-Speed Equipment **42.**

Effective Reminder Systems   *43*

Calendars You Should Keep **43.** How to Make Up the Calendars **44.** How to Use the Tickler Card File with Calendars **45.** Types of Reminders **46.** How to Prepare a Contact Reminder File **50.**

2. **Developing Good Typing and Information-Processing Skills   51**

Timesaving Equipment and Accessories   *51*

Typewriters and Accessories **51.** Word Processing Systems **52.** Integrated Voice-Data Terminals **55.** Telecommunications Interfaces **55.**

Basic Typing Rules   *56*

Following the Standard Rules for Spacing **56.** Typing Numbers and Fractions **56.** Making Special Characters Not on Your Keyboard **57.**

Timesaving Typing Procedures   *58*

How to Organize Work and Plan Ahead **58.** How to Type on Printed Forms and Ruled Lines **59.** How to Get the Same Number of Lines on Each Page **59.** How to Draw Lines on Work in the Typewriter **60.** How to Type Above and Below the Line of Type **60.** How to Center Headings **61.** How to Use the Tabulator **61.** How to Feed Numerous Sheets of Paper **62.** How to Address Envelopes Quickly **63.** How to Type Rush Telegrams and Memos **64.** How to Type Small Cards **65.**

How to Type Narrow Labels **65.** How to Type Stencils and Masters **65.**

Carbon Copies and Photocopies 66

Modern Photocopy Equipment **66.** Multiuses for Photocopies **66.** Keeping a Photocopy Log **67.** Selection of Carbon Papers **67.** Shortcuts in Using Carbon Papers **68.** How to Type on Carbon Copies Only **69.**

Correcting Typing Errors 70

How to Break Poor Typing Habits **70.** How to Correct Typewriter Errors **70.** How to Make Corrections on Carbon Copies and Stencils **71.** How to Make Corrections at the Bottom of a Page **72.** How to Make Corrections on Bound Pages **72.** How to Make Corrections with a Computer or Word Processor **73.**

Basic Office Papers 75

Cotton-Content Papers **75.** Sulfite-Bond Papers **76.**

Taking and Transcribing Dictation 76

Dictation and Transcription Equipment **76.** How to Take Dictation **77.** How to Transcribe Dictation **78.** Typing and Dictation Shortcuts **79.**

3. **Preparing and Publishing Reports 81**

How to Research a Report 81

Using Outside Sources **81.** Using Outside Information **82.** Using Computer-Assisted Research **83.** Finding Basic Sources of Information **84.**

How to Organize and Write a Report 90

Formal and Informal Reports **90.** Parts of the Report **93.** Use of Appropriate Language **95.** Types of Report Binders **96.** Checklist of Things to Remember **96.**

How to Prepare the Manuscript   97

Studying the Preliminary Draft **97**. Selecting the Right Paper **97**. Using Proper Spacing and Margins **98**. Numbering Pages, Titles, and Outlines **98**. Using the Right Footnote Style **100**. Selecting Levels of Heads and Subheads **104**. Setting Up the Title Page and Table of Contents **106**. Preparing Tables and Illustrations **106**. Preparing and Checking the Manuscript **111**.

How to Handle Typesetting and Printing   113

Arranging for Design and Typemarking **113**. Making Typesetting Arrangements **113**. Checking Proofs **114**. Arranging for Printing and Binding **114**.

How to Copyright the Report   115

Copyright Law **115**. Fair-Use Guidelines **116**. Copyright-Registration Procedure **117**.

4. Handling Mail and Electronic Messages   118

Conventional-Mail Processing   118

Handling Incoming Mail **118**. Handling Outgoing Mail **124**. Selecting Addressing and Mailing Equipment **126**. Maintaining Mailing Lists **128**. Handling Bulk Mailings **128**. Maintaining Efficiency in the Mail Room **129**.

Domestic Telegraph Service   132

How Domestic Messages Are Sent **132**. Classes of Domestic Service **132**. How to Type a Telegram **133**. How to Send the Same Message to Multiple Addresses **134**. Counting Charges for Telegrams **134**.

International Cable Service   135

How Messages Are Sent to Foreign Countries **135**. Classes of International Service **136**. Registered Code Addresses **137**. Counting Charges for Cables **137**. Economizing on Telegrams and Cables **138**.

High-Speed Messaging   *139*

Facsimile Transmission **139.** Telex Service **140.** Teletex Service **142.** Private Services **143.** Electronic-Mail Transmission **143.** Satellite Transmission **144.**

5. **Using Postal Information to Save Time and Money**   146

Domestic Postal Service   *146*

Sources of Information **146.** Mailable Items and How to Dispatch Them **146.** Size and Weight Standards **148.** Classes of Domestic Service **149.** Special Services **152.**

Private Delivery Services   *155*

Types of Air and Ground Services **155.** How to Use Private Services **156.**

International Postal Service   *156*

Sources of Information **157.** Postal Union Mail **157.** Parcel Post **159.** Special Services **159.**

Special Mailing Guidelines   *160*

Using Zip Codes to Speed Mail Delivery **160.** Following OCR Addressing Requirements **161.** How to Reduce Postage Costs **161.**

6. **Using Effective Telecommunications Practices**   164

Using the Telephone Efficiently and Courteously   *164*

Observing the Rules of Telephone Courtesy **164.** How to Be More Effective on the Telephone **165.**

Placing and Receiving Calls   *166*

Placing Calls **166.** Answering and Screening Calls **167.** Transferring Calls **168.** Handling Wrong Numbers **169.**

Principal Telephone Services   169

Operating Companies **169**. Station-to-Station and Person-to-Person Calls **170**. International Direct-Distance Dialing (IDDD) **170**. Out-of-Town Calls **171**. Wide-Area Telephone Service (WATS) **172**. Messenger Calls **173**. Appointment Calls **173**. Teleconference Calls **173**. Videoconferences **174**. Mobile Calls **174**. Special Business Services **175**.

Telephone References Books   177

The Telephone Directory **177**. Compiling a Desk Telephone Book **177**.

7. **Making Meeting Arrangements   179**

Making Arrangements for Meetings   179

Notifying Meeting Participants **179**. Preparing the Agenda **181**. Organizing Meeting Materials **181**. Securing a Meeting Room **182**. Preparing the Meeting Room **182**. Making Accommodations for Visitors **183**.

What to Do at the Meeting   183

Relaying Telephone and Other Messages **183**. Reading the Meeting Minutes **184**. Following Parliamentary Procedure **184**. Taking the Meeting Minutes **185**.

Maintaining the Book of Minutes   187

Typing the Meeting Minutes **187**. Correcting the Meeting Minutes **188**. Indexing the Minute Book **188**.

Meeting with Assistants and Coworkers   189

Preparing for the Meeting **189**. Conducting the Meeting **189**. Preparing Notes or Minutes **190**.

Assisting with Seminars and Conferences   190

Preparing Programs and Announcements **190.** Handling Registration Details **191.** Maintaining Files and Records **192.**

8. **Making Travel Arrangements   194**

Preparing for the Business Trip   194

Use of Travel Agents **194.** Use of Company Travel Departments **196.** How to Get Information about Transportation **197.** Special Secretarial Duties **199.** Traveling with Your Employer **203.**

Making Travel and Hotel Reservations   204

Checklist of Information You Need **204.** How to Prepare Time and Route Data **205.** What to Do about Delays in Getting Reservations **205.** Securing the Tickets **205.** Making Hotel Reservations **207.** Making Air-Travel Arrangements **208.** Making Train-Travel Arrangements **210.** Making Auto-Travel Arrangements **211.**

Foreign Travel and Pleasure Trips   213

Use of Travel Agents **213.** Securing a Passport **213.** Securing a Visa **214.** Special Secretarial Duties **214.** Travel Security **217.** Customs Information **218.** Guide to Travel Information **218.**

9. **Keeping Company Books and Records   220**

How to Keep Office and Company Records   220

Handling Petty Cash **220.** Maintaining Office Payroll Accounts **223.** Handling the Checkbook and Bank Statement **226.** Keeping Travel and Entertainment Records **231.** Handling Official Financing Statements **234.** Filing Contracts and Other Legal Documents **235.** Maintaining Securities and Property Records **238.**

How to Keep Office and Company Books   241

System of Bookkeeping **241.** Basic Rules of Double-Entry Bookkeeping **242.** Cash Journal **243.** General Ledger **246.** Subsidiary Ledger **246.** Balance Sheet **249.** Income (Profit and Loss) Statement **250.** Computer-Assisted Bookkeeping **251.**

How to Handle Billing and Collections   252

Calculating Charges **252**. Preparing Invoices **254**. Using Computers in Billing Clients **255**. Following Up Overdue Accounts **255**.

10. **Maintaining Good Human Relations and Proper Etiquette   259**

Etiquette in the Office   259

Your Professional Image **259**. Daily Greetings and Use of First Names **261**. The New Employee **261**. Having Refreshments in the Office **263**. Etiquette and Safety in Office Lines and Parking Lots **264**.

Receiving Visitors   264

Receiving and Greeting Callers **264**. Finding Out the Purpose of a Call **265**. Making a Caller Comfortable **266**. Announcing a Caller **267**. Greeting Callers Your Boss Will See **268**. Handling Callers Your Boss Will Not See **269**. Handling Telephone Calls During a Meeting **271**. Seeing a Caller Out **272**.

Managing Personal Skills and Human Relations   272

Working for and with Others **272**. Initiating and Managing Projects **274**. Managing Time and Money **275**. Interviewing and Supervising Assistants **277**. Observing the Rules of Confidentiality **279**. Handling Human Relations Problems **280**.

Handling Social-Business Responsibilities   286

Making Arrangements for Theater Tickets **286**. Handling Presents and Holiday Cards **287**. Preparing Invitations **289**. Keeping Records of Donations **291**. Sending Expressions of Sympathy **293**.

Ordering Social and Business Cards   295

Using Social Visiting Cards **295**. Using Informals **296**. Using Business Cards **296**. Ordering Cards **298**.

PART TWO
HOW TO WRITE EFFECTIVE LETTERS AND MEMOS

11. Mechanics of Business Correspondence 301

How to Set Up Letters and Memos 301

Letter Style **301**. Memo Style **301**. Punctuation Style **307**.

Principal Parts of Letters 308

Dateline **308**. Reference Line **308**. "Personal" Notation **308**. Inside Address **309**. Attention Line **311**. Salutation **312**. Subject Line **314**. Body **314**. Complimentary Close **315**. Signature Line **315**. Identification Line **321**. Enclosure Notation **321**. Mailing Notation **322**. Copy-Distribution Notation **322**. Postscript **322**. Heading on Continuation Pages **323**.

Principal Parts of Memos 323

Guide Words **323**. Body **323**. Signature Initials **324**. Identification Line **324**. Enclosure Notation **324**. Copy-Distribution Notation **324**. Postscript **325**. Heading on Continuation Pages **325**.

Envelopes 325

OCR Addressing **325**.

Forms of Address 327

General Rules **327**. Rules for Companies **328**. Rules for Men **328**. Rules for Women **329**. Rules for Prominent Persons **331**.

How to Select and Order Stationery 332

Type and Size of Paper **332**. Letterhead Design **332**. Continuation Sheets **333**. Envelopes **333**. How to Order Stationery **334**.

12. Valuable Aids for Productive Letter Writing   336

Planning a Letter   336

Using Appropriate Language   336

Stilted and Trite Expressions **336.** Unnecessary Words and Phrases **343.** Favorite Words and Expressions **344.** Short Words and Sentences **344.** Various Shades of Meaning **345.** Words That Antagonize **345.** Nondiscriminatory Language **346.** A Positive Approach **348.**

For a Better Letter Beginning   349

Make the Opening Short **349.** Go Straight to the Point **349.** Avoid Stilted Openings **351.** Include the Reader's Name **351.** Refer to a Previous Contact **352.** Use a Pleasant Phrase **352.** Use "Who, What, When, Where, and Why" **352.** Use Other Techniques of the Experts **352.**

For a Better Ending   353

Avoid Stilted or Formal Endings **353.** Suggest Only One Action **353.** Use Dated Action **354.** Use Positive Words **354.**

Form Letters   355

Using Form Letters **355.** Using Model Form Letters and Paragraphs **355.** Using Processed Form Letters **356.** Personalizing Processed Form Letters **358.** Using Memo Forms **358.**

13. Model Letters and Memos   360

Categories of Correspondence   360

Letters and Memos the Secretary Signs **360.** Letters and Memos Your Employer Signs **361.** Letters and Memos Written in Your Employer's Absence **362.**

Model Business Letters and Memos   363

Acknowledgments **363.** Adjustments **366.** Apologies **368.** Appointments **369**. Appreciation **372**. Collection **375**. Complaints **377**. Credit **379**. Employee Communications **380**. Follow-ups **383**. Goodwill **384**. Inquiries **385**. Introductions **386**. Orders **388**. Recommendations **389**. Reminders **390**. Requests **390**. Reservations **393**. Sales Promotion **394**.

Model Social-Business Letters and Invitations   395

Acceptance **395**. Birthday Greetings **397**. Condolences **397**. Congratulations **399**. Declinations **402**. Invitations **405**. Seasonal Good Wishes **406**. Thank Yous **407**.

PART THREE
HOW TO WRITE CORRECTLY

14. **Correct Word Usage   411**

Parts of Speech and Rules of Grammar   411

Parts of Speech **411**. Grammatical Terms **414**.

Troublesome Words and Phrases   426

15. **Spelling and Word Division   477**

Rules of Spelling   477

Plurals **477**. Combinations of i and e **480**. Doubling the Final Consonant **480**. Words Ending in Silent e **481**. Words Ending in ie **481**. Suffixes -able, -ous **482**. Words Ending in -able, -ible **482**. Words Ending in -sede, -ceed, -cede **483**. Suffixes -ance, -ence **483**. Suffixes -ise, -ize **483**. Words Ending in c **484**. Words Ending in y **484**. Prefixes dis-, mis- **484**.

How to Improve Your Spelling   485

Helpful Mnemonics for Accurate Spelling **485**. List of Commonly Misspelled Words **486**.

Rules of Word Division   488

Division of Word at the End of a Line **488**. Syllabication and Pronunciation **489**. Basic Rules of Word Division **489**.

16. Punctuation   492

Principal Marks and Rules of Punctuation   492

Comma: The Secretary's Troublemaker **492.** Period: The Most Familiar Punctuation Mark **497.** Semicolon: The Compromise between Period and Comma **499.** Colon: Its Important Uses **500.** Dash: A Useful Substitute **502.** Exclamation Point: A Stranger in the Secretary's Work **503.** Interrogation Point: A Question **503.** Quotation Marks: How to Use Them **504.** Apostrophe: Its Principal Uses **506.** Hyphen: A Useful Aid **507.** Parentheses or Brackets: When to Use Them **508.** Leaders and Ellipsis Points: Invaluable Aids **510.** Virgule (Solidus): For Special Occasions **511.**

17. Capitalization   512

Rules and Principles of Capitalization   512

Abbreviations **512.** Acts, Bills, Codes, Laws **513.** Courts, Judges, Cases **514.** Education **515.** Enumerations **516.** Foreign Names **517.** Geographic Terms **517.** Governments and Political Terms **518.** Headings and Titles **521.** Historical Terms **522.** Holidays, Seasons, Feast Days **522.** Hyphenated Compounds **523.** Leagues, Treaties, Pacts, Plans **524.** Lists and Outlines **524.** Military **524.** Money **525.** Music, Drama, Paintings, Poetry, Film, Radio **525.** Nouns and Adjectives **526.** Organizations and Institutions **527.** Peoples, Races, Tribes **527.** Personal Titles **528.** Personification **530.** Planets **530.** Political Parties, Fractions, Alliances **531.** Quotations **531.** Religious Terms **532.** Resolutions **533.** Series of Questions **533.** Sports and Games **533.** Trade Names **534.**

PART FOUR
THE SECRETARY'S HANDY INFORMATION GUIDE
18. Quick-Reference Guide to Facts and Figures   537

Study Outline for CPS Exam **537.** Marks of Punctuation and Mechanics **539.** Roman Numerals **539.** Abbreviations **540.** Correct Forms of Address **578.** Standard Proofreading Marks **604.** Corrected Galley Proofs **605.** Tables of Weights, Measures, and Values **606.**

Tables of Metric Weights, Measures, and Values **612.** Mathematical Tables **615.** Greek Letter Symbols **617.** Interest Tables **617.** Flowchart Symbols **620.** U.S. Area Codes and Time Zones **622.** International Time Chart **623.** International Time Differentials **624.**

19. Glossary of Important Business Terms   625

Business Law **625.** Business Management **629.** Accounting and Finance **634.**

Index   641

Complete Secretary's Handbook

sixth edition

─PART ONE─

Techniques for General Secretarial Duties

1. Using Effective Filing and Follow-up Techniques
2. Developing Good Typing and Information-Processing Skills
3. Preparing and Publishing Reports
4. Handling Mail and Electronic Messages
5. Using Postal Information to Save Time and Money
6. Using Effective Telecommunications Practices
7. Making Meeting Arrangements
8. Making Travel Arrangements
9. Keeping Company Books and Records
10. Maintaining Good Human Relations and Proper Etiquette

Chapter 1

Using Effective Filing and Follow-up Techniques

BASIC FILING SYSTEMS

The basic filing systems are alphabetical, geographical, numerical, decimal, and chronological. Some offices use a combination of systems such as alphanumeric. The following paragraphs explain briefly how to use each one. For a description of filing information in a nonpaper form, refer to **COMPUTERS AND OTHER AUTOMATED PROCEDURES,** page 36.

Since requirements differ from office to office, and others may have to use your system in emergencies, you may want to prepare a file manual for your office explaining the system and the steps involved in (a) preparing material for filing, (b) filing it, and (c) retrieving it from the files. However, the files should not routinely be open to everyone. Every filing system needs adequate controls and safeguards. (See **Controlling Material Taken from the Files,** page 27.)

Alphabetical Filing

Most conventional filing is alphabetical, numerical, or a combination of both. A secretary ordinarily files papers according to name or subject, using one of the basic systems of filing or an adaptation of it. For some records, a name file under an alphabetical system should be used; for others, a subject file arranged under a numerical system is more appropriate. Thus secretaries in a lawyer's office may use the numerical system for litigated cases, with alphabetical cross-reference index cards by name of parties to the litigation. They may also have an alphabetical file with a folder under the name of each client for correspondence that does not relate to litigated matters. Secretaries to sales managers will probably have an administrative file classified according to subject and another file classified according to name for correspondence with district managers and salespersons. Each office should devise a system that is most appropriate for the type of activity involved. However, experts recommend simple systems such as alphabetic or numeric over more complex systems such as subject or geographic whenever possible.

Name file. The easiest and quickest method of filing is to classify material according to name and to file it alphabetically. This system should be used whenever possible, because no cross-index or list of files is necessary. Rules for indexing and alphabetizing names are given on pages 13–20.

1. Folders. Make a folder for each correspondent or name, if there is sufficient material to justify a separate folder. From three to ten papers justify starting a folder. Arrange the papers within the folder by date with the latest date on top.

2. Miscellaneous folder. Make a miscellaneous folder for each letter of the alphabet and place it behind the last name folder under the particular letter. File any material for which there is no separate name folder in the miscellaneous folder alphabetically rather than by date. This keeps all papers relating to a particular name together. When they reach the required number, three to ten, make a separate folder.

3. Voluminous correspondence with the same person. If correspondence with the same person or firm is voluminous, separate it into date periods. You may obtain folders with printed date headings (figure 1), or you may type the dates on your labels.

4. Correspondents with the same name. On folders for correspondents with the same name, use different-colored labels. The distinctive color is a signal to use extra precaution in filing or in looking for filed material. Thus if you use blue labels and you have a folder for *Abernathy, Edgar, Sr.,* with a salmon label, you know immediately that you also have a folder for *Abernathy, Edgar, Jr.,* with a blue label.

Subject files. Some material does not lend itself to classification by name and must be classified by subject. The installation of a subject file requires great care. Do not attempt to choose the subject headings until you are thoroughly familiar with the material that is to be filed in your office. The list should be comprehensive and yet simple enough to avoid confusion. Subject headings must be specific, significant, and technically correct. Select nouns whenever possible, for they are more specific than other words such as adjectives.

Figure 1. Alphabetical Name File Arranged in Four Positions

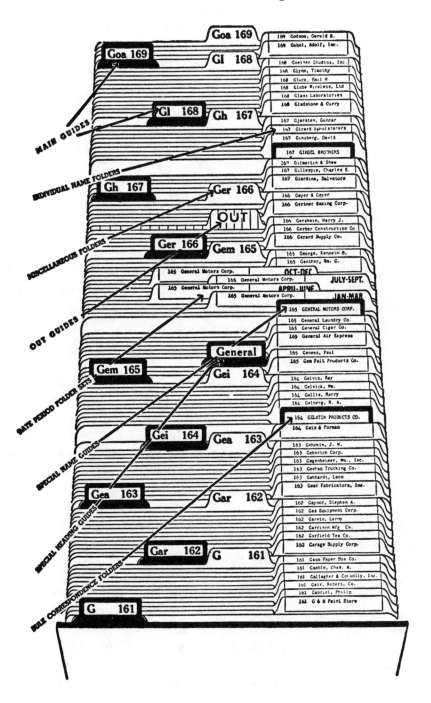

Expand subject files by adding other main subjects or by subdividing those already in use. If necessary, subheadings may be further subdivided, but for a secretary's purposes, a breakdown into main headings and subheadings is generally adequate.

1. Arrangement of subject files. Subject files may be filed alphabetically or they may be arranged in any logical order and filed according to a numbering system. Secretaries generally prefer the alphabetical system in which subject folders are arranged alphabetically, with subheadings filed alphabetically under each main heading.

In a subject file that has main headings and subheadings, you will have a three-position arrangement as follows:

a. *Alphabetical guides.* They may be cardboard separators with the letter of the alphabet at the left.

b. *Main subject guides.* They may be cardboard separators with metal or transparent plastic tabs into which the names of the main subjects can be inserted. These tabs should be in the center. Or a "miscellaneous folder" may be used as a main subject guide, as described in "d."

c. *Individual folders.* Use right-position tabs for these folders. Folders with precut tabs are available with tabs of varying widths (half cut, one-third cut, and so on).

d. *Miscellaneous folder for each main heading.* Label the miscellaneous folder like the guide and use a label different in color from that on the regular folders. Place the miscellaneous folder behind all of the other folders. The miscellaneous folder may be used instead of the main subject guides. In that case, the folder should have a center-position tab and should be placed in front of the subhead folders.

If the subject file has main headings, subheadings, and further breakdowns, use guides instead of folders for the subheadings and a four-position, instead of a three-position, arrangement.

2. Folders in the subject file. Arrange the papers in a subject folder by date, with the latest date on top. In the miscellaneous folder, material is filed alphabetically by subject rather than by date. When sufficient papers (three to ten) on a particular subject are accumulated in the miscellaneous folder, make a separate subject folder and add it as a subheading.

Type both the main heading and the subheading on the file labels. For convenience in filing and finding, type the subheading on the first line and the main heading on the second line, indented two spaces or in parentheses. If you have a red and black ribbon on your typewriter, you could type the main heading in red to distinguish it more readily from the subheading.

   3. Index to subject file.   For subject files, it is generally advisable to keep either an alphabetical list or a card index of the subjects: to prevent filing material under a new heading when you already have a folder for the subject and to enable a substitute, an assistant, or your employer to locate things in the file. A card index is easy to organize and flip through. However, a list prepared by computer also can be easily maintained. Changes are especially easy to edit in, and an updated list can be printed out at any time.

   a. *Alphabetical list.* Type in one alphabetical list the main headings and subheadings, with the main headings in full caps and the subheadings in initial caps. After each subheading, type in parentheses the main heading under which the subheading is classified. Leave sufficient space between the items to permit additions of new subjects. *Keep the list up to date.* An alphabetical list will usually be adequate when the files are not extensive and additions are infrequent. Here is the arrangement of an alphabetical list of subject files:

> Applications (Personnel)
> CONTRACTS
> EXPENSES AND EXPENSE ACCOUNTS
> FORM LETTERS
> Holidays (Personnel)
> Hotels, Reservations (Travel)
> INSURANCE
> INVESTMENTS
> Itineraries (Travel)
> Leases (Contracts)
> MEETINGS
> Minutes (Meetings)
> PERSONNEL
> TRAVEL

   b. *Card index.* If you use a card index instead of a computer printout, make an index card for each subject heading and subheading. Show for each subheading the main heading under which it is classified. When a subject heading is not self-explanatory, describe on the card the material covered by it. Also, make cross-reference cards for subjects on which there is insufficient material to justify a separate folder and for subjects under which material might logically have been classified but for which you chose another heading. Thus as the secretary to a department head, you may have a main heading "PERSONNEL." Since you have only a few papers relating to "Lunch Hour," you decide to file this material in the miscellaneous "PERSONNEL" folder. Make an index card for the subject "Lunch Hour" and indicate on the card that the material relating to it is filed in the miscellaneous "PERSONNEL" folder. File all of the cards alphabetically.

The card index is usually preferable for extensive, growing files, because it is easily kept up to date.

Combined name and subject file.   If you have only a name file and occasionally have material that should be filed by subject, or if you have a subject file and occasionally have material that should be filed by the name of the individual, you can combine the occasional folders with your main file. For example, in a name file, you might include a folder labeled "Applications" to receive the few applications that you keep in your files. Put a cross-reference sheet under the name of the applicant in the miscellaneous folder for the letter with which the surname begins. Or in a subject file, you might include a folder labeled with a person's name, which would actually be a subject.

Subject-duplex file.   Some material filed by subject is further identified by numbers. This additional coding is important when the files are expanding rapidly with numerous subdivisions. Under this system, main subject headings are given a base number (such as 100) and subheadings are given auxiliary numbers and/or letters (such as 100.1). The folders are then positioned in numerical sequence (100, 100.1, 100.2, and so on). As in the case of a straight numerical system, described below, the subject-duplex system necessitates maintaining an alphabetical computer list or auxiliary card index.

Numerical Filing

The numerical filing system requires numbers on the file folders, which are arranged sequentially. This is an indirect method of filing since it must be used in connection with a cross-index that shows what the number stands for. The index can be prepared by computer and printed out on paper, or an index card can be made for each folder and the cards arranged alphabetically. (See also **Subject-duplex file,** page 8.)

Types of numeric systems. In a *consecutive-number file system,* guides and folders are filed in ascending order (1, 2, 3, and so on). Although this is a simple system and the easiest to learn, all of the added file folders pile up at the end. In a *terminal-digit file system,* numbers are divided into units, for example, 45-67-89. The digits on the right (89) may refer to the file drawer; those in the center (67) may refer to the folder number; and those on the left (45) may refer to the order of papers in the folder (45-67-89, 46-67-89, 47-67-89, and so on). In a *coded-number file system,* the numbers and letters identify a specific person or product, for example, license plate numbers, social security numbers, and so on.

Advantages and disadvantages. The advantages of the system are the rapidity and accuracy of refiling, the opportunity for indefinite expansion, and the ability of data-processing systems to work more effectively with numbers. The disadvantages are having to maintain the auxiliary card index or computer list and having to make two searches, one of the index and the second of the files, every time papers are withdrawn or filed.

The numerical system is used mainly in files where each of the jobs, clients, or subjects has a number that acts as an identification mark (for example, insurance policies, medical records, requisitions, orders, bills, invoices); for the filing of confidential records; for handling a rapidly growing file; and in files where extensive permanent cross-reference is necessary.

Geographic Filing

Setting up a geographic system. Under the geographic filing system, material to be filed is often classified first according to the name of the state, then according to cities or towns, and last according to the names of companies and correspondents in each city or town. But in some organizations, the breakdown may also include countries or regions. Office-supply stores have standard sets of guides. This type of file also requires a cross-index. A name card or revised computer list may be prepared showing the customer name. The customer cards or the names on a computer printout would be maintained in alphabetical order.

Use of the system. This system is often used by sales organizations in which a review of the activity in any given territory is of more importance than the name of a company or individual. The geographic system would also be useful in activities such as market research, direct-mail advertising, and weather forecasting.

Decimal Filing

The decimal filing system is based on the Dewey decimal system used in some public libraries and in some highly specialized businesses.

How to classify records. All of the records in an office are classified under ten or fewer principal headings, which are numbered 000 to 900. Each heading is divided into ten or fewer subheadings, which are numbered from 10 to 90, preceded by the applicable hundreds digit. Each subheading may be subdivided into ten or fewer headings, which are numbered from 1 to 9, preceded by the appropriate hundreds and tens digits. If necessary, these headings may be further subdivided and numbered from .1 to .10, and so on, under the appropriate full number.

The following example illustrates a breakdown of books on Useful Arts under the Dewey classification used in libraries:

Useful arts	600
Engineering	620
Canal engineering	629

The secretary is seldom called upon to install a decimal system of filing. Should it become necessary, consult books describing the Melvil Dewey system, which can be obtained at most public libraries.

Chronological Filing

Advantages of an auxiliary file. Many secretaries find still another type of file, the basic chronological file, to be useful in addition to, not instead of, other filing systems. This auxiliary file contains carbon copies, in chronological order, of all outgoing letters, memos, notices, and reports. A chronological file is useful when trying to locate material the content of which has been forgotten. When, for example, your employer asks, "What was it we asked the city for about eight months ago?" you can simply look at the correspondence in the chronological file for the period in question.

Using the chronological file for review. A chronological file, also known as a "reading file," is a convenient way of recalling what went on during a given period. For example, when your employer has been out of town for a week, a quick look at the chronological file will help to bring him or her up to date on what has happened during that time.

BASIC FILING EQUIPMENT

Information that is retained on paper can be stored in a variety of containers of all sizes and colors. In fact, modern office designers consider the files as well as furniture and other items in planning for efficient use of space and effective color coordination to enhance productivity. The cost of required space for filing cabinets is also a factor, in addition to the cost of the cabinets themselves. Drawer files, for example, require more space than open shelves. For information about other means of storing nonpaper data, refer to **COMPUTERS AND OTHER AUTOMATED PROCEDURES,** page 36.

Standard Office Files

The traditional office file is a drawer-style letter- or legal-size cabinet. (Since legal-size paper is no longer accepted in some jurisdictions, there is a movement away from legal-size file material and containers.) *Vertical files* are upright units of one or more drawers. *Lateral files,* often with fewer drawers, are wide versions of the drawer-style cabinet. Most standard drawer files are available in decorator colors and may have locks; insulated, fireproof drawers; and suspension systems. They are designed to hold standard letter- or legal-size file folders and guides.

Open Files

To save space and provide for easy, visible filing and retrieval, some offices use open-shelf filing. Shelf units are usually in bookcase style, with shelves and no doors. Reference-shelf files, however, have doors that will lower like a countertop in front of each shelf. Some terminal-digit files are motorized, with a hanging (suspension) folder design. Rotary types have numerous floor-to-ceiling shelves. Open files are designed to accommodate either letter- or legal-size file folders and guides. Since the folders are immediately visible on open shelves, color coding can be used effectively to help the file clerk locate material quickly and easily spot misfiles.

Portable Files

Some file cabinets are on casters to enable one to move the unit from one place to another. Such rollaway files may have one drawer and one shelf or two drawers. The top half may have a lid rather than a pull-out drawer. The supplies for these units usually consist of the traditional letter- and legal-size folders and guides, but some are portable units for electronic data-processing materials. See **EDP Files,** page 13.

Safety Files

The purpose of a safety file is to protect materials from theft, fire, humidity, and other damaging elements. Thus any floor, shelf, or desk-top container that has locks and protective insulation could be considered a safety file. Because it may be of any size, the type of file material it will hold depends on its size and shape.

Tray Files

Tray files often look like narrow, flat drawers that hold cards or papers positioned in a flat, usually overlapping manner. Since the contents positioned in this way are open for immediate viewing, tray files are also called "visible files." (However, any file that positions the material for immediate viewing, such as a three-ring binder, is considered a visible file.) Some power-driven card units have trays on shelves that can be elevated or lowered to the level of the file clerk. These units are called "elevator files." Visible tray or elevator files often have cards or sheets in transparent pockets. Familiar sizes are 3 by 5 inches, 4 by 6 inches, and 5 by 8 inches. Guides are available along with the cards and transparent pockets.

Rotary Files

Both large and small rotary files are available. Large, motorized, carousel-style files (such as terminal-digit open files) will accept standard file folders and guides. Other rotary files are small, desk-top units that have a rotating wheel. An example of this is the rotary address file, in which small cards are cut or punched to fit around a circular cylinder or wheel.

Cabinets and Containers

A variety of boxes and other cabinets and containers are used to store supplies. Some large cabinets with doors have shelves as well as a section with a rod for hanging clothes. Some containers are simply fiberboard or cardboard boxes with a lid and a place to affix a label. Such containers might be used to store odd-sized material or inactive file folders. Those that are letter- or legal-size boxes will accommodate standard file folders and guides.

Specialized Files

Some files have special characteristics, such as the random file. This is a keyboard-activated file. Printed or typed cards have metal teeth on one edge that fit over a magnetic rod. When certain keys are depressed, one or more cards are pushed up. Other files are designed especially for odd-sized material. Art and blueprint files, for instance, accommodate drawings, blueprints, and artwork. The style may be open shelves with vertical dividers, flat drawers, or cubes that hold rolls of paper. See also **EDP Files,** below.

Combination Files

Any file cabinet or container that combines two or more purposes is a combination file. Some units, for example, may have a general storage compartment, shelf space, and drawer space. The type of supplies that will fit in a combination unit depends on the size and shape of the storage areas. See **Cabinets and Containers,** page 12; **Portable Files,** page 11.

EDP Files

Some electronic data-processing files are designed to hold computer printouts. Other containers are used to file magnetic media such as diskettes. For a description of these types of storage devices, refer to **COMPUTERS AND OTHER AUTOMATED PROCEDURES,** page 36.

INDEXING AND ALPHABETIZING

Basic Indexing Rules

Indexing, as applied to filing, is the arrangement of the names on the folder tabs or on cards for filing purposes. The folders or cards are then arranged in alphabetical order. You must know how names are indexed before you can consider them for alphabetizing.

Individual names. Individual names are indexed by the surname first, next the name or initial, and then additional names or initials.

> *Name*
> L. Vosburgh Lyons
> James G. Mellon
> R. S. Andrews

Index as
Lyons, L. Vosburgh
Mellon, James G.
Andrews, R. S.

Business concerns, organizations, and institutions.   When organization names are composed of names of individuals, follow the order that applies to individual names; otherwise, each word comprising the name is considered in the order in which it appears.

Name
James G. Mellon & Son
J. P. Goode, Inc.
Myron, Bache & Adams Co.
National City Bank
National Development Co.

Index as
Mellon, James G., & Son
Goode, J. P., Inc.
Myron, Bache & Adams Co.
National City Bank
National Development Co.

When an institutional name contains the name of the type of institution, such as "*Bank* of America" or "*University* of Illinois," the distinctive word is used first for filing purposes.

Name
Bank of America
University of Illinois

Index as
America, Bank (of)
Illinois, University (of)

Basic Alphabetizing Rules

Basic rules.   Although authorities differ in certain instances, the following rules for alphabetizing are widely accepted in the business world. Alphabetize by words, according to the first word in the name *as indexed*. When the first word of two or more names is the same, alphabetize according to the second word, then according to the third, and so on.

Index and File as
Brown, Albert A.
Brown, George
Brownell, Edward

Names of unequal length. The basic rule of alphabetizing by words results in the following simple rules: When two or more names are of unequal length but contain the same word or words and are spelled the same up to and including the last word of the shorter name, index and file the shorter name first.

Order
Brown, G.
Brown, George
Brown, George A.
State Bank
State Bank and Trust Company

Precedence of letters. Follow these rules in indexing and alphabetizing letters.

1. Letters used as words. One or more single letters used as words are treated as words. The group beginning with letter names is arranged alphabetically and precedes word names.

Order
A A Club
A C E Letter Co.
AWVS
Abbey Coat Co.
Admiration Cigar Co.

2. Ampersand symbol. The ampersand symbol (&) is not considered a letter and is disregarded in determining alphabetical sequence.

Index and File as
A & B Co.
Abernathy Stores, Inc.
Adams Hardware, Inc.
Adams & Rawlins, Inc.

Hyphenated names. Treat names composed of letters, words, or syllables joined by one or more hyphens as one word. When the hyphen is used instead of a comma in a firm name, the individual parts of the name are treated as separate words. You know that the hyphen replaces the comma when the names of two individuals make up the firm name.

Index and File as
Evers-Harper & Co. (hyphen used instead of comma)
Evers, Warren D.
Ever-Sharp Products Corp.
Up-Stairs Dress Co.
Upton-Smith, Edward L.

Abbreviations.   Abbreviations, such as *Chas., Co., Geo., Jas., St.,* and *Wm.,* are alphabetized in the same sequence as if spelled in full. Spell out on file labels for ease in filing.

Names
St. John's Church
Jas. Sanders
Jane Sanders
Wm. Smith
Willis Smith

Index and File as
Saint John's Church
Sanders, James
Sanders, Jane
Smith, William
Smith, Willis

Sometimes an abbreviated name is the actual legal name of the person or company. In this case, use the abbreviated spelling in filing.

Compound firm names.   When a firm name consists of a compound word that is sometimes spelled as one word, sometimes as two or more words, index as written but treat as one word in alphabetizing.

Index and File as
Lockport Engine Co.
Lock Port Fisheries
Lockport Mansions, Inc.
New Amsterdam Bakery, Inc.
New York City Bank
Newark Rubber Co.

North, R. S.
North East Commodities, Inc.
Northeastern Burlap Co.

Opinions differ about whether compound geographic names, such as New York, should be treated as one or two words in alphabetizing. Adopt a rule and follow it uniformly. In the example above, compound geographic names are treated as two words.

Sr., Jr., II, III.   You may retain designations that follow names, such as *Jr.* or *III* (Third), in indexing and filing and alphabetize according to the designation. The order is as follows: II (Second), III (Third), Jr., Sr. But some organizations ignore seniority terms and arrange identical names by address instead.

Index and File as
White, John, II
White, John, III
White, John, Jr.
White, John, Sr.

Surnames with prefixes.   When individual surnames are compounded with prefixes, such as *D', De, Del, De la, Di, Fitz, L', La, Las, Los, M', Mc, Mac, O', San, Santa, Ten, Van, van der, von,* and *von der,* index as written and treat as one word in alphabetizing, disregarding the apostrophe, the space, or the capitalization, if any.

Index and File as
Damata, J.
D'Amato, P.
D'Arcy, A. C.
De Lamara, A. D.
De La Mare, A. D.
Madison, R. L.
McIntyre, A. C.
Mean, Robert A.
Tenants' Committee, Inc.
Ten Eyck, E. M.

Articles, prepositions, and conjunctions.   Disregard articles, prepositions, and conjunctions in determining alphabetical sequence. The words in parentheses in the following examples are disregarded.

Names
F. A. Madison
The Marine Bank
Geo. Mathews
Society of Arts and Sciences
Society for the Prevention of Cruelty

Index and File as
Madison, F. A.
(The) Marine Bank
Mathews, Geo.
Society (of) Arts (and) Sciences
Society (for the) Prevention of Cruelty

Articles, prepositions, and conjunctions in foreign languages.
Consider an article in a name in a foreign language as part of the word that immediately follows it; treat prepositions and conjunctions as separate words in determining alphabetical sequence.

Names
C. H. Deramer
Der Amerikaner
Societe des Auteurs et Peintres
Societe des Auteurs, Musiciens et Compositeurs

Index and File as
Deramer, C. H.
Der Amerikaner
Société des Auteurs et Peintres
Société des Auteurs, Musiciens et Compositeurs

Words ending in "s."   When a word ends in "s," index and file as spelled regardless of what the "s" denotes (whether possession, with or without the apostrophe, or a singular or plural ending).

Index and File as
Girl Scout Council
Girls' Service League
Smith, John
Smith's Delicatessen
Thompson, R. S.

Names containing numbers.   When a name contains a number, alphabetize as if the number were spelled in full. Spelling out the names on the file labels facilitates the filing.

Names
28 Sutton Place, Inc.
2059 Third Ave. Corp.
The "21" Club

Index and file as
Twenty-eight Sutton Place, Inc.
Twenty Fifty-nine Third Ave. Corp.
(The) "Twenty-one" Club

Exception: Numbered streets and branches of organizations numbered consecutively should be arranged in numerical sequence. Thus Branch Number 4 precedes Branch Number 5, although if the numbers were spelled out and alphabetized, Branch Number Five would precede Branch Number Four.

Government offices. Index and file names of government offices under the names of the governing body, with the names of the departments, bureaus, or institutions as subtitles.

Federal
United States Government
   Treasury (Dept. of)
      Accounts (Bur. of)

State
Mississippi (State of)
   Education (Dept. of)
      Rural Education (Div. of)

County
Suffolk (County of)
   County Clerk

City
Memphis, Tennessee
   City Planning Commission

Titles. Titles are disregarded in indexing and filing but are usually written in parentheses at the end of the name.

Exceptions: If the name of an individual contains a title and a first name, without a last name, consider the title as the first word.

Names
Dr. J. C. Adams
Sister Mary Brown
Madame Celeste

Miss Helen Marsh
Count Carlos Sforza

Index and File as
Adams, J. C. (Dr.)
Brown, Mary (Sr.)
Madame Celeste
Marsh, Helen (Miss)
Sforza, Carlos (Count)

If a *firm name* contains a title, consider the title as the first word.

Index and File as
King Edward Hospital
Sir Walter Raleigh Tobacco Co.
Uncle Sam Produce Co.

Married women.   Index and file names of married women according to their married surnames, followed by their first names, unless they use their maiden names or are known by other names. Show the husband's initial or name in parentheses on the file label when it is convenient or important to have this additional information.

Name
Mrs. Robert E. (Ada R.) Brown
Mrs. Albert S. (Mary L.) Brown

Index and File as
Brown, Ada R.
    (Mrs. Robert E. Brown)
Brown, Mary L.
    (Mrs. Albert S. Brown)

AIDS TO FAST FILING AND FINDING

Using Timesaving Equipment and Techniques

An efficient secretary will quickly learn how to apply a few simple, timesaving techniques to filing duties. Most of the following will not only save precious minutes each day but will make your job much easier.

1. Visit showrooms and write to suppliers to request free sales literature to get ideas on new and effective filing materials and equipment, filing systems, and efficient office layouts.

2. Learn the pros and cons of different systems thoroughly (including standard and custom-designed commercial systems as well as advanced techniques such as microfilming, computer storage, and automated storage and retrieval systems), before you set up a new system or revise the present system in your office.

3. Avoid fatigue, which cuts work speed and performance, by using filing techniques and aids such as (a) stools with rollers, so that you can sit down during extended periods of filing; and (b) tables with rollers or trays that attach to file drawers, to keep material for filing at arm's reach. Keep heavy documents where it isn't necessary to lift or carry them far; store seldom-used materials in the higher and lower drawers or on top and bottom shelves; and always work from the side, not the front, of a file drawer.

4. File daily. Large stacks of accumulated filing can complicate the task and make it tiresome.

5. Simplify the step of sorting and organizing the material to be filed by using sorting trays, racks, or carts, whichever suits the type and volume of work you have. Use rubber fingers if you must leaf through large stacks of correspondence. Different-colored carbons, according to subject, will also speed the sorting process.

6. Use supplies and equipment that encourage rapid visual location. Examples are (a) visible files, including trays, holders, stands, looseleaf books, and desk-top organizers, along with transparent guides, binder and shelf clips, and pockets—all for quick visual identification of contents; and (b) color-coded files, both file folders and storage containers, for instant recognition of files and contents and easy-to-spot misfiles. Circular, rotating files, and open-shelf filing also permit fast and easy location and retrieval, especially in combination with color coding.

7. Avoid mishaps, such as (a) toppling a file cabinet by pulling out more than one drawer at a time; (b) spilling the contents of a folder by not resting it properly upon removal or by not using both hands while filing material in it or retrieving material from it; or (c) ruining a folder while pulling it out by grasping only the tab.

8. Keep the size of folders manageable—open new ones if necessary. Leave several inches for such expansion in each file drawer and on each shelf.

9. Use a guide for every six to eight folders and place folders *behind*

the guides. Investigate the use of file and desk-drawer dividers to aid further in compartmentalizing and organizing contents.

10. Speed the labeling process with products such as pressure-sensitive labels, preprinted tabs, and continuous-feed labels for typing. Some tabs are removable, and some have transparent windows for reuse, which means it is a simple matter to salvage and use old folders again merely by a quick tab change or by inserting a newly typed label.

11. Always position records in their folders face up with the top toward the left; the document with the most recent date goes in front. Fold oversized papers with the data on the outside.

12. Staple an envelope on the inside of a file folder when you have small clippings or pictures that might otherwise become bent or lost.

Typing Index Tabs and Labels

Basic rules.   For best results in typing tabs, guides, and folder labels, observe the following rules:

Use the briefest possible designations. Abbreviate, omitting punctuation whenever possible. Index tabs need to be legible only at normal reading distance. Guide labels should be legible at two to three feet. File-drawer labels should be legible at six to ten feet.

Use initial caps whenever needed. Full caps, especially in elite and pica type, do *not* increase the legibility of label designations; they decrease the amount of light background in the vicinity of the letters and make reading more difficult. Do not underline.

Folder labels.   The most important part of a folder label is the eighth of an inch immediately below the scoring (the place at which the label is folded when it is placed on the folder tab). Frequently, this space is the only part visible in the file. Therefore, write in the first typing space below the scoring. Typing should begin in the first or second typing space from the left edge of the label, except for one or two character designations. If this is done, all folder labels in the file drawer will present an even left margin.

Use initial caps and indent the second and third lines so that the first word of the first line will stand out.

In typing labels for a numbered subject file, leave space between the number and the first word; type the subject in block form. Avoid exceptionally long file numbers if possible. For proper arrangement of various label designations, see figure 2.

Figure 2. Proper Arrangement for Label Designations

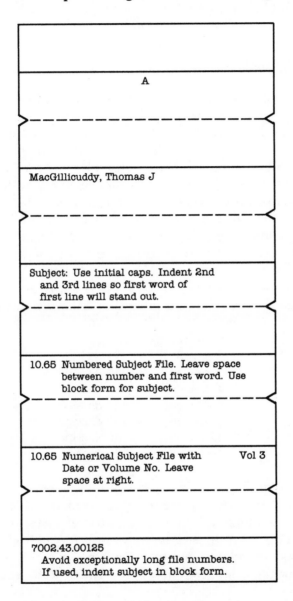

A
MacGillicuddy, Thomas J
Subject: Use initial caps. Indent 2nd and 3rd lines so first word of first line will stand out.
10.65 Numbered Subject File. Leave space between number and first word. Use block form for subject.
10.65 Numerical Subject File with   Vol 3 Date or Volume No. Leave space at right.
7002.43.00125 Avoid exceptionally long file numbers. If used, indent subject in block form.

Guide labels. For file-guide labels, use the largest type available. Begin the typing as high on the label as the guide tabs will permit. Center one- and two-character designations. Start all other designations in the second typing space from the left edge. Use abbreviations or shortened forms and omit punctuation, except for large numbers such as 10,000.

File-drawer labels. In preparing labels for file drawers, use the largest type available. Center the typing on the label and leave a double space above and below detailed reference information. It is better to print drawer labels because type is not legible at a distance.

Using Guides in the Files

Frequent guides make filing and finding easy. Therefore, it is usually advisable to put guides between at least every six to eight folders.

Alphabetic index guides.   Alphabetical index guides come in divisions of from twenty-five to two thousand. The twenty-five division has a guide for each letter from A to Z, with Mc added and XYZ combined in the last guide. Although in alphabetizing, names beginning with Mc are treated in regular alphabetical sequence (see page 17), Mc is included as a letter in a twenty-five-division index for the convenience of those who have more than three or four names beginning with Mc. The Mc guide precedes the M guide. In an index with more divisions, the Mc guide is in its proper alphabetical position, between the M and the N guides.

To determine which division you need, count the number of drawers of filing material. The following table shows the division required for a given number of drawers.

1 drawer	25 division
2 drawers	40 division
4 drawers	80 division
6 drawers	120 division
8 drawers	160 division
12 drawers	240 division
16 drawers	320 division

Tabs come in different sizes and positions, for example, third cut or fifth cut. This means that they are staggered from one side of the folder to the other side. You might, therefore, want to use a left-side tab for a main heading and all of the others to the right of it for subheadings.

Labels may be color coded to make it easier to identify material by subject. (Follow the rules given in **Typing Index Tabs and Labels,** page 22.)

Using Cross-References

When to use a cross-reference.   Frequently, material may be filed logically under one or more names or subjects. In those cases, file the paper under one name or subject and cross-reference under the other. For example, a letter from Mr. Remsen might relate to Ms. Abernathy. The most reasonable place to file the letter is under *Abernathy*, but a cross-reference should be made under *Remsen*. Write the cross-reference on colored cross-reference sheets, about $8\frac{1}{2}$ by 11 inches. They are available in most office-supply stores. (Cross-reference labels should be in a color different from the color of the labels on the regular folders.) *Use cross-reference sheets freely.* Each sheet should contain the information shown in figure 3. If Mr. Remsen has a regular folder, put the cross-reference sheet in it; if not, put it in the miscellaneous folder under R.

Permanent cross-reference. A permanent cross-reference is usually maintained when a name or subject can be filed under more than one designation. For example, a permanent cross-reference should be maintained under Simon, Franklin & Company to *Franklin Simon & Company*. When a permanent cross-reference is desirable, make a guide to serve as a cross-reference signal and insert it in its proper alphabetical position among the regular file folders. The back of an old file folder will serve this purpose. The cross-reference label should read:

Figure 3. Cross-reference Sheet

CROSS-REFERENCE SHEET

NAME OR SUBJECT:

Remsen, S. J.

REGARDING:

Recommendation, George Abernathy

DATE:

May 11, 19--

(see)

NAME OR SUBJECT:

Abernathy, George

Simon, Franklin, & Co.
See Franklin Simon & Company

Storing bulky materials.   Many secretaries must store odd-sized material or bulky objects (blueprints, film, and so on) in a special place. A cross-reference sheet in the regular files may be desirable for such cases.

When not to use cross-references.   There are instances when frequent reference or the need for full information immediately may preclude the use of a standard cross-reference procedure. A photocopy of the document in question placed in the regular files would be preferable for such situations.

Preparing Material for Filing

Checklist of things to do.   To prepare material for filing, do the following:

1. Check to be certain the material has been released for filing. (This may be indicated simply by a brief notation on the document or by a rubber-stamped FILE notice.)

2. If you have more than one category of files, segregate papers into the different categories: personal correspondence, business correspondence, documents, and the like. Then arrange items in each category in alphabetic order. For numeric files, code each item as described in number 6 below and arrange them sequentially. (Use one of the sorting aids described on page 21.)

3. Check through all papers that are stapled to see whether they should be filed together.

4. Remove all paper clips.

5. Mend torn papers with cellophane tape.

6. Note on the paper where it is to be filed. For a *name file,* underline the name in erasable colored pencil; for a *subject file,* write the main heading and subheading in the upper right-hand corner. Place guide or file number if used, in the upper right-hand corner. For *numerical coding,* refer to the card index and mark the assigned number in the upper right-hand corner. (*Note:* Because file copies sometimes must be photocopied later, some offices will not permit any writing on the file material. In that case attach self-sticking notes. Or, if permitted, use a nonreproducible blue pencil.)

7. Circle an important word or words in colored pencil to facilitate location of a particular paper when it is wanted. (*Note:* Refer to number 6 regarding writing on file material.)

8. Make necessary cross-reference sheets as each letter or paper is handled.

Controlling Material Taken from the Files

Using out folders and guides.   To control material taken from your files, use *out folders* or *out guides* the same height as the file folders but of different-colored stock, with the word *OUT* printed in all capitals on the tab. Out folders are often manila folders with the word *OUT* printed on the tab. Ruled spaces appear on the front for recording charge-out information. The out folder is substituted for the regular folder that is removed. Until the regular folder is returned, new correspondence is filed in the out folder.

When out guides are used, new material is accumulated elsewhere until the regular folder is returned. Out guides provide space on which to make an entry of the date, the material taken, who has it, and the date it should be returned. See figure 4. Place the guide in the files where the removed material was located. Some out guides have a pocket in which a charge-out slip (sometimes called a "requisition slip") can be filed. Copies of the slip can then be made, with one copy put in the guide pocket, another clipped to the file material that is removed, and a third copy put in the follow-up files, in case the user needs a reminder to return the material.

Secretaries in a private office do not put an out guide in the file every time they withdraw material for their employers. The guide is used under these circumstances: (1) Someone outside the immediate office wants the

Figure 4.   Out Card

DATE	MATERIAL	DATE REMOVED	TO BE RETURNED	CHARGE TO WHOM	REMARKS

material. (2) The employer expects to take the material out of the office. (3) The secretary expects the employer to keep the material a week or so.

Retrieving Lost Papers

Looking for misfiles.   When you, or someone else, has misfiled a paper and you have to find it, you can shorten your search by looking in the most likely places for misfiling it:

1. Look in the folders that precede and follow the folder the paper should be in.
2. Look under consonants that look alike either handwritten or typed—for example, *N, M, W, U,* and *V.*
3. Check under other vowels than the correct one. For a name beginning with *Ca,* look under *Ce, Ci, Co,* or *Cu.*
4. Abbreviations are easily misfiled. For example, an abbreviation of James Sanders may have been incorrectly labeled and filed under *Sanders, Jas.,* instead of *Sanders, James;* or an abbreviation of *Saint* may have been incorrectly labeled and filed under *St.* instead of *Sa.*
5. If more than one name is in the subject of the lost paper, look under each name, even though the paper should have been filed under the first name in the subject.
6. Look for a possible "charge-out" or "transferred" withdrawal that may not have been recorded.
7. As a last resort, check your sorter, behind the file cabinet or your desk, or even in the wastebasket.

Streamlining the Files

Use hanging folders and hanging pockets.   A suspension system keeps files orderly and uses file space efficiently.
1.   Adding metal frames to your cabinets.   Hanging folders and hanging pockets solve space problems for many secretaries. If your files did not come equipped with this feature, you can purchase metal frames in either letter or legal size, depending on the size of the cabinet drawer and the type of papers to be filed. The metal frame fits into the file drawer (from which the follow block has already been removed) and hanging folders and hanging pockets are ready to be dropped into place. The hanging folder serves as a guide card, folder, and separator all in one.

2. Using hanging folders. Although hanging folders have numerous advantages, you will not save space if you use too many in one drawer. Since two hanging folders take up one-half inch of space, a dozen of these folders would take up three inches of space, robbing you of more drawer space than you save by removing the follow block.

3. Using hanging pockets. Hanging pockets seem to be the most space saving of all divider devices. Pockets hold individual folders neatly in place and, unlike hanging folders, expand freely. If the material in your drawer is filed by subject, and your subjects are divided into four main categories, use four roomy hanging pockets in which to insert individual folders. Material that is numerically arranged can easily group itself in pockets by the tens or one hundreds, depending on the amount of material in each numbered section. Even alphabetically arranged material can be divided by means of a hanging pocket. Label one pocket "A to F," the second pocket "G to M," and so on. Material is never lost by slipping under other folders onto the floor of the drawer. Folders are held firmly in place and never slip or slide under one another.

Use special-purpose folders. Sometimes it is necessary to transfer important material temporarily to another location. Valuable documents should never be transported in an open file folder. A special-purpose folder with a clasp should be used. Many special-purpose folders have a metal or plastic fastener to secure the material inside. Others have a flap and cord that can be tied. Some of these folders have an expanding base and sides, too, so that more material can be added to the same folder. Another type of special-purpose folder has pockets in which you can insert magnetic cards and disks used in word processing. Since office suppliers have folders and filing cabinets for virtually every purpose, inquire whether something is available that precisely fits your needs.

Remove bulky follow blocks. If you are jamming records into a 26-inch file drawer that also contains a follow block about $\frac{3}{4}$ inch thick, you are losing between 1 and $1\frac{1}{2}$ inches of drawer space in each drawer. With four or five drawers in each cabinet, you are losing $7\frac{1}{2}$ inches of drawer space in each cabinet. Substitute hanging folders and pockets and portable drawer dividing units for the bulky follow blocks.

Use portable drawer dividing units. A portable drawer divider is another device to eliminate bulky follow blocks. The divider is a lightweight metal "skeleton" that separates and supports file folders and is easily inserted into a drawer. Its strong bottom stand holds folders upright and prevents loss through slipping.

This dividing unit serves other purposes too. It can be inserted into a desk drawer to hold miscellaneous papers, brochures, stationery, and other supplies. It can be used on the desk top, in lieu of a more elaborate desk-top organizer, to hold letters or magazines. It is adjustable, so that sections can be expanded or narrowed, as needed.

Eliminate magazines and bulky brochures.   File cabinets should not be piled high with old copies of magazines, brochures, and other printed material. Late issues of important periodicals should be on display for easy accessibility. After periodicals have been read by those who are interested, current issues should be substituted for them.

If it is necessary to keep dated printed matter for infrequent reference, it should be stored in a less accessible place. Material that must be kept filed and ready for quick reference should be stored as compactly as possible. Here are two ways of saving space through compact placement:

1. Narrow pamphlets and brochures, only a fraction of the size of the folder that holds them, should be stacked in double or triple rows, lengthwise, within the folder.
2. Printed matter that is clipped or bound on one edge should be equalized by alternating the papers within the folder: half of the bulky edges to the right side of the folder and half to the left.

Eliminate duplication.   Bulky files are greatly reduced when duplicate papers are removed from active files. Duplications often occur in the following areas: copies of memos and letters; galleys, page proofs, and paste-ups; reprints of published letters and reports; identical copies of published brochures.

1.   Unnecessary copies.   If you are in the habit of making two or three photocopies or carbon copies for each letter or report you type, consider reducing the number of copies you make. Unless your employer has need of extra copies for some special purpose, you may be cluttering your files with unnecessary copies of memos and routine letters. Condense and centralize your files wherever possible, to avoid overlapping. If you keep a "copy file" and a "follow-up file" in addition to your employer's complete file, you may be doubling the amount of work necessary to complete your tasks.

2.   Surplus copies of printed matter.   Unless you plan to distribute additional copies of brochures or reports, the filing of identical copies of printed matter is unnecessary. Many secretaries retain three copies of this type of material and send the remaining copies to storage spaces located in a remote part of the building.

Remove thick backings of clippings and photos.   Photographs and clippings that must be filed need support and protection against loss or tearing. Although cardboard backing is often used, it is unnecessarily thick for filing. Manila tag or another lighter backing is a better choice because it is sturdy and yet takes up less space. Celluloid envelope sheets are probably the best protection for photographs and clippings, and they are less bulky than even manila tag sheets, but they are more expensive.

Transfer little-used and odd-sized material. Odd-sized and bulky material such as blueprints or tape reels should not occupy valuable space in the regular files. Instead, they should be moved to suitable containers and merely cross-referenced in the regular files. Correspondence, papers, and records that cannot be destroyed but are referred to only occasionally should be transferred to storage to save floor space. Transfer files save time in filing and finding; they also release expensive equipment for active files. Some correspondence, such as standard inquiries or form-letter replies, should not even be retained. But if the inquiry represents a prospective customer or sale, the name and address should first be transferred to the appropriate mailing list maintained for this purpose.

Here is a list of ideas to facilitate the transfer of files that must be retained:

1. Plan the new file well in advance of the transfer date.

2. If the entire file is to be transferred, leaving only guides in the file drawers, prepare new folders for the new file beforehand. Prepare only those folders that will be definitely needed. Use a new color for folder labels and indicate the year as well as the title.

3. If the folders and the guides are to be retained in the file, prepare a new set of inexpensive folders to hold material in transfer drawers. Put titles on these folders identical with those in the current file and have them ready in advance of the transfer date.

4. If the space is available, keep the old files in the office for a few weeks until sufficient material for reference purposes accumulates in the new files.

5. Make sure ample storage space is available for the old files and that the transfer files or boxes fit the conditions in the storage location.

6. To avoid interference with general office procedures, plan to have the transfer operation done after hours. Plan for enough help to complete the entire job in one evening. For most efficient results, have two persons work on each drawer—one pulling out the folders and the other packing them in the transfer files. If folders

and labels have not been prepared in advance, have a typist do this work during the transfer operation.

7. Label all transfer files or boxes. Indicate contents of file, dates, and so on clearly on labels and affix them to the containers so that they can be easily read.

8. Pack transfer files or boxes tightly—two drawer-length transfer units will hold the contents of three filing cabinet drawers.

Develop a file-retention program.   Although it is necessary for a secretary to have a retention and disposal program for filing materials, it is not her or his responsibility to decide what should be kept and what should be destroyed. Keep a current copy of a guide to records retention in your office. (An excellent guide is available from the Electric Wastebasket Corporation, 145 West 45th Street, New York, N.Y. 10036.) However, legal advice should be secured concerning state and federal requirements before making any firm decisions about retention and disposal of files.

   1. Business matters.   If your company has established a procedure for the destruction of papers, you should be guided by this method. If no such policy exists, your employer should determine the period of retention for all types of documents and letters. How long a paper will be retained depends on legal considerations such as the statute of limitations or other requirements and your employer's desires.

   The preparation of any destruction schedule must take into account (a) the statute of limitations, (b) other laws that may apply to particular items, and (c) studies that have been made of how long business firms usually retain various types of papers. If space is at a premium and it is absolutely necessary to keep some types of correspondence for many years, some companies make microfilm copies, which take little space.

   Examples of records kept permanently are incorporation papers, journals and ledgers, and meeting minutes. Examples of records kept five to ten years are contracts that have expired, collection records, and evidence used in an insurance claim. Examples of records kept up to five years are meeting proxies, credit ratings of customers, and general correspondence. Examples of records kept up to one year are announcements, form letters, and duplicate copies of bank deposit slips.

   2. Personal matters.   Two factors will determine how long to keep personal papers and records: the statute of limitations and your employer's desires. Secretaries should compile for their own use a retention schedule that meets the employer's desires. To make the schedule, you should do the following:

a. List alphabetically all types of personal papers and records in the files.

b. Rule three columns to the right of the listed items.

c. In the first column, insert the statute of limitations requirements in your state or other legal requirements.

d. In the second column, show what you suggest as the period of retention. There are no established practices that can be used as guides for retention of personal papers as there are for business records.

e. Have your employer indicate in the third column his or her wish for the period of retention for each item.

f. Retype the schedule with just one indication of years—the time approved by your employer.

3. Storage-control schedule. When you put files into storage, type a transfer sheet, or storage-control schedule, for the active files. (Standard forms are available in office-supply stores.) List the following facts on your schedule:

a. File number on the storage box

b. Contents and date of contents

c. Location of storage box

d. Date to destroy contents

e. Date destroyed

f. Who authorized disposal

Safeguard your files and important documents. So much attention is given to filing systems that basic precautions for safety are often ignored in an office. As a separate record or as part of the retention records mentioned above, you should ask your employer to indicate which business and personal papers are confidential. All such items should be stored in cabinets with security locks, in bank safe deposit boxes, in a company safe, or in some other secure place approved by your employer.

Other considerations in filing and storing materials are fire, loss, humidity, and cleanliness. Each of these factors must be considered when selecting appropriate filing and storage equipment.

Use color coding to enhance your filing system. Color coding, as used in both folders/tabs and containers, can be applied to any filing system, and it can be as simple or as intricate as you like. Quick storage and retrieval and ease in spotting misfiles are the more obvious benefits of this technique.

Color can be applied numerically (black = 10; red = 20; green = 30) or by subject (black = Insurance; red = Real Estate; green = Investments). It can indicate action to take. For example, a yellow tab might indicate action completed; a red tab might indicate that follow-up action is needed. Some offices are using color to make evaluations as well (black = an interested, prospective customer; red = a potential, but difficult, customer; green = an unlikely prospect). The uses of color are almost limitless. Manufacturers of supplies and cabinets have complete systems already designed, and sales literature describing them is available free.

Determine if a file is really necessary. Files are intended to organize information so that it can be retrieved with a minimum of time and effort. Therefore, the temptation to overorganize is strong, and the secretary should view each new file critically. Before opening a proposed file, ask yourself these simple questions:

1. Will the proposed new file make it possible to locate information faster and easier than in present files?
2. How often will the file be used—often, occasionally, seldom?
3. Will the file require an increase in the number of carbon copies or photocopies (and thus in typing and copying time and costs) of certain correspondence?
4. Will the file increase the number of hours devoted to filing and related duties?
5. Will the file affect file-container and storage-space requirements?
6. Will the file require other new files (check-out, cross-reference, and so on) in order to maintain it properly?
7. Very simply, do the pros outweigh the cons?

HOW TO ORDER AND STORE SUPPLIES

Purchasing and Distributing Supplies

Secretaries often purchase and store supplies for themselves, their employers, and other coworkers. This involves a knowledge of what is needed and when, where to go to get it, and where to store it until time for use.

Requisitioning supplies. A large company will have a special department that orders and stocks supplies for use in offices within the company. In such cases, a secretary must complete a company order form, or requisition, and present it at the stockroom. Supplies may not always be available and requests should be made far enough in advance to allow for ordering if necessary. Your firm probably has its own requisition form to use; otherwise, standard forms from an office-supply store may be used. Follow the policy in your office concerning approval of requisitions. In some offices, the secretary is responsible for authorizing the purchase of office supplies.

Purchasing supplies outside. In a small office, a secretary may simply be asked to go to a local office-supply store and purchase (probably by charge account) the necessary supplies. At the time the supplies are ordered, you should keep a copy of the purchase order and check off items as they are received. Again, follow the policy in your office concerning authorization.

If you have doubts about quantities needed or length of time required on items that must be ordered, play it safe—order far in advance, several months if necessary, and order more than you believe is needed immediately. (See also **Inventory control,** below.)

Distributing supplies. It is usually a mistake for employees to help themselves to supplies. Lack of control inevitably causes confusion and unexpected depletion of some items. Try to develop a policy for checking the needs in your office periodically, perhaps weekly, so that you can order and distribute supplies according to a reasonable schedule. It would be inefficient to have to drop everything and rush out for supplies every time an employee ran out of paper clips or pencils. Also, keep a list of what supplies you distribute and to whom you distribute them. This will tell you, after a month or two, which employees use what supplies and how soon they are likely to run out of them.

Organizing and Storing Supplies

Inventory control. Some form of regular inventory control is needed, regardless of the size of the office. A typed list of supplies on hand and average quantity used during certain periods (monthly, for example) would be the simplest method. Such an inventory-control sheet would have several columns, recording the quantities left on hand at certain dates (such as at the end of each month). When the sheet indicated that a certain supply would be exhausted in another month, it would be time to reorder. As an example, the following entry would indicate on April 30 that it is time to reorder memo pads:

Item	Av. Qty. Used/Mo.	On Hand				
		Jan. 31	Feb. 28	Mar. 31	Apr. 30	etc.
Memo pads	12	48	36	24	12	etc.

Storage. Storage is frequently more of a problem than purchasing. Lack of organization will complicate the task of taking inventory periodically. Many of the same rules applied to the filing of regular correspondence can be used here. Seldom-used supplies, for example, should go on the top and bottom shelves or toward the back in a storage closet. Materials should be grouped for ease in locating and in estimating quantities. Mark packages for quantity as they arrive—don't trust your memory to hold until the end of the month. As supplies are removed during the month, cross out that quantity and jot the new balance on the front package. At the end of the month record the last balance on your inventory-control sheet.

COMPUTERS AND OTHER AUTOMATED PROCEDURES

Automated Information Storage and Retrieval

Automated filing equipment and procedures. The storage of information and its retrieval are processes that have been automated in many offices. Although there will always be certain materials that require manual filing and retrieval, vast quantities of information can be processed, stored, and located only by sophisticated equipment. Along with data-processing machines and the small-to-large computer installations, the larger company may well house sophisticated storage and retrieval devices. A detailed index that specifies the location of each file is usually maintained by computer. To retrieve a folder, a special electronic device is then activated by a keyboard operator to locate file containers and physically transport them to a predetermined location.

Large data-storage and retrieval centers are most common when an organization has a central filing department. If your employer would need something, you would probably ask the central department's operator for a file on a certain subject, which would be transported to you in a container conveyed automatically by machine. But smaller filing systems used in individual offices also may have automated features that do things such as rotate a circular file or move trays in and out. Check with nearby suppliers or write for sales literature about the latest equipment.

Information Processing by Computer

Desktop computers and word processors are commonplace in business, and a great deal of information is stored electronically.

Preparing the data. Data fed into a computer is called "input." Your raw facts and figures will likely be prepared for computer processing at a "dumb" terminal—a keyboard and display monitor connected to a large central computer—or an "intelligent" terminal—one that has its own memory and does not have to use the memory and processing capability of a central computer.

Most stand-alone computers and word processors store data on magnetic media: tape (such as a cassette) or more likely a diskette, which resembles a small phonograph record. Some terminals have a hard disk or a built-in Winchester disk for storing data, both of which have a storage capacity far greater than a removable tape or diskette. (See chapter 2, page 52, for a description of word processing systems.)

Printing out processed data. The results of the computer's work are either stored for later use or printed out or both. Output takes place with a printing device that resembles a typewriter without a keyboard. You can also view your work on the display monitor, or depending on your equipment, the output may be in a form such as a punched card (which then has to be translated into another form that you can read). Printers, however, "type" the data you want directly on paper (hard copy), ready for distribution.

Filing Diskettes and Printouts

Storing data on magnetic media. Information that you save, or store, on magnetic media such as a diskette must be given a file name so that later you can retrieve any one or more of the files that you stored. The instructions that accompany your computer or word processor and the particular software package that you use will tell you how to name your files. If, for example, you may use one to eight characters plus a three-character extension, you might name the revised Henderson report *HNDRSHRP.REV*.

Each time that you type a document such as a report, you will devise a file name and type the name for that document in response to the computer's instructions for creating a new file. With a felt-tip pen (never a hard pen or pencil point), write the same name on the blank label affixed to the diskette. The computer will retain a "directory" listing of all of the files you save on a particular diskette (or other media). To see a certain file from that diskette on the display monitor or to print out a hard copy of it, you must type the name you gave to the file in question and then press the appropriate keys to instruct the computer whether you want to print it out or view it on the monitor.

Storing the media and printouts.   Media such as diskettes must be stored in a safe, clean container. Special diskette files are available for this purpose, often containing locks to prevent theft or accidental loss or damage. For security reasons, confidential diskettes should be kept in a locked, inaccessible place. If confidential data are stored on a hard disk (which cannot be removed) or in the memory of a central computer (also used by other employees), you will no doubt be asked by your employer to use a password with such documents. Only those who know the password can then "call out" your file on a display monitor or print out a hard copy of it.

File containers for paper printouts include shelf-style pockets for storing binders and loose sheets and cabinets with hanging binder racks or printout drawers. Some printout storage devices are mounted on casters so that they can be wheeled from one place to another.

Storing Material in Reduced Form

Some equipment and processes store material in reduced form or size, such as microfilm or microfiche. *Micrographics* is the method of filing information by either microfilm or microfiche.

Microfilming.   Of the various processes of reduction, *microfilming* is the best known. With this method, documents are transferred onto a roll of film. After microfilmed documents are reduced and stored on film, they can be viewed on a screen when desired, and with certain equipment, they can be photocopied at the same time. Original, full-size files can then be destroyed, and only the film retained, with a savings in storage space of up to 98 percent. Moreover, the film is noncombustible, reducing the danger of loss through fire. Microfilm has special benefits in the storage and retrieval of extensive or continuous records, such as mailing lists, accounts receivable, personnel forms, and stock certificates or bulky items such as engineering drawings. It is also less expensive to mail microfilm than the original full-size documents.

Microfiche.   Similar to microfilm, *microfiche* is a method of storing microimages on sheets or cards. These sheets or cards can be examined through a viewer or produced by photocopier. One advantage of microfiche is that the sheets or cards can be filed conveniently in alphabetic file folders.

Analyzing Time and Cost Benefits

Determining need.   Automated procedures for handling information basically are intended to lower or control costs by reducing factors such as space and labor requirements and by increasing factors such as efficiency and output. Secretaries should be alert to signs that suggest a need for expansion: delays in processing, an increasing volume of work, and so on. They should periodically make studies of the steps involved in performing certain tasks manually, including how much time is involved. As soon as signs point to the possible need for automated procedures, it is none too soon to begin collecting information on new systems and to prepare a written report of the processing problems and requirements encountered. All of this will be helpful to your employer when the question of a new system arises and a justification analysis must be undertaken. (*Justification* is the process of determining if a new system or new procedure will prove profitable, that is, whether the expense can be justified.)

FOLLOW-UP FILING TECHNIQUES

Material That Needs Follow-up

The following items ordinarily call for follow-up:

1. Matters that are referred to other executives or departments for information or comment
2. Correspondence or memos awaiting answer
3. Orders for future delivery, both those that you receive and those that you place
4. Items that come up for periodic consideration, such as company reports of various kinds, tax matters, and contract renewals
5. Promises to be carried out in the future

Basic Follow-up Methods

In any tickler or follow-up system, one of two methods must be used: (1) the material to come up for action at a certain date must be placed in the tickler or (2) a notation or reminder of that material must be placed in the tickler while the material itself remains in its proper place in the regular files. The latter method is preferable for the secretary and is the only one described here.

Equipment for follow-up system. Numerous styles of equipment for follow-up purposes are on the market, but many secretaries for busy executives have found the follow-up system described here, or a variation of it, practical and efficient.

The only equipment necessary is a file drawer and file folders. Make a set of file folders consisting of (a) twelve folders labeled from January through December, (b) thirty-one folders numbered from 1 through 31, and (c) one folder marked "Future Years." If you have a heavy volume of follow-up material, it is advisable to have two sets of folders labeled by days—one for the current month and one for the succeeding month.

Tabbed guides also numbered 1 through 31 and removable separators labeled with the month will make it easier to locate a particular folder, but the guides are not necessary to the efficient functioning of the system.

Arrangement of folders for follow-up. Arrange the folders by day or by month.

1. Arrangement by day. Arrange the folders labeled by days in numerical order in the front of the file. Place in these folders the follow-up material for the current month. The folder labeled for the current month is at the back of the other monthly folders ready to receive any material to be followed up in the same month *next* year. Immediately following the numerical daily folders is the folder for the forthcoming month, followed by the folder for the succeeding month, and so on. Figure 5 is a diagram of the folders when April 16 is the current day.

2. Arrangement by month. A variation of the above plan is to arrange the files labeled by months in calendar sequence. Thus January is always the first month-by-month folder. Some secretaries prefer this arrangement because the folders remain in the same position. In this case, as the folder for each day is emptied, it is placed in position for the next month.

Operation of the Follow-up System

Make an extra copy of correspondence or memos that require follow-up, preferably on paper of a different color. Mark on the extra copy the date on which it is to be followed up. When there is no carbon copy or photocopy of material for follow-up, write a brief memo for the tickler file. For example, if you are supposed to remind your employer about a newspaper clipping on the thirtieth of the month, prepare a tickler memo for follow-up on the thirtieth, but file the clipping so that you can put your hands on it if your employer wants it before the thirtieth. The memo should indicate where the material is filed. File any pertinent papers in the regular files.

Figure 5. Diagram of Follow-up Files

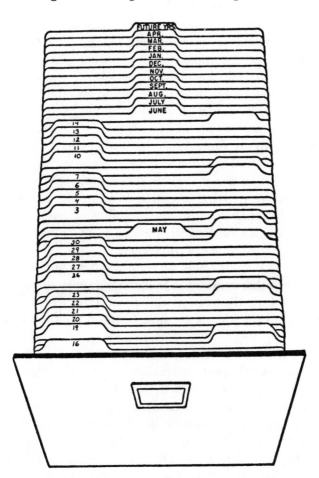

Place material that is to be followed up in the current month in the proper date folders. Each day transfer the empty daily folder to a position in back of the folder for the forthcoming month. Thus you always have thirty-one daily folders for follow-ups, part of them for the remaining days in the current month and part of them for the first part of the forthcoming month. Place material that is to be followed up more than thirty or thirty-one days in the future in the proper month folder, regardless of the day of follow-up. See figure 5, which is a diagram of the arrangement of folders on April 16. On that day, current material to be followed up from April 16 through May 14 is placed in daily folders: material to be followed up after May 14 is placed in the proper month folder. Material that had already been placed in the May folder will not be refiled in the daily folders until May 1.

On the first of each month, transfer the material from the folder for that month into the folders labeled by days. To avoid filing material for follow-up on Saturdays (if the office closes), Sundays, or holidays, reverse the folders for those days so that the blank side of the label faces the front of the file. (Some secretaries tape or staple a small pocket-size calendar to the front of the tickler file for checking weekend and holiday dates and making special notations.) The empty folder for the current month is transferred to the rear of the other month-by-month folders—or to its proper sequence if that arrangement is used.

Daily follow-up of material.   Each day when you examine your follow-up file, you will find that a large part of the correspondence has been answered without a follow-up. Destroy these copies or memos. If a heavy schedule keeps you from giving attention to all of the material in the daily folder, mark the less important items for follow-up on a later date. Move indefinite follow-ups forward from week to week until a definite date is established or until the matter is completed.

Follow-ups on a small scale.   When you have only a small amount of correspondence or other matters to follow up, a set of follow-up file folders is not necessary. Mark the copies with the follow-up date and file them chronologically in one folder, with those marked for the earliest follow-up on top.

Tickler card files for follow-up.   A tickler card file is as useful as follow-up file folders for most material, except correspondence. You can type a notation for yourself on a 3- by 5-inch card and place it in a tickler card file as easily as you can type a memo and put it in a file folder. But it is a waste of time to make a card notation of correspondence when you can make a photocopy so easily. Therefore, unless you have only a small amount of correspondence to follow up, and handle it as described in the preceding paragraph, use follow-up folders instead of a card tickler.

Use of Computers and High-Speed Equipment

There are times when the process of following up also requires the collection of massive amounts of information—too much for a secretary to begin searching for manually in the regular files.

Types of high-speed follow-up.   Follow-up systems that often require a fast method of data collection may involve business records, such as accounts payable and receivable. (See chapter 9.) Follow-up systems, in fact, are used with almost all items that require renewals or sequences of notices, such as invoices, purchase and job orders, leases and mortgages, various types of applications, tax and checks, records, bids, and insurance files, to name just a few. Often it is not enough for a secretary to be reminded to follow up something, such as past-due accounts. The facts related to some accounts must also be reviewed, and many companies have turned to high-speed equipment to locate such information instantly.

High-speed follow-up equipment. Some data-retrieval machines are electronically coded to locate and convey regular files in a matter of minutes or seconds. The computer is used regularly in offices of all sizes to process information, store it, and print it out later when follow-up action is needed. (See **COMPUTERS AND OTHER AUTOMATED PROCE-DURES,** page 36, for more information on automated storage and retrieval and information processing by computer.)

EFFECTIVE REMINDER SYSTEMS

Calendars You Should Keep

Office-supply stores have three basic styles of calendars: wall, desk, and pocket. *Wall calendars* are usually designed to show one day or one month at a glance and occasionally a full year or several years. *Desk calendars,* sometimes called diaries or journals, are available in a wide choice of sizes and types, including pads, book styles, combination memo-appointment, ring binders, spiral bound, and plastic or leather bound. They may be day-at-a-glance, week-at-a-glance, or month-at-a-glance versions. Most allow space for each day to write in appointments and memos. However, only certain styles have appointment spaces broken down into fifteen- or thirty-minute intervals. *Pocket calendars* are small versions of desk calendars that can be carried in one's pocket or in a purse.

Three essential calendars. You will probably decide on three general categories of calendar for your office.

1. Your own calendar. Either a standard desk calendar pad or a yearbook, with fifteen-minute or thirty-minute time divisions, would be a good choice in most situations. Many secretaries prefer desk calendars because the day's activities are then before their eyes constantly. To help you schedule your time during and after normal working hours, you might also keep a personal pocket/purse calendar to note special or additional work projects that might conflict with personal activities.

Enter notations of your own activities and business appointments as well as your employer's appointments and the things that you will have to remind him or her about. Enter any time-consuming task that must be done by a certain date sufficiently in advance to permit it to be done on time.

Always check each calendar—yours and your employers—early Monday morning. Scan the entire week so that you have in mind appointments and events planned several days ahead.

    2. Your employer's calendar.   Again, a standard desk calendar pad or a yearbook would serve most purposes. Many executives prefer a yearbook because its contents are not visible to callers. The calendar or yearbook must be large enough to enable you to note the caller's affiliation and purpose of the call.

    Enter all of your employer's appointments and the important days, such as a spouse's birthday. Do not enter items that are merely reminders to you, such as the date certain checks should be written. Although you enter reminders before the actual date on your own calendar, it usually is not necessary to do this on your employer's calendar. Watch your employer's calendar closely for appointments he or she makes without telling you.

    3. Your employer's pocket memo calendar.   Note in a small pocket memo book engagements that might conflict with future appointments your employer makes. This memo book is for your employer to take to meetings, luncheons, on trips, and the like, where questions of future appointments might arise.

How to Make Up the Calendars

    Preparing the calendar.   Keep a list of events that go on the calendars year after year (see checklist, page 45). Early in October, enter all of the recurring items, events, and engagements for the forthcoming year in the calendar for the next year. If your employer makes important engagements far in advance, you may have to make up the yearly calendars even earlier. In preparing calendars, work from the list and not from the current year's calendar, because the dates for the events change. For example, if board meetings are held on the first Monday of every month, the actual dates vary from year to year. In making an entry, be certain that the date is not a Sunday or a holiday. Enter notations of additional appointments or things to do as soon as you learn about them.

    Keep used calendars for one year—or longer if your employer wishes. Calendars are often necessary for reference at tax-preparation time or in verifying dates such as travel periods and special engagements.

    Using the calendar as a communications tool.   With a growing trend toward better teamwork in the modern office, the calendar provides a better-than-ever opportunity for employer-secretary and secretary-clerical assistant communication. When a good calendar-notation system is used, everyone becomes more aware of total office activities, and everyone works more closely in scheduling events that don't conflict with other work. Moreover, an expert secretary anticipates the needs of your employer and other personnel, and comprehensive calendar systems and tickler files are essential for this.

Checklist of recurring items. Following is a list of recurring items that a secretary usually enters on the appropriate calendars for each year. You may not be concerned with some of them and will probably add many others that apply specifically to your position. If dates usually call for presents or cards, enter reminders about ten days before the date as well as on the date.

1. Family dates such as anniversaries and birthdays
2. Holidays such as Thanksgiving and Memorial Day
3. Meetings such as board meetings
4. Payment dates such as insurance premium due dates
5. Renewal dates such as subscriptions to periodicals
6. Tax dates such as quarterly tax payments

How to Use the Tickler Card File with Calendars

The use of a 3- by 5-inch tickler card file will reduce the necessary work in preparing a calendar.

Basic materials. A tickler card file has a tabbed guide for each month of the year and thirty-one tabbed guides, one for each day of the month. The daily guides are placed behind the current month guide. Notes are made on cards, and the cards are filed behind the daily guide according to the date on which the matter is to be brought up. Be careful not to put a card on a weekend date. Check the next three days each Friday to avoid this.

Filling out the tickler card. Recurring items can be put on one card, and the card can be moved from week to week, month to month, or year to year. Thus if a certain check is made out each Friday, you can make one card and move it each week, instead of making fifty-two entries in the calendar. Furthermore, you can put all necessary information on the card so that you, or anyone else, can make out the check and mail it without referring to any other material.

For example, if interest on a mortgage is payable quarterly, the card would show (1) due dates, (2) amount of interest, (3) to whom payable, (4) where to send check, (5) brief description of property covered by mortgage, and (6) amount of mortgage. See figure 6.

Figure 6.   Interest-Payment Reminder

```
Int. due quarterly—15th of Jan., Apr., July, & Oct.

Amt. $400.   Make check to:  Estate of Harvey Adams
             Send check to:  Mr. Ralph Jones
                             Attorney for Estate of
                             Harvey Adams
                             75 Fifth Avenue
                             New York, N.Y. 10003

Mortgage for $40,000 on 71st Street Dwelling
```

Charge-out tickler files.   A common problem in many offices is the loss of material through lending practices. A tickler charge-out card could be prepared for each withdrawal. A supply of preprinted cards could even be placed in a conspicuous place for borrowers to select one to fill out at times when they remove material in the absence of the secretary (but some offices never allow material to be removed or filed by anyone else). Information should contain the (1) file caption, (2) name of borrower and his or her department, (3) dates of correspondence involved, (4) date of removal, and (5) date for follow-up. The completed card is filed behind the day of the month designated for follow-up, and another charge-out slip is placed in the regular files.

Checking calendars and tickler files daily.   A card tickler file does not take the place of a calendar for noting appointments. All engagements and appointments, even regularly recurring ones, should be entered on the calendar. Refer to both the calendar and the tickler file each morning.

Types of Reminders

An executive might want to be reminded from time to time of a particular matter until it has been acted upon. For example, he or she might want to be reminded to go over a certain file of material. This kind of item should be included from time to time in the typed schedule of appointments and things to do that you place daily on your employer's desk.

Using calendars and tickler files.   There are two ways of reminding yourself of the item:

1. Make a notation on your calendar at short intervals.
2. If you keep a tickler card file, note the item on a card and move the card from time to time.

Using reminder memos. Matters to come to your employer's attention in connection with any unscheduled but definite event are best handled by placing a reminder memo in an appropriately labeled folder for the event. For example, if your employer wants to be reminded to call on a certain customer the next time he or she goes to Chicago and the date of the trip has not been scheduled, make a folder marked "Chicago Trip" and put in it the necessary reminder memo. When the date of the trip is settled, give your employer the entire folder or include the item in a typewritten schedule of matters pertaining to the trip. If the event is of such rare occurrence that you would need a reminder that there is such a folder, do not use a folder but make the notation on your calendar or in the card tickler file as described here.

Reminders of appointments and things to do. Secretaries often compile a daily appointment list in addition to other reminders.

1. Daily appointment list. Each morning place on your employer's desk a "Today's List" of appointments and special things to be done. It is advisable to prepare this list at the end of the previous day's work. Make a copy for your own use.

Figure 7 illustrates a daily appointment list. Memo paper, about 6 by 9

Figure 7.   Daily Appointment Schedule

APPOINTMENTS FOR MONDAY, April 5, 19___

10:00 A.M.	Special Dictation——Speech for Ad Club
10:30	Conference——proposed personnel booklet
11:00	Mr. Simmons——new labor course
12:00	Employees' meeting——annual report on profit-sharing plan
1:00 P.M.	Luncheon at Ad Club with Y & R representatives
3:30	Mr. Dressler
4:00	Executive Committee meeting
5:00	Sales Staff meeting, through dinner

inches, is desirable for this purpose. At the time of each appointment, give your employer any material he or she will need for it. For example, before the 12 noon appointment shown in figure 7 hand your employer the material that has been prepared for making the report.

2.   Other reminders.   To remind your employer of some task, place the file on his or her desk. If your employer wants to do a certain thing in connection with the matter, attach a brief reminder to the file. For example, suppose that you were told, "I want to send a telex message to Robertson on Friday if we don't hear from him." On Friday, you would type a memo, "You wanted to send a telex message to Robertson" and attach it to the Robertson file before placing it on your employer's desk. If possible, draft the message to Robertson and attach it to the folder.

3.   Daily conferences.   Some executives make a practice of calling their secretaries into their offices daily to discuss pending matters and things to be done. A morning conference is an ideal way to keep open the channel of communication. For such a discussion, take with you a list of things to do and any material pertaining to them. Your employer will give you instructions on one matter after another.

Reminders showing appointments for a month.   Many executives like to see the month's engagements at a glance. There are calendars designed for this purpose, usually on cardboard of about 9 by 11 inches. The dates on this type of calendar show every Sunday in the month on the top row, every Monday on the next row, and so on, ending with every Saturday on the last row.

Figure 8 is an example of a four-week schedule, which is typed each week. Note that it lists holidays, evening social functions, and things to be done, as well as appointments. It also indicates days the secretary plans to be out of the office. The question marks indicate uncertainty. (WL stands for "Weekly Letter.") If the schedule is to remain on your employer's desk, he or she might like to have it mounted on cardboard to facilitate handling. Either staple or paste the corners to the cardboard. When your employer is planning to be away from the office for a week or so, he or she usually likes to know what is on the calendar for that period before completing any plans. Use the setup shown in figure 8 for this purpose.

Special reminders.   An executive may find it useful to have a 3- by 5-inch or 4- by 6-inch reminder card each evening when leaving the office. This contains not only a list of activities for the following day but also reminders of certain things that he or she should do at home. Figure 9 is a typical reminder card for an executive who lives in the suburbs.

.Figure 8.   Four-Week Schedule

APPOINTMENTS

Nov. 15 Mon. —   — WL-269
                — 12:00 Noon — Preliminary Meetg. — Cleve. Engrg. Soc.
                — 3:00 P.M. — Apex Bd. Meetg.

"   16 Tues. —   1:30 P.M. — Engineering

"   17 Wed. —   5:30 P.M. — Cath. Char. — Parlor B — Cleve. Athletic Club
                — 6:00 P.M. — ? Union Club—Ohio Pub. Expenditure Coun.—WTH

"   18 Thur. —   6:30 P.M. — Foremen's Dinner — Lake Shore Ctry. Club

"   19 Fri. — 12:15 P.M. — ?Amer. Trade Assn. Executives — Public Libr.
                — 6:? P.M. — Cleve. Engrg. Soc. Panel

Nov. 22 Mon. —   — WL-270

"   23 Tues. —   1:30 P.M. — Engineering

"   24 Wed. —   — Sandusky

"   25 Thur. —   — Thanksgiving

"   26 Fri. —   — Nancy away from office all day
              — Evening   — Apex Dance — Lake Shore Ctry. Club

Nov. 29 Mon. —   — WL-271
                —   — Check to W. Shaw

"   30 Tues. —   1:30 P.M. — Engineering

Dec. 1 Wed. —   — Sandusky

"   2 Thur. —   — Talk at Cincinnati — Wm. Campbell

"   3 Fri. —   —

Dec. 6 Mon. —   — WL-272

"   7 Tues. —   1:30 P.M. — Engineering
                — 6:00 P.M. — Loyal Service Club — Carter Hotel

"   8 Wed. —   — Sandusky

"   9 Thur. —   —

"   10 Fri. — 10:00 A.M. — VCMA Meeting — Hotel Cleveland

49

Figure 9.   Special Reminder Card

Reminder for WEDNESDAY, May 19 19—
Tell Mrs. Adams that her draperies will be delivered Mon.
Get exact dimensions of kitchen cabinet
  8:30—Parent-Teacher gathering at Westchester High
Pack bag for Dinner at Waldorf (White Tie)

10:30——Mr. John Brown
11:30——Portfolio Committee meeting
12:30——Luncheon for Ms. Loni Somes, Pres. Reynolds
           Inv. Assn., at Advertising Club
 2:30——Mr. Smith's office: 250 Broadway, Room 1200
           re: Texas bonds

Evening
 7:30——Reception, Grand Ballroom Waldorf-Astoria
 8:30——Dinner in honor of Dr. Thompson
           Chauffeur will return at 11:00, Park Ave. entrance

How to Prepare a Contact Reminder File

If your employer makes numerous contacts throughout the year, it is difficult for him or her to remember every one and the circumstances of the meeting. Yet it may be necessary to be able to recall names and connections. A contact reminder file is useful for this purpose.

Making up the file.   A looseleaf, leather, or plastic notebook, 5 by $7\frac{3}{4}$ inches or 4 by 6 inches makes a handy contact reminder file for recording the name of each person your employer meets, business and other affiliations, and the circumstances of the meeting. It is advisable to put on the record any personal items that might be helpful to your employer in recalling the individual. Thus if the person sent cigars or flowers at Christmas or a booklet published by his or her company, or if your employer sent the individual or someone related to the individual something special, make an appropriate notation on the record.

── Chapter 2 ──────────

Developing Good Typing and Information-Processing Skills

TIMESAVING EQUIPMENT AND ACCESSORIES

Typewriters and Accessories

Typewriters. Both electric and electronic typewriters are widely used in offices of all sizes in spite of the proliferation of word processors and desktop computers. Industry experts predict that of the two types—electric and electronic—the electronic machines will soon predominate, particularly since they have advanced technologically to compete even with some word processors and computers. Although electric models have many useful features such as self-correcting mechanisms, reverse underscore, and line finders, electronic models have some of the same timesaving features found on word processors and computers. Specific features vary from one model to another, but some or all of the following are possible:

1. Various types of memory are available for storing text: *document memory* (for storing a specified number of pages that can be recalled later); *phrase memory* (for storing common phrases that can be repeated later without retyping each time); *multiple-line memory* (for storing a specified number of lines that can be recalled later); *format memory* (for storing format instructions such as margin settings for repeated use). *Diskette storage*—the ability to transfer text to a diskette for permanent storage—is an add-on feature of high-level electronic typewriters.

2. A *display* is a small screen where you can see one or more lines that

you have typed. Some high-level machines can add on a full-size display screen similar to that of a computer or word processor for viewing part or all of a page.

3. A *spell-checker* is an electronic dictionary that will locate typographical errors and correct them as you specify.

4. Editing features such as *delete, insert,* and *search and replace* enable you to move, rewrite, add, or delete portions of text—before committing the words to paper—without retyping everything else.

5. *Automatic formatting* means that, with one or two keystrokes, the machine will automatically perform certain tasks: centering headings, aligning columns of numbers at the decimal points, underscoring, and so on.

6. Examples of other automatic functions are automatic *carriage return,* whereby the machine decides when to begin the next line, and automatic *paper feed,* whereby the paper will advance to any line down the page that you specify.

Accessories.   Electronic machines and some electric models have interchangeable typefaces. Usually, one typeface comes with the machine and additional faces must be purchased. Several types of ribbons are available. In addition to the traditional fabric ribbon, carbon film ribbons —single strike or multistrike—enable secretaries to produce clean, sharp copy. Important correspondence and reports that must be reproduced by photo-offset printing are often typed with carbon film ribbons. The correcting typewriter, which "lifts" errors from the page, has replaced correcting supplies in many offices. With noncorrecting typewriters, however, the secretary still has a variety of such supplies to draw from: correction fluid such as Liquid Paper, correction tape or paper such as KO-REC-COPY, and standard and electric erasers. Traditional correcting procedures are described below in **CORRECTING TYPING ERRORS,** page 70.

Word Processing Systems

Used broadly, the term *word processing system* could be applied to any machine or group of machines capable of handling text. This would include electric and electronic typewriters, magnetic-tape typewriters, computers, and dedicated word processors (computers that primarily handle text). But electric typewriters have no memory or display capability, and even high-level electronic models generally cannot match capabilities of a computer or word processor. Magnetic-tape machines are now considered nearly obsolete since they, too, have no display capability such as that of a computer or word processor. Therefore, *word processing* usually refers to the handling of text by a computer or word processor. The two main types of word processing systems are the stand-alone system and the shared system. (For more information on steps in word processing, see **How to Make Corrections with a Computer or Word Processor,** page 73.)

Stand-alone system. A stand-alone system may be a computer configuration of any size (such as a small portable computer, standard word processor, or a large mainframe computer). But to be considered a stand-alone system, it must be able to operate or function by itself. Therefore, it would have to have its own keyboard, display screen, hard disk or diskette drive mechanism, central computing logic, and printer. If it lacks one part of the configuration such as logic or memory capability, and has to be connected to a large central computer to function, it is not a stand-alone system. However, a number of stand-alone computers can be linked in some way to communicate with one another. In a local area network (LAN), for example, the computers communicate through direct wiring of one to another rather than over the telephone lines.

The following are the main parts of a stand-alone system:

1. Keyboard. Some keyboards are attached to the cabinet and others are thin, lightweight, detached, movable units, connected to the cabinet by a cable. The keys resemble those of the standard QWERTY typewriter keyboard, except there are additional keys used to perform editing and other functions.

2. Display screen. The television-like monitor shows the words you type as you type them. Size and colors of the screen display vary. Standard screens on the personal computer (PC), for example, usually display up to twenty-four lines of type up to eighty characters wide. Portable PCs have only about half of that capacity, whereas some larger workstation screens display up to sixty-six lines up to eighty characters wide. A popular screen display color is green letters on a black background, although some people prefer another combination such as amber or white on black.

3. Central processing unit (CPU). The brains of the configuration is the CPU. This is the control part of a system where the performance of various tasks is made possible. CPUs operate at different speeds measured in binary units, or bits. Thus a thirty-two-bit unit would normally work faster than an eight-bit unit.

In computer language, eight bits equal one *byte,* which is a character or space, and a thousand bytes is usually expressed as 1K. Hence if you read about a portable machine that has a memory of 64K, it can retain up to

64,000 bytes at one time. Therefore, if a page of text has two thousand spaces and characters, or bytes, the machine can hold thirty-two pages of text in memory at any one time.

4. **Storage.** Two types of storage are involved in a computer system. Internal storage, or memory, refers to the capacity in a system for retaining what you type while you're working on a document. This is known as "random-access memory," or "RAM." But RAM is temporary. To save your document, you must transfer it to permanent storage, for example, on a *diskette* (a magnetic medium that looks like a small phonograph record) or a separate larger capacity hard disk or built-in larger capacity Winchester disk. Otherwise, when you shut off the machine, everything that you typed, which is temporarily stored in RAM, will be wiped out.

Another type of memory is called "ROM," for "read-only memory." This is the information put into a machine during manufacture. Unlike RAM, the information in ROM can only be "read" by the machine; you cannot input your own data there and edit it as you can do with RAM.

5. **Printer.** The unit that automatically "types" the text that you see on the display screen in the printer. A great variety of printers are available, differing most significantly in speed and quality of type. Most letter-quality printers use ribbons like a typewriter and produce clean, sharp copy. Other printers form letters out of tiny dots (dot-matrix printers) and produce relatively inferior copy, although usually at much higher speeds.

Like actual typewriters, printers have a variety of features such as controls for spacing. Paper is fed into the machine by an attachment. *Sheet feeders* automatically insert individual loose sheets of paper into the printer. *Tractor feeders* have sprockets that pull up perforated, continuous-form sheets of paper that must be separated later.

Shared systems. There are two types of shared systems: shared logic and shared resource. A *shared-logic system* consists of "dumb" terminals (usually, only a keyboard and display screen) connected to a large central computer. In this case, the individual workstations "share" the logic and memory of the central computer. A *shared-resource system* also consists of individual terminals connected to a central computer, but each workstation has some memory and its own processing unit. Therefore, each terminal can function on its own when the central computer is temporarily down for repairs.

Time sharing. When a number of users share a computer simultaneously, it is referred to as "time sharing." Often the users are in various remote locations and access the central computing source over the telephone lines. Frequently, one organization owns the central computer and sells time to outsiders. Since delays are possible during times of heavy use, time sharing is less desirable for word processing than for other types of work.

Integrated Voice-Data Terminals

Voice-data integration is a term applied to the concept of transmitting both speech and data through the same network or to the idea of combining both speech and data in computer use. In either case, one objective of business users is to combine voice and data communications rather than have the expense of using or maintaining separate voice networks and data networks. In other words, rather than set up and maintain one network for text or other data transmission and another for telephone or voice communication, you would have a combined, or integrated, system capable of sending both types of messages.

Some of the use of voice-data capability today as an integrated function is through a device attached to office telephone systems. In voice-mail, for example, voice messages are converted into signals that are stored within a computer and later played for the receiver. Research in the area of voice-data operations is concerned not only with the record-and-playback function but with the conversion of text to speech. Since voice-data integration is a relatively young technology, it is not yet cost effective, and use is still somewhat limited to large organizations.

Telecommunications Interfaces

An *interface* is a link or connection between two systems. Computers and dedicated work processors often use the telephone lines to communicate with other computers and dedicated word processors. For this to work, the digital signals that a sending computer generates have to be converted to the analog signals that will travel over a telephone line. Then at the destination the signals have to be converted again from analog back to digital in order for the receiving computer to be able to accept the message.

A small device that will handle the conversion of signals is the *modem* (modulator-demodulator). By placing a telephone receiver on top of the modem, connecting the modem to the computer, and dialing the appropriate telephone number, a typed computer message can be converted into a form that will travel over the telephone lines. Communicating computers can thus send electronic messages, tap into *databases* (electronic libraries) to do research, and interact with a voice-mail system.

BASIC TYPING RULES

Good typing skills—with or without the benefits of word processing equipment—depend on a thorough understanding of basic typing techniques. The following sections describe the basic typing rules that every secretary should know.

Following the Standard Rules for Spacing

Usage has established the following standard rules for spacing:

No Space
Before or after a dash, which is two hyphens
Before or after a hyphen
Between quotation marks and the matter enclosed
Between parentheses and the matter enclosed
Between any word and the punctuation following it
Between the initials that make up a single abbreviation *(COD)*
Between the initials in a traditional state abbreviation *(N.J.)*

One Space
After a comma
After a semicolon
After a period following an abbreviation
After a period in a person's name *(R. A. Jones)*
After an exclamation mark used in the body of a sentence
Before and after "X" meaning "by" (3" X 5" card)

Two Spaces
After a colon
After every sentence
After a period following a figure or letter at the beginning of a line
   in a list of items

Never separate punctuation from the word it follows. For example, do not put a dash at the beginning of a line.

Typing Numbers and Fractions

Typing numbers in columns. When typing columns of arabic numbers, plan the spacing so that the right-hand edge is even (use the tabulator). Roman numerals are often aligned at the left margin.

3,078	VII
99·	XI
204	M
12	XIX
5	II

Typing numbers in letters or manuscript. Follow one of two standard rules:

1. Spell out numbers of less than one hundred and large round numbers—such as five hundred—except in paragraphs having large uneven numerals.
2. Spell out numbers one through ten except in paragraphs having other numbers above ten.

Rule 1 is often used in nontechnical and nonscientific matter and rule 2 is often used in technical and scientific matter.

Typing fractions. Fractions are hyphenated when the numerator and denominator are both one-word forms, such as *one-third* and *one-hundredth,* but omit the hyphen between the numerator and the denominator when either one or the other, or both, contain hyphens, such as *one twenty-fifth* and *twenty-five thirty-sevenths.*

Making Special Characters Not on Your Keyboard

Although modern equipment offers a wide variety of special characters—and you can custom order the characters you especially need—you also can overtype one standard character with another to form special characters that may not be on your typewriter keyboard.

¶	Paragraph mark	P and 1
÷	Division sign	colon and hyphen
£	Pound Sterling sign	f and t, or L and f
ç	Cedilla beneath "c"	c and comma
!	Exclamation sign	apostrophe and period
≐	Equation sign	hyphen—use ratchet detent lever and turn platen slightly
[	Brackets	underscore and diagonal
≠	Plus sign	hyphen and apostrophe; hyphen and diagonal
⌐	Caret	underscore and diagonal
§	Section sign	Strike lowercase s, backspace, roll platen forward, strike s again

§   Section sign   Strike lowercase *s*, backspace,
                                        roll platen forward, strike
                                        s again

TIMESAVING TYPING PROCEDURES

Word processing equipment is noted for the time you can save with it in editing documents. Instead of retyping a page or several pages each time you make a change, you merely type the correction or revision and let the computer readjust the rest of the copy accordingly. Then you can instruct the printer to print out the revised pages. However, some difficult tasks may be handled by electric or electronic typewriter rather than computer or word processor, and timesaving techniques are especially helpful in those cases. Sometimes the same procedures are useful in both typewriter and computer preparation. In both cases, for instance, it always pays to plan ahead and organize your work.

How to Organize Work and Plan Ahead

Most tasks are best handled when you have everything you need and you can work for long stretches without interruption. Frequent interruptions and disorganization where typing is concerned lead to disastrous results such as omissions, oversights, errors, and reduced speed and thus lower output. The section **Managing Time and Money,** page 275, in chapter 10 describes ways to accomplish more in less time, and the section **Typing and Dictation Shortcuts,** page 79, in this chapter also has some valuable timesaving tips. Two things in particular will help you save time in typing duties: organizing your work load and planning ahead, or scheduling.

Organizing your work.   With both typewriter and word processor preparation, know precisely what you will need before you begin typing. Arrange papers and other reference material you will have to consult on your desk in the order you will need it. Place everything within reach. Once you are seated by the typewriter, you shouldn't have to move away to reach for a file or search for an address. Similarly, have all of the tools you might need—correction supplies, paper, paper clips, diskettes, and so on—within arm's reach without moving away from the typewriter. Arrange your material in the order you plan to type each document, so that you can go from one project to another without interruption and without getting up from the keyboard between jobs.

Planning ahead.   At the beginning of each day, review your calendar (see chapter 1, page 43) several days ahead and schedule your work in logical categories. Except for rush work, you can segregate filing duties from typing duties, research from billing, and so on. Perhaps you have quiet periods during the day or on certain days when you could schedule typing for uninterrupted periods. Or perhaps you know that a report must be typed at the end of the week. By planning ahead, you can schedule the typing at the most advantageous time. You wouldn't, for example, want to start late in the day and then have to put everything away overnight and take it all out again the next morning. List your typing projects in order of importance and handle as many priority items as you can in one sitting. Until you become expert at scheduling your own work, don't hesitate to make up long, detailed work-to-do lists and to group and regroup various tasks until everything is scheduled in the most logical, efficient order.

How to Type on Printed Forms and Ruled Lines

Typing on printed forms.   When preparing to type on printed forms, check their alignment by holding several copies up to the light or against a window, before typing them.

Insert all of the forms, without carbon paper, in the machine and then insert the carbon paper as described on page 62.

If your "window test" proved that the printed material on the sheets was not correctly aligned, try sticking a pin through the forms at several points along the extreme margins (do this after inserting the carbon paper), lining up the forms accurately as you do so. Then you can make frequent "pin checks" and adjust the forms as you type.

Use your variable line spacer to align the type so that the tails of the longer letters (*y, p, g,* and the like) rest on the lines printed on the form.

Typing on ruled lines.   When typing on ruled lines, make certain that the typing is adjusted so that the bases of letters that extend below the line of the type such as *y, g,* and *p* just touch the ruled line. This is particularly important in filling out forms and documents that have a lot of ruled lines.

How to Get the Same Number of Lines on Each Page

In typing jobs that run four or more pages, it is desirable, and sometimes necessary, to have the same number of typewritten lines on each page except the first and last. If you are using a computer, the page length can be determined in advance for all pages, and the computer will automatically end each page at a predetermined point. With a typewriter, some machines have a page-end indicator or a numbered strip at the left edge of the platen. With a numbered strip, try the following:

1. Feed each page into the machine in alignment with the number 1.
2. Note the number on which you begin typing the first line of your model page. Start all pages on the same number.
3. Note the number on which you type the last line of your page. Finish all pages on the same number.

If your typewriter does not have a numbered strip:

1. Type the first sheet.
2. Lightly mark the next sheet with pencil.
3. Indicate the first line by having your pencil mark in line with the bottom edge of the first line of type so that you can align your machine on the mark.
4. Make the second pencil mark about four lines before the final line of type so that you can see the pencil mark as it comes out of the carriage. You will then know you have four more lines to type to complete the page.

How to Draw Lines on Work in the Typewriter

Vertical lines are used in some tables, although the trend is to avoid them. To draw vertical lines with a typewriter, release the platen as for variable spacing. Roll the platen up while holding a pencil or pen point firmly at the desired spot, not through the ribbon. Some typewriters have a special place to insert a pencil when drawing lines. Remember to hold the pencil firmly. Brace it against the machine, if you like. Or you can hold the pencil or pen point in the fork of the ribbon guide while rolling the platen. Horizontal lines are easily drawn with the underscore key.

How to Type Above and Below the Line of Type

Subscripts (typed below the line of type) and superscripts (typed above the line of type) are used in chemical formulas, to express degrees of temperature, and to refer to footnotes. With a word processor, depending on your software and printer capabilities, you may be able to designate raised or lowered letters with one or two keystrokes. To accomplish this manually on a typewriter, use the line-retainer lever, sometimes called the "line-position reset." When this lever is used, the platen can be revolved to any point to write the subscripts or other characters. When the lever is engaged again you will be able to return the platen to precisely the same spacing position at which you were originally typing.

The line-retainer lever is not the same as the variable line spacer. Although the variable line spacer will permit you to revolve the platen freely, it will not permit you to return the platen automatically to the same relative spacing position.

Always use this automatic line finder when feeding typed material back and forth in preference to rolling the material into position without using it. The use of the line finder not only permits much quicker positioning but also helps to prevent carbon smudges and wrinkling.

How to Center Headings

Computers, word processors, and many typewriters center headings automatically with one or two keystrokes. But if your typewriter does not center headings automatically, follow this procedure: Count the letters, spaces, and punctuation marks in the heading. Subtract one-half the number from the point on the typewriter scale that coincides with the center of the paper. (For example, if the paper extends from 0 to 102 on the scale, the center of the paper will be at 51 on the scale). The remainder will show the point on the typewriter scale at which the heading must begin. Thus if your heading contains 26 characters, and your center point is 51, your starting point will be 38, that is, 51 minus one-half of 26.

The starting point may also be determined by beginning at the center point and backspacing once for each two characters in the heading while spelling out the heading. In spelling the heading, include spaces and punctuation as though they were letters. This will place the machine at the proper starting point.

If part of the left margin is to be used for binding, the starting point will be moved toward the right by one-half the number of spaces cut off for binding. For example, if 35 is the starting point gauged by the entire width of the paper, and 10 spaces are to be allowed for binding purposes, the starting point will be 40.

How to Use the Tabulator

You should use the tabulator for more purposes than typing tables. Among the uses of the tabulator are paragraph indentations, placement of the dateline in letters, placement of the complimentary close and signature line, and arranging columns in tables. Tabulator points are usually set as part of the format instructions with a computer. With a typewriter, you can use the scale to judge positions of settings.

How to Feed Numerous Sheets of Paper

Paper is automatically fed into a printer one sheet after another with a sheet feeder or in perforated, continuous-form packs with a tractor feeder; after the document is printed, the attached sheets must be pulled apart at the perforations. With typewriters, paper must sometimes be fed into a machine in groups including numerous carbon sheets, although some offices no longer use carbon packs and instead make photocopies. But if carbon packs are needed, it can be difficult to insert numerous sheets of paper or bulky carbon packs in the typewriter. Try these methods:

1. To insert a bulky pack, release the paper feed and insert the paper sheets and carbon into the feed roll; then return the release lever.

2. Feed the paper sheets in without carbons, rolling the platen knob enough for the paper feed rollers to get a grip. Then insert carbon sheets one by one, making sure the shiny, or carbon, side faces you. Then twirl the pack into typing position.

3. Several sheets of paper and carbon may be inserted in the typewriter easily by placing them beneath the flap of an envelope. The platen, however, does not grasp a large pack as readily, and the

Figure 10. Device for Feeding Paper to Typewriter: Process of Making Device

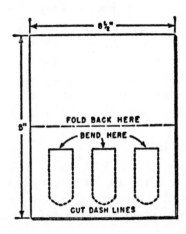

Figure 11.   Device for Feeding Paper to Typewriter, with Papers Inserted

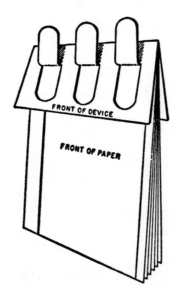

alignment is not as perfect as when the device described below is used.

4. When you have a very large pack to insert, try making this device (see figures 10 and 11):

   a. Fold a 5- by 8 $\frac{1}{2}$-inch strip of flimsy manila tag (an inexpensive file folder will do) across the center, lengthwise.
   b. Cut three U-shaped slots across the upper half of the folded strip, about one-half inch from the crease
   c. Lift up and bend backward the tongues formed by the slot.
   d. Insert the assembled sheets of paper in the folded strip.
   e. Feed the tongues from the U-slots into the typewriter. The platen grasps them more readily than it does a thick pack of paper.
   f. Remove the folded strip before beginning to type.

How to Address Envelopes Quickly

Some secretaries prefer to type envelopes with a typewriter rather than try to feed them into a printer. To address envelopes by typewriter, do the following:

Fold a piece of heavy paper through the center. Insert the folded end into the roller of the typewriter and roll it through until it extends about an inch above the front scale. Now insert the envelope at the front of the roller, behind the folded paper. (The flap of the envelope should be at the top, turned away from you.) Turn the roller back as many spaces as you need to bring the envelope to the proper position for addressing. Type the address and then turn the roller up enough spaces for you to lift out the envelope. The folded paper is then in place for the next insertion.

Chain feeding is a quick method of addressing numerous envelopes. Use the system described in **How to Type Small Cards,** page 65. The envelopes will pile up on the paper table in the same order in which they are typed. This saves you the trouble of re-sorting them.

When the flaps on the envelopes you are typing are thick or wide, your typing may be ragged. It is then better to chain-feed from the back of the platen. To do this, open the flap of the next envelope to be typed and insert it between the first envelope and the paper table, before removing the first envelope. A twirl of the platen knob removes one envelope and automatically brings the next one into position to be typed. Prepare your envelopes in chains of three when using this system.

How to Type Rush Telegrams and Memos

Telegrams and other rush messages are often sent by telex or facsimile (see chapter 4). If you must prepare an urgent message by typewriter, it is not necessary to remove other work. Just do the following:

1. Backfeed the paper and carbons that are in the machine until the paper shows a top margin of about two inches.

2. Insert the first sheet of the rush work behind the material you are typing, against the paper table, just as if nothing were in the typewriter.

3. To make carbons of the telegram, insert the second sheet of the telegram against the coated side of the carbon paper that is already in the machine. Thus the second sheet of the telegram is between the carbon and the second sheet of your letter. Do the same for each carbon that you have in the typewriter. (You must insert a sheet for each carbon in your machine to prevent the typing from showing on the carbon copies of your work.) For additional copies add carbon sheets in the usual manner.

4. Turn the platen knob until the telegram blanks are in position for typing.

5. After typing the message, backfeed until you can remove the telegram from the machine.

6. Forwardfeed to the point at which you stopped writing your letter or other work and continue with your typing.

How to Type Small Cards

It is easier to type a series of small cards by typewriter if you chain feed them from the front of the platen. After typing the first card, feed backwards until the card has a top margin of about three-quarters of an inch. Insert the next card so that the bottom of it will be held in place by the card just completed. Each succeeding card will be held in place by the card preceding it. The cards automatically pile up against the paper table in the order in which they are inserted in the machine.

How to Type Narrow Labels

By using this simple system, you will be able to type narrow labels by typewriter with both hands, thus avoiding typing with one hand while holding the label with the other:

1. Make a horizontal pleat about an inch deep in a sheet of paper.

2. Feed the sheet of paper into the machine in the regular way, maintaining the pleat so that the folded edge will be up when the material is in writing position. This pleat will form a shallow pocket.

3. When the pocket appears at the front of your platen, insert the label, or several of them, in the pocket.

4. Feed all material back so that you can type on the label.

How to Type Stencils and Masters

Each duplicating process—fluid, stencil, offset, and so on—uses its own stencil or master. Instructions for the use of each type accompany the package of stencils or masters. The following sections describe procedures in using a mimeograph stencil and an offset master.

Stencils.   Before you start typing a stencil, move your ribbon to the white or stencil position and clean your typewriter key faces with a cleaning brush and fluid. Next, place the stencil cushion sheet between the stencil and its backing sheet with the glossy side of the cushion sheet facing the stencil. Insert the packet into the typewriter and position it for typing according to the guide marks on the front of the stencil. (The face of the stencil has markings that show the area within which you must type.) Set the impression adjustment to a stencil or medium setting and begin typing as you normally would. (See also **How to Make Corrections on Carbons and Stencils,** page 71.)

Masters.   Paper masters for offset-press reproduction also have guide marks delineating the area in which you can type. Before inserting the master, clean the type faces on your machine with a stiff brush and wipe off any grease or oil on the platen that would stain or smudge the master. Use an offset carbon ribbon (or an offset typewriter ribbon or a standard carbon ribbon). If you use a carbon ribbon, put a backing sheet between the offset master and the platen. Insert the master carefully to avoid cracking and creasing it and use a low pressure setting on your typewriter. (See also **How to Make Corrections on Carbons and Stencils,** page 71.)

CARBON COPIES AND PHOTOCOPIES

Modern Photocopy Equipment

Copiers are made for any size operation, and some of the small copiers have features once common only to larger, more expensive machines. Photocopiers may be wet (using fluid) or dry (no fluid to change). Speed varies greatly depending on the model and size. Some copiers must be hand fed one sheet at a time; others will automatically feed large stacks of sheets at high speed. Certain models provide two-sided copying, digital quantity selection, reduction capability, sorting and collating, and computer-forms feeding. Some equipment already approaches facsimile capability (see chapter 4). Quality of copied material also varies from machine to machine. Some models reproduce material on low-quality paper, with a low-quality type image. Others use any type of paper and produce sharp, clear images, including extremely high art-quality reproduction.

Multiuses for Photocopies

The modern business office could not function without a photocopier. The following are the most common uses of copiers:

1. To make *exact* duplicates of an original

2. To make duplicate *file* copies (instead of carbon copies) or cross-reference copies

3. To make a number of copies—too few for a duplicator or offset press but too many for carbon copies

4. To save time when another method of duplication (carbon copies, mimeograph) would be more time-consuming

5. To inform others quickly and easily by sending them a copy of something

Keeping a Photocopy Log

To control costs and to assign costs to the appropriate accounts in bookkeeping, offices usually keep a record of copies made. You could develop a log for this purpose by typing a master form and thereafter making photocopies to use in the actual recording. The log might be an $8\frac{1}{2}$- by 11-inch sheet with ruled columns, or you might use a preruled page from a columnar (accounting) notebook. Column headings should include *Date, Number of Copies Made, By Whom, For (Purpose)*, and any other information required by your firm. Keep the log next to the copy machine with a sign posted on or next to the copier stating that all users *must* make a log entry.

Selection of Carbon Papers

Some copiers must use a special paper; others (plain-paper copiers) will accept almost any paper that you wish to use, such as regular bond typing paper. Carbon papers are different. There are basically two types of carbon papers: traditional wax carbon and solvent-coated carbon. The solvent papers usually last longer, give cleaner impressions, and produce more uniform copies. With traditional papers, select the heaviest carbon paper that will yield a sharp impression. Thin paper is required for making a large number of copies at once, whereas heavy paper, because of its durability, should be used if only one or two copies are needed. Carbon paper is offered in different weights and in a film or plastic grade, for example:

Type	Yield
Lightweight	1 to 10 copies
Medium weight	1 to 5 copies

Heavy	
weight	1 to 2 copies
Film (plastic)	1 to 10 copies

Depending on the manufacturer, the weights may be identified numerically, for example, no. 5 (one to eight copies) and no. 7 (one to four copies).

Carbon paper is made in several colors. Black is used universally; blue is the prevailing color for pencil carbon work. Carbon imprint shows up better on white, yellow, or pink sheets than on blue, green, russet, or cherry.

To avoid curling and wrinkling, keep carbons carefully in the desk, with the coated side down, out of the sunlight, and away from steam pipes. Film (or plastic) paper, being more durable, can be kept and used longer, and one can make up to ten copies at a time with it.

Some offices are concerned primarily with speed and convenience and not with any particular selection of color or weight in the preparation of carbon copies. Two popular products meeting those requirements are the treated carbonless paper (multiple sets not requiring any carbon paper between sheets) and the single sheet of tissue with a single sheet of lightweight carbon paper attached at one end. The best way to make a choice is to ask your local office-supply store to give you samples and prices of each that you can use to compare results.

Shortcuts in Using Carbon Papers

1. Take a small triangle off the upper left corner of the carbon paper so that when you take hold of the upper left corner, you are grasping the writing paper but not the carbon. Let the carbons extend slightly beyond the bottom edge of the copy sheets. This makes separating the copy sheets from the carbon easier. (Carbon paper can be bought with the corner already cut.)

2. To insert red figures or letters in the carbon copy of a report without removing the report from the typewriter, simply insert a small piece of red carbon behind the black carbon in the desired position, type the red copy, remove the red carbon, and proceed with the work.

   A sheet of heavier paper placed at the back of a carbon pack will prevent manifold paper from creasing and "treeing" with carbon lines.

How to Type on Carbon Copies Only

Occasionally, you may want to indicate some information on the carbons of a letter that you do not want to show on the original, or perhaps you want it to show on just one or two of several copies. If this is a matter of just a few words, insert a small scrap of paper over the original letter and an additional scrap over each of the carbons on which you do not want the notation to appear. Type the notation and then be certain to remove the scraps of paper. The notation will appear only on those copies before which you did not insert a scrap of paper. (If you use larger pieces of paper rather than small scraps you are less likely to overlook one when it is time to remove them.)

Even using a piece of paper over the original, you may get a slight indentation on it. To avoid that, try the following when you want to indicate something on the carbon copies but not the original. If the information is to appear at the top of the carbon copies:

1. Insert your paper in the usual way.
2. Use your paper-release lever to free the paper.
3. Move the carbon pack an inch or so above the original.
4. Return your paper release to the "tight" position.
5. Feed the material back and type in the information.
6. Feed the material forward again.
7. Use the paper-release lever and align the original with the carbon pack. Return the paper-release lever to the "tight" position and you are then ready to type your letter.

If the information is to be shown on the bottom of the carbon copies:

1. Position the machine exactly where you want the material to appear.
2. Use your paper-release lever.
3. Slip the original out of the machine without disturbing the carbon pack, engage the paper-release lever, and begin typing.

Caution: It is necessary to position the machine before removing the original because after the original is removed the first piece of carbon covers up the carbon copy of the letter you have typed. Do *not* try to remove the first carbon sheet. Its removal will smudge the carbon copies and drag them out of alignment.

CORRECTING TYPING ERRORS

Although a skilled typist makes few errors, some corrections are inevitable in most cases. With a computer or word processor, making corrections and other changes is easy, especially if a spell-checker is available to proofread, locate, and automatically correct the typos as you indicate throughout the document. Corrections by electronic typewriter also are relatively easy at least for the material held in the machine's limited memory capacity. But some corrections are not routine. For example, you may need to make a small correction later on a bound page. Or you may have to correct a typewriter-prepared mimeograph stencil. If you do make occasional errors, you can take two steps to correct them: (1) overcome poor typing habits and (2) acquire the art of making neat corrections.

How to Break Poor Typing Habits

For a week or two, make a notation of every typing error you make. Then study and analyze them. You will find repetition of the same type of errors—transposing certain letters, omitting letters, striking one letter in lieu of another one near it, and so on. Practice typing the word in which you made the error and words similar to it. Also, typing books usually have drills that can be used to try to break a bad habit.

How to Correct Typewriter Errors

Making erasures.   If you do not have a correcting typewriter and need to correct errors by erasure, use two erasers—a hard one and a soft one—or a combination eraser. Move the carriage as far to the side as possible so that paper and eraser fragments will not fall into the typewriter mechanism. Start with the soft eraser to remove the excess surface ink. Then change to the hard eraser to remove the imbedded ink. Finally, use the soft eraser again to smooth off the surface. When erasing, rub with short, light strokes. A sharp razor blade may be used on a good grade of paper to remove punctuation marks and the tails of letters.

If you accidentally move the roller or the paper, making it difficult to retype a letter on precisely the spot of the error, try using your stencil lever and make a test. The letter will strike the paper and leave a faint indentation but no black ink that must be erased again if your alignment is off.

Caution: Insert a plastic or steel eraser guard (on many typewriters, your typewriter scale often serves as a guard) between the carbon paper and the copy. The eraser guard is heavy enough to protect the other copies under it. If you use small pieces of paper back of each carbon sheet, you may accidentally leave one of them in your work.

Ask your purchasing department or local office-supply store about available correction supplies. A variety of products are available.

1. An eraser made of glass fibers will permit you to erase on the original without the impression of your erasure going through to the carbon. Be sure to move your carriage to the right or left when using the eraser, and do not handle the glass part of it.

2. Electric erasers, some battery operated, are available.

3. Special correction paper (or tape) is available for coating errors with a white (or other color) substance. (Self-correcting machines have a mechanism that "lifts" the ink of the error from the paper. Self-correcting typing paper and stationery can also be used with a self-correcting machine to improve the correction process even further.) Backspace to the point of the mistake, place the correction paper over the error, and retype the error. This whitens the incorrect letters and results in a blank space in which you can then type the correct word or letter. There is also a companion product for removing errors on carbon copies. These correction papers and tapes are available in different colors to match the color of the typing paper.

4. Correction fluid is popular for work where it is unimportant if the correction is noticeable (such as a rough draft) since it leaves a white blot on the paper (or colored spot, if colored fluid is being used on colored paper).

How to Make Corrections on Carbon Copies and Stencils

Correcting carbon copies.   Corrections on carbon copies are often much fainter than the rest of the typing. To avoid this, make the correction as follows: After the necessary erasure has been made, adjust the ribbon control indicator to stencil position. Put the carriage in the proper position and strike the proper key. This will leave the impression on the carbon copies, but the original will still be blank. Then switch the control indicator back to the ribbon, place the carriage in position, and again strike the proper key. This permits a perfect match of the typing on the original and will leave the typing on the carbon copies with an equal density of color.

Correcting stencils and masters.   Stencils and masters require a slightly different correction procedure.

1.   Stencils.   Be certain to proofread the entire stencil *before* you remove it from the machine (to avoid realignment problems later). Corrections can be made using a special stencil correction fluid. Lift off the film—if there is one—from the stencil sheet before applying the fluid or the film will stick to the stencil. Burnish the error with a paper clip before applying fluid if you are using a cushion sheet (see **How to Type Stencils and Masters,** page 65). Let the fluid dry before making your correction.

2.   Masters.   Proofread the entire master before removing it, since unnecessary handling may smudge or otherwise damage it. If there are any corrections to make, a white offset eraser will remove carbon-ribbon errors (see **How to Type Stencils and Masters,** page 65), but you should use an orange offset eraser immediately afterwards. Once you have removed the master, put a clean sheet of paper over it to protect it until you are ready to have it run.

How to Make Corrections at the Bottom of a Page

To erase on a line near the bottom of the page, do not remove the paper from the typewriter. Simply feed the sheet backward until the bottom edge is free of the platen. Make the erasure and turn the page back into position for typing. (Remember to use your automatic line finder when feeding sheets back and forth.) To erase on a line near the edge of the page, feed the sheet back until the bottom on the paper is free of the platen. Erase and turn the page back into position for typing.

How to Make Corrections on Bound Pages

Corrections can be made on pages that are bound at the top. Insert a blank sheet of paper in the typewriter, as though for typing. When it protrudes about an inch above the platen, insert between it and the platen the unbound edge of the sheet to be corrected. Turn the platen toward you until the typewriter grips the sheet to be corrected. You can then adjust the bound sheet to the proper position for making the correction.

How to Make Corrections with a Computer or Word Processor

The exact procedure to follow in making corrections or other changes with a computer or word processor depends on your equipment and the word processing software program you use. *Word processing software* is a set of instructions for performing text-editing functions. *Systems software,* on the other hand, is a set of instructions to direct the various devices in the computer configuration (such as a printer).

The word processing program and other program instructions are available on diskettes prepared for each type and brand of equipment. These diskettes are inserted into disk drives that "read" the information on the diskettes. To protect magnetic media such as diskettes, you must handle them with care and keep them free of dust. Do not touch the diskette surface or use them around magnets (which can disrupt or remove the data stored on them). The disk drive heads that "read" the diskettes should be kept clean as well. Some users clean them with a cleaning solution applied to a special head-cleaning diskette once a week (or more often).

Starting the program. When you are ready to work on a document, turn on your printer, monitor, and central processing unit (unless you are working at a terminal connected to a large central computer and central printer). Insert your systems diskette; or combined systems-word processing diskette into the left disk drive (if you have dual drives). Most users copy the systems data onto their word processing diskette so that they can start operations and begin the word processing program by inserting only the one diskette.

If your equipment also uses diskettes to store documents (rather than storing data on a separate hard disk or built in Winchester disk), insert a document disk into the right disk drive (of a dual-drive system). Then follow the instructions given with your software for activating your word processing program. Once the program is ready (you will see it on the display screen), you can begin typing or correcting the document. (Remember that procedures are slightly different from one machine to another and from one word processing program to another. Therefore, if you have a personal computer at home and use a word processor or computer at work, you may have to follow different instructions for each one.)

Editing a document. If your software has advance formatting provisions, specify what you want: margins, paragraph indentation, space between lines, tab settings, number of columns, position of page numbers, and so on. If you indicate all of these things in the beginning, the computer will automatically adjust your typing to fit the specifications you have chosen. Since a feature called "wrap" means that the computer automatically moves to another line when the typing reaches the right margin, you can continue typing, except to use the return key to begin a new line or paragraph. Your software also may enable you to use italics, bold-face letters, subscripts or superscripts, and other format elements simply by pressing one or two keys.

As you type, the words will appear on the display screen. With some software, it appears exactly as it will be printed on each page; with other software, the version you see on the screen will not completely fit the format specifications you indicated even though the printed version will match your format instructions.

Making corrections and revisions. With a computer or word processor, you can change a word or a line or a large block of copy simply by selecting what you want to change and deleting or moving it. With some software, you can delete a word simply by backspacing over it. For more extensive corrections you might press cursor keys (keys that move a tiny highlight left, right, up, or down on the screen) and, after highlighting the material to be changed, press other keys that automatically delete the highlighted text or insert it elsewhere.

Some equipment and some software are available with a small hand-held device called a "mouse." By rolling it around on a hard surface, you can move the cursor highlight and accomplish the same thing that you otherwise would do with the cursor keys. Although some secretaries believe that a mouse speeds the editing and correction process, others dislike taking their hands from the keyboard for any reason, believing that they are more likely to create new errors by doing so.

If your software has a search and replace feature, you can type a word you want to find and let the computer locate it. Then you can type the new version and let the computer correct it wherever it appears in the document. A spell-checker is an electronic library of words used by the computer to proofread your document. Some spell-checkers display each questionable word and give you the opportunity to type a corrected version, which the computer then uses to replace the incorrect version wherever it appears throughout the document.

Many other features are available with some software programs. A *help command,* for instance, can sometimes be activated by pressing one or two keys, thereby causing instructions in various areas (such as how to delete text) to appear on the screen. A *merge command* enables you to print two separate documents as if they were one. A *repaginate command* lets you see where the computer automatically ended each page and gives you the opportunity to change the line where the page ends to something else.

These and other timesaving features make correcting text a relatively simple process.

Saving text.   After you have made all of your corrections—or periodically during the editing process—you should transfer the work you are doing from the temporary RAM storage to permanent storage on a document diskette or a hard disk. With some software you can save your work at any time simply by pressing one or two keys. During a later typing session, if you want the text you saved to return to the screen, you must call it out by typing the file name that you gave to the document. The computer will then locate that particular document file on the diskette and show it on the screen.

Printing a document.   Your keyboard will have a "print" key that you press to activate your printer. First, however, you should double-check your format specifications and decide how many copies you want, if you want to print all or a portion of the document, and so on. The flexibility you have in making these decisions depends on the features of your software and the capabilities of your printer. Usually, after you start, you can pause or stop if you change your mind about something. When you have finished, follow your software instructions for making a backup copy of your document and then for terminating the typing session and turning off each piece of equipment. But before you remove and store your diskette in a diskette file, be certain that you have written on the diskette label the name of the document you were working on (follow your program instructions for naming a file). Use only a felt-tip pen to write on a diskette since a hard pen or pencil point could damage the magnetic surface.

BASIC OFFICE PAPERS

Secretaries use both letterhead stationery and plain cotton-content or bond paper in typewriter and word processor text preparation.

Cotton-Content Papers

Quality letterhead has a cotton content, usually 25, 75, or 100 percent cotton. It should be twenty-pound weight or higher, in a white or conservative light color. (See chapter 11, pages 332-35, for information on selecting and ordering stationery.) Lightweight paper used for carbon copies is also available with a cotton content. Quality cotton-content paper may be used for special typing projects, as well as for stationery, where appearance is important, although a high-grade bond is more common for nonstationery uses. Cost is a determining factor in many offices, and cotton-content paper is usually more expensive than bond paper. Also, the higher the cotton content, the more expensive the paper.

Sulfite-Bond Papers

The bond paper used for most typing and word processing projects is a sixteen- or twenty-pound weight. Bond paper is graded according to brightness and opacity. A No. 1 bond is the highest quality. It is often used in place of a cotton-content paper for general stationery. Lower quality bond (Nos. 4 or 5) might be used for duplicating, photocopying, and preparing rough drafts. Carbon-copy paper also is available in sulfite bonds, often in a seven- or nine-pound weight. Offices that are budget conscious should consider the lower quality but more economical bonds for all but the important work. Some firms are using lighter weight (less than twenty pound) papers for drafts and certain routine forms work to cut costs. Although heavier papers are more durable, this factor is not important in many applications.

TAKING AND TRANSCRIBING DICTATION

Dictation and Transcription Equipment

Dictation can be recorded on several forms of magnetic media such as cassettes, belts, and disks. These are *discrete media,* which means you can put them on and take them off the recording machine. You can also send them through the mail, erase and reuse them, and so on. *Endless-loop media* refers to a system that uses a continuous tape, which you don't remove. This is a stationary system unlike the discrete equipment and media.

Travelers like the portable cassette recorders, some of which are so small that they can be carried in one's pocket. Among the larger office systems, *shared recording* (also called *central recording*) is popular for economic as well as convenience purposes. In this situation, all units throughout a company are compatible, that is, they use the same media (which can therefore be ordered in economical quantities and put on any machine), and recorders and transcribers are interchangeable and can be moved from office to office or person to person with no retraining required. Small *work-group systems* integrate desktop dictation units and telephone answering capabilities. Connected to the office telephone system, this type of dictation process is used by persons who share secretarial support (rather than each person having a separate unit or system). *Central systems* are also connected to the telephone system and serve an entire organization. With a centralized configuration, someone can dictate by telephone and the secretary can transcribe later. Such a system may be integrated with word processing, electronic mail, and voice-data communications.

Dictating and transcribing units have numerous timesaving features. One model, for instance, has a digital display that shows where each letter begins and ends and how much tape is left. A search feature automatically locates and plays back instructions, and an alphanumeric readout shows how long each letter is—before it is typed. An insert feature lets you go back and make changes without erasing what you've already done. Another unique feature records and plays messages to callers who phone from anywhere in the world. Because modern technology changes rapidly, you should periodically request current sales information from suppliers to update your files and to remain aware of current innovations.

How to Take Dictation

Shorthand has been completely replaced by dictation and transcription equipment in many organizations. Yet, although many executives dictate by machine, and others write their letters in longhand, some secretaries occasionally must use shorthand. Observing a few simple rules will simplify the process.

1. Make it a practice right away in the morning to sharpen pencils (preferably medium soft lead) and have one or more shorthand notebooks ready, with rubber bands to secure completed pages. Have paper clips handy to clip certain pages together if desired. Finally, have special files or other pertinent material ready to take with you when your employer calls.

2. Use a colored pencil to write or mark special instructions in your notebook.

3. Leave space between letters or somehow keep them separate in your notebook—do not run one into another. There may be changes or copy to insert later and space will be needed then.

4. If your employer does not specify, ask about the type of item: letter, memo, or other; the number of carbon copies and to whom; the addressee's name and address; any other special instructions, such as if there is a "subject" line or enclosures.

5. During dictation, place your notebook on the desk or rest it in a

comfortable position for writing and flipping over filled pages without pausing. Date the first page at the bottom where it is easy to see when paging through the notebook later. Do not hesitate to speak up if the dictator is talking too fast or if you do not understand something. Most of the material you will record in shorthand, but an unfamiliar word is best written out in longhand. Remember that accuracy is of the utmost importance.

6. Take advantage of interruptions to reread your notes and make corrections.

7. After taking the dictation, double-check spelling of names, addresses, and unusual words, and complete your notes as soon as possible.

8. If you are having difficulty, it may be necessary to take a refresher course or at least work on troublesome words and symbols after hours.

9. When you are taking dictation by telephone, always read back your notes and repeat names, addresses, and special instructions.

10. When you are taking dictation at the typewriter, ask if the item will be long or short. Then proceed as if you are typing a draft, not stopping to make careful corrections while typing. Let the dictator read and revise the draft before typing the final copy.

How to Transcribe Dictation

Transcribing the notes, tapes, disks, belts, cassettes, and so on is just as important as taking the dictation. Most secretaries will want to begin as soon as possible, while everything is fresh in mind. If a transcription machine is used, it is necessary to be thoroughly familiar with it before beginning. Observing a few basic rules will simplify the entire process of transcribing.

1. Clear your desk and organize the necessary materials for transcription—stationery, envelopes, erasers, and so on. A copyholder or some support should be set up for the shorthand notebook, and the typewriter should be checked for a fresh ribbon and clean keys.

2. Reread all dictation (or listen to the tapes, disks, belts, cassettes, and so on), organize it in order of importance, and solve problems such

as paragraphing, missing punctuation, or errors in spelling before you begin typing. Most executives will expect their secretaries to polish and rephrase awkward passages.

3. Estimate the length of the letter so that it is positioned attractively on the stationery—this will take practice before you know how much typed copy comes from one of your notebook pages or from a transcription belt or tape.

4. If you cannot find a time of day to transcribe without interruption, have a colored pencil ready to mark the spot on your notebook where you stop each time. A transcription machine will automatically remain at the point where you stop it. When you complete a letter, draw a diagonal line through your notes or on the identification strip that accompanies a transcription belt or tape.

5. Follow your employer's preference for submitting the typed letter to be signed. You may place the addressed envelope over the typed letter along with carbon copies and enclosures and leave it face up on your employer's desk for his or her signature. However, some secretaries submit only the original letter, keeping the carbon copies from which they type the envelopes while waiting for the letters to be signed. After the letters are signed, proceed with filing and mailing, as described in chapters 1 and 4.

Typing and Dictation Shortcuts

Timesaving techniques cut costs and increase productivity. As long as they don't affect the quality of your work, your employer will be favorably impressed with your ability to cut corners and costs. Evaluate each job you undertake in terms of the number of steps involved. Can any steps be eliminated? You may be surprised at the number of shortcuts you can devise with a little ingenuity. For example, try these time savers in taking dictation:

1. To flip pages in your shorthand notebook faster, use a rubber finger on your left thumb and place it on the middle of the page with the other fingers under your notebook. After you have passed the center of the page, move your thumb up until the paper arches at the top. Slip your index finger under the page and grip the sheet between your thumb and index finger. You can now flip the page more rapidly when you reach the last line.

2. To locate telegrams quickly, fold the pages in your notebook that

have telegrams diagonally until they extend outside the book. You can also take your notes directly on a telegram to which you are replying.

3. To see dates of letters easily when paging through your shorthand notebook, place all dates at the *bottom* of the pages.

Also, try these time savers with your typing duties:

1. To type envelopes, drop the envelope between the letter and the platen before you remove the letter. By inserting it to the left of the paper guide, you can use your left margin stop.

2. To type a rush job when something is already in the typewriter, release the roller and backfeed the material already in the machine until you see a top margin of two inches. Insert the rush work back of the other material so that it will come out on top.

3. To judge quickly where to type addresses on form letters, when you prepare the stencil or master, make a pinpoint indentation where the address should begin. This faint impression will appear on all of the forms that are run from that stencil or master.

4. To type superior and inferior letters, use the ratchet-detent lever instead of the variable line spacer to release the roller in typing above or below a line. After you engage the lever, you can return the platen to the same line on which you were typing without having to make further adjustments.

—— Chapter 3 ——————————————

Preparing and Publishing Reports

HOW TO RESEARCH A REPORT

To gather information for a report, you need to know where to go. Even before deciding that, you need to have at least a rough outline of the report—a logical, orderly arrangement of the topics to be discussed in the report. During or after research, you or your employer may add, subtract, or rearrange the topics, but you nevertheless need a preliminary outline, or list, to follow in searching out information. The following sections suggest places to go.

Using Outside Sources

Places to go.   For research outside your own organization, you have several options. The most obvious place to go for most people is the library, usually the public library. In a medium-size or large city, a public library may have a fairly good reference room. If not, check your telephone directory for other nearby libraries in technical-vocational schools, colleges and universities, and research and other specialized institutions. If you are looking for books, don't forget bookstores—college bookstores, general commercial establishments, and so on.

Other places in your community and nearby communities may have the information you need too. Local, state, and federal government offices; schools and institutes; local clubs and civic groups; state or national trade and professional associations; and various other business, educational, and professional groups have magazines, books, reports, and other useful material on specialized subjects. They also have knowledgeable people who can answer questions. You need not be limited to nearby facilities either, unless you especially want to have face-to-face interviews or visit the establishment yourself. Otherwise, you can write or telephone any organization you choose anywhere you wish.

What to take along.   Use your yellow pages and consult out-of-state directories for possible sources. Then make a list of names, addresses, and telephone numbers. Always explain fully what you need when contacting anyone, and try to find out the name of the most appropriate person to speak with; you may have to start by asking for a particular department or by mentioning a logical job title.

Go to interviews well prepared with a list of questions, tape recorder, camera, and anything else you need. As a matter of courtesy, however, ask your subject if he or she objects to a tape-recorded interview or being photographed. For library work, arm yourself with a generous supply of paper and index cards. Use the cards to record each source you consult, so that later you can alphabetize the cards for ease in typing a bibliography.

Using Outside Information

You may use both inside and outside sources of information. Inside material and contacts are often overlooked, although they may be the best ones and the most readily available sources.

Inside sources.   Your own office files—or the files in another office—have a wealth of information. If you get to know other secretaries in your organization, you will likely find them eager to help you track down some elusive fact or figure. You, in turn, should be prepared to cooperate when they are on a fact-finding mission. Interviews, too, are not restricted to outside organizations. Your company probably has numerous experts in various departments who would be happy to answer questions. Your own organization also may have one or more libraries you could visit; perhaps your own office has a small library.

Chances are that your employer is not the only one in your organization who prepares reports. Find out what reports others in the company have written. No need to repeat work that someone else may already done. Don't hesitate to ask others for ideas either. People not only know about places to go, they know about other people, and such referrals can be timesavers. With a little persistence, you will soon have a long list of potential sources of information.

Using Computer-Assisted Research

Computers—in-house and outside—are commonly used to locate and print out information sources, as well as print out the information itself. If your own company has a computer, investigate whether you might be able to collect information with the help of your data-processing personnel. Otherwise, check whether any school, institute, or library in your area offers computerized search services.

Computer-search services.   Some organizations use computers to provide computer-research services for customers. Libraries that have a computer may also provide such services. The process commonly includes taking a list of key words, coding them, and feeding them into a computer. The computer then prints out a list of reference sources that pertain to the subjects identified by the key words. Computer-search services can save a lot of time and effort when you need to locate hard-to-find sources or a large number of sources. Ask at your local library or your local computer-search organization about the charges and how you should prepare the key words for them.

Databases.   With many computers (or microcomputers) or word processors, connected to a modem (modulator/demodulator), you can conduct research by telephone. A *modem* is a device that translates computer information into signals that can be sent by telephone. Thus instead of traveling to a library, you can use this equipment to "visit" electronic libraries called "databases," which have files of information stored in computers. A few sample databases are listed on page 89.

Since there are many databases, and the list is continually changing and growing, ask your local reference librarian for help in locating an up-to-date list of currently available database names, addresses, and telephone numbers. Computer magazines sold on newsstands frequently publish information about databases as well. Some database services provide access to numerous other databases that cover a wide variety of topics—DIALOG and System Development Corporation are two examples (see page 89–90 for addresses). Write to or telephone the sources you select as possibilities and ask about their requirements and charges.

Typically, there will be a subscription fee and/or an hourly rate. Access will be obtained by dialing a password and placing the telephone receiver on your modem. The modem will translate the signals that you receive from the database over the telephone lines into readable data. Depending on the database you access, you will likely receive a list of citations and/or abstracts from available sources of information on the topic you want to research. The database computer, then, checks its index the same as you would check a card catalog and selects books, articles, and other material that contain information about the topic you are researching.

Finding Basic Sources of Information

Using your ingenuity as a guide to information. A secretary needs a little ingenuity. The knowledge of where to look up information is a basic requirement, and one of the more obvious sources of all kinds of information is the library—your company library, the public library, state libraries, and the libraries of other companies and organizations, particularly research organizations. If you visit any of these facilities, do not be afraid that you will not know where to begin—simply explain your problem to the librarian and you will doubtless receive all of the help that you need.

However, many executives want the answer to a question "right now" and you do not always have time to go to the library. Use your ingenuity, then, and think of places to telephone. (The yellow pages of your telephone directory will serve you well on these occasions.) Perhaps your employer wants to know the foreign-exchange rate on a particular currency. Call a commercial bank that has a foreign department. If you need to find the technical term used to describe a certain item, call the manufacturer of, or dealer in, that item if one is available in your locality.

Using the latest available edition of a book. If your fact finding leads you to a particular reference book with a pattern of regularity, order a copy for your office or company library. If you have to go to a library, an idea of the scope of the books that are available in its reference department is necessary.

Using selected reference sources. The following sections list some of the reference books that you may find useful in your fact-finding missions. Ask your local reference librarian for other useful sources.

1. Encyclopedias and fact books. These reference works are invaluable as sources of a wide variety of descriptive information.

Columbia Lippincott Gazetteer of the World (Columbia University Press)

Economic Almanac (Conference Board)

Encyclopaedia Britannica (Encyclopaedia Britannica)

Encyclopedia Americana (Americana Corp.)

Facts on File (Facts on File)

Information Please Almanac (Houghton Mifflin)

International Encyclopedia of the Social Sciences (Free Press)

McGraw-Hill Encyclopedia of Science and Technology (McGraw-Hill)

New American Desk Encyclopedia (New American Library)

New Columbia Encyclopedia (Columbia University Press)

Statesman's Year-Book World Gazetteer (St. Martin)

Statistical Abstract of the United States (U.S. Government Printing Office)

Statistical Yearbook (United Nations)

Van Nostrand's Scientific Encyclopedia (Van Nostrand)

The World Almanac and Book of Facts (Newspaper Enterprise Association)

2. Atlases. An atlas provides detailed maps of places and often other information such as soil and climatic conditions.

Citation World Atlas (Hammond)

Goode's World Atlas (Rand McNally)

International World Atlas (Hammond)

North American Road Atlas (American Automobile Association)

Rand McNally Road Atlas (Rand McNally)

3. Dictionaries, word books, and quotation sources. Dictionaries give spellings, pronunciations, definitions, and other information; word books show spelling, word division, and often pronunciation; and books of quotations are collections of prose, verse, and proverbs from written and spoken sources.

Bartlett's Familiar Quotations (Little, Brown)

Black's Law Dictionary (West)

Dictionary of American Slang (Crowell)

Dictionary of Education (McGraw-Hill)

Dictionary of the Social Sciences (Free Press)

McGraw-Hill Dictionary of Scientific and Technical Terms (McGraw-Hill)

Oxford English Dictionary (Clarendon Press)

Roget's International Thesaurus (Harper & Row)

Stedman's Medical Dictionary (Scribner's)

Technical Terms (McGraw-Hill)

Webster's New World Thesaurus (Merriam)

Webster's Ninth New Collegiate Dictionary (Merriam)

Webster's Third New International Dictionary (Merriam)

4. Style books. Style books are intended to help you in matters such as proper capitalization, punctuation, citation form, and the treatment of written material in general.

Associated Press Stylebook (Associated Press)

The Elements of Style (Macmillan)

Government Printing Office Style Manual (U.S. Government Printing Office)

The Gregg Reference Manual (McGraw-Hill)

The Chicago Manual of Style (University of Chicago Press)

Manual of Style and Usage (New York Times)

Mathematics into Type (American Mathematical Association)

The MLA Style Manual (Modern Language Association)

The Practical Writer's Guide (New American Library)

A Uniform System of Citation (Harvard Law Review Association)

Words into Type (Prentice-Hall)

5. Directories. This type of reference is the best source of names and addresses (and other selected facts and figures) for different professions and fields of business.

American Book Trade Directory (Bowker)

American Medical Directory (American Medical Association)

Congressional Record (U.S. Government Printing Office)

Current Biography (Wilson)

Directory of Corporations, Directors, and Executives (Standard and Poor's Corp., McGraw-Hill)

Dun & Bradstreet Reference Book (Dun & Bradstreet)

The Federal Register (U.S. Government Printing Office)

The Foundation Directory (Foundation Center)

Gale's Encyclopedia of Associations (Gale Research)

Hotel and Motel Red Book (American Hotel Association Directory Corp.)

Kelly's Directory of Manufacturers & Merchants Directory (International Publications Service)

Literary Market Place (Bowker)

Martindale-Hubbell Law Directory (Martindale-Hubbell)

Million Dollar Directory (Dun & Bradstreet)

N. Y. Ayer & Son's Directory of Newspapers and Periodicals (Ayer)

National Directory of Addresses and Telephone Numbers (Concord Reference Books)

National Trade & Professional Associations of the United States (Columbia Books)

Official Airline Guide (Official Airline Guides)

Official Congressional Directory (U.S. Government Printing Office)

Official Guide of the Railways (National Railway Publications Co.)

Patterson's American Education (Educational Directories)

The Standard Periodical Directory (Oxbridge)

Standard & Poor's Register of Corporations, Directors and Executives (Standard & Poor's)

Thomas' Register of American Manufacturers (Thomas)

Ulrich's International Periodicals Directory (Bowker)

U.S. Government Manual (U.S. Government Printing Office)

Webster's Biographical Dictionary (Merriam)

Who's Who (various directories; Marquis)

Writer's Market (Writer's Digest)

6. Indexes. Indexes are guides to published material—titles, subjects, authors, dates of publication, and so on.

Applied Science and Technology Index (Wilson)

Biography Index (Wilson)

Book Review Digest (Wilson)

Books in Print (Bowker)

Business Books and Serials in Print (Bowker)

Business Periodicals Index (Wilson)

Congressional Record Index (U.S. Government Printing Office)

Cumulative Book Index (Wilson)

Education Index (Wilson)

Guide to American Directories (Gale Research)

Guide to Reference Books (American Library Association)

Index to Legal Periodicals (Wilson)

Monthly Catalog of U.S. Government Publications (U.S. Government Printing Office)

New York Times Index (New York Times)

Paperback Books in Print (Bowker)

Public Affairs Information Service Bulletin (Public Affairs Information Service)

Reader's Guide to Periodical Literature (Wilson)

Social Science Index (Wilson)

Vertical File Index (Wilson)

Wall Street Journal Index (Dow Jones Books)

7. Business and financial publications. For current business and financial facts, check some of the following newspapers and periodicals.

Barron's, National Business Financial Weekly

Business Week

Commercial and Financial Chronicle (semiweekly)

The Conference Board Business Record (monthly)

Consumer Reports (monthly)

Current Industrial Reports (quarterly or throughout the year)

Dun & Bradstreet Reference Book (bimonthly)

Dun's Review and Modern Industry (monthly)

Economic Indicators (monthly)

Federal Reserve Bulletin (monthly)

Forbes (biweekly)

Fortune (monthly)

Harvard Business Review (bimonthly)

Monthly Labor Review

Moody's Investors Service, for example: *Bond Record, Manual of Investments, Industrial Manual,* and *Handbook of Common Stocks*

Nation's Business (monthly)

The New York Times (daily)

Prentice-Hall Federal Tax Guide (annual)

Standard & Poor's Corporation, for example: *Corporation Records, Bond Guide,* and *The Outlook*

Survey of Current Business (monthly)

Value Line (loose-leaf service)

Wall Street Journal (daily)

8. Securities. Facts about investments (stocks, bonds, and so on) are available through the publications of various securities services such as the following.

Moody's manuals: *Bank and Finance, Industrial, International, OTC Industrial, Public Utility,* and *Transportation*

Standard & Poor's publications: *Corporation Records, Bond Guide, Stock Guide, The Outlook, Industry Surveys,* and *Stock Market Encyclopedia*

Value Line's report: *Investment Survey*

Wiesenberger Financial Services guide: *Investment Companies*

9. Taxes. Many organizations (for example, H&R Block) publish year-end income tax instruction books, but two publishers in particular have extensive tax services.

Prentice-Hall, Inc., Englewood Cliffs, N.J. 07632

Commerce Clearing House, Inc., P.O. Box 5490, Chicago, Ill. 60680

10. Databases. The following are a few well-known examples of the many available databases in the United States.

CompuServe Information Service (general service: CompuServe, 5000 Arlington Center Boulevard, Columbus, OH 43220)

DIALOG (numerous databases: Lockheed Information Systems, 3460 Hillview Avenue, Palo Alto, CA 94304)

Dow Jones News/Retrieval Service (financial data: Dow Jones & Co., P.O. Box 300, South Brunswick, NJ 08540)

The Information Bank—NYTIS (newspapers and periodicals: New York Times Information Service, Suite 86035, One World Trade Center, New York, NY 10048)

LEXIS (legal data: Mead Data Central, 200 Park Avenue, New York, NY 10016)

SDC Search Service (numerous databases: System Development Corporation, 2500 Colorado Avenue, Santa Monica, CA 90406)

The Source (general service: Source Telecomputing Corporation, 1616 Anderson Road, McLean, VA 22102)

HOW TO ORGANIZE AND WRITE A REPORT

Formal and Informal Reports

Formal reports. A formal report, usually typed on $8\frac{1}{2}$- by 11-inch paper, has all or most of these parts in the order shown:

1. Cover
2. Flyleaf (blank page between cover and title page)
3. Title page (see figure 12)
4. Letter of transmittal (on company letterhead)
5. Table of contents (see figure 13)
6. List of illustrations and tables
7. Abstract (summary of the report)
8. Introduction
9. Background information
10. Data analysis
11. Conclusions and recommendations
12. Appendix
13. Notes
14. Glossary
15. Bibliography
16. Index

Figure 12.   Title Page of a Formal Report

PROPOSAL TO STANDARDIZE
COLLECTION PROCEDURES

Submitted to
Andrea T. Webster
Manager, Accounting Department
Rice Electronics
1103 Northern Boulevard
Chicago, Illinois 60607

Submitted by
Randall H. Rice, Executive Assistant
Management Consultants, Inc.
743 Third Avenue
Chicago, Illinois 60606

May 17, 1988

Figure 13.   Table of Contents

Contents

Abstract vii

Introduction 1

I.   Scope of Collection Activity 4

    Staff 4

    Procedures 5

II.   Review of Current System 7

    Policies and Practices. 7

    Success Rate. 8

    Analysis of Problems. 10

III.   Use of a Standardized System. 14

    Functions in Standardized System 14

    Advantages and Disadvantages 17

    Projected Success Rate 19

Conclusions and Recommendations 23

Appendix: Activity Flow Chart 25

Notes. 28

Tables and charts are sometimes collected after the appendix or grouped and labeled as an appendix rather than scattered throughout the report body.

Informal reports. Short, informal reports are often prepared on memo stationery without any of the preliminary pages (such as title page and table of contents) that are found in a longer, semiformal or formal report. Although the informal report does not have end matter (such as the appendix and bibliography), supplementary material such as a chart or a pamphlet may be attached to the memo. The short, informal report resembles a regular correspondence memo (see chapter 13) in almost every respect, except that it may use short one- or two-word topic subheads in the body.

Parts of the Report

Your office may follow a particular pattern in both formal and informal reports. File copies can be used as guides in that case. Otherwise, observe the guidelines in the following sections.

Title page. Usually, the title page is the front cover, but if a report is enclosed in a binder, the title page is the first page beneath the cover. The items of information on the title page are (1) the title of the report, (2) to whom submitted, (3) by whom submitted, and often (4) the date submitted. See figure 12. Keep the title short—fewer than ten words, if possible. For spacing and arrangement of items, follow the example of figure 12.

Letter of transmittal. The letter of transmittal is placed after the title page. It is usually typed the same as you would type any letter (see chapter 13) on regular company letterhead. The letter should briefly, in about two paragraphs, explain the purpose and scope of the report and the sources of information used. It may acknowledge special help received and refer to special authorizations or requests. The author may also include some other pertinent information or comment, such as calling attention to an important finding, especially pertinent information not included elsewhere in the report.

Preface. Some writers prefer to include a one-page preface instead of a transmittal letter. The preface would contain essentially the same information but would be typed like a regular text page with the heading "Preface" instead of a chapter title.

Table of contents. The table of contents consists of the numbers (if any) and titles of the chapters or topics and the number of the page on which each begins. Prepare the table of contents after the final draft of the report has been completed and the pages numbered. In typing, follow the example of figure 13.

List of illustrations. If the report has a list of illustrations and tables, prepare it in much the same style as the table of contents, with figure and table numbers, titles, and possibly leaders guiding the reader to page numbers on the right. If there are numerous exhibits, it may be preferable to have two lists, one for illustrations such as photographs and graphic matter and one for straight tabular matter such as tables and lists. The illustrations themselves may be scattered appropriately throughout the report, used as appendixes, or collected at the ends of chapters (or all of them after the last appendix). No matter where you position them, *be certain that each one is mentioned in proper numerical order in the text discussion.*

Abstract. The report may include an abstract. This is a condensed summary of the report, briefly stating the objective and summarizing the results of the research and the author's conclusions. It may vary in length from a few paragraphs to more than a hundred pages. Many writers like to have short abstracts typed as a list of a half dozen to a dozen numbered points.

Body. The body of the report—the discussion and analysis of the findings—includes the introduction, the background, and each succeeding section of the data analysis, all developed logically to the final section, the conclusions and recommendations. Follow the instructions in **HOW TO PREPARE THE MANUSCRIPT,** page 97, for spacing, footnote and reference style, use of subheads, and preparation of illustrations.

Appendix. Some reports have supplementary supporting material —additional related information, tables, charts, and so on—that should be collected in a final chapter or section called the "Appendix(es)." Text-type discussion in the appendix should be typed like the material in the body of the report. Illustrative material such as a table should be set up as described in **Preparing Tables and Illustrations,** page 106.

Notes. If the report does not place footnotes at the bottom of each text page, number and collect them in a special section called "Notes." Type them as described on page 100.

Glossary. If a number of technical terms are used in a report, a glossary of brief definitions may be desirable. This alphabetical list of terms is typed either as a separate section after the notes section or as one of the appendixes before the notes section.

Bibliography. A bibliography is prepared from the 3- by 5-inch cards used during research to record each source of information. It is arranged alphabetically as described on page 102.

Index. Many reports omit the index, but if one is used, it should be prepared as follows: Underline key words in the final draft of the report. List these words or phrases on index cards, a *separate* card for each new word or phrase, with the page number(s) where the key words appear. Then group the cards by like categories before alphabetizing them. For example, assume that you have three cards, each with a word or phrase pertaining to "energy" but appearing on three different pages: (1) source of energy, page 9; (2) energy, page 17; (3) energy sources, page 19. Since you would have listed *each* page on a *separate* card, you now need to combine the three cards into one index entry:

Energy 9, 17, 19

To become more familiar with the appearance of an index, examine the indexes in reports previously prepared in your office and look at the indexes in several books, including this one.

Use of Appropriate Language

Words. Many writers have trouble selecting clear, concrete, specific words. Thus you read about a *good* employee instead of an employee who is a *programming expert.* Or someone refers to a machine that saves *time* each day instead of a machine that saves *fifty minutes* each day. Or you read that a new product will be released *soon* instead of on *September 8, 19—.* (See chapter 12 for more about appropriate language.) Sometimes the writer simply picks the wrong word, for example, saying *infer* when *imply* is meant (see chapter 14 for a list of misused words). Reports that are vague and imprecise are weak and uninformative. Whether you are writing the original copy or correcting someone else's work, look for a myriad of problems in word choice.

Sentences. Poor word choice can lead to weak, clumsy, or otherwise ineffective sentences. Short, simple sentences usually are stronger and clearer than long, rambling monologues. Contrary to prevalent thought in some offices, big words and long, complex sentences do *not* indicate more intelligence or better education; they merely reveal pompous, amateurish, and often tedious writing habits.

Try to use the active voice whenever you can *(I believe)* instead of the often weaker, stuffier passive voice *(It is believed that).* Then let your sentences (and paragraphs) slide one into another: *Sales have been declining; however, the sluggish economy is only partially responsible* (not *Sales have been declining. The sluggish economy is only partially responsible).* Use transition words such as *however, in fact,* and *therefore* to good advantage when movement from one sentence to another sounds abrupt, stiff, and awkward without them.

Avoid a lot of "there is" and "it is" beginnings. Instead of *There is a trend toward multifamily housing occurring today,* try *A trend toward multifamily housing is occurring today.* Making such changes may help you cut out unnecessary words too. For example, instead of "the year of 1987," simply say "1987." Don't delete words and sentences that are helpful in making the discussion flow smoothly and interestingly, even if they appear superfluous at first glance.

Generally, try to follow the requirements of the communication. A memo report, for instance, might use a more conversational style than a formal report, which must be objective and straightforward. But all reports—as well as any other type of writing—should be written in a style and tone appropriate for the reader.

Types of Report Binders

Staple short, informal reports in the upper left-hand corner or use a paper clip to secure the pages of a short memo report. Fasten formal reports along the left-hand margin or across the top, but preferably on the side. Use brads, paper fasteners, or staples for fastening. Many formal reports, especially long ones, are presented in special holders, binders, or folders; sometimes they are laced together on the left side with a plastic comb. Check at your local office-supply store for samples.

Checklist of Things to Remember

The longer the report, the more things you need to check before it is released. Some secretaries make up a list of everything they want to remind themselves to double-check. They go down this list one item at a time, crossing out or checking off each item when it is completed. For example:

1. Has the report been read carefully, word for word, for sense and proper language?
2. Have all typographical and other errors been corrected on the original and on all copies?
3. Are the pages numbered correctly?
4. Are margins, paragraph style, and other spacing matters attractive and consistent?

5. Has a consistent style of headings and numbering been followed throughout the report?

6. Have all statistics been checked against their sources?

7. Have all cross-references been checked?

8. Are footnotes in proper sequence with corresponding references in the text, and are the data consistent with the facts in matching bibliography entries?

9. Are mathematical tables and computations accurate?

10. Are proper names spelled correctly?

11. Are the pages arranged in proper sequence?

12. Are all pages firmly attached in the binding?

HOW TO PREPARE THE MANUSCRIPT

Studying the Preliminary Draft

Before typing a report in final form, read over the entire handwritten or rough draft with these purposes in mind:

1. To see that each sentence makes sense and that all sentences have been arranged logically in paragraphs. If you cannot understand something in a report someone else has written, ask the meaning of the sentence or paragraph and have it clarified.

2. To correct mistakes and improve the writing style where needed.

3. To identify or supply the headings and subheadings, so that you can visualize the report in final typewritten form. Headings help to bring out the organization of the report and to disclose weaknesses in the arrangement of the material.

4. To confirm that all parts of the report are there and in the right position, including the preliminary pages, footnotes, illustrations, and end matter.

Selecting the Right Paper

Reports are usually prepared on plain white paper, $8\frac{1}{2}$ by 11 inches, twenty-pound substance. Occasionally, long reports are written on legal-size paper (8-by-13 or $8\frac{1}{2}$-by-14 inches), but letter-size paper is preferred.

Use a good quality paper for the original. Lightweight paper may be used for duplicate originals when several copies are made by typewriter; however, most duplicates are made by photocopier or by one of the duplicating processes (large quantities are usually printed). If the report is in memo form, the first page will be written on memo stationery.

Using Proper Spacing and Margins

Deciding on single or double spacing.   Formal reports are usually double-spaced. However, if the report is to be duplicated or numerous copies are to be mailed, single spacing will save labor, paper, and postage. Use a double space between paragraphs of both single-spaced and double-spaced material.

Indent and single-space quoted or extracted material that runs eight lines or more. If the report has much quoted material, you may want to double-space the report to make the single-spaced quoted material stand out. (Remember that in a published report, every quote requires a footnote or other form of citation, and substantial quotes—such as more than one hundred words from an article or more than three hundred words from a book—require permission to quote from the copyright owner.) If the report manuscript is to be typeset, double-space everything, including quoted extracts.

Reports in memo form are usually single-spaced, unless they are very short (only one or two small paragraphs), in which case they may be double-spaced.

Setting margins for an attractive appearance.   Use ample and uniform margins at top, bottom, and side of about $1\frac{1}{4}$ inches on both sides and 1 to $1\frac{1}{4}$ inches top and bottom. Never use less than a 1-inch margin, *exclusive* of the part of the page that is used for binding. Thus if $\frac{3}{4}$ of an inch is used for binding, the bound edge (left side or top) should have a margin of $1\frac{3}{4}$ inches instead of 1 inch.

The first page of the report, of each chapter, and of each part such as the abstract should have a two- to three-inch margin at the top.

The left margin of indented material should be set even with the paragraph indentation of the main part of the report, usually five to ten spaces.

Numbering Pages, Titles, and Outlines

Numbering the pages.   Number the pages of the front matter starting with the table of contents and ending with the abstract—the pages that *precede* the report proper—with small roman numerals such as i, ii, iii, iv, and v. Number all pages of the report proper beginning with the introduction and ending with the index with arabic numerals, starting with 1. Place all numbers in the center of the page, one-half inch from the bottom, or place all numbers in the upper-right corner *except* on pages that open a new chapter or division of the report (use bottom-of-page numbers on opening pages). The pages of a report that is bound on the left side often use the right-hand corner position for page numbers.

Numbering appendixes. Most writers precede appendixes with a letter or number: Appendix A, Appendix B; or Appendix I, Appendix II; or Appendix 1, Appendix 2. Capital letters are often preferred when chapters have numerals. Each appendix also has a title (Appendix A: Interest Tables).

Numbering within the report and proper indentation. A report may use numbering and lettering schemes, in addition to headings, to simplify the reading. There are no fixed rules, but the following three patterns are among those commonly used. Notice that whatever the scheme, topics of equal importance are given equal emphasis in the arrangement. Follow the scheme consistently throughout the report.

Pattern 1	*Pattern 2*	*Pattern 3*
I	I.	I. . . . .
1.	1.	A. . . . .
(a)	A.	1. . . . .
(b)	B.	2. . . . .
(1)	(1)	(a) . . . .
(2)	(2)	(b) . . . .
II	2.	B. . . . .
	II.	II. . . . .

Observe the following rules within the numbering and lettering scheme:

1. Follow roman and arabic numerals with a period.

2. Do not use a period after a number or letter in parentheses.

3. Use a double space between paragraphs carrying a number or letter just as you would other paragraphs.

4. Determine how far you will indent each of the groups in your numbering and lettering scheme, indenting each successive group several spaces more than the preceding group, and maintain the same indentation plan throughout the report. Notice in the

examples of three patterns how II is aligned under I, (b) under (a), and so on.

5. Indent the first line in a main paragraph five to ten spaces. Indent the first line in an indented paragraph five spaces more than its own left-hand margin, or use the block form.

Using the Right Footnote Style

Using a notes section or bottom-of-page footnotes. If there are many footnotes in a report, number them consecutively, from 1 on. In a report that is divided into chapters, begin with footnote 1 in each chapter. Place the footnote (called a "superior figure" because it is typed raised above the normal line of type rather than "on line") at the end of the sentence in the text to which the footnote applies. Do not place numbers in the middle of sentences. In a double-spaced paragraph, it would look like this:

Only one real solution is offered: [1] To . . .

In a single-spaced paragraph it could be written as follows:

Only one real solution is offered:/2/ To . . .

If there are only a few footnotes in the report, you may use asterisks, daggers, or other similar characters instead of numbers.

Notes may be collected at the end of each chapter or at the end of the report in a separate "Notes" section. If you use bottom-of-page footnotes instead, place the footnote to the text at the *bottom* of the page on which the superior figure appears. Place the footnote to a table, however, at the bottom of the table. (See **Using the right reference-list style,** page 103, for another option.)

To separate a bottom-of-page footnote from the text, allow two lines of space below the last line of text, make a rule with the typewriter about two inches long, and then allow another line of space before typing the footnote. Precede the footnote with its corresponding number or symbol typed as superior numbers or on line. (The trend is to use numbers on line—not raised—with the actual footnote, unlike the corresponding number in the text, which is typed as a superior number in double-spaced copy.)

Examples of different types of footnotes are given below. Underscore what you want to appear in italic when the report is being typeset.

1. Citation of a book. Follow the style in notes 1 and 2:

1. Robert Semenow, *Questions and Answers on Real Estate,* 8th ed. (Englewood Cliffs, N.J.: Prentice-Hall, 1975), 111.
2. A. T. Watts, *The Fuel Factor,* 2 vols. (New York: Watson Press, 1982), 1:17.

2. Citation of an article. Follow the style in notes 3 to 5:

3. R. H. Lubar, "Plan for Tax Reform," *Fortune,* March 1986, 92–96.
4. Morris Stevens, "Synthetics," in *The Plastic World,* ed. Barbara Carter and John Reubens (Baton Rouge, La.: Microplastics Laboratories, 1981), 91.
5. Daniel Westerkamp, "Seeing Is Believing," *Journal of Middle Managers* 40 (April 1979): 100–101.

3. Acknowledgment of credit (usually an unnumbered note at the bottom of the first page of a chapter). Follow this style:

Acknowledgment is made to Charles Berg for the data on housing.

4. Citation of an unpublished paper. Follow the style in notes 6 and 7:

6. A. T. Watts, "Indian Culture: A Lost Art" (M.A. thesis, University of Arizona, 1977), 401–2.
7. Marlene Lake, Foreword to "Data Processing at Benson," mimeographed (Washington, D.C.: Benson Industries, 1985), iv.

5. Short references and ibid. Follow the style in notes 8 to 11:

8. Watts, "Indian Culture," 403.
9. Ibid., 401.
10. Lubar, "Plan for Tax Reform," 93; Watts, "Indian Culture," 400; idem, "The Fuel Factor," 76.
11. Lubar, "Plan for Tax Reform."

Some writers do not put footnotes at the bottoms of the text pages. They may collect only straight or source citations in a "Notes" section but leave expository notes at the bottoms of the text pages. In this case, the source notes at the end of each chapter would be numbered (starting with 1 in each chapter), and the expository notes at the bottoms of the pages might be lettered (starting with *a* in each chapter). The following list illustrates the difference between expository and straight source notes.

1. **Expository notes.**   Follow this style for the expository notes:

a. Percentages are based on the 1980 census.

b. This system has been in operation only two years, however, as explained in D. R. Thompson, *A Comparative Study of the X-L40 and the X-L400,* Highland Digital Manufacturers Studies in Data Processing, vol. 2 (Madison, Wis., 1979), 81.

2. **Source notes.**   Follow this style for the source notes:

1. Melanie Clarke, *Credit and Collection Systems,* rev. ed. (Philadelphia: Newhouse Publications, 1981), 214–19.

2. Jason Stowe and Ryan McConnell, "The Credit Chase," *Collection News Quarterly* 12, no. 2 (August 1982): 7–15.

Using the right bibliography style.   The bibliography often contains a list of all recommended publications on the subject of the report, including all sources cited in the footnotes. If it does not include all sources cited in footnotes, it is called a "Select," or "Selected," Bibliography. (Other titles are sometimes used for this section such as "Work Cited" and "Works Consulted.")

Bibliography entries are arranged alphabetically. Each entry is double-spaced in a manuscript to be typeset (the same as the footnotes) but may be single-spaced otherwise, with a double space between entries. Underscore anything you want to be in italic if the report is being typeset. If any entries are cited in the notes section(s) of the report, be certain that the data in notes and bibliography entries are the same, even though the style of typing differs.

1. **Books.**   Follow this style for book titles:

Watts, A. T. *The Fuel Factor.* 2 vols. New York: Watson Press, 1982.
Semenow, Robert. *Questions and Answers on Real Estate.* Englewood
    Cliffs, N.J.: Prentice-Hall, 1975.

2. **Articles.**   Follow this style for articles:

Lubar, R. H. "Plan for Tax Reform." *Fortune,* March 19, 19—, pp. 92–96.

Stevens, Morris. "Synthetics." In *The Plastic World,* edited by Barbara Carter. Baton Rouge, La.: Microplastics Laboratories, 1981.

Westerkamp, David. "Seeing Is Believing." *Journal of Middle Managers* 40 (April 1982): 100–115.

————."Satellite TV Breakthrough." *Madison Herald,* 29 May 1979.

3. Unpublished material. Follow this style for unpublished material:

Lake, Marlene. Foreword. "Data Processing at Benson." Mimeographed. Washington, D.C.: Benson Industries, 1978.

Watts, A. T. "Indian Culture: A Lost Art." M.A. thesis, University of Arizona, 1980.

The form in which the author's name is cited in the bibliography should be the form in which it appears on the title page of the published book being cited. Thus if the name on the title page is Robert Semenow, the form in the bibliography should be "Semenow, Robert." If, however, the name on the title page is R. Semenow, the form in the bibliography should be "Semenow, R." If an item has two or more authors, it is not necessary to reverse any names, except the one that appears first, which is reversed to aid alphabetical arrangement *(Dawes, Elaine, and Thomas Markham).*

If a bibliography contains more than one item by the same author, arrange them alphabetically according to title and use a long dash (as illustrated above for the David Westerkamp entry) instead of repeating the name each time. However, *do* repeat the name if a coauthor is added.

Bibliographies may be further classified according to the types of printed material: books, book reviews, pamphlets, indexes, guides, reference works, and the like, and some reports use subheads in the bibliography and group similar references in the appropriate categories.

Using the right reference-list style. Some reports use a name-date reference style. For example, a sentence in the text might read: "This system has been in operation only two years, however (see Thompson 1979: 17)." You might, then, have only a name-date "Reference" section in the report—no "Notes" section—or there still may be a "Notes" section at the end of each chapter (or one large section after the appendixes). The alphabetical entries in the reference section will look like this when a name-date citation style is used in the text:

> Thompson, D. R. 1979. *A Comparative Study of the X-L40 and the X-L400.* Highland Digital Manufacturers Studies in Data Processing. Vol. 2. Madison, Wis.

Notice that the date appears *immediately after* the name. If there should be two 1979 entries, both by Thompson, you would arrange them alphabetically and label the first one 1979a and the second one 1979b.

Selecting Levels of Heads and Subheads

The body of a report is usually divided into topics and subtopics with headings. Most writers already have a list of topics used in conducting research. Often these topics form the basis of the headings and subheadings in the report. In setting up the headings, keep this in mind: Topics of equal importance should be given equal emphasis.

Emphasis.   Emphasis is shown in typed material by centering and by the use of caps, spacing, underlining, or a combination of these techniques. Headings of the same relative importance should be identical in form.

Patterns of headings.   In typing a long report, make a pattern of the style of headings that you intend to use throughout the report. For example:

> FIRST-LEVEL SUBHEAD (centered)
> Second-Level Subhead (flush left)
> *Third-Level Subhead.* (underlined, indented with paragraphs, and
>   followed by period, with text sentence immediately following the
>   period)

If the report requires more breakdowns, select as many of the following as you need (but keep in mind that too many levels are distracting and can make material very complicated to read):

> FIRST-LEVEL SUBHEAD (centered)
> <u>SECOND-LEVEL SUBHEAD</u> (underlined and centered)
> Third-Level Subhead (flush left)
> <u>Fourth-Level Subhead</u> (underlined and flush left)

Fifth-Level Subhead. (indented with paragraphs and followed by a
period, with text sentence immediately following the period)

Sixth-Level Subhead. (underlined, indented with paragraphs, and
followed by a period, with text sentence immediately following
the period)

Seventh-level subhead. (indented with paragraphs and followed by
a period, with text sentence immediately following the period)

Eighth-level subhead. (underlined, indented with paragraphs, and
followed by a period, with text sentence immediately following
the period)

Use a triple space between a centered or flush-left heading and the text that precedes it; use a double space between the heading and the text that follows. You may treat subheads that are indented like paragraphs (called "run in" heads when a text sentence immediately follows the period) the same as a line of text, with no additional space preceding it, or you may use a double space before typing the run-in head.

Wording of headings. Headings should be short, striking, and descriptive of the topic being discussed. If it is impossible for a heading to be lively and descriptive at the same time, select the descriptive heading.

Headings should be uniform in grammatical construction if possible. Thus if a subheading is introduced with a participle, other subheadings under that topic ideally would all be introduced with a participle. All important words should be capitalized in a heading that uses both upper-case and lowercase letters but not conjunctions, prepositions, and articles.

Note the effective use of short, imperative sentences in the following headings from a report outlining a plan for strengthening a company's marketing program.

IMPROVE THE PRODUCT LINE
Pretest New Products
Shorten the Length of the Line
Reduce Percentage of Low-Volume Items
Improve Colors in Lower Price Lines

STRENGTHEN FIELD SELLING EFFORTS
Clarify Territorial Boundaries
Relieve the Overburdened Sales Force
Improve the Sales Compensation Plan
Develop More Appealing Displays
Improve Field Supervision

Setting Up the Title Page and Table of Contents

Typing the title page.   When an item on a title page is written on more than one line, divide the material at a logical point. Adjectives and articles are not separated from the word they modify, a preposition is not separated from its object, and a line does not end in a conjunction. Thus the title "The Participation of the White-Collar Worker in Modern Labor Unrest" should not be divided between "Collar" and "Worker," although this division makes a more even distribution of the letters in each line. That title should be written as follows:

THE PARTICIPATION OF THE WHITE-COLLAR WORKER
IN MODERN LABOR UNREST

The items on the title page are centered horizontally on the available space, exclusive of the part taken up by binding or fastening. With a left side fastening, allow $\frac{3}{4}$ inch for binding. The centering point on the typewriter scale is then moved seven spaces to the right of the actual center for pica type and nine spaces for elite.

Separate each item on the title page by at least four line spaces to give the page a balanced appearance, but use only two spaces between the lines of an item. Figure 12 is an example of a well-balanced title page.

Typing the table of contents.   Center the table of contents horizontally and vertically. Double-space a short table of contents; single-space a long one. List the chapter or topic numbers at the left, space three times, and follow with a list of the titles. List the page numbers on the right-hand margin.

If desired, use periods as leaders to guide the reader's eye across the space between the title and the page number. Space once between each period. To align the periods, always begin the first dot of the leaders at an even number on the typewriter scale.

Figure 13 shows the arrangement of chapter topics on a sample table of contents.

Preparing Tables and Illustrations

Setting Up Tables.   Although tables are more difficult to set up than most other pages, there are various techniques that help to simplify the task as described in the following sections. The finished tables may be typed at appropriate places in the text, or they may be typed separately and placed at the ends of chapters or used as appendixes or simply collected in order after the last appendix. Regardless of their position, *be certain that each table is mentioned in the text discussion* in the order numbered.

1. How to use measurements for typing tables. The following information will be helpful in planning the arrangement of a table when you need to make manual computations for typewriter preparation.

6 line spaces equal 1 inch, measured vertically.
10 spaces of pica type equal 1 inch, measured horizontally.
12 spaces of elite type equal 1 inch, measured horizontally.
A sheet of paper $8\frac{1}{2}$ by 11 inches has 85 spaces of pica type on a horizontal line.
A sheet of paper $8\frac{1}{2}$ by 11 inches has 102 spaces of elite type on a horizontal line.
A sheet of paper $8\frac{1}{2}$ by 11 inches has 66 vertical line spaces.

2. How to plan the arrangement. Before beginning to type a table, carefully plan the arrangement. Keep these thoughts in mind:

a. Tables usually have three parts: a number and title, column cross-headings, and a stub (the list of items running down the left side), which is equivalent to a column in planning the arrangement.

b. The figures are aligned on the right, words on the left (see figure 14).

c. Columns can be centered by gauging the center by the longest item in the column. Notice how, in figure 14, "Shares" is centered in relation to the number with the most digits, and "Held" is centered under "Shares."

3. How to determine vertical spacing. Allow one line space between the title and the subtitle, if any, or at least two line spaces between the title and the column cross-headings. Allow at least two line spaces between the column cross-headings and the items in the column. If the table is short, double-space between the items in the body to give the typed page a more balanced appearance. Very short tables are often typed without any rules. A longer table may have three (or more) rules, as shown in figure 14, before and after the cross-headings and after the last line in the table body.

4. How to type headings of tables. Center the title and subtitle of a table in the same manner that you would center any other heading. Remember to make an allowance if part of the left margin is to be used for binding. You may also type the title and subtitle flush left if preferred.

Figure 14.   Table Showing Proper Alignment of Words and Figures

Table I. Classification of Stockholders

December 6, 19—

	Stock-holders	Percent	Shares Held	Percent
Women	31,402	41.60	2,254,582	24.07
Men	23,285	30.84	2,161,751	23.08
Fiduciaries	14,658	19.42	1,488,444	15.89
Joint accounts	3,024	4.00	96,898	1.03
Institutions	1,164	1.54	230,773	2.46
Corporations and partnerships[a]	829	1.10	237,124	2.53
Nominees	511	0.68	2,319,731	24.77
Brokers	266	0.35	295,987	3.16
Insurance companies	233	0.31	204,729	2.19
Investment trusts	118[b]	0.16	76,459	0.82
	75,490	100.00	9,366,478	100.00

Source: Stock ledger, Philips, Henderson, and Evans.

Note: Women stockholders outnumber men by almost 11 percent.

[a] An analysis of corporations versus partnerships is shown in table II.

[b] The number of trusts declined between 1985 and 1988 but is expected to increase by early 1990.

The titles of other illustrations such as photographs or charts are called "legends" or "captions." A *caption*, if used at all, is the actual title or headline, often set above the illustration. A *legend* is an explanation, often set beneath the illustration. Many authors combine the two and set both together beneath the illustration, for example:

Fig. 1. Flowchart under Reorganization. The revised chain of command can be seen in this flowchart of division chiefs and department heads.

5. Where to position footnotes to tables. Type footnotes, as shown in figure 14, immediately under the body of the table. Notice that the source note precedes all other notes, and a general note precedes lettered or numbered footnotes. The letters or numbers in the table body are set as superior (raised) figures. The letters or numbers with the actual footnotes may be set raised or on line.

6. How to make top and bottom margins even. Here is what you do to make both margins the same:

a. Figure the number of line spaces on the paper that you are using.

b. Count the lines in the table and add the number of lines and spaces to be covered by the title and subtitle.

c. Subtract the total from the number of line spaces on your paper.

d. Divide the difference by two. The result is the number of line spaces to allow for the top and bottom margins.

7. How to make the side margins even. Calculations to center copy on a page are generally handled automatically with a computer, word processor, or electronic typewriter. Depending on your computer software program, for example, you may be able to specify margin settings through advance format instructions. To make such calculations manually (as with an electric typewriter), follow these directions:

a. Figure the number of spaces across the paper that you are using. If part of the left margin is to be used for binding, subtract those spaces from your count.

b. Count the number of characters in the longest line in each column, including the stub as a column, and total them.

c. Subtract the total found in step 2 from the number of spaces found in step 1. This gives the number of spaces that are available for left and right margins *and* to separate the columns.

    d. Decide how many spaces you want between each column. This varies with the amount of available space.

    e. Multiply the number of spaces to be put between each column by the number of columns, *not* including the first column.

    f. Subtract the result found in step 5 from the result found in step 3, and divide by 2. This gives the number of spaces to be allowed for each side margin.

    8. Where to set the tabulators. Tab settings are also determined and set easily with electronic equipment. With an electric typewriter, before beginning to type a table, set your tabulators as follows:

    a. Set the left-hand margin at the point found in step 6 above. This is the point where the stub or left-hand column begins.

    b. Space once for each character in the longest line of the stub, space once for each space that separates the columns (see step d), and then set the first tabulator key.

    c. Beginning at the point where the first tabulator key was set, space once for each character in the longest line of the second column, space one for each space that separates the columns, and then set the second tabulator key.

    d. Follow the same procedure until the tabulator key is set for the starting point of the last column.

    Handling other illustrations. Artwork and photographs that are to be printed should be prepared on a separate sheet, with a circled note in the margins showing the text page number where the figure is first mentioned (be certain that mention is made of *each* figure in the text and always in the order numbered).

    1. Photographs. Halftones (photographs) are best submitted to a printer as black-and-white glossy prints, unless the report is to be printed in color. If desired, you can put small lines (crop marks) in the white border, using a grease pencil that will rub off, to show the portion of the photograph that you want to use.

    2. Line drawings. Line drawings (charts, graphs, and so on that do not have tonal values like a halftone) may consist of pen-and-ink drawings or computer art. Clear, dark lines on a clean white background are needed for sharp reproduction.

    3. Marking instructions. With both line drawings and halftones, mark instructions to the printer on a tissue or acetate overlay sheet, but do *not* press down on the surface of the illustration or you will leave a crease that may show up in reproduction.

4. **Working with an artist.** If you retain an artist to prepare the illustrations, explain carefully the size, quality, and general characteristics desired as well as the intended means of reproduction (for example, black and white offset printing or full-color letterpress printing). The artist must have this information to prepare the artwork in proper form for the printer to use. Any problems because of poor communication in this respect could result in costly printing charges.

Preparing and Checking the Manuscript

Preparing the manuscript. The following rules should be observed in preparing manuscript copy that will be typeset:

1. Use $8\frac{1}{2}$ by 11-inch white bond. Make carbon copies or photocopies, but always send the original to the printer.
2. Use a carbon ribbon (as opposed to fabric) for sharp, clean copy if the manuscript is to be photographed for reproduction, that is, if it must be "camera-ready."
3. Keep the typewritten line to about six inches.
4. Use double spacing.
5. Keep the right-hand margin as even as possible, to help you later in estimating the length of the copy.
6. Indent paragraphs at least five spaces.
7. Type headings and subheadings in the position they are to occupy on the final printed page: centered, flush left, or indented with the paragraph.
8. Leave a margin of at least one inch on all four sides and keep each page as nearly uniform in length as possible.
9. Set off six or more lines of quoted material from the rest of the text (a) by single spacing the extracted material and (b) by indenting all of it from the left margin or from both the left and right margins.
10. Type footnotes double spaced and full measure (width) separate from the manuscript or in a notes section, unless there are very few, in which case they may be typed at the bottom of the text

page if desired. Type footnotes, reference lists, and bibliographies as described on pages 100–104.

11. Cross-references to material appearing in other parts of the manuscript should read "see page 000" when you submit the manuscript to the printer. But be sure to insert the actual pages later when the material has been typeset in final page form with page numbers.

12. If you need to write instructions to the printer on the manuscript, circle your comments in the margins. If you need to write instructions on a finished page that is ready to be photographed, use a light-blue pencil since this color will not reproduce, but take care in any event not to damage the page.

See page 104 for guides to proofreading and marking copy.

Checking the manuscript.   After you have typed the manuscript, read it line for line, looking not only for typing errors but other problems that may have escaped everyone during the writing stage.

1. Look for typing errors and missing copy.
2. Check whether punctuation, capitalization, spelling, abbreviations, and so on are consistent.
3. Recheck the pages to be certain none is missing or out of position. For copy to be typeset, see that all inserts are numbered and their position noted in the text.
4. Check the chapter titles and subheads in the table of contents against the actual titles and heads in the body of the manuscript; the wording should be consistent.
5. Double-check quoted material and illustrations to be certain that permission for their use has been obtained and that no required credit lines are missing.
6. On double-spaced manuscript to be typeset, you can make *short corrections* by crossing out the incorrect word and writing the correct word above it.
7. On double-spaced manuscript to be typeset, you can make *long corrections* by typing the revised material on a separate page and at the point of correction writing in the margin to "Insert page _____ here." On the revised page, make a note to "Insert on page _____."
8. When you have instructions for the typesetter or printer, write

them in the margin and circle them. Typesetters know they are not to set anything circled in the margin.

9. If you want to break up a long paragraph into two paragraphs, insert a paragraph sign where you want a second paragraph to begin. If you want to make one paragraph out of two separate paragraphs, simply run a line from the end of the first one to the first word of the second one.

10. To separate two words accidentally typed as one, draw a vertical line between them.

11. To retain material crossed out, put a row of dots beneath the crossed-out words and circle the word *stet* in the margin (but retype the crossed-out copy if it will not be completely legible).

12. To indicate that you want a word set in all capitals, draw three lines under it. Two lines would mean that you want *small* capital letters. One line would mean that you want the word set in italics. A wavy line would mean that you want it set in a bold type.

For further markings you may want to make, refer to the proofreader charts on pages 604 and 605.

HOW TO HANDLE TYPESETTING AND PRINTING

Arranging for Design and Typemarking

If the material to be printed needs a special shape, appearance, and arrangement of copy, you may need to have a professional artist design something for you and your employer to approve. This person would also mark your manuscript for specific typefaces, type sizes, column widths, spacing, and so on. Perhaps your company has an art department with people qualified to do such work. Otherwise, you could look in the yellow pages for local art talent. (Advertising agencies provide such services, although individual freelance artists often charge less.) Before you retain someone, explain your project to several prospects, ask for cost estimates (try to get two or three), and emphasize your deadlines; once you select someone, ask to see a *layout* (a rough sketch of the proposed design).

Making Typesetting Arrangements

Your yellow pages will list local printers and typesetters. Most printers provide typesetting too, so you may be able to arrange for both functions under one roof. As with the design and typemarking, here, too, try to find two or three prospects and ask for quotes on the job. Keep in mind that *cold type* refers to typesetting by a typewriter process (for example, computer) and usually includes photocomposition, or photographic processes, as well (for example Photon). *Hot type* refers to typesetting by use of metal (for example, linotype), where letters or lines of type are dropped into metal trays called "galleys." Cold type is often selected when speed and economy are important considerations. *Hot type* is sometimes preferred when quality is the principal consideration, but you should examine samples from both types of composition, since any difference may be imperceptible. Stress your deadline and explain precisely what you will do and what you expect the typesetter-printer to do. (In case that you have to do your own design and typemarking, ask the printer to help you select typefaces and show you how to mark the manuscript properly.)

Checking Proofs

The printer will supply one to three sets of proofs after the manuscript has been typeset. Long sheets not yet divided into pages are called "galley proofs" or "galleys." Exact pages are called "page proofs." Your job will be to proofread the galleys or pages (or both), correct them (using the proofreading guides on pages 604 and 605), and return them to the printer as soon as possible.

What to look for.   Look not only for typographical errors but for missing copy and missing or misplaced pages. Check whether all credit lines are there. Double-check the position of footnotes, figure captions and legends, titles and subheads, and so on. Facing pages (side by side) should end on the same line, without a *widow* (a very short line) falling at the top of the next page. Verify page numbers and anything else that might be missing or contain an error. Check that no more than two successive lines on a page end with hyphens. Look for distracting white "rivers" of space running throughout pages. But try to confine your markings to problems or errors created by the typesetter. If you start rewriting and rearranging copy at this stage, such new *author's alterations* could be expensive. Make all of such changes *before* sending the manuscript to the printer.

Arranging for Printing and Binding

You may be using the same establishment for typesetting, printing, and binding. If not, you must again check your yellow pages and secure quotes from two or three firms for each process. (It would be helpful to know if other customers are pleased with the work of a printer, typesetter, or binder that you are considering.)

Choosing a printer. For more economical work, you may choose a firm offering *photo-offset lithography,* a process that uses a plate prepared photographically. The quality of reproduction, particularly of photographs, may be slightly lower than with other printing processes such as letterpress, although quality varies in offset printing depending on the size and capabilities of the offset press. *Letterpress* uses a relief principle—the type and photographs are on raised surfaces called "cuts." Letterpress is used for both low-quality and high-quality work.

Checking the press proof. The printer will give you a negative proof or a press proof of your project before it is printed. This is your last chance to look for problems. Check the proof for errors missed during earlier stages and check for proper arrangement of pages, illustrations, and copy. Keep in mind that new revisions you might like to make will be even more costly at this late stage.

HOW TO COPYRIGHT THE REPORT

Copyright Law

Since January 1, 1978, all published and unpublished works that are fixed in a copy or phonorecord are subject to a single system of statutory protection. Registration of a work in the Library of Congress Copyright Office, although not necessary to have a valid copyright, is necessary for bringing a court action in regard to infringement.

The maximum total term of copyright protection for works already protected by federal statute before 1978 is now seventy-five years; a first term of twenty-eight years from the date of the original copyright plus a renewal term of forty-seven years. You must apply for renewal within one year before the first twenty-eight-year term expires. Copyrights already renewed that were in their second term between December 31, 1976, and December 31, 1977, have been automatically extended to last the full seventy-five years. (Ask the Copyright Office for Circular R15 and renewal Form RE.)

The new law sets a single copyright term with no renewal requirements. Works existing on January 1, 1978, but not copyrighted and not in the public domain are subject to automatic federal copyright protection.

The term of protection under the new law is a life-plus-fifty-years system (the same as most other countries have). This means that protection applies for the life of the author(s) plus fifty years after the death of the last surviving author. Protection for works made for hire and anonymous or pseudonymous works applies for seventy-five years from publication or one hundred years from creation, whichever is shorter.

All copyright terms will run through the end (December 31) of the calendar year in which they would otherwise expire. The renewal period for works copyrighted between 1950 and 1977 will run from December 31 of the twenty-seventh year of the copyright until December 31 of the following year.

Works in the public domain are not protected under the new law, and copyright that has been lost on a work cannot be restored, for example, if it did not meet requirements such as containing the proper copyright notice or if the terms of protection expired before renewal could be made.

Fair-Use Guidelines

The 1976 copyright law lists four criteria that are used to determine whether copying material from some source without permission or payment is fair:

1. The purpose and character of the use, including whether such use is of a commercial nature or is for nonprofit educational purposes
2. The nature of the copyrighted work
3. The amount and substantiality of the portion used in relation to the copyrighted work as a whole
4. The effect of the use upon the potential market for, or value of, the copyrighted work

Section 107 of the 1976 law states that "the fair use of a copyrighted work, including such use by reproduction in copies or phonorecords or by any other means specified by that section, for purposes such as criticism, comment, news reporting, teaching (including multiple copies for classroom use), scholarship, or research, is not an infringement of copyright." The 1976 law does not include guidelines for classroom copying, but systematic reproduction and distribution of single or multiple copies of books and periodicals by libraries (instead of their purchase) is forbidden. Spontaneous copying for classroom use must not exceed the number of students in a course, each copy must bear a copyright notice, and the amount copied must be brief.

Copyright-Registration Procedure

Copyright notice.   For copyright to be valid a proper notice must be published in a printed work. This notice must include (1) the letter *c* in a circle (and may also include the word *copyright* or the abbreviation *copr.*), (2) the year of first publication of the work, and (3) the name of the copyright owner *(Copyright © 1988 by Prentice-Hall, Inc.).* A United States citizen whose work includes a proper copyright notice also receives protection in all other countries that are members of the Universal Copyright Convention.

Information and forms.   Free registration forms are available from the Copyright Office, Library of Congress, Washington, D.C. 20559. Ask for instructions on the proper procedure for registering a work and the applicable fee to submit. Specify what kind of work—book, magazine, artwork, and so on—you want to register. For more information, consult a handbook such as Donald F. Johnson's *Copyright Handbook* (New York: R. R. Bowker, 1978), which provides the text of the copyright act of 1976 and includes sample registration forms and fair-use and reproduction guidelines.

Chapter 4

Handling Mail and Electronic Messages

CONVENTIONAL-MAIL PROCESSING

Although many messages are sent by telex and facsimile or through electronic-mail and voice-mail systems, most offices still send and receive a heavy volume of mail conventionally. Large organizations have mail departments that receive and distribute incoming items and meter and mail outgoing material. But many secretaries include mail processing among their daily duties.

Handling Incoming Mail

Categories for sorting the mail. Before opening the mail, quickly sort it into piles of (1) correspondence, (2) bills and statements (if you can distinguish them from the correspondence at a glance), (3) advertisements and circulars, and (4) newspapers and periodicals. Next you should separate the personal matters from business mail and separate business mail into outside and interoffice. Finally, set aside all priority matters requiring immediate attention. If your office has many more obvious categories of incoming mail, such as purchase orders or receipts, you may want to consider some of the sorting devices, usually in the form of racks or trays, available from most office-supply stores.

Letters marked "Personal" or "Confidential." Never open letters marked "Personal" or "Confidential" unless your employer has specifically asked you to do so. It is also advisable to assume that a letter written in longhand is personal, even if not marked as such, unless you know the correspondent and your employer has asked you to open the letter. If practical, hand deliver any letter you receive that is marked "Personal" or "Confidential."

Opening the mail.   Give the correspondence your first attention. Use a hand or electric letter opener, taking care not to slash the contents. Immediately attach the enclosures to the letters, making certain that no enclosures are left inside the envelopes.

Open packages carefully, too, and place any letter that is enclosed with your other correspondence. But place the mailing label from the box with the contents. Always check all contents against your purchase order and do not accept material that you did not order or should not be receiving.

Some mail may be sent to you in error. If you do not know the forwarding address, cross out the incorrect address, write "Not at this address" on the envelope, and put it back in the mail. (Note that only first-class mail is forwarded without reapplying postage.)

If the address of the sender is on the envelope but not on the letter, attach the envelope to the letter. Otherwise, put the envelopes aside until all of the mail is completely processed and you know that you will not have to check the envelopes for overlooked contents or addresses. (Do not destroy envelopes when the postmark date is significant.) (If a letter is undated, the postmark date should be recorded. Some offices require that all mail be rubber-stamped with the date and time received.)

Sorting the mail.   Sort the letters into three piles: (1) those that require your employer's attention, (2) those that require the attention of someone outside your office, and (3) those that require your attention. This applies also to interoffice memos.

As you sort the letters, double-check the enclosures. If any are missing, look in the envelope that was put aside for this purpose. If the enclosure cannot be found, make a notation on the letter to that effect. When the nature of the enclosure is such that the letter cannot be answered without it, put the letter in the pile that requires your attention.

Attach large enclosures in back of a letter, small enclosures in front of it. Loose items such as cash should be put in their proper place (such as a cash box) and the amount and location noted on the letter, with your initials.

Mail requiring your employer's attention.   Strive to have the mail ready before your employer gets to the office or as quickly as possible thereafter. Since the file of previous correspondence relating to a current letter will facilitate action, attach the incoming letter to the file, and type copies of incoming letters that are written in longhand, if not easily read.

Arrange your employer's mail in the order of importance, with the most important on top. Ask if your employer would like you to use prioritized, color-coded folders. Most executives with many outside activities also like to have the mail relating to personal matters segregated from that relating to company business. For handling the mail when your employer is out of the office, see pages 123–24.

Ask if you should annotate the mail—underline or otherwise designate the key points in lengthy letters and perhaps jot down useful facts on them. For instance, if a letter asks your employer to speak at a luncheon, you might underscore the time, place, and so on and in the margin of the letter point out any conflicting appointment. Depending on your copier, nonreproducible blue pencils may sometimes be used to underscore or circle words without leaving marks that will show if the letter is photocopied. But some offices will not permit any marking on letters. In that case, attach self-sticking, removable slips (available from office-supply stores).

Mail requiring attention by others.   When sorting the mail, place in separate piles correspondence that your immediate office cannot dispose of without information or assistance from someone else in the organization and correspondence that should be routed to others.

1.   Action requested slips.   Office-supply stores have standard self-sticking, removable slips that have places to check the action you wish to have taken, for example:

( )   For your information
( )   For your action
( )   For your approval
( )   For your comments
( )   Please forward
( )   Please return
( )   Please review with me
( )   Please file
( )   _____

Check the action you want taken, staple the form to the incoming correspondence, and forward it to the individual to whose attention it is directed. If necessary, attach pertinent files or previous correspondence.

2.   Routing slips.   If several people should see the correspondence, use standard routing slips or devise one similar to the one shown in figure 15. If you use slips that already have the names on them, place the numerals 1, 2, 3, and so on in front of the names on the slip in the order that each person should receive the mail.

If you attend to part of a letter before sending it to someone for

Figure 15.　Routing Slip

Date: 3/5/——		
(To be routed in the order numbered)		
2 Mrs. Edwards	*ORE*	*3/7*
1 Mr. Roberts	*LR*	*3/6*
4 Mr. Jones	*B.J.*	*3/10*
3 Ms. Nelson	*E.N.*	*3/8*
Mr. Ellis		
5 File		
Please initial, date, and forward.		

further attention, mark the paragraph that has had attention. Write the date and "done" or "noted" in the margin and initial.

Daily mail record.　Keep a simple daily record of all mail sent out of your office for action by another person. This applies to telegrams and reports as well as letters. The purpose of the record is twofold: It serves as a check on the receipt and disposition of mail that gets misplaced and for follow-up, if necessary.

For the daily mail record, use looseleaf sheets with vertical columns headed *Date, Description, To Whom Sent, Action to Be Taken,* and *Follow-up.* See figure 16. If you keep the record with pencil or pen instead of typing it, the sheets should have lines drawn between entries. Double-space between each entry on the typewriter.

Under *Description,* note the date of the communication, name of sender, and the subject matter. In the *Action to Be Taken* column, note the action that was checked on the slip that you attached to the communication before forwarding it. Write the deadline date for disposition in the follow-up column if it is necessary to follow up to see that proper action is taken. When the matter has had the necessary attention, draw a line through the entry.

Figure 16.   Daily Mail Record

DAILY MAIL RECORD				
Date	Description	To Whom Sent	Action to Be Taken	Follow-up
3/5	Spellman, Preface to Corp. Sec'y, 3/3	L. Rogers	Approval	3/8
3/5	Brown of U. of Wis. request for free copy of Credits & Collections 3/3	Andrews	Reply	

In some organizations, certain department heads receive all of the mail of the department so that they may assign the correspondence to the appropriate person for reply. In such cases, the daily mail record is particularly important.

Mail requiring your attention.   When sorting the mail, include in a separate pile the letters that you will answer for your employer's signature, as well as those that you will write over your own signature. See chapter 13.

When you take action your employer should be aware of, type an explanation of what you did, attach it to the original letter, and put it on your employer's desk for review. Most of the matters that you handle on your own will likely be routine (such as answering a routine inquiry or thanking someone for sending something you requested), and you would not report to your employer about such items.

Newspapers and periodicals.   Select newspapers and periodicals that your employer likes to read. Unwrap, flatten out, and put them in a folder labeled "Newspapers and Periodicals." Put the folder on his or her desk or in a briefcase if your employer prefers to take material of this kind home.

Send the other newspapers and periodicals to the persons in the organization who need them or put them on the shelves for reference. If your employer is paying for a periodical that he or she does not want, that is not needed by someone in the organization, or that is not valuable as reference material, ask if you should cancel the subscription.

Advertisements and circulars. Do not routinely discard all so-called junk mail. The educational value of advertisements and circulars is often overlooked. They are frequently a convenient and free source of information about things such as availability and trends in new products and procedures, or reminders of important meetings and other business-related events. Some of this material will doubtless interest your employer or another department in your company. For example, a lawyer is usually interested in the advertisement of law books; executives are always looking for cost-cutting ideas. If an order blank is enclosed with an advertisement, clip it to the advertisement.

Frequently, in the advertisements you will find solicitations for contributions. Put them in a separate folder and handle in the manner described for charitable contributions on pages 291–93.

Bills and statements. Bills and statements are filed until a certain time of the month designated for payment. Therefore, do not open them until you have disposed of the other mail. In fact, if you are particularly rushed and there is a large stock of them, you might put them in a "pending" folder until you have time to attend to them.

Procedure when your employer is away. The manner in which you should handle the mail when your employer is away from the office depends on office policy and your employer's personal preference. You can adapt the procedure recommended here as needed.

1. If your employer makes a practice of telephoning the office each day, sort the correspondence according to company matters and outside matters. Also jot down the gist of each letter so that you can report readily.

2. Telephone or send a telegram or telex about anything urgent that requires immediate personal attention if your employer does not call you.

3. Acknowledge all correspondence, whether personal or business (see page 362), if your employer is to be away more than a few days.

4. Dispose of as much of the mail as possible by covering the subject of the letter in your acknowledgment or by referring letters to other people in the organization for reply.

5. Copy all mail that requires your employer's personal attention and forward the copies.

6. Number consecutively the packets of mail that you send to your employer (1 of 4, 2 of 4, 3 of 4, 4 of 4). In this way, he or she can tell whether or not all of the mail that you send has arrived. Number-

ing the packets is particularly important when your employer is traveling from place to place.

7. If your employer is on a vacation and does not want mail forwarded, hold the letters that require personal attention and indicate in your acknowledgment when a reply might be expected.

8. Keep the accumulated mail in folders marked "Correspondence to Be Signed," "Correspondence Requiring Your Attention," "Correspondence to Be Read" (letters that have been answered but in which your employer will probably be interested), "Reports," and "General Reading Material" (miscellaneous items of advertising and publications that your employer might want to read).

Handling Outgoing Mail

Getting signatures on outgoing mail.   When you give letters to your employer to be signed, separate those that were dictated from those that you or someone else wrote for your employer's signature.

The most usual method of giving dictated letters to someone for signing is to remove the carbon copy and insert the flap of the envelope over the original letter and its enclosures. Many executives are interested only in the letters, however, and consider the envelopes a nuisance. The practice of giving your employer letters without envelopes also has this advantage: You can get the letters out for signature more quickly, because you can address the envelopes from the carbon copies or after the letters are returned to you. But do not file the carbon copies until after the letters are signed and you have made the necessary late changes on the copies.

Assembling the mail.   When the mail has been signed, bring it back to your desk and assemble it for actual mailing. Check each letter for these things:

1. Has the letter been signed?

2. Are all enclosures included?

3. Are the inside address and the envelope address the same?

4. Has your employer marked further corrections or changes?

5. Has your employer added a postscript in ink that you should add to the carbon copies (unless it is a personal comment)?

6. Does the envelope address use the two-letter state abbreviation and is the address surrounded by white space, so that the post office's

optical character reader (OCR) can sort the envelope automatically?

When everything is ready, organize the mail into like categories to prepare
for folding and inserting.

Folding and inserting letters in envelopes.   Since paper clips can
jam postal equipment, it is preferable to staple enclosures or insert them
loose in the fold of the letter. But if you must use paper clips, insert the
folded letter upside down so that the paper clip is at the bottom. In all other
cases, fold and insert the letter as follows:

1.   Folding letters.   Letters written on full-size letterheads for
insertion in long envelopes should be folded as follows: one fold from the
bottom, about one-third of the way up; a second fold from the bottom to
within one-sixteenth of an inch of the top. Insert in the envelope, top up.

Letters written on full-sized letterheads for insertion in short envelopes should be folded as follows: one fold from the bottom to within
one-quarter of an inch of the top; a second fold from right to left, about
one-third of the way across; a third fold from left to right within
one-quarter of an inch of the right edge. Insert with the right edge up.

Letters written on half-size letterheads should be folded as follows: one
fold from right to left, about a third of the way across; a second fold from
left to right, leaving about one-sixteenth of an inch between the edges at the
right. Insert in a small envelope with the right edge up.

Letters should be inserted into envelopes so that when the letter is
removed from the envelope and unfolded, the type side should be up.

2.   Inserting enclosures.   To insert like items quickly, open and
flatten the flaps of several envelopes. Hold the envelopes with one hand and
the enclosures with the other, sliding enclosures in, one after the other.
However, if you have different enclosures for the envelopes, handle them
separately to avoid slipping an enclosure into the wrong envelope. (For
further details on handling enclosures, refer to the following section.)

Handling enclosures.   Generally, follow these rules for inserting
enclosures, but avoid using paper clips, as explained in the preceding
section:

1.   Enclosures the size of the letter.   They are easily folded and
inserted, with their accompanying letters, into commercial envelopes of the
ordinary size. If the enclosure consists of two or more sheets, staple them
together but do not fasten the enclosed material to the letter. Fold the
enclosure, then fold the letter, and next slip the enclosure inside the last
fold of the letter. Thus when the letter is removed from the envelope, the
enclosure comes out with it.

2. Enclosures larger than the letter. They include booklets, pamphlets, prospectuses, catalogs, and other printed material too large to fit into a commercial envelope of ordinary size. They are generally mailed in large manila envelopes. Enclosures of this kind may be handled in one of the following ways:

a. The letter is inserted with the enclosure in the large envelope, which is sealed. In this case first-class postage is charged for both the letter and the enclosure.

b. A combination envelope is used. This is a large envelope with a flap that is fastened by a patent fastener of some kind but not sealed. A smaller envelope of commercial size is affixed on the front of this envelope in the process of manufacture. The letter is inserted into the small envelope and the flap is sealed. Postage is affixed to the large envelope at third-class rates and to the small envelope at first-class rates.

c. The enclosure may be sent, unsealed, in one envelope and the letter, sealed, in another.

d. A letter may be enclosed with a parcel if postage is paid on the letter at the first-class rate. (See page 150.)

3. Enclosures smaller than the letter. When enclosures are considerably smaller than the letter, staple them to the letter in the upper left-hand corner, on top of the letter. If the enclosure cannot be stapled (such as coins), tape the objects to a card, or place them in a small, marked envelope, and then staple the card or envelope to the letter. If two or more such enclosures are sent, put the smaller one on top.

Selecting Addressing and Mailing Equipment

The volume of work in an office changes as the organization expands its operations. One of the first places an increase becomes evident is in the level of mail activity. Whether or not the organization has a separate mailing department, it must be well equipped to handle the processing of outgoing mail properly and efficiently.

Postal equipment. A postage scale and a postage meter are usually the first pieces of equipment an office selects for the mail room. Scales may be purchased in an office-supply store, but a postage meter must be leased from a manufacturer that has a product approved by the U.S. Postal

Service. Application to use metered stamps can be made through your local postmaster.

The U.S. Postal Service then provides a license and record book. After paying in advance for the amount of postage desired, your local post office will set the machine, so you can meter mail up to the amount paid. The record book provides a place to record the amount of postage used and the current balance shown on the meter. Usually, you must take the meter to the post office to be reset. However, with the computerized remote postage meter resetting (CMRS) system, users who qualify and maintain an account with the post office can reset their own meters using a one-time combination with each resetting. The design stamp you use must be approved by the post office, and metered mail must be deposited in bundles separate from mail with postage stamps.

Other mailing equipment.   Organizations that process a lot of outgoing mail may need automatic or semiautomatic folding and inserting machines as well as collators. An efficient mail room also has sorting trays and racks and mail bag holders. When the volume of repeat mail—mail sent periodically to the same address—is large, some type of addressing equipment is needed. Although a small list could be maintained on multiple sheets of address labels (see **Maintaining Mailing Lists,** page 128), a longer list would require special equipment.

Making a study of mail room needs.   To help your employer select the best equipment for your needs, make a list of the factors characterizing your mail volume—how much, how often, to whom, and so on. Then write to manufacturers of addressing equipment for current product information. Collect sales literature on all types of addressing equipment.

Many mailing lists are maintained by computer. Others are processed by machines that use metal address plates. Some machines that operate on the same principle use cards to record and print out addresses. Magnetic tape typewriters are also used to store names and addresses, which can then be printed out on envelopes or press-apply labels.

Costs vary, depending on the medium for recording and storing the addresses. A metal plate, for instance, may cost more than a card, but it will also last longer. However if your addresses change frequently, perhaps permanency is not as important as economy. Or perhaps the quality of the impression is more important than economy. For example, a magnetic-tape typewriter address or a computer address printout will appear to be individually typed. For executives to make good judgments, they need to have all of the facts pertaining to the cost of putting an address on the list, the cost of making address changes, and the cost of printing out the addresses, as well as the speed in addressing, the quality of the address after printing, and any other factors that are important in your type of work.

Maintaining Mailing Lists

Large lists. Offices that do a lot of mailing may maintain their lists by computer or on automatic addressing machines (described in **Selecting Addressing and Mailing Equipment,** page 126) that operate at high speeds and can re-sort and select specific names for any mailing. If an outside service maintains the list, you usually submit incoming address changes as they arrive or perhaps weekly. Since mailing to obsolete addresses is expensive and wasteful, lists must be kept up to date at all times.

Small lists. Most secretaries type and maintain very small office lists on computer diskettes, labels, cards, or, less frequently, sheets of paper. Labels come in gummed rolls or sheets or individually. The sheets of labels are perforated so that you can tear off only the labels you need and use the rest later. You could type a master set and thereafter have photocopies made on additional gummed sheets. For medium- and small-volume mailers who want to convert to the zip + 4 codes on computer or word processor lists, the Postal Service will correct diskette lists of three hundred and fifty to fifty thousand names at no charge.

Some secretaries—even when they type labels—maintain a permanent list of 3- by 5-inch cards that can be filed alphabetically or any other way the secretary desires. Different-colored cards can be used to designate specific groups; for instance, salmon cards might signify local addresses. Sheets should be used only for very small lists such as a board of directors. No matter what method best suits your needs, set aside a time each week, or use slack moments throughout the day, to update your list so that you can use it on a moment's notice.

Handling Bulk Mailings

Large-volume mailings are usually sent at bulk rate, unless speed is critical, so only a regular first-class mailing would be possible. Otherwise, the most economical choice is bulk-rate mailing.

Because postal rates and regulations change frequently, you should consult your local post office for details concerning second- and third-class bulk mailings. Generally, one has to pay an annual fee and apply for a permit to mail this way. Envelopes must either have precanceled stamps affixed or have the envelopes printed with a bulk permit stamp. Then the mail must be sorted by zip code, tied in bundles, properly labeled, and delivered to the post office. All of these steps take time, and the secretary should be aware of the entire process in scheduling a mailing, arranging for help in preparing the bundles, and computing the savings (if any) over first-class mail. See chapter 5 for a description of the classes of mail and applicable regulations.

Maintaining Efficiency in the Mail Room

The well-equipped mail desk.   Your job of getting out the mail does not get simpler if you have a mailing department—at least not in every respect. You still have to decide the best method of sending out *your* mail. Although a knowledge of the basic postal rates, and ways to use them properly, is essential (see chapter 5), a well-equipped mail desk can prevent actual mail handling from being wearisome tasks.

1. Supplies and equipment.   Devices and supplies that can end some of the drudgery include electronic postage scales, postage meters, rubber stamps, colorful press-apply mailing labels, and a variety of mailing envelopes and package-sealing tapes. If you regularly send letters with special classifications, purchase a rubber stamp with the necessary information, such as "Priority Mail" or "Special Delivery."

Postage meters not only eliminate stamp licking but eliminate the need for keeping loose stamps, protect postage against loss and waste, and eliminate stamp borrowing. The equipment will also seal envelopes while applying postage. The record book maintained with a postage meter provides an additional accounting record and basis for cost evaluation.

2. Planning and record keeping.   To be certain that your mail goes out when you want it to, learn the post office's schedules for outgoing mail. If you have a company mail room, learn its schedules, capabilities, and any regulations that would affect your mailings. If you handle your own outgoing mail, plan your work to allow time to meet any outside postal schedules. For purposes of control and accurate bookkeeping, keep good records of what you send, to whom, why, and the cost of postage used. Have a sheet on your mail desk to record such information as soon as you prepare something for mailing—before you forget. Good records are important not only for the bookkeeper to know where to post expenses but also for purposes of reviewing how much it is costing to do certain things. (See **How to cut rising mail-room costs,** page 130.)

Five ways to speed post office processing.   You can speed your letters on their way faster if you take these steps:

1. Place the correct zip code in the address and leave white space

around the address as required for OCR sorting at the post office. (See page 161, chapter 5.) FIM and zip + 4 bar codes should be used with business-reply mail (consult your local post office for details).

2. One of the preliminary steps in the post office processing of mail is to sort the local mail from the out-of-town mail. Unless your daily mail is limited to just a few pieces, the way it leaves your office is important to fast handling. Stack and tie your mail in local or out-of-town bundles with addresses facing the same direction.

3. When you send a special class of mail, such as special delivery or priority mail, to the post office, place these letters in special bundles placed on top of the other mail. The postal employees can then spot them more easily.

4. You can save as much as a full day in delivery by getting your mail out in the morning, instead of late in the afternoon. Although this is not always practical for all mail, you should try to see that out-of-town mail is sent as early in the day as possible.

5. Keep in mind the pickup times at your local collection box for timing your mailings.

How to cut rising mail-room costs.   The costs of communicating by mail increase each year, but here are ways that you can combat rising mail-room expenses:

1. Double-check to be certain that everyone on your mailing list *must* receive a copy of your communication, and regularly update your mailing list to eliminate obsolete or inaccurate addresses.

2. If you find that you often mail several letters every couple of days to the same person, look into the possibility of combining mailings into one letter.

3. Try to eliminate unnecessary enclosures.

4. Use routing slips instead of mailing numerous carbon copies or photocopies.

5. Consider microfilm if continual bulk mailings are a problem in your office.

6. Compare the costs of a telex or facsimile message instead of a first-class letter.

7. Consider first-class-presort mail, which can save several cents a letter.

Figure 17. Mailroom-Security Checklist

Checklist for better mailroom security

The Postal Inspection service offers this checklist for better mailroom security. Your suggestions of ideas and methods to make the job go safely and smoothly are welcome.—Editor

( ) Mailroom personnel screened.

( ) Location, furniture and mail flow provide maximum security.

( ) Access limited to authorized personnel.

( ) Distribution delays are eliminated.

( ) Postage and meter protected from theft/unauthorized use.

( ) High value items locked overnight.

( ) Accountable items verified and secured.

( ) Registered, Express and insured services properly used.

( ) Control of address labels maintained.

( ) Labels securely fastened to mail items.

( ) Postage strips overlap labels.

( ) Labels and cartons do not identify valuable contents.

( ) Return address included and duplicate address in carton.

( ) Presort and ZIP + 4 savings taken when applicable.

( ) Parcels packaged properly.

( ) Containers and sacks used when possible.

( ) Outgoing mail proper-

ly delivered to postal custody.

( ) Employee parking separated from dock area.

( ) Lost and rifled mail reported to post office.

( ) Supervisor can see all employees and work areas.

( ) Contract delivery services screened.

( ) Unnecessary stops by delivery vehicle are eliminated.

( ) Procedures established for handling unexplained packages.

( ) Periodic testing done for loss/quality control.

Source: U.S. Postal Service, *Memo to Mailers* 20, no. 4 (April 1958): 8. Used with permission.

8. Note also that zip + 4 can save about a half-cent a letter.

9. For express mail, compare costs of private services (see chapter 5) with postal express service.

10. Check at your post office whether you qualify for the carrier-route presort discount.

11. When possible, use the telephone for local contacts.

12. Use only the service you need; for example, do not pay for special delivery if regular first-class mail will arrive just as soon.

13. Keep your messages brief and to the point—long-windedness costs money in extra postage.

14. Guard against unauthorized use of postage and supplies.

Mail-room security.   Abuse in the mail room is a problem in many organizations. Confidential mail is not protected, postage is taken for personal use, and valuable equipment and supplies are stolen. To help organizations eliminate abuse, the Postal Service has devised a checklist of twenty-four points, as illustrated in figure 17. A periodic check such as this can prevent potential problems from arising.

DOMESTIC TELEGRAPH SERVICE

How Domestic Messages Are Sent

You can send a domestic telegram through your telex network, by facsimile, or by computer. Users who don't have the volume to warrant this type of transmission can telephone Western Union and send a traditional telegram.

Territory covered by domestic telegraph service.   Western Union domestic telegraph service includes messages sent to any point in the continental United States, Canada, Mexico, and Saint Pierre and Miquelon Islands. Messages sent to Hawaii and other points overseas are classified as cablegrams.

Classes of Domestic Service

Since rates and requirements change from time to time, consult Western Union for current data pertaining to the following classes of domestic service. (See also **Counting Charges for Telegrams,** page 134.)

Fast telegram.   The fast telegram is quicker than any other class of service. It usually is hand delivered two to five hours after being called in. The charge is based on a minimum of fifteen words, with an additional charge for each word in excess of fifteen. The address and signature are not counted as words. Code may be used.

Mailgram. Mailgrams are sent from Western Union to the post office nearest the addressee and printed out individually. Charges are based on a minimum of one hundred words with an additional charge for additional words. The address and signature do count as words in a mailgram. Preferential treatment is given to mailgrams, ensuring their delivery in the next regular mail after being received at the post office —either the same day or the next morning, depending on time of arrival and schedule of mail deliveries.

Night letter. A night letter is slightly less expensive than a fast telegram. Delivery is made on the morning of the next day or the morning of the next business day in the case of a business message. A message phoned in one day will be received at its destination the next day (or business day) between 8 A.M. and 2 P.M. A night letter may be filed at any time up to 2 A.M. The charge is based on a minimum of one hundred words, with an additional charge for each group of five words in excess of one hundred. The address and the signature are not counted as words. Code may be used.

Money orders. Money orders can be sent through Western Union. The sender may call in and charge the order to Visa or MasterCard or take cash, a check, or money order to the local Western Union office. There is no limit on amount sent if cash is used. Call Western Union beforehand to determine the amount currently accepted by check.

Ships in port. You can send a telegram to a ship in port the same as if it were a land-based location. Include the full name of the passenger, the name of the port and pier, the steamship line and name of the ship, the stateroom number (if known), and the departure time.

How to Type a Telegram

Most companies simply telephone their messages to Western Union, but a copy of the message should be typed for the office files. Ask Western Union for blank forms to use as file copies. However, if you prepare typed copy for delivery to Western Union, the following guidelines are useful.

1. The number of copies depends on the requirements of your company. Four may be needed if the telegram is to be picked up by a messenger: the original for pickup, a carbon copy or photocopy

for confirmation by mail, a carbon copy or photocopy for your files, and a carbon copy or photocopy for the accounting department (or for your telegraph account file if you pay your employer's telegraph bill).

2. Check the class of service in the form provided on the telegraph blank—domestic service in the upper left corner, international service in the upper right corner. Also type the class of service two spaces above the address.

3. Type the date and hour in the upper right corner, two spaces above the address.

4. Omit the salutation and complimentary close.

5. Double-space the message.

6. Do not divide words at the ends of lines.

7. Type as you would any other material. Use all capitals only for code words.

8. In the lower left corner type: reference initials; how the message is to be sent—"Charge," "Paid," or "Collect"; address and telephone number of the sender, unless printed on the blank.

9. If the telegram is to be charged, type the name of the charge account in the space provided on the blank.

How to Send the Same Message to Multiple Addresses

If you want to send the message to a number of people, type the telegram text only once. List the names and addresses on a special sheet obtainable from Western Union (or on a plain sheet). Above the list type "Please send the attached message to the following twelve (whatever the number is) addresses."

Counting Charges for Telegrams

Addresses.   No charge is made for essential material in one complete address. A charge is made for alternate names or addresses. No charge is made for notations such as *personal* and *will call.* The telegram may be addressed to the attention of a specific individual without charge.

Signature and address of sender.   No charge is made for the name of the sender. The city and state from which the message is sent are included in the dateline free of charge, but a charge is made for the sender's street address if it is to be transmitted. The signature may include the company name and the name of the individual sending the telegram without charge, but a charge is made for the name of a department added to such a signature.

Cities, states, and countries.   In the message itself, names of cities, states, and countries are counted according to the number of words they contain. For example, *New York City* is three words, *United States* is two. Running the words together as *Newyork* does not affect the count. If the names are abbreviated, they count as one word. Thus *NYC* is one word.

Abbreviations.   Abbreviations that do not contain more than five letters are counted as one word. They should be written without spaces or periods—*COD, UN, FOB.*

Initials.   If separated by a space, initials are counted as separate words, but if written without spaces, they are counted as one word for each five letters or fraction thereof. Thus *R L* is counted as two words, but *RL* is one word.

Personal names.   Personal names are counted in accordance with the way they are usually written. Thus *Van der Gren* is counted as three words, *Van Dorn,* as two words; and *O'Connell,* as one word.

Mixed groups of letters and figures.   Mixed groups of letters, figures, and the characters $, /, &, #, ' (indicating feet or minutes), and " (indicating inches or seconds) are counted at the rate of five characters, or fraction thereof, to the word (if there are no spaces between them) in messages between points in the United States and between points in Mexico. Thus *one hundred* is counted as two words, but *10* is counted as one word; *$34.50,* as one word (the decimal is not counted); *44B42,* as one word, but *1000th* (six characters) is counted as two words. In messages sent to Canada and Saint Pierre and Miquelon Islands, each figure, affix, bar, dash, and sign in a group is counted as a word.

Punctuation marks.   Punctuation marks are not charged for, but the words *stop, comma,* and the like are counted.

Compound words.   Compound words that are hyphenated in the dictionary are counted as one word. Thus *son-in-law* is one word. Combinations of two or more dictionary words are counted according to the number of words of which they are composed. Thus *highschool* and *Newyears* are each counted as two words.

INTERNATIONAL CABLE SERVICE

How Messages Are Sent to Foreign Countries

You can send cablegrams as well as telegrams by telex or facsimile. But if the volume doesn't warrant this type of service, you can also telephone

Western Union or one of the international carriers such as ITT World Communications, RCA Global Communications, Western Union International, or MCI International.

Classes of International Service

Full-rate message (FR).   This is the standard fast service for messages in plain or secret (coded or ciphered) language. The charge per word varies according to the destination. There is a minimum charge of seven words. Since both the address and the signature are counted in the charge, users frequently obtain a registered code address and signature. See **Registered Code Addresses,** page 137.

Letter telegram (LT).   Letter telegrams (sometimes known as night letters) provide an overnight service (to certain countries) designed for messages of some length that need not arrive before the next day. Letter telegrams may be written in plain language only; however, registered code addresses may be used. The charge for the letter telegram is less than for a full-rate message, with a minimum charge of twenty-two words. The address and signature are counted in the charge as well as the indicator "LT," which must be inserted before the address. Letter telegram messages are delivered generally after 8 A.M. local time the day after filing. Certain Pacific and European countries have special rules.

Radiograms.   A full-rate cablegram can be sent to ships at sea in plain language or code. Give the name of the passenger (in full since there may be more than one with the same last name), his or her stateroom (if known), the ship, and the marine radio station in the address (write the station as one word). Type *INTL* above the addressee's name.

> INTL
> Walter Scott
> Stateroom 61B
> SS LIBERTE
> Newyorkradio (Via ITT)

Addresses and signatures are counted as in other international messages. Messages may be filed with an international carrier directly or with Western Union.

Radio photo service.   Radio photo service covers the transmission of photographs by radio. Among the types of material suitable for transmission are financial statements, machine drawings, production curves, fashion designs, architectural designs, typewritten matter, printed matter, affidavits, contracts, signatures, and business and legal papers of all kinds. Photo service is available to the public through some international carriers such as RCA Global Communications.

Special services.   One service, *reply prepaid (RP)*, means that you are paying in advance for a reply from your addressee overseas. *Paid confirmation (PC)*, accepted in some countries, means that you are paying for notification of the date and time of delivery. Confirmation costs the equivalent of seven additional words at the full-rate message price. *FS* typed before a name means that you are requesting forwarding to a person who has moved. *NUIT* typed before a name means that the message should be delivered even after business hours.

Registered Code Addresses

A charge is made for both the address and the signature in all messages sent to foreign countries. However, a registered code address and signature may be used. They obviate the expense incurred in using full addresses and signatures. Registered code addresses must be arranged locally. Contact one of the international carriers or Western Union.

Counting Charges for Cables

International carriers each have their own rates and procedures for counting charges. The following is an example of one such procedure:

Paid-service indicator (PSI).   Except for full-rate messages, which have no PSI, this is the first billable word.

Addresses.   In a registered cable address, the name of the person or company and the street are counted as one word regardless of the number of letters. The country may be indicated free of charge, and the city of origin, date, and time are free.

Signature.   A charge is made for each word. A cable need not be signed or it may be signed with a code signature. (Signatures are preferred to let the addressee know to whom to reply.) The signature is the last billable word.

Word count.   To count words for a cable, follow these rules:

1. A group of characters (letters, numbers, or mixed) is charged as one word if it does not exceed ten characters total.
2. A group of more than ten characters is counted at a rate of one chargeable word for each ten characters or less.

3. Isolated signs (? . , : " −) equal one word each if not part of a word group (some regulations state that one should not use symbols in cablegrams but should spell out each one).

Economizing on Telegrams and Cables

Plans for economy.   In trying to reduce costs in the use of telegraph service, consider three things: (1) the urgency of the message, (2) time differentials, (3) the wording of the message.

    1.   Urgency of message.   In some cases, delivery on the same day may be essential; in others, delivery on the morning of the following day would be satisfactory. The fastest service is the most expensive and therefore should be used only when urgency is a factor.

    2.   Time differentials.   Consider the variations in standard time in different parts of the United States and in different countries in choosing the class of service by which to send a message. The ITT World Communications time chart is shown in chapter 18. When passing a line to the left, subtract one day. When passing a line to the right, add one day. The simplified chart illustrated in chapter 18 was also compiled by ITT World Communications. It shows how to calculate time in foreign countries when you know eastern standard time. The following is an illustration of how money can be saved by considering time differentials:

> At 3:30 in the afternoon a secretary in San Francisco is told to send a nineteen-word telegram to New York City. Since it is 6:30 in New York City and the people to whom the message is being sent have probably left the office for the day, the secretary suggests sending a night letter. By considering the time differential, the secretary saves her company money without affecting the delivery time of the telegram. (Chapter 18 contains a map that shows the location of time zones in the United States.)

    3.   Wording of message.   Money can be saved by exercising a little care and ingenuity in the wording of a message. Although terseness should not be carried to the point that the message is not clear, complete sentence structure is not necessary. Verbs, nouns, and adjectives are the important words. In the following example a twenty-five-word fast telegram was nearly cut in half by deleting unnecessary words and expressing the same thought clearly in only fifteen words.

> *Twenty-five words:* WE ARE IN NEED OF PRICE AND DELIVERY SCHEDULE ON YOUR AEC-1400 PROCESSOR. WE BELIEVE YOUR

QUOTATION OF 14 AUGUST CONTAINS A TWO-DIGIT ERROR. *Fifteen words:* REQUEST NEW PRICE AND DELIVERY SCHEDULE ON AEC-1400 PROCESSOR. AUGUST 14 QUOTE IN ERROR.

HIGH-SPEED MESSAGING

With some types of high-speed transmission, messages can be sent in mere seconds to virtually anywhere in the world that is reached by telephone lines or satellite. Among the older high-speed technologies are telex and facsimile transmission; younger forms of rapid messaging include electronic mail and voice-data systems.

Facsimile Transmission

Facsimile refers to both the name of a machine and a process by which exact copies of documents can be converted into signals that can be sent over the telephone lines to a receiving terminal. At the destination a facsimile *transceiver* (a machine that can send or receive) converts the signals back into a readable form that is a precise duplicate of the original. Both text and graphics of almost any sort can be sent by facsimile.

How to send a facsimile message. Facsimile, or fax, machines look like compact copiers. To send a message, you place the document in a tray or around a cylinder. The machine then scans the material, and light and dark areas are converted into signals that can travel over the telephone lines to a compatible machine at the receiving terminal. When you are ready to send the message, you dial the telephone number at the receiving terminal and push the transmit button. However, facsimile can transmit only what is already prepared, since there is no keyboard. Therefore, you would prepare the message on a typewriter, computer, or word processor and add any needed graphics before putting the finished document on the facsimile machine.

Types of facsimile machines. There are four classifications of machines: Group I machines, which use a slower analog conversion process, have speeds of four to six minutes a page. Group II machines also use the analog technique but transmit at two to three minutes a page. Group III machines use a faster digital process to convert documents into code that can be transmitted at speeds of twenty seconds to a minute a page. Group IV machines, which are still being developed, also use the digital technique and are expected to transmit a page in seconds. Although digital equipment usually costs more, the transmission costs are less.

The newer transceivers can be programmed to store data so that it can be sent automatically whenever you choose, whether or not you are there at the time. The Group III machines have more advanced features than the early generation facsimile, for example: document reduction, programmable capability, automatic feed and cut, unattended operation, and telephone-line or satellite transmission.

Facsimile machines are convenient and simple to use, and transmission of one page costs less than sending a first-class letter and much less than using overnight express or placing a long-distance telephone call. All you need to operate the machine is a telephone, since the facsimile itself has its own scanner and printer. Although newer machines are generally compatible (that is, a receiving machine is likely to accept the sender's transmission without problems), facsimile paper is not so compatible. Thus paper manufactured to work on one machine might not work on another.

Facsimile services.   Businesses that do not own a facsimile machine can send messages nevertheless through a facsimile service. Some of the international carriers provide this service, as well as other local service establishments (check your yellow pages). For occasional use, you would take the document you want to transmit to the service bureau, much the same way that you might deliver a telegram to be sent to Western Union. However, because the document would be sent by converting it into signals that travel over the telephone lines, you would retain the original. Rates vary among the service organizations and change from time to time. Request current information and inquire whether you can send occasional individual documents or whether you must subscribe to a full service.

The United States Postal Service uses facsimile machines as well as other transmission methods in its INTELPOST service (see chapter 5, page 160). INTELPOST can be used to reach specified locations where the document can then be picked up or delivered by regular mail. Some private delivery services and other types of organizations also offer facsimile service in addition to the physical transportation of material.

Telex Service

Telex is another form of high-speed message transmission and, like facsimile, is an older technology.

How to send a telex message.   Whereas you cannot prepare a message on a facsimile machine—only send it—you can both type and send a telex message on machines commonly known as "teleprinters" or "teletypewriters." Telex is a keyboard-to-keyboard type of message transmission. The machines have typewriter-like keyboards on which you type the message, which means that you are limited to text, whereas facsimile can send exact copies of graphics as well as text.

Also, telex messages must be prepared in all capital letters, and the quality of the printout is often inferior. A teleprinter will code your message on a punched paper tape, which is fed into a reader device. Before word processors were widely used, your message was coded onto a punched tape as you typed. Therefore, you could not correct errors before sending the message. You had to type several Es or other letters after an error and then retype the word. With word processors you can now type and correct the copy on diskettes and then punch the tape from the corrected message. Using a corrected diskette, the tape that is coded to transmit the message can be error free.

After typing the message, you dial the telex number at the receiving terminal and press the appropriate transmission control. The typed message is then converted to signals that will travel over the telephone lines and at the destination it is converted back and printed out on a receiving teleprinter in normal, readable text.

Although all telex terminals are compatible, you must follow the instructions supplied by Western Union or one of the international carriers to use the teleprinter properly and to format your message correctly. These instructions will include guidelines for using the *answerback mechanism,* a code by which a sender and receiver identify each other. When you are ready to transmit, for example, you will press a "Call" button and then dial the telephone number designated by the telex service you are using. This will in turn activate your machine's answerback mechanism. Once both parties are correctly identified, the transmission can continue. For further details on procedures, see **Telex services,** below.

Telex I and II.   Since telex, established by Western Union, has been used for many years, the equipment is relatively standardized, and the cost of transmission is less than it is for some of the newer technologies and services such as electronic mail. Telex I is the original telex, and Telex II is the current name for TWX (Teletypewriter Exchange).

Although Telex I machines use a different code than Telex II machines, a Telex I user can transmit to a Telex II user without difficulty. Telex I transmits at a speed of about sixty-seven words a minute. Telex II transmits about one hundred words a minute. Telex I messages are billed on a pulse rate (one pulse = one character), and Telex II messages are billed by the minute.

Telex services.   A telex service is a network of subscribers who are interconnected. Your terminal may be directly connected to the service you choose, or you may have a private leased line. You can subscribe to a telex service through any communications carrier. Since the industry deregulated, Western Union has been able to connect you with overseas numbers and the international carriers have been able to connect you with domestic numbers.

Telex subscribers are provided with a telex number, and you should follow the service's instructions for transmitting messages on your own communicating teleprinter or the one supplied by the service. Usually, the system will prompt you, line by line, what to type: the receiver's name and the company name, street address, city, state or province, country, and zip or postal code, followed by your own name, country, and telex number. After that, you will be told to type the text, or the body of your message.

Write to the international carriers and Western Union and request current rates and guidelines for subscription. If you are already a telex subscriber, you will be listed in the annual *U.S. Directory for Telecommunications Subscribers* (free to telex subscribers). This directory lists the company name, address, carrier, telex number, and telex answerback for all telex subscribers.

Some services enable you to dial into the carrier of your choice with a computer and a modem. Through some services, for example, subscribers can have access to the full telex network using their computers rather than teleprinters. In this way you have all of the editing capabilities of any computer or word processor and can, at the same terminal, transmit your message through a telex network.

Telex messages can be prepared by subscribers and then delivered at a later designated time. This is sometimes referred to as a "store-and-forward service." In other words, you can store incoming messages in the carrier's central computer until you are ready to retrieve them or have them forwarded to an electronic "mailbox" for later pickup.

Teletex Service

Teletex service was introduced by Western Union in 1983 in selected cities in the United States and between those cities and West Germany, where it was first developed. This is a high-speed transmission service (forty-five times the speed of telex) for high-volume users. Teletex users can also transmit messages to telex subscribers.

Unlike telex messages, Teletex messages look like a traditional business letter, with uppercase and lowercase letters and better print quality. Teletex has a wider range of features too, including accents and diacritical marks. Contact Western Union for current rates and procedures.

Teletex messages can be prepared on word processors or computers that are specially equipped to send and receive such messages automatically. Therefore, the messages can be edited before sending them to their destination over the telephone lines. Teletex use is dependent upon manufacturers of the word processing equipment meeting the standards (such as compatibility) required by the Consultative Committee for International Telegraph and Telephone.

Private Services

Leased-channel service. Some very high-volume users need an exclusive communications line between their organization and one or more overseas offices. Such a line can be leased from an international carrier for a monthly charge plus, in some cases, an additional message-unit charge. Leased channels are used to transmit a wide variety of messages, including teleprinter, voice, facsimile, and electronic mail.

Tie-line service. Tie lines, also known as "tie trunks," are direct ties between two points. A tie line may, for instance, link two or more private branch exchanges or connect an organization directly with Western Union. Tie lines are usually leased from common carriers such as AT&T.

Electronic-Mail Transmission

Electronic mail (E-mail) is a relatively young technology that is still evolving. It primarily refers to a computer-based system whereby one computer sends a message to another. Since computers can store data, an incoming message is said to be filed in an electronic "mailbox." A *private electronic "mailbox"* means that only the intended recipients can read their own mail. A *bulletin-board system* means that messages are available for all users to read. Although passwords can be used to maintain confidentiality in electronic mail, some systems have no such security measures.

Types of E-mail systems. Large organizations today often aim for greater integration of computer and word processing operations, facsimile transmission, telex, and other messaging. Combining E-mail with other operations is a logical step in that direction, although the use of this system is dependent on receivers having compatible computer equipment to accept one's messages. Also, installation costs are high if firms do not already have the necessary equipment. But once the equipment is in place, there are usually savings in copying, long-distance delivery, and other traditional costs.

Some E-mail systems are *centralized,* consisting of a number of terminals connected to a large central computer. Others rely on a *network system* with a number of independent terminals each of which can send and receive messages on its own. A *node-to-node stand-alone electronic-mail system* is an independent computer capable of communicating with another compatible computer by using a modem and the telephone lines to send messages back and forth. A *local-area network (LAN)* is a network of computers that are wired to one another and communicate with one another directly (instead of using the telephone lines). *Voice-mail systems* also send, receive, and store messages and can be accessed from almost any telephone in the world (see **Integrated Voice-Data Terminals,** page 55, in chapter 2). Experts predict that voice and electronic mail will eventually be be integrated, with electronic mail ultimately becoming voice mail.

Public data networks.   These services function as a clearinghouse for the electronic messages of subscribers and offer third parties access to large databases. An example is MCI Mail. By way of a "switching technique," subscribers to certain data networks can call the network by telephone and then reach any other computer that is part of the data network. Because charges and procedures differ among the services, it is necessary to request current information including rates, types of service, and instructions on use of the service.

How to use E-mail.   To use E-mail you need a computer terminal or a communicating word processor. With the right equipment you can create a message of any length at any time of the day and send it to another terminal by using a modem and the telephone lines. If you use a service, follow the instructions provided for accessing the network. Usually, you must type certain words and codes to learn if there are messages waiting. You may also receive information such as who sent the message, how long it is, and when it was sent. With some systems, you are informed by a beep or some other signal as soon as a new message arrives. You can retrieve your messages from a remote location by telephone, much the same as you can pick up messages on an answering machine from a remote location. If you are at your computer terminal, you can read your incoming messages, store them until later, or immediately create replies.

When you create the messages you want to send on a computer or communicating word processor keyboard, you can edit them and print out a hard copy at your own terminal. Editing with E-mail software, however, is much more limited than with word processing software. An instruction guide is provided with the software, and some programs also have an on-screen "help" command.

Satellite Transmission

Some types of transmission cannot take place directly over the terrestrial telephone lines and satellites are used in those cases. INTEL-

SAT, an acronym derived from the International Telecommunications Satellite Consortium, is a communications satellite that can handle telephone, radio, and television transmission. The marine version of INTELSAT is INMARSAT. Through INMARSAT a properly equipped ship or offshore rig can contact any telex subscriber in the world. INMARSAT service is an automatic telecommunications service that operates similar to a telex service.

── Chapter 5 ──────────

Using Postal Information to Save Time and Money

DOMESTIC POSTAL SERVICE

Sources of Information

The *Domestic Mail Manual* covers regulations and information about rates and postage, classes of mail, special services, wrapping and mailing requirements, and collection and delivery services. The manual and loose-leaf supplementary service are sold on a subscription basis. For it and other postal publications for sale, write to the Superintendent of Documents, U.S. Government Printing Office, Washington, DC 20402.

The *National Five-Digit Zip Code and Post Office Directory* lists all post offices arranged alphabetically by states. It is sold in some post offices and can be ordered from Five-Digit Zip Code Directory Orders, Address Information Center, 6060 Primacy Parkway, Suite 101, Memphis, TN 38188–9980.

Other booklets and brochures are available free of charge from your local post office. A newsletter, *Memo to Mailers,* is available free from the U.S. Postal Service, P.O. Box 999, Springfield, VA 22150–0999.

Mailable Items and How to Dispatch Them

The following list shows the class of mail by which to send each item:

Item	*How to Send*
Bills and statements of account	First class
Birth announcements	First class

Bonds: negotiable	Registered first class
nonnegotiable	First class or certified first class
Books	Fourth Class

(Special rates apply to books. The book may be autographed. Mark the package "Special Fourth-Class Rate: Books.")

Catalogs	Third, fourth class

(Special rates apply to printed catalogs individually addressed and not weighing more than ten pounds. Each piece must be clearly marked "Catalog.")

Checks: filled out	First class
canceled	First class
certified	Registered first class
endorsed in blank	Registered first class
Circulars	Third class
Currency	Registered first class
Documents: no intrinsic value	Certified mail
with intrinsic value:	
(a) signed original	Registered first class
(b) copies	First class
Drawings	Third class
Form letters	Third class

(Check with the post office for the category of third-class mail suited to your needs.)

Greeting cards	First class
Jewelry	Registered first class

(Limit of liability is twenty-five thousand dollars—less if commercial or other insurance is also carried.)

Letters: carbon copies	First class
duplicate copies	First class
for delivery to addressee only	Registered or certified first class
form (See Form letters)	
handwritten or typed	First class
Magazines	Second class
Manuscript: without proof sheets	Fourth class insured

(Mark the package "Special Fourth-Class Rate.")

accompanied by proof sheets	Third or fourth class, depending on weight

(Corrections on proof sheets may include insertion of new matter as well as marginal notes to the printer. The manuscript of one article may not be enclosed with the proof of another unless the matter is mailed at the first-class rate.)

Merchandise (see Packages)	
Money orders	First class
Newspapers	Second class
Packages: up to sixteen ounces	Third class
sixteen ounces and	
over	Parcel post
containing messages	(see page 152)

(Packages may be sealed if they bear an inscription authorizing inspection by the postmaster. Packages containing articles valued at not more than five hundred dollars may be insured, but if they contain articles valued at more, they should be sealed and registered. First-class postage will then apply, and the liability limit is twenty-five thousand dollars.)

Periodicals	Second class
Photographs	Third class

(Wrap with a cardboard protection and mark the envelope "Photograph—Do Not Bend." Photographs may be autographed.)

Postal cards	First class
Postcards	First class

(To be mailed at postcard rates, cards must be $3\frac{1}{2}$ by $5\frac{1}{2}$ inches minimum and $4\frac{1}{2}$ by 6 inches maximum. If a card is enclosed in an envelope, it cannot be mailed at the postcard rate. Cards carrying a statement of a past-due account cannot be mailed at the card rate because they must be enclosed in an envelope.)

Plants, seeds, cuttings, scions,	Third class or parcel post de-
bulbs, and roots	pending on weight
Printed matter:	
less than sixteen ounces	Third class
sixteen ounces and over	Fourth class
Stock certificates:	
negotiable	Registered first class
nonnegotiable	First class or certified
Tapes and cassettes:	
personal	First class
nonpersonal	Special fourth class

(Mark packages for contents to avoid damage to magnetic surfaces. Mark fourth-class sound packages "Sound Recording.")

Typewritten material	First class

(See also Manuscript.)

Size and Weight Standards

Minimum-size standards. The following minimum-size standards apply to all mailable matter: All mailing pieces must be at least 0.007 inch thick, and all mailing pieces (other than keys and identification devices) that are 0.25 inch thick or less must be (1) rectangular, (2) at least $3\frac{1}{2}$ inches high, and (3) at least 5 inches long. Anything less than the minimum size is prohibited from the mails.

Nonstandard mail. First-class mail weighing one ounce or less, and single-piece rate third-class mail and certain international mail weighing one ounce or less are nonstandard and subject to a surcharge in addition to the applicable postage and fees unless they meet the following size standards: (1) length not greater than $11\frac{1}{2}$ inches, (2) height not greater than $6\frac{1}{8}$ inches, (3) thickness not greater than 0.25 inch, and (4) an aspect ratio (ratio of height to length) between 1:1.3 and 1:2.5 inclusive. Length must not be less than 1.3 or greater than 2.5 times the height.

Classes of Domestic Service

Express mail®. Express mail offers reliable expedited delivery of high-priority shipments within the United States and to selected foreign countries (see **INTERNATIONAL POSTAL SERVICE, page 156**). The fastest service, it provides several options for both private and business customers who require several options for both private and business customers who require reliable overnight delivery of letters and packages.

The three classes of domestic express service are Express Mail Next Day Service, Express Mail Custom Designed Service, and Express Mail Same Day Airport Service. All express shipments are insured at no additional cost. To use *Express Mail Next Day Service,* take your shipment to any designated Express Mail Post Office by the time designated at the facility. Your mailing will be delivered by 3 P.M. of the next day, or it can be picked up by the addressee at a designated destination post office as early as 10 A.M. the next business day. *Express Mail Custom Designed Service* is available only on a scheduled basic between designated locations. Mailers must complete a service agreement (Form 5631) that sets up the place and date of shipment. *Express Mail Same Day Airport Service* is available between designated airports for same-day delivery. Mail must be delivered at an airport facility during times specified by the Postal Service. For more information, consult your postmaster or customer service representative.

First-class mail. First-class mail consists of single letters, cards, presort first-class mail, zip + 4 first-class mail, and first-class zone-rated (priority) mail.

   1. **Letters and cards.** First-class mail (under twelve ounces) receives expeditious handling and transportation and free forwarding (for one year) and return and may not be opened for postal inspection. Any

mailable matter may be sent as first-class mail. Postal cards (Postal Service), postcards (commercial), personal correspondence, matter wholly or partially in writing or typewriting, bills, and statements of account must be mailed as first-class mail. When first-class mail is included with second-, third-, or fourth-class matter, postage at the first-class rate is required for the letter. The package should be marked "Letter Enclosed."

First-class mail will be delivered overnight locally and to certain designated areas if properly addressed (including zip code) and deposited in time. The designated overnight delivery areas are dependent on transportation accessibility and scheduling. Second-day delivery is scheduled for locally designated states nationwide to which transportation is available for consistent achievement of two-day delivery. Third-day delivery encompasses all remaining outlying areas nationwide.

2. Presort first-class mail. The Postal Service offers a presort rate that is less than the regular rate for letters and postcards. The presort rate is charged on each piece that is part of a group of ten or more pieces sorted to the same five-digit zip code or of a group of fifty or more pieces sorted to the same three-digit zip code prefix. To qualify, a mailing must consist of at least five hundred pieces. Mail that cannot be separated to five or three digits is counted toward the minimum volume but does not qualify for the lower rate. Carrier-route rates apply to each piece that is part of a group of ten or more pieces properly sorted to the same carrier route, rural route, highway contract route, post office box section, or general delivery unit. Each mailing must have a minimum of five hundred pieces. Customers are required to pay an annual fee and secure a mailing permit.

3. Zip + 4 first-class mail. This category of postage discounts consists of letters and postcards that are part of a mailing of at least five hundred pieces of a zip + 4 presort mailing or at least two hundred fifty pieces of a zip + 4 nonpresort mailing. The city-state-zip + 4 code line of the address must be located within an area 1 inch from the left edge of the mailing piece and 1 inch from the right edge. The bottom line of the address must be at least $\frac{5}{8}$ inch from the bottom edge, and the top line must be no more than $2\frac{1}{4}$ inches from the bottom edge. Ask at your local post office for details on having your hard-copy (paper) diskette mailing lists converted to zip + 4 free of charge.

4. First-class zone-rated (priority) mail. First-class zone-rated (priority) mail is first-class mail weighing more than twelve ounces, and rates are based on zoned distances. Except to APOs and FPOs, the maximum weight limit is seventy pounds, and the maximum size is 108 inches, length and girth combined.

Priority mail may be registered or insured or sent COD or special delivery if the charges for these services are paid in addition to the regular priority mail rate.

Second-class mail (newspapers and other periodicals).   Second-class mail includes newspapers and other periodicals issued at least four times a year. A publisher or registered news agent who mails at the second-class rate must have a second-class permit obtained from the post office.

To qualify for second-class rates, publishers and news agents must normally distribute primarily to paid subscribers (for additional information, contact your local post office). Second-class publications may not be designed primarily for advertising purposes. They must be formed of printed sheets and may not be reproduced by stencil, mimeograph, or hectograph processes.

The regular second-class postage rate varies depending on the distance mailed, the advertising portion of the publication's content, and whether the publication is mailed to an address within the country of publication. Ask at your local post office for details concerning bulk-rate mailings and special privileges such as the nonprofit rate.

Requester publications, whether free or by paid subscription, must have at least twenty-four pages but no more than 75 percent advertising. Mailers must produce a legitimate list of people who requested the publication.

Third-class mail (advertising mail and merchandise weighing less than one pound).   Third-class mail consists of circulars, booklets, catalogs, and other printed materials not required to be sent as first-class mail. It also includes merchandise, farm products, and keys. Each piece is limited in weight to less than sixteen ounces. There are two subcategories: single-piece rate and bulk rate.

Third-class mail is subject to postal inspection but may be sealed if clearly marked "Third Class" on the outside. It is advisable to designate the contents on the wrapper, such as "Merchandise" or "Printed Matter." Writing, except something in the nature of an autograph or inscription, is not permitted on third-class matter. "Do not open until Christmas," or a similar legend, may be written on the wrapper; other directions or requests may not. Corrections of typographical errors may be made.

Bulk rate requires a bulk-mail permit and is applicable to mailings of pieces separately addressed to different addresses in quantities of not less than two hundred pieces or fifty pounds. The pieces must be zip coded, presorted, and bundled or sacked. Ask at your local post office for sacking requirements for the various categories (such as carrier route) and the requirements for nonprofit organizations.

Fourth-class mail (parcels).   Parcels weighing one pound or more (except special or library-rate) are mailable as fourth-class mail. Generally, parcels weighing a maximum of seventy pounds and measuring up to 108 inches in girth and length combined can be mailed anywhere in the United States (ask at your local post office for exceptions). When mailing larger parcels, you should contact your post office for appropriate mailing instructions. Be certain packages are securely prepared for rough handling.

Do not seal the package unless it bears an inscription that it may be opened for postal inspection. No communication may be enclosed with a parcel unless additional postage is paid. Invoices and customer's orders that relate entirely to the articles may be enclosed. When articles are being returned for repair, exchange, or credit, no communication, such as "Please credit my account," may be included unless additional postage is paid, but the sales slip may be enclosed. Seasonal greetings may be enclosed.

A letter may be enclosed with a parcel if postage is paid on the letter at the first-class rate and on the package at the parcel-post rate. The mail will be dispatched as fourth-class matter. Beneath the postage and above the address, write the words "First-Class Mail Enclosed."

Special-handling postage entitles fourth-class mail to the same handling as is given to first-class mail but not to special delivery by the office of destination. Nor does special handling ensure the safe delivery of the mail.

Rates vary among parcel post, single pieces, bound printed matter, all zone rated, as well as for nonzone-rated items charged by the pound such as books (special fourth-class rate) and filmstrips (library rate).

Special Services

Business-reply mail.   Senders who want to encourage responses by paying the postage for those responses may use the business-reply service. Application is made by filling out U.S. Postal Service Form 3614 and paying the annual permit fee. A charge is imposed on each reply letter or card that is returned. Payment for returns is usually made by deduction from an advance account deposit by the mailer or by cash as returns are delivered. If an advance deposit is made at the post office, the mailer must pay an accounting charge plus the per-piece-returned rate. Ask for current requirements at your local post office.

Business-reply mail must be identified as such in large letters on the address side of the envelope. Also appearing on the same side must be the permit number, the name of the post office issuing the permit, and the endorsement "No Postage Necessary if Mailed in the United States." The envelope must also carry the words "Postage Will Be Paid by Addressee" or the inscription "Postage Will Be Paid by" over the name and address of the person or business firm to which the mailing is being returned.

Registered mail. A high-security service is available for all items mailed as first-class mail and is the safest way to send valuable and irreplaceable articles. Registered mail is accounted for during each phase of mail processing and delivery. Registry fees include proof of mailing and proof of delivery and are based on the value of the article. A return receipt showing delivery information and restricted delivery service are available for additional fees. Indemnity protection is available up to twenty-five thousand dollars.

Registered mail must be sealed. Mail without intrinsic value may be registered for the minimum fee or certified (see **Certified mail,** below). Priority mail also may be registered, and registered mail may be sent COD.

Certified mail. Certified mail service is available for all mailable matter of no intrinsic value mailed as first-class mail and provides proof of mailing and delivery. A return receipt showing delivery information is available for an additional fee. Restricted delivery service is also available for an additional fee. Certified mail does not offer indemnity protection and is not available for international mail.

Insurance. Most first-, third-, and fourth-class mail may be insured. Insurance service provides indemnity protection against loss and damage up to five hundred dollars for merchandise. Indemnity levels are based on a graduated fee schedule. No record of insured mail is kept at the post office where mailed, but return receipts and restricted delivery services are available for those parcels insured above twenty-five dollars.

Collect on delivery (COD). COD is a merchandise payment system that permits customers to mail an article for which they have not been paid and have the price of the article as well as the postage collected from the addressee. COD service includes indemnity and is available for first-, third-, and fourth-class mail. Fees are graduated and are based on the amount to be collected (five hundred dollar limit) or the indemnity protection desired. COD service is not available for international mail.

The sender of a COD parcel must guarantee return postage. COD mail may be sent special delivery or special handling if fees applying to those services are paid in addition to postage and COD charges.

Special delivery. Special delivery is available for all classes of mail except bulk third class and Express Mail. It is available at offices served by city carriers and within a one-mile radius of any post office, station, or branch, except contract stations, branches, or community post offices. This mail is given immediate delivery during prescribed hours. Consult your local post office on its availability at the destination office. It receives preferential handling in processing and fast delivery at the destination post office. It is also delivered on Sundays and holidays. Special delivery fees vary depending on the class of service used and the weight of the article.

Special delivery mail bearing the correct postage and fees can be deposited at all points that first-class mail can be deposited. However, it is recommended that special delivery be deposited at postal facilities to ensure the best service. Customers should use special delivery sticker labels, which can be obtained free from the post office, to identify the mail properly.

Special handling.   Special handling provides preferential handling to the extent practical in dispatch and transportation for third- and fourth-class mail but does not provide special delivery at the destination. It is available for a fee based on weight and the class of mail.

Domestic money orders.   Postal Service money orders are a safe and convenient way to send money through the mail and may be purchased at all post offices. They are available in amounts up to seven hundred dollars nationwide. Should your money order be lost or stolen, it will be replaced. Money orders can be redeemed at many banks, stores, and businesses, as well as at all post offices.

Mailgram service.   Mailgram is a Western Union service that enables you to send a message to virtually any address in the continental United States and Canada for delivery on the next business day. Your message is transmitted to a serving post office close to the recipient and is delivered by a regular carrier the next business day. See page 133, chapter 4.

Self-service postal centers. Self-service postal centers are customer-operated vending and mailing equipment located in U.S. Postal Service post office lobbies, shopping centers, college campuses, and so on. These centers provide complete mailing information and services for letters and parcels as well as sales of stamps, envelopes, postal cards, stamp booklets, parcel insurance, and individual stamps. Most centers are open twenty-four hours a day, seven days a week. All postal items in U.S. Postal Service machines are sold at face value. Contact your local post office for the location of the nearest U.S. Postal Service self-service equipment.

Post office lockbox and caller service.   Post office lockbox and caller service are premium services provided for the convenience of the public at an additional charge. These two services, provided in addition to available carrier or general delivery, afford customers privacy and permit them to obtain their mail at their convenience. Lockboxes are accessible during the hours the lobby is open and caller service during the hours that window service is available. Both services make use of the traditional post office box number as the address.

Philatelic mail order service.   The Philatelic Sales Branch provides mail order service for current postage stamps, postal stationery, and philatelic products, such as commemorative mint sets and *Stamps and Stories.* A fee catalog of all items available can be obtained by writing to the Philatelic Sales Branch, Washington, DC 20265–9998.

First-day cover service. To obtain first-day issue cancellations, customers should send self-addressed envelopes to the post office of the official first-day city. Customers may purchase their own new stamps from their local post offices, affix them in the upper right-hand corner of the envelopes, and submit them for cancellation service. Alternatively, customers may request the post office to affix the stamps (limit of fifty covers); such requests must enclose a check or money order to cover the value of the postage affixed. Cash will not be accepted. Covers bearing customer-affixed stamps will be given preferential service. Canceled covers will not be returned in protective envelopes even when furnished by the customer. All requests must be postmarked no later than fifteen days after the date of issuance for stamps and no later than the date of issuance for stationery items. A schedule of upcoming issuances can be obtained by writing to the Philatelic Sales Branch.

PRIVATE DELIVERY SERVICES

Types of Air and Ground Services

Private delivery services perform many of the same functions as the U.S. Postal Service. Some of these organizations transport material throughout the United States and in many foreign countries. Others serve primarily a local market. Some of them have even added other message services such as facsimile and electronic mail, whereas others such as bus lines and airlines handle only letter and package delivery and consider it a sideline or secondary function.

A full-service organization might offer ground and air delivery, telex and facsimile, electronic mail, and messenger service and would additionally place Western Union and other messages for you. Sometimes such organizations do not have their own delivery vehicles but act as an intermediary and simply send your material through another service. Because the services, regulations, and rates vary so widely from one service to another, you should develop a file of private services and update it periodically. Check your yellow pages and call the organizations operating in your area for current data.

Federal Express is an example of a large service that provides domestic and international delivery. Its domestic services include Zapmail (two-hour delivery), Priority 1 (10:30 A.M. next business day), Courier-Pak Overnight Envelope (10:30 A.M. next business day), Overnight Tube (10:30 A.M. next business day), Overnight Box (10:30 A.M. next business day), and Standard Air (one- to two-day service). One of the most familiar ground- and air-transport services is United Parcel Service. It lists Next Day Air and 2nd Day Air delivery options as well as nationwide ground-transportation services. Some delivery services such as Emery advertise that they will ship almost any size anywhere on a next-day-delivery basis.

Firms that specialize in delivery services almost always offer pick up and delivery. This is not necessarily the case, however, with bus lines, airlines, and other companies. When a service has an office in your area, you may also deliver your packages. Some of the private delivery services provide free mailing envelopes and cartons.

How to Use Private Services

Most large services will open a company account for you. Thereafter, when you have a letter or package to send, you only have to telephone the service and request pickup. The organization will charge the cost to your account number and bill you later.

Caution is in order when using any delivery service. Although fast delivery services are necessary when you have an urgent shipment, such services, which are expensive, are sometimes purchased needlessly. A package that might take two to three days to arrive if it were mailed the conventional way on Friday does not need expensive overnight service if it is going to an office that won't open again until Monday. Since there are so many options today (U.S. Postal Service, private delivery services, Western Union, international carriers, and so on), it pays to shop around.

INTERNATIONAL POSTAL SERVICE

Foreign or international mail is mail deposited for dispatch to points outside the United States and its territories and possessions. Foreign mail is classified as postal union mail, parcel post, and Express Mail International Service. Since international regulations are complex, with numerous variations depending on the foreign destination, call your local post office for rates, customs, and packaging requirements for the particular country, or refer to a current issue of the *International Mail Manual*.

Sources of Information

International mail regulations, rates, services, wrapping and mailing requirements, and customs information are described in the *International Mail Manual,* a manual and looseleaf supplementary service sold on a subscription basis. For it and other publications for sale, write to the Superintendent of Documents, U.S. Government Printing Office, Washington, DC 20402. Contact your local post office for free booklets and brochures.

Postal Union Mail

Postal union mail is divided into LC mail and AO mail. *LC mail* (letters and cards) consists of letters, letter packages, aerogrammes, postcards, and postal cards. *AO mail* (other articles) includes printed matter, matter for the blind, and small packets.

Letters and letter packages. Personal handwritten or typewritten communications having the character of current correspondence must be sent as LC mail. Unless prohibited by the country of destination, articles acceptable as postal union mail also may be sent at the letter rate of postage. Rates vary according to the country of destination and for surface or air transport. Merchandise that is liable to customs duty may be forwarded in letters or letter packages to many countries, prepaid at the letter rate of postage. Check with the post office regarding the appropriate form to be filled out and label(s) to be affixed.

Aerogrammes. Aerogrammes consist of sheets that can be folded in the form of an envelope and sealed. They can be sent to all foreign countries at a uniform rate. Messages are to be written on the inner side of the sheets, and no enclosures are permitted. Aerogrammes may be registered.

Aerogrammes with printed postage and airmail markings are sold at all post offices. The ones manufactured by private concerns, if approved by the U.S. Postal Service, are also accepted for mailing after the required postage has been affixed.

Postcards and postal cards. Only single cards without an envelope are acceptable in international mail; reply-paid cards and folded (double) cards are not accepted without an envelope. The maximum size is $4\frac{1}{4}$ by 6 inches and the minimum size is $3\frac{1}{2}$ by $5\frac{1}{2}$ inches. Rates vary according to the country of destination and for surface or air transport. Add "PAR AVION" to the left side of the front of the card.

Printed matter.   Printed matter is paper on which letters, words, characters, figures, images, or any combination thereof, not having the character of a bill or statement or actual or personal correspondence, have been reproduced in several identical copies by any process other than handwriting or typewriting. Computer-prepared material is considered printed matter. The three classifications are regular printed matter, books and sheet music, and publishers' periodicals. *Regular printed matter* consists of all printed matter other than the books, sheet music, and publishers' second-class publications. Rates vary according to the country of destination and for surface and air transport. Customs forms may be required in some countries (inquire at your local post office).

Printed matter may be sealed if postage is paid by permit imprint, postage meter stamps, precanceled stamps, second-class indicia. Write "PRINTED MATTER" on the wrapper and specify the type of printed matter, such as "BOOKS" or "SHEET MUSIC," since special rates apply to these categories. Write "PAR AVION" for air service.

Matter for the blind.   Material admissible in international mail as matter for the blind includes books, periodicals, and other matter in Braille or special type; embossing plates; and voice recordings and special paper for the blind. The weight limit is fifteen pounds. Packages must not be sealed. Write "MATTER FOR THE BLIND" in the upper right corner and add "PAR AVION" for air service. Rates vary according to country of destination and for air transport. Surface rates are free.

Small packets.   This class of postal union mail is designed to permit the mailing of small items of merchandise, commercial samples, or documents that do not have the character of current and personal correspondence. Tapes, cassettes, and similar items may be sent as small packets.

Rates, which are lower than for letter packages or parcel post, vary according to the country of destination and for surface and air transport. Write "SMALL PACKETS" (in a language familiar in the destination country) near the area of postage and add "PAR AVION" for air service. All small packets require customs forms (some countries will not accept small packets).

You may enclose a simple invoice and a slip showing the names and addresses of the sender and addressee of the packet but not any letter, note, or document having the character of actual personal correspondence; coins, bank notes, paper money, postage stamps (canceled or uncanceled), or any values payable to the bearer; platinum, gold, or silver (manufactured or unmanufactured); or precious stones, jewelry, or other precious articles.

Parcel Post

Parcel post may be sent to almost every country in the world, either by direct or indirect service. The parcels are sent from the United States by surface vessel or by airplane to a port in the country of destination or to a port in an intermediate country to be sent from there to the country of destination. In the latter case, the parcels are subject to transit charges in the intermediate country. Merchandise is permitted but not written communication having the character of current and personal correspondence.

The customs and other restrictions and regulations vary with the country of destination. Rates, too, vary according to the country of destination and for surface and air transport. Add "PAR AVION" to the back side of the parcel and Label 19 on the address side. Before preparing a parcel to be sent to a foreign country, consult postal authorities or the *International Mail Manual.*

Pack parcels in canvas or similar material; double-faced, corrugated cardboard boxes; solid fiber boxes or cases; thick cardboard boxes; or strong wooden boxes of material at least half an inch thick. It is permissible to use heavy wrapping paper or waterproof paper as the outside covering of a carton or box, but it may not be used as the only covering of the contents. Boxes with lids screwed or nailed on and bags sewed at the openings may be used, provided they conform to the special provisions of the country of destination.

Special Services

Special services are available only to certain countries (inquire at your local post office), and rates for most services vary according to the country of destination. *Special handling* entitles surface parcels, printed matter, matter for the blind, and small packets to preferential handling between the mailing point and the United States point of dispatch. *COD* and *certified mail* are not available for international mail. *Certificates of mailing,* however, furnish evidence of mailing but no insurance against loss or damage. *Insurance* is available only for parcel post. For added security, *registered mail* is available to most countries but only for letters and letter packages, small packets, matter for the blind, and printed matter. The indemnity limit is $20.40 (except $200.00 to Canada). *Restricted delivery* limits who may receive an item. *Recall* and *change of address* services enable a sender to ask for an item to be returned or its address changed. *Special delivery* offers faster delivery of postal union mail according to the regulations of the country of destination.

Other services are *Express Mail* for high-speed delivery to and from about a dozen countries, *reply coupons* to prepay mail from other countries, and *money orders* for safe transmission of money to certain countries. *INTELPOST* enables users to send copies of documents electronically to forty-eight countries. Customers may pick up the message within an hour or a copy will be delivered in the country's regular mail. Both text and graphics can be sent. *I-SAL* (International Surface Air Lift) is an accelerated bulk-mail system for publications, direct-mail pieces, and other printed materials to sixty-one countries. Delivery is usually seven to fourteen days from shipment. *International priority airmail* is available anywhere except Canada. Mail must be sorted for this service, which saves one day on delivery as a result. Regular *air mail* provides four- to seven-day delivery to most countries.

SPECIAL MAILING GUIDELINES

Using Zip Codes to Speed Mail Delivery

To ensure rapid processing of your mail, follow these guidelines in the use of zip codes. See also **Following OCR Addressing Requirements,** page 161.

1. Always use the two-letter abbreviation of a state plus the zip code. (See chapter 18 for a list of state abbreviations.) Capitalize both letters of the abbreviation; do not put periods between the letters (for example New Jersey is NJ). Do not use any punctuation between the state abbreviation and the zip code or between the city designation and the state abbreviation.

2. Use only two spaces between the state abbreviation and the zip code and place the zip code on the same line as the state abbreviation.

3. Use only approved city, street, and place-name abbreviations. (See chapter 18 for a partial list of approved street and place-name abbreviations.)

4. Use zip + 4 (the nine-digit zip code) to facilitate automation. (Inquire at your post office about free zip + 4 updating of mailing lists by the Postal Service.)

A zip code directory is available for reference in every post office, or copies may be purchased (see address on page 146). Directories published by commercial firms are sold in bookstores.

Following OCR Addressing Requirements

Your local post office may have free brochures on addressing requirements to ensure that your mail can be rapidly processed by postal optical character readers (OCRs) and bar code sorters (BCSs). To be processed by this equipment, postcards must be a minimum of $3\frac{1}{2}$ inches high and $5\frac{1}{2}$ inches long and 0.007 inch thick and a maximum of $4\frac{1}{4}$ inches high and 6 inches long and 0.25 inch thick. Envelopes must be a minimum of $3\frac{1}{2}$ inches high and 5 inches long and 0.007 inch thick and a maximum of $6\frac{1}{8}$ inches high and $11\frac{1}{2}$ inches wide and 0.25 inch thick.

The envelope address must be typed within a rectangular OCR read area as follows:

Sides of rectangle: 1 inch from left and right edges
Bottom of rectangle: $\frac{5}{8}$ inch from bottom edge
Top of rectangle: $2\frac{1}{4}$ inches from bottom edge

Type styles such as script, italic, artistic, or other unusual styles and some dot matrix print cannot be processed on an OCR. Ask at your local post office for Publication 25, *A Guide to Business Mail Preparation*, which explains more about OCR addressing requirements. See also figure 18.

How to Reduce Postage Costs

Money can be saved by knowing how and when to use the various types of mail service. Here are a few suggestions to reduce postage costs.

1. Use business-reply envelopes instead of stamped, self-addressed envelopes. These envelopes are often used with sales letters to make it easier for a prospect to buy. With bills or statements, a self-addressed envelope may be enclosed but usually without prepaid postage.

2. Mail early in the day to get the fastest service possible. This is especially important for first-class mail to distant points, which must meet plane schedules.

Figure 18. OCR and Bar Code Read Areas

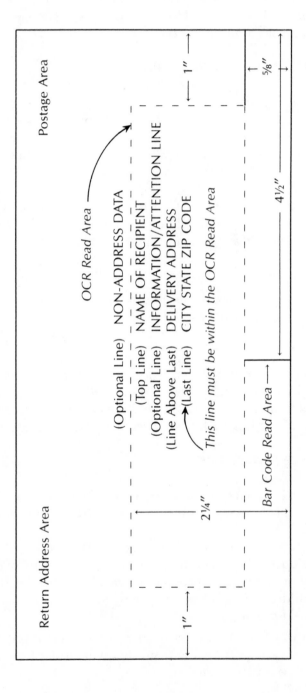

3. Eliminate special delivery if letters will reach their destination in time for the first mail delivery.

4. Economies are possible if you know how and when various classes of mail can be used.

5. If you have several letters for the same person, put them in one envelope.

6. Send all material to the same branch office in one envelope. Postage is paid on so much per ounce or fraction, and combining fractions saves ounces. Saving is also made on envelopes.

7. Write communications to branch offices on smaller or lighter weight memo paper. This reduces the weight of the mail going to branch offices.

8. Pack priority mail and other parcels in the lightest weight materials possible without sacrificing sturdiness.

9. Give thought to the weight of paper and envelopes used for normal correspondence. Reduced weight need not mean sacrifice of quality.

10. Do not send paper clips or clasps through the mail.

11. When you send a letter with material that does not require first-class postage, use specially constructed envelopes that have one part for the first-class letter and another part for the lower class material.

12. Consider whether telex, facsimile, or some other process (see chapter 4) might be less expensive than traditional mail. A telephone call also might be more economical.

13. Compare the costs of private services. See **PRIVATE DELIVERY SERVICES,** pages 155–56.

14. Investigate the savings with presort mail and zip + 4 (ask about having your list converted to zip + 4 free of charge by the Postal Service).

15. Consider document reduction such as microfilming (see chapter 1, page 38).

— Chapter 6 —

Using Effective Telecommunications Practices

USING THE TELEPHONE EFFICIENTLY AND COURTEOUSLY

When you greet visitors at work, they form an impression of you and your company by the way you look and act (see chapter 1). Essentially, the same thing happens when you speak over the telephone. Callers will form an initial impression from the sound of your voice (cheerfulness, attentiveness, boredom, irritation, and so on) and your apparent willingness (or lack of it) to help them. Unfortunately, many people cannot "hear" themselves and are completely unaware of problems in their telephone conversations.

Observing the Rules of Telephone Courtesy

The following simple rules constitute the basis of courteous and efficient telephone usage:

1. Answer calls promptly and return missed calls promptly.
2. When you leave your desk, arrange for someone to take your calls. Leave word where you can be located by telephone and when you will return.
3. Keep pad and pencil handy.
4. In asking a caller to wait, ask, "Will you please hold the line while I get the information?" and wait for the reply. When you return to the telephone, thank the caller for waiting. But if it will take you some time to get the information, offer to call back.
5. If you have to put down the receiver for any reason, do so gently.

But do not put it down with an open line when the caller might overhear other office conversations.

6. Do not interrupt or be impatient. Listen attentively, and do not make the other party repeat because of inattention on your part.

7. Do not try to talk with a cigarette, pencil, or chewing gum in your mouth. Speak slowly and enunciate clearly.

8. When you have finished talking, say something such as "Thank you, Mr. Smith," or "Good-bye" pleasantly and replace the receiver gently. But let the caller hang up first.

How to Be More Effective on the Telephone

To become more effective in your telecommunications, make these guidelines a habit:

1. Plan your telephone conversation before placing your call. Know your facts and the points you want to cover. If necessary, have an outline of them before you while you talk. Also have all records and other material before you, especially with out-of-town calls.

2. When making a business call, identify yourself without waiting to be asked who is calling.

3. When making a number of calls on a line serving several people, try to space your calls so that others may have a chance to use their telephones.

4. When you make a call, wait for six or seven rings before hanging up.

5. When you are making a call for your employer, be sure that he or she is ready to speak as soon as the person you are calling is on the line.

6. Before you start a lengthy explanation or conversation with a busy person, ask if the time is convenient. Then keep your telephone conversation brief but not to the point of curtness. Take time to address people by their names and titles. Use expressions of consideration such as "Thank you" and "I beg your pardon." A phrase such as "Yes, Mr. Adams" shows greater respect than "I see." Avoid slang and expressions such as "Yeah," "Uh-huh," and "Uh-uh."

7. When you receive a call for someone who is not in the office, make

a note of it and do not forget to give the person the note. (Place it on the person's desk right away if practical.)

8. Never ask a caller to wait while you get information and then stay away from the telephone so long that he or she hangs up before you return.

9. Don't chat with a friend who calls you during business hours; telephone abuse is a serious problem in the business world. Never chat with someone who calls your employer, except to respond politely to questions and comments.

10. Keep short summaries of important incoming calls (Call Sheet) for your employer, especially when he or she is away from the office.

PLACING AND RECEIVING CALLS

Placing Calls

Placing calls for your employer.   Many executives prefer to place and receive calls without intervention of the secretary. In some offices, however, the secretary always places the employer's calls. When you place the call, you may get the person called on the line before connecting your boss. Assume that you are calling Ms. Nelson for your employer Mr. Owens. When you get Ms. Nelson's secretary on the line, you might say, "Is Ms. Nelson there, for Mr. Owens of XYZ Company?" The other secretary will put Ms. Nelson on and trust to your good judgment to see that Mr. Owens comes on the line promptly. Never keep the person called (or your employer) waiting needlessly. (When a secretary calls your employer, you reciprocate the courtesy.) When Ms. Nelson comes on the line, say to her, "Here's Mr. Owens, Ms. Nelson," and establish the connection between the two at once.

If you call a close friend of your employer or a person to whom deference is due, connect your boss as soon as you talk to the secretary at the other end of the line. Tell him or her that the person called will be on the line immediately and let your boss receive the call without further intervention from you. Some secretaries follow this procedure at all times. If you are uncertain about the procedure your boss would prefer, don't hesitate to ask, and then make it a policy to handle all calls that way thereafter.

Placing your own calls.   Maintaining a pleasing tone of voice, follow these guidelines when you place calls. (See also **Observing the Rules of Telephone Courtesy,** page 164, and **How to Be More Effective on the**

Telephone, page 165; also refer to the various types of calls described in **PRINCIPAL TELEPHONE SERVICES,** pages 169–77).

1. Do not call information for a number except when you cannot find it in the telephone directory (there is usually a charge for information).

2. Give the person you are calling ample time to answer before you hang up.

3. When the person called answers, identify yourself immediately: "This is Kay Edwards of Prentice-Hall." Or, where appropriate: "Good morning, Mr. Brown [or simply 'Mr. Brown'], this is Kay Edwards of Prentice-Hall."

4. If the person who answers the telephone is not the one you want or does not identify himself or herself, ask pleasantly for the person you want and announce your name. "May I speak to Mr. Brown, please? Kay Edwards [of Prentice-Hall] calling."

5. When you do not want any particular person, state your wishes in a nice way, preferably in the form of a request: "The rug department, please." Or: "I'd like some information about_____." Or: "Would you please take an order for_____?"

Answering and Screening Calls

Answering incoming calls.   When you answer your employer's telephone, convey a friendly, helpful attitude to the caller. First identify yourself.

1. *When there is no switchboard:* "Prentice-Hall, Kay Edwards."

2. *When the operator has previously answered the call:* "Advertising Department, Kay Edwards speaking." If several people have the same extension, just answer, "Advertising Department. May I help you?"

3. *Your own telephone:* "Kay Edwards." Or: "Good morning. Kay Edwards speaking."

4. *Another person's telephone:* "Mrs. Brown's office." When desirable, also give your own name, for example, "Mrs. Brown's office, Kay Edwards speaking."

When you answer someone else's telephone, and the person called is not available, offer to take a message. Make a record of the caller's name, affiliation, telephone number, and the time of the call. See that the person called gets the message immediately on return (leave it on the person's desk if practical).

When you answer your employer's telephone and a secretary tells you that "Ms. Nelson of ABC is calling Mr. Owens," ask the secretary to wait a moment and announce the call to your boss, who will then pick up the telephone and wait until Ms. Nelson is connected. Or perhaps the other secretary has learned that you are cooperative and thus puts Ms. Nelson on the line at the same time that you connect the call with your employer.

Screening calls.   If you are expected to screen calls, a polite way of asking who is calling is, "May I tell Mr. Owens who's calling?" Or: "May I ask who's calling?" A legitimate caller seldom objects to giving his or her name. Almost all callers not only volunteer their names but also briefly state their business.

If the caller insists on withholding his or her name, you might say, very politely, "Mr. Owens has someone with him at the moment. If you're unable to give me your name, it might be best for you to write to him and mark your letter 'personal.' I'll make certain that he gets it right away." Finding out the purpose of a call is especially important when someone telephones for an appointment.

If you are not familiar with the names of people who have legitimate business with your employer, it is better for you to err by putting through a few unnecessary calls than by delaying or rejecting important ones. Or you might say that your boss is not available at the moment and ask for the caller's telephone number. Then investigate the call and, if necessary, check with your employer. If he or she wants to talk, call the party back in a few minutes. If you learn that the call is a nuisance call, handle it yourself.

Transferring Calls

Never transfer a call if you can handle it properly yourself or can have the appropriate person take care of it. If you cannot take care of the call yourself, handle it in one of the following ways:

1. Say that you will refer the matter to the appropriate person. In some cases, you will want to indicate that the person calling will be called back, but in other cases this will not be necessary: "That's something Ms. Rogers handles. If you like, I'll tell her about it, and I'm sure she'll look into it right away." Or: "That's something Ms. Rogers handles. If you like, I'll ask her to call you back."

2. Offer to transfer the person calling to someone who can take care of the call: "That's handled by our Credit Department. If you like, I'll connect you."

3. If you do not know who should handle the matter, tell the person calling that it is not handled by your department but that you will refer it to someone who will take care of it: "That's not handled in this department. But if you like, I'll check with the appropriate persons and ask someone to call you back." When you transfer a call, make sure that the person calling knows what you are doing in case the caller is accidentally cut off. Signal the switchboard operator slowly. Explain the situation so that the operator will not have to ask the person calling to repeat the information: "Will you please connect Mr. Smith [or 'this call'] with Ms. Rogers in the Credit Department?" Wait for the operator's reply to be sure he or she understands correctly.

4. If you offer to transfer a caller who is annoyed because he or she has already been transferred several times, apologize, ask the caller to give you his or her telephone number and name, and say that you will get the appropriate person to return the call as soon as possible. You must then see that anything you have promised the caller receives prompt attention.

Handling Wrong Numbers

You get a wrong number. If you place a call and receive what appears to be a wrong number, immediately check the telephone number, for example: "I beg your pardon, but is this 353-2000?" If it is evident that some error was made, express regret, even if you were not responsible. If the call was placed through a long-distance operator, and it is obvious that the operator made an error in dialing, report it immediately so that you will not be charged for the call.

Someone calls you by mistake. Inform the caller politely that he or she has reached a wrong number, and suggest that the caller recheck the number dialed. If your calls come through a switchboard operator who connects a call to you through error, signal the operator and politely ask to have the call transferred to the appropriate person. See Transferring Calls, page 168.

PRINCIPAL TELEPHONE SERVICES

Operating Companies

Local and short-distance toll calls in the United States are handled by seven regional Bell operating companies (BOCs): U.S. West, Pacific Telesis,

Southwestern Bell, Bell South, Bell Atlantic, Nynex, and Ameritech. The BOCs also provide inbound 800 service and outbound WATS service (see **Wide-Area Telephone Service [WATS],** page 172).

Long-distance service is provided by "other common carriers" (OCCs), sometimes called "specialized common carriers" (SCCs), such as AT&T, MCI, Sprint, and Allnet. In areas where *equal access* applies, you can dial 1 plus long distance without adding any special access codes, no matter which common carrier you choose for your long-distance service. Rates and specific services (private lines, voice-data, and so on) vary, however. Some carriers provide billing aids such as codes that you can assign to your customers. Each time you call a specific customer, then, using the code for that customer, the call is charged to that account and appears as such on your telephone bill.

Station-to-Station and Person-to-Person Calls

A *station-to-station call* is made when the caller is willing to talk with anyone who answers the telephone. A *person-to-person call* is made when the caller must talk to a specific person and asks the operator to connect him or her with that particular person, department, or extension telephone. Rates for these calls are higher than those for station-to-station calls.

Although a station-to-station call is less expensive, in a few cases, it is more economical to make a person-to-person call. If the person with whom you want to speak is extremely difficult to locate, use the person-to-person call, for the time spent in locating the person may run up the cost of station-to-station calls higher than the cost of a person-to-person call. But first determine if the party has a free 800 number that you could call.

Determining rate variations.   Reduced rates apply at certain times daily and all day on Saturday and Sunday to various points. Reduced rates are also in effect at night and on Sunday on calls to many foreign countries. The rules of the long-distance service you use and the time at the dialing point govern the application of reduced rates. Consult the front pages of your telephone directory to find out when they are applicable or ask the common carrier you are using for a printed rate schedule.

International Direct-Distance Dialing (IDDD)

The IDDD service is available from certain cities in the United States to many countries overseas. To place a call to any of the participating countries, you dial the international access code, country code, city code, and then the local telephone number, which could be a two- to seven-digit number. Check with the common carrier you use for specific information.

Operator-assisted international calls cost more than direct-dial calls, just as they do within the United States, and rates vary among the common carriers. Certain periods, for example, evenings and Sundays, have reduced rates. Although the time of the call is determined where the call is placed, keep in mind that there is a time differential. You might call someone at 6 P.M. local time, but the caller might be awakened at 3 A.M. somewhere else (refer to the international time charts in chapter 18, page 623).

Travelers often use their credit cards in the more than one hundred countries that accept them. One can also place collect calls from other countries. *Teleplan* is an agreement among certain countries whereby hotels limit surcharges on international calls.

Out-of-Town Calls

Direct dialing of long-distance station-to-station calls is possible throughout the United States. Check your local telephone directory for a list or map of area codes. See also the map of area codes in chapter 18, page 622. In some locations it is necessary to dial "1" (or some other digit) before dialing the area code and number.

If you reach a wrong number by direct dialing, contact an operator immediately and explain what happened to make certain that there is no charge for the call.

When you place a calling-card call. From most phones, dial 0, the area code, and the telephone number you want. After you hear a dial tone, enter your calling-card number and security code (if any). To make additional calls do not hang up. Simply press # (or other) button and enter the next number without reentering your calling-card number. With rotary telephones, you usually dial 0, the area code, and the number, and an operator will come on the line to ask for your calling-card and security number.

To make a person-to-person call on your calling card, you usually dial 0, the area code, and the telephone number and wait for the operator. Give your calling-card number and state that you want to make a person-to-person call. If the call is to be collect, give your own name and stay on the line until the call is completed. When a call cannot be completed at once, the operator will follow it up at your request.

If you do not know the out-of-town number you want to call. Dial 1 (in some locations), then the area code, and next 555-1212. When the operator answers, give the city you want to call and then ask for the telephone number of the party you want to call. (There is usually a charge for information). If the person has a free 800 number, dial 1 (in some locations) and then 800 followed by 555-1212.

Charges on out-of-town calls.   Keep a record of all out-of-town calls so that you can verify the telephone bill and the bookkeeper can allocate the charges to the proper customer or other expense account. Your company may require certain forms to be filled out on long-distance calls. Be careful to observe these requirements when you place a call through the company exchange (switchboard). You can also get the long-distance charge on a call at the time you make it if you ask the operator for it.

If a call must be placed from an outside telephone, have the operator charge the call to your office telephone, use a calling card, or place the call collect. Calling-card charges will appear on the next telephone statement. With a collect call, the person receiving the call, if he or she accepts it, will then pay the charges.

Telephone abuse.   Companies are always seeking ways to reduce expenses, and cutting daily abuse is a necessary step. Your employer may require the use of access codes for long-distance calls. In other words, only authorized employees know the code that is needed to make a long-distance call on the office telephone.

You can help your employer lower expenses by using free 800 numbers when calling outside or wait for a leased line to open up. (Some secretaries become impatient and simply dial a regular long-distance call, which is more expensive.) You can help, too, by protecting your calling card. Do not give it to an operator in a public place where someone might overhear it. Also, consider the hours when you call for maintenance service (charges may be higher after certain hours or on weekends). These and other measures will help your employer prevent telephone abuse and cut costs.

Wide-Area Telephone Service (WATS)

There are two types of WATS service, inbound (or inward) and outbound (or outward). An *inbound line* is used when a large number of calls are coming in from a wide area. Callers use your free (to them) 800 number then. If a customer calls you collect instead, you should advise the caller to hang up and call again on your firm's 800 number.

An *outbound line* is used when your firm makes a lot of calls to a particular area. If your company has a central telephone system, you will probably have to dial some code such as "7" to use the WATS line (just as you have to dial "9" with some systems to get a regular outside line).

WATS calls are billed at rates that differ from your regular telephone rates. Sometimes they are less expensive, but even if not, a firm may want a WATS line to conduct telemarketing (selling by telephone) more efficiently and to encourage customers to phone in orders.

Messenger Calls

If it is necessary to reach someone who does not have a telephone, the operator at the called point may be authorized to send a messenger for the person desired. Whether or not the call is completed, the caller pays the cost of the messenger's service, which is in addition to the regular person-to-person charge for the call.

Appointment Calls

In placing a person-to-person call, you may specify a certain time that you will talk with a person. The telephone operator will try to put the call through at the exact time. The charge is the same as for a person-to-person call. The advantage of an appointment call is that it saves time. Usually, you make arrangements with the person in advance so he or she will be standing by at the selected time.

Teleconference Calls

Teleconference, or audioconference, service makes it possible for an executive to be connected simultaneously with a number of other stations. Some firms use this procedure to avoid transportation, hotel, and other travel costs. No special equipment is required. Suppose that your employer needs to discuss a contract provision with three other people (usually, any number up to ten) who are in different cities. By means of a conference call, your employer and the other people can talk by long distance as though they were grouped around a conference table.

Your employer also can speak to a gathering of employees in different cities instead of to individuals. The telephone company will install loud-speaker equipment appropriate for the number of listeners. A control dial permits volume adjustment.

In arranging a conference call, dial 0 and explain that you want to make a conference call. Give full details—names, telephone numbers, time, and date—to the operator who handles the connection. In computing charges for conference calls, each party called at a different number is treated as a separate person-to-person call.

Your firm may also have computerized dial-in conference equipment that can connect twenty or more persons at the same time. If you have such a dedicated system in-house, follow the instructions provided by the manufacturer for connecting the parties simultaneously.

Teleconferencing is best used for short conferences, for example, no more than one to two hours. The teleconference may be tape recorded, or you may be asked to "listen in" and take minutes (see chapter 7, page 185). If your office is equipped with a speakerphone, whereby sound comes through a speaker rather than the receiver, you can have both hands free to take notes while listening.

Videoconferences

Videoconferencing is more expensive than teleconferencing since cameras and other equipment are needed. In its simplest form, a video-conference might consist of two connections, each with a picturephone (a telephone that includes a small screen on which each caller can see the other while talking). But sophisticated videoconferences require wide-screen monitors, sometimes several cameras, and often a large conference room where many conference attendees can be seated. Since the transmission equipment is usually expensive, videoconferencing is not widely used, and firms that do use it often rent the necessary facilities rather than purchase and maintain their own.

If you are asked to assist in preparations for a videoconference, your duties may include typing a list of requirements (number of participants, date and time desired, and so on) to present to the organization that rents videoconference facilities to users. You may also be expected to take minutes (see chapter 7, page 185) and later distribute a videotape or hard copy (paper) of the proceedings to attendees.

If your employer is arranging the conference, you will need to follow the same guidelines as for other meetings: organize meeting folders of pertinent material for your employer to take along, arrange for catered or self-service refreshments during the break (if any), and so on. For more details about meeting arrangements and meeting conduct, see chapter 7.

Mobile Calls

You can make local and long-distance calls to automobiles, trucks, aircraft, boats, and ships. Dial 0 and ask for the mobile, marine, or high seas operator, and give the number and party you want to reach (see chapter 4, pages 135–36, for information regarding the sending of cables and telegrams by telephone). Mobile numbers are listed in your regular telephone directory.

More and more executives are using mobile telephones in their cars. Whereas older mobile equipment was hampered by overloaded channels, creating long waits, new cellular radio technology has opened the door to more network subscribers. This technology uses small geographic cells, representing transmission centers, that can divide into even more small cells as calls increase.

To use a mobile telephone, a small radio-computer must be mounted on the vehicle. Users then can telephone anyone within the area covered by the mobile telephone company. Since users can call into a public telephone network with a mobile telephone, calls can be made worldwide from a mobile unit.

Special Business Services

Switching systems.   Two common office telephone systems are the key, or pushbutton, system and the exchange, a modern version of the old office switchboard. With the key system, telephones in different offices are interconnected and are also connected to outside lines. With an exchange, switching devices interconnect the telephones and provide access to outside lines.

The newer equipment is digital, that is, it transmits data in discrete steps based on binary digits (bits); older equipment uses a continuous analog signal. Since computers operate on a digital system, offices that want to integrate functions find that the digital telephone system is more readily linked to various kinds of computer activity.

Types of exchanges.   Office telephone exchanges are classified according to type (manual, computerized, and so on): *PBX* is a private branch exchange—a basic switching facility within an organization. *PMBX* is a private manual branch exchange—one that is operated manually. *PABX* is a private automatic branch exchange—one whereby the switching is achieved automatically by the equipment. *CBX* is a computerized branch exchange—one whereby functions are directed by a computer.

How an exchange functions.   With an exchange—unlike a key system, or group of interconnected pushbutton telephones—the switching occurs in a central mechanism that users activate by dialing codes, such as dialing "7" or some other number to use a WATS line. An exchange is usually able to accommodate more telephones than a key system and is therefore common in large organizations. An operator may receive calls and make the connections with the appropriate persons, or the system may allow direct dialing without operator intervention. A variety of configurations are possible, and your particular system may differ in some respects from that in other organizations.

Special features of an office telephone system.   Office systems often have many features such as those described in the following sections. In addition, your system may have a *recorder* that keeps track of calls (to whom, by whom, time, and cost). If you have computerized switching, your firm may be using the telephone lines to handle *electronic mail* (see chapter 4, page 143). Some equipment automatically dials calls by the most economical means (such as by WATS line); this type of automatic selection is called *least-cost routing (LCR)*. With *direct inward dialing (DID)* you can dial an in-house number from outside and bypass the central exchange. Some equipment is designed for *voice-data* functions—sending text and graphics as well as permitting traditional voice communications. Nearly all office systems use either separate *intercom* equipment or have an intercom system operated through the office telephone system. Secretaries use the intercom button on their telephones regularly to buzz their employers to signal incoming calls, visitors, and so on.

Answering machines and services.   For a fee, usually monthly, trained operators provide answering services for businesses and individuals. One simply lets the operators know what to do—take messages, refer callers to another number, and so on. Automatic answering machines connected to one's office or home telephone will record messages from callers and play your own messages to callers. A remote feature allows you to dial your own number from another location and activate the machine so that it will play back all messages to you over the telephone.

Leased lines.   Private lines are needed by some companies when the volume of calls is especially large. A common carrier such as AT&T will install a line between the firm and the desired geographic area for the exclusive use of the company. Lines can be leased domestically or internationally. Usually, there is a flat monthly rate for the line, often with an additional charge for message units. *Tie lines* are private lines too; they often connect exchanges of a firm in two locations. A *foreign-exchange line (FX)* is used to place or receive calls as though you were in another location. A firm thus might give the appearance of being located in a particular city when it really is using a foreign-exchange line.

Automatic dialers.   Special units can be purchased that will store telephone numbers you program into their memory. At any time thereafter, you can simply press a button and the number will be dialed automatically. Numbers are stored on different mediums, depending on the unit, for example, a magnetic tape, a coded plastic card, and so on.

Call sequencers.   Some mechanisms indicate which incoming call is the next in line, often by a flashing button. Advanced versions process unanswered calls after a specific number of rings and monitor incoming traffic.

Remote-call forwarding.   Business people who travel may have calls forwarded to them. Before leaving the office, for example, your employer would dial a simple code followed by the number where he or she could be reached. Calls would be automatically forwarded. At each stop this procedure could be repeated, and calls would literally follow the traveler from one stop to another. Some businesses use remote call forwarding as a means of maintaining a listed telephone number in another city, with calls by customers to that number forwarded to the business at its home site.

Paging devices.   Business people who are away from the office but want to be reached in emergencies often use pocket devices such as "beepers." These devices, which are effective within a specified range, signal the user to call the office.

Plug-in headset.   Secretaries who frequently take dictation over the telephone often use a plug-in headset. This device can be attached to your telephone to free your hands for note taking or typing. Modern versions are lightweight and easy to use.

TELEPHONE REFERENCE BOOKS

The Telephone Directory

Whereas the white pages in a telephone directory list all of the business and personal telephones in your community, except unlisted numbers and newly installed telephones, the yellow pages consist of advertisements of products and services that you may be able to use in conducting research and shopping for things needed in your office. Most directories include other useful information, for example, a map of area codes and a partial list of zip codes. If you make frequent calls to cities other than those listed in your local telephone directory, you can obtain directories for those areas through your local telephone business office. Inquire about the charges, which may differ from one city directory to another.

Compiling a Desk Telephone Book

Some telephone numbers you will call very often in your work. The handiest way to keep these numbers readily available is in a small desk telephone book. Numerous sizes and styles are for sale in stationery and office-supply stores.

In addition to numbers called frequently on company business, the following numbers should be kept in your desk telephone book:

Airlines	International carriers
Amtrak	Travel agency
Car-rental agency	Equipment-repair service
Express office	Private delivery service
Messenger service	Building manager or
Post office	superintendent
Emergency calls (Fire,	Residences of employees in your
Police, Ambulance, etc.)	office
Office-supply store	Weather
Western Union	

Personal numbers for your employer. Also keep in your desk telephone book the following personal numbers for your employer:

Bank	Theater ticket agency
Broker	Dentist
Garage	Doctors
Organizations to which he or	Family (residence and
she belongs	business)
Restaurants	Florist
Services (dry cleaner,	Friends he or she calls
tailor, etc.)	frequently
Stores he or she	
trades with	

Make a new book from time to time when additions, deletions, and changes make your list illegible.

Chapter 7

Making Meeting Arrangements

MAKING ARRANGEMENTS FOR MEETINGS

A secretary is often involved in meetings as a participant, an organizer, a coordinator, an assistant to someone attending or conducting the meeting, or a stenographer taking minutes. Since small to large meetings occur every day in business, secretaries must be familiar with the numerous aspects of meeting arrangements. Although this chapter describes face-to-face meetings, teleconferences (see chapter 6, page 173) are used in some organizations.

Notifying Meeting Participants

Type of notice.   Letting meeting participants know the details about time and place is usually the secretary's job. How you notify people depends on the type and size of the meeting. Notice of an informal meeting among a few persons could be handled in a variety of ways, for example, by telex or telephone, with follow-up letters or memos. For a very large meeting such as a convention, it would be necessary to use printed forms. Numbers, then, largely determine the method of notification you use (the bylaws of some organizations may specify the form that must be followed).

Details in notice.   Always include full details in your notice and see that the notices are sent far enough in advance to ensure that recipients have time to make travel and other arrangements necessary to attend. The details should include the name of the person or organization calling the

Figure 19. Sample Meeting Proxy

PROXY

I hereby constitute (name), (name), and (name), who are officers or directors of the Corporation, or a majority of such of them as actually are present, to act for me in my stead and as my proxy at the (meeting) of the stockholders of (company), to be held in (location), on (date), at (time), and at any adjournment or adjournments thereof, with full power and authority to act for me in my behalf, with all powers that I, the undersigned, would possess if I were personally present.

Effective Date _____

Signed (stockholder) _____

Address _____

City _____ State _____ Zip Code _____

PLEASE BE CERTAIN TO INCLUDE YOUR ADDRESS AND SIGNATURE AND THE DATE OF SIGNING. THANK YOU.

---

meeting and the date, time, place (not only the city and street address but the building room number), and purpose of the meeting. Some meetings such as a stockholders' meeting, must follow a prescribed policy in issuing a "call," or notice. The wording of such a notice, which will be given to you by the corporate secretary, must adhere to state statutes or corporate regulations, and a proxy must be enclosed (see figure 19). Other types of meetings, too, may require proxies in order to have enough votes to constitute the quorum required to conduct business.

For a relatively small meeting, if a preliminary agenda is available, enclose a copy of it (or anything else the participants should review beforehand). Add a statement or enclose a reply slip requesting that each person indicate *by a specific date* if he or she will attend. Some notices also include a request for topics to be discussed at the meeting (see **Preparing the Agenda,** page 181).

If a few of the same people attend regular meetings, maintain their addresses by computer or, manually, on index cards. For a small group, you could prepare multiple sets of mailing labels to avoid retyping each time. No matter how you maintain the list, keep it up to date at all times. (For more about mailing-list maintenance, see chapter 4, page 128.)

Preparing the Agenda

The person responsible for preparing the agenda may be the corporate secretary, in the case of a corporate meeting. The conference secretary or person chairing a meeting may be responsible in other situations. For departmental meetings, the head of the department may take care of this. If you work for the person who prepares the agenda, you can be very helpful in collecting office information, organizing topics, and typing and mailing copies to meeting participants.

Typing the agenda. Agenda topics, typed on $8\frac{1}{2}$- by 11-inch paper, are usually arranged in the order they will be discussed at the meeting. Procedures vary from office to office, but you will likely be expected to type at least one rough draft for the chair or corporate secretary and perhaps several if the agenda must be revised a number of times before it is complete.

Order of business. The agenda might contain some or all of the following items—in this order:

1. Call to order
2. Reading and approval of previous meeting's minutes
3. Treasurer's report
4. Other reports
5. Old business
6. New business
7. Committee appointments
8. Nominations and election of new officers
9. Announcements
10. Adjournment

Stockholders' meetings and certain other formal meetings have a designated order that must be followed. For formal meetings, examine previous agendas in the files and follow the order indicated by the corporate secretary or legal counsel.

Organizing Meeting Materials

Your employer will no doubt need to take along to a meeting various papers and supplies, and you can assist in organizing this material beforehand.

Meeting folder.   Most material, except for bulky reports and odd-sized documents, can be placed in a regular file folder or in several folders. Use different-colored labels or in some way color code the folders to help your employer locate papers quickly during the meeting. Collect essential correspondence and other material pertaining to the topics on the agenda as well as material pertaining to something new that your boss may want to introduce at the meeting. (After the meeting, be certain to return all material to the files.)

Supplies.   For an out-of-town meeting, extra supplies may be helpful —writing paper, envelopes, stamps, paper clips, cellophane tape, pencils, pen and ink, dictation belts or tapes, and so on. Some of these items may be helpful at a local meeting, too, although a well-prepared meeting room has paper and pencils at each place around the conference table.

Securing a Meeting Room

The conference room.   Some secretaries help to secure the meeting room. If the meeting is to be held in a hotel or motel instead of company offices, you will need to telephone appropriate sites and request information on sizes, availability when needed, and rates. Or your employer might ask you to reserve a conference room for an approximate number of persons at the XYZ Motel near the airport from which most participants will be arriving and leaving. You should confirm the approximate number of participants, so that the facility can reserve an appropriate size room.

Meals.   If morning or afternoon refreshments are desired, ask if the facility can provide them. Otherwise, inquire about delivery service from a nearby delicatessen or coffee shop. Your employer will let you know whether you should reserve a table in the dining room for lunch or whether you should ask the hotel to serve an appropriate selection from the menu to the participants in the conference room.

Equipment.   Determine what special equipment must be rented —display boards, projectors, tape recorders, and so on—and ensure that the facility (or other suppliers) will deliver everything needed and set it all up in adequate time before the meeting. Check whether an operator is needed for any of the equipment.

Preparing the Meeting Room

Meetings held in your own facilities usually can be checked out and even arranged at your convenience well in advance of the meeting. In a hotel or motel conference room, you may have to wait until another meeting adjourns to check the room.

Supplies.   If the facility does not provide supplies, your company will have to provide pencils and pads. Put one of each at every place around the table. Ask to have a pitcher of water and glasses delivered and located on the table. If smoking is permitted, ashtrays should be on the table. Visual aids and projection equipment, as well as any other equipment, should be set up and ready for use.

There should be a place for guests to put coats, hats, and other supplies, and enough chairs should be positioned around the table. Check the temperature and lighting; if you discover a problem, contact the hotel representative immediately. Finally, if a delicatessen or the hotel will be delivering refreshments, arrange to have a table set up at one side of the room or in an adjacent room or lobby. Participants can then interrupt the meeting whenever they please and serve themselves.

Making Accommodations for Visitors

Hotel rooms.   Sometimes it is necessary to make overnight hotel accommodations for out-of-town participants. The most convenient arrangement usually is to reserve a conference room and individual rooms for participants all in the same hotel or motel. A facility near the airport is a great convenience for incoming guests. Be certain to find out if spouses will accompany the participants. If numbers are indefinite or names are unknown, ask the hotel to reserve a block of rooms for an estimated number of guests.

Travel.   Occasionally, you may have to make partial travel arrangements as well for the participants. Usually, this is limited to car rental, taxi, or limousine service to and from the airport. Again, make reservations far enough in advance to ensure that ground transportation will be available. (See chapter 8 for further details on travel arrangements.)

WHAT TO DO AT THE MEETING

Relaying Telephone and Other Messages

Telephone calls.   Follow your employer's preference in handling calls and messages. Unless you are expected to put through important telephone calls, treat each call as if your employer were out of town. Handle what you can yourself, refer the caller to another available executive, or take messages and indicate that your boss will return the call after the meeting has adjourned.

Messages.   Urgent messages should be typed and quietly handed to the intended recipient. Wait to see if the person gives you a reply or asks you to handle the problem. If you are attending the meeting along with the other participants, perhaps to take the minutes, ask the secretary filling in for you to handle things the same as you would. If you are taking minutes, you cannot be interrupted or leave the meeting room.

Reading the Meeting Minutes

When you read the minutes.   If you are the recording secretary, you may be expected to read the previous meeting's minutes. Do so clearly, at a moderate pace, and in a voice loud enough for everyone to hear. There may be a tape recorder on the table recording the meeting proceedings. Be certain that you are speaking so that your voice will record properly.

When someone else reads the minutes.   Check the typed minutes carefully before you release them to anyone else. Also, check to see that all essential documents are attached—treasurer's report, budgetary information, and so on.

Following Parliamentary Procedure

Rules of order.   A book of parliamentary procedure called *Robert's Rules of Order* is a must for anyone who frequently is involved in preparing agendas and minutes and assisting with the organization and conduct of business. This book covers the rules concerning:

1. Introduction of business
2. General classification of motions
3. Motions and their order of precedence
4. Committees and informal action
5. Debate and decorum
6. Vote
7. Officers and the minutes
8. Organization and meetings
9. Officers and committees
10. Miscellaneous rules and practices.

Basic principles.   There are four basic principles of parliamentary procedure:

1. Majority vote prevails.
2. Participants may consider only one topic at a time.
3. Participants have equal rights and obligations.
4. The person chairing the meeting must conduct the proceedings objectively and ensure each participant's rights.

Business is transacted by way of motions. In formal proceedings, a person who wants some measure approved addresses the chair ("Madam Chairman" or "Mr. Chairman") and gives his or her name. After being recognized the person states: "I move that . . ." Another participant must second the motion before the chair can ask for a vote. First, however, the chair asks if there is any discussion. Depending on the formality, the vote may be made by ballot, roll call, show of hands, standing, voice, or general consent. Motions are handled in the order of precedence (importance). The chair is also responsible for declaring a motion (not a person) out of order.

Taking the Meeting Minutes

Minutes of a formal meeting must be accurate and complete, although not necessarily verbatim (except for resolutions, motions, and so on). Before you start, review minutes from other meetings and notice organization, amount of detail, phraseology, and so on.

1. Quickly prepare a seating chart to help you identify speakers during the meeting.
2. Have a copy of the agenda and other documents handy in case you need to check facts and figures.
3. Summarize general discussions but record resolutions, amendments, important statements, decisions, and conclusions verbatim. Figure 20 is an example of forms you could devise to help you record information. Even though a tape recorder may be used to back up your notes, don't rely on it to supply a lot of things you miss. It could be malfunctioning during the meeting without your knowledge.
4. Record the name of each person who makes or seconds a motion or who proposes any action or opinion.
5. Signal the chair if you miss anything or need additional information. You might arrange in advance for some sign to indicate that

Figure 20. Form for Recording Motions

MINUTES
(meeting name and date)

Motion No. 1_____

_____

_____

_____

Proposed by:_____   Seconded by:_____
For:_____   Against:_____

Motion No. 2_____

_____

_____

_____

Proposed by:_____   Seconded by:_____
For:_____   Against:_____

Motion No. 3_____

_____

_____

_____

Proposed by:_____   Seconded by:_____
For:_____   Against:_____

Motion No. 4_____

_____

_____

_____

Proposed by:_____   Seconded by:_____
For:_____   Against:_____

Motion No. 5_____

_____

_____

_____

Proposed by:_____   Seconded by:_____
For:_____   Against:_____

Motion No. 6_____

_____

_____

_____

the chair should repeat something or to request clarification of something.

MAINTAINING THE BOOK OF MINUTES

Typing the Meeting Minutes

Rough draft.   After the meeting, while everything is fresh in your mind, listen to the tape recording of the proceedings, correct your notes as needed, and prepare a double-spaced rough draft of the minutes. Submit this draft to your employer before preparing the final copy. After the rough draft is approved and complete, prepare the final version.

Final copy.   The final copy of the minutes should be prepared in a style consistent with previous minutes. But if you have no previous copy to follow, these guidelines may help:

1. Center the heading in all capitals. The heading should consist of the name of the group or company.

2. Give the day, date, hour, place, presiding officer, and type of meeting in the first paragraph. Indicate whether a quorum was present.

3. If it is a small meeting, list the names of those attending in a column or double column under the first paragraph.

4. Double-space the text and triple-space between individual items and topics. Single-space resolutions.

5. Use above-paragraph subheadings or margin captions. Type margin captions as follows:

ADJOURNMENT   A motion for adjournment was made by David Michaels and seconded by Regina Novak, and the meeting was adjourned at 4:10 P.M.

6. Indent paragraphs (not essential if side captions are used) ten spaces and indent resolutions fifteen spaces.

7. Use all capitals for *WHEREAS* and *RESOLVED* and capitalize *That* when it follows *RESOLVED (RESOLVED That)*. Use uppercase and lowercase letters for *Board of Directors* and *Corporation* (for whom the minutes are being written).

8. Use uppercase and lowercase letters for sums of money and put

the amount in parentheses after it: *Four Hundred Dollars ($400.00)*.

9. Use margins of about $1\frac{1}{2}$ inches.

10. State the time of adjournment and the date for the next meeting (if any) in the last paragraph.

11. Add two signature lines at the bottom of the page for the secretary (on the left) and the chair (on the right).

12. Attach pertinent documents such as the treasurer's report.

Correcting the Meeting Minutes

At each meeting, the minutes of the previous meeting are read; sometimes corrections are pointed out at this time, and you will need to correct the minutes accordingly.

Procedure. Draw a red pencil mark through each incorrect line. Write the correction above the red line and specify in the margin at which meeting the correction was made. For large corrections—too large to write above the red line—type the new material on a separate page and note in the margin that a correction appears on a sheet at the end of the minutes. Such corrections need to be signed by the secretary and chair the same as the actual minutes.

Indexing the Minute Book

Minutes are kept chronologically in a minute book, often a three-ring binder, so that you can easily locate the minutes of a certain *date*. But what if your employer asks for the minutes that cover a specific *topic*, date unknown? An index of topics is the answer if this is likely to happen.

Preparing an index. You can set up your index on 3- by 5-inch cards arranged alphabetically by *topic*. As soon as you finish typing the minutes, prepare a card for each topic (first check whether a card is already in the index file for that topic). If you maintain the index by computer, add an entry for each topic on the appropriate document file (you will probably include the same information that you would put on an index card). Use cross-references if topics might be described in more than one way. Put the topic heading in the upper left corner. In the center of the card, put the date and location of the minutes (7/14/88—Book 2—p. 31). If the same topic comes up at a future meeting, simply add the new date and location to the same card.

MEETING WITH ASSISTANTS AND COWORKERS

Secretaries sometimes schedule daily or weekly conferences with assistants or trainees. Sometimes members of a secretarial staff also meet regularly or occasionally and discuss office practices or special projects.

Preparing for the Meeting

If you are attending, but not conducting, the meeting, review any preliminary information you are sent and prepare notes on the subject so that you can contribute ideas when appropriate or at least respond intelligently during the discussion. The secretary conducting the meeting may distribute pencils and paper, but to be safe, come prepared with your own supplies.

If you are conducting the meeting, decide where to hold it—probably in your office or in the general secretarial offices. You will be expected to continue to take incoming calls and greet visitors, unless another secretary handles this for you during your meeting. Since many secretaries must maintain office activity as usual, particularly in a small office, they schedule conferences with assistants or other secretaries early in the morning, before normal business activity accelerates, or during the lunch hour. Consider the needs in your office, and select the best time for your situation.

Although secretarial meetings are often brief and informal, you should have an outline of what you want to discuss. Perhaps you want to review an assistant's problems in a particular area or perhaps you want to discuss a special project such as mailing-list conversion with other secretaries. If you want suggestions and other contributions from the others, let them know in advance what will be discussed so that they can prepare for it. You will likely set up the time and date in person if you work in the same office, so a personal reminder the day before the meeting may be adequate, rather than the written follow-up notices that are sent with certain other types of meetings. You may want to tell your coworkers to bring pencils and paper, but have extra supplies available in case they forget. You may also want to remind them to have someone take their incoming calls if necessary, and indicate how long they should arrange to be away from their desks.

Conducting the Meeting

Although an office secretarial meeting is usually informal, you should guide the discussion. Instead of calling the meeting to order, you might simply check to see that everyone is there and say, "let's start by talking about . . ." When you ask for responses, acknowledge people one at a time and stick to your agenda or order of topics. If everyone talks at once, or if the discussion strays off course, stand up if necessary to get their attention and then remind them that time is limited, that certain things have to be discussed or decided, and that therefore it is necessary for them to speak one at a time.

Instead of formal voting, you may just "agree" on a certain division of labor or certain procedures to follow. In the case of an assistant, you may simply give daily or work assignments and suggest solutions to problems or ask if there are any problems the assistant wants to discuss. But give the assistant or other participants a chance to speak and listen carefully to their comments. At the end, summarize the discussion and any decisions so that there will be no misunderstandings later.

Preparing Notes or Minutes

Everyone at an office secretarial meeting should take notes, especially if work assignments are made or decisions reached on work procedures. Formal minutes are not needed for a routine office meeting; however, if you are conducting the meeting, take notes and keep a typed summary of each meeting in a special secretarial-meeting folder. If problems ever arise later, you may need to refer to such notes to verify that you gave someone a certain work assignment on a particular day or that you and your coworkers agreed on a certain policy or division of labor for a special project.

ASSISTING WITH SEMINARS AND CONFERENCES

Secretaries to executives attending seminars and conferences are expected to help their employers prepare folders of meeting material to take along and to assemble supplies such as stationery and address lists (see figure 23 in chapter 8). Secretaries to persons arranging or conducting a meeting have additional duties. They may, for example, help in preparing a program, processing registrations, and, generally, setting up and maintaining various files pertaining to the event.

Preparing Programs and Announcements

A program committee is usually appointed in arranging a seminar or conference to select program topics and issue invitations to prospective speakers. If you are secretary to the person responsible for preparing the program and any related announcements, you will probably have two tasks—drafting the program and coordinating the typesetting, printing, and distribution of it.

The size of the program and the announcements may vary. For a large conference, there may be one or more preliminary mailings followed by a package including the program and various registration forms. Some programs are large—the size of a small booklet; others are no more than a one- or two-sided $8\frac{1}{2}$- by 11-inch sheet, with or without a cut-off registration form. Either way, you may have to prepare numerous drafts since program topics and speakers may change several times before a final selection is made.

Investigating printing needs. Based on the preliminary information your employer gives you, contact about three printers who are capable of preparing the materials and, if you don't have other arrangements, mailing the packages. (Or you may prefer to use a separate mailing house.) Ask for estimates and present the written bids to your employer for approval and selection of one. Also investigate whether any airlines would be willing to print and mail the material in return for free advertising in the packages or being designated official airline for the conference.

Planning to meet deadlines. One of the most important aspects of program and announcement preparations is the deadline. You must work out realistic dates with the printer to allow for typesetting, proofreading, corrections, printing, and mailing—all scheduled to allow participants time to decide whether to attend, to make arrangements in their own companies, to mail in advance registration fees, and so on. This entire process involves close coordination with the program committee, which may want to delay printing longer than is desirable in hopes of confirming more names of speakers or tentative topics. Keep your employer well informed of deadlines and put all dates on your and your employer's calendar. (For further information about typesetting, proofreading, printing, and so on, review chapter 3.)

Handling Registration Details

Depending on the type and size of the conference, registration may be complex or simple. Some organizations devise registration cards that can be filed alphabetically (by name) like index cards. Matching lists of data are often set up by computer and coded according to program session, meals registration, and so forth. At any time, then, you can print out a list of persons registered for a particular session or planning to be present at a certain meal.

Advance registration procedures. Although the procedure for processing registration varies according to the type and size of meeting, advance mail registration (as opposed to on-site conference door registrations) usually involves several steps. Each incoming check must be compared to the registration form to be certain the amount is correct (bill the registrant for any balance due), and the registration must be marked or stamped paid with the amount and the date *before* the check is deposited.

Maintaining Files and Records

Records for committee needs. Be prepared to work with the various conference committees to be certain that you are handling the registrations to meet all needs and that you have kept the records needed for you to provide any information needed by each committee. For example, the facilities committee will need to know if a particular session has so many registrations that a larger room is needed. Or perhaps the program committee will want to divide it into two groups and secure another speaker. If a session doesn't have enough registrations, they may want to cancel it. The meals committee will need to know how many luncheon, dinner, or banquet tickets have been distributed to be able to order enough meals and arrange for adequate dining- or lunch-room facilities. The budget committee will need to know how much registration money has come in and what bills have been paid or are due.

Records for the bookkeeper. Before you start processing registration checks, discuss procedures with the bookkeeper to be certain that you are providing the information needed for him or her to record transactions in the books of account and to provide satisfactory supporting documents. (See chapter 9 for more about bookkeeping procedures.)

Confirmation packets for registrants. You must also send a confirmation to each person who registers in advance. This often consists of a printed packet including confirmation card, luncheon or dinner tickets, and other materials that the person must have. If time is short, you may have to hold the packet for the person to pick up at the door at the conference site. (Most on-site registration booths have a place for advance registrants to check in and another place for latecomers who have not yet registered or paid.)

Data and tally records. If you are maintaining records by computer, pertinent information must be entered (name, date and amount paid, sessions registered for, session dates and times, and so on) for each registrant. But even if you keep records by computer, maintain another file of registration cards or forms and keep up-to-the-minute tally sheets of numbers registered for each session, each meal, each tour, and any other scheduled event. Before you file a registration card or enter the data in the computer, add a tally mark to each tally sheet (one for each session, meal, and so on). Also, set up file folders for copies of each type of correspondence—speakers' correspondence, hotel or convention-site correspondence, travel correspondence, and so on. Finally, ask your employer if there are any other files or records that are needed.

Chapter 8

Making Travel Arrangements

PREPARING FOR THE BUSINESS TRIP

Use of Travel Agents

A travel service is indispensable in making plans for both domestic and foreign business travel. A company may be able to open an account with an agency and be billed once a month, thus avoiding the nuisance of paying for numerous tickets throughout the month. Many firms use company credit, or travel cards, which serve essentially the same purpose. Either way, the monthly (or other) billing provides a good record for the accounting department.

What a travel agent will do for you.   A travel agent will procure all of the necessary tickets, plan an itinerary, arrange hotel accommodations, arrange to have a rented car awaiting the traveler at his or her destination, and perform many other services such as arranging sightseeing tours that will save you time and worry. You can make one telephone call and be sure of getting the best schedule and best routing, even though more than one airline or other transportation is involved. The travel agent represents all companies and is partial to none.

In the case of foreign travel, the agent will tell you what documents are needed (passport, visa, police and health certificates, and so on) and how to exchange dollars for foreign currency and will assist in getting traveler's checks or a letter of credit. He or she will arrange for a foreign representative of the agency to meet the traveler on arrival if desired, take care of baggage, and see the traveler through customs.

The agent will have a rental car waiting for the traveler at the destination and arrange personal and baggage insurance and even provide rain insurance (a sum designed to console in the event that rain mars the trip). He or she will help the traveler take advantage of money-saving foreign travel rates, such as promotional, excursion, or group rates, and arrange for interesting side trips to points of interest or special events in the particular area in which the traveler will be.

Working with an agency. Even if your company has an account with a travel agency, it may be your responsibility to act as liaison between the agency and your employer. You would then see that the desired arrangements are made without any inconvenience to your employer, and a reliable agency can be of immense help to you. Since travel agencies are linked to the airlines by computer, an agency can instantly find for you the lowest fare on a scheduled flight to your destination. Some travel agents specialize in corporate clients (who have different needs than vacation travelers have) or have a division dealing exclusively with business travelers.

The travel agent will also provide the information you need about current and upcoming special rates on certain airlines, arrangements for car or limousine or regular departure times to and from airports by the courtesy vehicles provided by many hotels, helicopter or other shuttle service where available, and connecting rail schedules in some cities. You can tell the agent about any special needs of your employer too: physical disability, seating preference on airplanes, nonsmoking or dietary requirements, preference for early or late arrivals, and so on.

What you should tell the travel agent. Get to know an agent who can work with you on a regular basis, someone who understands and appreciates your needs. When you ask an agent to arrange a trip for your employer, specify the number in the party, names, ages, sexes, and, if the trip includes a foreign country, citizenship. Also indicate where your party wants to go, dates of departure and return, mode and class of travel, and the approximate amount that can be spent. The travel agent will be able to tell you the classes of travel and rates that fit your budget on a particular airline or steamship, on the trains here and in foreign countries, and at hotels.

When your employer cannot decide on a definite itinerary. A traveler abroad who has all reservations made and confirmed in advance travels with the greatest ease and comfort. It sometimes happens, however, that it is impossible for your employer to know where he or she will be able to go and when. If plans are uncertain, give the travel agent the names of the places in which your employer expects to need hotel reservations, approximate dates, and how much per day he or she will spend for hotel expenses. The agent will do the following things:

1. Send you the name of a desirable hotel in each place
2. Write to each of the recommended hotels asking them to give your requests their best attention
3. Advise the agent's foreign correspondent in each city of the approximate date of arrival

Fees.   Usually, the traveler pays no additional fee for most services of a travel agency. However, if plans are canceled the agent may charge for the services rendered and to cover out-of-pocket expenditures such as long-distance telephone calls or telegrams. In some cases, the agent also charges for railway transportation arrangements but not in the case of prearranged vacation package trips.

How to select a travel agent.   If you have not had experience with a qualified travel agent, select one who is a member of a national organization with a grievance committee, should you ever have cause for recourse. Find out what fees and service charges may be assessed, if the agency has worldwide branches, and if someone from the agency has been to the various places to which your employer travels.

The American Society of Travel Agents, 711 Fifth Avenue, New York, NY 10022, familiarly known as ASTA, has members in the principal cities of the United States and Canada. The members may be recognized by the ASTA emblem, which they are permitted to display if they are in good standing. You can get the name of an ASTA member situated near your office by writing to the executive offices of the association, located in New York City. There are also many reliable agents that are not members of ASTA, but the code of ethics of this association is high and its members, therefore, are usually dependable and efficient.

Use of Company Travel Departments

Large firms have usually maintained their own travel offices or departments. They have traditionally served as a liaison between the traveling employee and the airlines, railroads, and so on or an outside travel agency. Now that the desktop computer has become common in organizations of all sizes, the potential for many companies to deal directly with airlines has increased. Another option that firms are exercising is the movement to designate company travel departments as branch agencies of a regular travel agency. With the right computer software, a company travel department can be linked through travel agencies directly with airline reservation systems. When airline ticket printers become common in company travel departments, firms will be able to print tickets on demand and even provide seat selection.

How to work with a company travel department. Secretaries who work for firms that have in-house travel offices should prepare the same itinerary and other information for the in-house travel personnel as they would for an outside travel agent: time, date, destination, airline or other preferences, shuttle and courtesy or rental-car needs, hotel preferences, personal disabilities or special requirements, and so on. If the company travel office has several employees, try to work closely with one in particular who will become familiar with your boss's preferences and needs.

How to Get Information about Transportation

Your employer will usually tell you which mode of transportation he or she intends to use. Sometimes certain information is needed to make a choice, such as:

1. What airline or railway may be used
2. Time schedules
3. Plane and train accommodations (such as dining and sleeping facilities)
4. Car-rental arrangements at destination
5. Costs
6. Baggage facilities

If your organization has a travel department, let the appropriate person know your employer's preferences and preliminary itinerary. The department will provide a schedule or several schedules, if alternatives are available. If you must secure the information on your own, contact a travel agent.

Checklist for handling preparations. When arranging a business trip for your employer, here is what you should do:

1. Get transportation information from your company travel office or a travel agent and submit a time-and-route schedule to your employer.
2. Ask the company agent or outside travel agent to make transportation and hotel reservations. (If it is necessary to write for reservations on your own, follow the sample letters on pages 393–94.)

Figure 21. Travel Itinerary

FROM	TO	VIA	DATE & TIME	ARRIVE (EST)	ACCOMMODATION	MEAL SERVICE	CAR RENTAL	HOTEL
N.Y.	Boston	Amtrak	5/6–11:30P	5/6–5:15A	Car 106 Room A Train 467	--	Hertz--Ford	Parker House
Boston	N.Y.	Eastern	5/8–3:30P	5/8–4:45P	Flight #633	Snacks	--	Home
N.Y.	Washing.	Eastern	5/13–8:30A	5/15–9:47A	Flight #431	Breakfast	Avis--Buick	Shoreham
Washing.	Atlanta	Eastern	5/15–2:50P	5/15–7:32P	Flight #565	Dinner	--	Atlanta-Baltimore
Atlanta	Cleveland	Eastern	5/19–5:50P	5/19–10:32P	Flight #732	Dinner	--	Carter Hotel
Cleveland	Chicago	United	5/22–6:10P	5/22–7:10P CST	Flight #501	Dinner	Hertz--Chevrolet	Stevens Hotel
Chicago	New York	United	5/28–12:00N	5/28–4:00P	Flight #622	Snacks	--	Home

All Standard Time one hour earlier than Daylight Time.

Checking Out Time—3:00 P.M.

3. Confirm that tickets have been sent or will be available at the counter before departure.

4. Prepare the travel itinerary and appointment schedule.

5. Assemble business data and supplies to be taken on the trip.

6. Prepare baggage identification labels and furnish baggage information.

7. Make financial arrangements for the trip.

8. Give the hotel confirmations and tickets to your employer.

9. If there are to be any formal occasions, such as dinners and conventions, try to find out what type of formal attire your employer will need.

Special Secretarial Duties

When you make travel arrangements for your employer, there are also many secretarial tasks relating to the necessary preparations for the trip.

Preparing the itinerary and hotel information. Type an itinerary showing points of departure and arrival; airline or railroad; dates and times of departure and arrival; accommodations; available car-rental facilities; and hotels. Figure 21 is an illustration of an itinerary.

Type the itinerary on strong, durable paper in triplicate—a copy for your employer, a copy for his or her family, and a copy for your file. Also make a copy for anyone in the organization who needs and is entitled to it. If you are working with a company travel office or a travel agency, the agent may prepare the itinerary.

Some secretaries type the itinerary and schedule of appointments in a small, top-bound notebook. You can do this by backfeeding (see page 64) the pages of the notebook into the typewriter. You can also put other information and reminders in the notebook. If it is spiral-bound, your employer can also use it for writing memos to send to you and to various executives in the company.

Compiling an appointment schedule. Prepare a schedule of all appointments your employer has on the trip. Include in the schedule the following: city and state; date and time; name, firm, and address of the individual with whom your employer has an appointment; telephone number; and any remarks or special reminders about the visit. Figure 22 is an illustration of a schedule.

If your employer has previously met any of the individuals with whom he or she is to do business, make a notation of the circumstances of the

Figure 22. Appointment Schedule

Appointment Schedule May 8-28

City & State	Date & Time	Appointment	Address	Phone	Remarks
Boston MA	5/7-5:30P	Williams-McGregor & Co.	125 South St.	543-3485	
	5/8-10:00A	Brown, Jones & Brown	348 South St.	211-1257	
	1:00P	Norris, at Copley Plaza, Merry-Go-Round		366-2764	Luncheon
Washington DC	5/13-11:00A	Sen. Snow	Sen. Off. Bldg.	840-4884	

meeting. You will have this information available if you keep the "contact reminder" file described on page 50.

Assembling data for business appointments. Place together the papers relating to each matter your employer will handle on the trip, for example, letters or memos concerning the problem to be discussed and also any other pertinent information. Use a rubber band or large paper clip to bind together the papers pertaining to each matter, and clearly label each packet.

Packing supplies for the trip. Make duplicate lists of the stationery and supplies that your employer needs when going on a business trip. Use the lists as checklists when you pack the supplies so that you will not forget anything. The list in figure 23 suggests items that might be needed.

Handling the baggage. Your employer may want to know the baggage allowance that will be checked without charge on the railroad or plane ticket and the limitations on the dimensions of baggage. You can usually find all of this information in the timetables. People who travel a lot usually increase their personal insurance coverage to compensate for damage and losses since airlines and other transportation company insurance is minimal.

Prepare identification labels for each piece of baggage, including a duplicate set that can be placed *inside* each piece. (Many people, for security reasons, do not want their names and addresses to show on any outside labels or luggage tags.) Labels are available at ticket offices and baggage counters. Keep a supply on hand.

For short trips some executives use a carry-on combination suitcase and briefcase or an attaché case with a divider that snaps down on one side. With clothes under the divider, a traveler can go from plane to appointment without having to stop at a hotel and unpack. Then, too, there is no time wasted waiting for luggage at the airport.

Arranging for travel funds. A businessperson uses one of the following plans for keeping a supply of funds while traveling.

1. Travel advances. Some companies reimburse employees later; others provide advance funds for traveling executives. With information supplied by your employer, you will be able to fill out the necessary company forms required for release of the advance.

2. Personal checks. A person who travels extensively usually has credit cards from the hotels where he or she stops or has a major national credit or charge card such as Visa, MasterCard, or American Express. It is then easy to cash checks at the hotels.

3. Traveler's checks. These checks are usually available in denominations of ten, twenty, fifty, one hundred, one thousand, and five thousand

Figure 23.   Checklist of Supplies for Trip

☐ Stationery of all kinds	☐ Pens and pencils
☐ Envelopes, plain	☐ Erasers
☐ Envelopes addressed to the company	☐ Clips
☐ Large manila envelopes	☐ Scissors
☐ Memo paper	☐ Rubber bands
☐ Stenographer's pad	☐ Blotters
☐ Legal pads	☐ Cellophane tape
☐ Carbon paper	☐ Calendar
☐ Address book	☐ Mail schedules
☐ Legal folders	☐ Pins
☐ Business cards	☐ Bottle opener
☐ Dictation equipment	☐ Ruler
☐ Dictation belts, tapes, or disks	☐ Band-Aids
☐ Computer tapes or diskettes	☐ Travel guides and maps
☐ Computer equipment	☐ Itinerary
☐ Mailing folders or boxes for dictation and computer media	☐ Appointment schedule
☐ Cash	☐ Timetables and schedules
☐ Personal checkbook	☐ Tickets
☐ Office account checks	☐ Passports, visas, etc.
☐ Expense forms	☐ Stamp pad & rubber stamps
☐ Other office forms	☐ Postage stamps
☐ Pertinent files	

dollars. Citibank of New York and Bank of America sell their own travelers checks; other banks usually sell American Express Traveler's Checks. You can purchase them direct from the American Express Company. To purchase traveler's checks for your employer at his other bank, fill out the bank's application form, which provides a space for the total amount of checks and the denominations desired. Your employer may have to sign the checks in the presence of the bank's representative. This practice is not always required but is advisable for safety. Some banks also allow you to mail in signature cards if you have an account there. If the account is particularly valuable, the bank's representative may come to your office; otherwise, your employer must go to the bank.

4. **Letters of credit.** A person traveling to a foreign country usually buys a letter of credit from his or her bank if funds of one thousand dollars or more are needed. You can fill out the application, but as in the case of traveler's checks, your employer must complete the transaction in the presence of the bank's representative. A letter of credit testifies to the holder's credit standing, serves as a letter of introduction to leading banks, and can be drawn against at banks in every part of the world until the face amount of the letter of credit has been exhausted. Many travelers find it advisable to purchase both traveler's checks and a letter of credit when planning a trip to a foreign country.

Building your own travel- and hotel-information library. Even though you may work with a company or outside travel agent, keep a reference shelf of roadmaps, timetables, and flight schedules for quick reference when you have a general question such as the usual time required for a direct flight between New York and Chicago. Whenever you are planning to take a trip, go to an airport, railroad station, hotel, or travel agency and pick up current schedules and timetables. If your employer travels frequently, consider purchasing one or more of the directories listed on page 207. Other useful references are the *Official Airline Guide* and *The Official Railway Guide*. Keep in mind, however, that schedules and rates change continually, and you must contact a company or outside travel agent for up-to-the-minute information.

Traveling with Your Employer

Basic rules of conduct. Some work cannot be handled by temporary office assistants in another city or foreign country. In these situations, it is more practical for the secretaries to travel with their employers.

Travel arrangements. Your employer will specify where you are to go and when. In some cases, your transportation and hotel arrangements may be identical; in other cases, you may not visit all of the same places or stay as long as in certain places.

Conduct. A business trip involves just that—business. Although you may have free time when you can shop, sightsee, take in a play, or enjoy a meal at an interesting restaurant, it is assumed that you are there to work.

Your days may be spent gathering information for your boss, checking further travel plans, typing, taking notes at meetings, organizing your employer's travel files, preparing and processing correspondence, and so on. Major hotels supply various rental equipment, or your company may have a branch in the city where you can secure office space to use a typewriter or word processor. When you arrive at a hotel with your employer, or drive together, he or she will take care of the tipping. Otherwise, handle this as if you were traveling alone. However, keep track of all business expenditures so that you can be reimbursed later.

Much of the time your employer may be entertaining clients or business associates. After work, you should then assume that you are on your own. But secretaries are part of the business team, representing their companies, and must dress and otherwise conduct themselves as they would at the office or at business-social events. If you are in a foreign country, respect the customs and follow proper rules of etiquette (thoroughly study the customs of the country before you leave on the trip).

MAKING TRAVEL AND HOTEL RESERVATIONS

Checklist of Information You Need

Today's business executive usually travels by plane, but circumstances may necessitate using an overnight sleeper. Therefore, before making reservations for the trip, you will have to know not only where your employer plans to go but also the method of transportation he or she prefers. You need the following information to make travel and hotel reservations, whether you use a travel agent or make the arrangements on your own:

1. Destination
2. Desired departure time (morning, afternoon, evening, or night)
3. Desired arrival and departure times for stopovers
4. Preferred transportation (plane, train, or automobile)
5. Travel accommodations desired (such as first class)
6. Whether or not a rental car is desired and vehicle preference
7. Whether or not connecting shuttle service is needed
8. Hotel preference and accommodations desired at destination

How to Prepare Time and Route Data

Sometimes companies have a particular airline that they want employees to use (it may provide discounts or other services). Otherwise, if there is more than one airline servicing the city that your employer is planning to visit, list some of the major airlines with departure and arrival times and submit the schedule so that your employer can determine which one is the most convenient.

In some cases, railway transportation may be more convenient or desirable. If traveling by train is more convenient, prepare a schedule showing information about departure and arrival times, railway lines to be used, and ticket information.

If the contemplated trip has several laps, submit the information for each lap on a separate sheet. This information is also helpful when making reservations.

List some of the major car-rental facilities available in each city on the itinerary, unless your company always uses a particular rental facility.

Planes and trains are usually scheduled on standard time at the place named in the timetable—eastern standard, central standard, and so on. (See page 622 for a time-zone map.) Call the change in time to your employer's attention.

What to Do about Delays in Getting Reservations

Frequently, you cannot get space when you want it. The travel agent will then keep trying and notify you if the space later becomes available. In this case, also put in your request for another airline or railroad. Be certain to cancel any other reservation you may have made when the space you want is confirmed. Often, in cases of delay, travel agents can be helpful in making numerous contacts and securing space that someone else has canceled.

Securing the Tickets

Company accounts and credit cards. Travel agents often make it easy to obtain and pay for tickets. Most companies whose personnel travel extensively open accounts with an agency (or with an airline). Often employees use a company credit card. Individuals who make many trips can open similar accounts on the basis of their personal credit. Those who don't have accounts can use one of the popular credit or charge cards such as Visa, MasterCard, or American Express.

Payment by check.   Even if your employer does not want to use a credit card or an account with a travel agency or airline, if time is available you can telephone an agent or the airline, make your reservation, and request that the ticket be mailed. Immediately on receipt of the ticket in your office, send a check. The ticket, however, is not valid until the check is received. When you make an arrangement of this kind, you must be sure that there is ample time for receipt of the ticket by you and, in turn, receipt of the check by the travel agent or airline.

Canceling reservations.   Should your employer change plans before you mail a check, simply return the unused ticket. Even if you charge the ticket with a credit card, the unused portion must be returned for the crediting procedure to begin. Always request a credit receipt to keep in your files until the credit appears on your monthly charge-card statement. If time is short, you can telephone a cancellation and follow up with a confirming letter.

How to check the tickets.   Always be sure to check any tickets carefully against the information you gathered in making the reservation. With plane tickets, look for these points.

1. Are the flight numbers correct?
2. What about time of departure?
3. Is the plane leaving from the airport from which you assumed it was leaving?
4. Is the city of destination the city to which your employer wants to travel?
5. Is the reservation on the airline you assumed it was on?
6. Is the ticket complete?

Tickets list major airlines by codes that are standard in the industry (although with mergers and name changes, codes may change, too, from time to time), for example:

AM	Aeromexico		AS	Alaska Airlines
OC	Air California		AZ	Alitalia
AC	Air Canada		AQ	Aloha Airlines
AF	Air France		HP	American West
JM	Air Jamaica		AA	American Airlines
EI	Air Lingus		BN	Braniff
TE	Air New Zealand		BA	British Airways
FJ	Air Pacific		BR	British Caledonian

CP	Canadian Pacific		OZ	Ozark Airlines
CI	China Airlines		PW	Pacific Western
CO	Continental Airlines		PA	Pan American World
DL	Delta Air Lines			Airways
EA	Eastern Airlines		PI	Piedmont
AY	Finnair		PS	PSA
HA	Hawaiian Air		QF	Qantas Airways, Ltd.
IB	Iberia Airlines		RC	Republic Airlines
FI	Icelandic Airlines		SN	Sabena World Airlines
JL	Japan Air Lines		SK	Scandinavian Airlines
KL	KLM			(SAS)
KE	Korean Air		SQ	Singapore
LH	Lufthansa German		SR	Swissair
	Airlines		TP	TAP
MX	Mexicana		TW	Trans World Airlines
ML	Midway		UA	United Airlines
NY	New York Air		AL	U.S. Airlines
NW	Northwest Orient		RG	Varig Airlines
	Airlines		WA	Western Union
OA	Olympic Airways			

With train tickets, before giving the tickets to your employer, check them carefully for information similar to that for the plane tickets. Check these points: time, date, destination, train number, accommodations, and railway station. Make sure that the ticket is complete.

Making Hotel Reservations

Directories. If you are using a company or outside travel agent, the agent will take care of hotel reservations according to your specifications or will make suggestions regarding hotel accommodations. Some firms negotiate with certain hotels for lower rates. But if your employer has no hotel preference, is not familiar with the hotels in a city where he or she expects to stop, and is not using a company travel department or travel agent, you can get detailed information by consulting the latest editions of *Hotel and Travel Index* and *Official Hotel and Resort Guide,* published by the Ziff-Davis Publishing Company, One Park Avenue, New York, NY 10016, and *The Hotel/Motel Red Book,* published by the American Hotel and Motel Association, 888 7th Avenue, New York, NY 10019. Also, Rand McNally and other organizations publish maps and travel books, available in bookstores. The number of rooms and the price enable you to judge the class of hotel. Or you can call a local hotel association or write to the Chamber of Commerce in the city of destination.

Reservation service.   Some credit- and charge-card organizations (such as American Express), certain associations, and larger hotel and motel chains provide a nationwide reservation service. Some airlines provide both flight and hotel reservation services. Information in the folders offered to members of the American Automobile Association guides the traveler to good hotels, inns, overnight guest houses, and motels in the United States, Canada, and Mexico.

Making the reservations.   When making a hotel reservation, give the company or outside travel agent the name of the person for whom the reservation is to be made, the time of arrival and probable time of departure, and the type of accommodations desired. Also inquire about the checkout time and include this information in the memo that you give your employer before the trip. The reservation can be made by telephone or letter. When you speak directly to someone at the hotel, get the person's name and the reservation number in case you need to make further contact to change the reservation.

Confirmations.   Always get confirmations of hotel reservations in writing or by wire and attach them to the copy of the itinerary that your employer takes along (see figure 21). This applies whether you make the reservation or whether it is made by someone in the place to which your employer is going. Specify to the travel agent that you want the room held. When you make a reservation yourself by credit card, you can ask for a "guaranteed" reservation.

Rooms for a large meeting.   If you must reserve rooms for a large meeting, such as a conference, it is best to speak directly with the sales manager at one of the larger hotels in the city where the meeting is scheduled. Hotels provide valuable assistance in arranging for group reservations, in selecting appropriate meeting rooms and other facilities, and in handling the many other details that are involved.

Exchange services.   Some firms participate in exchange services, such as the Great Exchange operated with the support of Pan Am. Travelers from foreign countries are housed in employee homes and apartments while visiting the United States, and company employees are housed in homes overseas while on a foreign trip. Ask your travel agent for more details.

Making Air-Travel Arrangements

Where to get information about airplane travel.   You can get general information about air travel from travel agents, the airlines themselves, and in the *Official Airline Guide.* For up-to-the-minute schedules and rates, you must telephone a company or outside travel agent with a computerized service or telephone the airlines directly. Remember to inquire about available ground transportation and courtesy vehicles. You may also need to find out whether helicopter service is available.

The best published sources of airline information are the *Official Airline Guides,* published by Reuben H. Donnelly, 2000 Clearwater Drive, Oak Brook, IL 60521. The North American edition lists cities in the United States, Canada, and United States possessions alphabetically. Under each city the airlines servicing that city are listed, together with the page numbers for the respective airline schedules. The guide index also indicates the availability of a car-rental service and/or air-taxi service for each city. International flight information is also included. Guides, issued twice monthly, may be obtained through yearly subscription or by purchase of single copies.

Group travel.   If your task involves arranging air travel for a large group—perhaps for a conference—contact your company travel department or an outside travel agent. If you are seeking only preliminary information, write to several major airlines and inquire about their special services for conference travel. Some will offer a number of attractive packages, including reduced group rates and block reservations from selected cities. Some will even do a promotional mailing, free of charge, to everyone registered for the conference or to prospective attendees.

Airline clubs.   Some major airlines have airline clubs. For an annual membership fee, travelers are offered special lounges at airports, conference rooms with telephones, and other services. Write to or telephone well-known national and international airlines for further information.

Finding out what accommodations your employer wants.   Many companies require their officials to travel at the economy rate if expedient. Most flights have both first class and coach, or economy, sections. Exceptions are shuttle flights, such as those between Washington and New York. These flights usually have only one class of travel. Reservations are not available, but the airline guarantees passage even if a second plane has to be placed in service for the scheduled flight.

Always find out if meals or snacks are available on the flight you are inquiring about. On most flights during a meal hour, meals or so-called snacks are available. The traveler can usually get a cocktail without charge at meal time in first class but must pay for it in coach service.

How to make the reservations.   Whether you deal with your company's travel department or an outside agent, be prepared with full facts before you make your contact. When you telephone a travel agent or airline reservation clerk, get the name of the person to whom you are talking (and give that person your name), so that if you must call again to clarify any part of the itinerary, you will be able to speak with the same person.

Explain clearly what reservations you want. Give the reservations clerk or travel agent the following information:

1. Points of departure and destination
2. Date and time of departure desired
3. Flight number (if known)
4. Class of accommodations desired
5. Any special needs (such as wheelchair or nonsmoking section)

The airline may offer a supersaver or an excursion rate, but if you inquire about this, also ask for any restrictions on this type of fare.

When your employer plans to make several stopovers on the trip, give the company or outside travel agent the approximate times he or she will depart from, and arrive at, various stops and the accommodations desired. If one lap of the trip is to be by train, the agent will also make that reservation for you, as well as car-rental and shuttle needs. Remember to reconfirm any lap of the trip before departure directly with the airlines.

Making Train-Travel Arrangements

Where to get information about trains. You can get information about travel by train from company and outside travel agents, directly from Amtrak, and in *The Official Railway Guide.* (Remember that rates and schedules in timetables or in a published guide will not have up-to-the-minute changes.)

The Official Railway Guide, issued monthly by the National Railway Publication Company, 424 West 33rd Street, New York, NY 10001, contains all of the schedules or timetables of Amtrak and all other passenger railroads in the United States, Canada, and Mexico, with sample fares and a description of the accommodations on each train. It also shows connecting bus and suburban rail lines and mileage between stations and contains maps of individual roads. It can be subscribed for by the year or single copies can be purchased.

Finding out what accommodations your employer wants. Your employer might travel in the coach section on a plane, but he or she is not likely to travel by coach on a train. Each timetable gives the accommodations or "equipment" offered by the scheduled trains or gives a reference to a page where that information can be obtained. You can tell from this whether the train carries a diner, club car, observation car, and the like and the type of sleeping accommodations carried.

Sleeping accommodations in first class may vary, but some of them include:

1. *Bedroom.* A private room containing lower and upper berths, the lower berth serving as a sofa for daytime use; toilet facilities are in the same room only in some bedrooms.

2. *Roomette.* A private room, intended primarily for single occupancy, sometimes with a bed folding into the wall and containing a sofa seat for daytime use; toilet facilities are usually in the same room.

Special cars are also available on some trains for handicapped persons. Tell your travel agent about any special needs you have.

How to make the reservations. The procedure for making train reservations is similar to that for obtaining plane reservations. An intelligent idea of what you want before you telephone your own company travel office, a travel agent, or Amtrak or some other railroad will help immeasurably.

Be sure to give complete and clear information on the point of departure and destination, time, train number or name, and the accommodations desired. For long-distance travel, trains are very limited, and you might not have a choice of time. This is also a good reason to make train reservations far in advance. When the exact reservations that you want are not available, ask the travel agent to suggest something that is available.

Making Auto-Travel Arrangements

Where to get information about automobile travel. You can get information about car rentals from your company or an outside travel agent and directly from the car-rental agencies. Also, the American Automobile Association provides various services for its members.

If your employer travels by automobile a great deal, he or she may find it advantageous to be a member of the American Automobile Association, which has a travel service available to plan any trip a member wants to take by motor vehicle. The headquarters is located at 8111 Gatehouse Road, Falls Church, VA 22042. To secure travel service, telephone or mail your request to the nearest branch of the association, and routings will be forwarded to you, or get them by calling in person at the nearest branch. Other auto clubs are also open to membership and provide a variety of services. Such organizations assist members by:

1. Advising them how to go, where to stop, and what to see
2. Preparing a special route map
3. Providing last-minute information on weather and highway conditions
4. Assisting in selecting and securing motel and hotel accommodations in advance of the trip
5. Providing emergency road service
6. Providing bail and arrest bonds
7. Providing accident insurance
8. Offering an auto-theft reward
9. Offering discounts on car-rental and other travel services

Members of some clubs also receive road maps, travel guides, or directories covering outstanding points of interest.

Airlines, railroads, hotels, and numerous other organizations now provide information about and assistance in arranging car rentals too.

Finding out what car-rental arrangements are needed. Your employer's preliminary itinerary and appointment schedule will suggest stopovers where a car may be needed. Ask about:

1. Specific places where a rental car or limousine is desired
2. Preferences for rental agencies
3. Preferences for make and size of car
4. Method of payment to be used
5. Dates and times car is needed
6. Whether drop-off in another city is desired

Some rental agencies provide a computer printout of directions to numerous local destinations. Ask your travel agent which ones provide this service in the cities your employer will visit.

How to make the reservations. On a trip involving several stops, your employer may prefer to travel from city to city by car or to have a car available for appointments within a particular city. Foreign travelers sometimes prefer a chauffeur-driven car, especially if they are on a tight schedule and are very unfamiliar with the foreign city. Some of the major car-rental facilities at each stop should be listed on the itinerary you prepare, unless your company requires that employees use a particular agency. If you know that a car will be needed, your travel agent can telephone in advance for reservations and have a car waiting at the airport or train station. On arrival, your employer need only show a driver's license. Payment is usually made with one of the major credit cards.

FOREIGN TRAVEL AND PLEASURE TRIPS

Use of Travel Agents

A company or outside travel agent is essential in making foreign travel arrangements. Follow the guidelines on the use of a travel agent at the beginning of this chapter.

Securing a Passport

Application for a passport, which should be made well in advance of the trip, may be executed before a clerk of a federal court, a state court authorized to naturalize aliens, an agent of the State Department, or a post office authorized to grant passports. Passport agents of the State Department are located in New York City, San Francisco, Chicago, Los Angeles, Boston, and New Orleans. In Washington, D.C., applications are executed in the Passport Division of the Department of State.

It is possible to travel to Canada, Mexico, and some Caribbean islands without a passport. For requirements, ask your travel agent or call the Passport Agency of the Department of State (in the white pages under U.S. Government).

Procedure. The following is a brief summary of the essential requirements for making application for a passport when the applicant is a native American citizen or a naturalized citizen.

A native American citizen must submit a previous U.S. passport or a birth certificate with the application, to prove citizenship. Birth certificates must show that the birth was recorded within one year from date of birth. If this certificate is not obtainable, the applicant must submit an affidavit executed by a person who has personal knowledge of the place and date of birth. If an affidavit of a relative or attending physician cannot be obtained, an affidavit of some other reputable person, preferably a blood relation, with knowledge of the facts should be submitted. The person must have known the applicant for several years. The affidavit should state how knowledge of the place and date of birth was acquired.

The traveler must establish his or her identification to the satisfaction of the passport agent. This may be done by presentation of one of the following documents containing the signature of the applicant and either a photograph or a physical description of the applicant:

1. Prior U.S. passport
2. Certificate of naturalization
3. Driver's license
4. Federal, state, or municipal government identity card

Two standard passport photographs must be submitted, along with the current passport fee.

A passport is valid for ten years after which it is necessary to apply for a new one. Passports may be renewed by mail if issued within the previous eight years. A renewal fee is required.

A naturalized citizen must present his naturalization papers and be identified in the same manner as a native-born citizen.

Applications of persons going abroad on business in pursuance of a contract or agreement with a federal government agency must be accompanied by a letter from the head of the firm or, in his or her absence, from the person in charge. The letter must state the position of the applicant, destination (or destinations), purpose of the trip, and approximate length of stay.

Securing a Visa

After the traveler gets a passport, the next step is to get visas for the countries that require them. Your travel agent will tell you whether or not a visa is required. Generally, the passport must be presented and a visa form filled out. The various countries have a number of special requirements, such as additional photographs, police and health certificates, vaccinations, and inoculations. Usually, there is a visa fee. Since the length of time required for processing a visa varies with the country, one should apply well in advance of a trip.

Your employer may ask you to consult the *Congressional Directory* for addresses of overseas consular offices. The U.S. Government Printing Office in Washington, D.C., sells a publication, *Key Officers of Foreign Service Posts* (subscription or single copy), that lists all embassies, legations, and consulates general (as well as giving other information, such as key officers).

Special Secretarial Duties

When your employer travels abroad *on business,* you have certain duties that you do not have in planning a pleasure trip. In addition to handling the duties pertaining to a business trip in this country, you should do the following:

1. Ask your travel agent or the consulates about the special require-ments imposed on *commercial* travelers but not on *pleasure* visitors. This is most important.

2. Compile a list of officers and executives of each firm with whom your employer does business in the foreign countries to be visited. A looseleaf notebook, about 6 by 4 inches, is convenient for this purpose. (See also the contact reminder file on page 50.)

3. Compile pertinent data on all recent deals completed with each firm, together with data on pending deals. You should have a manila folder for each company or individual to be visited.

4. Write letters for your employer's signature requesting letters of introduction from banks, individuals, business houses, and the like to their foreign offices. Such introductions are very helpful to a commercial traveler. The following is a form that you can adapt to your own purpose:

Mr. Alexander N. Genettes
Second Vice-President
Guaranty Trust Company
140 Broadway
New York, NY 10006

Dear Mr. Genettes:

On April 24 I am leaving for Europe on a business trip. I will call on publishers and booksellers in London, Paris, Zurich, Brussels, Amsterdam, Copenhagen, Oslo, Stockholm, and probably Barcelona. A letter from you to your correspondents in each of these cities might be helpful to me, and I would appreciate it very much if you would supply me with such a letter.

I expect to gain a good deal of firsthand information on general conditions in all of these countries, as well as more specific data on books and publishing matters. I will be glad to make available to you on my return any information that may interest you.

Sincerely yours,

Kenneth M. Winston
Manager, Foreign Division

5. Write letters to the firms on whom your employer expects to call and announce his or her travel plans, the dates of the proposed stay in the city concerned, your employer's local address, and the like. These letters are written over your employer's signature or in the name of the president of the firm. Although you might not draft these letters, you must remind your employer to dictate them well in advance of the trip.

6. Write an announcement of the planned visit to different trade or professional magazines published in the city or country to be visited. The announcement should give the address where your employer can be reached while there, as well as the dates of the proposed visit. If you use a skilled travel agent, he or she will prepare an itinerary of the entire trip and make extra copies for distribution.

7. Write a letter for your employer's signature six weeks or two months in advance of the trip to:

   Travel Officer, International Trade Service Divisions
   Special Services and Intelligence Branch
   Department of Commerce
   Office of International Trade
   Washington, DC 20230

   This letter should state the purpose of the trip and should include the itinerary. The Department of Commerce sends airgrams, via its bulletins, to all foreign offices announcing the visit.

8. Get a letter of authority, addressed "To Whom It May Concern," from the president or other person authorizing your employer to represent the firm. This is especially valuable in dealing with immigration or customs authorities.

9. Assemble data on the trade conditions, political aspects, geography, climate, customs, and the like of each country to be visited. If your employer makes frequent trips abroad, you should also accumulate such material throughout the year from trade journals. Mark with colored pencil the items of interest. Films are also available that contain information about these matters. Ask your local reference librarian to help you compile a list of current distributors and addresses.

10. If your company subscribes to the Dun & Bradstreet credit service, get a card from them authorizing your employer to call on

their foreign offices for credit information. This is a service that Dun & Bradstreet offers to its subscribers.

Travel Security

Theft—of both money, luggage, and other property—is all too familiar to both domestic and foreign travelers. Travel agents often recommend precautions in particular cities nationally and internationally. In addition, there are a number of general guidelines the traveler can observe.

1. Do not travel with more than two hundred dollars in cash. Prepay travel and hotel costs as much as possible. If you use credit cards, take as few as possible. Completely destroy the carbon copy used in charge forms—your card number shows on it and can easily be retrieved from a wastebasket by a thief. Check the sequence of your traveler's checks (some thieves steal only a few, hoping you won't notice).

2. Be certain that your personal insurance covers travel losses.

3. Keep your luggage with you at all times, and do not use expensive designer luggage that will readily attract a thief. Also use combination locks and luggage tags that conceal your name and address.

4. Inquire at the hotel about safe or unsafe areas to walk and avoid dark streets and parks.

5. Avoid using pocketbooks and similar small cases. But if you must carry a purse or small case, stay away from the curb where motorcycle thieves can snatch the object and quickly speed away. A woman can carry a shoulder bag tucked under her arm and held tightly by the strap. Men can use a money belt or, if necessary, only a front pocket. Wrap your wallet with a heavy rubber band to prevent a pickpocket from easily sliding it out of your pocket.

6. Keep your passport with you but in a guarded or inaccessible pocket, not in an open pocket or hip pocket, and never leave it laying on a hotel or restaurant table.

7. Do not wear much jewelry, especially expensive jewelry or something an inexperienced thief might assume is expensive.

8. Never enter a rental or any other car without checking the back seat to see if someone is hiding there, and park your car in a

well-lit place. If you go to a garage or parking lot where you must leave it with an attendant, take the trunk key with you. Store items only in the trunk of your car and, when available, use a hotel safe for jewelry and other valuables, important computer disks, and so on.

9. Have your hotel room made up during breakfast and hang a do-not-disturb sign out the rest of the day. Turn on the television and set the volume on low.

10. Keep your room key with you even when you leave the hotel.

11. In a hotel room, use the chain lock and the dead bolt (if any). Never open the door unless you know the person who is there.

12. As a precaution in case of theft, photocopy airline tickets and other documents with numbers before you leave. Keep one copy at the office and another in your suitcase; carry a third copy with you, apart from the original documents.

13. If you are robbed, call the police immediately, especially in a foreign country where it is difficult or impossible to file a claim after you have gone.

Customs Information

Anyone going to a foreign country should know in advance the U.S. customs laws and regulations covering purchases made in a foreign country and brought into the United States. A competent travel agent will usually supply you with this information, as well as with details about customs requirements in countries to be visited.

Printed information.   Whether or not you use a travel service, send for *Know Before You Go, GSP and the Traveler, Customs Hints for Non-Residents,* and *Customs Hints for Returning U.S. Residents.* These pamphlets, available from the U.S. Treasury department, Bureau of Customs, Washington, D.C., furnish the traveler with the general information needed about U.S. customs laws and regulations. Other useful pamphlets, available from the Superintendent of Documents in Washington, D.C., is *Your Trip Abroad,* a Department of State publication, and *Health Information for International Travel.*

Guide to Travel Information

An intelligent person traveling for pleasure is always interested in material about the places he or she is going to visit. An enormous number of travel books, guides, and other material have been published and can be obtained in libraries, bookstores, at travel bureaus, railroads, airlines, automobile associations, and hotels. Ask your employer the type of information that interests him or her. Then consult *Books in Print* or the *Cumulative Book Index* under "Voyages and Travel" and other classifications for titles. You can also get advice from your local bookstore, which will usually obtain for you any book it does not have on hand.

Because many travel guides undergo frequent revisions, always find out the date of the latest edition before acquiring a travel book.

Types of travel material. The following classifications of travel material will help you work out with your employer what he or she may want to take on the trip: (1) handbooks for foreign countries, (2) condensed guides for more than one country, (3) books on subjects of regional interest, (4) books on sports in various regions, (5) histories, (6) books about cities, (7) books that tell where to eat, and (8) books to read for entertainment.

Chapter 9

Keeping Company Books and Records

HOW TO KEEP OFFICE AND COMPANY RECORDS

Handling Petty Cash

Certain small, miscellaneous expenditures cannot easily or practically be handled by check. If a package arrived with ten cents postage due, for example, you wouldn't write a check for such a small amount. You would no doubt pay it with cash from the office petty cash fund. Other examples of small expenditures usually paid from petty cash are taxi fares, occasional office supplies, delivery charges, meals, gifts, shipping costs, postage supplies, minor repairs, office refreshments, and cleaning supplies.

Establishing a petty cash fund. The person authorized to write and sign checks—for example, the manager—draws and cashes a check for a small amount, perhaps twenty-five or fifty dollars—enough to last a certain period such as a month. The cash is usually placed in a metal box called the petty cash box, which is then stored in a safe place. Some secretaries lock the cash box in their desk drawers.

Making payments from petty cash. The secretary in charge of the petty cash fund keeps a record of every expenditure on small printed forms (available at most office supply stores) called "petty cash vouchers." The form may be as brief and simple or as detailed and complex as you like. A common form of voucher is shown in figure 24. You can even devise your own form and make photocopies. Be certain the voucher you use has a place for you to initial it, to signify approval of the expenditure, and a place for the person receiving the cash to sign his or her name, to signify receipt of the specified amount. The voucher should also clearly indicate *what* the

Figure 24.   Petty Cash Voucher

```
┌─────────────────────────────────────────────────────────┐
│                                                         │
│              PETTY CASH VOUCHER                          │
│                                                         │
├─────────────────────────────────────────────────────────┤
│                                                         │
│   Date ___June 4, 1988___      No. _69_                 │
│   Paid to __John Simmons__    $14.65                    │
│   For __taxi-to sales seminar__                         │
│                                                         │
│                                                         │
│   Approved by:            Payment Received by:          │
│                                                         │
│   ___E.C.K.___          ___John Simmons___              │
│                                                         │
└─────────────────────────────────────────────────────────┘
```

expenditure is for. Some offices want the voucher to state not only the nature of the expenditure (for example, postage) but the number of the account to which the expense will be charged later in the cash disbursements journal (for example, 201—postage).

Keep any receipts you receive whenever you make a payment from the fund. Some payments, such as carfare, will not have any proof of payment other than the voucher. But if you purchase a box of paper clips, the store will give you a cash register or written receipt. Attach any additional proof of payment, such as a receipt, to the voucher. Finally, file all vouchers (with additional receipts) numerically in a file folder. Daily—or at least frequently—verify the balance in the cash box. The total of the vouchers plus the remaining cash in the box should equal the amount of the check that was cashed and deposited in the box at the beginning of the period plus any cash that was in the box at that time.

Replenishing the fund.   When the fund is getting low, or at the end of a specified period such as a month, prepare a *record of transactions* for your employer. Even if your office does not use a formal, printed analysis sheet for this purpose, break down the expenditures by category so that they can be recorded in the company's cash disbursements journal. Figure 25 is an example of a petty cash transactions record that can be typed on regular $8\frac{1}{2}$- by 11-inch bond paper. After your employer reviews the record

Figure 25. Petty Cash Transactions Record

PETTY CASH TRANSACTIONS RECORD
April 1 to 15, 1988

Date	Voucher	To	Receipts	Payments	Supplies	Taxi	Postage	Meals	Delivery	Misc.
4/1	—	Balance	$27.10							
4/2	30	Ronald Sayles		$4.10		$4.10				
4/7	31	Joe's Market		5.49				$5.49		
4/11	32	Postal Carrier		0.23			$0.23			
4/13	33	Markam Window Serv.		5.00						$5.00
4/13	34	Cole Manfg.		1.70						1.70
4/14	35	Office Suppliers		0.79	$0.79					
4/14	35	D. T. Uphol. Shop		7.00						7.00
4/15	—	Balance	$ 2.79							

of transactions and replenishes the fund, place the record in the voucher file folder, in front of the group of vouchers listed on the transactions record. If only a few vouchers are involved, you may be able to staple them behind the petty cash transactions record sheet. As soon as the fund has been replenished, the entire process begins all over again.

Handling petty cash: the secretary's responsibilities. Treat the handling of petty cash the same as you would any other financial record-keeping duty—with utmost accuracy and attention to detail. Never permit anyone to borrow from the fund, and if ever you doubt whether an expense is legitimate, don't hesitate to ask for approval before you process the transaction.

Maintaining Office Payroll Accounts

Wherever people are employed, payroll records must be maintained. Although large organizations have special departments that handle payroll and accounting functions, in other companies, this duty is frequently assigned to a secretary or administrative assistant. Payroll records involve: (1) wages and salaries paid to employees and (2) payroll and withholding taxes paid to the federal, state, and local governments. Federal requirements apply nationwide, but you should contact state and local authorities for information about records required and payments due in your state and local jurisdiction.

Setting up payroll records. For payroll record keeping, many offices use printed employee compensation cards or a payroll book with pages similar to the printed cards. Earning cards, such as the one shown in figure 26, and payroll books are available in most office-supply stores. But complete payroll-record systems are also available for organizations that have a large number of employees. Many of these commercial systems consist of multiple sets, whereby carbon copies are automatically made each time an employee's check is written. One carbon is made directly on an earnings card and another on a payroll summary slip. Whether you use this system or a single record card or payroll book, the objective is the same: for each employee you need to record, for each pay period: (1) total hours worked, (2) gross earnings, and (3) deductions.

In simple terms, for hourly employees, the amount due to them at the end of a pay period is "total hours worked times the hourly rate of pay in your organization minus all deductions." Payroll data for each employee is then combined and transferred to a payroll journal. In addition to the columns shown in figure 26, a page in the payroll journal might have a column to record the check number of each employee's paycheck and

Figure 26. Employee Compensation Record

EMPLOYEE COMPENSATION RECORD

NAME —————
ADDRESS —————
PHONE —————

SOC. SEC. NO. —————
DATE OF BIRTH —————
RATE ————— NO. OF EXEMPTIONS —————

Pay period ending	Hours worked									Earnings				Deductions						Net pay
	S	M	T	W	Th	F	S	Total regular hours	Over-time	At regular rate	At over-time rate	Total	Social security	Fed- income tax	State income tax	Group insurance	U.S. bonds	Other	

QUARTERLY TOTALS

224

columns for tax-exempt wages. Standard payroll journals are available in most office-supply stores.

Organizations that have anything from a small desktop computer to a large computer feed the various information described in this chapter into the computer, where it is stored until time to compute earnings and taxes due to the government. At that time, the computer, instead of the secretary or payroll clerk, computes earnings and withholdings. Nevertheless, the requirements are the same as far as the employee or the government is concerned, no matter who or what records and computes data.

For employees who are on a wage basis, hours worked is a key factor in computing earnings and deductions. To determine the total hours worked, you must collect time cards or time books from the employees and others who are responsible for recording hours worked. Some employees use time cards that are punched in a time clock, and others fill out their time slips by hand. Sometimes, a supervisor or foreman keeps a time book in which the hours worked are recorded for all employees. In large organizations, electronic time recorders record a variety of payroll data and provide more accurate records for the payroll department. Other employees are on a salary and are paid an established amount regardless of regular or overtime hours worked. Your employer will provide all of the information you need to know about your organization's hourly and overtime rates, annual salaries, and the method for determining gross pay and deductions.

Processing payroll taxes.   The payroll cards (or payroll book) on which you record hours worked, gross earnings, and deductions will provide the information you need to compute the amount of periodic payments to the government for payroll taxes. Although state and city requirements vary, as do company insurance and retirement plans, federal law requires two principal deductions from each employee's gross earnings: (1) social security (FICA) taxes and (2) income taxes. Some employers must also pay federal unemployment taxes. Rates as well as the bases for each tax change, often from year to year, and you should request current information from the Internal Revenue Service (IRS) each year.

Income taxes must be withheld from each employee's paycheck above a certain minimum. That minimum depends on the number of withholding allowances claimed by the employee and his or her marital status. Employees file Form W-4 with their employers showing how many exemptions they claim.

Social security taxes are deducted from wages (up to a certain ceiling) paid to an employee during the year. The employer then matches this amount when submitting withholdings to the federal government.

Federal unemployment taxes must be deposited by employers who paid a certain amount of wages in any calendar quarter, or who at any time had one or more employees for some portion of at least one day during each of twenty calendar weeks. However, no deduction is made from the employee's paycheck for these taxes.

Paying payroll taxes to the federal government.   Employers must deposit payroll taxes with the federal government if their total liability —income tax withholding plus employer-employee social security tax —exceeds a specified amount. Circular E, *Employer's Tax Guide,* available free from the IRS, gives current details about how much to withhold and when and where deposits must be made. To make each deposit, fill out Form 8109, *Federal Tax Deposit Coupon,* and deposit it, with your employer's check for the total deposit due, in the bank where the check is drawn or in a Federal Reserve Bank (follow the instructions in Circular E). These reports are made during the month following the end of each calendar quarter (in January, April, July, October), unless the withholdings are significant, in which case they must be deposited more frequently.

Form 941 must be filed quarterly for accounting for social security taxes and federal withholding taxes. At the end of each year, in January, employers must file Form 940, *Employer's Annual Federal Unemployment Tax Return.* This form shows total wages paid, taxable wages, and gross federal unemployment tax. In addition to the forms listed here, employers may also have state and local reports to file.

Since the facts and figures for all of these reports come from the firm's payroll records, the maintenance of thorough and accurate payroll records is essential. Furthermore, payroll information is strictly confidential, and secretaries who maintain data about employees' wages and salaries must protect and secure such records at all times.

Handling the Checkbook and Bank Statement

Except for petty cash expenditures, all major payments must be made by check. The secretary's duties vary depending on the size of the firm and the office, but professional secretaries are always prepared to assume responsibility for reconciling bank statements, organizing bills for payment, preparing supporting documents, and even filling in the check stubs and writing checks for the employer's signature.

Writing checks and filling in stubs.   When a bill arrives, it should be checked for accuracy and initialed by the person authorized to approve payment. After approval, it may be your job to write the check and fill in the stub.

Your employer will probably use a large, desk-size checkbook with three prenumbered checks per page and large stubs. Such books have a reorder form enclosed for your convenience when the supply of checks is running low. Always verify the information on your checks after a new order arrives.

When you write each check, also enter on the stub the same basic information: (1) date, (2) payee, (3) amount, and (4) purpose of the payment. Some offices also record the number of the account on each stub. If rent is listed in the cash disbursements journal as account number 601, for example, you would then also note "601" on the check stub when paying the rent. Full data is important because expenditures recorded in the cash disbursements journal are taken from the data on the check stubs.

State the name of the payee accurately. Omit titles such as *Mr.* or *Dr.*, except a check made payable to the wife of Edward Jones would require the title *Mrs.* (Mrs. Edward Jones). However, a check made payable to Edna Jones would need no title. Capitalize principal words in the amount but write cents as a fraction, unless the entire amount is less than one dollar:

One Hundred Fifty-Two and No/100 . . . . Dollars
Only Sixty-Five Cents . . . . ~~Dollars~~

Notice that the word *Only* precedes the amount in cases of less than one dollar and the printed word *Dollars* is crossed out. Avoid spaces where someone might alter the check. In other words, write figures close to the dollar sign ($20.00, not $ 20.00).

To find the current bank balance, you simply subtract the amount of each check you write from the previous balance and add any new deposits, the same as you would do in your personal checkbook. If you spoil a check, cross out the signature and write "Void" across the face of both the check and the stub in large letters. Then staple the voided check to the back of the stub, and when the canceled checks arrive with the next bank statement, add it to the group of canceled checks and note the voided check number on the bank statement.

Remember to add back the amount of any check written for which you issue a stop payment. Perhaps you learn that a check is lost in the mail, and you want to be certain that it isn't cashed illegally. You should then telephone the bank immediately and ask it to stop payment on the check (usually, there is a charge for this service that will appear on your next statement as a debit). Give the bank the date, the payee's name, the amount, and the check number.

In the case of electronic funds transfer, deductions and additions occur without normal check writing or submission of deposit slips. For example, some items are not paid by check but are automatically deducted from one's account (such as insurance premiums). Deposits, too, are sometimes made automatically. For funds to be automatically transferred, the holder of the bank account must sign an authorization slip with the bank so that the transfer of funds can take place on a regular basis. These items also appear on the monthly bank statement.

Making deposits.   Always examine checks carefully before making deposits. Look for postdating (checks that are dated ahead), discrepancies between figures and written amounts, or problems with the signature. Then endorse each check (see figure 27) and list it individually on the deposit slip (1) by the name of the drawer, (2) by transit number, or (3) by the place where it is payable.

The endorsement should be made across the left end on the back of each check. It should correspond *exactly* with the name of the payee. If the name of the payee is not correct, endorse the check as it is made out and then write the correct name under the endorsements.

Endorsements may be restrictive, blank, or specific. Figure 27 shows each type.

1.   Restrictive endorsement for deposit of checks.   A restrictive endorsement restricts or limits the endorsee's use of the funds represented by the check. When the check is endorsed to a bank for the credit of the

Figure 27.   Endorsements of Checks

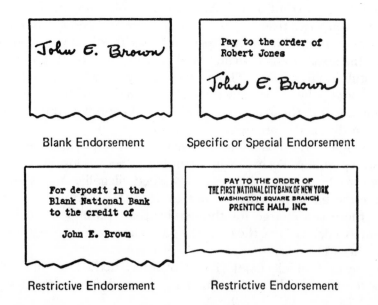

Blank Endorsement   Specific or Special Endorsement

Restrictive Endorsement   Restrictive Endorsement

payee, it does not require a manual endorsement. A rubber stamp or typewritten endorsement is acceptable.

The usual phrasing for a restrictive endorsement is "Pay to the order of _____ Bank for deposit only. John E. Brown." If the name of the payee is incorrect, type the name as it appears on the face of the check, and then stamp or type the endorsement for deposit.

Always use a restrictive endorsement on a check that is to be deposited by mail.

2. Blank endorsement. To endorse a check in blank, the payee simply signs his or her name on the back of the check, thereby making it negotiable without further endorsement. Anyone may then cash the check. Do not endorse a check in blank on the typewriter. The endorsement should be written in ink by the payee of the check or by someone authorized to endorse checks for the payee. Never endorse a check in blank until you are ready to cash or deposit it.

3. Specific endorsement. A specific or special endorsement specifies the person to whom the check is transferred. Thus John E. Brown, the payee of a check, endorses it "Pay to the order of Robert Jones. John E. Brown." The check is then payable only to Robert Jones. A specific endorsement must be signed by the payee or someone authorized to endorse checks for the payee, but the other part of the endorsement may be written on the typewriter.

How to reconcile bank statement and checkbook. Upon receipt of the bank's statement, reconcile the balance shown by the bank with the balance shown by your checkbook as of the date of the bank statement. Your bank statement will include a printed form that you can use for the reconciliation. Although the form style differs from one bank to another, the basic steps are the same (figure 28 shows the principal steps in a bank statement reconciliation):

1. The bank statement shows all withdrawals against and deposits to the credit of an account. When a statement is sent to you, the canceled checks may be arranged in the order in which the items appear on the statement. Compare the amount entered on the statement with the amount on the check. If there is a discrepancy, call the bank immediately.

2. Arrange the canceled checks in numerical order if you receive them. Some banks will retain the checks on microfilm if a customer requests it, in which case you receive only the bank statement.

3. Beginning with the first check, compare the amount of each

Figure 28.   Bank Statement Reconciliation

Bank Statement Reconciliation

June 30, 19___

Balance per bank statement		$1,385.45
Add: Deposit mailed June 30, not shown on bank statement		865.80
Subtotal		$2,251.25
Deduct: Checks outstanding		
#734	$200.00	
#742	16.50	216.50
Reconciled balance per bank		$2,034.75

canceled check with the corresponding stub in the checkbook. If the amounts are in agreement, put a check mark in front of the amount on the check stub. (If they are not in agreement, you have likely made an error and will have to adjust your balance accordingly.) Also compare the name of the payee on the check with the name on the stub.

4. Make a list of the outstanding checks—those that have not been paid, as indicated by the stubs that do not have check marks on them. Show the numbers and the amounts of the check on this list.

5. Record and subtract any bank service charges and/or bank debit memos. *(Debit memos* are notification of bank charges such as the charge for printed checks or correction of errors.) Bank service charges are generally of relatively small amount and can usually be accepted as accurately computed. However, if the amount of the service charge seems unusual, call the bank and ask to confirm its accuracy.

6. Check the deposits shown on the bank statement against those shown on your stubs. Make a list of deposits not shown on the bank statement. Deposits mailed the date the bank statement was closed and thereafter will not be credited on the current bank statement. If deposits that the bank should have received are not entered on the statement, get in touch with the bank immediately.

The reconciled amount should be the same as the balance shown by your checkbook after you subtract service charges and debit memos (see Step 5).

Many banks offer a no-service-charge checking account if a minimum balance is maintained in the account. If your employer is still paying service charges, you should determine whether a no-service-charge account can be established.

If your checkbook balance and the bank balance are not reconciled after you have taken the foregoing steps, you have made an error in your stubs (or, although rare, the bank has made an error). Check carefully the addition and subtraction on each stub and, also, the balance carried forward from stub to stub. This will reveal any error you have made and you can then adjust the final stub to show the correct balance.

After the reconciliation has been made, okay and initial it. Put the reconciliation, the bank statement, and the canceled checks on your employer's desk unless previously instructed to do otherwise.

Handling supporting documents. For every check you write, a written document should be produced to "support" the check, that is, to substantiate the amount of the check, its purpose, and so on. The most common supporting document is an invoice. When you receive a bill for something you purchased, keep a copy of the invoice. Mark the document "paid" and indicate the date and check number. If no supporting document is available, type a memo starting the purpose of the check and, again, mark it paid, with the date and check number. All of these documents should be filed in a paid bills folder or binder. Depending on the practice in your office, file the documents (1) numerically according to the paid check number you mark on each item or (2) alphabetically according to the payee's name.

Keeping Travel and Entertainment Records

Most companies require that employees document and report all travel and entertainment expenses. This step is necessary whether a traveler received travel funds in advance or whether someone is requesting reimbursement for out-of-pocket expenses. The forms used to report travel and entertainment data vary widely, although certain basic data is common to all of them. Figure 29 illustrates a simple combination travel-entertainment expense form. Office-supply stores sell other standard forms—some providing room to record much more detail—and many companies have their own forms especially designed to suit their needs.

Recording the data. The person who takes the trip or does the entertaining will supply the rough notes (and receipts) you need to fill out the report form. Many executives take a copy of the form with them, fill it out in pen and ink, and give it to the secretary to type. If it is your job to fill in the form from scratch, follow these basic steps:

Figure 29. Expense Report Form

EXPENSE REPORT

Name _____   Period Covered _____

Title _____   Department _____

Date	Transportation		Living Exp.		Enter-tainment	Phone Telegr. Postage	Misc.	Daily Total
	Auto	Plane	Train	Hotel	Meals				
Total									

Item	Current Month	Previous Month	Year to Date
Mileage			
Expenses			
Budget			

Source: Mary A. De Vries, *The Prentice-Hall Complete Secretarial Letter Book* (Englewood Cliffs, N.J.: Prentice-Hall, Inc., 1978).

1. Organize the receipts and notes into the categories listed on the form you will be using to record the data, for example, meals, hotels, and so on.

2. Double-check dates, names of places and persons, and all other facts and figures.

3. If any receipts or paid bills are missing for expenses such as hotels or car rental (there won't be any for miscellaneous expenses such as tips or taxi fare), let the executive know. In certain instances, you may be able to write for a copy of some missing bill.

4. After you are certain all receipts and notes pertaining to all expenditures have been properly grouped by category (for example, telephone, plane fare), list each expense in the proper column on the report form and add the amounts of the individual listings to arrive at a total for each category.

5. Ask your employer if he or she has any final items to add. If not, type the figures on a clean form, making as many copies as required in your office.

Following IRS regulations.   Since federal rules and regulations change from year to year, always keep on file the latest information. IRS publication 463, *Travel, Entertainment, and Gift Expenses,* is available free from any office of the Internal Revenue Service. This publication lists a number of travel expenses that the government considers legitimate, that is, as the "ordinary and necessary expenses incurred in traveling away from home for your trade or business":

1. Meals and lodging
2. Air, rail, and bus fares
3. Baggage charges
4. Cost of transporting sample cases or display materials
5. Cost of maintaining and operating your automobile
6. Cost of operating and maintaining your house trailer
7. Reasonable cleaning and laundry expenses
8. Telephone and telegraph expenses
9. Cost of a public stenographer
10. Cost of transportation to or from the airport or station to hotel, from one customer or place of work to another

11. Reasonable transportation costs from place of obtaining meals and lodging to place of work while away from home

12. Other similar expenses incident to qualifying travel

13. Reasonable tips incident to any of these expenses

But travel expenses do not include entertainment expenses while away from home. Business entertainment expenses are a separate category, and meals, for example, must be accounted for separately. A percentage is deductible "only if they are ordinary and necessary expenses of carrying on your trade or business," according to the IRS. An example is taking a client to the theater.

In both cases—business travel and business entertainment—the IRS requires that the person making a business trip or entertaining for business purposes must *prove* each expenditure with timely receipts and other documents showing amounts spent, dates, places, reasons for the expenditure, and relationship of person or persons visited or entertained. Regulations are strict, and accurate records and supporting documents are essential. The secretary's role is highly important in helping her employer collect the necessary supporting material, organize it, and record the facts and figures on acceptable travel and entertainment expense report forms.

Handling Official Financing Statements

Businesses that sell goods on credit have financing statements that debtors must sign to signify agreement to the terms of the sale. Such statements provide information about the transaction including:

1. Name and address of seller

2. Name and address of buyer

3. Goods sold

4. Terms of sale (number of installments, amount of each installment payment, interest rate and other charges, period of agreement, and so on)

Often the sales agreement has numerous additional terms and conditions explaining matters such as what will happen if the buyer defaults on the payments.

A *security agreement* identifies the seller's interest in a transaction. When buyers pledge something of value *(collateral)* such as an automobile in return for a loan, they are in effect promising to give up the automobile to the seller if they fail to repay the loan. But sellers sometimes want additional protection. For example, they might want assurance that a buyer won't sell the car pledged as collateral or pledge it to another lender. To deal with such problems, a comprehensive set of laws called the Uniform Commercial Code has been adopted by most states in whole or in part.

Uniform Commercial Code (UCC). The UCC covers commercial transactions such as the sale of goods. It also covers a variety of other business matters such as investment securities, bank deposits, and secured transactions. Article 2 of the UCC covers contracts involving the sale of goods, and Article 9 covers transactions in which the seller has a security interest.

Article 9 pertains primarily to personal property and fixtures, for example, the sale of an office copier on credit. If a business sells a copier on credit, it usually retains an interest in the copier until the final payment has been made by the buyer. If the buyer fails to make the payments, the seller can repossess the copier, provided that the seller's security interest has been *perfected*. This means that a document known as a "financing statement" was filed with the appropriate governmental agency. In effect, it gives added protection to sellers who might sign an agreement with a buyer who then pledges the same collateral to someone else or who sells the pledged collateral before the contract has been paid in full.

Financing statements. Check the applicable statutes in the place where the collateral is located to determine the place of filing a financing statement. Then write to the designated governmental agency and request a UCC-1 Financing Statement form. This form is fairly standard in the states that have adopted the UCC, but check for variations in your particular area. Other forms may also be needed such as a UCC-2 (duplicate) to file with another agency (if required) or a UCC-3 (amendment) if you want to change the original UCC-1 statement.

UCC financing statement forms are usually brief, and the secretary primarily fills in the blanks: debtor's name and address, lender's name and address, and items sold under a credit arrangement. The statement is then signed by the seller (secured party) and the buyer (debtor) before it is mailed to the designated agency for official filing. (Be sure to keep a copy for the office files.)

Filing Contracts and Other Legal Documents

A legal *contract* is an enforceable agreement between two or more parties. It must include a promise to give something, to do something, or to refrain from doing something; a *consideration* (something of value promised

Figure 30. Agreement between Two Corporations with Seals Attested

THIS AGREEMENT, entered into on the _____ day of

_____, 19—, by and between _____ CORPORATION,

a corporation organized and existing under and by virtue of the laws

of the State of _____, and having its office at

_____, _____, hereinafter referred to as

"_____," and THE _____ COMPANY, a corporation

organized and existing under and by virtue of the laws of the State

of _____, and having its office at _____,

_____, hereinafter referred to as "_____,"

WITNESSETH:

WHEREAS_____

_____; and

WHEREAS_____

_____

_____.

NOW, THEREFORE, in consideration of the premises

_____

_____.

IT IS AGREED:

1. _____

_____

_____.

2. _____

_____.

(*Continued on following page*)

IN WITNESS WHEREOF the parties hereto have on the day and year first above written caused these presents to be executed in their behalf and in their corporate names respectively by their proper officers hereunto duly authorized and their respective corporate seals to be hereto attached by like authority.

(Corporate Seal)   _____CORPORATION

                                              By _____
ATTEST: President

_____
                    Secretary

                                              THE_____COMPANY
(Corporate Seal)

                                              By _____
ATTEST: Vice President

_____
                    Secretary

(Number page in center, one-half inch from bottom.)

Source: Besse May Miller, revised by Mary A. De Vries, *Legal Secretary's Complete Handbook,* third edition, (Englewood Cliffs, N.J.: Prentice-Hall, Inc., 1953, 1970, 1980).

or given); parties who are legally capable of contracting; and a reasonable agreement among the parties as to what the contract means.

Although a contract does not have to be in writing to be valid, it usually is a typed, computer-prepared, or printed document signed by all parties. The form of a legal document will depend on the issuer and what the instrument involves (sale of goods, labor contract, and so on). A fill-in-the-blank form may suffice in many cases. In others, a highly complex and detailed document prepared by an attorney may be required.

Typing the document. Figure 30 illustrates a relatively standard form used in some law offices that can be adapted to other general needs. To prepare this type of agreement, type the document double-spaced on $8\frac{1}{2}$- by 11-inch white bond paper. The specific terms of the agreement are described in the middle of the form. The exact wording should be specified by the firm's attorney or by your employer.

Make a duplicate *original* for each signing party and a copy for the files, as well as any additional copies requested by your employer. All parties must sign the document, and, if required, the corporate seals of the corporate parties to the agreement must be affixed and attested to by the corporate secretaries.

Some legal instruments also require an *attestation clause* to make them legal. This is a statement signed by witnesses that the parties to the agreement signed and sealed the document in their presence. An *acknowledgment* is a signed statement by the person who executes a legal instrument that the instrument is genuine. It is sworn before a notary public. The acknowledgment is prepared according to requirements in the state where it is to be recorded or used. Acknowledgments and similar legal requirements are usually prepared by an attorney.

Maintaining Securities and Property Records

To report dividend and interest income and capital gains and losses for tax purposes, federal, state, and local governments require that certain records be kept. Although state and local requirements vary from one place to another, federal regulations are the same everywhere. In the case of a corporation with large and diverse holdings, the record keeping is usually under the management of specialists in the financial area. But in many other offices the secretary may keep similar records for the company or for one or more executives in the firm. Two types of transactions in particular involve ongoing record keeping: securities transactions and real estate transactions.

Securities records.   To keep track of sales and purchases of securities, you need to record every transaction as it occurs. Often the data are maintained by computer, and current listings can be printed out at any time. If you need to keep records and files manually, you can use a standard form from an office-supply store or devise your own form. Individual records of transactions must be kept for each security. These records may be maintained on cards, loose sheets in a file folder, or sheets in a three-ring binder. Figure 31 is an example of a format that could be used on a card or columnar sheet (headings can vary according to the amount of detail your employer wants to have recorded).

You should also maintain a list of all investments or one list of all stocks owned, another of all bonds owned, another of mutual funds, and so on. The column headings on each sheet (or card) should include the following:

1. Name of stock (or bond, mutual fund, and so on)

Figure 31. Record of Securities Transactions

SECURITIES TRANSACTIONS

Name of Security _____

Exchange Where Listed _____

Broker _____ Telephone _____

Address _____

Location of Security _____

No. Shares	Certif. No.	Purchase or Sale	Date	Price/ Share	Broker's Commis.	Tax	Total Price	Net Receipt	Cap. Gain (Loss)	
									Short Term	Long Term

Figure 32. Real Estate Records

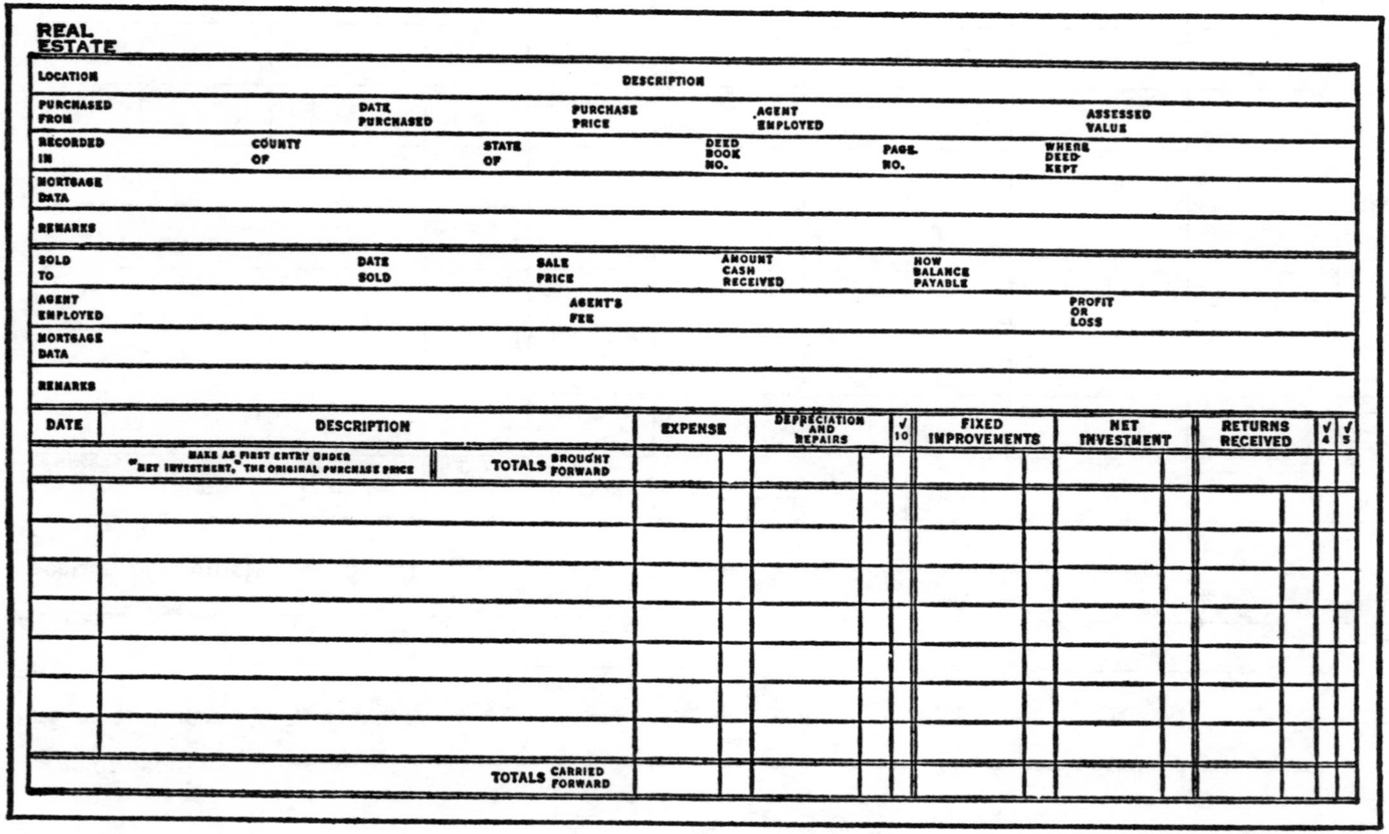
REAL ESTATE

LOCATION			DESCRIPTION		
PURCHASED FROM	DATE PURCHASED	PURCHASE PRICE	AGENT EMPLOYED		ASSESSED VALUE
RECORDED IN	COUNTY OF	STATE OF	DEED BOOK NO.	PAGE NO.	WHERE DEED KEPT
MORTGAGE DATA					
REMARKS					
SOLD TO	DATE SOLD	SALE PRICE	AMOUNT CASH RECEIVED	HOW BALANCE PAYABLE	
AGENT EMPLOYED		AGENT'S FEE			PROFIT OR LOSS
MORTGAGE DATA					
REMARKS					

DATE	DESCRIPTION		EXPENSE	DEPRECIATION AND REPAIRS	√ 10	FIXED IMPROVEMENTS	NET INVESTMENT	RETURNS RECEIVED	√ 4	√ 5
	MAKE AS FIRST ENTRY UNDER "NET INVESTMENT," THE ORIGINAL PURCHASE PRICE	TOTALS BROUGHT FORWARD								
		TOTALS CARRIED FORWARD								

Source: Prentice-Hall Editorial Staff, revised by Mary A. De Vries, *Private Secretary's Encyclopedic Dictionary,* third edition (Englewood Cliffs, N.J.: Prentice-Hall, Inc., 1984).

2. Description

3. Number of shares (or face value)

4. Total cost (no. of shares times the cost per share)

5. Current market value

A separate income (dividend or interest) record is also necessary with columns listing:

1. Name of stock (or bond, mutual fund, and so on)

2. Date of income

3. Amount received

4. Current total

Real estate records.   Individuals and companies that have real estate holdings on which rental income and loss must be reported need reliable records to use in computing taxes due and in determining the profitability of the holdings. Although this type of information may be processed by a special department in a company, in some firms the secretary may be responsible for recording purchases, sales, and costs such as insurance, mortgage interest, and miscellaneous repair bills. Figure 32 can be used for this purpose. Record all expenses such as building maintenance and real estate taxes in the "Expense" column. Depreciation and repairs such as plumbing repair are recorded in a separate column.

HOW TO KEEP OFFICE AND COMPANY BOOKS

System of Bookkeeping

The *system of bookkeeping* used in an office refers to the method of recording and classifying transactions. *Accounting,* on the other hand, is much broader and more complex than bookkeeping, and it includes the analytical work such as interpreting financial data. Secretaries who work in organizations that do not have a separate accounting and bookkeeping staff often help with some of the mechanical aspects of bookkeeping and may even assist in certain accounting functions, such as preparing periodical financial reports.

The bookkeeping system used in most offices is called "double-entry bookkeeping." With this system, all transactions are recorded twice (in two accounts). The two basic types of books in which the transactions are recorded are called "journals" and "ledgers." The purpose of each type is explained in the following sections.

Basic Rules of Double-Entry Bookkeeping

To simplify the process of recording transactions in one of the books of account, numbers are often assigned to individual accounts, and the accounts are then arranged in numerical order in the general ledger. Each account has a debit (left-hand) column and a credit (right-hand) column. The principal behind double-entry bookkeeping is that each amount is entered in both a debit and a credit column, and the total of all debit balances must equal the total of all credit balances.

Debit and credit entries.   To help you decide whether to record an amount in a debit or credit column, remember these two basic rules:

1. *Debit entries* increase assets and expense accounts and decrease capital, income, and liability accounts.
2. *Credit entries* increase capital, income, and liability accounts and decrease assets and expense accounts.

An *asset* refers to something owned that has a money value such as furniture or cash on hand. A *liability* refers to something that is owed such as bills to be paid or taxes that will be due for payment. Assets minus liabilities equals the *capital,* that is, the difference between what a business owns and what it owes. Table 1 shows the type of entries you would make for transactions that either increase or decrease an account. The sections **Cash Journal,** page 243, and **General Ledger,** page 246, explain how to put the basic principles of double-entry bookkeeping to actual use.

Table 1
Type of Entries for Each Class of Accounts

Class of Account	Type of Entry	
	When the Transaction Decreases the Account	When the Transaction Increases the Account
Asset	Credit	Debit
Liability	Debit	Credit
Capital	Debit	Credit
Income	Debit	Credit
Expense	Credit	Debit

Cash Journal

Journals are books of original entry—the first place you record a transaction. It doesn't matter whether you call one of these books the cash journal or cash receipts journal or the cash payments journal or cash disbursements journal. When cash journals are used, one—the *cash receipts journal*—is for all transactions involving the receipt of cash, and the other—the *cash payments journal*—is for all transactions involving the payment of cash. When such special journals are used, very few transactions remain. Those that are left are then entered in a *general journal*. Finally, entries from all of the journals are posted in the ledgers, the books of final entry. Both of these records may be kept by computer. The Internal Revenue Service requirements are discussed later in the section **Computer-Assisted Bookkeeping,** page 251.

The cash receipts journal. During the month, you would record each item of cash received. Each amount would be recorded in *two* columns—a credit column and a debit column. Figure 33 shows how income would be recorded in a cash receipts journal. (A check is placed in the check-mark column later when amounts are posted to the ledger.)

At the end of the month, you would total all columns in the cash receipts journal (called "cross-footing"). The sum of debit columns always must equal the sum of the credit columns, or a mistake has been made. Column totals would then be posted to the ledger as described in the **General Ledger** section, page 246.

The cash payments journal. You would handle the recording of cash payments the same as cash receipts. Individual entries first would be recorded on a daily basis in the cash payments journal—each amount recorded in a debit column and repeated in a credit column. At the end of the month, columns would be totaled, with each total posted to the appropriate ledger account, as described below in the section **General Ledger,** page 246. Figure 34 shows how to record cash payments in the journal. (Again, a check is placed in the check-mark column at the time each amount is posted to the ledger.)

General journal. A general journal is used for the transactions that cannot be made in the cash receipts or cash payments journal (or in another special journal such as a sales journal or a purchases journal). This journal is also used to make adjusting and closing entries at the end of the accounting period. A bookkeeper, or accountant, frequently closes the books and makes any required adjusting entries. Entries from the general journal are posted to the ledger at the end of each month, just as they are posted from any of the special journals.

Figure 33. Cash Receipts Journal Entries

CASH RECEIPTS JOURNAL April, 19— PAGE 6

Invoice	Date	Received From	✓	Income, Cr.		Total Receipts Dr. (101)	Bank Dep.
				(102) Prod. Repairs	(103) Prod. Sales		
00271	Apr. 5	E. Smith Co.		35.00		35.00	
00272	6	J. Morris			100.00	100.00	135.00
00273	9	W. Weiss & Co.		16.00	214.00	230.00	230.00
00274	14	R. Feldman		72.00	160.00	252.00	252.00
00275	26	A. Etiozni		111.00	200.00	311.00	311.00
				234.00	694.00	928.00	928.00

244

Figure 34. Cash Payment Journal Entries

CASH PAYMENTS JOURNAL ___April 19___ PAGE ___4___

Ck. No.	Date	Paid to	For	✓	Amount, Cr.	Office Exp., Dr. (204)	Other, Dr. Item	Other, Dr. Amount
140	Apr. 1	V.C.Industries	office rent		700.00		(300) rent	700.00
141	6	Office Suppliers	lamp		60.00	60.00		
142	11	Office Suppliers	stationery		98.00	98.00		
143	30	Postmaster	postage		18.00		(260) postage	18.00
					876.00	158.00		718.00

General Ledger

Ledgers—both subsidiary (see **Subsidiary Ledger,** below) and general—are books of final entry, unlike the journals, which are books of original entry. The *general ledger* is the book where miscellaneous accounts are kept.

Figure 33 shows how cash receipts would be recorded in a cash receipts journal. At the end of the month, columns would be totaled to prepare for transfer to the general ledger. Figure 35 shows how the *receipts* would be posted in the ledger, and figure 36 shows how the *payments* would also be posted in the ledger. (The notation "CR6" in the "Post Ref." column of figure 35 refers to page 6 in the cash receipts journal. The notation "CP4" in the "Post Ref." column of figure 36 refers to page 4 in the cash payments journal.)

The process of listing ledger accounts, showing the balance of all debits and all credits, is called "taking a trial balance." In ledgers, as in journals, the sum of all debits must equal the sum of all credits. If a discrepancy appears, look for an error in addition or in posting. Remember that each amount must appear in a debit column and in a credit column. In other words, one must post each amount twice, and failure to do this will result in a difference between the sum of all debits and the sum of all credits.

Subsidiary Ledger

Your organization may use special ledgers as well as a general ledger. For example, some firms use an accounts receivable ledger and an accounts payable ledger. In the *balance form of account,* a special ledger has three columns: debit, credit, and balance. The third column—balance—would show, for example, how much a customer owes in total as of a certain date—the balance owed, in other words.

The number and types of ledgers (and journals) you use depends on the type of business your employer is engaged in and how complex your bookkeeping and accounting needs must be. The more complex the business, the more likely that you will have a separate accounting department to handle both the mechanical and analytical functions. Nevertheless, a secretary should be prepared to assist others who perform these functions, and a good place to start is with a general understanding of double-entry bookkeeping and a working familiarity with the principal books of original and final entry.

Figure 35.   Posting to the General Ledger from the Cash Receipts Journal

GENERAL LEDGER

			Cash (101)			PAGE __1__		
DATE	DEBIT	POST REF.	AMOUNT	DATE	CREDIT	POST REF.	AMOUNT	
19– Apr 30		CR 6	928.00					

			Income from Product Repairs (102)			PAGE __2__		
DATE	DEBIT	POST REF.	AMOUNT	DATE	CREDIT	POST REF.	AMOUNT	
				19– Apr. 30		CR 6	234.00	

			Income from Product Sales (103)			PAGE __3__		
DATE	DEBIT	POST REF.	AMOUNT	DATE	CREDIT	POST REF.	AMOUNT	
				19– Apr. 30		CR 6	694.00	

247

Figure 36. Posting to the General Ledger from the Cash Payments Journal

GENERAL LEDGER

Cash (101)   PAGE 1

DATE	DEBIT	POST REF.	AMOUNT	DATE	CREDIT	POST REF.	AMOUNT
19— Apr. 30		CR 6	925.00	19— Apr. 30		CP 4	876.00

Office Expenses (204)   PAGE 4

DATE	DEBIT	POST REF.	AMOUNT	DATE	CREDIT	POST REF.	AMOUNT
19— Apr. 30		CP 4	158.00				

Rent (308)   PAGE 5

DATE	DEBIT	POST REF.	AMOUNT	DATE	CREDIT	POST REF.	AMOUNT
19— Apr. 30		CP 4	700.00				

Postage (260)   PAGE 6

DATE	DEBIT	POST REF.	AMOUNT	DATE	CREDIT	POST REF.	AMOUNT
19— Apr. 30		CP 4	18.00				

Balance Sheet

The two major financial statements are the balance sheet and the income, or profit and loss, statement (see page 250). A balance sheet shows the financial status of a business on a particular date. Your employer may prepare a balance sheet at the end of each month or at the end of each quarter or only at the end of the year. The format is the same in any case, and your duties in typing or preparing a balance sheet by computer are also the same regardless of the time of year it is prepared.

Basically, a conventional balance sheet lists the assets of a company on the left (debit) side of a page and the liabilities and capital on the right (credit) side. The sum of the left and right sides should be equal, or in balance. The heading of a balance sheet gives the name of the business, the name of the statement (Balance Sheet), and the date of the report.

Assets are usually listed in the order of liquidity, with current assets first and fixed assets last. In other words, the current assets are more *liquid*, that is, they are more easily converted into cash. *Fixed assets* refers to permanent property used in the business. Liabilities that mature first are listed first and those that mature last are listed last. Thus current liabilities would be positioned before long-term liabilities. A balance sheet is really a summary of the general ledger accounts. Figure 37 is an example of the proper arrangement of assets and liabilities in an *account form* of balance sheet. Notice that accounts are arranged on the page so that the left and right sides end on the same line.

Figure 37. Balance Sheet

ADDISON RESEARCH CLINIC

Balance Sheet

December 31, 19—

Cash	$ 2,000.00	**Liabilities:**			
		Accounts payable			$ 4,000.00
Accounts receivable	1,600.00	Notes payable			12,000.00
Office equipment	900.00	Total Liabilities			$16,000.00
Buildings	75,000.00	**Stockholders' equity:**			
		Capital stock	$74,000.00		
Land	20,000.00	Retained earnings	9,500.00		83,500.00
	$99,500.00				$99,500.00

Income (Profit and Loss) Statement

An income statement shows the results of operating a business at the end of a specified period—whether a company made or lost money. Figures for this important financial statement are taken from the journals and ledgers. Thus before this statement, or the balance sheet, for that matter, can be prepared, the journals and ledgers must be completely up to date.

A simple, short form of income statement will show what a company received, what it spent, and what it earned (assuming it received more than it spent). Management, owners, creditors, and others are very much interested in the economic picture revealed by the statement. Figure 38 shows an income statement covering the month of November. This type of statement can be prepared on regular $8\frac{1}{2}$- by 11-inch bond paper. But office-supply stores also carry standard forms that can be filled in by the secretary or anyone else in charge of such report preparation.

Figure 38. Income (Profit and Loss) Statement

BENNINGTON INDUSTRIES

Income Statement

For the Month Ended November 30, 19—

Income:		
Net sales		$125,000.00
Dividends		4,000.00
Total Income		$129,000.00
Expenses:		
Cost of goods sold	$90,000.00	
Selling expenses	8,000.00	
Administrative expenses	6,000.00	
Interest expense	100.00	
		104,100.00
Total Expenses		$ 24,900.00

Computer-Assisted Bookkeeping

People and machines work together to perform many routine tasks in the business world. It is not surprising that computers are a prominent feature in offices that handle accounting and bookkeeping functions. Computers can process vast amounts of accounting data, and few organizations with extensive accounting work could manage without them. Electronic data-processing equipment can be used in almost every phase of accounting operations. But the computer is especially valuable in processing payrolls, inventories, accounts receivable, and accounts payable. It is also used frequently to process the data needed to post journal entries to the ledger accounts.

An electronic data-processing system can not only store and compute figures, it can maintain all of the records pertaining to payroll work, and it can even prepare the employees' paychecks. In addition, it can produce data for management to use in making decisions, for example, reporting labor costs for a particular project, time requirements, and so on.

Although individuals—not machines—analyze accounting transactions and adjustments, the computer can actually take figures and print the journals, post to the ledgers, and print the income statement, the balance sheet, and other financial reports. With its sophisticated computational capability, the computer is an essential tool in forecasting profits or losses and in revealing trends or reversals in trends. Now that desktop computers are well within the financial reach of the small business operation, many secretaries are benefiting from the assistance of electronic data-processing equipment in numerous accounting and bookkeeping duties, from computing gross pay to reconciling the monthly bank statement.

IRS requirements. According to the Internal Revenue Service, if you keep your records in an automatic data-processing (ADP) system, the system must include a method of producing legible records that will provide proof of your tax liability.

An ADP system is acceptable if it complies with the following guidelines:

1. It must print out your general ledger and its source references for the same period as your tax year. It must also periodically print out any subsidiary ledgers.

2. It must provide an audit trail so that details (invoices and vouchers) of the summary accounting data may be identified and made available on request.

3. It must provide a way to trace any transaction back to the original source or forward to a final total. If printouts of transactions are not made when they are processed, your system must be able to make a record of these transactions.

4. It must have adequate storage facilities for machine-sensible data media, printouts, and all supporting documents. These records must be kept in the same way as records under a manual accounting system. You need not keep punched cards if the information is on magnetic tapes or disks or is recorded in some other way.

5. It should have available a full description of the ADP part of the accounting system and the controls you use to ensure accurate and reliable processing.

HOW TO HANDLE BILLINGS AND COLLECTING

Calculating Charges

Collecting money that is owed to your firm should be a preplanned function, even if your office is responsible only for occasional, miscellaneous collections. Firms that handle a huge number of transactions usually have a department especially geared to prepare and mail invoices and process receipts. But in smaller firms or firms that handle a limited number of bills and receipts, the secretary may assist in calculating charges, preparing and mailing invoices, and processing incoming payments.

How to develop a system.   One of the first steps is to develop a system for calculating charges if your office doesn't already have one. To do this, list the factors or materials that you expect someone to pay for: time, telephone calls, photocopying costs, supplies, merchandise, and so on. Some offices assume that some of these things are absorbed in the daily operating overhead. For instance, office stationery would not be charged to a particular customer in normal circumstances. Therefore, you need not keep track of the number of sheets of stationery used to type letters to a particular customer. On the other hand, perhaps your office does assign long-distance telephone charges to specific accounts. Professional persons, such as lawyers, keep track of time, telephone, photocopying, and other costs pertaining to a specific client's needs.

Once you have established which costs must be borne by a customer/ client, you can set up a notebook, file folder, or card file for recording time and expenses. Some firms have a file folder for each client in which the secretary keeps:

1. Telephone message slips with time and charges noted on each slip (ask the operator to give you time and charges for each call)
2. Copies of telegrams sent, with charges
3. A record of all time spent on behalf of a client—broken down by employee (manager, secretary, and so on)
4. A record of materials (such as photocopies) provided for work on behalf of the client
5. A record of postage and other mailing expenses
6. Copies of any paid bills pertaining to other expenses incurred on behalf of a client

Many secretaries use calendars with fifteen-minute divisions to note time spent for each client. When it is time to bill the client, perhaps at the end of the month, they add up the total time spent per client. Similarly, many secretaries keep a tally sheet by the office photocopy machine on which they note all copies made per client. At the end of the month, or when it is time to prepare a bill, total photocopies are added together for each client.

Some modern equipment and systems automatically indicate charges per customer. With some telephone systems, for instance, you can precede each call with a customer code, and the telephone bill will then reflect charges per customer. Certain electronic postal equipment similarly provides a miniaccounting system. By way of a postage charge-back system, internal mailing costs can also be assigned to the office or department doing the mailing.

How to compute the charges. Choose the method of record keeping (cards, record sheets, file folders, and so forth) that best suits the type of work or service your office provides. Even if you use a computer to maintain expense records, you will have to collect some material manually to determine what figures are to be fed into the computer. Once you have the totals, the rest is a matter of simple arithmetic. For example, if your employer expects you to charge each client ten cents a copy for photocopies, you simply multiply that rate by the number of copies made for a particular account. Postage is normally charged at cost. If you spent seventeen dollars sending a packet of supplies, and your office assigns such costs to the customer, you would simply add seventeen dollars to other items on the customer's bill. Perhaps your employer charges fifty dollars an hour for his or her time and ten dollars an hour for your time. If your employer worked one hour on behalf of a particular client and you worked two hours, the part of the bill pertaining to labor would be seventy dollars.

In other situations, charges are calculated for merchandise simply by adding the firm's established price for the goods, plus postage and handling. Regardless of your company's type of work or policy in determining charges, accuracy is vital. A mistake could cost the firm money—or anger a good customer.

Preparing Invoices

Office-supply stores have a variety of standard forms that can be used to bill customers. But organizations that regularly send out bills have their own invoices printed usually with the company's name and address in a prominent position. Some organizations have both invoices (sent periodically or immediately at the time of completing work or making a sale) and statements (sent at the end of each month, showing the balance the customer/client owes as of that date). These forms may be multiple carbonless sets, whereby the top copy (original) is sent when a charge is due, the second copy is sent one month later as a follow-up notice, and the third copy is sent two months later as a second follow-up notice. (The final copy is the office file copy.) After that, if not before, chances are that the company will take more serious steps to collect, such as sending a series of collection letters.

Guidelines for preparing invoices. In large firms invoices are prepared with special billing machines or by computer. In manual preparation, to avoid problems later, observe a few basic rules.

1. When you type each invoice, be certain all copies are aligned if you use multiple sets. (See chapter 2: **How to Type on Printed Forms and Ruled Lines,** page 59, and **How to Feed Numerous Sheets of Paper,** page 62.)

2. Have all calculations made *before* you start typing, including any discount notices or terms (interest charges for late payment are usually printed on the invoice in advance but companies sometimes offer discounts for early payment such as 2%/10 days, meaning that the customer may deduct 2 percent from the bill if payment is made within ten days from the invoice date).

3. Double-check your figures *before* you start typing. Look for oversights such as failure to add an outstanding balance from the previous month to the current month's charges.

4. Organize the material so that you type the most urgent bills first—the ones you want to go into the mail immediately.

5. If you do not use window envelopes (a great time saver), double-check each envelope address against each inside address on the invoices.

6. Set tab stops at appropriate places on your typewriter to speed the typing process, and observe the many typing tips in chapter 2.

7. Follow the procedures described in chapter 4 for folding and inserting in envelopes (page 125).

8. File the office copies of the invoices—and the carbon copies that represent the second and third notices—in a follow-up file for further action in thirty days or when payment is received.

Using Computers in Billing Clients

The office that bills a substantial number of clients or customers daily, weekly, or monthly may use a computer to prepare invoices. Even with the aid of modern calculators, punched-card machines, magnetic-tape typewriters, and various addressing and mailing machines, the job of billing would be too time-consuming when vast numbers are involved. However, the computer has relieved the problem of processing thousands, or even hundreds of thousands, of bills.

Computer programs.   Especially prepared programs are designed to put the raw data into the computer at the time of a sale or as service costs are known. Even a small firm with a desktop computer would be able to feed into the computer figures such as hours worked, cost of time, cost of material, and so on. When it is time to bill a customer/client, the computer can compute the cost of time, material, and other provisions and print out the list of charges for each account.

How much or how little the computer does depends on the computer itself—its capabilities—and the program used to put data into it *(input)* so that later it can print out the results *(output)*. In any case, computer-assisted billing clearly eliminates most of the drudgery and tedious routine of the billing function.

Following Up Overdue Accounts

What do you do when someone doesn't pay the bill you send? Follow-ups are an everyday occurrence in the business world. In collection matters, follow-ups may be handled in a number of ways, depending on the number of clients.

Follow-up collection systems.   Statements and follow-up invoices can be prepared by computer when large numbers are involved. For the small office using manual billing methods, three common systems used in collections are the ledger system, multiple-invoice system, and tickler-card system.

1. With the *ledger system,* suitable only when the number of accounts is few, you would make notations concerning steps to be taken—or steps already taken—directly in the ledger. No other card file or follow-up folder would be maintained.

2. With the *multiple-invoice system,* you would keep on file duplicate copies of each invoice. If someone hasn't paid at the end of thirty days, for example, you can simply send a second or third notice —until it is apparent that more drastic steps must be taken to collect the overdue account. When a payment is received, the unused duplicate invoices for that particular customer are destroyed. With this system, duplicate invoices may be arranged numerically in a file folder, so you can quickly retrieve and destroy surplus copies when a check arrives and no further follow-up is needed.

3. The *tickler-card system* requires that a card be typed for each delinquent account. Information on each card would include the customer's name and address, amount due, terms, due date, and follow-up action to date. Such a file is divided into thirty-one compartments, one for each day of the month. Each customer's card is filed behind the date on which further action is to be taken. The secretary must inspect the cards behind the current compartment each day and take the required action for each situation. The disadvantage of this system, as is the case with all tickler-card files, is that it involves an extra step of preparing cards in addition to typing invoices.

Other follow-up action.   Sometimes routine follow-ups, such as sending duplicate copies of invoices every thirty days, fail. Usually, the next step is to write letters. Often a series of four to six letters is written, each letter worded more strongly than the previous one. (Chapter 13, page 376, gives an example of a collection letter.) Some offices use standard collection notices available in office-supply stores (see figure 39). Telephone calls —when the number of delinquent accounts is limited—are often effective in collection procedures. Some firms even try calling on the customer in person. Mailgrams and telegrams, too, are used to create a sense of

Figure 39.   First-Notice Collection Form

```
┌─────────────────────────────────────────────────────────────┐
│                    YOUR COMPANY NAME                          │
│                    Address/Telephone                          │
│                              |                                │
│                              |                                │
│  JUST A FRIENDLY REMINDER ...|  If your check is already in   │
│                              |  the mail, please disregard    │
│  TO:                         |  this notice. If not, your     │
│                              |  prompt payment will be        │
│                              |  greatly appreciated.          │
│                              |  Thank you!                    │
│                              |                                │
│                              |                                │
│                              |  Invoice No.: _____   │
│                              |                                │
│                              |                                │
│                              |  Date Due: _____   │
│                              |                                │
│                              |                                │
│         FIRST NOTICE         |  Amount Due: _____   │
└─────────────────────────────────────────────────────────────┘
```

urgency. Often, when a series of collection letters is used, the final letter demanding payment by a specified date is sent by registered mail. Such letters firmly insist on payment within a set period such as ten days or two weeks. The customer is told that the matter will be turned over to a lawyer or collection agency if payment is not forthcoming. Both agencies and attorneys that specialize in these matters will attempt to collect the delinquent account for a percentage of the amount that is due. As a final resort, the firm can always arrange for the attorney to sue the debtor.

Standard collection statements.   Letters, telegrams, printed notices, telephone calls, and personal visits all make use of standard collection statements. How harshly or how gently each statement is worded depends on the firm's relations with the customer, the customer's attitude and intentions, the past-due amount involved, and how long overdue the account is. Each office follows a standard procedure and uses some or all of the following statements at some time:

1. You apparently forgot/overlooked your payment.
2. Please let us know if your check is in the mail.
3. May we have your check promptly?

4. Protect your credit standing by sending in your check immediately.

5. We will be happy to fill your order as soon as your past-due account is settled.

6. We value your friendship too much to resort to legal action. Won't you send us your check today?

7. Let us know if you are experiencing difficulty in making your payments. We may be able to devise a payment plan especially for you in this instance.

8. Urgent that we receive your payment by _____.

9. We must receive your check no later than _____ to avoid action by our attorney.

10. Unless we receive your full payment by _____, this matter will be turned over to the XYZ Collection Agency.

11. Payment by _____ will prevent repossession of your _____.

12. Failure to send your check has left us no choice but to instruct our attorney to proceed immediately with legal action.

Pros and cons of collection efforts.   Although it may seem that all of the possible collection steps involve more time and expense than an overdue account is worth, organizations nevertheless must have a system to discourage delinquency and make reasonable efforts to collect the payments that are essential for the firm to remain in business. The secretary who helps prepare the letters, telegrams, printed notices, and so on plays a vital role in maintaining the financial well-being of his or her employer.

— Chapter 10 —

Maintaining Good Human Relations and Proper Etiquette

ETIQUETTE IN THE OFFICE

Your Professional Image

Image—the portrait of ourselves that we present to others—is far more important than most people realize. Good skills and quality work are essential, but a poor image can cloud even the most perfect technical abilities (typing, filing, and so on).

Your image will affect the receptiveness of coworkers to your ideas and requests—something that can be crucial when you need help or generally want to advance in your career. Clients and customers, too, will respond positively or negatively to the image you convey through dress, attitude, poise, courtesy, ethical actions, and so on. Some of them may gain their first impression of your company through you.

In general, human relations experts recommend a helpful, cheerful, positive, and confident attitude combined with a neat, clean, conservative, and businesslike personal appearance. Specifically, they recommend that you develop as many of the following attributes as possible:

1. Develop healthful eating habits to help you look and feel better.
2. Use your dress, hair style, and so forth to convey confidence and professionalism. Experts say to dress for the job you want. To advance in many companies, this often means well-tailored businesslike suits or dresses with jackets and an attractive and practical

hair style. In other words, dress as though you are attending a business meeting, not a rock concert or the opera.

3. Pay attention to your body language. Stand straight and walk with a confident stride. Avoid frowns and shifting, nervous glances. Look others directly in the eye when talking. Work hard to eliminate undesirable hand or other body movements and distracting habits such as chewing on a pencil.

4. Don't be tardy. Employers rank this high among their pet peeves.

5. Be courteous to *everyone* and take time to reply to any question or request, even when you are disagreeing with someone or are extremely busy and would prefer to avoid interruptions.

6. Be open to two-way communication. Always be willing to exchange ideas and learn from others.

7. Learn to accept new ideas and challenges with an air of excitement and enthusiasm rather than with debilitating fear and insecurity—it shows.

8. Learn how to work effectively under pressure. Don't interrupt your concentration with worry. Set a good pace and keep your mind on the work.

9. Have a positive attitude toward life in general and avoid negative responses that create friction at work. This includes cheerfully accepting extra work and staying late when necessary.

10. Develop a team attitude (in terms of cooperation but not at the expense of individual initiative) and be willing to accept help and delegate work to assistants.

11. Display your skills and talents—let others know what you can do. Your boss will be surprised and pleased to learn that you have untapped potential.

12. Be willing to change course or admit an error. In other words, be open to the demands of the moment. Don't avoid action or try to stay in the middle of the road simply because you are afraid you may be criticized later if you are wrong or if others disagree.

13. Never be cynical and sarcastic. It suggests an attempt to hide feelings of inferiority and insecurity.

14. Develop initiative. Become active rather than passive in offering suggestions, in asking necessary questions, and in handling tasks on your own.

15. Develop your leadership abilities. Learn how to delegate tasks,

supervise assistants, and organize and manage projects on your own.

16. Read, listen, inquire—whatever is needed to become familiar with your job, your office, and your company—so that you will appear alert and knowledgeable in the presence of others.

Daily Greetings and Use of First Names

Greetings to coworkers.   There is no need to be unsure about whether you should greet certain people whom you do not know personally —those from another office getting on the elevator with you, a door attendant, an elevator operator, or the company president. The courtesy of saying "Good morning" or "Good night" to someone is universally acceptable in business. But this does *not* mean that you should try to promote a conversation with the company president.

Use of first names.   Most modern offices are informal, and the use of first names among fellow employees is the usual practice. But even in such offices, there are situations in which it is proper to use a title *(Mr., Mrs., Miss, Ms.)* and the person's last name. The most important rule is simple: Follow the practice that has been established in your office. Generally, however, it is traditional to observe these common guidelines:

1. Addressing your supervisor.   You should never address your boss or immediate supervisor by first name unless that person has informed you specifically that it is all right to do so. Even then, you should use a title in addressing the person in the presence of visitors. (Your boss or supervisor should extend that same courtesy to you.)

2. Addressing executives.   You should never address a person of executive rank by first name, unless he or she tells you to do so. Addressing executives by title is the only practice that is accepted as conventional etiquette despite the informality that might exist in the office.

3. Addressing older men and women.   It is not unusual for an older employee to prefer to be addressed by title by younger coworkers. Even if others in the office refer to an older employee by first name, it is best to wait before you take the same liberty if you are new in the office.

The New Employee

Helping a new employee.   A new secretary or any other new employee appreciates it when coworkers provide a friendly reception and help familiarize the newcomer with the strange surroundings. Giving a new employee a helping hand with his or her work also ensures that the employee will become productive more rapidly. It encourages the new employee to appreciate your company and to want to stay with it. But even if there were not these practical reasons for making a new employee feel at home and for helping someone get started in a new job, business etiquette requires such efforts.

Most large companies, and many smaller ones, have an orientation program for new employees, but this program does not take the place of personal friendliness and assistance from a coworker.

Introducing newcomers to coworkers.   Make a point of seeing that new employees are properly introduced to the people with whom they will be dealing. It will help if they are also given some idea of what each person does. Names and faces are then easier to remember and new workers get a general idea of how their jobs fit in with others.

Inviting newcomers to lunch.   Be certain to invite new employees to join you and other coworkers for lunch. This is a particularly good way to help someone new feel at home and part of the team. Take advantage of this time to find out the newcomer's interest in work-related matters and cooperative efforts such as car pooling.

Scheduling periodic conferences.   For the first week or two, schedule daily ten- to fifteen-minute conferences to discuss both routine work and special projects and to answer any questions the newcomer has. After this initial period, you may want to schedule weekly conferences until the newcomer is thoroughly familiar with the work. Such brief meetings will help eliminate confusion and save time in the long run by increasing the newcomer's familiarity with the work and with office procedures, thereby lessening the prospects of time-consuming mistakes and later problems.

Observing the rules when you are a newcomer.   A newcomer should observe certain rules of etiquette. If you are the newcomer, here are a few suggestions that may help you get a practical and congenial start on a new job.

1.   Don't be a show-off.   It is rude and useless to try to impress old-timers by telling them how much better your previous employer handled matters or to point out mistakes you see them making. Once you have established a working relationship with the other workers and with your boss, your suggestions will stand a much better chance of being accepted instead of resented.

2.   Don't be too friendly too soon.   Use some restraint in your first few days on a job. Give those already on the job a chance to make the friendly advances. You not only avoid giving the impression that you are pushy and forward but also avoid forming alliances that you may later regret.

3. Know what to do when you are invited to lunch. On your first day, a few persons may ask you to have lunch with them. Generally, you are expected to pay for your own lunch, even if your immediate supervisor is in the group. If your immediate supervisor invites you to have lunch with him or her alone, generally the superior pays for your lunch.

Having Refreshments in the Office

Taking daily breaks. Having coffee, tea, or another beverage is an established practice in American business, but a few cautions are in order.

1. Be neat. Coffee crumbs, coffee stains, cluttered ashtray, cigarette ashes, and unwashed coffee cups are unsightly.
2. Observe common table manners when eating and drinking at your desk.
3. Don't let your refreshments interfere with business. The excuse for a break is that it increases efficiency, but the practice of taking refreshments at work can be harmful to business if not used with discretion. If a coworker, a business caller, or an executive comes to your desk while you are taking a break, you should give your full attention to the caller, and you should never keep a visitor waiting while you finish eating or drinking.
4. Don't "stretch" your pause for refreshments with a second cup of coffee, an extra helping of food, or even some chewing gum.
5. Do not pause while you are taking a break to attend to personal grooming at your desk unless you are clearly alone. Application of makeup, combing of hair, filing of nails, and so on are most properly attended to in the restroom.
6. Follow the practice in your office regarding the purchase of refreshments. Often coworkers take turns in going out to get refreshments for everyone or in making coffee in the office. If there is no office coffee fund, employees should pay for their own refreshments or take turns purchasing coffee for the office coffee machine. It is perfectly proper to ask for payment from anyone who fails to pay you in advance or fails to reimburse you.

Providing refreshments for visitors. If guests arrive while you are having coffee, and your desk is near the area where they are visiting, it is usually appropriate to offer them a cup of coffee (or other beverage) also. If guests are already waiting, postpone having your refreshments until you are alone.

Each office has its own practice. In some small, professional offices, the secretary or the executive always offers the visitor a cup of coffee. In other large business reception rooms, no effort is made to offer refreshments to the numerous callers coming and going.

Etiquette and Safety in Office Lines and Parking Lots

Etiquette in office lines.   In many business situations, employees must line up and await their turns. Although no one enjoys having to wait, rules of etiquette *must* be followed in getting on and off elevators; lining up in the cafeteria or lunchroom; waiting for the drinking fountain; punching the time clock, morning and afternoon; and so on. Time clocks create a double problem. Latecomers must rush down the hall, without regard for their own safety or that of others, to punch the clock just before it changes from 9:00 to 9:01 a.m. In the afternoons, the rush for first place in the line to punch out is not only a breach of etiquette but is a violation of traditional company safety rules.

Safety in the parking lot.   Many employees tend to forget their manners, as well as their own safety and that of others, in a wild dash to get to work on time or to be the first one out of the parking lot. If you calmly continue working for five to ten minutes after quitting time, you will find that you can get out of the parking lot easily and just as soon as if you had rushed to join the traffic jam.

RECEIVING VISITORS

Receiving and Greeting Callers

Methods of receiving callers.   Organizations have different methods of receiving callers. In large companies, all callers go to a reception room or desk where a trained receptionist takes care of the preliminaries and advises the secretary that a caller has arrived. (Each morning it is helpful to give the receptionist a list of callers you expect during the day.) The secretary then goes to the reception room, introduces himself or herself, and escorts the visitor to the office, if the caller has an appointment. Do not attempt to carry on a conversation at this time, but do respond cordially to any remarks or questions.

In small companies the telephone operator may double as receptionist, or a messenger or some other person who has been trained in the preliminaries may greet the visitor.

How to greet a caller.   Formality is appropriate in greeting an office caller. You should say, "How do you do?" or "Good morning," or "Good afternoon"—not merely "Hello." Let the caller make the first gesture toward shaking hands. If your desk is at the entrance of the office or in a convenient or conspicuous location, you need not rise to speak to a caller unless he or she is a person of considerable importance or much older than you. After your greeting, if the caller does not volunteer any information, your next move is to ask, "May I help you?"

If a talkative caller is making small talk with you when an important businessperson enters the office to keep an appointment, but the caller does not notice the businessperson, try to draw the conversation to a pause or a close gracefully, without appearing to silence the talk. If you cut into the conversation abruptly, you will embarrass both people.

Finding Out the Purpose of a Call

A secretary is usually expected to ask why a caller wants to see his or her employer, not only when the caller comes to the office unexpectedly but when telephoning for an appointment. If a visitor presents a card, you may be able to tell the reason for the visit from the card; also, in many cases, you may know the purpose of the visit from previous correspondence or visits. The "voice with a smile" is never more useful than when you are trying to get information from a caller or when you are refusing to let the person see your employer. This duty requires discretion, tact, and patience. Fortunately, a visitor who makes a call in good faith rarely objects to telling the purpose of the visit.

Greeting a caller.   You might say something such as, "Good morning, Mrs. Jones. I'm Mr. Brown's secretary. He's busy at the moment, but is there anything I can do for you?"

Or: "Good morning. I'm Mr. Brown's secretary. He's not in the office now, but is there anything I can do for you?"

Or: "Good morning, Mrs. Jones. I'm Mr. Brown's secretary. What can I do for you?"

Or: "You're waiting to see Mr. Brown? I'm Sarah Edwards, Mr. Brown's secretary. Can I be of any help?"

1. Caller states business.   Assuming that the caller's business is of interest to your boss, you might say, "I'm afraid I can't arrange a definite appointment right now because I don't know what additional commitments Mr. Brown has made since I last saw him. But if you'll let me have your telephone number, I'll call you either later today or surely tomorrow morning and arrange an appointment for you. I know Mr. Brown will be glad to see you."

Or you may arrange a definite appointment on the spot; you may take the caller in to see your employer; you may arrange for the caller to see an assistant; or you may handle the matter yourself. Each situation will be different, and you should make a judgment as the occasion requires.

2.   Caller refuses to state business.   You might say something such as, "I'm afraid I'm not free to make appointments without letting Mr. Brown know what visitors want to discuss. Could you give me a general idea?"

Or: "Unfortunately, Mr. Brown is only able to see people by appointment. Since I make all of his appointments, I'll need to know what you would like to discuss with him."

Or: "Could you let me know what you want to see Mr. Brown about? That's the first thing he always asks me to find out."

3.   Caller still refuses.   You might say something such as, "I'm very sorry, Mrs. Jones, that I can't help you, but those are our office rules, and Mr. Brown expects me to observe them. Without some indication of the business you want to discuss, I'm afraid there's no way I can help you."

Or: "In that case, Mrs. Jones, perhaps you could write Mr. Brown a note. Just tell him briefly what you want to see him about and ask for an appointment."

Making a Caller Comfortable

Show callers where to leave their hats, coats, briefcases, and any other articles that are not needed for the appointment. Offer to hang up their coats.

When callers have to wait, ask them to have a seat. If they have to wait any length of time, provide newspapers and magazines. If callers deserve special attention, ask, "Is there anything I can do for you while you're waiting?" If they would like to look up something in the telephone directory or make a call, offer to look up a number, but do not insist. Point out a private telephone, if there is one, and be sure not to show any unnecessary interest in a private discussion.

Do not begin a conversation with waiting visitors, but if they show an inclination to talk, respond. Choose topics in which they are likely to be interested, but avoid controversial issues. Never tell your employer's friend a story you know that he or she would enjoy telling. If a visitor asks questions about the business, reply only in generalities.

Announcing a Caller

When your employer is ready to receive a guest, you may do one or two things. If the caller is known to your employer and has visited the office before, you may nod and say something to the effect that "Mr. Wilson is free. Won't you go right in?" However, if it is the caller's first visit, or if the caller is an infrequent visitor, go along to the door of your employer's office, step to one side, and say, "Mr. Wilson, Mr. Smith." *Or:* "Mr. Wilson, this is Mr. Smith."

When older people, dignitaries, or women are announced in a business office, it is usually considered proper to mention the guest's name first. The name mentioned first is the person being honored. For instance, should a church dignitary visit your employer, the polite announcement would be: "Bishop McLeish, Mr. Wilson." (Refer to the chart in chapter 18, pages 578–603, for the proper titles by which to announce officials and dignitaries.)

Callers with an appointment.   If you have a receptionist, give her a list of appointments each day. She will then be in a position to handle your callers courteously and efficiently.

When a caller with an appointment arrives, notify your employer immediately unless he or she is in a conference that cannot be interrupted. You might say something over the intercom such as, "Mrs. Carter is here for her ten o'clock appointment. May I bring her in?" If the caller is already in your office, near your desk, it is better to go into your employer's office and announce that the caller has arrived. When your employer is ready, say, "Will you come with me, Mrs. Carter?" and introduce her as described above.

1.   When a caller must wait.   If your employer has to keep a caller with an appointment waiting, explain the delay, for example: "Mr. Grant has someone with him at the moment, but he'll be free in a few minutes. Will you have a seat?" If the delay will last for any length of time, tell the caller the approximate time that it will be necessary to wait. The caller can then decide whether to wait or make a later appointment. (If you know in advance that your employer is not going to be able to keep an appointment promptly, you should notify the caller before the person leaves his or her office.)

2.   When your employer is called away.   You can say something such as, "Good morning, Mr. Hughes. Ms. Smith was called into the plant about ten minutes ago. She should be back any minute now. Do you mind waiting?"

If an unexpected emergency will keep your employer out of the office for more than a few moments, you might explain the absence this way: "Good morning, Mr. Hughes. I'm afraid that Ms. Smith was called to the office of the chairman of the board a little while ago. I'm not sure when she will be back. I tried to reach you, but your secretary said that you had already left. Would you like to wait, or would you prefer to come back or talk with someone else?"

Callers without an appointment.   Usually, when a person your employer will see calls at your office without an appointment, you know the person well enough to greet him or her by name: "Good morning, Ms. Douglas. It's nice to see you again." You might briefly inquire about her family or ask about her recent vacation. Then ask the nature of the unexpected visit. After you learn the purpose of the call, if you have the least doubt about whether your employer wants to see visitors, ask.

If your employer is busy, ask the caller to wait, explaining approximately how long it will be. Unless the unexpected caller is someone your employer is always especially eager to see, the delay may make the caller realize that it is better to make an appointment. You might limit the unexpected caller's visit by saying something such as, "Mr. Roberts has another appointment in ten minutes, but he'll be glad to see you in the meantime."

Perhaps a crowded schedule makes it inconvenient for your employer to see the unexpected caller at that time. Explain the situation, assuring the caller that a visit at any time other than the present would be most welcome. Offer to make a future appointment if your employer is interested.

Greeting Callers Your Boss Will See

Calls by friends of your employer.   Some visitors are important clients or friends whom your boss will almost always see.

1. How to announce the caller.   When a friend of your employer calls, announce the person over the intercom, and, if your employer is free, escort the visitor to your employer's office right away.

2. What to do when your employer is away.   If a visitor arrives without an appointment and your employer is out, do everything possible to make the caller comfortable (offering newspapers and the like) until your employer arrives. If your employer is not expected, express his or her regret at not seeing the caller and ask if the caller can return another time. Never ask a visitor to wait in your employer's office, unless he or she has told you to permit this. Do everything you can to make your employer's friend feel welcome, but never be *overly* friendly.

Calls by office personnel. In many business organizations today, top officials keep an "open door" to the office personnel. The secretary must usually make the appointments, but if the open-door policy prevails, the secretary does not inquire about the purpose of the appointment.

Always treat officers and executives of the company with respect, but it is not necessary to stand up every time an officer enters your office. However, you should offer the caller a chair if he or she has to wait.

Occasionally, you can save time for your employer and also do a favor for a young, new employee who wants to see your employer. In an appropriate situation you might say something such as, "What's on your mind, Joe? Anything I can do?"

If Joe hedges, you might say, "Do you want to sit down and tell me about it? Maybe I can help."

If Joe tells you about it, you might say, "I'll be glad to talk to Ms. Abbott about this, and then we'll let you know what can be done."

Or you might go to Ms. Abbott and say, "Joe Brown, a new member of the Mailing Department, has a problem he needs your advice about. If you can see him for a minute, I think you could be of help."

Or you might say to Joe, "It could be a mistake, Joe, for you to discuss that with Ms. Abbott. It would mean that you were going over the head of your immediate supervisor. Why don't you tell Mr. Jacobs [the immediate supervisor] how you feel. I have a feeling he will do anything he can to straighten things out for you."

Use your own judgment in each situation, but if a caller does not want to confide in you, do not urge the person to do so.

Handling Callers Your Boss Will Not See

When you know that your employer is not interested in the purpose of the visit or is too busy to see the caller, you might say something such as, "I wish I could be more helpful, but Ms. Evans is concerned with some emergencies and will be involved for some time; therefore, she has to limit her engagements to matters directly connected with business activity. It will be quite a while before this situation changes, and the only thing I can suggest is that you take up your matter with her in writing."

Or you might ask the caller if you or another person could be of help. If the caller has sales material or samples to distribute, offer to take the samples and show them to the appropriate person at an opportune time.

Callers soliciting contributions. When a caller states that his or her business is to solicit a contribution, you might say, when applicable: "Unfortunately, the demands on Mr. Lewis are so numerous that he's forced to limit his contributions to charitable causes he has contributed to for years, and he just is not able to add to that list. I'm sure you can understand his situation." However, if you have any doubts about your employer's wishes, ask what he or she prefers in regard to new solicitations.

Callers you refer elsewhere.   When you find the purpose of a caller's visit involves a matter that should be taken up with another person in the organization, you might say something such as, "That's something handled for Ms. Johnson by Mr. Smith. I'll be glad to make an appointment for you, or if he's not busy now, I'm sure he'll be happy to see you right away."

Or: "I wonder if you could take this up with Mr. Smith of our Sales Department. He's more familiar with the matter than Ms. Johnson and can be of more help to you."

If the caller agrees to see Mr. Smith, get Mr. Smith on the telephone and explain the situation. Then say, "Mr. Smith will be glad to see you now. Just go to the fourth floor and tell the receptionist that Mr. Smith is expecting you." Or, if necessary, tell the caller, "I'm afraid that Mr. Smith can't see you this morning, but he asked if you could come in at eleven o'clock tomorrow."

If the caller objects because he cannot see your employer personally, tell him that the instructions are made by your employer and you have to abide by them.

Problem callers.   Persistent and emotional callers pose a problem for both the secretary and the executive.

1. Persistent callers.   Some callers simply will not accept any explanation you give for being unable to see your employer. A few may become rude or even threatening. Most problem callers are more persistent and annoying than dangerous, and with them you should be just as persistent—but polite—in making the explanations and suggestions described in the previous section. In other words, insist that you are not authorized to change procedures. But always assure the caller that he or she can write your employer a letter and that you will be certain your employer sees it.

2. Threatening callers.   Should a caller become threatening, speak *privately* with your employer or ring for security if your company has such a system. Do not attempt to cope with someone who is abusive and potentially dangerous.

3. Emotional callers.   Certain situations are emotional, although not abusive or threatening. Perhaps a man who has just lost his job is extremely upset. Female secretaries should secure male assistance—your employer or another person—in calming an emotionally troubled male caller. If the emotional caller is a woman, a female secretary may be able to calm the troubled visitor. If not, consider asking another—preferably mature—female employee to help.

Handling Telephone Calls during a Meeting

How to interrupt a conference.   Try to avoid interrupting a conference, but if it is essential to enter a room where your employer is in conference, do so quietly and unobtrusively. Type on a slip of paper any message that must be delivered to someone in the conference room. If you want instructions, type the questions. Your employer can the handle the matter with a minimum of interruption. If it is essential to announce a caller to your employer while he or she is in conference, simply take in the visitor's card or type the name on a slip of paper.

When a visitor overstays an appointment, buzz your employer on the intercom to announce another appointment. In some offices, the executive has a concealed bell that can be rung unobtrusively when he or she wishes to terminate a conference. The secretary can then enter the room and remind the executive about the next appointment.

How to handle telephone calls for a visitor.   When there is a telephone call for a visitor, ask the person calling if it is possible for you to take the message. If so, type the message on a sheet of paper, addressing it to the visitor, and also type your name, the date, and the time at the bottom of the sheet. No visitor should be required to decipher strange handwriting.

If the person calling insists on speaking to the visitor, go into the conference room and, with a glance that takes in both your employer and the visitor, apologize for the interruption: "Excuse me, Mr. Howard (looking at the visitor), Mr. Davis is on the telephone and wants to speak with you. Do you want to take it here?" (Indicate which telephone to use.) If he says yes, put the call through. Often, however, the visitor says that he will call back, in which case you give the message to the person calling and type out the telephone number as a reminder for the visitor.

If several people are in conference with your employer and you must deliver a message to one of them, type it and take it to that visitor, just as you would to your employer. If the visitor is wanted on the telephone, also type on the message: "Do you want to take the call in the outer office?" The visitor can then leave the conference without disturbing the others.

Seeing a Caller Out

You may find it necessary to remind your employer that it is time for the next appointment—a cue to the visitor that it is time to leave. Or if your employer warns you in advance that your assistance may be needed in cutting a visit short, you might interrupt politely with a reminder that it is time for your employer to leave or to attend some other meeting. As visitors prepare to leave, help them collect their articles and show them to the door, saying "Good-bye" with a pleasant smile. If your building is large and a visitor is a stranger, you should in most cases point the way to or escort the person to the elevator or lobby.

MANAGING PERSONAL SKILLS AND HUMAN RELATIONS

Working for and with Others

Working for one person.   In the modern office the employer-secretary relationship is—or should be—a matter of teamwork. Each person must respect what the other contributes to the smooth and successful functioning of the office. One of the best ways to foster such respect is to keep the channel of communication open. Talk often and try to keep your employer well informed about office activities. Similarly, try to keep informed about your employer's activities and needs. As the occasion arises, volunteer to do nonroutine tasks and openly demonstrate your willingness to participate in the successful functioning of the office.

Often it is necessary to put personal preferences and opinions aside to develop an effective working relationship. Secretaries who work for one person must recognize their responsibility in cooperating with and assisting their employers. This may mean supporting—in the office and outside —policies and practices with which you personally disagree. However, it is perfectly appropriate to make recommendations and offer ideas for your employer's consideration.

Learn to accept criticism graciously and gratefully. Use it as a means to become more capable and successful. Similarly, if you see an error your employer has made, point it out tactfully. For example, if your boss makes a mathematical error in a report, and you discover the correct figure, and if it is a minor error, correct it, but avoid any reference to it at all. If it is important, point out your change, and ask if your boss would mind checking it. But if your boss finds an error in a report prepared by a typist working under you and asks who did it, tell him or her but add that it is your responsibility. (If the error is indicative of a recurring problem, this may be an opportunity to discuss corrective steps with your assistant. If a slow assistant prevents you from completing assignments quickly, do not report this to your boss; find out why the assistant is slow and help him or her along, and if that does not solve the problem, get another assistant.)

Be prepared to overlook personal traits in your employer that annoy you. If the relationship is going to work, it will take your full attention just to be supportive and cooperative and to do your part to ensure that the relationship works for the benefit of your company at all times.

Working for more than one person.　　Even when you work for two or more people, the combination should be viewed as a team. Everyone still has the same overall objective: to contribute to the successful operations of the company.

Secretaries who work for several executives must be particularly adaptable. After all, each executive has his or her own personality and method of working. One person may be more demanding than another. One may expect you to work more independently than another. You will have to adjust your work habits to each situation.

One of the major problems concerns scheduling. If two rush jobs reach you at once, which person do you favor? Unless one executive is the superior and another the subordinate, you should avoid any appearance of favoritism. Explain any conflict that arises to *each person* and ask *all of them* for assistance in resolving the situation. It is important that each one be aware of your work load and any serious problems in scheduling. But try to avert potential problems by anticipating task and time requirements and organizing your work to accommodate each person's needs.

Working with other departments.　　In large companies, many of your contacts will be with coworkers in other departments. The training department may need to work closely with the sales staff, or the public relations office may need to work closely with the mail department. Sometimes one department is faced with a rush job and needs to call on another department for assistance and cooperation.

Be certain to contact the appropriate person in each department, and try to develop good relations with that person. When someone frequently helps you, try to reciprocate and at least make a point of expressing your appreciation at every occasion.

Avoid antagonisms that could develop when one department appears to be giving priority to someone else's request. Try to find out why. Perhaps the secretary with the priority work would be willing to let your job go first. Perhaps there was simply a misunderstanding in handling your work. Someone may be preoccupied with a personal problem and is creating a problem for you unintentionally (always look behind the scenes before you make a hasty judgment). At any rate, aim to *discuss* problems and encourage a spirit of good human relations in your dealings with coworkers in other offices and departments.

Initiating and Managing Projects

Becoming an initiator.   Busy executives need secretaries who can work independently. They simply don't have time to decide every thing that needs to be done around the office or to help the secretary start each project. The secretary who can work on her own is a great asset in any organization.

To become an initiator, you need to become a thinker and have a bit of imagination. As you observe activity in your office, stop to think whether everything is being handled in the most efficient, logical manner. You may decide that the filing system needs streamlining or that the storeroom needs reorganizing or that better records of incoming and outgoing mail should be kept. Naturally, you're not looking for work just for the sake of looking for work. The question is whether some change or new procedure would truly improve operations. If it would and it is nothing requiring your employer's approval, start the project on your own. Think it through (pros and cons), plan the steps you must take, and then simply begin.

Your ideas may involve more than changes you can make on your own. Learn to state the needs and benefits you visualize in clear, persuasive language, so you can present your ideas to your employer. Not all of your proposals may be accepted, but if your ideas are realistic, many of them will be. If they are accepted, again, develop your own plan and simply begin. If you need the cooperation and assistance of others, find ways to motivate them as well.

Coordinating and managing projects.   Leadership qualities are important when it comes to coordinating and managing projects. Some of the most essential qualities are the ability to organize, to set priorities and standards, to delegate work, to solve problems, to motivate others, and to schedule work and meet deadlines.

1. Coordination.   Coordinating a project means making everything and everyone work together effectively to achieve some ultimate common goal. If your special project is to produce a newsletter, you need to coordinate the work of writers, artists, photographers, typesetters, printers, and so on. In other words, you need to work out each aspect of production, so everything and everyone will pull together at the right time in the right way.

2. Management. Managing a project means controlling and directing all aspects of it. To manage effectively, you need to plan the various steps, secure the assistance you need, and delegate each phase of activity to the appropriate people, setting stands and guidelines and supervising their work throughout the project. You need to schedule everything to meet your deadline and to ensure that everyone else completes his or her task as required. This means constant communication. You must decide on and explain the standards to be followed (the scope and quality of work required—the yardstick for you and others to use in deciding whether all facets of the work are being performed satisfactorily). As problems arise, you need to deal with them, working out solutions and making decisions, often instantaneously. Generally, you need to oversee the entire project and make it work. One thing management instructors often fail to mention: you also need to have some fun.

Managing Time and Money

Managing your own time. The way you manage your own time depends in part on the type of work you do. But generally, experts say that you must, first, be very critical about each thing that you do and, second, learn how to do high-priority work better. Managing your time more successfully may involve some drastic changes in your habits. Here are some steps that will get you started.

1. Set goals and write down everything you want or need to do.
2. Set priorities; that is, arrange your goals in order of importance.
3. Plan your time by scheduling each task and setting deadlines, using calendars, planners, checklists, and anything else that will help.
4. Delegate work to assistants to allow more time for important matters.
5. Learn to say no to wasteful, unnecessary intrusions.
6. Control interruptions by discouraging unnecessary visiting and by reorganizing and rescheduling your work to fit quiet and busy periods.
7. Develop better communications to avoid repeating conversations and having to redo work.
8. Avoid time-wasting, unproductive squabbles with coworkers.

9. Look for ways to improve the processing of mail, correspondence, and other recurring items.

10. Take time to do each job right the first time, since it will take much more time to do it all over later.

11. Group your activities; for example, run all errands in one trip.

12. Organize each task before you start it, so you won't have to stop midway because of something you forgot.

13. Make use of downtime, such as when a telephone call is on hold, by planning future activities.

14. Schedule work according to your physical strength, doing the hardest jobs when you have the most energy.

15. Simplify tasks, for example, using the telephone instead of taking off time for a personal visit.

16. Avoid procrastination by starting with something you like to do.

17. Work on ways to improve your concentration and shut out nuisance distractions.

18. Make better use of available technology (machines, services, and so on) to simplify otherwise tedious, time-consuming manual tasks.

Learning to be cost-conscious.   Increasing costs threaten businesses of all sizes, and wasteful habits are taboo. Since secretaries use and often purchase so many of the supplies in an office, they must be as concerned as their employers about managing money and materials. Learning to be cost conscious should be the goal of every secretary.

Here are some things that will help you eliminate waste and establish better control over office expenditures:

1. Learn to control expenditures by budgeting and anticipating your needs and expenses over selected periods such as a month or a quarter.

2. Keep accurate records to compare costs and usage from one period to another, to forecast future needs and costs, and to determine priorities.

3. Order supplies for extended periods, when practical, to take advantage of bulk discounts.

4. Organize your work to avoid duplication and unnecessary waste of stationery, supplies, and so on.

5. Use credit wisely to avoid unnecessary finance charges in purchasing supplies, and shop where returns are accepted and money is refunded.

6. Deal only with reliable suppliers who provide quality products and stand behind their goods.

7. Avoid unnecessary correspondence and mailings, grouping frequent communications whenever possible.

8. Eliminate unnecessary long-distance telephone calls and fast-delivery service (such as telegrams) for messages that are not urgent.

9. Read available books and articles on money management and purchasing.

10. Remember that "time is money" in business and become time conscious as well as cost conscious.

Interviewing and Supervising Assistants

Finding and interviewing new employees.   Many secretaries help their employers find and interview new employees.

1.   Where to find prospective employees.   Recruits can be obtained from many sources. Consider the ones most likely to have the type of employee you need, for example:

a. Employment agencies

b. School placement offices

c. Employment/unemployment bureaus

d. Newspaper advertisements placed by you or the applicant

e. References from outside sources

f. Contacts previously made by interested applicants

g. Your company's personnel department

2.   How to conduct an interview.   You must plan ahead for the interviews to find out what you want to know about the applicant and also to provide information to the applicant—all within the time set aside for the meeting. These are the basic steps involved:

a. Set a mutually convenient time.

b. Prepare a detailed, written description of the company and the job, listing specific tasks the applicant will have to perform.

c. Devise skills tests if applicable, such as a typing test, when prepared tests are not available.

d. Draw up a list of specific questions you want to ask (your company may have a standard application form, but this list is necessary in addition) and take notes throughout the interview; be a good listener.

e. Make certain that the applicant is comfortable and at ease, and try to encourage him or her to volunteer information and indicate relative interest in skills and job duties.

f. If possible, review a completed application before the interview so that you can use the interview to clear up problems.

g. If you interview several prospective employees, follow the same procedure with each one so that your comparison will be meaningful and fair.

h. Summarize and type the results and present them to your employer along with any recommendations or comments that you have, after all of the interviews are complete.

Training and supervising assistants.   Once the new worker is hired, the job orientation and training begin. The new employee should be made to feel at home and acquainted with not only the immediate office but general company policy and facilities as well.

Training will require (1) careful instruction and explanation of duties —presented at a pace the employee can digest—and (2) practice sessions where actual tasks are first completed under your direct supervision, often with step-by-step explanations as work proceeds. It will become evident when direct, constant supervision can be relaxed.

Once the worker is functioning alone—with the exception of occasional questions—you should still check his or her work occasionally for errors and general quality, as well as for efficiency and overall performance. (Some secretaries schedule daily, then weekly, ten- to fifteen-minute conferences to review work loads and answer questions.) If further guidance or discipline is required, do not hesitate to provide it. Remain alert to dissatisfaction and actively encourage open communication that will prevent such problems. Develop the same spirit of teamwork that characterizes the ideal employer-secretary relationship.

It is important throughout the worker's employment to provide motivation. An employee who has no incentive to do better probably will not. Job satisfaction is essential in any position. Compliment the new employee frequently. If criticism is necessary, offer it in a positive, constructive manner that encourages the person to work harder and gain—not lose—confidence.

Here are some of the things to cover in your training sessions:

1. Supplies—location and use
2. Forms—location and use
3. Correspondence—company practice, with samples
4. Typing aids—how-to instructions such as chain feeding and inserting carbon packs in machine
5. Style—correspondence, reports, and so on
6. Machines—care and operation
7. Filing—procedures and location
8. Telephone—use and courtesy
9. Available facilities such as purchasing department and cafeteria
10. Company—review of product/service, personnel, and so on
11. Grammar and writing skills
12. Mail—handling incoming and outgoing
13. Other duties and office procedures

In spite of all efforts to find and select the right candidate and give proper training, there is always the chance that the person will not work out. The employee may be unable to produce work of adequate quality. If further training will not solve the problem, you will be forced to advise your employer, who may ask you to discharge the employee. It will be necessary to tell the person as gently as possible that she or he is being released. You could indicate that the employee may want to pursue further training or education or that she or he would be more suited for a different type of job or office. Be as tactful, but direct, as possible and wish the person well.

Observing the Rules of Confidentiality

All organizations need to maintain a certain degree of privacy and confidentiality. The ones that deal with sensitive material or must constantly safeguard against giving an advantage to competitors have special policies and procedures in this regard. Secrecy is important even within a company office or department.

How to act when you are away from the office. As a rule, when you are away from the office, never discuss with others matters about your employer, the nature of your work, or matters about your company except in generalities ("I'm a secretary; yes, I love my job"). Assume—even if you are not told—that all conversations about specific people and projects are taboo, that everything is confidential unless you have been told otherwise. In other words, it's fine to tell someone that you work for an accounting firm, but it would be a serious breach of confidentiality to discuss your work pertaining to one of your employer's clients. Similarly, it would be fine to tell someone that you work in the file department of a clothing manufacturer, but it would be grounds for dismissal to tell anyone what you read in one of the files.

How to safeguard office material. Employers must be able to trust the people who work for them. No business could function effectively if secretaries and others knowingly or unwittingly violated the all-important rule of confidentiality.

In addition to not discussing office matters, you should make it a practice to protect the material with which you work: keep confidential papers on your desk turned over and locked in the files the rest of the time; keep your shorthand notebook and other notes in your desk when not being used; keep tapes and diskettes with word processing and other document files locked in their file containers; keep outsiders *out* of your employer's office when he or she is away; don't discard carbon copies or photocopies that you don't intend to use without shredding them; and keep your desk, files, and other storage areas locked, with the keys well hidden from possible intruders.

Handling Human Relations Problems

What to do about gossip. A grapevine is a trail of office gossip passed from one employee to another by word of mouth. The smart secretary regards grapevine news with caution. If you hear through this source something that seems to be important news and that directly affects you and your job, directly question your employer about it. *Never* spread grapevine information. Passing on unfounded rumors can lead to unfortunate consequences and can involve you in embarrassing situations.

Remember that a rumor can have serious consequences when it gets outside the company. Even when you have no reason to doubt what you hear, strictly avoid making office matters public. Discussing the matter with a close friend in a restaurant is the same as making the news public, because you never know who may overhear you.

What to do about personal borrowing and lending.   In the area of personal borrowing and lending, a breakdown of scrupulous courtesy can cause irreparable ill will among those in the office who must work together. In general, it is advisable *not* to borrow if you can possibly avoid it.

If you must borrow, be sure to make it a practice to return what you have borrowed as quickly as possible. Delays lead to forgetfulness and to accidents or actual loss of things—with the inevitable disagreeable feeling on the part of the individual who was kind enough to lend you his or her belongings.

1. Borrowing money. From a practical standpoint, discretion, responsibility, and trustworthiness rank above courtesy when borrowing money—without these qualities, there is no courtesy in the transaction. Do not borrow money, even very small sums, from coworkers or people who do business with your company if you can possible avoid it. If you must borrow lunch money, for example, be sure you return it promptly.

Borrowing a large sum of money from a coworker or someone doing business with the company is frowned on in all business organizations. Even if a friend, out of kindness, offers you a loan, don't accept it. Banks, not friends or business associates, are appropriate sources for such purposes.

2. Lending money. If a coworker has been remiss in returning a loan, you will show more consideration by tactfully reminding him or her of the debt than by nursing a secret annoyance. Never mention the debt to others. Although a large amount of money cannot simply be forgotten, and you may have to resort to legal action to recover it, use such measures as a last alternative since it will, at the least, put a strain on your working relationship. The wisest policy is: "neither a borrower nor a lender be."

How to deal with office politics.   *Office politics* is a general term that usually refers to games that people play to get ahead at work or perhaps to get by with something questionable.

1. Unethical practices. Competition is healthy and desirable in most circumstances, but when the motivation to gain recognition and get ahead causes irrational, unethical behavior, it is clearly unhealthy. Honest, hard work, in the spirit of teamwork and cooperation, is the only ethical way to secure a raise or promotion. This type of challenge to a coworker is natural and common. But unfair schemes and secret ploys to discredit competing coworkers are unthinkable to an honest, responsible person.

2. The unethical coworker. If you are forced to deal with a coworker who is acting questionably in efforts to gain some favor or recognition above you, do not be pushed into using similar strategy.

Continue to work honestly and responsibly and see that your actions are fair and open for all to see. If necessary, regularly point out to your employer what you have done in your work and what you are planning to do so that any efforts by someone else to claim credit for your achievements or to sabotage them will soon be exposed. (Send your boss copies of letters and reports you write; type a summary of an idea you have—with your name on it; and so on.) You may have to be patient, but keep in mind that there is something to the cliché that if you give people enough rope, they will hang themselves.

    3. Office politics.   The term *office politics* implies something shady to many people, but it also refers to legitimate maneuvers to make your worth known. Don't hesitate to use honest, ethical strategies to help get a raise, get a promotion, and generally enhance your status in your company. For example, develop a reputation as a cooperative, understanding coworker by being a good listener and volunteering to help others in appropriate situations; demonstrate your worth to your employer—particularly, when you are seeking a raise or promotion—by regularly making your achievements known (in writing when possible) and by periodically preparing a new, detailed job description that illustrates your merits; regularly engage in independent inquiry and study to become better informed and to polish your abilities in specific areas of work; develop your initiative to the fullest and take advantage of opportunities to handle matters on your own. Generally, work hard to enhance your competence and subtly make your employer and others aware of your expanding responsibility and capability.

    How to cope with injuries and illnesses.   Since office workers are vulnerable to accidents and illnesses and since these occurrences are typically unexpected, a secretary may have to make some fast decisions when something happens.

    1. What to do for an injured coworker.   Injuries and illnesses at work should be handled the same as you would handle them outside the office. The first concern must be the injured employee. Quickly give whatever first aid you can offer and then immediately summon appropriate help. With a minor illness or injury, it may be sufficient to accompany the coworker to a company nurse or doctor. With a serious accident, it will be necessary to call an ambulance instantly. If you must leave the office to accompany the injured person somewhere, ask a coworker to cover for you. Since every situation will vary, you will have to use your own judgment each time. But in each case, remember that the employee's safety and well-being come first.

    2. How to help a coworker during the recovery period.   Employees who have been ill or in an accident will need your help during their recovery. Offer to take over some of their tasks and let them know that you and others will do what you can to help handle their work loads until they are fully recovered. Your employer will no doubt divide the work among certain members of the staff or bring in temporary outside help. If you are given extra duties, it may be an inconvenience and a strain to handle the increased work load. But unless the request is unreasonable or impossible (in which case you should ask to hire temporary help), do what you can without complaining. One day the tables may be turned, and you may need the cooperation and help of your coworkers to keep your job secure while you are recovering.

How to handle personnel problems.   Every office, large or small, is a potential trouble spot where human relations are concerned. Even in the highly automated office where tasks involve person-machine more than person-to-person contact, there are problems that a secretary may face.

1. Serious conflicts.   How do you handle a situation where you and another worker are in strong disagreement? First, you should remember that it is necessary to continue working each day with your coworkers. Arguments seldom solve anything. The sensible route is to take time to listen and try to understand the other side—before it becomes a conflict. If possible, seek a no-fault resolution. If you still disagree, do not change your opinion, but do not let it anger you that someone else has a different viewpoint. If you are in charge, you are entitled to put your decision into effect if it concerns office procedures. If it is a matter of concern to your employer, let him or her make the final decision. The important thing to remember is that patience, understanding, and a friendly attitude will go a long way in preventing disagreements from becoming battles. Although some conflict cannot be avoided, there are things you can do to minimize the probability. Stress is a cause of many forms of conflict, and you can help combat it—even encourage harmony—by staying calm and level-headed when you are the one under pressure. Often it is a matter of understanding *yourself* better.

Make a list of your strengths and weaknesses and find ways to emphasize your strengths and overcome your weaknesses. Chances are that modifying your own behavior in this way will help to reduce incidences of conflict. You may be able to encourage others—subtly—to emphasize their strengths and overcome their weaknesses too; if you can't, learn to empathize with them and accept their weaknesses, but do not let them provoke you into unwanted conflict. Perhaps you simply need to work harder to win over diffident or uncooperative coworkers. If you run into disinterest or even the "cold shoulder" treatment, don't let it dissuade you.

Examine the communications function: make a list of ways to avoid misunderstandings by making your written and spoken messages clearer, by asking questions when you need more information, and by speaking only for yourself—never for others without their authorization.

2. Problems of others.   One of the most difficult situations arises when a secretary either is asked for personal help or is in a situation where it seems necessary to offer assistance. If the person in trouble is a coworker, and possibly a good friend as well, the secretary will doubtless feel compelled to offer help and comfort. There is a dangerous point that may be reached. A good rule to remember is that you never really help someone by covering for errors or problems. If someone has a drinking problem, for instance, or some emotional problem affecting his or her work, do not play doctor or psychologist and do not help the person hide it from your employer. Rather, help the person find professional guidance outside —quickly.

If the individual with a problem is your employer and you are asked to offer suggestions, do the same thing. Otherwise, if the problem is extremely serious and is clearly jeopardizing the company's welfare, you should carefully consider advising your employer's immediate superior that a threatening problem exists. (But proceed cautiously—perhaps the superior is part of the problem.) If the problem is minor, or at least not a threat to the company, what you do depends on how much it disturbs you. You can try to ignore it or ask for a transfer to another office. In any case, do *not* participate in anything illegal or immoral even if it seems the only way to save your job or help an employer in trouble. If you cannot reason with your employer, or if his or her superiors are also involved, you may *as a last resort* have to resign your position in that office or even in the entire company

Every situation that presents itself is different in some way, and your response will have to be dictated by the seriousness of it and your own involvement. Certainly, you should not seek out individuals with problems and should not attempt to involve yourself as an amateur psychiatrist or counselor.

3. Employee grievances.   Management often establishes a grievance committee or arranges for some individual to hear the grievances of employees. The theory is that employees who are given an opportunity to air their complaints and work out solutions with management will be less likely to become disgruntled or quit their jobs. You can apply this same policy to your assistants—arrange for a certain period each week for employees with grievances to talk them over with you. But if no attempt is made to solve the problems or to explain fully what can and cannot be done and why, the entire process will be a waste of everyone's time.

4. Sexual harrassment. Both men and women may be subject to pressure from their superiors to grant sexual favors in return for job security, a promotion, or something else the employee deems important. This road is fraught with dangers, and no one should submit to any pressure of this sort—*ever.*

How you handle such a situation depends on the incident, your objectives, and your sense of social justice. In serious cases, employees have brought charges against their superiors on grounds of sexual harrassment. Unfortunately, most employees in such or similar situations have probably been fired for refusing to submit or have resigned rather than try to deal with the problem.

An essential first step in cases of unwanted sexual advances is to be extraordinarily firm and clear in your *initial* response. Don't wait; give absolutely no hint that you are unsure or may change your mind. *Very clearly* state that under *no* circumstances could you *ever* consider an involvement *of any sort* with someone at work, that it is *completely* beyond your ability in every possible way even to imagine or discuss the possibility —*no matter what the consequences.*

If the person appears willing and perhaps eager to drop it in light of your strong position, help him or her save face by changing the subject and never mentioning it again—to anyone. But if the person continues with bribe or even threats, increase the firmness of your position. If that fails to bring it all to a halt and you are in physical danger, get out quickly and seek immediate help if necessary. In fact, serious threats and certainly physical abuse require immediate police assistance.

In cases of undeniable sexual harrassment, as opposed to some casual pass or nonserious flirtation, you have to decide what steps you want to take, legal or otherwise. Each situation will be different. It may be enough in certain cases to make clear that unless it all stops *immediately* you will have no choice but to report it; in other cases, this will be insufficient, and you will actually have to report it. If you sense that the problem will continue, keep a private written record of what was said or done, including the time and place. Then speak to your supervisor unless the threat comes from your supervisor. In that case speak to your supervisor's boss. If that fails to produce results, take your notes to the personnel director. Finally, if all else fails, file a complaint with the Equal Employment Opportunity Commission. Remember that employers are responsible for an occurrence of sexual harrassment in their companies. Above all, remember that sexual harrassment is a crime that cannot be ignored—for your own safety and well-being and for that of your coworkers.

5. Performance problems. Some problems affect or involve an employee's ability to perform. Perhaps the employee's productivity or output is low. Perhaps the quality of the employee's work is below standards. If the reasons are unknown, a performance appraisal is in order. This may involve having employees record each step they take in their jobs—what they do and how long it takes to do it. A review of their education, background, and specific job qualifications may be needed. Finally, it may be desirable to interview the employees, pointedly asking questions that will reveal their attitudes, understanding of work requirements, and so on.

Many things cause performance problems, and the first step is to isolate the factors that directly contribute to the problems. For instance, outmoded equipment could lead to poor performance on the job. In other cases, however, equipment and working conditions might be perfect, but the employees might have problems at home interfering with their performance at work. These situations can be delicate, and you need to work *with* the employees, encouraging their cooperation and participation, in solving the problem. Any criticism that must be given should be phrased positively and constructively (for example, "A little more practice, Joan, and I think you'll be doing letter-perfect work," *not* "You're still making mistakes, Joan").

HANDLING SOCIAL-BUSINESS RESPONSIBILITIES

Making Arrangements for Theater Tickets

The secretary's chief responsibility when an employer entertains at the theater is reserving the tickets. That is a difficult chore unless the tickets are ordered far in advance. Theaters, telephone services, and ticket agencies are listed in the telephone directory, and newspapers carry advertisements of current plays. Many hotels also have information on, and facilities for, the purchase of theater tickets, tours, and other forms of entertainment.

Using ticket agents.   On short notice, a ticket agent may be helpful. An account at an agency simplifies the problem somewhat. Establish a contact at the agency and make all purchases through the same person if possible. Specify the event and the date, and the agent will deliver the tickets to you or at the theater box office. You may also specify which seats you want. An additional charge by the agency is added to the original cost of each ticket. Many agencies will allow you to charge the tickets with one of the major credit cards.

Purchasing tickets at the box office.   Tickets can also be purchased at the box office, but the problem of getting good seats on short notice—or getting any seats at all—remains no matter where or how you purchase the ticket. Many box offices accept credit cards.

Using a telephone service.   In major cities, you can also call a telephone service—such as Ticket Central in New York, Teletron in Boston, and Top Ticket in Houston—for tickets and charge them with one of the major credit cards. Often you can specify the area, such as orchestra, but usually not the specific row or seat desired. Ask where you may pick up the tickets—usually at the box office. Also ask whether there is a service charge.

Sending tickets through the mail.   Some people prefer to have the tickets in advance rather than pick them up at the box office. If you send tickets through the mail to anyone, always include the numbers of the seats in your letter of transmittal. This information on the copy of your letter is useful if the tickets are lost.

Typing information for your employer.   When you give the theater tickets to your employer, enclose them in an envelope with the following information typed on it:

1. Day of the week and date of performance
2. Curtain time
3. Name and address of theater
4. Name of show
5. Seat numbers

Handling Presents and Holiday Cards

Helping with extra holiday duties.   Your calendar has a notation (see page 45) to bring holiday lists to your employer's attention. The time depends on shopping conditions in your locality. For example, allow about six weeks before Christmas. Many private secretaries assist in the selection of cards and address and mail them. Some secretaries make suggestions for presents and help select and prepare them for mailing.

Preparing the holiday gift list.   Figure 40 is a suggested form to use in bringing the list of Christmas gifts to your employer's attention. The form is self-explanatory. The employer makes additions or deletions, approves the gifts suggested by you or decides on something else, and indicates the price range. In addition to Christmas, there are other holidays such as Hanukkah that are celebrated about the same time. It is important to be aware of the days and knowledgeable about the various customs. To

Figure 40.   Christmas List

	CHRISTMAS LIST 19-- (Mr. Hambro)				
Name	Gift yr. before last	Gift last yr.	Amt. spent	Suggestion	Amt. to spend?
Mr. & Mrs. Nelson	cocktail glasses	gourmet cheese	$60	handcrafted vase	
Allen Pierce	humidor	manicure kit	$18	leather stationery case	

avoid duplication in your list, you should keep a similar card record for those people to whom your employer gives gifts at other times of the year.

Wrapping and mailing gifts.   Appropriate holiday cards, in preference to visiting cards, are usually sent with holiday gifts. When you plan to have a store gift-wrap and mail gifts, take the cards with you when you do your shopping. If a gift is to be mailed, comply with the request of the Postal Service and mail early during busy holiday seasons such as Christmas. This is especially important if the packages are to be sent abroad.

Handling money gifts.   All executives have a certain number of service people to whom they give gifts of money each Christmas. If you help your employer handle money gifts, make a list of those to whom your employer gives money and ask him or her to indicate the amount. The list will include household employees, elevator operators, doormen and women, janitors and building superintendents (but not building managers) of apartment houses and office buildings, mail carriers, and any others who perform services throughout the year and are not tipped. The amount given household employees is usually based on salary and length of service; the amount given apartment house employees, on the rent; the amount given others, on length of service. Some executives also give money to relatives and members of their families.

If the amount of money is small, twenty-five dollars or less, use crisp new bills; for a larger amount, write a check. No matter what the amount or to whom given, insert it in a Christmas envelope printed for that purpose.

Preparing card lists.   Keep an alphabetical list of the names and addresses of people to whom your employer sends holiday cards. If your employer sends personal cards to some people and sends cards jointly with his or her spouse to others, keep separate lists. Your employer may also have a select list of cards that he or she prefers to sign. In addition, you may have to keep a separate list of customers or clients who receive company or firm cards.

When a card is received from someone who is not on the list, add the name below the regular list so that the next year, your employer can decide whether to add that person to the list. If he or she makes new contacts during the year, add them to the list, indicating where the contact was made. Your employer will cross out any names that should not be on the list.

It is important to note changes of address. Many of the addresses will be in your address book; you should compare your list with them before addressing the cards. As cards are received, it is advisable to compare addresses shown on the envelopes with the ones on your list. Check the names on the list as you address the cards. The same list can be used for several years if there are not many additions.

Keeping records of birthdays.   Keep a card record of those who receive presents on other occasions such a birthdays. The record should show the present given on each occasion and the approximate cost. Your employer will want to know what presents were given to a particular person on other occasions as well as on previous birthdays before making a decision about another birthday present.

Selecting gifts for wedding anniversaries.   Presents on wedding anniversaries follow a tradition—each anniversary is associated with a different substance or jewel. Gift stores and jewelry stores have lists of the substance or jewel currently associated with each anniversary. Merchants' associations may revise the list from time to time, so check for any recent changes before making a purchase.

Preparing Invitations

Formal invitation.   The formal invitation is written in the third person and is engraved, partially engraved, or handwritten. Envelopes are always handwritten. With a partially engraved invitation, spaces are left open to write in the guest's name, time, date, and nature of the event. Paper for a formal invitation is often heavy white or light cream stock.

Figure 41.   Formal Invitation

Miss Michele Green, president
The New Company
requests the pleasure of your company
at a reception
in honor of Mr. Walter Arlington
on Friday, the fourth of August
at half past six o'clock
at 1200 Seventh Avenue
Houston

RSVP Card Enclosed   *Black tie*

Printers and stationery stores have books with sample paper and sample lettering. A white or ivory card may be used for partially engraved invitations, and heavy white or cream writing paper may be used for handwritten invitations. The invitation often uses block lettering and should be presented in a standard format. The letters *RSVP* in the lower left-hand corner mean that a reply is expected. Figure 41 is an example of a formal invitation showing the placement and spelling of date, hour, and address.

Formal reply. The reply (and envelope) to a formal social invitation must be handwritten and follow the same form as the invitation. Thus you would reply in the third person and repeat essential data, as shown in figure 42. Use personal writing paper and fold it in half the same as the invitation itself. A reply to a social-business function may be typed on business letterhead.

Informal invitation. The informal invitation can be typed or handwritten on folded note paper or calling cards. Figure 43 shows an example of a preprinted fill-in invitation. Printers, stationery stores, and

Figure 42.   Formal Reply

Mr. and Mrs. James Forrest
accept with pleasure
the kind invitation of Miss Greene
to be present at the reception
in honor of Mr. Walter Arlington
on Friday, the fourth of August
at half past six o'clock
at 1200 Seventh Avenue
Houston

---

office-supply stores have examples of informal, printed invitations, partially filled in. An informal social-business invitation such as for a business luncheon is commonly typed as a social-business letter on business letter-head.

   Informal reply.   Your reply to an informal invitation depends on the format of the invitation itself. The RSVP notice in figure 43 gives a telephone number, indicating that you should reply by phone. Most of the informal business invitations that come into the office are not sent on printed cards or note paper but are typed as a traditional letter. Replies are then sent in the same letter format on business stationery. An example of this type of acceptance letter is shown on page 395.

Keeping Records of Donations

   How to handle requests for donations.   Records of donations or contributions must be kept (1) to support the allowable income tax

Figure 43.   Informal Invitation

David Cross

requests the pleasure of your company

at _____ *Dinner* _____

on _____ *Saturday, April 9, at 8 o'clock* _____

at _____ *The Cross-Country Inn* _____
_____ *44 Lakeside Boulevard* _____
_____ *Burlington* _____

RSVP

471-9033

---

deduction and (2) for your employer's information. But the secretary is also concerned with record keeping for nontax purposes.

At certain times of the year, numerous organizations make drives for donations. It may be advisable to accumulate the requests in a folder and give a batch of them to your employer at an opportune time. If the request comes from a new organization, try to find something about it and present the details to your employer. Never destroy a request for a donation unless your employer has told you to do so. Some people, particularly those in public positions, make a practice of responding, at least in a small way, to nearly every request. See page 404 for a letter regretting inability to make a donation.

How to keep a record of donations.   When your employer is considering whether to make a certain donation, he or she is interested in knowing (1) the amount donated to a specific organization the preceding year and (2) the total amount of donations for the current year. Note on each request, before giving it to your employer, the amount donated the previous year. Give the running record of donations for the current year to your employer with each request. At the end of the year, make an alphabetical list of organizations to which contributions have been made. When your employer makes a pledge payable in installments, enter the due dates on your calendar or in your card tickler (see page 45).

Sending Expressions of Sympathy

How to send expressions of sympathy. Sympathy to the family of a deceased friend or acquaintance is usually expressed by (1) flowers, (2) a letter of sympathy, (3) mass cards, or (4) contributions.

1. Flowers. It is customary to send flowers to a bereaved family, except to an Orthodox Jewish family. It is appropriate to send them fruit baskets. A visiting card, with the engraved name struck out in ink and bearing a few words of sympathy, may accompany the flowers. Usually, however, the secretary orders the flowers by phone and the florist supplies the card and writes the name of the person sending the flowers. The florist will ask you the name of the deceased, where the funeral is to be conducted, and the date and time of the service.

Flowers are appropriate at a memorial service—as for someone lost at sea—or when the deceased is to be cremated. Cut flowers are not appropriate for a funeral service. Some kind of floral piece, a spray or a wreath, is preferable.

2. Letters of condolence. Letters of condolence are sent to a family of any faith. See page 398 for an example.

3. Mass cards. Mass cards may be sent to a Roman Catholic family by a Catholic or a non-Catholic. You may obtain them from any priest. It is customary to make an offering to the church at the time of asking for the card. Although a Roman Catholic might ask a priest to say a mass for a non-Catholic, it is not in good taste to send a mass card to a non-Catholic family.

4. Contributions. Many families request that, instead of flowers, friends send contributions to charities or other organizations in which the deceased was interested. The organization sends the family a notice of the contribution. Your employer may want to write a short note to the family of a close friend or relative and tell them that he or she is sending a donation in their name even though the gift is later announced by the organization.

How to acknowledge flowers and mass cards. The secretary needs to be concerned not only with the acknowledgment itself but with the records pertaining to the replies.

1. Files to keep. In case of the death of a member of your employer's family, write descriptions of floral pieces on the back of each accompanying card. Keep separate files for fruit baskets, mass cards, and letters. Arrange all in alphabetical order. Make a separate notation of people who have sent both flowers and mass cards and of those who have written and also sent fruit baskets, flowers, or mass cards. Prepare separate lists (see figure 44).

2. Types of acknowledgments. Authorities differ about whether good taste permits a typed acknowledgment or an engraved acknowledgment card. If there are few acknowledgments to write, undoubtedly your employer should write them in longhand. However, in the case of a

Figure 44.   Lists for Acknowledgment of Cards and Flowers

List No. 1		
	FLOWERS	
Name and Address (Alphabetical)	Kind of Flowers	Remarks
Brown, Mr. and Mrs. R.S. (Catherine and Bob) 275 E. 86th St. New York NY 10017	Spray, calla lilies	See Mass list
Jones, Mrs. A. (Mary) 79 W. Adams St. Boston MA 03201	Iris, white stock	Also wire from Mr. Jones (Tom)

List No. 2		
	MASSES	
Name and Address (Alphabetical)	Particular form of card; how many masses	Remarks
Brown, Mr. and Mrs. R.S. (Catherine and Bob)	Society for the Propagation of the Faith	See Flowers list
Murphy, Thomas E. (Tom) 44 Fifth Ave. New York NY 10017	6 masses	

prominent person, when hundreds of people send flowers, mass cards, letters, and so on, the task of acknowledging each by a handwritten letter is too formidable. Engraved acknowledgment cards may be used to acknowledge letters of sympathy, flowers, mass cards, or fruit baskets from persons who are unknown to the bereaved but should not be sent to close personal friends.

Also make a list of the names and addresses of those who performed outstanding services, such as doctors and nurses; priest, rabbi, or minister; editorial writers; and the like. Your employer may want to send letters of appreciation to them.

From these lists it is simple to handle the acknowledgments. The first column gives you the proper salutation (Dear Mary); from the information in the second column, you can make a special comment in your acknowledgment of the type of flowers, mass card, and so on; the column headed *Remarks* gives you other information you may need. A thank you letter should also be sent to those who gave memorial contributions to organizations. The notices from the organizations tell who made the contributions.

Your employer will select from the lists the friends to whom he or she wants to write in longhand and will dictate acknowledgments to some of the others. You can then draft and type acknowledgments to the rest of the names on the lists.

ORDERING SOCIAL AND BUSINESS CARDS

Using Social Visiting Cards

The use of visiting cards has declined considerably, but they remain traditional in formal settings.

Visiting cards should be of medium-to-heavy white card stock. A woman's card is about $3\frac{1}{2}$ by $2\frac{1}{2}$ inches. A man's card is about $3\frac{1}{4}$ by $1\frac{1}{4}$ inches. The engraving should be in black. When ordering for an executive, be sure to order some matching envelopes so that they may be sent with flowers or gifts. (Anything mailed, however, must meet the $3\frac{1}{2}$- by 5-inch minimum requirement of the Postal Service.)

Initials should be avoided as much as possible, and one's given name must be written in full. It is better to write out the entire name, usually centered on the card. *Mr., Mrs., Miss, Dr.,* or a military title is the only title that should be used before the name. (Single women may omit *Miss* if desired.) Unlike a business card, the visiting card of a married or widowed woman uses the husband's full name. If a name is very long, *Senior* or *Junior* may be abbreviated and capitalized, but it is preferable to write the word out in all lowercase letters. It is a matter of choice whether an address is engraved on the personal visiting card, although it is unusual to include the address. If used, the house address appears in the lower right-hand corner. (See **Using Business Cards** for social amenities for business cards.) Stationery stores and printers have samples of card stocks and typefaces.

Using Informals

Along with the decline in the use of social visiting cards came an increase in the use of *informals,* larger cards on which one can write a short message. Although the design depends on preference, an executive's name is usually engraved (but may be printed) in black ink on white or cream-colored stock exactly as it appears on a visiting card. Instead of a name, one may use a monogram in the upper left corner. Since informals are used in the mails, they must be $3\frac{1}{2}$ by 5 inches or larger. Foldover note paper, folded to $3\frac{1}{2}$ by 5 inches or more, is used much the same as an informal and has become even more popular than informals for thank yous, informal invitations, and other forms of social correspondence.

Using Business Cards

All executives who call on clients or customers or who make business calls for any reason carry business cards. You should be aware of, and able to make suggestions about, the social amenities for business calling cards. How do they differ from a social visiting card? What is the wording for them? Are they sent with gifts from an executive to customers or clients?

Size of business cards.   The business card is usually about $3\frac{1}{2}$ by 2 inches.

Style for executives and other personnel.   On the executive level, a business card often has the executive's name in the middle of the card and his or her title and the firm name in the lower left-hand corner, either one above the other. The address and possibly telephone/telex number are then in the lower right-hand corner. If the business is in a large city, the street address and the city are used, but the state may be left out. If the company offices are in a small town, the name of the state is written on the same line as the town, no street address being necessary. Some very prominent executives omit their titles from the card; only the executive's name and the name of the company appear on it.

High-level executives may prefer a conservative type style, such as traditional block or Roman, engraved in black on quality parchment or white card stock. Some executives today prefer a more informal, modern look.

Initials and abbreviations, although not correct on social calling cards, may be used on business cards. However, the word *Company* should be written out unless the abbreviation *Co.* is part of the registered name of the firm. A title such as *Mr.* does not precede the executive's name on a business card as it does on a social card, but *M.D.* or military rank may follow the name.

On business cards of company representatives below the executive level, the firm name is usually imprinted or engraved in the center of the card and the individual's name, title, and department in the lower left corner. The address and the telephone/telex number may be in the lower right-hand corner. Sometimes the person's name and title will be centered and the firm name will be in the left-hand corner and the firm address in the right-hand corner. The precise arrangement depends on personal preference to a great extent.

Cards used by salespersons or other representatives to advertise a company or a product frequently carry a trademark or emblem, or an eye-catching design, and the printing or engraving may be done in color. A calendar or advertising matter may appear on the back of the card. The telephone number is always on a card of this type.

Doctors and dentists frequently put their office hours on their cards. Printers and stationery stores have numerous examples of card stock, typefaces, and designs ranging from ultraconservative to ultramodern.

Business cards for women.   The business card used by a woman is the same as a man's, and her personal title *(Miss, Ms.,* or *Mrs.)* is included only if it would otherwise not be clear that she is female.

When having cards printed with a title, women in business follow the rules for addressing women in other situations. Thus a card might read *Edna Hill, Edna Wright,* or *Edna Hill-Wright.* A woman with a professional title may use either her maiden name or her married name combined with her first name and her title. For instance, when Dr. Laura Rogers marries John Edwards, she may call herself "Dr. Laura Edwards" or "Dr. Laura Rogers." On her business cards, she may use either "Laura Rogers, M.D.," or "Laura Edwards, M.D." (See pages 329–31.) Military titles may also be used. Secretaries who represent their employers at meetings should have their own cards printed, following the suggstions given here.

Correct use of business cards with gifts.   Traditionally, an executive did not enclose a business card with a gift, even though the gift was going to a client or customer, unless it accompanied a gift to a new business. Otherwise, the giving of a gift was thought to be a social gesture, requiring a social visiting card. This rule is now honored more in the breach than in the observance. However, presidents or board chairmen of large corporations often have special cards printed for enclosure with holiday gifts. It mentions the company name and the name of the executive sending the gift but in no way resembles a business card. Today, many executives personalize their regular business cards by striking out their engraved name on the front and writing a note on the front or back, signing it with their first name only. Some executives prefer to use "informals" or foldover note paper for short messages (see page 296).

Ordering Cards

How and when to reorder cards. Do not forget to put a reorder reminder with your employer's business calling cards. It usually takes ten days or two weeks (perhaps longer to get engraved cards). Until you have been working for your employer long enough to know his or her wishes, you should get approval before reordering. For instance, your employer may want to change the style of the card or some of the information on it. Stationery stores and printers have a wide selection of card stock and typefaces, if you are ordering for the first time or need to revise the style and information on a card.

—PART TWO———

How to Write Effective Letters and Memos

11. Mechanics of Business Correspondence
12. Valuable Aids for Productive Letter Writing
13. Model Letters and Memos

—— Chapter 11 ————————————

Mechanics of
Business Correspondence

HOW TO SET UP LETTERS AND MEMOS

Letter Style

The standard styles in which letters are set up are:

1. Full block (figure 45)
2. Block (figure 46)
3. Semiblock (figure 47)
4. Official (figure 48)
5. Simplified (figure 49)

Read each of the letters for an explanation of its distinguishing characteristics.

Memo Style

Memo formats vary as do the sizes of memo stationery. But most styles omit the inside address, salutation, complimentary close, and signature and substitute guide words such as *To, From, Subject,* and *Date.* Figure 50 illustrates a common format and provides further information on memo styles.

Figure 45. Full-Block Style. The distinguishing feature of the full-block style of letter is that all structural parts of the letter begin flush with the left margin. There are no indentations. The initials of the person dictating are not included in the identification line. Open punctuation may be used in the address and signature.

[LETTERHEAD]

July 16, 19—

Ms. Sheila Jones
The Modern School for Secretaries
12 Harrington Place
Greenpoint, NJ 07201

Dear Ms. Jones:

You asked me to send you examples of letter styles being used in offices throughout the country.

This letter is an example of the full-block style of letter, which has been adopted as a standard at Prentice-Hall. We have reproduced it in our Employee Manual so that everyone will be familiar with the form and the instructions for its use.

Since Prentice-Hall is a leading exponent of modern business methods, we naturally use an efficient letter form. This style saves time and energy.

As you can see, there are no indentations. Everything, including the date and the complimentary close, begins at the extreme left. This uniformity eliminates several mechanical operations in typing letters.

Our dictaphone typists always use this form unless the person dictating instructs otherwise. The person dictating is at liberty to alter the form if a change is desirable for business reasons.

Since this person's name is typed in the signature, it is not considered necessary to include his or her initials in the identification line.

Sincerely,

Martha Scott
Correspondence Chief

hc

Figure 46. Block Style. The distinguishing feature of the block style of letter is that the inside address and the paragraphs are blocked, flush with the left-hand margin. The salutation and attention lines, if any, are aligned with the inside address. The dateline and reference line are flush with the right-hand margin. The typed signature is aligned with the complimentary close. Open punctuation may be used.

[LETTERHEAD]

July 16, 19—

Your reference 12:3:1

Mrs. Jane Carter
The Modern School for Secretaries
12 Harrington Place
Greenpoint, NJ 07201

Dear Mrs. Carter:

You asked me if there is any one letter style that is used more than the others. Probably more business concerns use the block style than any other, because its marginal uniformity saves time for the typist. Many companies are adopting the full-block style, however, because it saves even more time than the block. This letter is an example of the block style.

As you can see, the inside address is blocked and paragraph beginnings are aligned with the left margin, as they are in the full-block form. Open punctuation may be used in the address.

The dateline and reference line are flush with the right margin. The dateline is two lines below the letterhead, and the reference line is two lines below the dateline. The complimentary close begins slightly to the right of the center of the page. Both lines of the signature are aligned with the complimentary close.

I do not advocate including the initials of the person dictating in the identification line, because his or her name is typed in the signature.

Sincerely,

Mary A. De Vries
Managing Editor

cf

Figure 47. **Semiblock Style. The distinguishing feature of a semiblock style of letter is that although the inside address and salutation begin flush with the left-hand margin, the first line of each paragraph is indented five to ten spaces. The dateline and reference line are flush with the right-hand margin. All lines of the typed reference are aligned with the complimentary close. Open punctuation may be used.**

[LETTERHEAD]

July 16, 19—

Ms. Paula Anderson
The Modern School for Secretaries
12 Harrington Place
Greenpoint, NJ 07201

Dear Ms. Anderson:

Thank you for your letter requesting a semiblock style letter to add to your correspondence manual. Most companies have a definite preference in letter style. Some leading business corporations prefer that all letters be typed in semiblock style. This style combines an attractive appearance with utility. Many private secretaries, who are not usually concerned with mass production of correspondence, favor it.

This style differs from the block form in only one respect—the first line of each paragraph is indented five to ten spaces. As in all letters, there is a double space between paragraphs.

The dateline is flush with the right margin, two to four lines below the letterhead. The complimentary close begins slightly to the right of the center of the page. All lines of the signature are aligned with the complimentary close. Open punctuation may be used in the address.

Because the name of the person dictating is typed in the signature, his or her initials are not necessary in the identification line.

Sincerely,

Nancy Davis
Chairperson, Business
Education Department

cf

Figure 48.   Official Style. The distinguishing feature of the official style letter is that the inside address is placed below the signature, flush with the left-hand margin, instead of before the salutation. The identification line and enclosure notations, if any, are typed two lines below the last line of the address. Open punctuation may be used. This style is especially appropriate for personal letters in business.

[LETTERHEAD]

July 16, 19—

Dear Miss Kennedy:

Every correspondence manual should include a sample of the official style.   It is used in many personal letters written by executives and professional persons and looks unusually well on the executive-style letterhead.

The structural parts of the letter differ from the semiblock arrangement only in the position of the inside address.   The salutation is placed two to five lines below the dateline, depending on the length of the letter.   It establishes the left margin of the letter.   The inside address is written in block form, flush with the left margin, from two to five lines below the final line of the signature.   Open punctuation may be used in the address.

The identification line, if used, should be placed two lines below the last line of the address, and the enclosure mark two lines below that.   Because the name of the person dictating is typed in the signature, it is not necessary for the letter to carry an identification line.   The typist's initials may be on the carbon of the letter but should not be on the original.

Sincerely yours,

(Mrs.) Leslie Thomas
Correspondence Secretary

Miss Janice Kennedy
The Modern School for Secretaries
12 Harrington Place
Greenpoint, NJ 07201

Figure 49. Simplified Style. The distinguishing feature of the simplified style of letter is that the salutation and complimentary close are omitted. There are no indentations and everything is typed flush left. The initials of the person dictating are not included in the identification line. Open punctuation may be used in the inside address.

[LETTERHEAD]

July 16, 19—

Mr. William Wyatt
The Modern School for Secretaries
12 Harrington Place
Greenpoint, NJ 07201

SIMPLIFIED LETTER FORMAT

You asked for an illustration of the simplified letter style, Mr. Wyatt. This letter is an example of the modern, easy-to-type simplified format.

Unlike the other styles, this one omits the salutation and complimentary close. But it resembles the full-block format in that the structural parts are all positioned flush left. The subject line is typed in all capitals, flush left, without the word SUBJECT. The signature, too, is typed in all capitals, flush left, in one line.

Businesses that choose this style of letter, Mr. Wyatt, typically mention the recipient's name in the opening and closing paragraphs.

CYNTHIA R. RITTER—OFFICE MANAGER

ml

Figure 50. The Memo Format. The memo format allows fast and easy typing. Information is easily filled in at predetermined positions in the heading. The body is typed in block fashion. The initials of the person dictating are not included in the identification line.

[LETTERHEAD]

To: _____Susan Eddington_____   From: _____Lois Stanford_____

Subject: _____Memo Format_____   Date: _____July 16, 19—_____

Memo styles vary from simple notes to standard multiple-copy forms, sold in office supply stores, to company-designed memo letterheads. Most forms include guide words such as To, From, and Date at the top of the page. Some also include a subject line at the top and a signature line at the bottom of the page.

Paragraphs are usually typed flush left, with no indentation. The sender's initials may be typed below the last paragraph. Other notations such as the enclosure notation are positioned the same as in a traditional letter.

                                    LS

rr

Enc.

Punctuation Style

Either mixed or open punctuation may be used in the structural parts of a letter. *Mixed punctuation* means punctuation marks after the city in the inside address and after the complimentary close. *Open punctuation* means the omission of punctuation marks after these parts. Many firms with word-processing equipment use open punctuation to reduce keystrokes. Whether open or mixed punctuation is used in the address, a colon follows the salutation.

PRINCIPAL PARTS OF LETTERS

Dateline

The position of the dateline on the page depends on the style of letter used and the length of the letter. The dateline is usually typed from two to four lines below the letterhead (or more if the letter is very short). It should be flush with either the right- or left-hand margin, depending on the style of the letter.

How to type the dateline.   The following suggestions should be kept in mind when typing the dateline:

1. Date the letter the day it is dictated, not the day it is typed.
2. Type the date conventionally, all on one line (September 15, 19—). But note that the military and some other organizations place the day first (15 September 19—) and omit the comma.
3. Do not use *d, nd, rd, st,* or *th* following the day of the month (*not* September 15th).
4. Do not abbreviate or use figures for the month (*not* Sept. 15 or 9/15).
5. Do not spell out the day of the month or the year.

Reference Line

If a file reference is given in an incoming letter, include a reference line in your reply. Place your own reference beneath the incoming reference.

How to type the reference line.   When letterheads include a printed reference notation, such as *In reply please refer to,* type the reference line after it. Otherwise, type the reference line two lines beneath the date.

April 20, 19—

Your File 3476

Our File 2785

"Personal" Notation

A letter or envelope should not be marked "Personal" or "Confidential" as a device to catch the attention of a busy recipient. These words should be used only when no one but the addressee is supposed to see the letter.

How to type the "personal" notation. Type the word *Personal* or *Confidential* flush left four lines above the inside address (or two lines below the reference line), which is at the top of the letter. You may underline the notation to make it more noticeable.

Inside Address

What the inside address contains. The inside address includes the name and address of the addressee. In addressing an individual in a company, the inside address contains both the individual's name and that of the company and may also contain the individual's business title.

> John Jones
> The Mississippi Electrical Power
>   and Light Company
> 148 West Tenth Street
> Jackson MS 39201

Where to type the inside address. Begin the inside address at the left-hand margin of the letter, not less than two or more than twelve lines below the dateline. The exact position of the first line of the address depends on the length of the letter. The inside address should not extend beyond the middle of the page. Carry over part of an extremely long line to a second line and indent the carry-over line three spaces. Single-space the address even if the body of the letter is double-spaced.

How to type the inside address. Follow these guidelines in typing the inside address:

1. The inside address should correspond exactly with the official name of the company addressed. If *Company, Co., The, Inc.,* or *&* is part of the company's official name, use the form shown by the company title. Punctuate the name according to the company's official style.

> ABC Company Inc.
> ABC Company, Inc.
> ABC Co., Inc.

2. Do not precede the street number with a word or a sign or with a room number.

70 Fifth Avenue (*not* No. 70 Fifth Avenue or #70 Fifth
   Avenue)
70 Fifth Avenue, Room 305, (*not* Room 305, 70 Fifth Avenue)

Use a *post office box number* in preference to a street address, if you
know it.

3. Spell out the numerical names of streets and avenues if they are
   numbers of twelve or under. When figures are used, do not follow
   with *d, st,* or *th.* Use figures for all house numbers except *One.*
   Separate the house number from a numerical name of a thor-
   oughfare with a space, a hyphen, and a space. Authorities give
   different rules for writing addresses, but the following are widely
   used forms.

> 23 East Twelfth Street
> 23 East 13 Street
> One Fifth Avenue
> 2 Fifth Avenue
> 234 - 72 Street

4. Never abbreviate the name of a city, unless the abbreviation is
   standard, such as *St. Louis* and *St. Paul.* For the names of states,
   territories, and United States possessions, use the abbreviations published by the U.S. Postal Service (see chapter 18, page
   566).

5. Use no more than two spaces between the last letter of a state
   name and the first digit of the postal zip code.

6. Even if there is no street address, put the city, state, and zip code
   on the same line.

7. Do not abbreviate business titles or positions, such as president,
   secretary, and sales manager. *Mr., Mrs., Miss,* or *Ms.* precedes
   the individual's name even when the business title is used. But
   do not use two titles referring to the same thing (*not* Dr.
   Morris Anderson, M.D.). If a person's business title is short,
   place it on the first line; if it is long, place it on the second
   line.

> Mr. James E. Lambert, President
> Lambert & Woolf Company
> 1005 Tower Street
> Cleveland, OH 44900

> Mr. George F. Moore
> Advertising Manager
> Price & Patterson
> 234 Seventh Avenue
> New York NY 10023

However, the modern trend is to omit the business title if it makes the address run over four lines. For example, many business writers would omit *Advertising Manager* in the above example.

8. In addressing an individual in a firm, corporation, or group, place the individual's name on the first line and the company's name on the second line. When addressing a letter *to the attention of* such individual, place the person's name in an attention line two lines below the address.

9. Do not hyphenate a title unless it represents a combination of two offices (secretary-treasurer) or if it contains the word *vice* (vice-president).

10. When writing to the officer of a company who holds several offices, use only the title of the highest office, unless letters from the officer are signed differently.

11. If a letter is addressed to a particular department in a company, place the name of the company on the first line and the name of the department on the second line.

12. Type the names of two or more persons in an inside address, one above the other, with no space between them.

> Ms. Janice Smith
> Mr. Rod Boyleston
> Computer Consultants, Inc.
> 1811 First Avenue
> Milwaukee WI 12346

Attention Line

Business letters addressed to a firm are often directed to the attention of an individual by the use of an attention line, in preference to addressing the letter to the individual. This practice ensures that the letter will be opened promptly by someone in the firm even if the person to whom it is directed is not available.

How to type the attention line.   Type the attention line two lines below the address. The word *of* is not necessary. The attention line has no punctuation and is not underscored. When a letter addressed to a firm has an attention line, the salutaiton is general, for example: *Gentlemen,* or *Ladies,* or *Ladies and Gentlemen,* because the salutation is to the firm, not the individual. It is permissible to direct the letter to the attention of an individual without including his or her first name or initials, if they are unknown.

Preferable:	Attention Walter R. Richardson
Permissible:	Attention Mr. Richardson

Salutation

Where to type the salutation.   Type the salutation two lines below the inside address, flush with the left-hand margin. If an attention line is used, type the salutation two lines below the attention line.

How to type the salutation.   Capitalize the first word, the title, and the name. Do not capitalize *dear* when *my* precedes it, but do capitalize *my,* thus *My dear Mr. Jones* (formal).

Use a colon following the salutation. A comma is used only in personal or informal social letters, particularly those written in longhand.

How to select the right forms of salutation: An informal salutation is used in business letters whether or not the letter writer is acquainted with the addressee, thus *Dear Mr.* instead of the more formal *My dear Mr.* and the antiquated *My dear Sir.* (See the chart in chapter 18, pages 578–603, for the correct salutation to use when addressing people in honorary or official positions.)

1. Never use a designation of any kind after a salutation.

   Dear Mr. Roberts: (*not* Dear Mr. Roberts, C.P.A.:)

2. Never use a business title or designation of position in a salutation (except in references to high officials: *Dear Mr. President* for the president of the United States).

Right:	Dear Mr. Adams:
	Dear Mr. Secretary: (U.S. Cabinet)
Wrong:	Dear Secretary: (business firm)
	Dear Secretary Ames: (business firm)

3. If a letter addressed to a company is directed to the attention of an individual, the salutation is to the company (for example, *Ladies and Gentlemen*), not to the individual.

4. Follow a title with the surname.

Dear Professor Ames: (*not* Dear Professor:)

5. The salutation in a letter that is not addressed to any particular person or firm, such as a general letter of recommendation, is *To Whom It May Concern*. Note that each word begins with a capital letter.

6. The salutation in a letter addressed to a group composed of men and women is *Ladies and Gentlemen;* to a married couple, *Dear Mr. and Mrs. Marsh*. Several alternative salutations may be used for professionals who are husband and wife and for a professional woman married to an untitled man:

   Dear *Dr.* and *Mrs.* Marsh:
   Dear *Drs.* Marsh: (if both are doctors)
   Dear *Dr.* and *Mr.* Marsh: (if he is untitled; the professional person is mentioned first)

7. When the gender is unknown, use the person's first name in the salutation.

Dear M. L. Watson:

How to address women.   Follow these rules in letters addressed to women:

1. Do not use *Miss* as a salutation unless it is followed by a name.

Dear Miss Brown: (*not* Dear Miss:)

2. If the letter is addressed to a firm of women, the salutation is *Ladies* or *Mesdames*. Do not use "Dear" or "My dear" with either of these salutations.

Ladies:
Mesdames:

3. The salutation to two women with the same name is:

Dear Mss. Smith: (married or unmarried)
Dear Mesdames Smith: (unmarried)
Dear Miss Smith and Mrs. Smith: *or* Ladies: (one married and the
   other unmarried)

Use *Mss.* unless you know that the reader would prefer *Mesdames, Misses,* or
Miss / Mrs.

Subject Line

Subject lines make it necessary for the writer to devote the first
paragraph of his or her letter to a routine explanation of the subject of the
letter; they also facilitate the distribution of mail to various departments
and expedite subject filing.

How to type the subject line.   Center the subject line two spaces
beneath the salutation unless the full-block or simplified style of letter
(figures 45, 49) is used; then type the subject line flush with the left-hand
margin. Never place the subject line before the salutation. It is part of the
body of the letter, not of the heading.

Sometimes the subject line is preceded by *In re* (legal field) or *Subject.*
The trend is to omit these words, except in legal letters. No punctuation
follows *In re* but a colon follows *Subject.* The important words in a subject
line are capitalized. The line also may be typed in all capital letters or
underlined, but the trend is to omit the underlining.

Body

How to type the body.   Follow these suggestions for the body of a
letter:

1. Single-space the body unless the letter is very short. Single-space a
   short letter if half-sheet letterheads are used.
2. Double-space between paragraphs.
3. When the block or simplified style of letter is used, begin each line
   flush with the left-hand margin.
4. When an indented style (such as the semiblock or official letter) is
   used, indent the first line of each paragraph five to ten spaces.
5. Always indent paragraphs when a letter is double-spaced.

How to set up enumerated material in the body of the letter. These guidelines apply to itemized lists in letters:

1. Indent five spaces from the left margin of the letter—more if necessary to emphasize the indentation.
2. Precede each item with a number, followed by a period (or enclose the number in parentheses).
3. Begin each line of the indented material two spaces to the right of the number.
4. Single-space the material within each item but double-space between items.

How to write dates. Usually, in the body of the letter, a date is written as *March 5*. When the day precedes the month, write out the day: *fifth of March* or *5th of March*.

Complimentary Close

Where to type the complimentary close. Type the complimentary close two lines below the last line of the letter. Begin it slightly to the right of the page, except in the full-block or simplified style. It should never extend beyond the right margin of the letter. In letters of more than one page, at least two lines should be on the page with the close.

How to type the complimentary close. Capitalize only the first word. Follow the complimentary close with a comma. (This is often preferred practice even when open punctuation is used in the inside address.)

How to select correct forms of complimentary close. As with salutations, the preferred practice today is to use a warm, friendly complimentary close, thus: *Sincerely, Sincerely yours, Cordially, Cordially yours, Regards, Best regards, Best wishes*. When writing to a company, *Sincerely* is preferable to *Cordially*. (See the chart in chapter 18, pages 578–603, for the correct complimentary close to use in letters to persons in official or honorary positions.)

Signature Line

What the signature contains. The signature to a business letter may consist of the typed name of the company, the signature of the writer, and the typed name of the writer and his or her business title. Some authorities recommend using the firm name when the letter is contractual. (For the use of *I* or *we* in letters, see chapter 14, page 451.) The trend is to omit the firm name, except in a signature to formal documents. Also, the typed name of the writer should be omitted if it appears *on the letterhead*. The inclusion in the signature of the writer's business title or position indicates that he or she is writing the letter in an official capacity.

Firms of attorneys, certified public accountants, and the like frequently sign letters manually with the firm name, particularly if the letter expresses a professional opinion or gives professional advice.

Where to type the signature. When the firm name is included in the signature, type it two lines below the complimentary close, the writer's name four lines below the firm name, with the writer's position either on the same line or on the next line. When the firm name is not included, type the writer's name and position four lines below the complimentary close.

Align the signature with the first letter of the complimentary close. The lines of the signature should be blocked, unless an unusually long line makes it necessary to have a carryover line (which would be indented three spaces). No line of the signature should extend beyond the right-hand margin of the letter.

> David Hillsborough
> Research Coordinator and
> Activities Director

How to type the signature. Follow these rules for the correct style of typed signature line and the accompanying handwritten (signed) signature:

1. Type the firm name in capitals, exactly as it appears on the letterhead.

> Sincerely yours,
>
> ACCOUNTING SERVICE COMPANY, INC.
>
> *Keith Norwood*
>
> Keith Norwood
> Treasurer

Never use the title *Mr.* unless it is necessary to show that the signer is a man.

Leslie Carter

(Mr.) Leslie Carter

2. Type the signature exactly as the dictator signs his or her name. (Do not type the name and title if this information is already printed at the top of the letter along with the letterhead address.)

Right:

Richard P. Miller

Richard P. Miller
President

Wrong:

Richard P. Miller

R. P. Miller
President

3. Business titles and degree letters follow the typed signature. No title precedes either the written or typed signature except *Miss* or *Mrs.* (unless *Mr.* or *Ms.* is necessary to clarify gender).

Bernard Frost

Bernard Frost, Ph.D.

Paula Addison

(Mrs.) Paula Addison

How to type signatures for women. These guidelines apply to the signatures of women:

1. An *unmarried woman* may precede her typed signature with *Miss* in

parentheses or omit it. (If she omits it, you should assume she wants to be addressed as *Ms.*)

Nora Kingston   *Nora Kingston*
(Miss) Nora Kingston   Nora Kingston

2. A *married woman* may omit her title, thereby indicating that she prefers to be addressed as *Ms.* or, by using it, indicate that she prefers you use *Mrs.* in addressing her. Her signature line also indicates whether she prefers that you use her maiden name, married name, or both of them combined. With her married name or maiden and married names combined, she may precede her typed signature with *Mrs.* in parentheses. She may also type her full married name (with husband's first name) in parentheses beneath the handwritten signature; this form is compulsory for formal social usage.

Janet Houston
Janet Houston

Janet Farraday-Houston
Janet Farraday-Houston

Janet Houston
(Mrs.) Janet Houston

Janet Farraday-Houston
(Mrs.) Janet Farraday-Houston

Janet Houston
(Mrs. Arnold K. Houston)

Janet Farraday
Janet Farraday

3. A *widow* signs her name as she did before her husband's death (follow the forms for a married woman, above).

4. Assuming that a *divorcee* does not use her maiden name, she may sign her first name, with or without the initial of her maiden name, and her former husband's surname. The typed signature is the same as the written signature and may be preceded by *Mrs.* in parentheses, or she may omit the title to indicate that she prefers to be addressed as *Ms.* The typed signature also may combine her maiden name with her former husband's surname without a first name (formal social usage) or use her first name with maiden name and her former husband's surname (with no title or, if she prefers, preceded by *Mrs.* or *Miss*). If she uses her maiden name, she may use *Miss* or omit the title to indicate that she prefers to be addressed as *Ms.*

Right:

Eleanor M. Davis

(Mrs.) Eleanor M. Davis

(Mrs. Montgomery Davis)

Eleanor Montgomery Davis

(Miss) Eleanor Montgomery Davis

(Mrs.) Eleanor Montgomery Davis

Eleanor Montgomery
Eleanor Montgomery

Eleanor Montgomery
(Miss) Eleanor Montgomery

Wrong:

Eleanor M. Davis
(Mrs. John R. Davis)

How to type the secretary's signature. When you sign your employer's name to a letter, place your initials immediately below it.

Hiram R. Jones
rg
Hiram R. Jones
President

When you sign a letter in your own name as secretary to your employer, do not include his or her initials unless another person in the organization has the same name. Always precede your employer's name by a title.

Right:

Elizabeth Mason
Secretary to Mr. Nelson

Wrong:

Elizabeth Mason
Secretary to Mr. R. S. Nelson

Identification Line

The identification line shows who dictated the letter and who typed it. The only purpose of the identification line is for reference by the business organization *writing* the letter. The writer's name is typed in the signature.

How to type the identification line. Unless company rules require otherwise, type nothing but your initials in the identification line and do not show them on the original of the letter.

If your company requires it, type the initials of both the writer and the stenographer flush with the left-hand margin, two lines below the last line of the signature. If the official style of letter is used (figure 48), the identification line is typed two lines below the inside address. When the person who signs the letter has not dictated it, type his or her intials first, those of the person dictating next, and those of the transcriber last.

JC:MK:ul

Enclosure Notation

How to type the enclosure notation. When a letter contains enclosures, type the word *Enclosure* (or *Enclosures*) or the abbreviation *Enc.* (or *Encs.*) flush with the left-hand margin two lines beneath the identification line. If there is more than one enclosure, indicate the number. If the enclosures are of special importance, identify them. If an enclosure is to be returned, make a notation to that effect.

RPE:es   RPE:es

Enclosure   Enc. 2

RPE:es

Enc. Policy 35-4698-M (to be returned)

RPE:es

Enc. Cert. ck. $2,350 (Mtge., Nelson to Jones)

Mailing Notation

How to type the mailing notation.   When a letter is sent by any method other than regular mail, type a notation of the exact method on the envelope (see page 326), and make a similar notation *on the copy* of the letter flush left two lines beneath the enclosure notation or, if none is used, two lines below the identification initials. (Some companies type the notation on the original as well as the carbon copy.)

Copy-Distribution Notation

How to type carbon-copy, photocopy, and reprographic-copy notations.   When a copy is to be sent to another person, type the distribution notation flush with the left-hand margin two lines below all other notations.

> cc: Mildred Parsons
> pc: Mr. S. A. Williams
> rc: Linda Caruthers

The abbreviation *cc* is used on a carbon copy. *Copy, c,* or *pc* is used when the copy is a photocopy; *rc,* when it is a reprographic copy.

How to type the blind-copy notation.   Type the blind-copy notation *bc* in the same position as a carbon-copy notation *on the copies only*. This indicates that the addressee of the letter does not know that a copy was sent to anyone.

> bc: Samuel Felshner

Postscript

A postscript is an added thought unrelated to the body of the letter (*not* something you simply forgot to type in the body itself).

How to type the postscript.   When it is necessary to add a postscript, type it two lines below the identification line or the last notation on the letter. If you use a semiblock (indented) style of letter (figure 47), indent the left margin of the postscript the same as the paragraphs in the body. Type it flush left if you use a full-block (figure 45), block (figure 46), or simplified (figure 49) format. You may include or omit the abbreviation *P.S.* Use *P.P.S.* with a second postscript. Type the writer's initials immediately after the last word in the postscript.

Heading on Continuation Pages

If the letter runs to two or more pages, use a plain sheet for the additional page, without a letterhead but of the same size and quality of paper as the letterhead. (Your company may have special stationery for the continuation pages.) There is no need to use the word *continued* at the bottom of the first page. The fact that no signature appears at the end of the page makes it obvious that another page follows.

How to type the continuation heading. The heading should contain the name of the addressee, the number of the page, and the date, and the margins should be exactly the same as those for the first sheet. Leave two or more lines between the continuation heading and the body of the letter.

David Jones   2   May 5, 19—

Mary Brower
September 12, 19—
page two

You should have at least two lines of the body of the letter, exclusive of complimentary close, signature, and so forth on the continuation sheet.

PRINCIPAL PARTS OF MEMOS

Guide Words

A memo heading is often printed at the top of the page just beneath the name and address. This heading consists of guide words such as *Date, To, From,* and *Subject.* Instead of typing a dateline, inside address, salutation, subject line, and so on, as you would do with a traditional letter, you simply fill in the appropriate information after each guide word (see figure 50). Major words in the subject line are capitalized the same as they are in a letter (see page 314).

Body

How to type the body. Follow these guidelines for typing the body of a memo:

1. Type the body of a memo single-spaced or double-spaced, depending on its size, the same as the body of a letter (see page 314).
2. Paragraphs may be indented but are often typed flush left like a block letter (see figure 50).
3. Since the memo has no salutation, the first paragraph is typed two or more lines after the last line of guide words.

Signature Initials

How to type the signature initials. One style of memo has a preprinted line at the bottom of the page for the writer to include his signature, but most memos omit the signature line. Some writers, however, like to have their initials typed two lines beneath the last line of the body, positioned slightly to the right of the page center. Others do not want their initials *typed* on the memo, but they include their handwritten initials in this position.

Identification Line

How to type the identification line. Type the identification line flush left two lines beneath the last line of the body or two lines below the signature initials, whichever is last. Follow the instructions for using an identification line in a letter on page 321.

Enclosure Notation

How to type the enclosure notation. Type the enclosure notation flush left two lines beneath the identification line. Follow the instructions for using an enclosure notation in a letter on page 321.

Copy-Distribution Notation

How to type the copy-distribution notation. Type the copy-distribution notation *(cc, c, pc, copy, rc)* flush left two lines below all other notations. Type the blind-copy notation *(bc)* only on the file copy and the copy of the intended recipient. Follow the instruction for using a copy-distribution notation in a letter on page 322.

Postscript

How to type the postscript. Type a postscript—flush left or indented the same as the paragraphs in the body—two lines below the last notation. Follow the instructions for using a postscript in a letter on page 322.

Heading on Continuation Pages

How to type the continuation heading. Type the heading on a memo continuation page the same as you would for a letter. Follow the instructions on page 323.

ENVELOPES

OCR Addressing

How to type the address. Figures 51 and 52 show commonly used styles of address on envelopes (note the use of all capitals and omission of punctuation as preferred by the U.S. Postal Service for optical character reading).

Figure 51. Envelope Showing Correct Placement of Personal Notation.

```
┌─────────────────────────────────────────────────────────┐
│                                                          │
│   [RETURN ADDRESS]                                       │
│                                                          │
│                                                          │
│      PERSONAL                                            │
│      ─────────                                           │
│               MR RS JACKSON                              │
│               NORTHERN MANUFACTURING CO                  │
│               25 W 79 ST RM 600                          │
│               MILWAUKEE WI 12345                         │
│                                                          │
│                                                          │
└─────────────────────────────────────────────────────────┘
```

Figure 52.   Envelope Showing Correct Placement of Attention Line and Special Delivery Notation.

```
[RETURN ADDRESS]


                                    SPECIAL DELIVERY

        FTM: 0021-1-86
        NORTHERN MANUFACTURING CO
        ATTN MR. RS JACKSON
        25 W 79 ST RM 600
        MILWAUKEE WI 12345
```

The items in the envelope address are usually the same as those in the inside address (see page 309). It is important that you use the official post office abbreviation of the state (see chapter 18, pages 566–68) followed by the zip code. The name of a foreign country is written in capitals as the last line in an address on the envelope but with only initial capitals in the inside address. For a list of postal address abbreviations, consult the national zip code directory, available to the public for reference in most post offices.

Although companies have their own preferred style of address, and the envelope address should include the same data as the letter's inside address, the Postal Service recommends the following: that you write the address in block style at least 1 inch from the left edge and at least $\frac{5}{8}$ inch from the bottom edge; that you put unit numbers such as a suite immediately after the street on the same line; that you put a box number before a station name; and that you type the address in all capitals without punctuation.

With window envelopes, the insert should show at least $\frac{1}{4}$ inch space at the left, right, and bottom edges of the window.

Where to type the personal notation.   Type a personal notation in all capitals to the left of and two lines above the address block. It may be underscored. See figure 51.

Where to type the attention line: Type the attention line immediately beneath the company name or left of the address block on any line above the second line from the bottom of the address. See figure 52.

Where to type the mail instruction. Type mail instructions such as *SPECIAL DELIVERY* in all capitals about two lines below the postage area. See figure 52.

Where to type account numbers. Nonaddress data such as account numbers or dates should be placed immediately above the first line in the address block. See figure 52.

FORMS OF ADDRESS

General Rules

Follow these guidelines in addressing men, women, and firms. (For the correct forms of address to those who hold official or honorary positions see the chart in chapter 18, pages 578–603.)

Titles. Always precede a name by a title, unless initials indicating an academic degree or *Esq.* follow the name. The use of a business title, a position, or *Sr., Jr., II, III,* after a name does not take the place of a title. (Some writers omit the comma before the abbreviations *Jr.* and *Sr.* in a name, but you should follow the style used by the person in question.)

> Mr. Ralph P. Edwards III, President (*not* Ralph P. Edwards III,
>   President)

Degrees. Initials or abbreviations indicating degrees and other honors are sometimes placed after the name of the person addressed. Use only the initials of the highest degree; more than one degree may be used, however, if the degrees are in different fields. List the degree pertaining to the person's profession first, for example, *John Jones, LL.D., Ph.D.,* if he is a practicing attorney by profession. A scholastic title is not used in combination with the abbreviation indicating that degree, but another title may be used in combination with abbreviations indicating degrees.

> Dr. Roberta E. Saunders (*preferred*) or Roberta E. Saunders, Ph.D.
>   (*not* Dr. Roberta E. Saunders, A.B., A.M., Ph.D.)
> Dr. Ralph Jones (*preferred*) or Ralph Jones, M.D. (*not* Dr. Ralph
>   Jones, M.D.)
> The Reverend Perry E. Moore, D.D., LL.D. (*degrees pertain to field
>   other than title indicates*)
> Professor Lola Markham (*not* Professor Lola Markham, Ph.D.)

Esquire. The abbreviation *Esq.* may be used in addressing prominent attorneys or other high-ranking professional men and women who do not have other titles. *Mr., Mrs., Miss,* or *Ms.* does not precede the name when *Esq.* is used. In fact, no other title is used with *Esq.*

> The Honorable Richard P. Davis (*not* The Honorable Richard P.
>   Davis, Esq.)
> Allison D. Wells, Esq. (*not* Ms. Allison D. Wells, Esq.)
> Nathan Rogers, Jr., Esq. (*not* Mr. Nathan Rogers, Jr., Esq.)

Note: The title *Esquire* is commonly used in England and its colonies. There it is the proper title to use in addressing the heads of business firms, banking executives, doctors, and the like (Robert E. Meadfe, Esq., M.D.; Laurence D. Goode, Esq., M.D.).

Rules for Companies

Use the single-sex designations *Messrs.* or *Mesdames* only if the companies consist solely of men or women. *Messrs.* or *Mesdames* may be used in addressing a firm—but not a company—of men or women only when the names denote *individuals.* Do not use *Messrs.* or *Mesdames* as a form of address for the corporations or other business organizations that bear impersonal names.

> American Manufacturing Company (*not* Messrs. American
>   Manufacturing Company)
> Mesdames Marvin, Tobin, and Smart (*not* Mesdames Marvin, Tobin,
>   and Smart, Inc.)
> James Marshall & Sons (*not* Messrs. James Marshall & Sons)

Rules for Men

Titles: Use the title *Mr.* when a man does not have a professional or honorary title such as *Dr.,* unless initials indicating a degree or *Esq.* follow the name.

> Mr. John Wyatt
> Professor John Wyatt
> John Wyatt, M.D.
> John Wyatt, Esq.

Rules for Women

Firm composed of women. In addressing a firm composed of women either married or unmarried, use *Mesdames* or *Mmes.*

Mesdames Cooper and Hill

Unmarried woman. Use *Ms.* unless you know that the woman prefers *Miss.*

Ms. Donna Devane

Married woman. In formal social usage, a married woman is addressed by her husband's full name preceded by *Mrs.* In business, she may be addressed either by her husband's first and last name preceded by *Mrs.* or by her first name and her maiden name preceded by *Mrs.* or *Ms.* or by her first name and her maiden name preceded by *Ms.* or *Miss.* Use *Ms.* with her first name and married last name unless you know that she prefers another form. Some women combine their maiden and married names, with or without a hyphen (Mrs. [or Ms.] Janice Evans-Sloane).

Married name:	Mrs. William Mackenzie *(formal social or business)*
	Ms. Carol Mackenzie *(business)*
	Mrs. Carol Mackenzie *(business)*
Maiden name:	Ms. Carol Neitzer *(business)*
	Miss Carol Neitzer *(business)*
Maiden and married names:	Ms. Carol Neitzer-Mackenzie *(business)*
	Mrs. Carol Neitzer-Mackenzie *(business)*

Widow. In formal social usage, a widow is addressed by her husband's full name preceded by *Mrs.* In business, follow the rules for a married woman.

Divorcee. If a divorcee retains her married name, the title *Mrs.* is preferable to *Miss.* (If she uses her maiden name, she may use either *Ms.* or *Miss.* In business she may be addressed by her first name combined with her married last names preceded by *Mrs., Miss,* or *Ms.* or by her maiden name preceded by *Miss* or *Ms.* Use *Ms.* with her married name unless you know that she prefers another form. In formal social usage, she is addressed by her maiden name combined with her married name preceded by *Mrs.* (no first name.).

Married name:	Ms. Margaret Weeks *(business)*
	Mrs. Margaret Weeks *(business)*
Maiden name:	Ms. Margaret Barkley *(business or informal social)*
	Miss Margaret Barkley *(business or informal social)*
Maiden and married names:	Ms. Margaret Barkley Weeks *(business)*
	Miss Margaret Barkley Weeks *(business)*
	Mrs. Margaret Barkley Weeks *(business)*
	Mrs. Barkley Weeks *(formal social)*

Wife of a titled man. Do not address a married woman who has no title by her husband's title. Address her as *Mrs. Robert E. Adams* or *Mrs. R. E. Adams.* If she is addressed jointly with her husband, the correct form is *Dr. and Mrs. Robert E. Adams, Judge and Mrs. Irving Levey.*

Professional women. Address a woman with a professional title by her title followed by her first and last names. A married woman may use her maiden name or maiden and married names combined in practicing her profession if she prefers.

When writing to a professional woman and her husband jointly, as husband and wife and in social correspondence, include the woman's title: *Dr.* John Williams and *Dr.* Mary Williams, *Drs.* John and Mary Williams. When a professional woman is married to a man without a title, keep the woman's title: *Dr.* Mary and *Mr.* John Williams (the titled person preceding the untitled person). If possible, however, follow the style preferred by the man and woman as shown in previous correspondence with them.

Man and woman. When writing to a man and woman in their individual capacities, address them by their respective titles, placing one name under the other.

Mrs. Lynda Russell
Mr. Adam L. Matthews

When you do not know whether an addressee is a man or a woman, omit the title in the inside address of a letter and use the person's first name in the salutation.

M. L. Dorsey
1133 North Avenue
Prescott AZ 86301

Dear M. L. Dorsey:

For the correct form of addressing women holding honorary or official positions, see page 332 and the chart in chapter 18, pages 578–603.

Rules for Prominent Persons

Persons with name unknown. You should make every effort to learn the name of the person addressed, as well as his or her title. (For those few instances in which the name is omitted, see the forms of address chart in chapter 18, pages 578–603.) If you know the title only, address the person by the title prefaced by *The*. For example, *The Lieutenant Governor of Iowa*. The formal salutation would be *Sir* or *Madam*.

Acting official. When a person is acting as an official, the word *Acting* precedes the title in the address but not in the salutation or spoken address. For example, *Acting Mayor of Memphis, Dear Mayor Blank*.

Former official. A person who has held an official position and is entitled to be addressed as *The Honorable* is addressed as *The Honorable* after retirement. The title itself, such as *Senator* or *Governor,* is not used in the address or salutation. Even a former president is called *Mr.* An exception to this practice is the title of *Judge*. A person who has once been a judge customarily retains the title even when addressed formally. Retired officers of the armed forces retain their titles, but their retirement is indicated as, for example, *Lieutenant General John D. Blank, USA, Retired*. (The military omits periods in designations such as *USA,* although they are often retained in traditional usage such as formal social correspondence.)

People with scholastic degrees. In many cases, the name in the address is followed by the abbreviation of a scholastic degree. (In the case of more than one degree, list the one pertaining to the person's profession first.) If you do not know whether the addressee has the degree, do not use the initials. Also, do not address a person by a scholastic title *(Dr.)* unless he or she actually possesses the degree that the title indicates *(Ph.D.)*.

Spouses. The wife of an American official does not share her husband's title. When they are addressed jointly, the address is, for example, *Ambassador and Mrs. Blank*. Nor does a husband share his wife's title. When they are addressed jointly, if he does not have a title, the contemporary forms of address are *Ambassador* Ruth Blank and *Mr.* J. W. Blank (the titled person preceding the untitled person), *Ambassador* Ruth and *Mr.* J. W. Blank, *Ambassador* and *Mr.* Blank. (See page 330 for guides to addressing a husband and wife when both are doctors and when the wife is a doctor and the husband is not.)

Women.   Women in official or honorary positions are addressed just as men in similar positions, except that *Madam* replaces *Sir,* and *Mrs., Miss,* or *Ms.* replaces *Mr.* Use *Ms.* unless you know that the woman prefers *Mrs.* or *Miss.*

HOW TO SELECT AND ORDER STATIONERY

Type and Size of Paper

Letter.   Traditional business letterhead is $8\frac{1}{2}$ by 11 inches and most envelopes, files, and business machines are geared to accommodate this size. It is referred to as "letterhead size," although letterheads in other sizes are used, as shown here in inches:

Baronial	$5\frac{1}{2}$ by $8\frac{1}{2}$
Executive, or Monarch	$7\frac{1}{4}$ by $10\frac{1}{2}$
Official	8 by $10\frac{1}{2}$
Standard	$8\frac{1}{2}$ by 11

Memo.   Memo sizes vary much more than letter sizes, from small note paper to the regular $8\frac{1}{2}$ by 11 inches. The half-sheet, or memo size, is $5\frac{1}{2}$ by $8\frac{1}{2}$ inches. Standard forms of almost any size can be purchased from office suppliers. Some officers decide on an appropriate size for their communications and have their own memo letterhead printed using the same design as found on their company letterhead stationery. In selecting a size for memo stationery to be sent outside the firm, be certain to consider the size of the envelope into which it must fit.

Letterhead Design

General characteristics.   Businesses use letterheads to convey a desired image. The typography, logo (emblem), color, and arrangement of these items may be conservative, bold, or anything else a firm desires. The basic company stationery, used by most offices, may be white or colored stock (such as light beige or blue) and have black or colored type on the letterhead. The typical size is $8\frac{1}{2}$ by 11 inches.

Executive stationery. Letterheads for the personal use of top executives typically possess dignity, and their chief characteristic is simplicity, attained by black or some other conservative color engraved copy on pure white or cream paper of heavy substance and high quality. In addition to the company letterhead, the full name of the office is engraved at the left margin, with the title of the office the executive holds directly underneath it. The size of the sheet is sometimes smaller than standard letterhead. The two common types of paper are *laid* (with a pattern of parallel lines that give a ribbed appearance) and *wove* (with a smooth, soft finish).

An executive may use his or her business letterheads for all business correspondence. Personal stationery, informals, and foldover note paper are used for personal and social correspondence such as answers to formal invitations, letters of condolence, or answers to letters of condolence from personal friends. Personal writing paper may be engraved with the residence address alone, with both the executive's name and residence address, or with a monogram (common on foldover note paper). Personal stationery is usually the Executive, or Monarch, size ($7\frac{1}{4}$ by $10\frac{1}{2}$ inches) for men; personal stationery for women is usually smaller, although both men and women use the Executive size for social-business messages.

Continuation Sheets

Continuation sheets are frequently referred to as "second sheets." Technically, the reference is inaccurate. Second sheets are papers used for making multiple copies of letters and other documents.

Continuation sheets should be of the same size and quality as the letterhead. Some firms print their name and address in small type at the top of the continuation sheet, near the left-hand margin. Order these sheets when you order the letterhead paper. After you have placed two or three orders for stationery, you will be able to judge more accurately the proportion of continuation sheets to letterheads that you use.

Envelopes

Envelopes should be of the same quality and stock as the letterhead. The most popular sizes for business are:

No. 5 $\frac{1}{2}$ (Baronial)	4 $\frac{5}{8}$ by 5 $\frac{15}{16}$
No. 6 $\frac{3}{4}$ (Commercial)	3 $\frac{5}{8}$ by 6 $\frac{1}{2}$
No. 7 (Executive, or Monarch)	3 $\frac{7}{8}$ by 7 $\frac{1}{2}$
No. 9 (Official)	3 $\frac{7}{8}$ by 8 $\frac{7}{8}$
No. 10 (Standard)	4 $\frac{1}{8}$ by 9 $\frac{1}{2}$

Numbers $6\frac{3}{4}$, 9, and 10 accommodate $8\frac{1}{2}$- by 11-inch letterheads. The Executive, or Monarch, size is used with a letterhead size of $7\frac{1}{4}$ by $10\frac{1}{2}$ inches. The No. $5\frac{1}{2}$ Baronial is also sometimes used by business executives for personal stationery.

How to Order Stationery

Judging quality. The quality of paper may be judged by its appearance and use characteristics.

Determining weight. Paper weight (called "basis weight") is measured by the ream, which consists of five hundred sheets cut to a given standard size for that grade. The weight of the ream may be sixteen pounds, twenty pounds, twenty-four pounds, or more (or less). (Figure 53 indicates the most practical weights for various uses.) Stationery is usually selected in a twenty-pound weight or more. Lighter weights are often used for airmail stationery and for making carbon copies.

Placing orders. Get a written quotation that specifies the *weight* and *content* of paper and the kind of *engraving or printing* that will be on it. In placing your order, specify:

1. The quantity in sheets
2. The weight
3. The content (cotton, watermark rag, or good grade sulphite bond)
4. The grain: parallel to writing for typewriters; perpendicular to writing for duplicating processes (you may want to discuss this with your printer)
5. That the letterhead shall be printed on the "felt" side of the paper, or the top side (all but a careless printer will do this automatically)
6. The size

Figure 53.   Weights of Paper for Various Uses

Weight of Paper	
Use	*Substance Weight (In order of preference)*
Executive letterheads	24, 20
Company letterheads	24, 20
Personal or semibusiness letterheads	24, 20
Airmail letterheads [and carbon copies]	13, 9
Second-page letterheads	Same as letterhead
Branch office and salesperson's letterheads	20, 16
Circular or form letters	20, 24
Hotel, fraternal, or club letterheads	24, 20

Courtesy Hammermill Paper Company

7. The color
8. The previous order number if this is a repeat order
9. The supplier's reference number if it is an initial order
10. A sample letterhead from a previous printing, if available.

── Chapter 12 ──

Valuable Aids
for Productive Letter Writing

PLANNING A LETTER

Plan your communication as a whole before you start to write the first paragraph. A simple procedure follows:

1. Read carefully the letter you are answering and underscore in red or blue pencil the main points in it (if your office policy does not allow marking on original letters, make a photocopy or jot notes on a separate piece of paper).
2. Tell yourself the purpose of the letter.
3. Jot down an outline of what your answer should contain.
4. Collect all of the facts you need to reply.
5. Try to visualize your reader and adapt the letter to the recipient.

USING APPROPRIATE LANGUAGE

Stilted and Trite Expressions

A key objective in good letter writing—as in any writing—is to avoid stilted or worn-out expressions. To illustrate the improvement that results when stilted or trite phrases are eliminated, consider the following example of a business letter as originally written and then as rewritten:

Stilted and verbose language.   Notice the stiff, out-of-date style in this example.

Dear Sir:

Replying to your kind favor of the 15th inst. in which you inform us that the enameling sheets ordered by you have not come to hand, beg to advise we have checked up on this shipment and find same left our factory March 10 and should have reached you March 13. For your information wish to state that we are now tracing through the express company. If the shipment does not arrive by March 19, kindly wire us collect, and we will duplicate same.
Regretting the inconvenience caused you, we are,

Yours truly,

Clear and straightforward language.   Here the outmoded style has been transformed into a concise, businesslike, modern style:

Dear Mr. Bradley:

The shipment of enameling sheets that you asked about left our factory on March 10. It should have been delivered to you not later than March 13, so we have asked the express company to trace the shipment immediately.

If you do not receive the sheets by March 19, please call us collect, and we will start another shipment at once.

We are sorry that this delay occurred and assure you that we will do everything possible to expedite delivery.

Sincerely yours,

List of trite terms.   Here is a list of expressions that are stilted or trite and hence are not good usage and should be avoided.

acknowledge receipt of. Use *We received.*

advise. Used with too little discrimination and best reserved to indicate actual advice or information. Often *say* or *tell* is better—or nothing.

Poor: We wish to *advise* that your order was shipped April 7, 19—.
Better: Your order was shipped April 7, 19—.

and oblige. A needless appendage.

> *Poor:* Kindly ship the enclosed order *and oblige.*
> *Better:* Please ship the enclosed order *immediately.*

as per; per. Correctly used with Latin words *per annum* and *per diem.* Otherwise, *a, according to,* and the like are preferred.

> *Allowable:* Five dollars *per* yard
> *Better:* Five dollars *a* yard
>
> *Poor: As per* our telephone agreement
> *Better: As we agreed* by telephone; or *in accordance with* our telephone agreement
>
> *Poor: Per* our contract
> *Better: According to* our contract

ascertain. A more pompous way of saying *find out.*

> *Poor:* Can you *ascertain* the reason for the delay?
> *Better:* Can you *find out* the reason for the delay?

at all times. Often used with little meaning. Better to use *always.*

> *Poor:* We will be happy to talk with you *at all times.*
> *Better:* We will *always* be happy to talk with you.

at this time. Also unnecessary in most cases. Try *at present* or *now*—or nothing.

> *Poor:* We wish to advise that we are out of stock of handkerchiefs #1000 *at this time.*
> *Better:* Handkerchiefs #1000 are out of stock *now.*

at your convenience; at an early date. Trite, vague, and unnecessary in most cases. Be specific.

> *Indefinite:* Please notify us *at an early date.*
> *Better:* Please let us know *by return mail* (or *within ten days;* or *by the first of next month*).
>
> *Vague:* We would appreciate hearing from you *at your convenience.*
> *Better:* We would appreciate hearing from you *by return mail* (or *by the tenth of June*).

beg. Do not use old-fashioned expressions such as *beg to state, beg to advise,* and *beg to acknowledge.*

> *Poor:* In answer to yours of the 10th inst., *beg to state* . . .
> *Better:* In answer (or reply) to your letter of May 10, *we are pleased* . . .

consummate. A more pretentious word for *complete.*

> *Poor:* After we *consummate* the arrangements . . .
> *Better:* After we *complete* the arrangements . . .

contents carefully noted. Contributes little to a business letter.

> *Poor:* Yours of the 5th received and *contents carefully noted.*
> *Better:* The instructions outlined in your letter of June 5 have been followed in every detail.

duly. Unnecessary.

> *Poor:* Your request has been *duly* forwarded to our executive offices.
> *Better:* We have sent your request to our executive offices.

enclosed please find. Needless and faulty phraseology. The word *please* has little meaning in this instance. The word *find* is used improperly.

> *Poor: Enclosed please find* sample of our #1989 black film ribbon.
> *Better: We are enclosing* a sample of our #1989 black film ribbon.

encounter difficulty. A more pompous and dramatic expression for *have trouble.*

> *Poor:* If you *encounter difficulty* finding volunteers . . .
> *Better:* If you *have trouble* finding volunteers . . .

enlighten. A pretentious way of saying *tell.*

> *Poor:* Ray will *enlighten* you about it.
> *Better:* Ray will *tell* you about it.

esteemed. Too flowery and effusive.

> *Poor:* We welcomed your *esteemed* favor of the 9th.
> *Better:* Thank you for *your letter* of April 9.

favor. Do not use the word *favor* in the sense of letter, order, or check.

> *Poor:* Thank you for your *favor* of October 5.
> *Better:* Thank you for your *letter* of October 5.

forward. Do not use for *send.*

> *Poor:* Please *forward* a brochure to my office.
> *Better:* Please *send* a brochure to my office.

have before me. A worn-out expression.

> *Poor:* I *have before me* your complaint of the 10th.
> *Better: In answer* (or *reply*) to your letter of November 10 . . .

hereto. Often needless.

> *Poor:* We are attaching *hereto* a copy of our contract covering prices on linoleum.
> *Better:* We are attaching a copy of our contract covering prices on linoleum.

herewith. Often redundant.

> *Poor:* We enclose *herewith* a copy of our booklet.
> *Better:* We are pleased to enclose a copy of our booklet.

in re. Avoid. Use *regarding* or *concerning.*

> *Poor: In re* our telephone conversation of this morning . . .
> *Better: Regarding* our telephone conversation of this morning . . .

in the event that. Use *if* or *in case.*

> *Poor: In the event* that you are in the city Thursday . . .
> *Better: If* you are in the city *Thursday* . . .

initiate. A pompous substitute for *start* or *begin.*

> *Poor:* She plans to *initiate* work on the project tomorrow.
> *Better:* She plans to *start* work on the project tomorrow.

inquire. A pompous substitute for *ask.*

> *Poor:* May I *inquire* how many attended?
> *Better:* May I *ask* how many attended?

it is requested that. Simply say *please.*

> *Poor: It is requested that* you meet us at the restaurant.
> *Better: Please* meet us at the restaurant.

line. Do not use in place of *merchandise* or *line of goods.*

> *Poor:* Our salesman Joe Whitman will gladly show you our *line.*
> *Better:* Our salesman Joe Whitman will gladly show you our *merchandise* (or *line of goods*).

our Ms. Becker. Use *our representative Ms. Becker* or just *Ms. Becker.*

> *Poor: Our Ms. Becker* will call on you next Tuesday, May 10.
> *Better: Our representative Ms. Becker* will call on you next Tuesday, May 10.

procure. Simply say *get.*

> *Poor:* Did you *procure* the supplies?
> *Better:* Did you *get* the supplies?

recent date. Vague and unbusinesslike. Better to give the exact date.

> *Vague:* Your letter of *recent date* . . .
> *Definite:* Your letter of *June 2* . . .

render. Do not use for *do* or *offer.*

> *Poor:* We would like to *render* our assistance.
> *Better:* We would like to *offer* our assistance.

same. A poor substitute for one of the pronouns *it, they,* or *them.*

> *Poor:* Your order of the 5th received. Will ship *same* on the 10th.
> *Better:* Thank you for your order of March 5. We expect to ship *it* to you by the 12th of this month.

state. Often too formal. Better to use *say* or *tell.*

> *Poor:* We wish to *state* . . .
> *Better:* We are pleased to *tell* you (or *let you know*) . . .

take pleasure. A trite expression. Use *are pleased, are happy,* or *are glad.*

> *Poor:* We *take pleasure* in announcing our fall line of shoes.
> *Better:* We *are pleased* to announce our fall line of shoes for women.

thanking you in advance. Discourteous and implies that your request will be granted.

> *Poor:* Kindly mail me any information you may have about removing crabgrass. *Thanking you in advance* for the favor, I remain,
> *Better:* I would appreciate any information you may have about removing crabgrass.

under separate cover. Meaningless. Better to be specific and give the method of shipping.

> *Poor:* We are sending you *under separate cover* a copy of our pamphlet "How to Grow Lawns."
> *Better:* We are pleased to send you *by third-class mail* a copy of our pamphlet "How to Grow Lawns."

valued. Too effusive and suggestive of flattery. Better to omit.

> *Poor:* We appreciate your *valued* order given to our salesman Ryan McCall.
> *Better:* We appreciate the order you gave our salesman Ryan McCall.

wish to say; wish to state; would say. All are examples of needless, wordy phraseology. Simply omit.

Poor: Referring to your letter of the 10th, *wish to say* that we cannot fill your order before the first of December.

Better: In answer to your letter of March 10, we will be able to fill your order about December 1.

Unnecessary Words and Phrases

Many letter writers add unnecessary words to their phrases because of an erroneous idea that the padding gives emphasis or rounds out a sentence. For example, letter writers frequently speak of *"final* completion," *month of* January," or *"close* proximity." The completion is obviously final or it is not complete. January is obviously a month. Incidents in proximity are obviously close. Here is a list of padded phrases frequently used in business letters and other writing. The italicized words are completely unnecessary and should be omitted.

It came *at a time* when we were busy.
Leather depreciates *in value* slowly.
During *the year of* 19—, prices fell.
It will cost *the sum of* one hundred dollars.
At a meeting *held* in Philadelphia, the bylaws were amended.
We will ship these shoes *at a later date.*
In about two weeks' *time,* the tourist season begins.
In order to reach our goal, we must work harder.
The mistake *first* began because of a misunderstanding.
A *certain* person by the name of Bill Jones is here.
The *close* proximity of these two incidents surprises me.
It happened at *the hour of* noon.
We see some good in both *of them.*
In *the city of* Columbus, residential housing is scarce.
The body is made *out* of steel.
During the *course of the* campaign, four candidates withdrew.
Perhaps it may be that you are reluctant.
Our uniform *and invariable* rule is to reward senior employees first.
Someone *or other* must be responsible.
We are now *engaged in* building a new plant.
By *means of* this device we are able to detect surface lesions.
All that is necessary *for you to do* is to use common sense.
We have discontinued *the policy of* the late renewal penalty.
Will you please *arrange to* send the booklets.

Two words with the same meaning.   Some letter writers think that if one word does a job, two words add emphasis. Actually, the second word makes the thought less effective. Here are a few examples of "doubling."

> sincere and good wishes
> first and foremost
> appraise and determine
> experience together and contacts in
> deeds and actions
> optimism and encouragement
> refuse and decline
> unjust and unfair
> advise and inform
> at once and by return mail
> immediately and at once
> demand and insist
> right and proper
> obligation and responsibility

Favorite Words and Expressions

Avoid acquiring favorite words or expressions. They become habitual and your letters sound cut and dried. Some writers unintentionally overuse their pet expressions:

> *Poor: For your information,* the meeting will be Friday, August 11, 19—. A copy of the agenda is enclosed *for your information.*
> *Better:* The meeting will be Friday, August 11, 19—. A copy of the agenda is enclosed.

Short Words and Sentences

Word length.   Some people think that using a large vocabulary of big words will mark them as learned, but when short, simple words will do the job as well, it merely marks them as pretentious. This does not mean that an extensive vocabulary is not an asset; the more words that writers know, the more clearly and forcibly they can express themselves. But they should never choose words of many syllables over those with few syllables unless there is an important reason for doing so. For example, in a business letter, there is seldom a justifiable reason for using *ultimate* for *final, prerogative* for *privilege, transpire* for *occur, commence* for *start, terminate* for *end,* or *converse* for *talk.*

Sentence length.   Since the aim of a business letter is to transfer a thought to the reader in the simplest way with the greatest clarity, avoid long, complicated sentences. Break up overlong, stuffy sentences by making short sentences of the dependent clauses. Here is an example of one overlong, stuffy sentence.

> Believing the physical union of the two businesses to be desirable and in the best interests of the stockholders of each corporation, the Boards of Directors have given further consideration to the matter and have agreed in principle upon a new plan that would contemplate the transfer of the business and substantially all of the assets of the A Company to B in exchange for shares of common stock of B on a basis that would permit the distribution to the A Company stockholders of one and one-half shares of B common stock for each share of A Company common stock.

Rewritten in four shorter sentences, this becomes:

> The Boards of Directors of both companies thought a merger desirable and in the best interests of the stockholders. They finally agreed on a new plan. The business and substantially all assets of the A Company will be transferred to B in exchange for B common stock. A Company stockholders will get one and one-half shares of B common stock for each share of A Company common stock.

Various Shades of Meaning

Use different words to express various shades of meaning. In this case a large vocabulary is helpful. The writer with an adequate vocabulary writes about the *aroma* of a cigar, the *fragrance* of a flower, the *scent* of perfume, and the *odor* of gas, instead of the *smell* of all of these things.

Words That Antagonize

Words that carry uncomplimentary insinuations not only are tactless but often defeat the purpose of your letter. Never use a word that might humiliate or belittle the reader. Here are some expressions *to avoid* in letters:

> claim
> complaint
> defective
> dissatisfied

> error
> failure
> inability
> inferior
> mistake
> neglect
> poor
> trouble
> unfavorable
> unsatisfactory

For example, do not say "You *failed* to enclose the prospectus you mentioned." Say "The prospectus you mentioned was not enclosed."

Nondiscriminatory Language

Sexism.   Avoid all forms of sexist language. For example, use asexual words such as *people, civilization,* or *humankind* for *mankind; salesperson* for *salesman,* and *businessperson* or *business people* for *businessmen.*

> The workshop is especially useful to business people (*not* businessmen).

Do not refer to personal characteristics (instead of professional capabilities) in women.

> The program is run by William Parker, manager, and Jeanne Troy, executive assistant (*not* William Parker, manager, and his lovely assistant Jeanne).

Use first and last names and personal titles of men and women in the same way (See **FORMS OF ADDRESS,** page 327, in chapter 11.)

> Mr. Rod Boylston and Ms. Amelia Steiner (*not* Mr. Rod Boylston and Amelia).

Refer to adults as men and women in describing a group or use neutral terms such as *staff* or *committee.*

> The men and women (*not* the men and girls) from the West Coast office will host this year's banquet.

Use the term *spouse* or *spouses,* not *wife* or *wives,* in general references.

> Employees and their spouses (*not* wives) are excluded from the
> contest.

Do not use *his* in general references; use *his and her* or *their.*

> Each candidate must manage *his or her* (*not* his) own campaign. *Or:*
> Candidates must manage *their* own campaigns.

Avoid comments that refer to a person's sex.

> The speaker (*not* woman speaker) will discuss high-tech
> management.

Racial and ethnic bias. Eliminate language that reveals or focuses on racial and ethnic characteristics. Delete remarks that reinforce negative attitudes and draw attention to racial and ethnic backgrounds.

> Marilee Jefferson is a chemical engineer (*not* a black engineer) at
> ABC Industries.

Delete remarks that humiliate members of a racial or an ethnic group.

> The company's English-language workshop is designed for Mexican
> and Puerto Rican employees (*not* disadvantaged minorities).

Do not divide people into general white and nonwhite groups; identify the specific heritages.

> The new training program is for black, Mexican-American, and
> Asian (*not* nonwhite) employees.

Do not unwittingly suggest that members of a certain heritage usually are the opposite of some admirable trait.

> Foy Chan is a capable manager (*not* an open and honest manager,
> which might imply that people of his heritage are often secretive
> and dishonest).

Delete comments that stereotype all members of various racial and ethnic groups.

Some people are very ambitious *(not* the Japanese are very ambitious).

Handicap bias.   Eliminate remarks that draw attention to a person's handicap or unintentionally demean the person. However, even though you should avoid comments that unnecessarily draw attention to a disability, do not foolishly pretend it does not exist when circumstances necessitate dealing with it.

Nora, let's discuss ways to make the files more accessible *(not* Just ask Jane if you need something from the files).

Do not perpetuate negative attitudes and draw unnecessary attention to a disability; make any essential reference to a disability incidental.

Una Macauley, who has multiple sclerosis *(not* the MS victim Una Macauley), will head the orientation seminar for handicapped employees.

Avoid comments that stereotype all people with handicaps or a certain type of handicap.

Roy has exceptional hearing *(not* Roy has exceptional hearing because he can't see).

Do not use words and phrases that are demeaning even if common. For example, say *disabled* or *handicapped,* not *crippled; emotional difficulties,* not *insanity; seizure,* not *fit; slow learner,* not *retarded;* and *speech and hearing impaired,* not *deaf and dumb.*

The cafeteria should be made more suitable for handicapped employees *(not* cripples).

A Positive Approach

Always use a positive (and tactful) approach in letters. The following examples show how much more forceful and effective a positive approach is than a negative one:

Negative: We cannot quote you a price until we have seen the specifications.
Positive: We will be glad to quote you a price as soon as we have seen the specifications.

Negative: We cannot ship these goods before August 8.
Positive: We will ship the goods on or shortly after August 8.

FOR A BETTER LETTER BEGINNING

The opening of any letter must get the reader's attention immediately. (See figure 54) The following sections describe eight concrete suggestions that will help you develop a technique of starting a letter, even a routine letter, in a natural and interesting manner.

Make the Opening Short

Long paragraphs are uninviting and discourage many readers; therefore, the opening should be short. Refer to figure 54 for examples.

Go Straight to the Point

Beating about the bush does not capture the reader's attention. Start talking, just as if you were taking your part in a conversation. This does away with the practice of restating the contents of a letter that you are answering.

When to use a restatement.   A brief restatement sometimes makes it easier for your correspondent to find his or her letter in the files. Or the restatement might relieve the reader of having to refer to a copy of the letter. In these cases, a brief restatement is desirable. Your guide should be: does the restatement serve any useful purpose? Consider this example of a reply to a man who wants to buy an oil burner:

> In reply to yours of the 15th in which you state that you would be interested in receiving more complete information as to our STEADY-HEAT Oil Burner, since you are considering installing a burner in your home, we are enclosing a booklet . . .

The reader knows that he is considering installing a burner and knows that

Figure 54. Chart Showing Openings and Closings for Various Types of Letters.

	Openings	Closings
Appreciation	It was generous of you to give me so much of your time yesterday, and I appreciate your co-operation.	Thank you for your help. We're ready to serve you in every way possible.
Appreciation for messages of congratulations	I appreciated your comments about my efforts to guide the new Credit Management program.	Thanks for your thoughtful note.
Replying to requests for information booklets, and samples	The information you requested concerning the STEADY-HEAT Oil Burner is in the enclosed booklet.	When we can be of further help, please let us know.
Congratulations	I was pleased to read in this morning's paper of your appointment yesterday to the state supreme court.	You have my sincere congratulations added to all others that you must be receiving.
Complaints	Unfortunately, my last case of mayonnaise reached me in damaged condition.	I will keep the damaged case until I receive further instructions from you.
Adjustments or answering complaints	We are glad that you notified us promptly that some of your books have not yet arrived.	We very much regret the delay and hope that it will not cause you serious inconvenience.
Asking a favor	I know you must be busy with vacation time nearly here, but I have a small favor to ask of you.	I hope you'll be able to find time in your busy schedule to join us. Everyone is eager to see you again.
To Applicants	We appreciate the interest shown by your application for a position on the Prentice-Hall sales staff.	The best of luck to you, both in finding the right job and in making the most of it.

he wrote for information about the Steady-Heat burner. The date that he wrote the letter is of no interest. Why not open the letter with:

> The enclosed booklet "Better Heat with Steady-Heat" will provide the information you requested about the STEADY-HEAT burner.

Avoid Stilted Openings

Participial phrases and stilted expressions bore readers and exhaust them before they reach the point of the letter.

Artificial	*Natural*
Replying to your letter of July 9 in which you request that we send you samples of our WEAREVER fabrics, we are asking . . .	Thank you, Mr. Edwards, for your request for samples of our WEAREVER fabrics.
In accordance with the authority contained in your letter of April 9th, the records of this office have been amended to show the date of your birth as January 4, 1943, instead of January 4, 1945.	In answer to your letter of April 9, we have corrected our records to show the date of your birth as January 4, 1943, instead of January 4, 1945.
It is with the deepest regret that I must decline your kind invitation to speak at the luncheon meeting of the Secretarial Association to be held on April 18.	I'm very sorry that I must decline your invitation to speak at the Secretarial Association's luncheon on April 18.

Include the Reader's Name

The use of the reader's name in the opening sentence personalizes a routine letter. There is no discourtesy in the use of a person's name even in the first letter that is written. The use of the name in the illustrations below (see **Use a Pleasant Phrase,** page 352) makes those opening sentences more interesting to the reader. When overdone, however, the use of the name sounds too familiar. Do not use the name more than once in a short letter of two or three paragraphs.

Refer to a Previous Contact

In your opening, take advantage of a previous contact with your reader, either by letter or in person. Reference to a mutual interest or contact requires no particular skill, but it tends to get a letter off to a good start.

> It was a pleasure to have such an interesting visit with you during
>   my trip east last week.
> Thanks to you, Mr. Barrett, my stay in Cleveland was delightful.

Use a Pleasant Phrase

Use any appropriate statement that may trigger an agreeable attitude. Even if you are going to disagree with the reader later, don't put the bad news in the first sentence. This device is particularly helpful in adjustment letters. Here are three pleasant opening sentences:

> We appreciated your letter, Ms. Adams.
> You are very patient, Mrs. Jones.
> Your interest in better business letters, Mr. Johnson, makes writing
>   to you a pleasure.

Use "Who, What, When, Where, and Why"

When you have good news that you know will interest an individual or group, follow newspaper style and tell your reader who, what, when, where, and why in the opening. This technique is particularly effective in sales or promotional letters. Here is an illustration:

> June [when] is that eagerly awaited month when motoring
> Americans take to the highways for their annual vacations [why].
> Wherever [where] you may be planning to go this summer, our
> new travel information bureau [who] will be happy to assist
> [what] you.

Use Other Techniques of the Experts

The experts devote considerable time and effort to developing techniques that help them write attention-capturing openings. Some additional techniques they have developed are:

1. Use of a question
2. Statement of an unusual or not commonly known fact
3. Telling of an interesting story
4. Use of a quotation
5. Reference to a famous name

FOR A BETTER ENDING

The closing of your letter frequently influences the reader to do what you ask—or it might have the opposite effect. The closing should add something definite to the letter or it should not be there. (See figure 54.) The following sections describe four techniques that will help you to write closings that add to the persuasiveness of your letters.

Avoid Stilted or Formal Endings

A dull closing sentence can ruin an otherwise effective letter. For example, here is the last paragraph of a letter soliciting club memberships. The job was finished—and it was a good job—with the first paragraph. But the writer weakened the appeal of the selling paragraph because he could not resist the temptation to add this old-fashioned sentence in the closing paragraph:

> Thanking you for your kind consideration of the advantages of membership in our organization, and trusting you will see your way clear to acceptance of this invitation, we remain . . .

Suggest Only One Action

Tell the readers the *specific* action that you expect them to take. If they are given a choice of several things to do, they will probably do nothing. Concentrate on *one* action and do not mention others.

In the following closings, the alternative suggestions tend to confuse the reader; the specific suggestions are impelling and produce action.

Alternative Suggestions	*Specific Suggestions*
Write us a letter or telegram or send the enclosed card right now.	Send the enclosed card today.

If it is convenient for you to see me, please drop me a note or call me at 356-4920.

When it is convenient for you to see me, please call me at 356-4920.

Please mail this payment to arrive at our office within five days. Or if you aren't able to do that now, send us a postdated check for the same amount.

Please mail this payment to arrive at our office within five days, which would be by Saturday, May 7, 19—.

Use Dated Action

If you expect the reader to take certain action in the future, use *dated action.* That is, tell the reader that you expect the action by a given date or within a certain number of days, not "in the near future."

The experience of an insurance company illustrates how an indefinite date can weaken a letter. The company had difficulty getting reports from examining physicians. The letters asked the doctors to return the report blanks "as soon as possible," but the company found that on an average it had to write 3.7 follow-up letters to each physician. The company then switched to dated action and called for the return of the blanks by a specific date. As a result, the average number of follow-up letters for each report was reduced to 2.1.

Here are two examples of dated-action closings:

For us to handle this claim promptly for your patient, we will need your preliminary report by the *end of this week, July 13, 19—.*

An *immediate reply* will enable us to complete the draft of the contract by Friday.

Use Positive Words

Negative words anywhere in a letter weaken it, because they show the writer's lack of confidence. They are doubly harmful in the closing. *Hope, may, if,* and *trust* tend to defeat the purpose of any business letter. Compare the following negative closings with the positive revisions.

Negative

If you will okay the card, we will gladly send you a copy of the bulletin. *Trusting* you will do this . . .

Positive

Your copy of this interesting bulletin is waiting for you. Just okay and mail the card.

Now is the time when our customers are stocking up for summer business. We *trust* you will join them by placing your requirements on the order blank enclosed.

If you would like to have our salesperson call with samples, please so advise.

Now is the time when our customers are stocking up for summer business. You can join them by placing your requirements on the order blank enclosed.

Ted Mead, someone you are going to like, will be around next Monday morning to show you samples and service your order.

FORM LETTERS

Using Form Letters

Keep a file of form letters and form paragraphs to be used in recurring situations that require almost the same letter. You can save samples of both outgoing and incoming letters and create your own examples to add to them. Some secretaries keep such samples in a "Forms" file folder. Others prefer a three-ring binder with dividers for sales letters, announcements, and other major categories. You can also maintain a forms file by computer. A good index is needed, however, so that you can easily select forms that you want to "call out" for editing and printout. Form letters are entirely satisfactory when no attempt is being made to slant the letter toward a particular reader. Often they are better than an individually composed letter, because more time and thought are given to their preparation. Rewrite form letters from time to time to keep them current and up to date.

The secretary is concerned with two types of form letters: (1) model forms (those that you use as a guide in typing individual letters) and (2) processed forms (those for which all or most of the letter is preprinted, often with the inside address and salutation typed in the blank space left on each printed form).

Using Model Form Letters and Paragraphs

A list of routine letters that the secretary writes and examples of them are given in chapter 13. These letters may be used as models. Make copies of the letters that you are likely to need and keep them in your form-letter file. Analyze your correspondence to see what other types of model letters you need. Select one you have already written to meet the need and correct and improve it to conform with the principles explained in this chapter. Then place it as a model in your form-letter file.

You will find, also, that model paragraphs can be used in many letters. For example, if you answer, instead of merely acknowledge, a letter received in your employer's absence, your opening paragraph could be the same in each letter. Place the paragraph in your form-letter file. But be careful not to use the same opening paragraph in frequent letters to the same person.

Using Processed Form Letters

Situations that can be covered by processed form letters vary with the secretary's position. The factors that determine which letters might be processed are (1) frequency of use, (2) purpose of the letter, and (3) the probable reaction of the recipient. Difference of opinion exists about the effectiveness of form letters, but if properly handled and personalized, there can be no logical objection to them. When the letter is purely routine or when the recipient is interested only in the information it contains, a preprinted letter can be used to advantage. Obviously, form letters save time and money. Refer to figure 55 for a list of questions that will help you decide when to use a processed form and whether your forms are effective.

Figure 55.   Form-Letter Effectiveness Checklist.

	Yes	No
Is the form letter designed so that a typist can make typed fill-ins easily?	( )	( )
Has a test been made to see whether a file copy of the letter is actually needed or whether the prescribed number of copies can be reduced?	( )	( )
Is the letter easily understood on the first reading?	( )	( )
Is it free of old-fashioned letter language, such as "reference is made to," "you are advised that," and "examination of our records discloses"?	( )	( )
Has a "usage" test been made to see whether it is practical to carry a printed stock?	( )	( )

(Continued)

Figure 55 *(Continued)*

Does the letter concern a routine business or
informational matter? ( ) ( )

Is there a mark to show the typist where to
begin the address so that it will show in the
window of an envelope? ( ) ( )

Will the supply on hand be used up in a few
months' time? ( ) ( )

Is the letter identified in any way, for example,
by a number printed in one of the corners? ( ) ( )

If you were the person receiving the form letter,
would you consider it effective and attractive? ( ) ( )

Has a test been made of typed letters to see
whether it is practical to replace any of them
with form letters? ( ) ( )

Has provision been made for reviewing all
requests for form letters to make sure that
unnecessary, poorly written, and poorly designed
letters do not slip into print? ( ) ( )

Do you have standards that you expect all form
letters to meet? ( ) ( )

Are form letters put into use by written instructions
explaining when they are to be used, enclosures
(if any) that should be made, and carbon-copy
requirements? ( ) ( )

Do you have a systematic way of numbering form
letters? ( ) ( )

When form letters become obsolete, are immediate
instructions issued to discontinue their use and
to remove old stock from supply cabinets and desk? ( ) ( )

Source: National Archives and Records Service, Records Management Division, General Services
Administration, Washington, D.C.
Note: A checkmark in the "No" column indicates the need for corrective action.

Personalizing Processed Form Letters

Form letters that are not prepared by computer may be duplicated by copier or by a stencil, spirit, or offset process. If you want to have the processed form closely resemble an individually typed letter, pick a process that provides clean, clear copy and avoid those that give images a fuzzy, blurred appearance. Also, you can improve the layout and appearance of processed form letters by typing in the dateline, inside address, salutation, and complimentary close on each form. In doing this it is important to match as closely as possible your typewriter ribbon's color and impression with the type on the processed form.

Automated typewriters will type letters at high speed. Some of these machines, such as the magnetic-tape models, produce individually typed, personalized form letters, combining a standard letter body with the individual names and addresses. Revisions and corrections are easily and quickly edited into the tape, and letter-perfect copy is produced with a minimum of time and effort.

Computers and dedicated word processors have greatly simplified the processing of forms. You can purchase software programs with hundreds of standard letters to choose from and with which you can merge your own mailing list of names and addresses. Or you can prepare your own electronic collection of forms, again merging the body of each letter you want to use with your list of names and addresses. Each letter, then, has essentially the same body but different selected information such as the inside address and salutation. The printer connected to the equipment will then print out letters that appear to be individually written and typed.

Whether form letters are prepared by one of the duplicating processes, by automatic typewriter, or by computer, these simple steps will help to personalize the letter:

1. Use a good quality paper.
2. Sign the letter with pen and ink.
3. Seal the envelope.
4. Send the letter by first-class mail.
5. Use postage stamps rather than metered envelopes.

Using Memo Forms

Memos are exchanged among the various offices, departments, and divisions within a corporation. More and more, companies are also using memos for external correspondence in placing orders, corresponding with business associates and well-known clients, and so forth. Memos, like letters, can be prepared in the same manner described above for model and processed forms. Some companies have specially printed stationery; others use inexpensive stationery without a letterhead; others use a special size of stationery. Figure 50 in chapter 11 illustrates a common memo format.

Routing a memo. If you want a *single* copy of a memo to go successively to each of several persons, address it this way:

1. Mr. S. Brown
2. Mrs. C. Smith
3. Ms. R. Jones

If you want the memo to come back, include your employer's name as number 4. Each person receiving the memo will strike out his or her own name, write the date on which the memo was read and action taken, and check the next name.

Unless material is confidential, do not use sealed envelopes for inneroffice memos, but mail memos going out of the office the same as you would mail a letter. Chapter 11 discusses envelope addressing (page 325) and other matters pertaining to the preparation and mailing of correspondence.

— Chapter 13 —

Model Letters and Memos

CATEGORIES OF CORRESPONDENCE

Letters and Memos the Secretary Signs

Your employer's wish is the principal factor in deciding which letters you might sign. If he or she expects you to use your own judgment, the determining factor is consideration for the recipient of the letter. A writer who expects a letter to be answered by an executive might be offended if it is passed to someone else in the office. In this case, it would be poor business procedure for you to write the letter over your signature. However, if the recipient is interested only in the information given in answer to the letter, you can safely write it over your own signature. As secretaries assume more responsibility in the modern business world, letter writing becomes an increasingly important daily activity.

Examples of letters that you will often write and sign include:

1. Acknowledgments
2. Adjustments in account
3. Appointments
4. Follow-ups
5. Inquiries

6. Orders
7. Reminders
8. Requests
9. Reservations

A pattern and models for each type of letter are illustrated in the following sections. The signature is the same in each case (see page 320 for examples).

(Your Handwritten Signature)
Secretary to Mr. Jones

Letters and Memos Your Employer Signs

Style and tone of letters. Familiarize yourself with the tone and style of your employer's correspondence. The aim in composing a letter for someone else's signature is to write it *exactly* as that person would have dictated it. Here are three rules:

1. Follow the executive's style as closely as possible without flagrantly disregarding the rules of good letter writing. Thus if the executive has a few pet phrases, use them, but if he or she has a habit of opening letters with long participial phrases, try a natural opening, and probably your employer will approve it.

2. Adapt the tone of your letter to the tone the executive uses when dictating. Thus if the letters come quickly to the point, compose letters in that tone; if the letters are gentle and courteous, use that tone. It is particularly important to know whether the tone of the letter should convey personal friendship, a formal business relationship, or some other attitude.

3. Use the same salutation and complimentary close that your employer would use. They change with the relationship existing between the writer and the addressee. Thus if the manager uses "Dear Bob" as the salutation to Senator Robbins, you would use the same salutation in letters that you write to him for your employer's signature.

Letters about company business. All of the rules of good letter writing described in chapters 11 and 12 are applicable here. One type of letter that you may send out in the company's name is the letter announcing to a firm or a customer that a donation is being given in its name to a hospital or charity in place of the usual Christmas gift.

Dear Mr. Jones:

On behalf of this company, I am happy to tell you that we are sending in your name a donation to the Children's Hospital in place of the personal gift we usually send at this season.

May the coming holidays bring to you and yours good health, happiness, and a full share of those things that make this world a better place in which to live.

Cordially yours,

Personal business letters.   Before you acquire the technical knowledge necessary to write letters about the company's business, you may be expected to handle the personal letters (such as congratulations, thank yous, and special greetings) that the amenities of business require.

You will write some of these letters for your employer's signature without instructions and others from a few words of instruction or from marginal notes that he or she makes on an incoming letter.

An effective personal letter must meet these requirements, in addition to those given in chapter 12 for any letter:

1. Be sure that your letter is opportunely timed. A note of congratulations, a message of condolence, or a letter of appreciation is far more effective if it is written promptly—that is, immediately after the event.

2. Make the tone of your letter personal, so that the message is tailor-made for the *individual* reader.

3. Be cordial and friendly but not gushy.

4. Select a salutation and complimentary close that harmonize with the friendly tone of the letter. Use the reader's name in the greeting unless the letter is addressed to an organization.

5. Write with a sincerity that lends conviction to your message.

6. Have your employer sign the letter. The recipient will value the personal touch of his or her signature.

Letters and Memos Written in Your Employer's Absence

Letters that you may be expected to write over *your* signature when your employer is away include the following. Refer to the models in this chapter for examples.

1. Acknowledgments
2. Apologies
3. Appointments
4. Appreciation
5. Follow-ups
6. Goodwill

7. Inquiries
8. Orders
9. Reminders
10. Requests
11. Reservations

MODEL BUSINESS LETTERS AND MEMOS

Acknowledgments

Acknowledgment without answer.   The pattern for these letters is simple:

1. Respond promptly and thank the writer for any information or material you received.
2. State that your employer is out of the city or away from the office, if that is the case, and give the expected date of his or her return.
3. Assure the writer that his or her message will receive attention when your employer returns.
4. If the delay may cause inconvenience to the writer, add a note of apology.

Do not refer to an illness or other difficulties when explaining your employer's absence from the office, unless the writer knows the circumstances. Say, "Because of Mr. Peter's absence from the office, he will not be able to attend. . . ."

Dear Mrs. Stevenson:

Thank you for sending Mr. James the information about the Denver project. He's away on business now, but I'll bring this to his attention as soon as he returns, and I'm certain he will contact you promptly.

Please accept my apologies for this unavoidable delay.

Sincerely yours,

Dear Mr. Ames:

Your letter of August 14 arrived the day after Ms. Tauber left on a two-week business trip. Since you indicated that it does not require an immediate answer, I'll hold it for prompt attention on her return.

Sincerely yours,

Dear Ms. Parker:

Thank you for contacting Mr. King about the new tax forms. He is attending a convention in Philadelphia this week and will return to the office next Monday. I'll be certain to bring your letter about the new tax forms to his attention at that time.

Sincerely yours,

Acknowledgment that also answers. The important factor in answering, as well as acknowledging, a letter is to know the facts. Here is a suggested pattern:

1. Respond promptly and identify the incoming letter.
2. State that your employer is away if that is the case.
3. State the facts that answer the letter and express appreciation if something was received.
4. If appropriate, or desirable, state that your employer will write when he or she returns.

Dear Mr. Frederick:

Your letter reminding Mr. Stone of his promise to speak before the ABC Club at lunch on Tuesday, December 20, arrived during his absence from the office.

He will return on Monday, and I will bring your thoughtful

letter to his attention then. I know that he is looking forward to speaking at the luncheon.

Sincerely yours,

Dear. Mrs. Florio:

Thank you for asking to see Mr. French about office equipment.

Mr. French will be out of the office for the next month. However, Mr. Rhinesmith is responsible for all company purchases, and you may want to contact him. His office is in Room 512, and he is usually available every morning from 10 o'clock until noon. If you want to call him for an appointment, his extension is 560.

I'll see that he has this correspondence, so you may refer to it when you call.

Sincerely yours,

Dear Mr. Roberts:

Your letter asking Ms. Ainsworth to speak before the ABC Club of Jackson on January 14 arrived a few days after she left town on a business trip.

However, after checking her schedule for January 14, I see that she is to make a special report to the Board of Directors on that day, and therefore it apparently will be impossible for her to address the members of your club at that time.

I know that Ms. Ainsworth will nevertheless appreciate your kind invitation and will write to you as soon as she returns to Nashville.

Sincerely yours,

Adjustments

Errors, misunderstandings, and changes in plans make it necessary for business people to write letters of adjustment. Many adjustments result from the use of charge cards, credit cards, and company or individual travel accounts. The example below pertains to a travel account, but the same pattern can be applied to adjustments in other types of accounts.

Letters of adjustment of travel accounts. Many companies and executives use travel accounts, and the charges for travel tickets, hotel accommodations, car rental, and other travel services are billed by itemized monthly statements. When services are involved, the statement is accompanied by a *record of charge* made at the time the service is completed. This record of charge shows the date and items of purchase, the signature of the purchaser, and the name and address of the service establishment.

Always check the items of the record of charge signed by your employer against the itemized monthly statement received. Also make certain that any travel ticket cancellations have been properly credited to the account. Letters that you will write usually fall into three classes: (a) when the amount of an item is incorrect, (2) when the total is incorrect, and (3) when a ticket cancellation has not been credited.

1. When the amount of an item is incorrect. The same procedure would apply if the total were incorrect.

   a. Give the person's name, the company, and the account number in which the travel card is issued.
   b. Describe the incorrect item and tell how it is incorrect.
   c. State what the item should be, giving any documentary information that you have.
   d. Ask for a corrected statement or enclose a check for the correct amount and ask that the error be rectified on the next statement.

Ladies and Gentlemen:

   ACCOUNT 365-809-112, A. D. BROCK, COMPUTERS, INC.

   Your statement of June 17 charges Mr. Brock's account for dining services at the Princess Hotel in Bermuda during the week of May 8 for $312.67. According to the record of charge, the total should be $302.67, or $10.00 less than the statement shows.

Enclosed is Mr. Brock's check for this month's statement, minus $10. Please credit Mr. Brock's account in full.

Sincerely yours,

2. When a ticket cancellation has not been credited. Follow these steps when a bill or statement fails to credit the amount of a ticket that was canceled.

a. Give the person's name, the company, and the account number in which the travel card is issued.
b. Give the date, point of departure, and destination of the original reservation.
c. Tell how and when it was canceled.
d. State the amount that has been incorrectly charged.
e. Ask for a corrected statement or enclose a check for the correct amount and ask that the error be rectified on the next statement.

Ladies and Gentlemen:

ACCOUNT 711–298–067–A, ANDREA R. ACE, WINSTON MOTORS

Your statement of August 15 to Ms. Ace includes a charge of $80 for a flight from New York to Washington. We originally scheduled this flight by telephone and received the tickets and your letter of confirmation on July 28.

However, on Ms. Ace's instructions, I canceled this flight by telephone on the morning of July 29 and returned the tickets to you in my letter of that date.

Enclosed is Ms. Ace's check for the amount of your August 15 statement, minus the charge for this flight. Please credit her account in full.

Sincerely yours,

Apologies

When there is an adequate and convincing explanation for a situation that requires an apology, a few words can be devoted to the explanation. If no justification exists, a frank admission of that fact usually has a disarming effect on the reader. Regardless of the circumstances, any situation that requires a letter of apology requires a tone of warmth and friendliness.

Letter of apology.   Whenever possible, follow an apology with a solution or means to rectify the situation.

Dear Ms. Morton:

I hope you will accept a sincere apology for my absence from the Credit Association meeting yesterday afternoon.

When I told you earlier in the week that I planned to be there, I fully intended to be. But a meeting of our own credit department staff yesterday afternoon lasted much longer than expected, and it was impossible for me to get away.

When I see Jim Davis at lunch tomorrow, I will ask him to bring me up to date on yesterday's developments.

Sincerely yours,

Explanation of oversight.   An oversight usually deserves an explanation as well as an apology. Sending a thoughtful letter to a customer or client is a good way to improve customer relations.

Dear Mr. Clemons:

I was sorry to learn that our shipment of booklets was delivered without the free self-inking address stamp. The stamp that was promised with your order is enclosed.

Usually, the booklets are shipped from our own facility, and our packers routinely insert a stamp with each order. But because your request was a rush order, we asked the printer to ship the booklets directly to you from their shop, bypassing our offices. Apparently, someone missed the instructions to include your stamp with the order.

Please accept our apologies for this oversight and any inconvenience it may have caused you. We appreciate your interest in our booklets and hope you will continue to find them a productive adjunct to your next mailing.

Sincerely yours,

Appointments

Here is the pattern that a letter arranging an appointment should follow:

1. Refer to the purpose of the appointment.
2. Suggest, or ask the person to whom you are writing to suggest, the time, place, and date.
3. Ask for a confirmation of the appointment.

These letters fall into three groups: (1) your employer asks for an appointment; (2) you ask someone to come in to see your employer; and (3) you reply to a letter asking your employer for an appointment.

Your employer asks for appointment. Whether the letter goes out over your signature or your employer's, keep it brief but be certain to provide all necessary facts.

1. You want to fix the time. Include the place, time, and date.

Dear Mr. Green:

Mr. Stone is attending a convention in Chicago next week. While he is there, he would like to discuss with you the revision of your book on tax reports.

Will it be convenient for him to call on you Tuesday afternoon, June 1, at two o'clock?

Sincerely yours,

2. You have to let the other person fix the time. If your employer is following a schedule, you might suggest a general time period such as within the next week or two; otherwise, leave it all up to the recipient.

Dear Mr. Roberts:

Ms. Gorman is returning from Washington on Friday of this week and would like to discuss with you the results of her sessions with the Labor Committee.

Will you please ask your secretary to telephone me and let me know when it will be convenient for you to see Ms. Gorman?

Sincerely yours,

You ask someone to come in to see your employer. You may find it necessary to specify a certain time, or you may be able to let the other person choose the time.

1. You want to fix the time. Again, give the place, time, and date.

Dear Mr. Morris:

Mr. Polinski would like to know if it would be possible to see you on Monday, February 27, at two o'clock in his office, Room 201, to complete arrangements for the rental of your summer cottage.

Please let me know whether this time is convenient.

Sincerely yours,

2. You let the other person fix the time. You may nevertheless want to suggest a general period such as "next week."

Dear Mrs. Elwood:

The papers in connection with the trust that you are creating for your daughter are now complete, except for your signature. Mr.

Watkins would like to know if you could come to his office early
next week to sign them.

Please telephone me to arrange a convenient time for you.

Sincerely yours,

Reply to letter asking your employer for an appointment. You
will either agree to the request or say no politely (see page 381). If you say
yes, you must again deal with the three basic facts of date, time, and place.

1. You fix a definite time. In this case, you give a specific time
rather than a general period.

Dear Ms. Smith:

Mr. Brown will be glad to see you on Monday, December 27,
at two o'clock in his office, Room 201, to discuss with you the
program for the annual convention.

Sincerely yours,

2. You let the other person fix the time. Here you give the
recipient a chance to suggest a time but you may want to indicate the week.

Dear Mr. Rhoades:

Mr. Ricotti will be glad to see you some time during the week
of March 3 to talk over the installation of the elevator in his
residence at 20 West Street.

If you will telephone me at 353-9200 we can arrange a time
that will be convenient for you and Mr. Ricotti.

Sincerely yours,

3. Your employer signs the letter. The facts that are stated remain unchanged even though your employer signs the letter. However, he or she may want to add a personal closing sentence.

Dear Mr. Boyd:

I will be happy to talk with you when you are in Minneapolis next week. Would it be convenient for you to come to my office at ten o'clock, Thursday morning, November 5? I believe this hour will give us the best opportunity to discuss your project without interruption.

It will be a pleasure to see you again.

Cordially yours,

4.   You have to say no politely.   The trick to writing these letters is to combine firmness with courtesy.

Dear Mr. Thomas:

Ms. Jarvis has considered very carefully all that you said in your letter of December 21. If there were any possibility that a meeting with you would be helpful, she would be glad to see you. However, she does not believe that would be the case and has asked me to let you know and to thank you for writing.

Sincerely yours,

Appreciation

A letter of appreciation is sent when someone does something helpful or commendable and is often used to promote goodwill. It should not discuss other business and should reflect genuine sincerity and honest gratitude, not merely the writer's desire to conform with the rules of etiquette. The letter should be brief, and the tone should be one of friendly informality. The factors that determine the suitable degree of informality are the following:

1. The extent to which the favor, service, or courtesy performed is personal

2. The degree of friendship existing between the writer and the recipient

3. The age and temperament of the recipient

For personal favor or service. In the case of an important favor such as filling in at the office during a long absence, you might offer to reciprocate or generally suggest that the recipient not hesitate to ask if ever you can be of assistance. However, appreciation for small favors and deeds also promotes good relations, and the overall tone and style of the letters are similar regardless of the magnitude of the situation.

Dear John:

Thank you so much for the ticket to the Annual Retailers' Convention and Forum. The exhibits were extremely interesting, and I particularly enjoyed the forum sessions.

It was thoughtful of you to remember me. My sincere thanks for your kindness.

Cordially,

For assistance to company, club, or association. It is important to acknowledge all forms of special assistance with a brief letter of appreciation.

Dear Ms. Noble:

It was generous of you to spend so much time with our organization yesterday. The material you brought and the suggestions you made will be of great help in our new organization plans in the Personnel Department.

We all appreciate your cooperation. My sincere thanks for your valuable help.

Sincerely yours,

For hospitality. When the thanks involve personal attention, the letter should have an especially warm, personal tone.

Dear Ned:

I want to thank you for your hospitality during my two-week stay in Chicago. I count the evenings spent in your home as highlights of my stay in your city.

Your personal knowledge of the Merchandise Mart and the time you spent with me in the Mart greatly enhanced the pleasure and fruitfulness of my trip.

Thanks so much for your kindness.

Best regards,

For message of sympathy. Keep letters pertaining to sympathy brief—usually, no more than one to three sentences.

Gentlemen:

The members of this organization appreciate your kind expression of sympathy on the sudden death of our treasurer, Thomas Thornhill. We feel keenly the loss of one whose ability and exceptional personal qualities have meant so much in the growth of this firm.

Please accept our sincere thanks for both your sympathetic message and your splendid tribute to Mr. Thornhill.

Sincerely,

For message of congratulations about a speech. If the circumstances provide the opportunity, say something nice about the other person or organization in addition to expressing appreciation.

Dear Andy:

That was a fine letter you wrote to me about my talk in Milwaukee last week, and I appreciate it ever so much.

Speaking to the members of your organization was a most enjoyable experience, and I am very glad that my remarks contributed in some small way to the success of your meeting.

Cordially,

For favorable mention in a speech.   You can easily adapt this letter if mention was instead made in an article or a book.

Dear Mr. Kennedy:

Thank you for the generous remarks you made in your speech before the Dry Goods Association yesterday about my part in the association's activities.

Coming from someone of your high standing among the business people of this state, the compliment was especially pleasing, and I'm happy to know that you approve of my work.

Sincerely,

Collection

Large companies usually have a separate department that handles the collection of past-due accounts. In other cases, collection problems fall to each individual office or department.

When a series of follow-up letters is necessary, the tone usually progresses in each succeeding letter from a casual reminder to a firm final demand for payment before taking legal action.

1. Know the facts of each collection problem before preparing your letter.
2. Always give your client or customer a chance to pay before announcing other action.

A casual reminder.   The first letter is usually short and friendly since the payment may have been overlooked and not intentionally ignored.

Dear Mrs. Stone:

Just a friendly reminder that your payment of $82.40 for the stationery you purchased on August 12 will be very much appreciated.

If your check is already in the mail, please disregard this notice and accept our thanks. If it is not, won't you take a moment to mail it today?

Cordially yours,

A firm reminder. When it is clear that something is amiss, the tone of the letter, although not overly harsh and threatening, hints at an adverse impact on the recipient's credit standing.

Dear Mrs. Stone:

Ninety days have passed, but we have not yet received your payment of $82.40 for stationery purchased on August 12.

Since we have received no reply from you concerning this purchase, we assume the balance due is correct and that your records agree with ours. Won't you therefore send us your check immediately and protect your credit rating?

Your cooperation and prompt reply will be very much appreciated, Mrs. Stone.

Sincerely yours,

A final appeal. This final letter before legal or other action is taken may be preceded by two other letters: (1) a discussion letter, asking the recipient to indicate, in confidence, whether he or she is having difficulties and (2) an urgent message that says the recipient must break his or her silence to avoid having serious action taken. If these efforts fail, the final appeal usually announces that a collection agency or attorney will take over shortly, and it gives the recipient one last chance to respond.

Dear Mrs. Stone:

Since you have not replied to any of my previous letters, I regret that we must take other steps to collect the past-due amount of $82.40 for stationery you purchased on August 12.

If we do not have your check within ten days, by January 1, the Morris Collection Agency will begin appropriate action in our behalf. I hope you will take this final opportunity to avoid further damage to your credit standing as well as the additional costs you may incur if legal action is required.

Send us your check by January 1, and the matter will be resolved before the Morris Collection Agency takes further action.

Sincerely,

Complaints

Anger and frustration breed many unjustified complaints. Such emotional outbursts usually involve unfair criticism and unreasonable requests for adjustments. Many complaints, however, involve actual errors and are proper and necessary.

Letters calling attention to an error in an account. In calling attention to an error in an account, avoid giving the impression that you are complaining. Keep the tone of your letter pleasant and remember not to use words that antagonize (see list of page 345). These letters fall into four classes: (1) when the amount of an item is incorrect, (2) when the total is incorrect, (3) when returned merchandise has not been credited, and (4) when an item not purchased is charged to the account.

1. When the amount of an item is incorrect. Here is a workable outline that covers the necessary points (follow similar steps when the total is incorrect):

a. Give the name and number of the account.

b. Describe the incorrect item, and tell how it is incorrect.

c. State your version of what the item should be, giving any documentary information you may have.

d. Ask for a corrected statement or enclose a check for the correct amount and ask that the error be rectified on the account.

Ladies and Gentlemen:

The September statement of Walter Northrup's account shows a charge of $30.00 for dinner for two on the evening of August 15. Evidently, this charge should have been posted to someone else's account since Mr. Northrup was out of town that evening.

I have deducted $30.00 from the total amount of the statement and am enclosing Mr. Northrup's check for $100.80.

Sincerely yours,

2.   When an item not purchased is charged to the account. These letters should include the following points:

a. Name and number of the account
b. Description of the item charged in error, including the price and the date charged
c. Any additional pertinent information that you have
d. A request that the charge be investigated
e. A request for a corrected statement

Ladies and Gentlemen:

The June statement of Mrs. Robert Walker's account no. 14825 shows a charge of $35.85 on May 15 for three boxes of envelopes. Mrs. Walker charged three boxes for $35.85 on May 10 and three boxes for the same amount on May 20, but she did not charge anything on May 15. The six boxes that she bought were properly charged to her account.

Naturally, Mrs. Walker is concerned that someone may have used her account without her permission. Would you please investigate and let her know what happened?

Sincerely yours,

3.   When returned merchandise has not been credited.   Follow the same pattern as when the amount of an item is incorrect.

Ladies and Gentlemen:

On May 4 James Novak, account number 15836, returned for credit a pen and pencil set that he purchased from you on May 2. The price was $27.50, including tax.

Mr. Novak's June statement does not show this credit. A credit slip was given to him, but unfortunately, it has been misplaced. Mr. Novak would therefore appreciate it if you would verify the credit and send him a corrected statement.

In the meantime, I am enclosing Mr. Novak's check for $146.25, which is the amount of the statement less the price of the returned merchandise.

Sincerely yours,

Credit

Letters pertaining to credit matters involve the reputations of companies and individuals. Accuracy, honesty, and fairness are therefore essential in providing information.

Providing credit information.   If the person or organization asking for information provides a special blank form, fill out the required facts on that form. Otherwise, compose your own brief letter. Be accurate, honest, and show consideration for the subject's feelings and needs.

Dear Mrs. Donnovan:

Our experience with Brewster Toyland has been generally satisfactory. They have paid most of our invoices within 30 days and the rest within 60 days. Their purchases have ranged from $75 to $400 a month.

Based on our two-year relationship with Brewster Toyland, I would not hesitate to extend credit to them on purchases up to $500.

If I can answer any further questions, Mrs. Donnovan, just let me know.

Best regards,

Requesting credit.   When requesting certain forms of credit such as a bank credit card, one might simply ask for a credit application. In other situations, one might collect recommendations from business sources and call on the supplier to present the backup information. Another common approach is to write a personal letter to the appropriate person in the firm from whom credit is desired.

Dear Mr. Blakely:

Along with our company's steady growth, our advertising department is facing continually increasing needs for additional printing and composition services. Since we are familiar with your reputation for quality work and prompt delivery, we would like to place some orders with you in the coming months.

Our department currently purchases from $2,000 to $4,000 worth of printing and composition each month. Would you be able to extend your usual credit terms to our department for amounts within this range? I'm enclosing the name of our bank and two organizations that have provided credit to us in the past.

Please let me know if you need additional information for us to establish an account with you. Thanks very much, Mr. Blakely.

Sincerely,

Employee Communications

Management sends company employees a variety of letters, memos, announcements, and other forms of communication. Many of these messages are sent in memo format; others may be prepared in letter format with a salutation such as "Dear Staff Member" or "Dear Employee." Some letters are factual and straightforward such as a transmittal letter; others may be motivational, intended to encourage employees to take certain action or adopt a certain attitude. Often they are written in a warm, personal, conversational, tone. One of the most common letters is the announcement (of a new employee, a promotion, a change in policy, and so on).

Announcement of staff appointment. This type of appointment —introducing a new employee or a new appointment—has a friendly, upbeat tone. Although the letter should not be effusive in its praise, the staff member is usually presented in the best light, with mention of commendable background details.

TO: Members of the Training Department

SUBJECT: Assistant Director Position

I'm very happy to announce the appointment of Joanne Pressman as assistant director of our Data Processing Training Department. Joanne will assume the post vacated by Roy Carter, who recently joined our Los Angeles training staff.

Joanne comes to us from New York, where she was senior training instructor in the Data Processing Division of Standard Equipment, Inc. She taught data processing for eight years and worked closely with the data-processing training director during the past two years. As a result, she is thoroughly familiar with the scope and responsibilities of her new position and is highly qualified to handle the many challenges of the position of assistant director.

I know that Joanne will welcome your help and cooperation in becoming familiar with our department and her new duties. We all wish her much success and feel very fortunate to have her as part of our team.

Letters that say no. Occasions inevitably arise when your employer has to say no to another employee. Perhaps a proposal is unacceptable; a request for a raise may be unrealistic; or it may be necessary to refuse someone's offer to help. The possibilities are endless. But all messages that say no should observe three basic rules.

1. If something is offered, thank the employee.
2. Explain—tactfully—why the offer or request is being turned down.
3. Try to encourage the employee in regard to future efforts or opportunities.

Dear Ms. Snow:

We have carefully considered your request for a salary increase of $4,000 in lieu of the $1,200 increase you were recently granted. However, I'm sorry to let you know that our company is unable to grant an increase of that size at this time.

Although your job record at Brandon Wholesalers is very satisfactory, you have only completed your first year with us. It is our current policy to offer salary increases up to $1,200 a year, but not beyond, to one-year employees in your job classification. But your next job and salary review is scheduled for June 1, and we will reevaluate your progress and the company's financial position at that time.

We hope you will continue to enjoy your work at Brandon Wholesalers, Ms. Snow, and we look forward to a long and mutually rewarding association.

Cordially,

Transmittal message.   People in business regularly send material back and forth. Sometimes a detailed cover letter is necessary to explain the reason for sending the material, what it is, and so on. Usually, though, material is routinely transmitted from one person to another with no detailed explanation. Brief transmittal messages are commonly typed in the memo format. Sometimes only a handwritten note is attached to the material or a routing slip. The traditional brief transmittal message should simply state what is enclosed. If it is necessary to tell the recipient why it is being sent, add a sentence or two of explanation.

TO: J. M. Aldine

FROM: A. J. Frastizi

ELECTRONIC PRODUCTS SURVEY

Here's the report you requested, Jim. Do let me know if you have any questions.

Follow-ups

If correspondence in your follow-up file (see Chapter 1) is not answered by the follow-up date, trace the letter for a reply. Your letter should cover the following points:

1. Identify the letter. Identification by date is not sufficient because your correspondent does not know what you are writing about.
2. Offer a reason for the recipient's failure to reply, without casting reflection on the recipient.
3. Enclose a copy of your original letter, unless it was very short. If so, simply repeat the contents in your follow-up letter.

Copy of original letter not enclosed. If you can briefly and adequately describe the unanswered correspondence, there is no need to enclose your original letter.

Ladies and Gentlemen:

On February 2 we ordered from you 200 copies of your latest bulletin, "Successful Selling Techniques," but we have not yet had an acknowledgment of the order.

Since our first order evidently went astray, please consider this a duplicate.

Sincerely yours,

Copy of original letter enclosed. Some things are too detailed to repeat in a new letter, and it is then better to enclose a copy of the original correspondence. Since the following example is a follow-up of a letter requesting a favor, it is written for your employer's signature. Notice that a reply is requested by a specific date.

Dear Ms. Roberts:

In the rush of work you probably have not had time to answer my letter of October 25 about using some of your selling ideas in our Real Estate Service, with credit to you. On the chance that this letter did not reach you, I'm enclosing a copy of it.

I would like to include your selling ideas in the next supplement of the service. This will be possible if I have your reply by December 15.

Thanks very much.

Cordially,

Goodwill

Letters of goodwill help build a favorable image of your company and develop good human relations both inside and outside the organization. Examples of such letters are letters of appreciation, offers of assistance, messages of congratulations, thank you letters, holiday and seasonal greetings, and letters of commendation. (For further examples see pages 396–407.)

1. Use any appropriate occasion to say something nice.
2. Write naturally and sincerely.
3. Do not use these letters for other business purposes; restrict your comments to the occasion.

Dear Ken:

Congratulations! I was really pleased—but not surprised—to learn about your promotion. I know you'll do an outstanding job, as always, and the company is truly fortunate to have you in charge of our field operations.

Best wishes, Ken, for a challenging and successful future in your new post.

Cordially,

Inquiries

Some letters simply and briefly inquire about a product or service or ask some other question. Letters that concern information received or requested include those that (1) supply information about things such as products and services, (2) acknowledge the receipt of information, and (3) answer inquiries about things such as delivery dates and prices. These letters should cover the following:

1. Identify the incoming letter and acknowledge any information received.
2. State that your employer is away if that is the case.
3. Provide the information requested, if possible.
4. Advise the writer that your employer will contact him or her upon return.

General inquiry. Most inquiries are brief, straightforward, and specific.

Ladies and Gentlemen:

Do you have a copier service representative in or near Jackson? If so, please send his name and telephone number.

Thank you.

Sincerely,

Reply to inquiries. Be as informative and specific as possible in your first reply.

Dear Mr. Jackson:

In Ms. Cole's absence I'm replying to your inquiry about our Model ABC office copier. This copier is in stock and available at $525. A brochure describing its many new features is enclosed.

We appreciate your interest, and I hope this will be of some help to you until Ms. Cole returns next Monday, September 20. She will be happy to call you then to answer any further questions you may have.

Sincerely,

Introductions

The letter of introduction may be prepared for direct mailing to the addressee or for delivery in person by the one introduced. In the latter case, the envelope should be left unsealed as a courtesy to the bearer. When there is sufficient time for the letter to reach its recipient before the arrival of the person introduced, the preferable practice is to send the note directly to the addressee.

The letter is ordinarily written in a spirit of asking a favor. It should include:

1. The name of the person being introduced
2. The purpose or reason for the introduction
3. All relevant and appropriate details, personal or business
4. A statement that any courtesy shown will be appreciated by the writer

The writer's acquaintance with the person introduced and with the recipient of the letter and also the purpose for which the letter is written determine its tone. When the writer is introducing a personal friend on both social and business bases, the tone is informal. When the writer is introducing a business associate for purely business reasons, the tone is more conservative.

A letter introducing a new sales representative is distinctly promotional. It often includes a summary of the new representative's qualifications and background for this work, as well as an assurance of the person's desire to cooperate with the reader.

Introducing a personal friend.   Although the tone is more informal in this letter, it nevertheless includes pertinent background information about the friend.

Dear Ed:

My good friend Paul Davison plans to be in Akron next week and will present this letter to you.

Paul is very much interested in developing a house magazine for Robert Gould & Company of Cleveland, where he is in charge of the Sales Promotion Department. I have told him that you publish one of the finest house organs I have ever seen and suggested that he drop in for a chat with you.

I know that you and Paul will like each other, and I'm sure you can give him some valuable suggestions. I will certainly appreciate anything you do to assist him, and I know that Paul will be sincerely grateful for your help.

It must be about time for you to make another trip to Cleveland, and I hope you will plan to have lunch with me at the club.

Cordially,

Introducing a business or professional associate. The introduction written for only business reasons omits the informal comments of the preceding letter.

Dear Ms. Bradley:

I'm pleased to introduce to you a very good friend, Arthur Truesdale, chief engineer for the Acme Fisher Company.

Mr. Truesdale is making a careful investigation of the heating and power plants of some of our largest industries before writing a report on the subject. He tells me that your company has one of the most modern plants in our country and that he would like very much to inspect it.

Since you both might profit from knowing each other, I'm writing this letter and will greatly appreciate whatever assistance you can give Mr. Truesdale.

Sincerely yours,

Orders

Placing orders.   When a firm does not use a printed order form or requisition blank, orders are often written in a memo format, although the traditional letter format also may be used.

1. Indicate that your letter represents an order (or request for refund).
2. Give the name and address to which the bill should be sent.
3. List items desired, with all pertinent order data (catalog number, color, and so on).
4. State where the order should be sent and indicate if a specific delivery date is desired.

TO: Art Supply Store

FROM: J. T. Watt, Purchasing Department

OUR ORDER JF-610903

Please send the following item and charge it to our account number 730–01–221163.

One (1) #47321 Easel, Walnut, $45.95

Please deliver to our letterhead address, attention R. M. Blake. We will need this item by March 25.

Thank you.

Ladies and Gentlemen:

On August 5 I placed an order for rental of two overhead projectors to be used at our company's September 6 seminar at the Hotel Franklin. The rental fee was paid in advance by our check number 7808 for $37.50.

The seminar has since been postponed indefinitely, and we want to cancel our order. Please acknowledge this cancellation by mail and send us our refund of $37.50.

Thank you.

Sincerely,

Recommendations

Recommendations, or references, are commonplace in our mobile society. Not only do business people recommend employees for new positions, they recommend products, services, and so on.

1. Provide as much helpful information as possible.
2. Be objective, honest, and tactful.
3. In requesting a reference from someone, be certain to show appreciation.

To Whom It May Concern:

Jennifer King was employed as our office manager from 1984 to 1987. During this time she was responsible for the management of typing, duplicating, communicating, filing, records management, and other office functions.

Ms. King supervised a staff of fourteen and is credited with raising employee morale and efficiency to the highest level ever experienced during my association with this company. At all times she demonstrated a thorough and expert knowledge of office skills and procedures and maintained a steady, constant flow of high-quality work.

Ms. King would be a great asset to any organization desiring smooth and efficient office functioning, and I am happy to recommend her for any position in the area of office management and administration.

Sincerely,

Reminders

Most reminders are brief, factual restatements of something someone has forgotten or may forget without the reminder. The memo format is ideal for such brief messages to coworkers and well-known business associates and customers.

1. State the facts.
2. Ask for a confirmation by letter or phone.
3. Be tactful and do not accuse the recipient of being forgetful.

TO: David Jocelyn

EDUCATION COMMITTEE REPORT

Just a reminder that the Education Committee report you're preparing is due April 9. Could you drop me a note indicating the status of your project?

Thanks, Dave.

Requests

Letters of request ask to have something done. Like inquiries, these letters should be specific.

1. Tell what you want and, possibly, why.
2. Indicate what the recipient should do.
3. Give all necessary facts.
4. Express appreciation if special effort is involved.

Request for missing enclosure. If you urgently need the material, give the recipient a deadline.

Dear Mr. Pearson:

Since Mr. Symonds is out of town this week, I'm acknowledging your letter of April 12 to him. You mentioned that you were including the proposed plans for new tennis courts; however, they were not enclosed.

Mr. Symonds will need the plans in order to discuss this matter with the Board of Trustees. Since they are meeting early next week, could you please send them by the next mail? Thank you very much.

Sincerely,

Request for favor. All requests must be persuasive to some degree. In a request for a favor, a positive, friendly, persuasive tone is particularly important.

Dear Nora:

If you could spare a little of your time and expertise, I'd like to enlist your help for our November 7 seminar, "Computer Networking."

We've decided to publish the remarks of each of the twelve scheduled speakers and mail them to the attendees shortly after the seminar. But experience tells me that most of the papers will need a close reading and some careful editing to clean up the usual typographical errors and smooth out the typically awkward language of nonwriters. Our budget, however, has no allowance for purchasing outside assistance, so we're seeking in-house talent. As editor of our company's house organ, you have precisely the expertise we urgently need. I know how busy you are, but perhaps you could oversee the editorial function and assign the actual copyediting to members of your staff.

Everyone greatly respects and values your work, Nora, so I can add many voices to my own in asking this favor. I'm sure you know how important the seminar is to our company, and we truly do need your help. May we count you in?

I'd appreciate a call (extension 812) from you by the end of this week. Many thanks.

Best wishes,

Letters granting requests.   A friendly acknowledgment expressing pleasure in granting a request builds goodwill.

Dear Mr. Milliken:

We're glad to send you with our compliments the booklet "A Dozen Ways to Build Business." Your copy is being mailed today in a separate envelope.

Your interest in this publication is appreciated, and we hope the booklet will prove useful to you.

Cordially yours,

Letters explaining delayed action.   When definite action cannot be taken immediately, a note of acknowledgment is a business courtesy.

Dear Mr. Hanley:

I will be glad to send you whatever information I have on mailing-list testing that is relevant to your problem. You are right that I have been interested in this aspect of promotional work for some time, and I have accumulated a considerable amount of material.

Unfortunately, I must leave this evening on a business trip to Boston and Providence, and I will be away from the office for the next three or four days. But as soon as I return, I will check over the mailing-list material and send you anything that I think may prove helpful.

Cordially yours,

Dear Bill:

Just a short note to tell you that I have received your letter of April 24 concerning requirements for the housing project. May I have a few days to think this over?

You will hear from me further within the week, and I hope it will be possible for me to be helpful to you.

Sincerely,

Reservations

Letters making travel reservations. Although many reservations are made by telephone, key points to cover in a letter are:

1. Name and position of person desiring reservation
2. Flight, train, and so on with date on which space is desired
3. Schedule of flight or train
4. Class or accommodation desired
5. Travel or credit card number (if any)
6. Confirmation

Ladies and Gentlemen:

Mr. Edward Henderson, president of Henderson Industries, would like to reserve coach space to Los Angeles on Flight 261 out of Chicago on Saturday, November 24. Our schedule shows that this flight leaves at 9:45 A.M., central standard time, for Los Angeles, and arrives at 2:45 P.M., Pacific standard time. Mr. Henderson's travel card number is 72910.

Please confirm the reservation immediately and tell me what the fare will be. Thank you.

Sincerely,

Letters making hotel reservations. When you write for hotel reservations for your employer, include the following information (as well as personal requests your employer may have such as a room on a certain floor or a guaranteed reservation):

1. Accommodations desired
2. Name of person for whom reservation is requested
3. Date and time of arrival
4. Probable date of departure
5. Credit card number (if any)
6. Request for confirmation

Ladies and Gentlemen:

Please reserve for Ms. Jane Bergman a living room and bedroom suite, beginning Friday, January 5. Ms. Bergman will arrive the afternoon of the fifth and plans to leave the afternoon of the tenth.

Please confirm this reservation and tell me what the rate will be. Thank you.

Sincerely yours,

Sales Promotion

In large companies, sales letters are usually prepared by specialists. In other situations, however, promotional letters may be written by your employer with your help.

1. The message should arouse interest and prompt the reader to take action.
2. Describe what is being offered and tell why the customer will benefit from it.
3. Pave the way for possible further contact.

Dear Mr. Samuels:

Have we got a new copier paper for you! It's a completely new lightweight grade of paper designed and manufactured especially for your equipment.

This remarkable new lightweight substance-16 paper runs just as efficiently as the heavier sheets you've been using. Moreover, it has the same top-grade, brilliant white characteristics of the heavier paper, and it has the opacity needed for quality copying. What does all of this mean? It means a big load off your budget: reduced paper costs *and* lower postage and mailing costs!

Phil Evans, our representative, will be in your city the week of July 14 and will contact you before then to arrange a convenient time to let you test samples of the new paper. In the meantime, I'm enclosing a booklet describing its many features and uses.

Best regards,

MODEL SOCIAL-BUSINESS LETTERS AND INVITATIONS

Acceptance

A personal letter accepting something should convey appreciation and enthusiasm. If certain details are not clear, the acceptance must deal specifically with these points. Otherwise, a brief note is sufficient.

Accepting invitation to a special event.   Use an enthusiastic and appreciative tone in responding to any invitation.

Dear Mr. Nash:

I'll be delighted to be a guest of the Rand-Niles Company on the happy occasion of its fiftieth anniversary dinner.

Our association has indeed been very close, and I wouldn't miss being with you for anything in the world.

I'm looking forward to seeing you at the celebration.

Sincerely,

Accepting speaking invitation.   Repeat the details conveyed in the invitation or query the writer if any essential information is not clear or was omitted.

Dear Mr. Scott:

I'm happy to accept your invitation to speak at the American Business Administrators' annual meeting on March 5 at two o'clock. I've always admired your organization and look forward to the opportunity to attend one of your meetings.

What do you think of the topic "The Relationship between Business and the College of Business Administration"? This is simply a suggestion. Since you did not indicate how long you want me to speak, I will limit my address to thirty minutes unless I hear otherwise from you.

I'm eager to meet you and the other members of your society. In the meantime, if you need any information from me for your program, do let me know.

Sincerely yours,

Accepting membership in professional or civic organization. Ordinarily, association membership is handled routinely, and one does not respond personally. But sometimes a special invitation is extended personally and thus should be acknowledged personally.

Dear Ms. Foley:

Your cordial invitation for me to join the American Business Writing Association pleases me very much, and I accept with pleasure.

I realize that your membership includes many recognized authorities on the subject of business writing, both in academic ranks and in business circles. I'm highly complimented to have the opportunity to become associated with such a group.

Sincerely yours,

Birthday Greetings

Greetings on special occasions should be warm and friendly, with the degree of informality depending on the relationship of the writer and recipient. In all cases, avoid remarks about the person's age and, generally, keep the message brief.

Dear Helen:

Here's wishing you a wonderful and joyous day on December 12 and much happiness on every day that follows. A very happy birthday, Helen!

Regards,

Condolences

In any letter written to express sympathy, sincerity and tact are the most important qualities. Avoid words or sentiments that could distress the reader. Do not philosophize on the meaning of death or quote scripture or poetry. A letter of condolence should not be long and involved. A decision about the length is based on (1) the degree of friendship between writer and reader, (2) the situation that prompts the letter, and (3) the tastes and temperament of the reader.

Formerly, all letters of condolence were written in longhand, but today such letters to business acquaintances who are not well known to the writer may be typewritten on business letterheads.

In the case of the death of an intimate friend, a handwritten letter, on personal writing paper or foldover note paper, is correct. Some executives prefer to write letters of condolence in longhand, whether to a business or social acquaintance. In these cases, you give your employer the paper, the correct address, and perhaps a necessary fact or two.

To a business associate of the deceased.   A letter pertaining to a business contact, unless a personal friend is involved, usually omits an offer of assistance during the time of bereavement.

Dear Mr. James:

It was with deep regret that I learned this morning of the sudden death of Walter Conroy. I thought of you immediately, for I realize how great the loss of your good friend and business partner of some twenty years will be to you.

All of us in the furniture business will miss Walter. We admired the combination of kindness and honesty that his life represented. But since the loss to you is most direct and personal, I wanted to send you these words of sincere sympathy on the death of a loyal friend and trusted associate.

Sincerely,

To the widow of an employee.   A letter to a member of the family of the deceased may be more personal in tone, and an offer of assistance is common.

Dear Mrs. Echols:

It was with a very real sense of loss that I heard today of the death of your husband. I valued his friendship for many years. I don't believe I've ever known another man who was so loved and respected by all who knew him. It was a privilege to know Jack, whose place in our company can never be fully taken by anyone else.

My heartfelt sympathy goes out to you and your family. If there is any way in which I can be of assistance in the weeks ahead, please do not hesitate to call on me.

Sincerely,

To someone with personal injury, illness, or property damage. Most unfortunate situations are potential objects of a sympathetic message. Because of the endless variety of difficulties, each letter has to be especially tailored to the individual's circumstances.

Dear Clyde:

I have been watching closely the reports in the paper each evening about your progress, and I am delighted at the news of your continued improvement. Tonight's item says that you and the doctors have won the fight, for which your many friends here are very thankful.

I hope that you will be feeling more and more like your former self from now on and that you will soon be returning home.

Sincerely,

Dear Mr. Beckman:

We were extremely sorry to learn that your warehouse was damaged by fire last night.

Perhaps there is some special service that we can perform in this emergency. If there is, please feel entirely free to call on us.

You have been a friend and customer of Maybank Brothers for many years, and we want to be helpful in any way possible.

Sincerely yours,

Congratulations

The outstanding qualities of an expression of congratulations are (1) brevity, (2) naturalness of expression, and (3) enthusiasm. Trite, stilted phrases indicate a lack of sincerity and destroy the individuality of the letter.

For professional or civic honor. All letters of congratulations should focus on the subject and never discuss other business.

Dear Mr. Dodge:

I read with mixed feelings the announcement of your election as president of Norwich University. I am delighted, of course, at this splendid tribute to your ability and achievements. But I am also keenly regretful that it will take you away from Highland. The place you hold in the life of this community will be hard to fill.

The purpose of this letter, however, is to congratulate you on the high honor that has come to you, which you so well deserve. You have my very best wishes for continued success in your new work.

Sincerely yours,

On outstanding community service. Appointments outside of business present excellent opportunities to send messages that promote goodwill.

Dear Ms. Morrison:

I read with pleasure of your appointment as director of the United Cerebral Palsy Fund Drive in the community.

When someone as busy as you are makes time to assist in the conduct of the affairs of the town, it's time for the rest of us to applaud the wonderful job she is doing.

Please accept my sincere admiration and every good wish for your success.

Sincerely,

On retirement. Keep the spirit of unselfish praise for the recipient, even though he or she may be completely leaving the business community.

Dear Walter:

I just learned of your forthcoming retirement from Scott Investment Company and wanted to congratulate you on your record of wise leadership that has given your company the stature it now has.

No one, on retiring from business, has ever taken with him as high a degree of respect and good wishes from so many devoted friends and associates as you have received.

Sincerely,

On a business anniversary. Letters to customers or clients on special occasions build goodwill. One should focus on the occasion, however, and strictly avoid any sales-promotion effort.

Dear Mr. Laughlin:

We're delighted to send you our sincerest congratulations on the fortieth anniversary of The Personnel Group. All of us at Brownley Suppliers feel fortunate to have had you as a customer for many of those years.

The Personnel Group is widely known and respected for its substantial contribution to our community. You truly have something to celebrate in this anniversary year. From its inception, The Personnel Group has made steady growth and progress, gaining many new friends with every year of service.

We all look forward to your continued success and heartily salute your well-earned position in our community.

Cordially,

On service to company. Employees are commonly recognized for ten, twenty, or more years with a company. A letter of recognition briefly offers congratulations and acknowledges the person's good work, devotion, special contribution, or anything else that is pertinent and appropriate. A gift may be sent if the recipient is a good friend or if the occasion is a special anniversary.

Dear Marie:

Congratulations and all good wishes to you on your twentieth anniversary at The Information Center!

Here's a little gift for you to help you celebrate this happy day. Considering your outstanding record of progress and achievement, as well as the countless friends you've made, I know this is a significant occasion for you.

Everyone shares my best wishes for continued success and satisfaction in your career. Have a very happy anniversary, Marie.

Cordially,

Declination

Letters of declination should include an expression of regret and an expression of appreciation for the invitation. An explanation of the circumstances that prevent acceptance helps to show that the regret is sincere. The message must combine cordiality with tact.

Declining invitation pending further thought. When it is necessary to think about something, keep the letter brief, indicate when you'll give your answer, and close with a positive remark.

Dear Bill:

Just a short note to tell you that I have received your letter of April 24. May I have a few days to think about this?

You will hear from me further within the week, and I hope it will be possible for me to be helpful to you.

Sincerely yours,

Declining invitation to banquet, luncheon, or entertainment. Adopt a tone of sincere regret in turning down a special invitation.

Dear John:

For several weeks I have expected that you would be holding the annual foundation banquet in June, and I've been keeping my fingers crossed in the hope that I could be present. Unfortunately, June 15 is out of the question for me. I'll be in Boston at that time attending a company sales conference.

My sincere thanks, nevertheless, for your gracious invitation. I hope this year's banquet will be the best yet; under your capable guidance, I am sure it will be.

Cordially,

Declining a speaking invitation. It is not only acceptable but it is flattering to the recipient for a declination to state that you would like to be considered on another occasion.

Dear Ms. Connors:

It was good of you to invite me to be your guest speaker at the monthly meeting of the National Office Management Association on March 18. I know I would very much enjoy being with you. However, on that evening I am scheduled to speak in Boston.

I appreciate your thinking of me. Should another occasion arise, please call on me. I would be very happy to address the members of your group another time.

Sincerely,

Declining invitation to serve on civic or professional committee or board. Be certain to convey the impression that the declination is not meant to suggest that the activity is unimportant.

Dear Mr. Cavanaugh:

Thank you for your kind letter of March 6 in which you invited me to become a member of your Committee on Professional Standards in Advertising.

I would like very much to accept the invitation; unfortunately, my present business duties will not permit me to give such an undertaking the time and consideration it deserves. I want you to know, however, that your invitation is deeply appreciated and that you and your associates have my very best wishes.

Yours sincerely,

Declining request to support charitable or other organization. These letters must be firm in saying no but simultaneously let the writer appear warm and considerate.

Dear Mr. Duval:

I just received your letter of December 15 inviting me to participate in the fund-raising program of the Human Welfare Association, and I appreciate your thought in writing to me.

There is no undertaking more deserving of financial aid or any to which I would more gladly contribute than that which you represent. At the same time, I must tell you that all of the funds I have available for such purposes have already been earmarked and that it just is not possible for me to do what you ask at this time. Later, perhaps—but at the moment I do not feel free to make either a current or future commitment.

Although I am not in a position to lend active support just now, I send you my best wishes for success in the fine work you are doing.

Sincerely yours,

Invitations

Many invitations are sent by letter in the business world. However, whether formal or informal, invitations must include all necessary facts.

To attend a social event. Include the usual facts of time, date, and place.

Dear Mr. Walker:

The Scott-Miller Company will observe its fiftieth anniversary at an informal banquet to be held in the Langley Hotel junior ballroom at seven o'clock on May 7, 19—.

We hope that you will attend as a guest of the company. Since you have played a substantial part in its progress, your presence on this happy occasion seems particularly appropriate.

The program following the dinner will be varied and entertaining, and we are sure that you will have a most enjoyable evening.

Cordially yours,

To give an address or informal talk. Include a reason why the person would be an appropriate speaker for the occasion.

Dear Mrs. Serenbetz:

The Board of Directors of the National Office Management Association has asked me to extend an invitation to you to be our guest speaker at the monthly association meeting, Monday, December 7, at the Waldorf-Astoria Hotel at 8:30 P.M.

We have had many inquiries from regional members for updated information in connection with the use and misuse of aptitude, vocational, and personality tests used in modern employment practice. We know of your research work in this field and hope that you will be able to honor us with an acceptance to speak to association members at this time.

I look forward to hearing from you.

Sincerely yours,

Seasonal Good Wishes

Written in mid-December, letters of seasonal good wishes emphasize (1) appreciation of the reader's friendship, confidence, and cooperation and (2) an expression of good wishes for the holiday season and the coming year. Ordinarily, the message of seasonal good wishes should not be more than 150 words. the tone and content are influenced by the relationship involved, but they should all have the essential qualities of informality, friendliness, and sincerity.

Dear Mr. Ramsey:

The association with you during the past year has been so enjoyable that I want to send you this word of good wishes for a happy and successful 19—.

I hope the coming year will afford more opportunities for pleasant contacts between your firm and mine and that I will have the pleasure of further visits with you from time to time.

Sincerely,

Dear George:

As we approach the end of 19—, I realize that the enjoyable association with you has contributed much toward making it a very pleasant year for me.

In sending you these words of thanks for your kindness on several occasions, I wish for you the happiest of holiday seasons.

May the New Year bring you continued health, happiness, and success.

Sincerely yours,

Thank Yous

The opportunities to build good relations by saying thank you are limitless. In most cases, a brief note is sufficient.

Dear Mr. Bentley:

It was a rewarding experience for me to tour your plant facilities last week. The efficiency gained by your new assembly robots is truly amazing.

I sincerely appreciated the time you spent with me, Mr. Bentley, and I want to thank you for making my trip so informative and enjoyable.

Best regards,

Dear Erin:

I sincerely appreciated your help in getting out our company newspaper during my stay in the hospital. The issue was one of the best ever, and I'm truly grateful for the time and careful attention you devoted to the project. It really took a big load off my mind.

Many thanks, Erin. I hope I can be of help to you some day too.

Cordially,

—PART THREE———

How to Write Correctly

14. Correct Word Usage
15. Spelling and Word Division
16. Punctuation
17. Capitalization

—Chapter 14————————

Correct Word Usage

PARTS OF SPEECH AND RULES OF GRAMMAR

Parts of Speech

Noun. A word that names a person, place, thing, idea, action, or quality. It may be preceded by the articles *a, an,* and *the* and may be plural, show possession, or be used as the subject of a sentence, as the object of a preposition or verb, or as a predicate noun after certain verbs. *See also* **Grammatical Terms, Collective noun.**

> The *letters* (plural) were perfect.
>
> The *secretary's* (possession) *supervisor* (subject) was pleased with the *letters* (object of preposition *with*).
>
> The secretary typed the *letter* (object of verb *typed*).
>
> She was an outstanding *secretary* (predicate noun).

Pronoun. A word that takes the place of a noun. *I, we, you, he, she, it,* or *they* are personal pronouns used as subjects or predicate pronouns. *Me, us, you, him, her, it,* and *them* are personal pronouns used as objects. *Who* and *whom* are relative pronouns used to refer to persons or animals, *which* to animals or things, *that* to persons, animals, and things. *This, these, that,* and *those* are demonstrative pronouns. *Each, none,* and *some* are examples of indefinite pronouns. *Myself, herself,* and *yourself* are examples of reflexive and intensive pronouns.

> *It* (personal pronoun as subject) is *she* (as predicate pronoun) *who* (relative pronoun) will be in charge.
>
> To *whom* (object of *to*) do *you* (subject) wish to speak?

This (demonstrative pronoun as subject) is my typewriter.

Each (indefinite pronoun as subject) secretary must prepare *herself* (reflexive pronoun referring back to subject) for greater responsibility.

The manager *himself* (intensive pronoun emphasizing the subject *manager*) will conduct the campaign.

Adjective. A word that modifies (describes or limits) a noun or pronoun. Adjectives usually add *-er* (comparative degree) or *-est* (superlative degree) to mean more or most; they also may be preceded by the words *more* or *most* to express a greater or lesser degree of something. An adjective that is placed after a verb is called a "predicate adjective."

The *alert* (descriptive adjective) secretary caught the error in time.

The *bimonthly* (limiting adjective) report is directed toward executive secretaries.

The new machines are *easier* (comparative degree) to operate than the old ones.

The new models are the *most reliable* (superlative degree) of all machines in the company.

Her salary was *substantial* (predicate adjective.)

Adverb. A word that modifies a verb, an adjective, another adverb, or a clause or sentence. Some adverbs have an *-ly* ending. Others add *-er* (comparative degree) or *-est* (superlative degree); they also may be preceded by the words *more, most, less,* or *least* to express a greater or lesser degree of something. Adverbs often can be identified in a sentence as the words that answer the question how, when, where, how much, or to what extent.

He searched the files more (comparative) *thoroughly* (modifies verb *searched*) the second time.

It was an *unusually* (modifies adjective *busy*) busy day.

The report was *exceptionally* (modifies adverb *well*) well written.

Unfortunately (modifies sentence), the disk was lost.

Verb. A word that expresses action or state of being. A *transitive verb* has an object; an *intransitive verb* does not. *Auxiliary,* or *linking, verbs* are words used with a principal verb to form a verb phrase. A *regular verb* adds -*d* or -*ed* to the present tense to form a past tense and a past participle. An *irregular verb* uses a completely different spelling of the present tense in its past and past-participle form. A verb must agree with its subject in number and person.

> The secretary *has* (transitive verb) a heavy work load (object).
>
> She *types* (intransitive verb) quickly (no object).
>
> He *passed* (regular verb: *pass, passed, passed*) the exam.
>
> You *write* (irregular verb: *write, wrote, written*) the introduction.
>
> Each student and teacher *was* (*was* agrees in number with the singular subject *Each*) given a chance to speak.

Preposition. A word that connects a noun or pronoun (object of the preposition) with another word(s) and shows the relationship between the two. Some prepositions are followed by a verb, an adjective, or an adverb. A prepositional phrase is a sentence fragment of two or more words beginning with a preposition and including an object and any modifiers of the object. It may be used as a subject noun, an adjective, or an adverb. Examples of prepositions are *to, of, for, in, on, with, about, between, among, concerning, since,* and *toward.*

> The secretary left *for* (preposition) New York (object).
>
> The orders came *from* (preposition) above (adverb).
>
> *To understand the issue* (prepositional phrase as a subject) is to understand the alternative solutions.
>
> The office *of the vice-president* (prepositional phrase modifying the noun *office*) is closed today.
>
> She worked diligently *to finish on time* (prepositional phrase modifying the adverb *diligently*).

It is better to end a sentence with a preposition than to use an awkward construction, but it is incorrect to place an unnecessary preposition at the end of the sentence.

> Where is the book *at* (unnecessary preposition)?
>
> Now we know what the candidate stands *for* (*not* Now we know *for* what the candidate stands).

Conjunction. A word that connects other words, phrases, clauses, or sentences. *Coordinating conjunctions* such as *and, or, nor, but,* and *for* connect equal elements (words, phrases, clauses, or sentences). The conjunction *and* is frequently misused to connect two verbs when the second verb should be

an infinitive, for example: "Try *to finish* (not *and finish*) the chapter."
Subordinating conjunctions such as *if, as, since, because, while, after, before,
when, unless, until, though,* and *although* join a dependent clause to an
independent clause. *Correlative conjunctions* such as *either-or, neither-nor,
so-as, as-as, whereas-therefore,* and *whether-or* are used in directly related
clauses within a sentence. *Conjunctive adverbs* such as *therefore, however,
moreover, furthermore, nevertheless, consequently,* and *accordingly* join two
elements and also function as adverbial modifiers.

> Mr. Jacobs *and* (coordinating conjunction) Ms. Holt will conduct the
> seminar.
>
> We will call *when* (subordinating conjunction) the equipment is
> ready.
>
> *Either* Ellen *or* (correlative conjunction) Linda should go.
>
> Postal rates are scheduled to increase next week; *therefore*
> (conjunctive adverb) we should complete the mailing by Friday.

Interjection. A word, usually independent of the rest of a sentence, that
expresses sudden or strong feeling. Other parts of speech such as exclamatory nouns can also be used as interjections. Some words used as interjections are really slang expressions.

> *Oh* (regular interjection)! Look at that!
>
> *George* (proper noun used as interjection)! Are you serious?
>
> *Whew* (slang expression used as interjection)! It's hot today!

Grammatical Terms

Adjective. *See* **Parts of Speech, Adjective.**

Adverb, *See* **Parts of Speech, Adverb.**

Agreement of verb with subject. A verb should always agree with its
subject in number and person. The rule is simple, but the number of the
subject is not always clear. Mistakes sometimes occur when two or more subjects are joined by *and* (*see* **Compound subject**); when two or more subjects
are joined by *or, nor,* and the like (*see* **Alternate subject**); when a noun or a
phrase intervenes between the subject and the verb (*see* **Intervening noun**)
and when a verb is followed by a predicate nominative (*see* **Predicate
nominative**).

Alternate subject. Two or more singular subjects in the third person
joined by *or, nor, and, not, but, either-or,* or *neither-nor* take singular verbs in
the third person.

> *Neither* power *nor* wealth *is* (not *are*) a substitute for health.

If two or more subjects differing in number or person are joined by *or, nor, and not, but, either-or, neither-nor,* the verb agrees with the subject nearer it. (You may also rephrase a sentence to avoid awkwardness).

> *Either* the women *or* the supervisor *has* (not *have*) to work late.

Antecedent. Also called "substantive." A noun or pronoun to which another pronoun refers.

> *Janice* (antecedent) organized the office library, but *she* (pronoun referring to noun *Janice*) plans to expand it for departmental use.

Appositive. A word that explains or identifies another word(s).

> Henry Southby, *sales manager* (appositive), has been promoted to vice-president, sales.

Article. The adjectives *a* and *an* are known as "indefinite articles"; the article *the* is known as a "definite article."

> *A* (indefinite article) book on *the* (definite article) subject of telecommunications is being published now.

Auxiliary verb. Also known as "linking verb." A verb that is used with a principal verb to form a verb phrase. Auxiliary verbs are *be, can, do, may, have, shall, will, must, ought,* and sometimes *let.*

> She *must* (auxiliary verb) attend (principal verb) the conference.

Case. The relationship of a noun or pronoun to other words. The *nominative case* (subject) denotes the person or thing (noun or pronoun) doing the acting in a sentence. The *objective case* (object of a verb or preposition) denotes the person or thing being acted upon. The *possessive case,* formed by adding an apostrophe (') or apostrophe and *s* (Ms. Burns' house; Carol's house), is used to show ownership.

> *She* (nominative case—subject) sent the report to *him* (objective case—object of the preposition *to*).
>
> The *president's* (possessive case) opening remarks were brief.

Collective noun. Singular in form, the name of a group or collection of people or things. Examples are *team, family, audience, community,* and *committee.* A collective noun takes a singular or plural verb according to the intended meaning.

> The American *family* has not disappeared in the twentieth century as predicted (singular verb *has* to emphasize the family as a unit).
>
> The *family* were registering to vote (plural verb *were* to emphasize the individual members).

Comparative degree. A means of expressing a greater or lesser degree of two persons or things. Adverbs and adjectives both use the comparative degree. *See* **Parts of Speech, Adjective; Adverb.**

Complement. A word or phrase used after a verb to complete the meaning of a sentence. *See* **Direct object; Predicate adjective; Predicate nominative.**

Compound personal pronoun. A word formed by adding *-self* or *-selves* to the possessive of a simple personal pronoun.

> She typed it *herself* (reflexive compound personal pronoun referring back to subject).
>
> The citizens *themselves* (intensive compound personal pronoun emphasizing the subject *citizens)* wanted higher educational standards.

Do not use a compound personal pronoun in place of the objective case of the pronoun.

> Best regards from George and *me* (not *myself).*

Compound predicate. Two or more connected verbs or verb phrases.

> She *typed and edited the report.*

Compound subject. Two or more connected subjects (which require a plural verb unless preceded by a singular indefinite pronoun such as *each* and unless the compound subject refers to a single person or thing).

> *Personal progress and success* depend (plural verb) on many things.

The *vice-president and treasurer* (single office) is (singular verb) out of town.

Each officer and member was (singular verb to agree with singular pronoun *Each)* present.

Compound term. Applies to two or more short words written together, joined by a hyphen, or written separately but expressing a single idea. Thus *editor-in-chief, businessperson,* and *attorney general* are all compounds. The authorities differ about whether many compounds should be written as one word.

Plurals: Form the plural of a compound word by adding -*s* to the most important noun in the compound: *editors-in-chief, sons-in-law, attorneys general.* See also chapter 15, **RULES OF SPELLING, Plurals,** page 477.

Consistency: When there is a choice, decide whether you want to hyphenate two or more words, write them as one word, or write them as separate words, and follow the form you choose consistently. If your company has a style manual, follow it.

Meaning: Use the form that conveys the proper meaning. Although your dictionary might show two or more words joined together or hyphenated, the meaning might differ from the meaning of the same words used separately.

The *take-off* was smooth. We will *take off* from Kennedy airport.

He is very *matter-of-fact.* As a *matter of fact,* I didn't go.

Usage: Do not hyphenate or join words together simply because they are frequently used together. Wait until the grammar experts accept them in compound form.

Adjectives: Hyphenate two or more words used as an adjective when they precede a noun: *two-story* house, *short-term* loan, *no-par* stock, *above-mentioned* law, *well-known* politician. Do not hyphenate compound adjectives that follow a noun.

The author is *well informed.*

The teacher is *civic minded.*

Do not hyphenate color variations used as an adjective, such as *navy blue* dress, *light grey* paint.

Fractions: Hyphenate fractions when the numerator and the denominator are both one-word forms, such as *one-third, three-fourths, one-hundredth.*

Nationalities: Hyphenate two or more words to indicate that the person or thing shares in the qualities of both, as in *Anglo-American, Sino-Japanese, Latin-American, Scotch-Irish.*

Coined phrases: Hyphenate coined phrases, such as *middle-of-the-road, pay-as-you-go, drive-it-yourself, ready-to-wear.*

Adverbs: Do not use a hyphen to connect an adverb and an adjective. Do not use a hyphen to connect an adverb ending in *-ly* and a past participle in phrases such as a *happily married* couple, *brilliantly colored* picture.

Titles: Do not hyphenate titles such as *rear admiral* and *chief of staff,* but do hyphenate *secretary-treasurer* and other coined compounds. Also hyphenate *ex-president, president-elect,* and *vice-president-elect.*

Conjunction. *See* **Parts of Speech, Conjunction.**

Coordinate conjunction. *See* **Parts of Speech, Conjunction.**

Dangling modifier. A word, phrase, or clause that is misplaced in a sentence so the connection between it and the word it is supposed to modify is not clear.

> *After finishing the report* (dangling), editing began (illogically seems to modify *editing*).
> *After finishing the report,* he began editing (correctly refers to *he*).

Dependent clause. Also called "subordinate clause." A group of words that has a subject and a predicate but cannot stand alone as a sentence.

> The receptionist *who works at the front desk* will direct you to the Sales Department.

Direct object. A noun or noun equivalent that receives a verb's action. It often answers the question "what" or "whom" after the verb.

> She typed (what?) the *letter.*

Double negative. The use of two negatives to express a negative thought is wrong. Some double negatives, such as *don't want no, doesn't need none, wouldn't never,* are obviously wrong, but the insidious double negatives occur with words that convey a negative idea, such as *hardly, barely, scarcely,* *but, but that,* rather than with words that are definitely negative in form, such as *no, more, never. See* **TROUBLESOME WORDS AND PHRASES, hardly; scarcely; but; but that; not.**

Expletive. A word such as *there* or *it* that fills the position of the subject while the real subject is in the position of the predicate noun. The verb should agree with the actual subject. To avoid a monotonous succession of expletives, rephrase sentences, placing the real subject in its usual position.

> *There* (expletive) are (plural verb to agree with real subject *cartons)* four cartons arriving today. *Better:* Four cartons are arriving today.

Future-perfect tense. *See* **Tense.**

Future tense. *See* **Tense.**

Gerund. A verbal noun, that is, a word derived from a verb and used as a noun. A gerund always ends in *-ing.* If a noun or pronoun precedes a gerund, it must be in the possessive case. A gerund may function as the subject, as the object of a verb or preposition, or as a predicate noun. When you have a choice between a noun form or a gerund, use the noun form. *See also* **Participle.**

> Your (possessive case, not *you) buying* (gerund as subject) the house was a good investment.
> Mr. Blakely enjoys *selling* (as object of verb *enjoys).*
> Her style of *supervising* (as object of preposition *of)* is effective.
> Her Learning is *experiencing* (as predicate noun).
> *Accepting* (gerund form) the position was an ill-advised move. *Better: Acceptance* (noun form) of the position was an ill-advised move.

Imperative mood. *See* **Mood.**

Indicative mood. *See* **Mood.**

Indirect object. A noun or noun equivalent that usually tells to or for whom (or what) something is done. It is placed before the direct object and helps it complete the meaning of the verb.

> The manager gave the *president* (indirect object) his *report* (direct object).

Infinitive. A verb form used as a noun, an adjective, or an adverb, usually preceded by *to.*

Tense: Use the present infinitive, not the perfect, after past conditions such as *would have liked, would have been possible.*

> It would have been possible *to reduce* (not *to have reduced)* the
>   cost at that time.

Split infinitive: It is best not to split the infinitive by placing a word or words between *to* and the verb.

> The company agrees *to increase* (not *to substantially increase)* the
>   salaries substantially.

Split infinitives are preferable to awkwardness or ambiguity.

> *Awkward:* Efforts *to unite firmly* bolters from the party were a failure.
> *Improved:* Efforts *to firmly unite* bolters from the party were a
>   failure.

Series of infinitives: If qualifying words separate infinitive phrases, repeat *to* in each phrase; if no qualifying words intervene, do not repeat *to.*

> *To punish* and *expose* the guilty is one thing; *to help* the unfortunate
>   is another.
> It is improper for the debtor *to take* an unearned discount and then
>   *to refuse* to pay the difference.

Interjection. *See* **Parts of Speech, Interjection.**

Intervening noun or phrase. The intervention of a noun between the subject and the verb will sometimes cause trouble if the intervening noun is different in number from the subject. Remember that the verb agrees with the subject, not the intervening noun.

> *Celluloid* used as handles on umbrellas and canes *is* (not *are)* of
>   high quality.

A phrase coming between a subject and a verb can sometimes cause trouble. The verb agrees with the subject of the main sentence, not with the subject of the phrase.

> The *community,* as well as the owners of the land, *is interested* in
>   development.

Intransitive verb. *See* **Parts of Speech, Verb.**

Irregular verb. *See* **Parts of Speech, Verb.**

Linking verb. *See* **Parts of Speech, Verb.**

Misplaced modifier. A word(s) positioned in a sentence so it is awkward or appears to modify the wrong word. *See also* **Dangling modifier.**

> She *only* (misplaced) ordered the paperback edition. *Better:* She ordered *only* the paperback edition.

Mood. A term referring to the form of a verb that indicates the attitude of the speaker or writer. The three moods are indicative (concerns a fact), subjunctive (concerns the imagined or conditional), and imperative (concerns a command or wish).

> *Indicative: Is* this your typewriter? This *is* my typewriter.
> *Subjunctive:* If we all *go,* no one will be available to answer the phone. I wish Doug *were* here.
> *Imperative: Take* the day off. *Have* a good time.

Nominative case. *See* **Case.**

Nonrestrictive clause. A subordinate clause that is not essential to the meaning of the sentence and is usually set off with commas.

> The lesson plan, *which was more detailed than I expected,* is published with a separate resource manual and reading list.

Noun. *See* **Parts of Speech, Noun.**

Objective case. *See* **Case.**

Omission of words. Words may be omitted from a sentence only if they can be supplied clearly and exactly from a parallel portion of the sentence. In two clauses, if one subject is singular and the other plural, do not omit the verb.

> *Wrong:* The sky was clear and the stars bright.
> *Right:* The sky *was* clear and the stars *were* bright.

Do not omit part of a verb phrase if it is different in form from the corresponding part of the parallel verb phrase.

> *Wrong:* The company always *has* and always *will give* recognition where it is due.
>
> *Right:* The company always *has given* and always *will give* recognition where it is due.

Do not omit an article, a personal or relative pronoun, or a preposition that is necessary to the grammatical completeness or to the clear understanding of a sentence.

> *Wrong:* He wrote to the chairman and president (two persons).
>
> *Right:* He wrote to the chairman and *the* president (two persons).
>
> *Wrong:* I have great sympathy but no confidence in that class of people.
>
> *Right:* I have great sympathy *for* but no confidence *in* that class of people.
>
> *Better:* I have great sympathy for that class of people but no confidence in them.

See also **Infinitive, Series of infinitives,** for omission of *to* in a series of infinitive phrases.

Participle. A verbal adjective, that is, a word derived from a verb that modifies a noun or pronoun. The present participle ends in *-ing (taking). See also* **Gerund.** The past participle ends in *-en* or *-ed (taken).* The past-perfect participle is preceded by the word *having (having taken).* A participle that incorrectly does not modify a noun or pronoun is called a "dangling participle."

> The *winning* (participle modifying noun) photograph (noun) was announced today.
>
> *Sending* (participle with object) her (object) the information, realized how much I had to learn.
>
> *Speaking* (participle modified by adverb) slowly (adverb), he repeated the instructions.

Do not use the present participle for the past-perfect participle, which expresses an action completed at the time indicated by the main verb.

> He *completed* the report on schedule, *having worked* (not the present participle *working)* unusually long hours.

Passive voice. *See* **Voice.**

Past-perfect tense. *See* **Tense.**

Past Tense. *See* **Tense.**

Person. Identifies the speaker. The *first person* is the one speaking. The *second person* is the one being spoken to. The *third person* is the person or thing being spoken about.

> *I* (first person) am responsible for incoming-mail distributions.
> *You* (second person) are responsible for outgoing-mail duties.
> *They* (third person) are responsible for all other mail functions.

Possessive case. *See* **Case.**

Predicate. The part of a sentence having the verb and other words that make a statement about the subject.

> Jill and her staff *have a heavy work load during conference registration.*

Predicate adjective. *See* **Parts of Speech, Adjective.**

Predicate nominative. A noun or pronoun following an intransitive verb (one that does not take an object), thereby completing, or helping to complete, the predicate. As its name implies, a predicate nominative is always in the nominative case. A predicate nominative is also called a "complement." All complements, however, are not predicate nominatives. Forms of the verb *to be (am, is, are, was, were)* do not take an object but are followed by a predicate nominative. A common error is the use of the objective case of a pronoun *(me, us, her, him, them)* as a predicate nominative.

> It was *I* (not *me*) to whom you spoke.
> It was *he* (not *him*) who delivered the papers.

A verb must agree with its subject and not with the predicate nominative. Difficulty is caused by the use of a singular subject and plural predicate nominative or vice versa.

> A valuable *by-product* (singular subject) of training conferences *is* (singular verb) the numerous *opportunities* (predicate nominative) afforded for management to observe the trainees' reactions.

Preposition. *See* **Parts of Speech, Preposition.**

Present tense. *See* **Tense.**

Present-perfect tense. *See* **Tense.**

Pronoun. *See* **Parts of Speech, Pronoun.**

Relative pronoun. *See* **Parts of Speech, Pronoun.**

Restrictive clause. A subordinate clause that is essential to the meaning of the sentence and should not be set off with commas.

> A copier *that can enlarge diagrams* would be useful in our office.

Split infinitive. *See* **Infinitive, Split infinitives.**

Subject. A word or group of words in a sentence about which a statement is made.

> *The company* has five hundred employees.
> *The sales staff and the research staff* worked together on the product-development project.

Subjunctive mood. *See* **Mood.**

Subordinate conjunction. *See* **Parts of Speech, Conjunction.**

Superlative degree. *See* **Parts of Speech, Adjective.**

Tense. The time of action expressed by a verb. The six tenses are present, past, future, present perfect, past perfect, and future perfect.

> *Present tense* (denotes action occurring now): I *write* slowly in longhand.
> *Past tense* (denotes past time): I *wrote* the message in shorthand.
> *Future tense* (denotes future time): I *shall write* to you as soon as the product is available.
> *Present-perfect tense* (denotes action completed at the time of speaking or writing and action that also may be continuing into the present): I *have written* a lot about that subject.
> *Past-perfect tense* (denotes action completed at some definite time in the past): I *had written* a novel by the time I was eighteen.
> *Future-perfect tense* (denotes action to be completed at a definite future time): I *will have written* the press release by the time you need it.

Do not use the future tense for action completed before a future time.

> She *will have finished* (not the future tense *will finish*) the book
> before next month.

Do not use the past tense for the present-perfect or past-perfect tenses.

> I *was filing* when he returned, but I *had been typing* (not the past
> tense *was typing*) the report before that time.

In dependent clauses, a permanently true fact is usually put in the present
tense even when the main verb is in the past tense. (This rule does not apply
to independent clauses or sentences with one verb).

> We *were taught* (past tense) in school that "Hamlet" *is* (present
> tense) Shakespeare's greatest tragedy.

The present tense may be used idiomatically to express future action in
some cases.

> My vacation *starts* (for the future tense *will start*) next Friday.

Use the progressive form, not the simple present, to express action in
progress.

> When I *write* in the morning, as I *am writing* (not the present tense
> *write*) now, I compose with more facility than in the evening.

After the future tense in a main clause, use the present tense in a dependent
clause.

> The chairperson *will open* the meeting as soon as the speaker
> *arrives*.

When using the past tense, you must use the past-perfect tense to refer to a
preceding event.

> He *pledged* the books he *had bought* (not *bought*) last week.

Transitive verb. *See* **Parts of Speech, Verb.**

Verb. *See* **Parts of Speech, Verb.**

Voice. The quality of a transitive verb that shows when the subject is acting (active voice) or being acted on (passive voice). Voice is ordinarily not troublesome, but do not mix the voices by shifting from active to passive illogically.

> The jurors *deliberated* for forty-eight hours before the judge
> discharged them (*not* before they *were discharged* by the judge).

The passive voice is less emphatic than the active.

> The publisher *rejected* the manuscript (*not* the manuscript *was*
> *rejected* by the publisher).

TROUBLESOME WORDS AND PHRASES

about. If you are being precise, use *at;* if you are approximating, use *about.* But if a sentence already indicates an approximation or estimation, *about* is redundant. Never use the combination *at about. See also* **Parts of Speech, Preposition.**

> He will be here *about* (approximately) nine o'clock and will leave *at*
> (precisely) noon.
> The program will begin *about* (not *at about*) 8:30 P.M.
> I estimate that we will sell two thousand (not *about* two thousand)
> copies.

above. Preferably used as an adverb or preposition rather than as an adjective or noun.

> *Permissible:* The *above* outline.
> *Preferable:* The outline given *above.* The preceding outline.

accede (vb.). When it is followed by a preposition, use *to.*

> He will probably *accede to* the demands.

accompany (vb.). Use *by* when a person accompanies another. Use *with* when the reference is to some intangible thing.

He was *accompanied by* his wife.

The angry tones were *accompanied with* a pounding on the desk.

according (adj.). Follow by preposition *to*.

> *According to* the instructions, we register here.

adapt, adopt (vb.). *Adapt* means to make fit or suitable, to adjust; *adopt* means to take as one's own, to accept formally.

Many companies *adapted* their plants to the needs of an expanding economy.

The company *adopted* the suggestions.

addicted to, subject to. *Addicted to* means devoted to persistently, as to a bad habit or indulgence; *subject to* means liable to or conditional on.

> Jones is *addicted to* alcohol.
>
> This arrangement is *subject to* approval by Mr. Jones.

adept (adj.). When it is followed by a preposition, use *in*.

> He is *adept in* science.

adequate (adj.). When it is followed by a preposition, use *for* when "enough" is meant, *to* when "commensurate" is meant.

That amount is *adequate for* (enough) her living expenses.

That amount is not *adequate to* (commensurate) the demands made on her.

adverse, averse (adj.). *Adverse* means in opposition, unfavorable; *averse* means having a dislike for. *Adverse* refers chiefly to opinion or intention; *averse* to feeling or inclination.

> His report was *adverse* to the interest of labor.
>
> He is *averse* to criticism from others.

advise, inform (vb.). Use *advise* in the sense of counsel, warn; use *inform* in the sense of acquaint, tell, communicate knowledge to.

I will *advise* him not to accept the contract as it now stands.

I will *inform* (not *advise*) them that the contract is full of loopholes.

affect, effect (n., vb.). The word *affect* is not used as a noun, except as a psychological term; *effect,* used as a noun, means result.

The *effect* of a sarcastic business letter is to harm business.

Affect, as a verb, means to influence, to concern, to change; *effect,* as a verb, means to cause, produce, result in, bring about.

Passage of this bill will *affect* (influence, concern) the entire country.

Passage of this bill will *effect* (bring about) the cooperation of all parties.

Affect is also used in the sense of assuming or pretending.

He *affects* a blustery manner to hide his shyness.

ago (adj.). When a qualifying clause is used after *ago,* begin the clause with *that,* not *since.*

It was ten years *ago that* (not *since*) the stores were consolidated.

agree (vb.). You agree *with* a person, *to* a proposal, *on* a plan.

I *agree with* you.

He *agreed to* the suggestion.

The union will not *agree on* a compensation plan.

Also, a thing may agree with another thing.

The photograph *agrees* with the painting.

agreeable (adj.). Usually, it is followed by *to* but may be followed by *with* when used in the sense of in conformity or in accordance.

The plan is *agreeable with* (in accordance) my understanding of what is expected of us.

alike (adj.). Do not precede it with *both*.

> They are *alike* (not *both alike*).

all (n., pron., adj., adv.). When it is used as a noun, *all* is either singular or plural, depending on the meaning.

> *All* (everything) *is* forgiven.
> *All* (several people) *are* forgiven.

When it is used with a pronoun, *all* is a noun and is followed by *of*.

> Number *all of* them.

When it is used with a noun, *all* is an adjective; *of* is not needed.

> Number *all* (of the) sheets.

all right. This expression should always be written as two words.

> Are you *all right* (not *alright*)?

allusion, illusion, delusion (n.). An *allusion* is a reference to something; an *illusion* is a false image; a *delusion* is a false concept or belief.

> In his speech he made an *allusion* (reference) to the president's last news conference.
> The mirrors gave the *illusion* (false image) of a larger room.
> The company's accounting system creates a *delusion* (false concept) about its profits.

amend, emend (vb.). *Amend* means to improve or to make right. *Emend* means to correct or alter.

> The senator wants to *amend* the constitution.
> The manager wants to *emend* the foreword to the report.

among. See **between; Parts of Speech, Preposition.**

amounts. Words stating amount (time, money, measurement, weight, volume, fractions) take a singular verb.

> *Five days is* the usual work week.
> *Three feet is* the correct measurement.
> *Five yards is* what I ordered.
> *Three-quarters* of a pound *is* enough.
> *Ten dollars is* more than I expected.

anger (n.). Anger *at* that which hurts or annoys, *toward* a person.

> She expressed her *anger at* having to work overtime.
> She expressed her *anger toward* the supervisors.

angry (adj.). Angry *at* a thing, *about* a situation, *with* a person.

> I am *angry at* the computer.
> I am *angry about* the tight schedule.
> I am *angry with* Louise for backing out.

annoyed (vb.). Annoyed *with* a person, *by* that which annoys.

> I am *annoyed with* her.
> I am *annoyed by* her carelessness.

anxious, eager (adj.). *Anxious* is frequently misused for *eager.* To be *anxious* is to be worried; to be *eager* is to anticipate enthusiastically.

> I am *eager* to hear the new director's address.
> He is *anxious* (worried) about the outcome of the election.

anyone (pron.), **any one.** Singular, followed by a singular verb and singular pronoun.

> *Anyone* who *is* interested in *his* work *makes* a point of getting to work on time.

Of the two forms, *anyone* and *any one,* the first is correct when *anybody* can be substituted in the sentence with no change in meaning. In other uses, *any one* is the correct form.

> If we send *anyone* (anybody), it should be Mr. Jones.
>
> If we send *any one* of the salespersons, it should be Mr. Jones.

anytime. As an adverb, written as one word.

appraise, apprise (vb.). *Appraise* means to estimate something. *Apprise* means to inform someone about something.

> He will *appraise* the property.
>
> She will *apprise* the manager of her progress.

apt, liable, likely (adj.). *Apt* suggests a habitual tendency; *liable* usually means exposed to a risk or unpleasantness. When the sense is simple probability, use *likely*.

> Business people are *apt* (have a tendency) to dictate letters carelessly.
>
> A businessperson who dictates letters carelessly is *liable* to lose (exposed to the danger of losing) his or her customers. (*Note:* Some authorities condemn "liable to do something," allowing only the prepositional instead of the infinitive phrase—"A businessperson is *liable to* the loss . . .")
>
> He is *likely* to (probably will) vote against the bill.

as (n., pron., conj., prep., adv.). Use *as . . . as* in affirmative statements; use *so . . . as* in negative statements and in questions implying a negative answer.

> This window display is *as* attractive *as* the last one.
>
> This window display is not *so* attractive *as* the last one.
>
> Could any ambitious young man be *so* foolish *as* to turn down the offer (implying a negative answer)?

Use *as* to express comparison when a clause containing a verb follows. *See also* like.

> Copy the report exactly *as* it is written.

As is overworked when used as a substitute for *since, for,* or *because.*

> *Since* (not *as*) the opposition showed no sign of yielding, the
> minority abandoned its position.

Avoid using *as to* in place of a simple preposition such as *of, about, among,*
upon.

> She has no conception *of* (not *as to*) the proper performance of her
> duties.
> The witness testified *about* (not *as to*) the defendant's early life.

as if, as though, like. *As if* is less formal than *as though. As though* is used in
the same sense, and like *as if,* it is followed by a verb in the subjunctive
mood. *Like* is widely used and misused in informal conversation (*like* I said),
but authorities still recommend that it be used as a preposition and with a
noun or pronoun that is *not* followed by a verb.

> She hesitated to begin the project *as if* she were afraid it would fail.
> He angrily rejected the proposal *as though* it were a personal
> affront.
> The president acts *like* a dictator.

assure, ensure, insure (vb.). *See* **ensure, insure, assure.**

averse. Not to be confused with *adverse. See* adverse.

aversion (n.). Aversion *to* a person, *for* acts or actions.

> He has an *aversion to* the director.
> He has an *aversion for* public speaking.

bad (n., adj.), **badly** (adv.). Use the adjective *bad* when it refers to the
subject and is simply joined to the subject by the verb. When the verb
denotes action, use the adverb *badly* to modify the action.

> He looks *bad* (describes "he").
> He was injured *badly* in the accident (describes how he was
> injured).
> He writes *badly* (describes how he writes).

balance (n.). Frequently misused for *rest* or *remainder*. *Balance* is a financial term and should be used only in reference to the difference between two amounts.

> She gave the *balance* of the money to the Red Cross.
> We expect to ship the *remainder* of the order next week.
> The *rest* of the audience enjoyed the program.

because. Frequently incorrectly used instead of *that* after "The reason . . . is . . ." *See* **Parts of Speech, Conjunction.**

> The reason the goods were delayed was *that* (not *because*) they
> were shipped to the wrong zone number.

beside (prep., adv.), **besides** (prep., adj., adv.). *Beside* means by the side of, close to; *besides* means additionally, in addition to.

> The letter is on his desk, *beside* (close to) the file.
> *Besides* (in addition to) these two bills, several others arrived late.
> We have these two bills and several others *besides* (in addition).

between. Use the objective case after *between*. *See* **Parts of Speech, Preposition.**

> *Between* you and *me* (never *I*).

Use *between* when reference is made to only two persons or things; use *among* when reference is made to more than two.

> The friendliness *between* the British foreign minister and the
> American secretary of state promoted harmony.
> The friendliness *among* British, American, and Israeli delegates
> promoted harmony.

Do not use *each* or *every* after *between* or *among* when *each* or *every* has a plural sense.

> Almost all of the audience went into the lobby *between* scenes (or
> *between each scene*).
> It is essential that harmony prevail *among* the departments (not
> *between every department*).

biannual, biennial (adj.). *Biannual* means twice a year, although not necessarily at six-month intervals; *semiannual* implies an interval of six months, *biennial* means once in two years. *(Biannually, biennially,* are the adverbial forms.)

> The association holds *biannual* (two a year) conferences.
>
> Congresspersons are elected *biennially* (every two years).

biweekly, bimonthly (adj., adv.). *Biweekly* means once every two weeks or twice a week; *bimonthly* usually means once every two months. But it is clearer to use *once every two weeks, once every two months. See* **semimonthly, semiweekly.**

blame (vb.). Blame a person *for* something; do not blame something on a person.

> *Blame* the administration *for* the present difficulty (not *Blame it on the administration).*

both (adj., pron., conj.). Plural, followed by a plural verb and plural pronoun. *Both* is unnecessary with the words *between, alike, at once, equally,* and should be omitted unless the omission of the other words is preferable.

> *Both* the Democrats and Republicans *are* eager (not *equally eager)* to prevent the spread of communism. *(Or:* The Democrats and Republicans are *equally* eager to prevent the spread of communism.)

bring, take (vb.). These words are opposites. *Bring* implies "coming" with some person or thing to another place; *take* implies "going" with some person or thing to another place.

> I will *bring* the book *with* me.
>
> I will *take* the book *to* his office.

but. When it is used in the sense of *except,* some writers incorrectly consider *but* as a preposition and follow it with the objective case. The case after *but* varies according to its usage. When *but* and the word that follows it occur at the end of the sentence, the word after *but* is in the objective case. *See* **Parts of Speech, Conjunction.**

> Everyone *but she* (not *her)* enjoyed the entertainment. *(She* did not enjoy it.)

I told no one *but him* (not *he*) about the change. (I told *him* about it.)

A common error is the use of *but* after a negative.

I *can* (not *cannot*) but object to the title.

When *but* is used in the sense of *except,* it may follow a negative.

No one but he went.
He accepted *none* of the shipment *but* the short coats.

But what is correctly used only when *except* could be substituted for *but.* The use of *but what* for *but that* is a colloquialism.

He said nothing *but what* (or *except what*) any honorable person would have said.

but that. A common error is the use of *but that* instead of *that* to introduce a clause after *doubt* (either the verb or the noun *doubt*).

There is no doubt *that* (not *but that*) the shipment will reach you tomorrow.

But that is not interchangeable with *that.* Notice the difference in meaning in the following sentences.

It is impossible *that* the signatories to the United Nations Charter will sanction the move. (They will not sanction it.)

It is impossible *but that* the signatories to the United Nations Charter will sanction the move. (They are sure to sanction it.)

It is not impossible *that* the signatories to the United Nations Charter will sanction the move. (They may sanction it.)

Unnecessary negative: When *but that* has a negative implication, the subsequent use of *not* is incorrect.

How do you know *but that* the apparent friendliness of our competitor may be (not *may not be*) an attempt to probe our methods?

cabinet (n.). When it is used to mean a body of advisors, *cabinet* is a collective noun. *See* **Grammatical Terms, Collective noun.**

can, could (vb.). *Could* is the past tense of *can*. *See* **Grammatical Terms, Tenses.** Use *can* with verbs in the present, perfect, and future tenses; use *could* with verbs in the past and past perfect tenses.

> I give/I have given/I will give what I *can*.
> I gave/I was giving/I had given what I *could*.

Use *could,* not *can,* when *would* is used in the main clause.

> He *would* stop in Cincinnati on his way west if he *could* arrange to meet you there.

A common error is the misuse of *could* for *might* in conditional sentences. *Could* expresses ability, *might* expresses permission or possibility. *See* **can, may.**

> If you have not bought the stock, you *might* (not *could*) as well forget about it.

can, may (vb.). *Can* denotes ability or power; *may* denotes permission.

> *Can* you (will you be able to) make shipment next week?
> *May* we (will you give us permission to) make shipment next week?
> I *can* (it is possible for me to) go to Alaska by plane. *May* I? (Do I have your permission?)

canvass (vb.), **canvas** (n.). *Canvass* means to scrutinize, discuss, solicit, not to be confused with *canvas,* a heavy cloth.

> You should **canvass** the neighborhood for support.

capital, capitol (n.). *Capital* is a city that is the seat of the government; *Capitol* is the building in which Congress meets or a building in which a state legislature meets. State capitols may be spelled either uppercase or lowercase, but the United States Capitol is spelled with an uppercase C.

> Washington, D.C., is the *capital* of the United States.
> I hope the repairs to the *Capitol* are completed when we visit Washington.
> The *capitol* at Albany is being repaired.

Capital has several other meanings, for example, accounting assets, but they do not cause confusion.

careless (adj.). Careless *about* appearance and dress, *in* the performance of an action.

> She is *careless about* her dress.
> He was *careless in* checking the machine.

class (n.). Pl., *classes. See* **Grammatical Terms, Collective noun.** For correct usage in the sense of "kind" or "sort," *see* kind.

coincident (adj.). When it is followed by a preposition, use *with.*

> His theory is *coincident with* the facts.

committee (n.). *See* **Grammatical Terms, Collective noun.**

common, -er, -est (adj.). Preferable to *more common, most common.*

common, mutual (adj.). *Common* refers to something that is shared alike by two or more individuals or species, as *common fear* of war, *common trait* of character. *Mutual* refers to something that is reciprocally given and received, as *mutual agreement, mutual respect.*

> They have a *mutual* (not *common)* desire to cooperate.
> A *common* (not *mutual)* effort ensured the success of the project.

Mutual can also be used in the sense of "having the same relationship to each other."

> We have *mutual* (or *common)* friends.

compare to, compare with. If you want to suggest a similarity or to state that a similarity exists, use *to.* If you want to indicate specific similarities or differences, use *with.*

> The speaker *compared* the new law *to* a plague. (The speaker merely suggested a similarity.)
> The speaker *compared* the British law *with* the American statute. (The speaker made a detailed comparison.)

complacent (adj.), -ency (n.); complaisant (adj.), -ance (n.). *Complacent* people are pleased with themselves or with things that affect them personally. A *complaisant* person is eager to please by compliance or indulgence.

> Don't let your *complacency* about your work keep you from knowing your shortcomings.
>
> If Congress were in a more *complaisant* mood, the president might be able to push the law through.

complement, compliment (n., vb.). *Complement* is that which is required to complete or make whole; *compliment* is an expression of admiration. The noun *complement* is followed by the preposition *of;* the verb *compliment* is followed by *on*.

> This department has its full *complement* (noun) *of* workers.
>
> A gold clip on your dress will *complement* (verb) your costume.
>
> His *compliments* (noun) *on* my article were gratifying.
>
> The president *complimented* (verb) him *on* the showing made by his department.

complementary, complimentary (adj.). The distinction in meaning is the same as that between *complement* and *compliment. See above.* The preposition *to* is used with *complementary; about* or *concerning* is used with *complimentary.*

> Practical experience is *complementary to* theoretical training.
>
> Two *complementary* colors mixed together make a third color.
>
> His review of the book was not *complimentary.*
>
> *Complimentary* remarks *about* a person's work are always appreciated.

compliance (n.). When it is followed by a preposition, use *with.*

> They are in *compliance with* the law.

comply (vb.). When it is followed by a preposition, use *with.*

> You should *comply with* the law.

concur (vb.). Concur *in* a decision, opinion, belief; concur *with* a person.

I *concur in* that decision.

I *concur with* you.

conducive (adj.). When it is followed by a preposition, use *to*.

The machine's rhythm is *conducive to* relaxation.

confidant (n.), *confident* (adj.). *Confidant* is a person to whom secrets are entrusted. *Confident* means assured and self-reliant.

He was her *confidant*.

She was *confident* the project would be approved.

conform (vb.). When it is followed by a preposition, use *to* or *with*.

The report *conforms to* Regulation 6-AR.

connect (vb.). Objects, places, or people are connected *with* one another *by* certain means.

Gimbels used to be *connected with* Saks *by* a bridge.

connection (n.). The phrase *in this connection* is never good usage; the phrase *in connection with* is considered trite and is overworked. There is no grammatical objection to it when it is the proper phrase to use, but a substitution is preferable. Try *about* as a substitute.

He talked to her *about* (not *in connection with*) the report.

conscious (adj., n.), **aware** (adj.). *Conscious* emphasizes inner realization; *aware* emphasizes perception through the senses.

He became *conscious* of the reason for his failure.

He was *aware* of stale air in the room.

consensus (n.). An erroneous expression frequently used is *consensus of opinion*. *Consensus* means agreement in matter of opinion; therefore, the expression is redundant.

A *consensus* (not *consensus of opinion*) was reached.

consist (vb.). Followed by *of* to indicate the material, by *in* to define or show identity.

> Margarine *consists of* (the materials) vegetable oils and coloring.
>
> The sinking-fund method *consists in* (may be defined as) the payment of a sum.
>
> His greatest asset *consists in* (is) his ability to understand.

contemptible, contemptuous (adj.). *Contemptible* means despicable, deserving of being despised. *Contemptuous* means scornful.

> The effort to bring pressure to bear on him was *contemptible* (despicable).
>
> His comments on the report were *contemptuous* (scornful).

continual, continuous (adj.). *Continual* means occurring in close succession, frequently repeated; *continuous* means without stopping, without interruption. The same distinction applies to the adverbs *continually* and *continuously*.

> *Continual* (frequent) breakdowns in the factory delayed production.
>
> The machinery has been in *continuous* (without stopping) operation for sixty hours.
>
> He is *continually* (frequently) asking for favors.
>
> He drove *continuously* (without stopping) for six hours.

correct (adj.). Not comparable. If anything is correct, it cannot be *more* correct. *More nearly correct* is allowable.

correlative (adj.). When it is followed by a preposition, use *with*.

> The two methods are *correlative with* each other.

could. *See* **can, could.**

council (n.), **counsel** (n., vb.), **consul** (n.). *Council* applies to a board or assembly and to the meeting of such a body; *counsel* means advice or to advise. *Consul* is a government representative looking after his country's interests in a foreign country.

> The *council* met last Wednesday.

His job was to *counsel* prisoners.

He held the position of U.S. *consul* in Argentina.

credible, credulous, creditable (adj.). *Credible* means believable; *credulous* means easily imposed on, believing too easily; *creditable* means praiseworthy.

He is not a *credible* witness.

The readers are indeed *credulous* if they believe the editorial completely.

His summation of the case was highly *creditable*.

damage, injury (n.). *Injury* is the broad general term; *damage* is especially an injury that impairs value or involves loss. *Injury* is impairment of utility or beauty and applies generally to persons, feelings, reputation, character, and sometimes to property. *Damage* applies to property only.

He collected insurance for *injury* to his back and for *damage* to this car.

data (n.). Plural and takes a plural verb and plural adjective pronoun. The singular form *datum* is now seldom used.

We have proved that *these* (not *this*) data *are* (not *is*) reliable.

dates from. The correct expression is *dates from,* not *dates back to.*

The artifacts *date from* the sixteenth century.

deduction, induction (n.). *Deduction* refers to reasoning by moving from the general to the particular. *Induction* refers to reasoning by moving from the particular to the general.

Deduction: All computers accept some form of symbolic data; therefore, the XL100 should accept symbolic input.

Induction: Having read thousands of business letters, most of which have one or more grammatical errors, I believe that most business people need further education in basic English composition.

defect (n.). Defect *in* a concrete object; defect *of* an intangible quality, such as judgment or character.

The failure to pick up speed is a *defect in* the machine.
The *defect of* his character is impatience.

depositary, depository (n.). *Depositary* is applied to the person or authority entrusted with something for safekeeping. It may also be used to apply to the place where something is deposited or stored. *Depository* is applied only to the place where something is deposited or stored.

The president is the *depositary;* the bank is the *depository.*

depreciate (vb.). Do not follow *depreciate* by the words *in value.* If anything has depreciated, its value is less.

The ring has *depreciated* (not *depreciated in value*).

did (vb.). Sometimes misused in place of *has* or *have. Did* represents past action; *has* or *have* represents action continuing to the present moment. The misuse usually occurs with *yet* or *already.*

Did you listen to "Town Meeting" yesterday (past action)?
Have you heard the results of the election yet (not *did you hear*)?
I *have* not heard (not *did not hear*) the results of the election yet.

differ (vb.). Used in the sense of unlikeness, *differ* is followed by *from;* used in the sense of disagreeing in opinion, it is followed by *with.*

My sales campaign *differs from* yours.
I *differ with* you about the value of your sales campaign.

different (adj.). Do not use it to show separate identity that has already been established.

Three secretaries (not *three different secretaries*) asked for a
Christmas vacation.

different from. This is the correct form; *different than* is sometimes used when followed by a clause.

My sales plan is *different from* yours.
The computer looked *different than* I thought it would.

differentiate, distinguish (vb.). *Differentiate* means to show specific differences in two or more things. *Distinguish* means to point out general differences.

> You can *differentiate* among the fabrics by texture and design.
>
> You can easily *distinguish* evergreens from deciduous trees.

direct (vb., adj., adv.). The adverb form is *direct* or *directly*. *Direct* is not comparable. If anything is direct, it cannot be *more* direct. *More nearly direct* is allowable.

disappointed (adj.). Disappointed *with* a thing or object; otherwise, disappointed *in*.

> I am disappointed *with* the car.
>
> I am disappointed *in* the outcome of the election.

disburse, disperse (vb.). *Disburse* means to pay out. *Disperse* means to cause to break up or spread out.

> He *disbursed* the payroll.
>
> The crowd *dispersed*.

disinterested, uninterested (adj.). *Disinterested* means impartial, without selfish motive or thought of personal gain. *Uninterested* means not interested or enthusiastic.

> The teacher stated the case in a *disinterested* (impartial) manner.
>
> He seemed *uninterested* (lacking in interest) in his work.

dissent (vb., n.). When it is followed by a preposition, use *from*.

> He *dissented from* the majority.

do (vb.). Principal parts: *do, did,* and *(has, had,* or *have) done. See* **Parts of Speech, Verb.** For the misuse of *did* for *has* or *have, see* **did.**

doubt if, doubt that, doubt whether. *Doubt if* should be avoided in business writing. *Doubt that* is the preferred expression in negative or interrogative sentences when little doubt exists. *Doubt whether* is usually limited to situations involving strong uncertainty.

> I *doubt that* we can meet the deadline.
>
> I *doubt whether* anything will come of it.

due to. Often misused for *owing to. Due* is an adjective and must be attached to a noun or pronoun, whereas *owing to* is now considered a compound preposition. *Due to* means caused by. Test your sentence by substituting *caused by* for *due to.*

> The labor movement is losing prestige *owing to* the methods of some of its leaders. *(Methods* is the object of the compound preposition *owing to.)*
>
> The success of the firm was *due to* (caused by) the ability of its president.
>
> The firm succeeded *owing to* (not *due to)* the ability of its president.

each (pron., adj., adv.). When it is used as a subject, *each* invariably takes a singular verb and pronoun even when followed by *of them* or the like.

> *Each* of the reports made by the committees *was* a tribute to the late president.
>
> *Each carries his* or *her* share of the load.

When *each* immediately follows a plural noun or pronoun, the verb is plural.

> The *officers each take* an oath.

When *each* refers to a preceding plural noun or pronoun, the number of a subsequent noun or pronoun depends on whether *each* comes before or after the verb. Use the plural when *each* precedes the verb, the singular when *each* follows the verb.

> The *employees each have their* own assignments (precedes the verb).
>
> The *employees are* responsible *each* for *his* or *her* own assignment (follows the verb).

For the use of *each* after *between* or *among, see* **between.**

each other, one another. *Each other* should be used when only two things are referred to and *one another* when more than two are referred to.

> Smith and I see *each other* often.
>
> It will be interesting for the four of us to see *one another* again.

The possessive of *each other* is *each other's;* of *one another, one another's.*

They did not spare *each other's* (two persons) feelings.

They did not spare *one another's* (more than two persons) feelings.

economics (n.). Usually plural in form but singular in meaning; hence, it takes singular verbs and singular pronouns. *See* **-ics.**

> Economics *is* of prime importance to every student of commerce.
> Several courses in *it* are required.

effect. *See* **affect.**

either (conj.). Singular, followed by a singular verb.

> *Either* of these sales plans *is* excellent.

Use *either* to designate one of two persons or things; use *any one* to designate one of three or more.

> You may choose *either* of the (two) new typewriters or *any one* of the (three) old typewriters.

either . . . or (conj.). The construction after correlatives should be the same; for example, if *either* is followed by a verb, *or* must be followed by a verb. The misplacement of *either,* a common error, frequently results in an unbalanced construction after the correlatives

> You are required *either to register* by the 15th *or to drop* the course (not *either are required to register . . . or to drop*).
> *Either you must go* today, *or you must wait* until next week (not *You must either go . . . , or you must wait*).

elicit (vb.), **illicit** (adj.). *Elicit* means to bring out. *Illicit* refers to something illegal.

> The ad *elicited* a negative response.
> The harbor was known for numerous *illicit* activities.

else (adj., adv.). A common error is to combine *else* with *but.*

> It was nothing *but* selfishness on his part (not *nothing else but*).

The possessive of *somebody else* is *somebody else's;* of *everyone else, everyone else's;* the same form is followed for other examples such as *anyone else* and *no one else.*

emigrate, immigrate (vb.). *Emigrate* means to go *from* one's own country to another for the purpose of living there. *Immigrate* means to go *into* a country or place for the purpose of living there. *Emigrate* is followed by the preposition *from, immigrate* by *to.*

> Thousands of Jews *emigrated from* (left) Germany and *immigrated to* (moved to) Israel.

eminent, imminent (adj.). *Eminent* means prominent, distinguished, and is applied to persons. *Imminent* means impending, threatening, close at hand, and is applied to events. *See also* **immanent, imminent.**

> He is an *eminent* lecturer.
> A struggle for power between the two nations is *imminent.*

ensure, insure, assure (vb.). *Ensure* means to make certain. *Insure* also means to make certain or to give or take insurance (generally by purchasing it). In the sense of "making certain," American writers tend to prefer *insure,* and British writers tend to prefer *ensure. Assure* means to guarantee and is used only in reference to persons.

> They campaigned an extra week to *insure* (or *ensure*) that the measure would pass.
> She *assured* them that the deadline would be met.

equally as. Often incorrectly used for *equally . . . with,* for *equally* by itself, or for *as* by itself.

> The Republicans are *as* (not *equally as*) guilty as the Democrats.

-ever. Compounds of *-ever—however, whichever, whoever, whatever—*are not interrogatives. A common error, particularly in speech, is to use these compounds as interrogatives with the thought that they add emphasis to the question.

> How (not *however*) did you find out?
> Who (not *whoever*) told you that?

every (adj.). Always singular. Followed by singular verb and singular pronouns.

> *Every* large company in the industry *files its* reports with the trade association.
>
> *Everyone was* trying to better *his* or *her* position.
>
> *Every one* of the students who participated in the demonstration put *himself* or *herself* in the position of insubordination.
>
> *Every one* but he *was* at the meeting.

everybody (pron.). Write as one word. Always singular. *Everyone* is preferred.

every (adj.) **one, everyone** (pron.). Write as one word only when *everybody* is meant. If *of* is used, the expression must be written as two words.

> *Everyone* (everybody) should attend the meeting.
>
> *Every one of* the department heads attended the meeting.
>
> All of the drawings are excellent; *every one* (*of* the drawings) deserves a prize.

See every for the correct number of verb and pronoun to use after *every one* or *everyone*.

everywhere (adv.). Always written as one word. *Every place* is commonly misused for *everywhere*. *See* **place.**

expect (vb.). Expect *of* a person; otherwise, expect *from*.

> The company expects loyalty *of* its employees.
>
> They *expect* tornados to come *from* the hurricane.

faced (vb.). When it is followed by a preposition, use *by* or *with*.

> She is *faced with* a difficult decision.

farther (adj., adv.), further (adj., adv., vb.). Use *farther* to refer to distance; use *further* to refer to time, quantity, or degree.

> Philadelphia is *farther* from Washington than from New York.
>
> We went *further* into the matter.

This distinction, however, is disappearing, and *further* is widely used in all instances.

fatal (adj.). Not comparable. If anything is fatal, it cannot be *more* fatal. *More nearly fatal* is allowable.

feel (vb.). Followed by a predicate adjective and not by an adverb *(see* **Parts of Speech, Adverb),** unless it is used in the sense of touching physically.

> I do not *feel well* (predicate adjective modifying *I).*
>
> He telephoned and said that he still *feels* very *bad* (not *badly)* (predicate adjective modifying *he).*
>
> The doctor *felt* the bruise *tenderly* (adverb describing how the doctor touched the bruise).
>
> I *felt sick* when I heard the news (predicate adjective modifying *I).*

few (indef. pron.). Either singular or plural, depending on the meaning. *See* **less** for the distinction between *less* and *fewer.*

> A *few is* enough.
>
> Many are called, but *few are* chosen.

final (adj.). Not comparable. If anything is *final,* it cannot be *more* final. *More nearly final* is allowable.

firstly (adv.). In formal enumerations, the use of *first, second, third,* or *firstly, secondly, thirdly,* and so on is a matter of personal preference. However, *first, second, third,* is preferable. Do not mix the forms (not *first, secondly, third).*

formally, formerly (adv.). *Formally* means in a formal manner; *formerly* means previously.

> He was *formally* initiated into the club.
>
> He was *formerly* president of this company.

former (adj.). Correct when used to designate the first of two persons or things; incorrect when used to designate the first of three or more.

> Smith and Jones were at the convention; the *former* gave an interesting talk.
>
> Smith, Jones, and Brown were at the convention; *Smith* gave an interesting talk.

fractions. *See* **amounts.** For the use of the hyphen in writing fractions, *see* **Grammatical Terms, Compound term,** *Fractions.*

-ful. The correct plural of words ending in *-ful,* such as *spoonful, handful,* is *-fuls: spoonfuls, handfuls* (not *spoonsful, handsful*). *See also* **Grammatical Terms, Compound terms,** *Plurals.*

full (adj.). Not comparable. If anything is *full,* it cannot be *more* full. *More nearly full* is allowable. The adverb form is *full* or *fully. See* **Parts of Speech, Adverb.**

further. *See* **farther.**

generally, usually (adv.). Use *generally* in a general sense or as a whole; use *usually* when you mean in the majority of cases.

> It was *generally* believed that the market would rise.
> The market is *usually* erratic in a presidential election year.

good. *See* **well.**

goods (n., pl.). Always takes a plural verb and plural pronouns.

> The *good were* damaged in transit before *they were* delivered.

government (n.). In the United States, *government* is construed as singular; in Great Britain, as plural.

> The United States *government is* sending *its* delegates to the meeting.
> Her Majesty's *government are* sending *their* delegates to the meeting.

group (n.). *See* **Grammatical Terms, Collective noun.**

guarantee (n., vb.), **guaranty** (n.). For the verb, always use *guarantee.* Business convention has established a specialized use of *guaranty* as a noun, which is illustrated in expressions such as *contract of guaranty, act of guaranty.* However, *guarantee* is never wrong, even in these expressions. A safe rule to follow is: when in doubt, use *guarantee.*

> The manufacturer's *guarantee* expires next year.

habitual (adj.). When it is followed by a preposition, use *with.*

It is *habitual with* him.

had (vb.). *Had . . . have* is sometimes carelessly used in inverted sentences when only *had* is required.

> Had I been (not *have been*) on the jury, I would have voted to
> acquit him.

An incorrect use of *had . . . have* occurs when the sentence has not been inverted.

> If I had been (not *had have been*) on the jury I would have voted to
> acquit him.

hardly (adv.). This word conveys a negative idea and should not be used with a negative. The error usually occurs when the speaker or writer decides to modify a negative statement.

> The company *can hardly* (not *cannot hardly)* take that attitude.

Hardly is used only in the sense of *scarcely*. The adverb of *hard,* meaning firm or solid, is the same as the adjective—*hard.* The following examples illustrate how the use of *hardly* changes the meaning of a sentence.

> His salary as president of the company is *hard* earned.
> His salary as president of the company is *hardly* earned.

he. Nominative case of third-person singular pronoun. For misuse of *he* instead of *him, see* **Parts of Speech, Pronoun.** For use after forms of the verb *to be (am, is, are, was, were), see* **Grammatical Terms, Predicate nominative.**

heavy (n., adj., adv.). The adverb forms are *heavy, heavier, heaviest,* or *heavily, more heavily, most heavily. See* **Parts of Speech, Adverb.**

help (n., vb.). Should not be followed by *but* when used in the sense of avoid.

> I cannot *help feeling* (not *help but feel*) that you are unwise.

her (pron.). Objective case of *she.* For use as an object, *see* **Parts of Speech, Pronoun.** For misuse of *her* instead of *she* after forms of the verb *to be (am, is, are, was, were), see* **Grammatical Terms, Predicate nominative.**

him (pron.). Objective case of *he*. For use as an object, *see* **Parts of Speech, Pronoun.** For misuse of *him* instead of *he* after forms of the verb *to be (am, is, are, was, were), see* **Grammatical Terms, Predicate nominative.**

himself. *See* **Grammatical Terms, Compound personal pronoun.**

hope (n., vb.). Sometimes incorrectly used in the plural after *no.*

> We have no *hope* (not *hopes*) of receiving payment.

When *hope* is used in the passive voice, the indefinite pronoun *it* is always the subject. The error usually occurs when *it* is omitted from the parenthetical expression *it is hoped*, especially in a clause introduced by *what.*

> This region is now experiencing what, *it is hoped* (not *what is hoped*), will be a short cold spell. *(What* is the subject of *will be.)*

I. Nominative case of first-person singular pronoun. For use of *I* instead of *me, see* **Parts of Speech, Pronoun.** For use after the forms of the verb *to be (am, is, are, was, were), see* **Grammatical Terms, Predicate nominative.** Avoid use of the editorial *we* instead of *I* in a letter written on behalf of a company. Use *I* when referring to the writer individually and *we* when referring to the company. *I* and *we* may be used in the same letter.

> *I* (the writer) will look after this order, and you may be sure *we* (the company) will ship it tomorrow.

-ics. A few English words end in *-ic—music, rhetoric, logic, magic*—but the normal form is *-ics.* Words ending in *-ics* are sometimes treated as singular and sometimes as plural.

> *Singular when used strictly as the name of a science or study: Politics* (the science of) *is* most interesting.
> *Singular when used with a singular noun complement: Politics is a game* at which more than two can play.
> *Plural when used loosely and when denoting qualities, usually preceded by his, the, such: Such politics* never *win* an election.
> *Plural when denoting practice or activity: Superb tactics were* responsible for our victory.

identical (adj.). When it is followed by a preposition, use *with* or *to.*

Your suit is *identical to* mine.

if (conj.). Often misused in place of *whether.*

I am not sure *whether* (not *if*) I can ship the goods on that date.

Avoid the use of *if and when.* Only in rare cases is *if and when* really better in a sentence than *if* or *when.*

He told the union members that *when,* or *if,* the Republicans gain control, conditions will change.

ignorant (adj.). When it is used in the sense of uninformed, follow by *in;* in the sense of unaware, by *of.*

He treats her as though she were *ignorant in* the subject.
I was *ignorant of* his interest in the matter.

ill (adj.). When it is followed by a preposition, use *with.*

He is *ill with* the flu.

immanent, imminent (adj.). *Immanent* means indwelling, inherent. *Imminent* means impending, threatening, close at hand.

Honesty and fairness are *immanent* in the president's character.
The passage of the bill is *imminent.*

immigrate (vb.). *See* emigrate.

impatient (adj.). Impatient *at* actions or characteristics; *with* persons.

I am *impatient at* delays.
I am *impatient with* Mark.

imply, infer (vb.). *Imply* means to suggest, insinuate, express vaguely. *Infer* means to draw from, deduce from, gather from, or conclude from.

Your letter *implies* that I have tried to evade payment of the bill.
I *infer* from your letter that you cannot grant an extension of time.

impossible (adj.). Not comparable. If anything is *impossible,* it cannot be *more* impossible. *More nearly impossible* is allowable.

in, into (n., prep., adj., adv.). *In* denotes position or location; *into* denotes action, motion from without to within.

> He was *in* the sales department but is now *in* the advertising department.
> Put this folder *in* (not *into*) the file drawer before locking it. (The folder itself is passive and takes no action.)
> We went *into* the room.

Do not use *into* for the words *in to* (adverb and preposition).

> He went *in to* the meeting. (You cannot go *into* the meeting.)
> He took her *in to* (not *into*) dinner.

inasmuch (conj.). Always written as one word.

infer. *See* **imply.**

inferior (adj.). Should be followed by *to,* not *than.*

> Their products are always *inferior* from every point of view *to* ours.

inform. *See* **advise.**

ingenious, ingenuous (adj.). *Ingenious* means clever, skillful; *ingenuous* means frank, innocent, trusting.

> He concocted an *ingenious* (clever) plan to avoid the law.
> He is very *ingenuous* (trusting, easily fooled) for a man of his age and background.

insofar as (conj.). *Insofar* may be written as one word or three; one is preferred.

interstate (n., adj.), **intrastate** (adj.). *Interstate* means between two or more states. It can also refer to a highway that crosses two or more states. *Intrastate* means within one state.

> He traveled *Interstate* 80 between Iowa and Illinois.
> They engaged in *interstate* commerce between New York and New Jersey.
> They engaged in strictly *intrastate* commerce in Delaware.

investigation (n.). When it is followed by a preposition, use *of.*

> The *investigation of* merger trends is almost over.

its (adj.), **it's.** *Its* is the possessive form of the impersonal pronoun *it. It's* is a contraction of *it* and *is* or *it* and *has* and is sometimes incorrectly used as a possessive.

> The company has expanded greatly in recent years; *its* success is
> attributable to *its* founders.
>
> *It's* too bad that the books will not be ready for delivery by
> September.
>
> *It's* (it has) been three months since we received that order.

jury (n.). *See* **Grammatical Terms, Collective noun.**

kind (n.). Pl., *kinds.* The explanation here applies also to *class, sort, type, size, breed, brand, quality, variety, species,* and similar words. The singular form is modified by *this* and *that,* not *these* and *those.*

> *This* (not *these*) *kind* does not grow readily; *that* (not *those*) does
> grow readily.

The expression *kind of* is followed by a singular noun unless the plural idea is particularly strong. The common error is inconsistency.

> The *kind of position* (not *positions*) that appeals to me doesn't
> interest her.
>
> The *kind of positions* I prefer *are those* that offer a lot of company
> benefits.

It is incorrect to follow *kind of* by *a.*

> What *kind of* (not *kind of a*) position do you want?

After the plural form *kinds of,* a singular or a plural noun may be used.

> The *kinds of* writing that *are* the most lucrative *are* novels and
> inspirational books.
>
> The *kinds of* books that they publish *are* novels and textbooks.

know, realize (vb.). *Know* means to perceive, to understand. *Realize* means to accomplish, to grasp fully, and implies a more thorough understanding than *know*.

> I *know* a better route.
>
> I *realize* the implications of our action.

latter, last (adj.). The word *latter* may be used to designate the second of two persons or things previously mentioned but should not be used where more than two have been mentioned.

> We are now conducting a special sale of suits and overcoats; the *latter* (not *last*) are particularly good value.
>
> We are now conducting a special sale of hats, suits, and overcoats; the *overcoats* are particularly good value.

Do not use the expression *the latter part of.* The correct expressions are *toward the end of, the last part of.*

> The book will be published *toward the end of* next month.
>
> The book will be published *the last part of* next month.

lay, lie (vb.). *Lay* means to put or set down, place, deposit. *Lie* means to rest, to be in a certain position or location. *Lay* takes an object; *lie* confines the action to the subject. Principal parts, *lay: lay, laid, laid, laying.* Principal parts, *lie: lie, lay, lain, lying.* The common error is the use of *lay* or one of its principal parts for *lie* or one of its principal parts. Thus *lay* is used incorrectly in place of *lie*. Remember that you must lay *something* down.

> *lay, laid, laid, laying:*
>
> You *lay* the *book* on the table, and it *lies* there.
>
> You *laid* the *book* on the table yesterday, and it *lay* there until Mary picked it up.
>
> I *lay* the *letters* in the same place on his desk each morning.
>
> I *laid* the *letters* on his desk before I left the room.
>
> The brickmason *has laid* the *stones* in an irregular pattern.
>
> The brickmason *is laying* the *stones* in an irregular pattern.

> *lie, lay, lain, lying:*
>
> I *lie* (not *lay*) in the sun for an hour every day.
>
> I *lay* (not *laid*) in the sun for an hour yesterday (past tense).

The book *has lain* (not *laid)* there for a month.

The book *is lying* (not *laying)* here where you laid it.

lead (vb.). Principal parts, *lead, led, led. See* **Parts of Speech, Verb.**

less (prep., adj., adv.). Use *less* only in the sense of a smaller amount. Apply *less* only to things that are measured by amount and not by size, quality, or number.

He has *less* (a smaller amount of) assets than liabilities.

The staff in the New York office is *smaller* (not *less)* than that in the Chicago office.

Fewer (not *less)* industrial accidents occurred this year than last.

liable (adj.), **libel** (n.). *See also* **apt.** *Liable* means responsible or obligated according to law. *Libel,* as a noun, means a written defamatory statement.

The company is *liable* for the damages.

He sued the writer for *libel.*

like (n., vb., conj., interj., prep., adj., adv.). Commonly misused in place of *such as* when the meaning is *for example.*

In his factory are a number of useful machines, *such as* (not *like)* cutters and stamps.

Use *like* as a preposition, *as* as a conjunction. *Like* takes an object; *as,* or *as if,* introduces a clause.

You are *like me* in your desire for perfection. (No verb follows *like.)*

He treats her *as if* (not *like)* she were ignorant.

I wish I could think *as* (not *like)* he (does). (The verb is understood.)

likely. *See* **apt.**

live (vb.). Live *in* a town, *on* a street, *at* a certain address, *by* means of a livelihood.

He lives *in* New York *on* Tenth Street.

He lives *at* 231 West Tenth Street.

He lives *by* selling family heirlooms.

loan (n., vb.), **lend** (vb.). Many authorities object to any use of *loan* as a verb. It is best to use the word only in connection with formal banking transactions—for example, placing a *loan* through a banker. For general purposes, use *lend*. Never use *borrow* to mean *lend*.

> Will you *lend* (not *loan*) me ten dollars?
> He *lent* (not *loaned*) me ten dollars.
> The bank *loaned* the money at 12 percent interest.
> *Lend* (not *borrow*) me a quarter, please.

loose (adj.). Means unfastened. Frequently confused with *lose* (verb), meaning to misplace.

> The handle is *loose*.
> Did you *lose* the pen?

majority (n.). Relates to the greater of two parts regarded as parts of a whole.

> A *majority* (greater number) of my hours are spent on the computer.

Plurality: In a contest, *majority* means more than half of the votes cast, whereas *plurality* means more votes than any other candidate received but less than half of the votes cast.

> Smith received a *plurality* but not a *majority* of the votes. There were 21,000 votes cast, and Smith received only 10,000. Jones received 7,000, so Smith's *plurality* was 3,000. A *majority* is necessary for election.

Number: Majority is singular or plural depending on the sense in which it is used. Thus when *majority* is plural, it is followed by a plural verb. When it refers to majority as a whole, it takes a singular verb.

> The *majority* (the majority as a whole) *is* against the new bill.
> A *majority* (the larger number as individuals) *are* against the new bill.

many a. Always takes a singular verb, even if it is followed by a compound subject.

Many a newspaper and magazine *has* published his work.

mass (n.). Do not capitalize it in reference to individual celebrations, but do capitalize it in reference to the eucharistic sacrament. A *mass* is offered or celebrated, not held.

They celebrated *mass* at 6 o'clock in the morning.

mathematics. *See* **-ics.**

may. *See* **can.**

may, might (vb.). When expressing possibility in a simple sentence, these words are usually interchangeable.

> I suggest that we settle the question now; otherwise it *may* (or *might)* cause trouble several years hence.
> We *may* (or *might)* decide to order a different make.

Might is the past tense of *may.* In using *may* or *might,* generally observe the proper sequence of tenses. With the present, perfect, and future tenses, use *may;* with the past or past perfect, use *might.*

> I give/I have given/I will give you the information so that you *may* understand the situation.
> I gave/I was giving/I had given you the information so that you *might* understand the situation.
> As we *have seen,* it *may be* wise to allow the debtor additional credit.
> I *have not heard* what happened this morning, but he *may have persuaded* her to adopt his view.
> The president *said* that we *might have* a holiday.
> The instructions *were* that, come what *might,* the task should be completed by the end of September.

Might is conditional. It is used in the main clause of a conditional sentence whether the condition is expressed or implied.

> Anyone *might* learn the facts from the report (if he read it).
> If the product is successful, it *might be* necessary to increase the size of the plant. (The increase is conditional on success.)

If the certificate fails to make provision for the issuance of stock in series, it subsequently *might be* amended to include that provision.

Might is used in the sense of *would perhaps* in a conditional statement.

With a little persuasion, Mr. Brown *might* (would perhaps) agree to that arrangement.

Might is used in the subjunctive to express a supposition.

He spoke *as though* he *might* sever his connections with the company.

May is used in prayer and benedictions. The subjunctive *might* denotes wish without expectation of fulfillment.

May God bless you.

See can, could, for the misuse of *could* for *might* in conditional sentences.

me (pron.). Objective case of *I.* For use as an object, *see* **Parts of Speech, Pronoun.** For misuse of *me* instead of *I* after forms of the verb *to be (am, is, are, was, were), see* **Grammatical Terms, Predicate nominative.**

might. *See* **may.**

minimal (adj.), **minimum** (n.). *Minimal* is that constituting the least possible. *Minimum* means the least quantity or value possible.

His contribution was *minimal.*
The *minimum* temperature was below freezing last year.

monopoly (n.). When it is followed by a preposition, use *of.*

They have a *monopoly of* the market.

more than one. Always takes a singular noun and verb, although the meaning is plural.

More than one *defendant is* involved.

most (n., pron., adj., adv.), **almost** (adv.). *Most* is used with an adjective to express the superlative degree. Do not use *most* for the adverb *almost*.

> He is the *most eager* of the boys.
> *Almost* all senators voted against the bill.

Most in many constructions also changes the meaning of the sentence when it is used incorrectly.

> I am *most ready* to go (more ready than others).
> I am *almost ready* to go (nearly ready to go).

mutual. *See* **common.**

myself. *See* **Grammatical Terms, Compound personal pronoun.**

neither (pron., conj., adj., adv.). Singular, followed by singular verb. The use of a plural verb after *neither* is a common error.

> *Neither* of these plans *is* satisfactory.

Use *neither* to designate between one of two persons or things; use *none* or *no* instead of *neither* to designate one of three or more.

> He decided that *neither* of the (two) plans suggested was satisfactory.
> He decided that *none* of the (five) plans was satisfactory.
> *No* report submitted to date covers the subject adequately.

neither . . . nor (conj.). It is always incorrect to use *or* with *neither*. The construction after correlatives should be parallel. The misplacement of *neither* frequently results in unbalanced construction after the correlatives.

> The plan meets the approval *neither of* the president *nor of* the treasurer.
> The plan meets the approval of *neither* the president *nor* the treasurer.

news (n.). Plural in form but singular in meaning.

> The *news is* good.

nobody (pron.). Always written as one word. *No one* is preferred. Use a singular verb with both *nobody* and *no one*.

> *No one is* working today.

none (indef. pron.). Either singular or plural, depending on the meaning.

> We asked for volunteers, but *none* of them *was* willing to go.
> I want *none* of them to go unless *they* want to.

no . . . or. When *no* precedes the first word or phrase in a series and is applicable to each, connect the words or phrase with *or*, not *nor*.

> *No* man, woman, *or* child can be happy without friends.
> Several of the families had *no* fuel to burn *or* money with which to buy it (no fuel, no money).

not (adv.). *Not* is often superfluous in a subordinate clause after a negative in the main clause. In each of the following sentences, *not* should be omitted.

> No one knows how much time may (not *may not*) be wasted in argument.
> Do you think there might (not *might not*) be some other cause at work here?

Not is correct when its use is necessary to convey the intended meaning, but usually a better construction is the substitution of *no* for *not*.

> Is it impossible for you to realize that *no* merger will be consummated?
> He does not believe that there are *no* extenuating circumstances.

nowhere (n., adv.). Always written as one word. Do not add an *s* to *nowhere; no place* is commonly misused for *nowhere*.

> I have gone *nowhere* today.

number (n.). Followed by a singular verb when used collectively, by a plural verb when used distributively.

A *number* of company rules and regulations (as a group, not specific) *discourages* employee initiative.

A *number* of the company's rules and regulations (certain ones in the group) *discourage* employee initiative.

odds (n., pl.). Always takes a plural verb.

The *odds are* against him.

off (prep., vb., adj., adv.). Never follow *off* by *of.*

He gave me 10 percent *off* (not *off of*) the list price.

oneself (pron.). Formerly *one's self* but now preferably written as one word.

Conducting *oneself* professionally is essential in business.

only (adv., adj.). The meaning that the sentence is intended to convey determines the position of the word *only.*

Only his assistant has authority to sign the payroll record.

His assistant has *authority only to sign* the payroll record, not to prepare it.

His assistant has authority to sign *only the payroll record* (or *the payroll record only*).

Each of these sentences conveys a different meaning. The first states that the assistant is the only one with authority to sign; the second, that the assistant has no authority beyond signing; and the third, that the assistant has authority to sign the payroll record but nothing else.

Only is sometimes erroneously used as a conjunction.

The *one* (or *only*) difference between your pen and mine is the different nib (*not* Your pen is the same as mine *only* that the nib is different).

oral (adj.). *Verbal* is often misused for *oral. See* **verbal.**

over (prep., vb., adj., adv.). The expression *over with* is erroneous; the *with* is superfluous.

Our annual sale is now *over* (not *over with*).

owing to. *See* **due to.**

people (n.). Singular in form but plural in meaning. The plural *peoples* is used when more than one race or nation is referred to.

The *peoples* of France and Italy share many economic goals.

Persons, people: When referring to a number of individuals, use *persons.* When referring to a group, use *people.*

Six *persons* were in the room.
Do you know the *people* who live next door?
The American *people* are democratic.

place (n.). Must be used as the subject or as the object of a verb or preposition. *Place* is commonly misused with *any, every, no, some,* after an intransitive verb. The adverbs *anywhere, everywhere, nowhere, somewhere,* are usually better.

Are you going *anywhere* (not *any place*) this afternoon?
I have looked *everywhere* (not *every place*) for the letter.
I have *no place* to go (object of the transitive verb *have*).
I have *nowhere* to go.
He is located in *some place* in the West (object of preposition *in*).
He is located *somewhere* in the West.

plurality. *See* **majority.**

practical, practicable (adj.). *Practicable* means feasible, capable of being put into practice; *practical* means useful or successful in actual practice. *Practical* may be used with reference to either persons or things, but *practicable* can be used only with reference to things.

Jones is a *practical* man. (He is a doer.)
The scheme is *practical*. (It will be successful when it is carried out.)
The scheme is *practicable*. (It can be carried out.)

precede, proceed (n.). *Precede* means to go in front or to surpass. *Proceed* means to continue, to come forth.

The president *precedes* the vice-president in the receiving line.
Proceed with the test.

precedence (n.). When it is followed by a preposition, use *of.*

The vice-president has *precedence of* the secretary of state.

precedent (n., adj.). When the noun is followed by a preposition, use *of* or *for.* When the adjective is followed by a preposition, use *to.*

He set a *precedent for* the others.
It is a *precedent* case *to* use as a guide.

preclude (vb.). An erroneous expression is *preclude the possibility of* since *preclude* means to render impossible.

She agreed to the review in an effort to *preclude* (not *preclude the possibility of*) a misunderstanding.

prescribe, proscribe (vb.). The word *prescribe* means to order as a rule or course to be followed or, in medicine, to order as a remedy. The word *proscribe* means to denounce or condemn a thing as dangerous, to outlaw.

What do you *prescribe?*
Destroying files is *proscribed.*

presently (adv.). Meaning soon, before long. A common error is the use of *presently* when *at present* is meant.

We expect to complete the book *presently* (soon).
At present (now) we are working on your book.

principal (n., adj.), **principle** (n.). The word *principle* is a noun only and cannot be used as an adjective. *Principle* means a fundamental or general truth, a rule. *Principal* is used in all other cases. As a noun, *principal* has a variety of meanings; as an adjective, it means chief, main, most important.

We have always acted on the *principle* (fundamental truth) that honesty is the best policy.
An agent may bind his *principal* to contracts entered into within the scope of his authority.

The loan, including *principal* and interest, amounted to $350.

The New England states have been our *principal* source of business during the past five years.

The *principal* of the school is here.

proceeds (n., pl.). Refers to a sum of money. Used in the plural and takes a plural verb.

The *proceeds* were substantial.

prove (vb.). Principal parts: *prove, proved, proved.* The use of *proven* for *proved* is increasing in the United States but is considered poor usage by some grammarians.

He *has proved* his case.

provided, providing (conj.). The use of *providing* as a conjunction is not always sanctioned, although it is commonly used. It is preferable not to use *that* after *provided* except where it is accepted usage in formal documents.

I will give you the order *provided* (or *providing*) you agree to my price.

quality (n.). Pl., *qualities. See* **kind.**

quarter (n., vb., adj.). When you are referring to the time of day, the correct expression is *a quarter to,* not *a quarter of.*

reaction (n.), **reply** (n., vb.), **response** (n.). *Reaction* means a response to stimuli. It should not be used to mean attitude, viewpoint, feeling, or response. *Reply* means a response in words. *Response* is a reply, an answer.

The injection caused a violent *reaction.*

She sent her *reply* by messenger.

The client's *response* was positive.

reason (n., vb.). When a sentence begins with "The reason is" or "The reason why . . . is," the clause giving the reason should begin with *that* and not with *because.*

Her *reason is that* (not *because*) she does not have the money.

The *reason why* the goods were delayed *was that* (not *because*) they were not shipped as scheduled.

reconcile (vb.). When it is followed by a preposition, use *with* or *to*.

> She *was reconciled to* a stressful week ahead.

regard (n., vb.). Do not use *regards* in place of *regard* in the expressions *in regard to, with regard to.*

regardless (adj., adv.), **regardless of** (prep.). *Irregardless* is not a word. Misuse perhaps is caused by confusion with the word *irrespective,* which means "without respect to" and is correct. *Regardless* takes the preposition *of.*

> We should acknowledge all orders *regardless* (not *irregardless*) *of* the amount involved.

relation(ship) (n.). When it is followed by a preposition, use *of, to,* or *with.*

> The *relation of* these parts is not clear.
> The *relationship of* the beneficiary *to* the insured is not close.
> Our strained *relations with* Russia are a source of worry.

resentment (n.). Resentment *at* or *for* an action, *against* a person.

> My *resentment against* him was *at* (or *for*) his rudeness to me.

retroactive (adj.). When it is followed by a preposition, use *to.*

> The law is *retroactive to* May 14.

riches (n., pl.). Always plural and takes a plural verb.

> The *riches* of life *are* not always monetary.

right (n., vb., adj., adv.). The adverb form is *right* or *rightly. See* **Parts of Speech, Adverb.** *Right* is not comparable. If anything is *right,* it cannot be *more* right. *More nearly right* is allowable.

round (n., vb., prep., adj., adv.). *Round* is not comparable. If anything is *round,* it cannot be *more* round. *More nearly round* is allowable.

same (adj.). Do not use as a pronoun. Businesspersons especially are guilty of the misuse of *same.*

> We will repair the spring and ship *it* (not *same*) to you.

scarcely (adv.). This word carries a negative idea and should not be used with a negative.

> There is *scarcely any* (not *scarcely no*) time left in which to fill the order.

seem (vb.). Followed by a predicate adjective and not by an adverb.

> The new machines *seem* strange (not *strangely*).

semimonthly, semiweekly (adj., adv.). Because *semi* means half, *semiweekly* means twice a week and *semimonthly* means twice a month.

set. *See* **sit.**

shall (should); will (would) (vb.). *Should* is the past tense of the auxiliary verb *shall; would,* of the auxiliary verb *will.* Traditionally, *shall* and *should* are used in the first person (*I shall*) and *will* and *would* in the second and third persons (*he will, they will*) to express simple futurity. To express determination, the order is traditionally reversed (*I will, he shall, they shall*). However, *will* and *would* are often preferred in *all* persons in contemporary American usage (*I will* instead of *I shall*) as sounding less stuffy.

she. Nominative case of third-person singular pronoun. For misuse of *she* instead of *her, see* **Parts of Speech, Pronoun.** For use after forms of the verb *to be (am, is, are, was, were), see* **Grammatical Terms, Predicate nominative.**

since (conj., prep., adv.). Do not use *since* to begin a clause after *ago.* Begin the clause with *that.* This error is more apt to occur when a parenthetical expression follows *ago.*

> It is more than ten years *ago,* as well as I remember, *that* (not *since*) the stores were consolidated.

Be certain that a phrase introduced by *since* is correctly attached to the sentence and is not a dangling participial phrase. *See* **Grammatical Terms, Participle.**

> *Since I prepared* the report, *new figures are* available.
> *Since preparing* the report, *I have found new figures* (not *Since*

preparing the report, *new figures are* available).

Since the preparation of the report, *new figures are* available.

sit, set (vb.). *Sit* means to rest when the subject rests. *Set* means to place an object. *Sit* never takes an object; *set* always does. Principal parts, *sit: sit, sat, sat, sitting.* Principal parts, *set: set, set, set, setting.*

He *sits* at his desk.

He *sat* at his desk from ten to eleven.

He *has sat* there for two hours.

He *is sitting* at his desk.

I *set* the thermos on his desk every morning.

I *have set* the thermos on his desk every day for a month.

I *set* the thermos on his desk yesterday, as usual.

I *am setting* the thermos on the table.

The thermos *sat* on the table for a week (past of *sit).*

The thermos *has sat* there for a week (present perfect of *sit).*

size (n.). Pl., *sizes. See* **kind.** *Size* is a noun; *sized,* an adjective. Either noun or adjective may form a compound adjective.

medium-size or *medium-sized* house

Because *size* is a noun and not an adjective, it is incorrect to omit the *of* in these and similar expressions.

that size *of* machine

so. For the correct use of *so . . . as, see* **as.**

some (pron., adj., adv.). For misuse of *some place, see* **place.**

somebody, someone (pron.). Always write *somebody* as one word. *Someone* is preferred. Write *someone* as one word when it is equivalent to *somebody;* otherwise, it is two words.

He will appoint *someone* of outstanding ability.

If *some one* person is designated to head the project, we can plan accordingly.

Singular, followed by singular verb and pronoun:

> I know *someone* (or *somebody*) *was* here while I was away, because
> *he* left *his* briefcase.

some time, sometime, sometimes (adv.). Either *some time* or *sometimes* may be used instead of *at some time,* meaning a point of time not specified. There is no distinction. The trend is to omit *at* and use *sometime.*

> I expect to be there *sometime* (or *some time*) in August.

Use *some time* when referring to an indefinite lapse of time. It is incorrect to use *sometime* in this sense.

> It will take *some time* to prepare the report.

Sometime may be used as an adjective to describe a former state. It is equivalent to *at one time having been.*

> Dr. Evatt, *sometime* minister of Australia, is speaking tonight.

Sometimes, written as one word, means at several indefinite times; on some occasions.

> *Sometimes* she works late.

somewhere (n., adv.). Always written as one word. *Some place* is commonly misused for *somewhere. See* **place.** *Somewheres* is not a word.

sort (n.). Pl., *sorts. See* **kind.**

species (n.). Singular or plural depending on the intended meaning.

> The *species is* well known.
> These *species are* being studied now.

spoonful (n.). Pl., *spoonfuls. See* **RULES OF SPELLING, Plurals,** page 477, in chapter 15.

stationary (adj.), **stationery** (n.). *Stationary* means standing still; *stationery* means writing materials.

Some loading platforms are *stationary,* but others are mobile.

Don't forget to order the office *stationery.*

straight (n., vb., adj., adv.). The adverb form is *straight. Straightly* is rare. *Straight* is not comparable. If anything is *straight,* it cannot be *more* straight. *More nearly straight* is allowable.

subject to. *See* **addicted to.**

substantive. *See* **Antecedent.**

such (pron., adj., adv.). Do not use *which, who, that,* or *where* with *such.* The correct combination is *such . . . as.* Frequently, the better usage is to omit *such* or change *such* to *the, that, those,* and the like.

Some people give only *such* things *as* (not *that*) they do not need.

Some people give only *those* things *for which* they have no need.

Do not use *such as* in place of *as* to introduce a prepositional phrase.

Radios that you have previously purchased from us, *as in* (not *such as in*) your last shipment, are out of stock.

suitable (adj.). Suitable *for* a use or purpose, *to* an occasion or requirements.

The machine is *suitable for* that work.

The machine is *suitable to* the requirements of your office.

superior (adj.). Should always be followed by *to,* not *than.*

It is *superior* from every point of view *to* the other material.

surround (vb.). When it is followed by a preposition, use *by.*

We are *surrounded by* buildings.

tactic (n.). Pl., *tactics.* Commonly used in the plural.

Her *tactics are* questionable.

than (prep., conj.). Never use after *more and more. See also* **different from.**

The Supreme Court has granted *more* (not *more and more*) powers to the federal government *than* was originally intended.

thanks (n., pl.). Always takes a plural verb.

> Our *thanks are* directed to all of you.

that (conj.). Use only one *that* to introduce a single clause. A common error is the use of a second *that* when a phrase or clause intervenes between *that* and the clause it introduces.

> I hope *that* when you have reconsidered the matter you will cooperate (not *that* you will cooperate).

that, which (rel. pron.). Use *that* to introduce a defining or restrictive clause; use *which* to introduce a nondefining, nonrestrictive clause, a comment, or an additional thought.

> Statutory requirements *that* fix a definite number of days for notice must be followed.
> The proposed amendments, *which* increase the value of the measure, were adopted unanimously.

them (pron.). Objective case of *they*. For use as an object, *see* **Parts of Speech, Pronoun.** For misuse of *them* instead of *they* after forms of the verb *to be (am, is, are, was, were)*, *see* **Grammatical Terms, Predicate nominative.**

there (n., pron., adj., adv.). Often used to introduce a clause in which the verb precedes the subject. The number of the verb is not affected by *there* but depends on the number of the subject.

> *There are* not sufficient *data* (plural subject) available.
> *There is* a *mass* (singular subject) of data available.

they. Nominative case of third-person plural pronoun. For misuse of *they* instead of *them*, *see* **Parts of Speech, Pronoun.** For use after the forms of the verb *to be (am, is, are, was, were)*, *see* **Grammatical Terms, Predicate nominative.**

time card (n.). Two words. *See* **Grammatical Terms, Compound term.**

toward(s) (prep., adj.). Either is correct, but the use of *toward* is more prevalent. *Towards* is the accepted British form.

try (vb.). Often erroneously followed by *and* with a verb in place of an infinitive.

Try to come (not *and come*) to New York.

type (n., vb.). Pl., *types. See* **kind.** The noun *type* should not be used as an adjective. It is incorrect to omit the *of* in these and similar expressions: type *of* machine, type *of* building, type *of* person.

uninterested. *See* **disinterested.**

unique (adj.). *Unique* is not comparable; it means the only one of its kind. You should not say *"most* unique," *"more* unique," or *"very* unique."

unqualified (adj.), **disqualified** (vb.). *Unqualified* means not having the right qualifications. *Disqualified* means deprived of the right qualities.

> He was *unqualified* for the job (not right for it).
> She was *disqualified* from the competition (made ineligible).

unquestioned, unquestionable (adj.) *Unquestioned* refers to that which has not been questioned; *unquestionable,* that which cannot be sensibly questioned.

> The statement was *unquestioned.*
> His loyalty is *unquestionable.*

unsatisfied, dissatisfied (adj.). *Unsatisfied* means not content and wanting more. *Dissatisfied* means unhappy.

> She is *unsatisfied* with the amount of the research.
> She is *dissatisfied* with her job.

us (pron.). The objective case of *we;* sometimes misused for *we.*

> Tell *us* what to do.
> They are not as efficient as *we* (are efficient) from the standpoint of accuracy.

valuables (n., pl.). Always used in the plural and takes a plural verb.

> Your *valuables are* safe.

variety (n.). Pl., *varieties. See* **kind.**

verbal (adj.). Relates to either written or spoken words. *Verbal* is used often carelessly in place of *oral* with reference to spoken words. To avoid confusion, use *oral* to mean spoken words and *written* to mean written words.

> A contract, whether written or *oral* (not *verbal)* is binding.
>
> He gave *oral* (not *verbal)* instructions.
>
> A few *verbal* (or *written)* changes (changes in words) are necessary.

verb. *See* **Parts of Speech, Verb.** For agreement of a verb with its subject, *see* **Grammatical Terms, Compound subject; Alternate subject; Intervening noun or phrase; Predicate nominative.**

very, very much. These words are overworked. Although they are acceptable modifiers, excessive use of them destroys the force of the words modified. *I am pleased* is as emphatic as *I am very much pleased.* Rather than using *very* or *very much,* selecting a stronger word is often the better alternative. Those who insist on using *very* and *very much* should observe correct usage. These terms are not interchangeable. The problem is whether to use *very* or *very much* before a passive participle. Use *very* when the passive participle has the force of an adjective.

> A *very delighted* crowd heard the news.

Use *very much* (or *much)* when the passive participle is used in the predicate with verbal force.

> I was *very much* (or *much)* delighted at the result of the game.
>
> I will be *very much* (or *much)* inconvenienced by the delay.

Exception: A passive participle that, although used as a verb, has lost its verbal force by common usage is preceded by *very.*

> I am *very* (not *very much)* tired of hearing about the matter.

viable, workable (adj.). *Viable* means capable of existence. *Workable* means practicable, feasible, capable of working or succeeding.

> The new company is a *viable* entity.
>
> The plan seems *workable* to me.

wait on. Do not use in place of *wait for.*

We have been *waiting for* (not *on*) her.

wake (vb.). Principal parts: *wake, waked,* or *woke* and *has, had,* or *have waked.* *See* **Parts of Speech, Verb.**

way (n., adj., adv.). Do not use *ways* in place of the singular *way.*

> This year's sales are quite a *way* (not *ways*) ahead of last year's.
> *Better:* This year's sales are *considerably* ahead of last year's.

we. Nominative case of first-person plural pronoun. For misuse of *we, see* **Parts of Speech, Pronoun.** For use after forms of the verb *to be (am, is, are, was, were), see* **Grammatical Terms, Predicate nominative.** For the correct use of *we* or *I* in letters, *see* I. *We* is frequently misused for *us* in apposition to a noun in the objective case.

> It is advisable for *us* (not *we*) citrus growers to organize an association.

well (adj., adv.), **good** (adj.). *Well* may be either an adjective or an adverb but is usually an adverb except when it refers to a state of health. *Good* is always an adjective.

> He *did* the job *well* (adverb, describing how he did the job).
> He looks *well* (predicate adjective, referring to state of health).
> The *situation* looks *good* to me (predicate adjective, describing the situation).
> The upswing in the stock market is a *good indication* that prosperity is still with us (adjective, modifying *indication*).

what (pron., adj., adv.). May be either singular or plural. In the singular, *what* stands for *that which* or *a thing that.* In the plural, *what* stands for *those* (persons) *who* or *those* (things) *that.*

> *Singular: What is* saved in price *is* likely to be lost in service and goodwill.
> *Plural:* My *reasons* for refusing the order *were what* I considered sufficient (*reasons* is the plural antecedent of *what*).

If *what* is singular in the beginning of the sentence, it remains singular. A common error is to make the second verb agree with a plural predicate nominative. In each of the following examples, *what* is definitely established as singular because it is followed by a singular verb. The second verb must also be singular, although it is followed by a plural predicate nominative, which is the complement to *what.*

> *What is* needed *is* houses at prices that the people can afford.
>
> *What seems* to be needed *is* stringent regulations.
>
> *What causes* the delay *is* the three transfers.

In each of the following examples, *what* is used in the plural sense. Test the sentence by substituting *those* (things) *that* for *what.*

> He is attempting to show by the chart *what appear* (not *appears*) to be the reasons for the decrease in sales (meaning "those reasons that").
>
> The company sold at discount only *what were* (not *was*) considered refrigerators of second quality (meaning "only those refrigerators that were considered").

when (n., pron., conj., adv.). Do not use *when* to define a word.

> A sentence is a complete thought (not *when you have a complete thought*).

Where is frequently misused for *when. Where* should introduce an adverbial clause of place; *when,* of time.

> *When* (not *where*) a proxy is given limited power, he must act within the limitations.
>
> A surplus exists *when* (not *where*) there is an excess in the aggregate value of assets over liabilities and capital.
>
> *Where* the company is building its new offices, a redwood forest once stood.

where (n., conj., adv.). Sometimes misused in place of *that.*

> I see in the paper *that* (not *where*) the corporation has declared a dividend.

Do not use *where* to define a word.

Perjury is the voluntary violation of an oath (not *where a person voluntarily violates an oath*).

Where should be used to introduce an adverbial clause of place, not of time; *see* when for an example.

which (pron., adj.). For use of *that* as a relative pronoun instead of *which, see* **that, which.**

while (n., vb., conj.). When it is used most precisely, *while* means "during the time that" or "as long as." It is sometimes incorrectly used as a substitute for *although, whereas,* or *but.*

> *Although* (not *while*) the report is due now, more research is needed.

who, whom (pron.). *Who* is the nominative cause and is used as the subject; *whom* is the objective case and is used as the object of a verb or preposition.

> He is the client for *whom* (object of *for*) I prepared the contract.
> Mr. Adams is the person *who* (subject) has charge of sales.
> *Whom* (object of *to see*) do you want to see?
> Mr. Edwards is the candidate *who* I believe will win. *(Who* is the subject of *will win; I believe* is parenthetical.)
> Mr. Edwards is the candidate *whom* I favor. *(Whom* is the object of *favor.)*

will. *See* **shall.**

would. *See* **shall.**

write (vb.). When an indirect object follows *write,* without a direct object, precede the indirect object by *to.* If a direct and indirect object follow, *to* is not necessary.

> I will write *to you* as soon as I can.
> I will write *you* (indirect object) a *letter* (direct object) as soon as I can.

wrong (n., vb., adj., adv.). The adverb forms are *wrong, wrongly. See* **Parts of Speech, Adverb.** *Wrong* is not comparable. If anything is *wrong,* it cannot be *more* wrong.

yourself (pron.). Pl., *yourselves. See* **Grammatical Terms, Compound personal pronoun.**

— Chapter 15 —————————

Spelling and
Word Division

RULES OF SPELLING

Plurals

Singular nouns.   Usually the plural is formed by adding *s*.

files   telephones   desks

In some cases, it is formed by adding *es*.

classes   churches   boxes

Words ending in o.   Words ending in *o* preceded by a vowel form the plural by adding *s*.

folios   trios   studios

Generally, words ending in *o* preceded by a consonant form the plural by adding *es*.

potatoes   heroes

A few form the plural by adding *s*.

solos   dynamos   memos

Some have both forms.

cargoes/cargos   mottoes/mottos   zeros/zeroes

Words ending in y.   Words ending in *y* preceded by a vowel form the plural by adding *s*.

attorneys   days

Words ending in *y* preceded by a consonant change the *y* to *i* and add *es*.

ladies   berries   countries   counties

Words ending in f or fe.   Some nouns ending in *f* or *fe* change the *f* to *v* and add *s* or *es*; some do not; some have both forms. There is no way to distinguish the groups. When in doubt, consult a dictionary.

roof/roofs   chief/chiefs   loaf/loaves
leaf/leaves   cliff/cliffs

Words ending in ch, sh, ss, or x.   Add *es* to form the plural of words ending in *ch, sh, ss,* or *x*.

church/churches   dish/dishes   glass/glasses   box/boxes

Irregular nouns.   Some words are spelled differently in the plural form; others use the same spelling in both the singular and plural forms.

child/children   corps/corps

Abbreviations.   The plural of an abbreviation is usually formed by adding *s*.

mfrs.   mos.   nos.

The plurals of some abbreviations are formed by repeating the abbreviation.

p., pp./page, pages   v., vv./verse, verses

Figures, letters.   Add *'s* only if *s* alone would be confusing.

    p's and q's   6's and 7's   Ph.D.'s and Ed.D's

In most cases, letters and numbers form the plural by adding *s* alone

    YWCAs   1980s

Compound terms. In general, the plural of a compound term is formed by making the most important word plural. The most important word is the word telling what the principal is. Following this general rule, military titles for the most part form the plural by adding *s* to the second word, which is usually the most important. However, *sergeant major* forms the plural on the first word because the rank is really a form of *sergeant*, not major. Civilian titles usually add the *s* to the first word, since the first word usually tells what the person is.

> *notaries* public (they are *notaries*, not *publics*)
> major *generals* (they are *generals*, not *majors*)
> *adjutants* general (they are *adjutants* (assistants), not *generals*)

The following are examples of forming the plural of a compound term by making the most important word plural:

aides-de-camp	*governors* general
ambassadors at large	judge *advocates*
assistant *attorneys* general	lieutenant *colonels*
attorneys general	*presidents*-elect
bills of lading	*rights*-of-way
brigadier *generals*	sergeants at arms
brothers-in-law	*sergeants* major
comptrollers general	*surgeons* general
deputy *chiefs* of staff	trade *unions*
general *counsels*	

When both words are of equal importance, both words take the plural form.

    coats of arms   men employees   women drivers

When no word is of importance in itself, the last word takes the plural form.

    forget-me-*nots*   jack-in-the-*pulpits*   pick-me-*ups*

When a noun is compounded with a preposition, the noun takes the plural form.

hangers-on   *listeners*-in   *passers*-by   by-*products*

When neither word in the compound term is a noun, the last word takes the plural form.

also-*rans*   go-*betweens*   write-*ups*   tie-*ins*

Compound nouns written as one word form their plurals regularly. Words ending in *-ful* are the only ones that cause trouble.

cup*fuls*   tablespoon*fuls*   bucket*fuls*

When it is necessary to convey the meaning that more than one container was used, write the compound as two words and add *s* to the noun.

5 *cups* full   2 *tablespoons* full   4 *buckets* full

Combinations of i and e

Learn the following rhyme to avoid mistakes in combining *i* and *e*. Use *i* before *e* except after *c*, or when sounded like *a* as in neighbor and *weigh*.

believe   receive   weight

Exceptions: either, neither, seize, weird, sheik, leisure, plebeian, financier, specie, conscience.

Doubling the Final Consonant

Double the consonant before a word ending that begins with a vowel if the word ends in a single consonant preceded by a single vowel and if the accent falls on the last syllable of the word. (For the purpose of this rule, words of *one syllable* are considered "accented" on the last syllable.) Confusion arises because *all* of these conditions must be met before the consonant can be doubled.

occur/occurred (all conditions are met)
bag/baggage (all conditions are met)

ship/shipped (all conditions are met)
commit/commitment (suffix does not begin with a vowel)
desert/deserting (word does not end in a single consonant)
appeal/appealed (final consonant not preceded by a single vowel)
offer/offered (accent does not fall on the last syllable)

Exceptions: Most of the exceptions are derivatives in which the syllabication changes and the accent of the main word is thrown back on the first syllable.

de fer′/def′er-ence   infer/inferable   transfer/transferable
re fer′/ref′er-ence   pre fer′/pref′er-ence

But the *r* is doubled when adding *-ed* or *-ing* to *defer, prefer,* and *refer.*

deferred/deferring   preferred/preferring   referred/referring

Words Ending in Silent e

Suffixes beginning with a vowel.   Words ending in a silent *e* usually drop the *e* before a suffix or verb ending that starts with a vowel. *See also* **Suffixes -able, -ous.**

bride/bridal   argue/arguable   guide/guidance
owe/owing   ice/icing   judge/judging
use/usable (*variant* useable)   sale/salable (*variant* saleable)

Exceptions: dye/dyeing, eye/eyeing, hoe/hoeing.
Suffixes beginning with a consonant.   Words ending in silent *e* usually retain the *e* before suffixes beginning with a consonant, unless another vowel precedes the final *e.*

hate/hateful   argue/argument   excite/excitement   due/duly

Exceptions: abridgment, acknowledgment, judgment, nursling, wholly.

Words Ending in ie

Words ending in *ie* drop the *e* and change the *i* to *y* before adding the *-ing.*

die/dying   lie/lying

Suffixes -able, -ous

Words ending in *e* preceded by *c* or *g* do not drop the final *e* before the suffixes *-able* or *-ous* but do drop the final *e* before the suffix *-ible*.

service/serviceable   manage/manageable   courage/courageous
advantage/advantageous   deduce/deducible   convince/convincible

Words Ending in -able, ible

If a word has an *-ation* form, it always takes the suffix *-able* instead of *-ible*.

application/applicable   reparation/reparable

Many words that do not have an *-ation* form also take the suffix *-able*, which is far more common than the suffix *-ible*. There is no rule distinguishing the groups. The following list includes common *-ible* adjectives. It does not include other forms of the same word made by adding a prefix. For example, *credible* is included in the list, but *incredible* is not.

accessible	descendible	gullible
adducible	destructible	ignitible,
admissible	diffusible	ignitable
apprehensible	digestible	impassible
audible	dirigible	impressible
avertible	discernible	includible,
coercible	discussible,	includable
cohesible	discussable	incontrovertible
collapsible	dismissible	indefeasible
collectible,	distensible	indefectible
collectable	divertible	indelible
combustible	divisible	inducible
compatible	edible	intelligible
comprehensible	educible,	invertible
compressible	educable	invincible
conductible	eligible	irascible
contemptible	exhaustible	irresistible
contractible	expansible	legible
convertible	expressible	negligible
corrigible	extendible,	omissible
corruptible	extendable	ostensible
credible	extensible	perceptible
deducible	fallible	perfectible
deductible	feasible	permissible
defensible	flexible	persuasible,
depressible	forcible	persuadable

pervertible	reprehensible	susceptible
plausible	repressible	suspendible
possible	resistible	tangible
preventible	responsible	terrible
preventable	reversible	vendible
producible	sensible	visible
reducible	suggestible	
remissible	suppressible	

Words Ending in -sede, -ceed, -cede

Only one word in our language ends in *-sede—supersede.* Only three end in *-ceed—proceed, exceed, succeed.* All of the others end in *-cede.* Remember also that *proceed* changes its form in *procedure.*

Suffixes -ance, -ence

When the suffix is preceded by *c* having the sound of *k,* or *g* having a hard sound, use *-ance, -ancy,* or *-ant;* when *c* has the sound of *s,* or *g* the sound of *j,* use *-ence, -ency,* or *-ent.*

convalescence	significant	negligence
indigent	extravagant	intelligence

If the suffix is preceded by a letter other than *c* or *g* and you are in doubt about the spelling, consult the dictionary.

Suffixes -ise, -ize

There is no rule governing the use of *-ise* or *-ize.* The words in the following list, and their derivatives and compounds, are spelled with *-ise.*

advertise	advise	apprise	arise	chastise	circumcise
comprise	compromise	demise	despise	devise	disguise
enterprise	excise	exercise	exorcise	franchise	improvise
incise	merchandise	premise	reprise	revise	supervise
surmise	surprise	televise			

The preferred American spelling for other such words is *-ize.*

apologize	criticize	realize	summarize

Words Ending in c

When a word ends in *c,* insert a *k* before adding a suffix beginning with *e, i,* or *y.*

picnic/picnicking/picnicked   traffic/trafficker/trafficking

Words Ending in y

Words ending in *y* preceded by a consonant usually change the *y* to *i* before any suffix or verb ending except one beginning with *i.*

modify/modifying/modifier/modification   worry/worrisome/worried
lonely/lonelier/loneliness

Exceptions: 1. Adjectives of one syllable have two forms in the comparative and superlative.

dry: drier/driest or dryer/dryest
shy: shier/shiest or shyer/shyest
spry: sprier/spriest or spryer/spryest

2. Adjectives of one syllable usually retain the *y* before *-ly* and *-ness.*

shyly/shyness   dryly/dryness   spryly/spryness

3. The *y* is retained in words with *-ship* and *-like* and in derivatives of *lady* and *baby.*

secretaryship   ladylike   ladyfinger   babyhood

Words ending in *y* preceded by a vowel usually keep the *y* before any verb ending.

buy/buying   employ/employment   delay/delayed

Exceptions: day/daily, pay/paid, say/said.

Prefixes dis-, mis-

Words formed by adding the prefix *dis-* are frequently misspelled because of doubt about whether the combined form has one *s* or two. If the word to which the prefix is added begins with *s*, the combined form has two *s's;* otherwise, the combined form has only one *s*. The same rule applies to the prefix *mis-*.

agree/disagree	appoint/disappoint	appear/disappear
regard/disregard	satisfy/dissatisfy	simulate/dissimulate
spell/misspell	apply/misapply	print/misprint

Note: The current trend is to write words with prefixes closed (*anticlimax*) unless the prefix precedes a proper name (*anti-American*), or when a double vowel might make the word difficult to read if the hyphen were omitted (*antiintelligence* versus *anti-intelligence*), or when a different meaning is intended (*re-form*, meaning to form again).

HOW TO IMPROVE YOUR SPELLING

Helpful Mnemonics for Accurate Spelling

One of the easiest ways to learn to spell a certain word is to make up a phrase that will call the correct spelling to mind. This device to aid the memory is called a *mnemonic*. A silly phrase or a little rhyme will often make a word stick in your mind even better than a sensible rule. Keep a list of these words and the phrase or rhyme you make up on your desk. Each time you must look up the spelling of a word, add the word to your list with your own phrase or jingle; the next time that word comes up, look at the list instead of in the dictionary. You will be amazed at how quickly you will learn to spell the words on the list.

A superitend*ent* collects *rent*.
All right is the opposite of *all wrong* (there is no word *alright* just as there is no word *alwrong).*
Only a *rat* would sepa*rat*e friends.
Perhaps he is only a compa*rat*ive *rat*.
A fri*end* sticks to the *end*.
My button is l*oose;* if I am not careful I will l*ose* it and then it will be l*ost*. Or: You g*oose*, your button is l*oose*.
Cut me a *pie*ce or *pie.*
An apartment l*ease* brings p*eace* from rent incr*ease*.
A letter is written on station*ery*. You st*a*nd still when you are station*ary*.
The princip*al* part is the m*a*in p*a*rt.
The para*ll*el lines are in the center of the word (think of the two *l*'s as parallel lines).

Super*sede* is the only word in the English language that ends in
    -*sede*.
She is irresis*ti*ble when wearing *li*pstick.
An *able* man is depend*able* and indispens*able*.

List of Commonly Misspelled Words

Certain words are more troublesome than others, and special attention is required to avoid misspellings. This list contains five hundred
problem words listed by frequency of spelling error.[1]

occurrence	livelihood	participant	reimburse
negligible	deficit	psychology	convenient
permissible	consensus	maintenance	disappoint
liaison	criticism	occurred	opportunity
acquiesce	adequate	congratulate	exaggerate
questionnaire	vendor	grievance	leisure
clientele	irrelevant	imperative	competitor
develop	privilege	environment	annoyance
likable	phase	definite	unanimous
collateral	benefited	acquaintance	procedure
supersede	cancellation	council	undoubtedly
forcible	advantageous	usable	oblige
conscientious	guarantee	negotiate	accessory
etiquette	legitimate	deteriorate	emphasize
deductible	influential	attorneys	conceivable
catalog[2]	consistent	edition	omitted
aggravate	jeopardize	mortgage	substantial
equipped	personnel	counsel	inquiry
harass	indispensable	efficiency	patronage
accede	recurrence	judgment	conscience
allotted	vacuum	occasion	effect
all right	possession	inconvenience	noticeable
discrepancy	precede	canceled[4]	appreciable
accessible	accompanying	concurred	accommodate
mischievous	eligible	itinerary	price list
percent	correspondents	calendar	stationery
existence	vicinity	convenience	applicable
interfere	forfeit	withhold	correspondence
occurring	analyze	justifiable	indebtedness
parallel	omission	prejudice	preliminary
regrettable	laboratory	recipe	stationary[5]
salable[3]	license	simultaneous	precision
siege	expedite	apparel	preferable
acknowledgment	advisory	defendant	accumulate
ascertain	bankruptcy	definitely	concession
allotment	commitment	conscious	excellent
criticize	repetition	unnecessary	familiarize
illegible	gauge	deferred	loose
inasmuch as	hazardous	interrupted	lose

remittance	advertisement	visible	concede
courteous	enterprise	immediately	neighborhood
pamphlet	analysis	incidentally	securities
recognized	allowable	receipt	announce
itemized	basis	applicant	assured
persuade	brilliant	commission	describe
accidentally	menus	succeed	absence
apologize	accrued	excellence	exceed
except	hesitant	excessive	advice
recommend	customer	independent	annual
similar	decision	quantity	available
eliminate	extension	quite	delegate
endeavor	grateful	specialize	development
manufacturer	reference	letterhead	economical
miscellaneous	argument	modernize	efficient
permanent	exercise	volunteer	practice
proceed	management	physician	principal
anxious	seized	achievement	career
affidavit	recently	beginning	column
enthusiasm	sufficient	confident	hardware
restaurant	architect	difference	height
amendment	vehicle	equipment	inventory
announcement	confidential	admirable	quiet
mileage	controversy	original	comparable
ninety	courtesy	recognize	compliment
attendance	anticipate	essential	endorsement
separate	bureau	facilities	investor
referring	fulfillment	casualty	corporation
bulletin	superintendent	magazine	disappear
legible	deceive	voluntary	intercede
thorough	personal	incurred	ninth
dependent	practical	altogether	apparent
embarrass	practically	fourth	description
preferred	referred	schedule	necessary
representative	minimum	extraordinary	shipment
strictly	overdue	beneficiary	adapt
surprise	particularly	capitol	pleasant
advisable	complement	premium	maximum
foreign	tariff	prominent	salary
formerly	appropriate	prosecute	significant
partial	debtor	ridiculous	throughout
brochure	freight	tragedy	depositors
dissatisfied	serviceable.	unfortunately	professor
emphasis	sincerity	volume	subscriber
respectively	writing	across	survey
nevertheless	receive	appearance	temporary
offense	whether	too	urgent
fascinate	advertising	bargain	acceptance
pursue	especially	bookkeeper	allowance
approximate	merchandise	expenditure	article
principle	preference	responsible	envelope
intelligence	assessment	satisfactory	experience
acquire	inducement	successful	respectfully

circumstances	campaign	finally	wholesale
concern	capital	knowledge	compelled
extremely	defense	forty	consequence
financial	desirable	handled	director
genuine	governor	length	employee
individual	paid	ordinary	associate
occupant	permitted	organization	appointment
response	previous	warehouse	appliance
valuable	probably	controlling	assignment
beneficial	purchase	initial	cordially
continuous	secretary	somewhat	pleasure
emergency	choice	address	accept
furthermore	choose	current	agreeable
hoping	it's	accuracy	almost
intention	requirement	believe	business
memorandum	appraisal	coming	budget
accordance	competent	committee	busy
among	compromise	their	conference
assistance	identical	there	eagerly
cannot	impossible	really	forward
consignment	library	submitted	government
renewal	manuscript	installment	typing
attention	medical	someone	authorize
realize	offering	worthwhile	client
responsibility	creditor	comparison	coverage
statistics	decide	reasonable	favorable
ultimately	devise	enclose	device
yield	favorite	expense	friend
affect	already	shipping	official
planning	arrangement	organize	remember
adjustment	usually	route	supervisor
advise	explanation	until	transferred
businessman	February	various	weather

1. Compiled by the Dictation Disc Company, 240 Madison Avenue, New York, NY 10016.
2. The spelling *catalogue* is acceptable.
3. The spelling *saleable* is acceptable.
4. The spelling *cancelled* is acceptable.
5 Meaning "immobile."

RULES OF WORD DIVISION

Division of Words at the End of a Line

To avoid a ragged right-hand margin, it is sometimes necessary to divide a word at the end of a line. But divide a word *only* when necessary. Try not to have two successive lines with a divided word at the end, and never have more than two. Never divide the last word on a page except in legal documents, where the word is sometimes divided to show continuity. Try to avoid dividing the last word in a paragraph.

Syllabication and Pronunciation

The correct division of a word depends on the breakdown of the word into syllables. American dictionaries syllabicate according to pronunciation and not according to derivation. If you do not know the proper division into syllables for a word, look up the word in a definition dictionary or a spelling dictionary. Spelling dictionaries that show pronunciation as well as word division are especially helpful because pronunciation is a basic guide to word division. For example, *pre-sent* means to give or introduce; *pres-ent* refers to a gift.

Basic Rules of Word Division

One-syllable words. Never divide words pronounced as one syllable.

> through (*not* th-rough)   drowned (*not* drown-ed)
> gained (*not* gain-ed)

Four-letter words. Never divide a four-letter word.

> only (*not* on-ly)   into (*not* in-to)

One-letter syllables. Never separate one-letter syllables from the rest of the word.

> around (*not* a-round)   alone (*not* a-lone)
> caf-e-te-ria (*not* cafeteri-a)

Divide a word with a one-letter syllable within the word after the one-letter syllable, except in the case of the suffixes *-able* or *-ible*.

> busi-ness   sepa-rate   medi-cal   con-sider-able   reduc-ible

Note: There are many words ending in *-able* or *-ible* in which the *a* or *i* does not form a syllable by itself. These words are divided after the *a* or *i*.

pos-si-ble   char-i-ta-ble   ca-pa-ble

Two-letter syllables.   Do not carry over a two-letter syllable at the end of a word.

caller (*not* call-er)   deeded (*not* deed-ed)
purchaser (*not* purchas-er)

Avoid separating two-letter syllables at the beginning of a word from the rest of the word.

eli-gi-ble (*not* el-igible)   begin-ning (*not* be-ginning)
atten-tion (*not* at-tention)   redeemed (*not* re-deemed)

Always keep three or more characters (including punctuation) on the top line or see that three or more are carried to the next line.

break-up, (Carry over the three characters *up,* to the bottom line.)

Consonants within a word.   When the final consonant in a word is doubled before a suffix, the second consonant belongs with the letters following it.

run-ning   occur-ring

Do not carry over to the next line single or double consonants in the root word.

call-ing (*not* cal-ling)   forc-ing (*not* for-cing)
divid-ing (*not* divi-ding)   fore-stall-ing (*not* forestal-ling)

When two consonants occur within a word, divide the word between the consonants.

gram-mar   expres-sive   moun-tain   foun-da-tion

Prefixes and suffixes.   Divide a word before or after (not within) prefixes and suffixes.

anti-climax (*not* an-ticlimax)   mini-computer (*not* min-icomputer)
over-confident (*not* ov-erconfident)   trust-worthy (*not*
                                              trustwor-thy)

Hyphenated compounds.   Avoid dividing a compound hyphenated word except where the hyphen naturally falls.

> father-in-law (*not* fa-ther-in-law)   self-applause (*not*
>   self-ap-plause)

Dashes.   Divide after a dash and keep the dash on the top line.

> typing—/ and proofreading (*not* typing / —and proofreading)

Abbreviations.   Do not divide abbreviations and acronyms.

> Ph.D. (*not* Ph.–D.)   YWCA (*not* YW-CA)
> isn't (*not* is-n't)   COD (*not* C-OD)

Numbers.   Avoid dividing numbers. If it is necessary to divide them, divide on the comma and retain the comma.

> $1,548,–345,000 (*not* $1,548,3-45,000)

Divide dates in the body of a letter between the day and the year, not between the month and the day. Avoid separating other number-word groups and separate numbers in lists only before the number.

> September 19, / 1988 (*not* September / 19, 1988)
> page 15 (*not* page / 15)
> 1100 West / Avenue (*not* 1100 / West Avenue)
> (1) typing, / (2) editing, and (3) spelling (*not* [1] typing, [2] / editing,
>   and [3] spelling)

Names.   Do not separate the initials of a name, and avoid separating initials, titles, or degrees from the name; also avoid dividing proper names.

> John / Devonshire (*not* John Devon-shire)
> A. C. / Davis (*not* A. / C. Davis)

Chapter 16

Punctuation

PRINCIPAL MARKS AND RULES OF PUNCTUATION

Comma: The Secretary's Troublemaker

Many people tend to overwork the comma. The trend is to curtail its use and omit it in many cases where its use was formerly mandatory.

Appositives. Use a comma to set off an *appositive*, that is, an expression that explains or gives additional information about a preceding expression.

> The president of our company, *Mr. Edwards,* is in Europe.
> My husband, *John,* is an electrical engineer.

But do not separate two nouns, one of which identifies the other.

> The *conductor Bernstein* returned to America today.
> The *witness Jones* testified that he saw the defendant.
> His *son Carl* graduates today (he may have more than one son, so do not set off with commas).

Cities and states. Use a comma to separate the name of a city from the name of a state and enclose the state in commas.

> Brown Company of Auburn, *New York,* has reduced turnover by 50 percent.

Compound predicates. Compound predicates are not separated by commas.

> The total number of children in high school is increasing *and* will
> continue to increase for several more years.

Compound sentences.   Use a comma to separate the two main clauses joined by the conjunctions *but, and, or, for, neither, nor,* or *either.* The comma precedes the conjunction.

> We appreciate your order of July 16, *but* we are unable to accept it
> because of our established merchandising policy.

The comma may be omitted before *and* if the clauses are short and closely connected in thought.

> The radios were shipped yesterday *and* the television sets will be
> shipped tomorrow.

Dash and comma.   Do not use a dash and comma together.

> He's very bright—or perhaps he's very lucky. *Or:* He's very bright,
> or perhaps he's very lucky. *Not:* He's very bright,—or perhaps
> he's very lucky.

Dates.   Separate the day of the month from the year by a comma. The trend is to omit the comma after the month if no day is given.

> The dividend is payable March 12, 1988, to the stockholders.
> On March 1988 the dividend is payable to the stockholders.

Ellipsis.   Use a comma to indicate that one or more words, easily understood, have been omitted. A construction of this type is known as an *ellipsis* (plural, *ellipses*). For a description of dots or other marks used to show omission of words, *see* **Leaders and Ellipsis Points: Invaluable Aids,** page 510.

> The employer contributed 60 percent; the employees, 40 percent.

Essential and nonessential phrases and clauses.   A restrictive phrase or clause (often introduced by *that* or *who*) is one that is essential to the meaning of the sentence and is not merely descriptive or parenthetic; it should *not* be set off by commas. A nonrestrictive phrase or clause (often introduced by *which* or *who*) is one that adds an additional thought to the sentence but is not essential to the meaning of the sentence; it *should* be set off by commas.

> The car *that was damaged* is being towed away.
> The lawyer *who argued the case* is a close friend of the defendant.
> Mr. Ransome, *who argued the case,* is a close friend of the defendant.
> The rule against lateness, *which has been in effect many years,* is strictly enforced.

Inseparables.   A frequent error is the separation of words that belong together and are interdependent, for example, separating a verb from its subject or object or predicate nominative or a limiting clause from its antecedent. In the following examples, the commas in brackets should be omitted.

> The rapid advancement of the company to its present enviable position in the publishing world [,] is attributable largely to the acumen and energy of its founders. (The comma separates the subject *advancement* from its verb *is.*)
>
> The revision combines with the first edition's thoroughness [,] a constructive viewpoint, a wide range of practices, and up-to-date methods. (The comma separates the verb *combines* from its objects *viewpoint, range,* and *methods*).
>
> The leeway allowed to the defendants in this trial, as in all others [,] where justice prevails, is in sharp contrast to the treatment accorded defendants in totalitarian countries. (The *where* starts a limiting relative clause modifying *others. See* **Essential and nonessential phrases and clauses,** page 493.)

Introductory words.   Use a comma to separate an introductory word from the rest of the sentence. Words ending in *-ly* are usually set off by a comma, as are words such as *however* and *for example.* The trend is not to set off brief introductory words such as *thus* and *yet. See also* **Parenthetical words and phrases,** page 495, and **Semicolon: The Compromise between Period and Comma, Before a conjunctive adverb,** page 499.

> *However,* the office will be closed.
> *Yes,* the meeting will be held as scheduled.
> *Thus* we took an earlier flight.
> *Usually,* the office is open on Saturday.

Names.   Do not use a comma between a name and *of* indicating place or position.

> Henderson Manufacturing Company *of* Phoenix, Arizona
> Mrs. Edwards *of* Robinson & Co.
> Ms. Steinberg *of* counsel

Place a comma between a name and *Inc., Sr.,* and *Jr.* when the person or company uses that style; omit the comma when the subject also omits it. (Do not place a comma before *II* or *III* in a name.)

> Lever Brothers, *Inc.*   R. G. Jones, *Sr.*   R. G. Jones III

Numbers.   Use a comma when writing figures in thousands *but not* in street, room, post-office-box, postal-zip-code, telephone, and book-page numbers.

> $15,800.65   1381 Vinton Avenue   P.O. Box 4671
>   zip code 07632   page 1159   3,800 cars

Oh.   Use a comma after *oh* if other words follow it.

> *Oh,* he returned the manuscript yesterday.

Parentheses and comma.   Use a comma after a closing parenthesis if the construction of the sentence requires a comma. Never use a comma *before* a parenthesis or an expression enclosed in parentheses.

> Our incorporators' meeting (the first meeting of our stockholders),
>   which is required by law, will be held November 15.
> Our incorporators' meeting (the first meeting of our stockholders)
>   will be held November 15.

Parenthetical words and phrases.   Use commas to set off parenthetical words or phrases like *I believe, for example, however,* unless the connection is close and smooth enough not to call for a pause in reading.

> *Furthermore,* credit obligations may be paid out of capital items.
> The economic condition of the country, *I believe,* is gradually
>   improving.

He was *perhaps* busy at the time.

That make of car is not expensive and *therefore* appeals to potential customers in the low-income brackets.

Participial phrases.   Do not separate a participle from the noun it modifies when the noun is not the subject and the expression is not closely connected with the rest of the sentence. The commas in brackets in the following sentences should be omitted.

The operators [,] *having agreed to arbitrate,* the union called off the strike.

The evidence [,] *being merely circumstantial,* the jury acquitted him.

Phrases with a common element.   Place a comma before a word or words that are common to two or more phrases but are expressed only after the last phrase. In the following examples the commas in brackets are frequently *omitted in error.*

The report was documented with references to many, if not all [,] of the recent court decisions on the question of interlocking directorates. (The words *of the . . .* are common to *many* and to *all*).

The sales manager's reports are clearer, more concise, more instructive [,] than those of the advertising manager. (The words *than those . . .* are common to *clearer, more concise,* and *more instructive.*)

Note: If the phrases are connected by a conjunction, the comma is omitted.

The sales manager's reports are clearer, more concise, *and* more accurate than those of the advertising manager.

Quotations.   Set off direct quotations by commas.

His reply was, "I am interested in the matter."

"I am not interested in the matter," he replied.

But if a question mark is needed at the end of the quotation, do not use a comma.

"What is the lowest price you can quote?" he inquired. (*Not:* "What is the lowest price you can quote?," he inquired.)

Quotation marks and comma.   Place the comma on the *inside* of quotation marks.

> When he spoke of "overtime," I thought he meant "over 35 hours."

Series.   Separate words and phrases in a series by a comma. (*See also* **Semicolon: The Compromise between Period and Comma, Series,** page 499. For use of the comma to show words omitted in a series, *see* **Ellipsis,** page 493.

> Thus we speak of buying goods on credit, of a merchant's credit, and of making a payment by credit.
> Its membership comprises manufacturers and wholesalers of silverware, watches, diamonds, and semiprecious stones.

But do not use a comma between two (not a series) parallel constructions joined by a conjunction.

> This amount is equal to the covered loss less (1) the coinsurance deduction and (2) the normal loss.
> He can ask for changes in the estimate or for a completely revised estimate.

Period: The Most Familiar Punctuation Mark

Sentences.   Place a period at the end of a declarative or imperative sentence.

> The contract was signed last week (declarative).
> Hold the shipment until next month (imperative).

Initials and abbreviations.   Place a period after certain initials and abbreviations. The periods are omitted between initials standing for agencies and other organizations and between the letters of many abbreviations (*see* the list of abbreviations in chapter 18, pages 540–77) and after letters used as a name. For other examples where the period should be omitted, *see* **Omissions,** page 498.

> Ph.D.   ibid.   Chas.   R. E. Smith   NASA   Mr. T

Outlines.   Place a period after each letter or number in an outline or itemized list unless the letter or number is enclosed in parentheses.

> A. Comma
>   1. Appositives
>   2. Cities and states
> (A) Comma
>   (1) Appositives
>   (2) Cities and states

Omissions.   Omit the period after contractions; roman numerals, except in an outline; sums of money in dollar denominations, unless cents are added; shortened forms of names and words in common use; and letters identifying radio and television stations.

ass'n	sec'y	volume II	George V	$50	$50.25
Ed	Will	ad memo	percent	photo	NBC

Periods and parentheses.   When an expression in parentheses comes at the end of a sentence and is part of the sentence, put the period *outside* the closing parenthesis; if the parenthetical expression is independent of the sentence and a period is necessary, place the period *within* the closing parenthesis.

> The creditor can get a judgment against him and garnishee his wages (see section 15).
> The creditor can get a judgment against him and garnishee his wages. (The law of garnishment is discussed in Section 15.)

But do not use a period when a complete declarative or imperative sentence is enclosed in parentheses *within another sentence.*

> The honorary chairman of the board (he retired from active duty several years ago) addressed the Quarter-Century Club.

Periods and quotation marks.   Always place the period *inside* quotation marks.

> Please explain what you meant by the expression "without reservation."

Semicolon: The Compromise between Period and Comma

Compound sentences.   A semicolon may be used to separate the parts of a compound sentence when the comma and conjunction are omitted.

> The adjustment has been made; the file has been closed.

Long, involved clauses.   Use a semicolon to separate long, involved clauses.

> A low rate of interest usually reflects easy conditions and an
> inactive industrial situation; a high rate indicates money
> stringency and industrial activity.

Punctuated clauses.   Use a semicolon to separate clauses that are punctuated by commas.

> On the other hand, if the turnover is low in comparison to the
> normal figure it shows just the opposite; that is, it indicates
> weaker sales policy and poorer purchasing ability and stock
> control than the average.

Series.   In enumerations or series of items, use semicolons to separate items that contain commas. (*See also* **Comma: The Secretary's Troublemaker, Series,** page 492.)

> The most important of these services are published by Moody's
> Investors Service, Inc.; Standard and Poor's Corporation; and Fitch
> Publishing Company, Inc.

Before a conjunctive adverb.   Use a semicolon before an adverb that serves the purpose of a conjunction. The conjunctive adverbs are *accordingly, also, besides, consequently, furthermore, hence, however, indeed, likewise, moreover, nevertheless, otherwise, similarly, so, still, therefore, thus.* The trend is to omit the comma after a conjunctive adverb preceded by a semicolon, unless it ends in *-ly,* and to omit the comma after short conjunctive adverbs such as *so* and *thus.* In the following examples the comma in brackets *should* be omitted in the first example and *may* be omitted in the second and third examples.

He told his secretary that he did not want to be disturbed; so [,] she
did not announce the chairman of the board, whom she did not
recognize.

He telephoned that he did not plan to leave until next week;
therefore [,] I did not consider it necessary to send the report to
him by airmail.

He will attend the meeting; indeed [,] he will be the main speaker
at the meeting.

Quotation marks and semicolon.　Place the semicolon *outside* quotation marks.

As stated in his report, "the department is expanding"; therefore
our advertising should reflect this development.

Parentheses and semicolon.　Use a semicolon after a closing parenthesis if the construction of the sentence requires a semicolon. Never use a
comma or semicolon before a parenthesis or an expression enclosed in
parentheses.

The current sales figures are ambiguous (in my opinion); however,
new data will be out this month.

Colon: Its Important Uses

Introduction to lists, tabulations.　The most frequent use of the
colon is after a word, phrase, or sentence that introduces lists, a series,
tabulations, extracts, texts, and explanations that are in apposition to the
introductory words.

The following is an extract from the report:
These conditions must exist:

But do not use a colon to introduce a series of items that are the direct
objects of a preposition or verb or that follow a form of the verb *to be*. In the
following example the comma in brackets should be omitted.

The requirements of a good secretary *are* [:] ability to take rapid
dictation and to transcribe it rapidly and accurately, ability to
spell correctly and to use the dictionary to the best advantage,
and familiarity with basic office procedures.

Note: A colon may precede a *formal tabulation* even when the tabulated words or phrases are the objects of a preposition or verb or follow a form of the verb *to be*.

> The requirements of a good secretary are:
> 1. Ability to take rapid dictation
> 2. Ability to spell correctly
> 3. Familiarity with basic office procedures

Pauses. Use a colon to show a pause between two closely related sentences.

> The secretary had one primary goal: she wanted to advance within the company.

Time and ratios. Use a colon to indicate clock time and to show ratios.

> 4:10 A.M.   8:1 ratio

Letter salutations. Business-letter salutations are always followed by a colon.

> Dear Mrs. Adams:

Footnotes. Use a colon to separate the name of the city and state of publication from the name of the publisher.

> 1. Gavin A. Pitt, *The Twenty-Minute Lifetime* (Englewood Cliffs, N.J.: Prentice-Hall, Inc., 1988), 20.

Bible references. Use a colon to separate the verse and chapter in biblical references.

> Matthew 10:4

Dash and colon. Do not use a dash with a colon.

> Look at this bulletin—it's amazing. (*Not:* Look at this bulletin:—it's amazing.)

Dash: A Useful Substitute

Principal use.   The dash is a more forceful mark than most other punctuation. It is used principally to set off explanatory or parenthetical clauses (*see also* **Parentheses or Brackets: When to Use Them, Explanatory expressions,** page 508), to indicate abrupt changes in the continuity of expression, and to set off a thought that is repeated for emphasis. But some writers use a dash unnecessarily and excessively when a comma or other punctuation would be more appropriate; such overuse causes a dash to lose its effectiveness and distracts the reader.

> The old typewriter—last year's model—is a better machine than the new one.
> He said that Monday would be fine—or did he say Tuesday?
> She returned my copy—the copy I thought was lost.

Series.   A dash may be used before or after a clause that summarizes a series of words or phrases, but a colon is more common *after* such a clause.

> "Wage and Hour," "Arbitration," "Union Contracts"—these chapters indicate only a few of the topics discussed in our *Complete Labor-Equipment Services* handbook.
> Our *Complete Labor-Equipment Services* handbook has six chapters: "Wage and Hour," "Employee Relations," "Union Contracts," "Labor Relations," "State Labor Law," and "Pension and Profit Sharing."

Dash and other punctuation marks.   A dash may be used after an abbreviating period. If the material set off by dashes requires an interrogation or exclamation point, retain the punctuation before the second dash. Do not use a dash with a comma or semicolon. Do not use a dash and colon together before a list of items (*see* **Colon: Its Important Uses, Introduction to lists, tabulations,** page 500).

> The check is now O.K.—he made a large deposit.
> The head of the personnel department—is his name Donovan or O'Donnovan?—said he thought there would be an opening next week.

Exclamation Point: A Stranger in the Secretary's Work

Exclamatory sentences.   Place an exclamation point after a startling statement or a sentence expressing strong emotion.

How incredible that he should take that attitude!

Exclamatory words.   Place an exclamation point after exclamatory words.

Oh!   Great!   Stop!

For emphasis.   If not used to excess, an exclamation point is a good device to lend emphasis or to drive home a point. It is used more frequently in sales letters than in any other business correspondence. But, like the dash, unless the exclamation point is used sparingly, it loses its effectiveness and distracts the reader.

Buy now!   And more than 1000 forms!

Interrogation Point: A Question

Interrogative sentences.   Place a question mark after a direct question but not after an indirect question.

Have you heard the decision that was made at the conference
(direct)?
Mr. Rogers asked me, "When will the book be ready for
publication?" (direct).
Mr. Rogers asked me when the book would be ready for publication
(indirect).

Requests.   Do not place a question mark after a question that is a request to which no answer is expected.

Will you please return the signed copy as soon as possible.

Queries.   A question mark enclosed in parentheses may be used to query the accuracy of a fact or figure. Other punctuation is not affected by this use of the question mark.

> The treaty was signed September 5(?), 1979

Series of questions.   A question mark is usually placed after each question in a series included within one sentence, and each question usually begins with a capital.

> What will be the significance of our landing on the moon if we still cannot get along with others? If our cultural endeavors have been sacrificed? If world peace is still unstable?

But the question mark may be omitted in a simple series.

> Who is responsible for (a) copyediting the book, (b) producing the artwork, and (c) preparing the production schedule?

Quotation marks with question marks.   *See* **Quotation Marks: How to Use Them, Placement of quotation marks,** page 506.

Quotation Marks: How to Use Them

Direct quotations.   Enclose the exact words of a speaker or writer in quotation marks, but do not enclose words that are not quoted exactly. The quoted material may be a word or several paragraphs in length.

> On July 15 he wrote, "Please consider the contract cancelled if the goods are not shipped by the tenth of next month."
> On July 15 he wrote that we should consider the contract canceled if the goods are not shipped by the tenth of next month.
> He wrote that he was "no longer interested" in the proposition.

But do not use quotation marks when the name of the speaker or writer immediately precedes the quoted material or in question-and-answer material.

> Mr. Edwards: In my opinion the machine is worthless.
> Ms. Roberts: Upon what do you base that opinion?

Paragraphs.   When quoted material is more than one paragraph, place quotation marks at the beginning of each paragraph but only at the close of the last paragraph. For omission of words in quoted material, *see* **Leaders and Ellipsis Points: Invaluable Aids, Ellipsis points,** page 510.

Definitions. Quotation marks may be used to enclose a word or phrase that is accompanied by its definition, although in material that is to be typeset and printed, the word being defined should be underscored and the quotation marks omitted. (Many writers underscore rather than use quotation marks even when the material will not be typeset or printed.)

> The party against whom garnishment proceedings are brought is
> called the "garnishee."
> "Bankruptcy insolvency" means that a debtor's total assets are less
> than his total liabilities.

Unique words or trade terms. Quotation marks may be used to enclose a word or phrase the *first* time the term is used in an unusual sense or with a special trade meaning. It is not desirable to use the quotation marks when the term is repeated, and one should be careful not to enclose terms when the sense or meaning is understood. (Many writers use quotation marks excessively and unnecessarily.)

> This "pyramiding" was carried to an extreme in the public utility
> field.
> In "spot" markets commodities are bought and sold in specific lots
> and grades with a definite delivery date specified.

Titles and names. Use quotation marks to enclose the titles of articles, chapters or part titles in books, unpublished works such as a thesis or conference paper, short poems, songs, and television and radio shows.

> "Heredity in Asian Cultures" (article or chapter title)
> "CAM and CAD Technology in the 1980s" (conference address)
> "Winter's Song" (short poem)
> "Star Spangled Banner" (song)
> "Highway to Heaven" (television show)

Note: Titles of books, periodicals, brochures and pamphlets, operas, paintings, plays and motion pictures, and long poems are underscored in typed material and italicized in typeset and printed material. Do not use quotation marks with or underscore the Bible or names of its books (Psalms) or other parts of it (New Testament); movements of a symphony, concerto, or other long composition or names of numbered compositions (Symphony no. 5 in

C Minor); parts of poems or plays (Scene 2); book series titles (Studies in American Literature) and book editions (Second Edition); common titles in a book (Appendix I); notices (No Smoking); and mottoes (One for All and All for One).

Single quotation marks.   Use single quotation marks to enclose a quotation within a quotation.

> Last week he wrote, "It is understood that delivery 'must be made on or before the 30th.'"

Placement of quotation marks.   Always place a period or comma *inside* quotation marks.

> The account was marked "paid," but he never received a receipt.
> The check was marked "canceled."

Always place colons and semicolons *outside* quotation marks.

> Turn to the chapter "Consideration for Stock"; the reference is in the first paragraph.

Interrogation and exclamation points come before or after the quotation marks, depending on the meaning of the text.

> Who is the author of "Up the Down Staircase"? (The entire question is not quoted.)
> He shouted, "I will never consent to those terms!" (The exclamation is part of the quotation.)

Apostrophe: Its Principal Uses

Possessives.   Use the apostrophe to indicate the possessive case of nouns. Do *not* use the apostrophe to indicate the possessive case of personal pronouns. (*See also* **Grammatical Terms, Case,** page 414, in chapter 14.)

> John's   Davis's   its   theirs

Contractions.   Use the apostrophe to denote a contraction or omission of letters. Place the apostrophe where the letter or letters are omitted.

it's for *it is*   *ass'n* for *association*   *'84* for *1984*

But omit the apostrophe in contractions formed by dropping the first letters of a word if the contraction has come into common usage.

phone   plane   though

Letters and symbols.   Use the apostrophe to form the plurals of letters and symbols. (*See also* **Plurals, Figures, letters,** page 478, in chapter 15.)

p's and q's   5's and 6's   #'s

Words.   Use an apostrophe to indicate the plural of a word referred to *as a word,* without regard to its meaning, but use the regularly formed plural if a meaning is attached to the word.

There are three *but's* in the sentence.
The *ayes* have it.
There are eight *threes* in twenty-four.
There are eight *three's* in the sentence.

Abbreviations.   Use an apostrophe to denote the plural or some other form of an abbreviation. (*See also* **Plurals, Figures, letters,** page 478, in chapter 15.)

three O.K.'s   O.K.'d   V.I.P.'s

Hyphen: A Useful Aid

Division of words.   Use a hyphen at the end of a line to show that part of a word has been carried over to another line. See chapter 15 for the principles governing the division of words at the end of a line.

Compound terms.   Use a hyphen as a connecting link in compound terms. (*See* **Grammatical Terms, Compound term,** page 417, in chapter 14.)

Series of hyphenated words.   In a series of hyphenated words having a common base, place a hyphen after the first element of each word and write the base after the last word only.

fourth-, fifth-, and sixth-grade pupils

Use a suspended hyphen in numerical descriptions. (Some writers do not insert a space after the first number and instead write the description closed.)

> 3- by 5-inch cards (suspended)
> 3-by-5-inch cards (closed)
> one- to two-year program (suspended)
> one-to-two-year program (closed)

Time.   Use a hyphen to indicate a span of time but do not use a hyphen with the words *from* or *between* in relation to a time period.

> The report covers the fiscal year 1985–86.
> The report covers the period *from* January 1985 *to* December 1986.
> The report covers the period *between* January 1985 and December 1986.

Parentheses or Brackets: When to Use Them

Brackets.   If your typewriter has a bracket key, use brackets to rectify mistakes in quoted material and to enclose parenthetical material *within* remarks already enclosed in parentheses. If necessary, brackets can be made by using the short diagonal and dash keys. *See* **BASIC TYPING RULES, Making Special Characters Not on Your Keyboard,** page 57, in chapter 2.

> "The fire occurred [*sic*] in 1985."
> Read Chapter 5 ("Real Estate Practice [legal implications] in New York") before you begin writing.

Explanatory expressions.   Use parentheses to enclose parenthetical or explanatory expressions that are *outside* the general structure of the sentence. Parentheses indicate a stronger separation than do commas or dashes. *See also* **Dash: A Useful Substitute, Principal use,** page 502.

> The place at which an incorporators' meeting (sometimes called the first meeting of the stockholders) is to be held is determined by statute in most states.

Figures.   Enclose a figure in parentheses when it follows an amount that has been written out in words and when the American equivalent of foreign currency is given.

> Under the will he received £100,000 ($280,000).
> The check is for seven thousand five hundred (7,500) dollars.
> The check is for seven thousand five hundred dollars ($7,500).

Note: If the figure is written *before* the word *dollars,* do not use the dollar sign; if the figure is written *after* the word *dollars,* use the dollar sign. (This rule also applies to the percentage sign.)

Questions and answers.   In testimony (question-and-answer material), use parentheses to enclose matter describing an action and, also, to indicate a person who has not previously taken part in the questions and answers.

> Q. (By Mr. Smith) Will you identify this handkerchief? (Hands the witness a handkerchief)

Enumerations.   Enclose in parentheses letters or numbers in enumerations run into the text. (In general writing it is often preferable to omit the numbers entirely, except in long or complex enumerations.)

> Stock may be divided broadly into two kinds: (1) common stock and (2) preferred stock.

Single (closing) parentheses.   Parentheses are usually used in pairs, but a single closing parenthesis may be used instead of a period to follow a letter or roman numeral in outlines. Usually, double parentheses (or a period) are preferred even in this case.

> 1) Parentheses
>   a) Brackets
>   b) Explanatory expressions

Punctuation in parentheses.   Commas, periods, and similar punctuation marks belong *within* the parentheses if they belong to the parenthetical clause or phrase. They are placed *outside* the parentheses if they belong to the words of the rest of the sentence. *See also* **Period: The Most Familiar Punctuation Mark, Periods and parentheses,** page 498.

> The boy ran as if a ghost (and, indeed, he may have been right) were following him.
> She reported the action at once. (She has a strong sense of civic responsibility.)
> He turned in a perfect examination paper. (What an example for the rest of the class!)

Leaders and Ellipsis Points: Invaluable Aids

Leaders.   A row of dots (periods) or short lines (hyphens) to lead the eye across a space in the line of writing to a related figure or words. Their principal use is in statements of account or other tabulations.

Accounts Receivable $1,425.72

Ellipsis points.   The marks used to show an omission from a sentence of a word or words that would complete the construction. The marks may be dots (periods) or asterisks. When you are quoting and want to omit words, use three consecutive asterisks (* * *) or dots (. . .) to indicate an omission of words. If a period would ordinarily follow the words omitted, you will then have four dots, one representing the period. Put a space before and after each dot except when the first dot represents a period.

> . . . according to Mr. Burns, but . . . the check is past due (words omitted at the beginning and in the middle of the sentence: three dots, equal space before and after each one).

> The report will nevertheless be delayed. . . . Let us hope it doesn't happen again (end of the sentence or other sentences or paragraphs missing: no space before first dot since it represents a period).

> I was wondering . . . (incomplete sentence: three dots, equal space after each one)

> The purpose of punctuation is clear. . . . and it should be respected (end of first sentence and beginning of next sentence missing: no space before first dot since it represents a period).

The same principles apply to extracts, which are blocks of copy set off from the rest of the text and indented.

In an extract the first complete (no introductory words missing) sentence is *not* indented and is *not* preceded by three dots—*if* it falls somewhere within the first paragraph you are quoting. But four dots *are* placed at the end of the sentence or paragraph to show that other words, a sentence(s), or another paragraph(s) is missing. . . .

. . . the second paragraph *is* indented and *is* preceded by three dots when the beginning words are omitted from a sentence that does *not* open that paragraph. Also, three dots are used as always when words are missing in the middle of any sentence . . . in any paragraph.

Virgule (Solidus): For Special Occasions

Principal use.   The virgule (also called "solidus" and "slash") is used most often in fractions, in identification numbers, in abbreviations, in place of the word *per,* in dates instead of a hyphen, between nouns of equal weight, to show a time span, and between lines of poetry that are run into the text. Usually, there is no space before or after the virgule unless it is used to separate lines of poetry. (Some authorities recommend that the hyphen instead of the virgule be used to show a time span and between nouns of equal weight.)

> 7/8 (fraction)   B/R-423   B/L (bill of lading)
> miles/hr.   1985/90   owner/operator   Thompson said:
> "But the rose's scene is bitterness / to him that loved the rose."

——Chapter 17——

Capitalization

RULES AND PRINCIPLES OF CAPITALIZATION

Abbreviations

Degrees and titles. Capitalize abbreviations of degrees and titles. Do not space between the letters. Some organizations are following the trend to write degrees and certain titles without periods and with no space (e.g., ScD).

> A.B.   Ph.D.   M.P.   Jr.   Lt. Col.

Initials of names. Capitalize initials of names. Space between the initials unless there are three initials.

> R. D. Ellis   R.D.M. Ellis   Mr. T   JFK

One letter. Capitalize abbreviations of one letter, except most units of measurement and minor literary subdivisions.

> F (fahrenheit)   p. 3 (page 3)   t (ton)

Time and years. Abbreviations such as *a.m.* may be lowercase or uppercase, but the trend is toward lowercase. Do not space between the initials. The abbreviation for *meridies* (noon) should be capitalized, because it is one initial—*M.* Do not use these abbreviations when the hour is written out; write *four o'clock in the afternoon* or *four o'clock,* not *four* P.M. Abbreviations for chronology such as *Ano Domini* are typed in all capitals and are usually typeset in small capitals.

P.M.   B.C.   PST (Pacific standard time)

Common abbreviations. Many common abbreviations may be lowercase or uppercase, but the trend is toward lowercase. Organization initials and well-known acronyms are usually capitalized (but not general shortcuts such as *po* for *post office*), and two-letter postal abbreviations are always capitalized. Do not space between the letters. (See the lists of abbreviations in chapter 18, pages 540–77, for examples.)

COD or cod   FOB or fob   NB or nb
SALT   YMCA   IBM   NY

Acts, Bills, Codes, Laws

Official title. Capitalize the official titles of specific acts, bills, codes, and laws; also capitalize the accepted title by which a law is generally known.

Securities Exchange Act, the securities act, the act
Civil Rights Bill, the bill
National Labor Relations Act, the act

But lowercase *bill* or *law* when used with the sponsor's name unless the formal title of the bill is given.

the Thomas bill, the Thomas wage-hour bill

General descriptive terms. Lowercase *bill* and *act* when they are standing alone; also lowercase abbreviated titles and general descriptive terms designating them.

the securities act
the rent-control bill
the wage-hour bill

Federal, state, and municipal codes. Lowercase federal, state, and municipal codes, but capitalize the formal titles of codes of law.

building code
Code of Criminal Procedure
Code Napoléon

Constitution. Capitalize *constitution* when it refers to the specific constitution of a country, but lowercase general references. Capitalize *constitution* immediately following a state name, but lowercase it when it precedes the state name and in general references.

> the U.S. Constitution, the Constitution of the United States, the
>   Constitution (of the United States), a national constitution
> the New Jersey Constitution, the constitution of New Jersey, the
>   state constitution, the constitution

Amendments to the U.S. Constitution. Capitalize amendments to the Constitution when they are referred to by number or by full title, but lowercase them when they are used as general terms or as parts of general descriptive titles.

> Eighteenth Amendment, the amendment
> prohibition amendment
> Child Labor Amendment, the amendment
> constitutional amendment

Courts, Judges, Cases

Full title. Capitalize the full title of a court, but lowercase *court* when it is standing alone or when it is used in a general descriptive sense. Always capitalize references to the Supreme Court of the United States, even when the word *Court* is standing alone.

> the federal courts
> Judge Mason's court
> U.S. Supreme Court, the Supreme Court, the Court
> Court of Appeals of New York, the Court of Appeals (capitalized to
>   distinguish from the U.S. court), the court
> Arizona Supreme Court, the supreme court, the court
> General Sessions
> magistrate's court
> traffic court
> night court

Judges, justices. Capitalize titles when they precede a proper name, but lowercase *chief justice, associate justice, justice, judge, magistrate, surrogate,* and so on when they stand alone.

> Magistrate Williams, the magistrate
> Associate Justice Donaldson, the associate justice
> Surrogate Brown, the surrogate

Reference to the judge. Capitalize *court* when it refers directly to the judge or presiding officer. Capitalize *Your Honor, His* (or *Her*) *Honor,* when they refer to the Court.

> The *Court* overruled the objection.
> In the opinion of the *Court* . . .
> If it please *Your Honor* . . .

Bar, bench. Capitalize *bar* and *bench* when they are part of a judicial body, but lowercase them in all other instances.

> American Bar Association, the bar
> Court of King's Bench, the bench

Cases. Capitalize the main words in the name of a case but not the abbreviation *v* or *vs* (versus).

> *White and Stone, Inc.* v. *City of Cleveland,* the *White* case

Education

Names of schools. Capitalize the names of schools or colleges and their departments, but lowercase the words *school, college,* and *department* when they are not part of a name.

> Washington Irving High School, the high school
> Dartmouth, the university
> Public School No. 1, a public school
> Department of History, the history department
> College of Liberal Arts, the college
> School of Business Administration, the business school

Classes. Capitalize the names of classes of a high school, college, or university, but lowercase the word when it refers to a member of a class.

> Freshman Class, a freshman

Degrees, chairmanships.   Capitalize academic degrees, scholastic honors, chairmanships, fellowships, and the like, whether abbreviated or written in full, if the person's full name is given. Lowercase these words when they are not part of a name or title.

John Smith, Ph.D.; John Smith, Doctor of Philosophy; the doctor of
   philosophy degree
LL.D., degree of doctor of laws, doctor of laws degree
M.A., master of arts degree
Robert Brown Fellowship, the fellowship
Sc.D., doctor of science degree, the doctorate

Courses, subjects.   Capitalize the official names of courses, but capitalize the names of subjects only when they are derived from proper names.

Education II, the education course
Modern History 309, the course in modern history
I am studying history, Latin, and English.

Enumerations

Preceded by a colon.   Capitalize the first word in each section of an enumeration that has been formally introduced if the enumerations are in a complete sentence. Lowercase brief items that do not make sentences, unless they are itemized.

A secretary uses the guide under these circumstances: (1) Someone
   outside the immediate office wants the material. (2) The manager
   expects to take the material out of the office. (3) The secretary
   expects to use the material for more than one day.
She listed the following as her qualifications for the position: (1)
   initiative, (2) intelligence, and (3) tact.
Her qualifications for the position are:
   1. Initiative
   2. Intelligence
   3. Tact

Not preceded by a colon.   Lowercase enumerations that are not preceded by a colon.

The disadvantage is offset to some extent by (1) the limited liability of shareholders and (2) the marketability of ownership in the company.

Foreign Names

General rule.   Usually articles, prepositions, and conjunctions (such as *du, de, la, le, von, van*) that constitute a part of foreign names are not capitalized unless the name is written without the given name or a title. However, some people with foreign names prefer capitals, and you should observe the person's preference.

> E. I. du Pont de Nemours
> Van Wort, the author
> Martin Van Buren (preferred spelling)
> Ludwig van Beethoven
> Dr. de la Bonne

Geographical Terms

Points of compass.   Capitalize names of points of the compass when they refer to a section of the United States, but lowercase them when they denote simple direction or compass points.

> the South, south of here, southern
> the Northwest, to the northwest, northwestern
> the East, moving east, eastern
> the West, a west window, western
> the Midwest, midwestern origin

Popular names.   Capitalize popular names of specific localities. But lowercase *ghetto, fatherland,* and the like.

> Corn Belt, Cotton Belt
> East Side, West Side
> the Delta
> the Loop (Chicago)
> Mississippi Valley, valley of the Mississippi
> the Continent (Europe), continental Europe, a continent
> New York ghetto

Regional terms.   Capitalize regional terms that are part of a precise descriptive title, but lowercase terms that are merely localizing adjectives.

> the Eastern Shore
> the South Shore
> South Jersey (definite regional term)
> northern China (localizing adjective)
> western New York (localizing adjective)

Coast.   Capitalize *coast* when it designates a specific locality or stands alone, but lowercase it when it is used with geographic designations.

> West Coast (U.S.), the coast
> New England coast, the coast
> Pacific Coast (U.S.), the coast
> Jersey coast, the coast
> Florida coast, the coast
> Gulf Coast (U.S.), the coast

Divisions of world or country.   Capitalize most political divisions and major parts of the world or a country but not adjectives derived from them.

> the Old World, the New World
> Far East, Near East
> New England states
> Roman Empire, the empire
> the Union (U.S.)
> West Africa, western Africa
> Arctic, arctic winter
> North Atlantic, northern Atlantic
> Orient, oriental
> Mississippi River, the river
> Mississippi and Arkansas rivers
> Tropic of Cancer, the tropics
> Central America
> central Europe (general), Central Europe (World War I political
>   division)
> the East (U.S. region), eastern U.S.

Government and Political Terms

Government, administration.   Capitalize *government* and *adminis-tration* when they are part of a title; otherwise, lowercase them.

Her Majesty's Government, the government in Britain
the U.S. government, the federal government, the government
the Reagan administration, the administration
the Tennessee government, the government of Tennessee, the
   government

Federal. Capitalize *federal* when it is part of a title. When *federal* is used as an adjective referring to institutions or activities of the federal government, use lowercase. Always use lowercase when *federal* is used as a general term.

Federal Register (title of publication)
the federal government
the federal courts
the federal principle of government

National. Capitalize *national* when it is part of a title or name of a political party (the word *party* is not capitalized); lowercase it when it is used as a general descriptive term. Also lowercase *nationals,* meaning citizens of a country.

National Labor Relations Board, the board
the National Socialist party, the party
national customs
The nationals were opposed to the legislation.

State. Capitalize *state* or *commonwealth* when it is part of a name; otherwise, lowercase it.

New York State, state of New York, the state
Commonwealth of Massachusetts, the commonwealth

City. Capitalize *city* when it is part of a name, but lowercase it when it is used in transposed form or when it stands alone.

New York City, the city of New York, the city

County. Capitalize *county* when it is part of a name, but lowercase it when it is used in transposed form or when it stands alone.

Westchester County, the county of Westchester, the county

District.   Capitalize *district* when it is part of a name, but lowercase it when it is used as a general term or when it stands alone.

> District of Columbia, the district
> Second Congressional District, the congressional district
> Third Assembly District, the district

Ward, precinct.   Capitalize *ward* and *precinct* when they are part of a name, but lowercase them when they stand alone.

> Ward 3, Third Ward, the ward
> Fifth Precinct, the precinct

Departments, boards, committees.   Capitalize the full title of governmental departments, boards, committees, commissions, bureaus, and so on, but lowercase *department, board, committee, commission, bureau,* and the rest when they are used alone in place of the full name.

> Police Department, the department
> Department of Justice, the Justice Department, the department
> Bureau of Standards, the bureau
> Council Finance Committee, the Finance Committee, the committee

Names of legislative bodies.   Capitalize the names of legislative, administrative, and deliberative bodies, both domestic and foreign.

> U.S. Congress, the Congress
> U.S. House of Representatives, the House
> U.S. Senate, the Senate
> Board of Estimate, the board
> House of Lords, the House
> Parliament (Br.), parliamentary

Lowercase general or incomplete designations of legislative bodies.

> the city council, Huntsville City Council
> the lower house, the House of Commons
> the senate (no specific state), Iowa State Senate, the Senate (Iowa)
> the assembly (no specific state), Delaware General Assembly, the
>   General Assembly (Delaware), the Assembly (Delaware)

Legislature. Capitalize *legislature* when it is part of the name of a specific body. Unless the exact designation is used, there is no need to capitalize *legislature* when it is used with the name of a state.

> Mississippi Legislature, the legislature
> Arkansas legislature (the exact designation is Arkansas General
> Assembly), the legislature

Headings and Titles

General rule. Capitalize all important words (nouns, pronouns, verbs, adjectives, adverbs) in headings and titles of books, articles, lectures, reports, and the like, and lowercase articles, conjunctions, and prepositions. (See chapter 3, page 104, for the preferred style of writing headings in reports.)

> Valuable Aids in Letter Writing
> Selecting and Operating a Business of Your Own
> This Is the Way It Was
> Trends in Productive Sales Techniques
> Substance before Style

Infinitives. Lowercase the *to* in an infinitive.

> How to Build a Better Vocabulary
> How to Establish and Operate a Retail Store

Prepositions. Prepositions of five or more letters may be capitalized but the trend is to lowercase them. Prepositions of less than five letters are always lowercased.

> Let's Talk about Children
> Life without Stress
> Computers for the Home
> Rules concerning Parliamentary Procedure

Break in title. Articles, prepositions, and conjunctions that immediately follow a marked break in a title, indicated by a colon or dash, are capitalized.

> Pick Your Job—And Like It
> Television: The Eyes of Tomorrow

Historical Terms

Eras. Capitalize designations of eras of history and periods in the history of a language or literature. But lowercase informal adjectives in phrases such as *early Victorian* and numerical periods such as *twentieth century*. Lowercase very recent designations such as *space age*.

Dark Ages	Stone Age
Middle Ages	the Exile
Christian Era	Roaring Twenties
the Diaspora	Medieval Latin
Elizabethan Age	antiquity
nineteenth century	baroque period
colonial period (U.S.)	ancient Greece
the Renaissance	a renaissance of poetry

Important events. Capitalize the names of important events. But lowercase *war* unless it is part of the name of a war.

> Missouri Compromise, the compromise
> World War II, the Second World War, the war
> Peace of Utrecht
> Battle of the Bulge, the battle
> Vietnam War, the war in Vietnam, the war

Documents. Capitalize the names of important historical documents.

> Magna Carta
> Declaration of Independence, the declaration
> Atlantic Charter, the charter
> Monroe Doctrine, the doctrine

Holidays, Seasons, Feast Days

Religious. Capitalize religious holidays and feast days.

Yom Kipper	Passover	Christmas Eve
Good Friday	Hanukkah	Lent

Secular. Capitalize secular and especially designated days and weeks. But lowercase descriptive days such as *primary day*.

Thanksgiving Day   Memorial Day
Clean-Up Week   inauguration day

Seasons.   Lowercase names of seasons, unless they are personified.

autumn   spring   summer
midwinter   Spring, with her arms full of flowers . . .

Hyphenated Compounds

General rule.   The capitalization of hyphenated compounds varies among authorities. The style indicated here is common in secretarial practice. But whichever style you adopt, be consistent.

Hyphenated words.   Capitalize the parts of a hyphenated word that would be capitalized if the word were not hyphenated.

no-par stock
English-speaking nations
Anglo-Saxon descent
ex-President Johnson

Titles and headings.   Capitalize all parts of hyphenated words in titles and headings, except (1) when the second word modifies the first word and (2) when the two parts are considered one word.

Spanish-speaking Students
Self-taught Writers
Sage of Twenty-second Street
Conference of Ex-Senators
Anti-intellectual Bias
Owner-Operator Guidelines
Nineteenth-Century Politics
Non-American Alliances

Compound numerals.   Lowercase the second part of a compound numeral, even in titles and headings.

Eighty-first Congress Convenes
One-fifth of Students on Strike
261 Sixty-second Street

Leagues, Treaties, Pacts, Plans

General rule. Capitalize the names of bodies, except adjectives derived from them or incomplete designations. Capitalize *treaty, pact,* and *plan* only when part of a specific title.

> United Nations
> General Assembly, the assembly
> Security Council, the council
> Secretariat
> Treaty of Versailles, Versailles treaty, treaty at Versailles, the treaty
> Marshall Plan, the plan
> Pact of Paris, the pact

Lists and Outlines

General rule. Capitalize the first word of each item in a list or outline.

> I. Office procedure
>   A. Typing
>   1. Typewriter and computer

Military

Names. Capitalize names of military services, but lowercase words such as *army* and *navy* when they stand alone, are used collectively in the plural, or are not part of an official title.

> United States Army, the army, the armed forces
> United States Navy, the navy
> United States Signal Corps, Signal Corps, the corps
> United States Marines, the marines
> National Guard, the guard
> Red Army, Russian army, the army

Branches, divisions. Capitalize titles of various branches or divisions, but lowercase general references such as *division.*

> First Division, the division
> Third Army, the army
> Company A, the company

Navy Militia, the militia
Second Battalion, the battalion

Titles. Capitalize a few titles of distinction that refer to a specific person, whether the title is standing alone or is followed by a proper name. Capitalize *Fleet Admiral* and *General of the Army* to avoid ambiguity. But generally lowercase military and naval titles when they are standing alone and are not followed by a proper name.

the Chief of Staff
the General of the Army, the general
the Admiral of the Fleet, the admiral
Admiral Rogers, the admiral
Captain Smith, the captain
the Adjutant General
the Judge Advocate General
the Paymaster General
Commander Roberts, the commander

Money

Checks. In writing checks, the amount of money is always written out with each word capitalized. In general writing, the amounts are usually not capitalized.

Two Hundred and No/100
We made two hundred dollars.

Legal documents. To ensure accuracy, in legal documents spell out amounts of money and capitalize each word in the amount.

Eight Hundred Twenty-Five Dollars ($825)

Music, Drama, Paintings, Poetry, Film, Radio

General rule. Capitalize the principal words in titles of plays, hymns, songs, paintings, and the like. Lowercase movements of a symphony, concerto, or other musical composition. Lowercase *trio, quartet, quintet,* and so on when they refer to compositions, but capitalize them when they are used in the name of performers. Usually, capitalize the first word in every line of poetry, although some modern poetry is not capitalized in the traditional style. In cases of irregularity, follow the poet's style.

"Rock of Ages" (hymn)
A Chorus Line (play)
"Cagney and Lacey" (TV show)
"Posies for a Parlour" (short poem)
Rodin's *The Thinker* (sculpture)
Beethoven's Fifth Symphony, Symphony No. 5 in C Minor
William Tell Overture
California Quartet (performers)
"I bridle in my struggling Muse in vain, / That seeks to launch into
  a nobler strain" (Pope).

Nouns and Adjectives

Names.   Capitalize the names of particular persons, places, and things (proper nouns).

John Smith   Washington, D.C.   Statue of Liberty

Common nouns used in names.   Capitalize common nouns and adjectives used in proper names.

the Liberty Bell

Words derived from proper nouns.   Lowercase words derived from the proper nouns that have developed a specialized meaning through use.

anglicize   japan varnish
italicize   bohemian
manila envelopes   roman type, Roman numerals

Epithets.   Capitalize common nouns and epithets used with, or as substitutes for, proper names.

the Canal (Panama Canal)   Peter the Great
the First Lady   Richard Coeur de Lion

Nouns with numbers or letters.   Nouns or abbreviations used with numbers or letters in a title are capitalized. In general writing, the trend is to lowercase common references such as *grade* and *article* (grade 6; article 7, section 5; room 102), although *room, suite,* and so on are capitalized in addresses, and *article, section,* and so on are capitalized in formal documents. Particular designations such as *Psalm 22* are always capitalized.

```
Sputnik I      World War II      Division IV
Ward 3         Class B           Precinct 4
grade 6, 6th grade          section 6, 6th section
```

Organizations and Institutions

Official names or titles.   Capitalize the official names of organizations and institutions. But lowercase the common noun when it is used in the plural with two or more names.

> Young Men's Christian Association, YMCA, the association
> Prentice-Hall, Inc.
> Ohio University, the university
> Ohio and Chicago universities, the universities
> Metropolitan Opera, the opera
> Independent Order of Odd Fellows, an Odd Fellow, the order
> Southern Railroad, the railroad
> Southern and Pennsylvania railroads, the railroads

Terms not part of name or title.   Lowercase terms referring to organizations or institutions if those terms are not part of a specific name or title, even when the terms stand for specific organizations or institutions. But in formal writing, such as contracts, capitalize the term that stands for a specific organization or institution.

> the parent-teacher association, Portland Parent-Teacher Association
> the chamber of commerce, Prescott Chamber of Commerce
> the board of directors (general), the Board of Directors (formal document)
> the company, Newcomb Engineering Company
> Pursuant to a resolution of its Board of Directors, XYZ Corporation, a corporation duly organized, hereinafter called the Corporation, has adopted . . .

Peoples, Races, Tribes

General rule.   Capitalize the names of peoples, races, and tribes. But lowercase terms that refer to color or localized designations.

```
Romans      Aryans          Caucasians
Jews        Negroes         whites
Malays      bush people     blacks
```

Personal Titles

General rule.   Capitalize professional, academic, military, and similar titles or designations preceding names, but lowercase them following names or used instead of names. See also rules for the military on page 524. Do not capitalize general descriptive titles such as *programmer* even before a name.

> District Attorney Bell, the district attorney
> Governor Jones, the governor
> Captain Davis, Capt. Mark Davis, the captain
> salesman Joe Brown, the salesman

President.   Capitalize *president* when it precedes a name; otherwise, lowercase it.

> Mr. Nelson, president of NAM; President Nelson; the president

National government officials.   Capitalize titles of cabinet members, heads of departments, and government dignitaries when the titles are used with names. *The Speaker* (of the House of Representatives) is usually capitalized, even when alone, to avoid ambiguity.

> Secretary of State George Schultz, the secretary of state, the
>   secretary
> Ambassador Jones, the ambassador
> Thomas O'Neill, Speaker of the House; the Speaker of the House

State or municipal officials.   Capitalize the titles of *governor, chief executive* (of a state), *lieutenant governor, mayor, borough president, senator, assemblyman, alderman,* president of any municipal body, and the like when they are used with proper names. Lowercase these titles when they follow a name or are used as general terms without reference to a specific official or office.

> Governor Smith, the governor
> Alderman Rogers; Mr. Rogers, president of the Harrisville Board of
>   Alderman; President Rogers
> Mayor Adams, the mayor
> Senator Waltham, the senator

Capitalize heads of state and city departments such as *police commissioner, city counsel, commissioner of education, attorney general, sheriff,* and subordinate titles such as *deputy sheriff, assistant attorney general,* when they precede names. Lowercase them when they follow a name or stand alone.

> Commissioner Edwards, the commissioner
> Assistant Attorney General Brown, the assistant attorney general
> Sheriff Lewis, the sheriff

Business and professional titles. Capitalize business and professional titles when they precede a name. Lowercase them when they follow a name or when they are used instead of a name of a specific office or official. In formal writing, such as contracts and minutes of meetings, titles referring to a specific officer of a specific company or organization may be lowercase or uppercase, but in such writing, you must capitalize *company, corporation,* and the like.

> Professor Stone, the professor
> Dr. Carvelli, the doctor
> Mr. Edgar Robbins, president of XYZ Company; President Robbins,
>   the president

Honor or nobility. Capitalize all titles of honor or nobility when preceding a name. (Some British titles are also capitalized when used without a personal name.) Lowercase them in all other instances.

> Queen Elizabeth, the queen of England
> Pope John Paul, the pope
> the Princess Royal
> the Duke of Kent
> His Excellency
> Your Grace

Acting, under, assistant. Capitalize the words *acting, under,* and *assistant* when they are part of a capitalized title that precedes a name. Otherwise, lowercase them along with the rest of the title.

> Acting Secretary of State Mackintosh, the acting secretary
> Under Secretary of Labor Collins, the under secretary
> Assistant Secretary of Education Monroe, the assistant secretary

Words in apposition. When a common noun precedes a name but is separated from it by a comma, the noun does not have the force of a title and is not capitalized.

> The secretary, John Doe, is on the executive committee.
> Secretary Doe is on the executive committee.

Compound titles.   Capitalize all parts of a compound title if any part is capitalized.

> Vice-President Bush
> Congressman-Elect Adamson

Lists of names.   In formal lists such as a mailing list, titles and descriptive designations immediately following the names should be capitalized.

> Ms. Adelaide Horton, President
> Prescott Information Bureau
> 1111 Main Street
> Prescott AZ 86301

Personification

General rule.   Personification gives some attribute of a human being to inanimate objects, abstract ideas, or general terms. Capitalize the things personified when emphasis is desired.

> The meeting was called to order by the Chair.
> "Low Spirits are my true and faithful companions" (Thomas Gray).
> The trees whispered in the wind.
> The waves roared as the hurricane approached.
> I heard the winds moaning in the moonless night.

Planets

General rule.   Capitalize the names of the planets and imaginative designations of celestial objects. But lowercase *stars, earth, moon, sun,* unless they are used in connection with other planets that are always capitalized.

Saturn   Leo   Mars
Milky Way   Big Dipper
This is a scientific treatise on the relation of Mars to Earth.
The earth is fertile indeed.

Political Parties, Factions, Alliances

Names. Capitalize names of political parties, factions, and alliances. Do not capitalize *party*.

Democratic party, the party, Democrats, democratic principles
rightists, leftists, the Left, the Right, Left Wing and Right Wing (of
    political parties), left wing of the CIO
Socialist party, Socialists (of the party), socialist (general) economy

Words derived from names. Lowercase words derived from the names of political parties, factions, and alliances.

Communist party, communism, communistic
Socialist party, socialism, socialistic
Democratic party, democratic, democracy

Quotations

Direct quotation. Capitalize the first word of an exactly quoted passage if it is a complete sentence, but lowercase quoted parts that do not form a complete sentence.

In his report the president said, "A member will not be permitted to
    remain in service after the normal retirement date without the
    special consent of the company."
What did he mean by calling my action "reprehensible"?

Indirect quotation. Do not capitalize indirect quotations.

In his report the president said that employees will not be
    permitted to remain in service.

Broken quotation. Do not capitalize the second part of a broken quotation, unless it is a complete sentence.

"If the order is not received by the first," he wrote, "we will be
   compelled to cancel it."
"If the order is not received by the first, we will be compelled to
   cancel it," he wrote. "We cannot sell the goods after that date."

Religious Terms

Church.   Capitalize *church* when it is part of the name of an edifice.

> Central Presbyterian Church, the church
> St. Peter's Catholic Church, the church
> the Roman Catholic church
> the Baptist church
> The First Lutheran Church, the church

Church dignitaries.   Capitalize the title of a church dignitary when
it is used before a name. Lowercase it in other instances.

> the Reverend John Smith, the reverend
> Pope John Paul, the pope
> Mother Angelica, the mother superior
> Cardinal Spellman, the cardinal
> Rabbi Feldman, the rabbi
> Father Williams, the father, the priest
> Deacon Jones, the deacon

Deity.   Capitalize all names and appellations of the one supreme God
(Lord) and of other dieties such as Zeus. (In Jewish literature the word *God*
as the name of *the* deity is spelled G-d.) Capitalize the personal pronouns *he,
his, him, thee, thou,* and so on when they refer to the deity only in cases
where capitalization avoids ambiguity. Do not capitalize the relative pronouns *who, whom.*

> God   Buddha   Allah
> In the Protestant religion, God is all-powerful, and it is he who
>   reigns supreme.

Bible.   Capitalize all names for the Bible and other sacred books.
Also capitalize books and versions of the Bible. Do not underscore or use
quotation marks. But lowercase adjectives such as *biblical.*

> New Testament   the Gospels   Talmud, talmudic

Denominations. Capitalize the names of all religious denominations.

Baptists   Mormons
Gentiles, gentile practices
Franciscan order, the order

Resolutions

General rule. In resolutions write every letter in *WHEREAS* and *RESOLVED* in capitals; begin *That* with a capital letter.

RESOLVED That . . . WHEREAS . . .

Series of Questions

General rule. When a series of questions is included in one sentence, each questions usually begins with a capital letter.

What must a secretary do to advance herself? Get a college
education? Take an evening course?

Sports and Games

College colors. Capitalize *gold, maroon, crimson,* and the like when they designate teams and refer to college colors.

The Crimson Tide triumphed over the Black and Gold.
Their uniforms are blue and orange.

Games and sports. Lowercase the names of sports and games, except when the names derive from proper names or are trade names.

football   Rugby   bridge
Monopoly   going to Jerusalem

Playing fields. Capitalize the names of playing fields and stadiums.

Yankee Stadium, the stadium   the Bowl
Madison Square Garden, the Garden (capitalized to avoid
ambiguity)

Cups, stakes.   Capitalize *cup, stakes, trophy,* and the like when they are part of a specific title; otherwise, lowercase them.

> Belmont Stakes, the stakes
> Davis Cup, the cup
> Atlantic Trophy, the trophy

Trade Names

General rule.   Always capitalize trade names and spell and punctuate them as the manufacturer does.

> Teletype   Kleenex
> Coca-Cola   Q-Tips Cotton Swabs

—PART FOUR————

The Secretary's Handy Information Guide

18. Quick Reference Guide to Facts and Figures

19. Glossary of Important Business Terms

─ Chapter 18 ─

Quick-Reference Guide to Facts and Figures

Study Outline for CPS Exam (page 537)

Marks of Punctuation and Mechanics (page 539)

Roman Numerals (page 539)

Abbreviations (page 540)

Correct Forms of Address (page 578)

Standard Proofreading Marks (page 604)

Corrected Galley Proofs (page 605)

Tables of Weights, Measures, and Values (page 606)

Tables of Metric Weights, Measures, and Values (page 612)

Mathematical Tables (page 615)

Greek Letter Symbols (page 617)

Interest Tables (page 617)

Flowchart Symbols (page 620)

U.S. Area Codes and Time Zones (page 622)

International Time Chart (page 623)

International Time Differentials (page 624)

STUDY OUTLINE FOR CPS EXAM

Professional Secretaries International (PSI) offers a Certified Professional Secretaries (CPS) certificate to qualified secretaries who pass an exam on diverse subjects. Applicants must fall within one of four categories:

secretary (experience completed); secretary (employed full time, experience to be completed); business educator (secretarial experience completed); or student (now enrolled, experience to be completed). Study materials are available from PSI, 301 East Armour Boulevard, Kansas City, MO 64111 −1299.

The following outline, reprinted with permission from *Capstone,* 1987, summarizes examination content in six key areas:

I BEHAVIORAL SCIENCE IN BUSINESS tests the principles of human relations and organizational dynamics in the work place. It focuses on needs, motivation, nature of conflict, problem-solving techniques, essentials of supervision and communication, leadership styles, and understanding of the informal organization.

II BUSINESS LAW measures (1) the secretary's knowledge of the principles of business law and (2) knowledge of the effect of governmental controls on business. Understanding of the historical setting in which these controls developed should be emphasized in preference to names and dates.

III ECONOMICS AND MANAGEMENT consists of 35% economics and 65% management. Emphasis is placed on understanding of the basic concepts underlying business operations. Key economic and management principles as well as the latest governmental regulations in business are included.

IV ACCOUNTING measures (1) knowledge of the elements of the accounting cycle; (2) ability to analyze financial statement accounts; (3) ability to perform arithmetical operations associated with accounting and computing interests and discounts; and (4) ability to summarize and interpret financial data.

V OFFICE ADMINISTRATION AND COMMUNICATION measures proficiency in subject matters unique to the secretary's position: (50% office administration) executive travel, office management, records management, and reprographics; and (50% written business communication) editing, abstracting, and preparing communications in final format.

VI OFFICE TECHNOLOGY covers the secretary's responsibilities created by data processing, communications media, advances in office management, technological applications, records-management technology, and office systems.

MARKS OF PUNCTUATION AND MECHANICS

´ (é)	Accent, acute	ˇ (č)	Haček
` (è)	Accent, grave	-	Hyphen
' or '	Apostrophe	—	Em dash
*	Asterisk	–	En dash
{ }	Braces	. . . . . .	Leaders
[ ]	Brackets	¯ (ō)	Macron
˘	breve	¶	Paragraph
ˆ	Caret	‖	Parallels
, (ç)	Cedilla	( )	Parantheses
ˆ or ⁀ or ˜ (ô)	Circumflex	.	Period
:	Colon	?	Question mark (*also,* Interrogation point)
,	Comma	" "	Quotation marks
†	Dagger	§	Section
¨ (ö)	Dieresis	;	Semicolon
‡	Double dagger	˜	Tilde
or . . .	Ellipsis points	___	Underscore
!	Exclamation point	/	Virgule (*also,* Solidus, Diagonal)

ROMAN NUMERALS

I	1	XI	11	XXX	30	CCC	300
II	2	XII	12	XL	40	CD	400
III	3	XIII	13	L	50	D	500
IV	4	XIV	14	LX	60	DC	600
V	5	XV	15	LXX	70	DCC	700
VI	6	XVI	16	LXXX	80	DCCC	800
VII	7	XVII	17	XC	90	CM	900
VIII	8	XVIII	18	C	100	M	1,000
IX	9	XIX	19	CC	200	MM	2,000
X	10	XX	20				

General Rules for Roman Numerals

1. Repeating a letter repeats its value: XX = 20; CCC = 300.
2. A letter placed after one of greater value adds thereto: VIII = 8; DC = 600.
3. A letter placed before one of greater value subtracts therefrom: IX = 9; CM = 900.

4. A dash line over a numeral multiplies the value by 1,000. Thus $\overline{X} = 10,000$; $\overline{L} = 50,000$; $\overline{C} = 100,000$; $\overline{D} = 500,000$; $\overline{M} = 1,000,000$; $\overline{CLIX} = 159,000$; $\overline{DLIX} = 559,000$.

ABBREVIATIONS

Abbreviations style varies considerably, but the trend is toward lowercase letters and few or no periods, unless the period is needed to distinguish an abbreviation (such as *in.* for *inch*) from an actual word (such as the preposition *in*). But always follow the preferred style in your office or profession. (For additional information about abbreviations, see chapter 17, page 513.)

General Abbreviations

A

@   at (referring to price)
a, amp.   ampere
a to oc   attached to other correspondence
aa   author's alteration (printing)
aar, AAR   against all risks
ac   alternating current
a/c   account
A/C   account current
a/cs pay.   accounts payable
a/cs rec.   accounts receivable
a.d.   before the day
a/d   after date
ad fin.   to the end *(ad finem)*
ad inf.   without limit *(ad infinitum)*
ad int.   in the meantime *(ad interim)*
ad lib., ad libit.   at one's pleasure; freely to the quantity or amount desired *(ad libitum)*
ad loc.   to *or* at the place *(ad locum)*
ad val., a/v   according to value *(ad valorem)*
adv. chgs.   advance charges
af   audiofrequency
agb   a good brand
a-h, amp-hr.   ampere-hour
aka   also known as
AM   amplitude modulation

an.   arrival notice (shipping)
anon.   anonymous
a/o   account of
ap   additional premium
a/p   authority to pay
a/r   all risks; against all risks (marine insurance)
as.   at sight
a/s   after sight
Ast, AST   Atlantic standard time
A/T   American terms (grain trade)
at. no.   atomic number
at. vol.   atomic volume
at. wt.   atomic weight
att.   attached
attn., atten.   attention
au.   author; astronomical unit
Au   gold
av., avdp.   avoirdupois
AV   authorized version
aw   all water (transportation)
a/w   actual weight
AWG   American wire gauge

B

b   born; brother
b of m   bill of materials
b/a   billed at
bal.   balance
bb   bail bond; break bulk
bbl   barrel(s)
b/c   bill for collection
B.C.   before Christ
bd   bank draft
b/d   barrels per day; brought down (accounting)
bdl   bundle
BE, B/E   bill of exchange; bill of entry
bf   boldface; brief (legal)
b/f   brought forward (bookkeeping)
b/g   bonded goods
B/H   bill of health
bhp   brake horsepower
bkpt   bankrupt
bkt.   bracket

bl   bale(s)
B/L   bill of lading
bm   board measure
bo   buyer's option; back order; branch office
b/o   brought over (accounting)
bp   bills payable; bill of parcels
b/p   blueprint
bpd   bank post bill; barrels per day
B/R   bills receivable; builders' risks
Bros.   Brothers
bs   backspace
b/s   bill of sale; bill of store (commerce)
bsk.   basket(s)
Bs/L   bills of lading
b7d, b10d, b15d   buyer 7 days to take up, etc. (stock market)
B/St   bill of sight
BTU   British thermal unit(s)
bu.   bushel(s)
bv   book value
bw   please turn page *(bitte werden)*
BWG   Birmingham wire gauge
bx.   box

C

©, copr.   copyright
c   carat; chapter(s); about *(circa)*
C   centigrade
C/   case(s)
ca   capital account; credit account; current account; chartered
   accountant; commercial agent; close annealed; about *(circa)*
CAF   cost, assurance, and freight
cal.   small calories; calendar; caliber
can.   cancelled; cancellation
cap.   capital; capacity
caps   capital letters
cart.   cartage
cb   cash book
cbd   cash before delivery
cc   carbon copy
cd   cord; cash discount; certificate of deposit
c/d   carried down (bookkeeping)
C/D   commercial dock; consular declaration
c&d   collection and delivery

cd. ft.   cord ft.
cert., ctf.   certificate; certification; certified
cf   compare
c/f   carried forward (bookkeeping)
c&f   cost and freight
cfi   cost, freight, and insurance
cfo   cost for orders
cg   centigram
cge. pd.   carriage paid
ch.   chain; chapter; channel (TV); chemical; chart; candle hours
chap., chaps.   chapter; chapters
chg.   charge; change
c&i   cost and insurance
cif   cost, insurance, and freight
cir.   circuit, circular; circulation; circumference
ck(s).   cask(s); check(s)
cl   carload lots; center line; centiliter (metric)
c/l   craft loss; cash letter
clt   collateral trust (bonds)
CLT   code language telegram
cm   centimeter
cm^2 square centimeter
cm^3 cubic centimeter
cm pf   cumulative preferred (stocks)
cn   credit note; consignment note; circular note
co.   company; county
c/o   carried over (bookkeeping); in care of; cash order
COD   cash, or collect, on delivery
col.   column
coll. tr., clt   collateral trust (bonds)
consgt.   consignment
coop.   cooperative
corp.   corporation; corporal; to the body *(corpori)*
cos   cash on shipment
cp   candle power; carriage paid
CPA   certified public accountant
CPLS   certified professional legal secretary
cpm (cps)   cycles per minute (second)
CPS   certified professional secretary
cr   class rate; current rate; company's risk
cr.   credit; creditor
cst, CST   central standard time
ct, CT   central time
ctge   cartage

ctn.   carton
ctr.   center; counter
cum.   with; cumulative
cum. pref.   cumulative preferred (stocks)
cur.   current
cv   chief value
cv db   convertible debentures (securities)
cv pf   convertible preferred (securities)
cvt   convertible (securities)
cw   commercial weight
cwo   cash with order
cwt   hundredweight

D

d   deci (prefix: one-tenth); died; daughter
da   deka (prefix: ten)
D/A   deposit account; documents against acceptance; discharge
   afloat
db   decible; debenture
db rts.   debenture rights (securities)
dba   doing business as (co. name)
dbk.   drawback
dbu   decibel unit
dc   deviation clause; direct current
dd   delivered at docks; demand draft; days after date (bill of
   exchange)
deb.   debenture
dec.   decision; decimal
def.   deferred (securities)
deg.   degree
dep. ctfs.   deposit certificates
df   dead freight
DFA   division freight agent
dg   decigram
dia., diam.   diameter
diag.   diagram; diagonal
dis.   discount
div.   dividend; division
dkg   dekagram (metric)
dkl   dekaliter (metric)
dkm   dekameter (metric)
dks   dekastere (metric)
dkt.   docket

dl   demand loan; deciliter (metric)
DL   day letter (telegraph)
dld   delivered
dlo   dispatch loading only
DLO   dead letter office
dls/shr   dollars per share
dm   decimeter
D/N   debit note
do. ·   ditto (the same); delivery order
dp   direct port
D/P   documents against (or for) payment
dr.   debit; debtor; drawer
D/R   deposit receipt
dr ap   apothecaries' dram
dr av   dram avoirdupois
d/s   days after sight
DSC   distinguished service cross
DSM   distinguished service medal
D.V.   God willing *(Deo volente)*
dw   dead weight
D/W   dock warrant
dwc   dead weight capacity
dwt   pennyweight(s); deadweight tons
dwtf   daily and weekly till forbidden
dy   delivery

E

ea.   each
eaon   except as otherwise noted
ed.   editor; edition(s); education
Ed. Note   editorial note
EDP   electronic data processing
edt, EDT   eastern daylight time
EE   errors excepted
e.g.   for example *(exempli gratia)*
emp   end of month payment
enc.   enclosure
end.   endorse; endorsement
eng.   engine; engineer; engineering; engraved
eo   by authority of his office *(ex officio)*
eod   every other day (advertising)
e&oe   errors and omissions excepted
eohp   except as otherwise herein provided

eom   end of month (payments)
Esq.   esquire
est.   estate; estimated
est, EST   eastern standard time
esu   electrostatic unit
et al.   and others *(et alii)*
et seq.   and the following *(et sequens)*
et ux.   and wife *(et uxor)*
ev   electron volt
et vir.   and husband
eta   estimated time of arrival
etc.   and the others; and so forth *(et cetera)*
ev   electron volt
ex   out of *or* from; without *or* not including
Ex B/L   exchange bill of lading
ex cp   ex coupon
ex div.   without dividend
ex int.   not including interest
ex n   ex new (excluding right to new shares—NYSE)
exp.   express; expenses; export

F

f   following (after a numeral); feminine
F   fahrenheit
faa   free of all average (shipping)
fac.   facsimile; fast as can
FAM   Free and Accepted Masons
faq   fair average quality; free at quay
faqs   fair average quality of season
fbm   fleet board measure
fd.   fund
FD   free discharge; free delivery; free dispatch
f&d   freight and demurrage (shipping)
Fed. Reg   Federal Register
ff   following (after a numeral); folios
ffa   free from alongside; free foreign agency
fia   full interest admitted
fig(s).   figure(s)
fio   free in and out
fit.   free of income tax; free in truck
fiw   free in wagon
fl. oz.   fluid ounce(s)
fln   following landing numbers (shipping)

fm   fathom(s)
FM   frequency modulation
fn.   footnote
fo   firm offer; free overside; for orders; full out terms (grain trade)
fob   free on board
foc   free on car; free of charge
fod   free of damage
fol.   folio; following
foq   free on quay
for.   free on rail
fos   free on steamer
fot   free on truck
FP   floating (or open) policy; fully paid (premium)
fpm   feet per minute
fps   feet per second
F/R   freight release
frof   fire risk on freight
frt.   freight
ft   full terms
ft.   foot *or* feet
ft.^{2} square foot
ft.^{3} cubic foot
ft./sec.   feet per second
fur   furlong
fv   on the back of the page *(folio verso)*
fwd   fresh-water damage; forward
fx   foreign exchange
FYI   for your information (interoffice use)

G

g   gram (metric)
G   gauss; giga (prefix: one million)
g gr.   great gross
G/A   general average (marine insurance)
gfa   good fair average
GFA   general freight agent
gi   gill
GI   government issue; general issue
gm   gram
GNP   gross national product
GPA   general passenger agent
gpm   gallons per minute
gr   gram; grain; gross

gr. wt.   gross weight

gro   gross

gs   ground speed (aviation)

gtc   good till cancelled *or* countermanded (brokerage)

gtm   good this month

gtw   good this week (becomes void on Saturday)

H

hc   held covered (insurance)

hdqs.   headquarters

hdwe.   hardware

HE   high explosive

hf, HF   high frequency

hfm   hold for money

hg   hectogram

hhd.   hogshead

hl   hectoliter (metric)

hm   hectometer (metric)

hon.   honorable

hp   horsepower

HQ   headquarters

hr.   hour

HR   House bill (federal); House of Representatives

hw   high water

HWOST   high-water ordinary spring tide

hyp.   hypothesis

Hz   hertz

I

IB   invoice book; in bond

ibid.   in the same place *(ibidem)*

ibo   invoice book outward

ic&c   invoice cost and charges

id   the same *(idem)*

i.e.   that is *(id est)*

ihp   indicated horsepower

imp. gal.   imperial gallon

in.   inch.

in.^{2} square inch

in.^{3} cubic inch

in loc.   in the proper place

in re   in regard to

Inc.   Incorporated

inf.   infinity; below (*infra*)
ins.   insurance
int.   interest
inv.   invoice
ips   inches per second
IQ   intelligence quotient
ital.   italics
iv   invoice value; increased value

J

j   joule (electricity)
JA   joint account
jg   junior grade
jnt. stk.   joint stock

K

k   carat; knot; kilo (prefix: one thousand)
kc   kilocycle
kd   knocked down
kg   kilogram
kl   kiloliter
km   kilometer
kv   kilovolts
kva   kilovolt-ampere
kw   kilowatt
kwh, kwhr   kilowatt-hour

L

l   line (*pl.,* ll) liter
L. Ed.   Lawyer's Edition
LA   Lloyd's agent
L/A   letter of authority; landing account
lat.   latitude
lb.   pound
lc   lowercase; letter of credit
LC   deferreds (cable messages)
L/C   letter of credit
LCL   less than carload lot
lcm   least common multiple
ldg.   loading; landing
ldg. & dely.   landing and delivery
lds.   loads

lf   lightface; ledger folio
lg. tn.   long ton
lge.   large
lin. ft.   linear foot
lip.   life insurance policy
lkg. & bkg.   leakage and breakage
LL   lease-lend
Ll. & Cos.   Lloyd's and Companies
lmsc   let me see correspondence
loc. cit.   in the place cited *(loco citato)*
log.   logarithm
long.   longitude
lr   lire
ls   place of the seal *(locus sigilli)*
lt   long ton
LT   letter message (cables)
ltd.   limited (British)
lt-v   light vessel (shipping)
lv.   leave
LW   low water
LWM   low-water mark

M

m   married; masculine; meter; milli (prefix: one-thousandth)
M   thousand; monsieur *(pl.,* MM); noon *(Meridie);* mega (prefix: one
    million)
ma   milliampere
m/a   my account
mar.   marine; maritime; married
max.   maximum
mb, mbar   millibar
mc   marked capacity (freight cars)
Mc   megacycle; marginal credit
MC   master of ceremonies; member of Congress
mcps   megacycles per second
m/d   months after date
M/D   memorandum of deposit
mdse.   merchandise
med.   medium; medicine; medical
mep   mean effective pressure
Messrs.   Misters (Messieurs)
mf, MF   millifarad (electricity)
mfg.   manufacturing

mfr.   manufacturer
mg   milligram
mG   milligauss
mh, mH   millihenry
MH   main hatch; Medal of Honor
MHz   megahertz
mi.   mile
mi.^{2} square mile
mi.^{3} cubic mile
min.   minute; minimum
min. B/L   minimum bill of lading
mip   marine insurance policy
misc.   miscellaneous
ml   milliter
Mlle.   Mademoiselle
mm   millimeter; necessary change being made (*mutatis mutand*)
MM, Messrs.   Messieurs
Mme.   Madam
Mmes.   Mesdames
mo   money order
mo.   month
mol. wt.   molecular weight
MP   member of Parliament; military police
mpg   miles per gallon
mph   miles per hour
ms(s)., MS(S)   manuscript(s)
m/s   months after sight; meters per second
Msgr.   Monsignor; Monseigneur
mst.   measurement
mst, MST   mountain standard time
mt   empty; metric ton
mt.ct.cp.   mortgage certificate coupon (securities)
mtg.   mortgage
mv   market value; millivolt
MW   megawatt
M   micro (prefix: one-millionth)

N

n   net; note (*pl.,* nn); number; nano (prefix: one-billionth)
n/a   no account (banking)
N/a   no advice (banking)
NA   not available
natl.   national

naut.   nautical
nb, N.B.   note well *(nota bene)*
nc   new charter; new crop
NCO   noncommissioned officer
ncup   no commission until paid
ncv   no commercial value
nd   no date
ne   not exceeding; no effects (banking)
NE   New England; Northeast
nes   not elsewhere specified
N/F   no funds (banking)
NG   no good
nhp   nominal horsepower
NL   night letter (telegraph)
NLT   night letter cable
NM   night message
N/m   no mark
no.   number
n/o   in the name of (finance); no orders (banking)
noe   not otherwise enumerated
nohp   not otherwise herein provided
nol. pros.   to be unwilling to prosecute *(nolle prosequi)*
nom.   nominative; nominal
nom. std.   nominal standard
non obst., non obs.   not withstanding *(non obstante)*
non pros.   does not prosecute *(non prosequitiur)*
non seq.   does not follow *(non sequitur)*
nop   not otherwise provided for
nos   not otherwise specified
np   net proceeds; nonparticipating (stocks); no place; no publisher
NP   notary public
npt   normal pressure and temperature
nr   no risk; net register
nrad   no risk after discharge
ns, n.s.   new series
NS   national society
N.S.   New Style (dates)
nsf   not sufficient funds (banking)
nspf   not specially provided for
nt   net ton
N/t   new terms
nt. wt.   net weight
*n*th   indefinite
ntp   no title page
Nv   nonvoting (stocks)

O

ob   died *(obiit)*
OB/L   order bill of lading
obs.   obsolete
oc   open charter; overcharge; over the counter; office copy
od   on demand
o/d   overdraft (banking)
oe   omissions excepted
OE   Old English
oo   on order
o/o   order of
op   out of print
op. cit.   in the work cited *(opere citato)*
opn.   opinion
or.   owner's risk (transportation)
o&r   ocean and rail (transportation)
os, o.s.   old series
o/s   out of stock
OS   on sample; one side
O.S.   Old Style (dates)
os&d   over, short, and damaged (transportation)
ot   on truck; overtime
O/t   old terms (grain trade)
ow   one way (fare)
oz.   ounce(s)

P

p   page *(pl.,* pp.)
pa   by the year *(per annum);* private account; particular average;
   power of attorney
PA   purchasing agent
PABX   private automatic branch exchange (telephone)
pam.   pamphlet
part.   participating (securities)
pat.   patent
PBX   private branch exchange (telephone)
pc   percent; post card; petty cash
P/C   prices current
pct.   percent; precinct
pd   per diem
pd.   passed; paid
PD   port dues
pfd.   preferred

p&i   protection and indemnity
pk.   peck
pkg.   package
pl   partial loss
p&l   profit and loss
pm   premium money
p.m.   afternoon *(post meridiem)*
PM   postmaster; Provost Marshal
pn   promissory note
p/n   please note
po   post office
por   payable on receipt
pp   parcel post
ppd.   prepaid; postpaid
ppi   parcel post insured; policy proof of interest
ppt   prompt loading
pr.   pair
pref.   preface; preferred
prin.   principal; principle
pro tem.   for the time being *(pro tempore)*
prox.   proximate; of the next month *(proximo)*
ps   public sale; picosecond
PS, P.S.   postscript
psf   pounds per square foot
psi   pounds per square inch
Pst, PST   Pacific standard time
pt.   pint
Pt, PT   Pacific time
pw   packed weight (transportation)
pwt   pennyweight
PX   please exchange; post exchange; private exchange (telephone)

Q

q   quintal (metric)
Q   question; query
qda   quantity discount agreement
qed, QED   which was to be proved or demonstrated *(quod erat demonstrandum)*
qq   questions; queries
qr.   quarter
qt.   quart(s)
qv   which see *(quod vide)*

R

r   reigned; recto
R/A   refer to acceptor; return to author
R/C   reconsigned; recovered
rcd.   received
rd   running days
RD   refer to drawer
re   in regard to
recd., rec'd.   received
ref.   referee; reference; referred
reg.   registered; regulation(s)
rep.   report
res.   residue; research; reserve; residence; resigned; resolution
rev. A/c   revenue account
rf., rfg.   refunding (bonds); radio frequency
rhp   rated horsepower
RI   reinsurance
r&l   rail and lake (transportation)
rl&r   rail, lake, and rail (transportation)
rm.   ream (paper); room(s)
rms, RMS   root mean square
r&o   rail and ocean (transportation)
rog   receipt of goods
rom.   roman (type)
rop   run of paper
rotn. no.   rotation number
rp   return premium; reply paid (cable)
rpm   revolutions per minute
rps   revolutions per second
RR   railroad
RSVP   please reply *(Répondez s'il vous plaît)*
Rt.   right(s) (stock)
r&t   rail and truck
rva   reactive volt ampere
RVSVP   please reply at once *(Répondez vite, s'il vous plaît)*
rw   railway
r&w   rail and water (transportation)

S

s   son; substantive; second
/s/   signed
s to s   station to station

sa   subject to approval; safe arrival; without year *(sine anno);* under
  the year *(sub anno)*

sanr   subject to approval no risk (no risk until insurance is
  confirmed)

s/b   statement of billing (transportation)

sc   small capital letters; same case (legal); namely, to wit *(scilicet);*
  salvage charges

s&c   shipper and carrier

sd   without a day being named *(sine die);* sight draft

sdbl   sight draft, bill of lading attached

SE   stock exchange; Southeast

sec., sect.   section

sec., secy., sec'y   secretary

seq.   the following; in sequence

ser.   series

SF   sinking fund

S&FA   shipping and forwarding agent

sgd.   signed

sh.   share

sh. tn.   short ton

shp   shaft horsepower

shpt.   shipment

sic   so; thus (to confirm a word that might be questioned)

sit.   stopping in transit (transportation)

sk.   sack

sl   salvage loss; without place *(sine loco)*

sn   shipping note

so.   seller's option; shipping order; ship's option

soc.   society

sol.   solicitor(s); solution

SOL   shipowner's liability

SOP   standard operating procedure

sp   supra protest; stop payment

spd   steamer pays dues

ss   namely *(scilicet)*

SS   steamship

s7d, s10d, s15d   seller 7 days to deliver, etc. (stock market)

SST   supersonic transport

st   short ton; let it stand *(stet)*

St.   saint

sta.   station

stat.   statute

std.   standard

stg.   sterling; storage

stk.   stock
str.   steamer
sup   above *(supra)*
supp.   supplement
supt.   superintendent
sv   sailing vessel; same year; under the word *(sub verbo)*
svp   if you please *(s'il vous plaît)*
sw   shipper's weights
swg   standard wire gauge
syn.   synonymous

T

t   metric ton(s)
T   tera (prefix: one trillion)
taw   twice a week (advertising)
tb   time base
tc   until countermanded
td   time deposit
TE   trade expenses
tel.   telegram; telegraph; telephone
tf   till forbidden (advertising)
tl   time loan
tlo   total loss only (marine insurance)
tm   true mean; trademark
tn.   ton
T/o   transfer order
tr.   transpose
t/r   trust receipt; tons registered (shipping)
trans.   transitive; translated; transportation; transaction
treas.   treasurer
ts   typescript
TT   telegraphic transfer
twp.   township
tws   time wire service (telegraph)
TWX   teletypewriter exchange

U

u   velocity; atomic mass unit
U, univ.   university
UA   underwriting account (marine insurance)
uc   uppercase
ud   as directed

ugt   urgent (cable)
uhf   ultrahigh frequency (TV)
ui   as below *(ut infra)*
ult.   of the last month *(ultimo)*
up.   under proof
us.   as above *(ut supra)*
ut   universal time
ut sup.   as above *(ut supra)*
u/w   underwriter

V

v   volt; versus; value; velocity
va   volt-ampere (electricity)
vc   valuation clause
vf   video frequency (TV)
vhf   very high frequency (TV)
vi   see below *(vide infra)*
vid.   see *(vide)*
viz.   namely *(videlicet)*
vol.   volume
vop   value as in original policy
vs   verse; versus
vt.   voting (stock)
vv   vice versa

W

w, W   watt (electricity)
wa   with average (insurance); will advise
wd.   warranted; word
wf   wrong font (typesetting)
wg   weight guaranteed; wire gauge
wh, Wh   watt-hour (electricity)
whsle.   wholesale
wi   when issued (stock exchange)
wk.   week
wl   wave length
w/m   weight and/or measurement
woc   without compensation
wp   without prejudice; weather permitting; wire payment; word
   processing
wpp   waterproof paper packing
wr   with rights (securities); warehouse receipt
w&r   water and rail (transportation)

wt.   weight
ww   with warrants (securities); warehouse warrant

X

x per   without privileges
x rts.   without rights (NYSE)
xcp   without coupon (NYSE)
xd   without dividend (NYSE)
xi   without next interest (NYSE)
xn   ex new
xp   express paid
xw   without warrants (securities)

Y

yb.   yearbook
yd.   yard
yd.^{2} square yard
yd.^{3} cubic yard
yr.   year

Z

z   zone; zero
zf   zero frequency
zhr   zero hour

Abbreviations of Months and Days

Jan.	January	Jul.	July
Feb.	February	Aug.	August
Mar.	March	Sept.	September
Apr.	April	Oct.	October
May	May	Nov.	November
Jun.	June	Dec.	December

Sun *or* S.	Sunday
Mon. *or* M.	Monday
Tues. *or* Tu.	Tuesday
Wed. *or* W.	Wednesday
Thurs. *or* Th.	Thursday
Fri. *or* F.	Friday
Sat.	Saturday

Abbreviations of Academic Degrees

A

A.B.   Bachelor of Arts
A.M.   Master of Arts
A.M.L.S.   Master of Arts in Library Science
Ar.M.   Master of Architecture

B

B.A.   Bachelor of Arts
B.Ag. *or* B.Agr.   Bachelor of Agriculture
B.Ar. *or* B. Arch.   Bachelor of Architecture
B.B.A.   Bachelor of Business Administration
B.C.   Bachelor of Chemistry
B.C.E.   Bachelor of Chemical Engineering; Bachelor of Civil
   Engineering
B.C.L.   Bachelor of Civil Law
B.D.   Bachelor of Divinity
B.D.S.   Bachelor of Dental Surgery
B.E.   Bachelor of Education; Bachelor of Engineering
B.E.E.   Bachelor of Electrical Engineering
B.F.   Bachelor of Finance; Bachelor of Forestry
B.F.A.   Bachelor of Fine Arts
B.Lit(t).   Bachelor of Literature *or* Letters
B.L.S.   Bachelor of Library Science
B.M.   Bachelor of Medicine
B.Mus.   Bachelor of Music
B.Pd. *or* B.Pe.   Bachelor of Pedagogy
B.P.E.   Bachelor of Physical Education
B.S. *or* B.Sc.   Bachelor of Science
B.S.Ed.   Bachelor of Science in Education
B.T. *or* B.Th.   Bachelor of Theology

C

C.B.   Bachelor of Surgery
C.E.   Civil Engineer
Ch.D   Doctor of Chemistry
Ch.E. *or* Chem.E.   Chemical Engineer
C.S.B.   Bachelor of Christian Science

D

D.C.   Doctor of Chiropractic

D.C.L.   Doctor of Canon Law; Doctor of Civil Law
D.D.   Doctor of Divinity
D.D.S.   Doctor of Dental Surgery
D.F.A.   Doctor of Fine Arts
D.Lit(t).   Doctor of Literature *or* Letters
D. es L.   Doctor of Letters (French)
D. es S.   Doctor of Science (French)
D.L.S.   Doctor of Library Science
D.M.D.   Doctor of Dental Medicine
D.Mus.   Doctor of Music
D.O.   Doctor of Osteopathy
D.S. *or* D.Sc.   Doctor of Science
D.Th. *or* D. Theol.   Doctor of Theology
D.V.M.   Doctor of Veterinary Medicine

E

Ed.B.   Bachelor of Education
Ed.D.   Doctor of Education
Ed.M.   Master of Education
E.E.   Electrical Engineer
Eng.D.   Doctor of Engineering

J

J.C.D.   Doctor of Canon Law; Civil Law
J.D.   Doctor of Laws; Juris Doctor; Doctor of Jurisprudence
Jur.D.   Doctor of Law

L

L.B.   Bachelor of Letters
L.H.D.   Doctor of Humanities
Lit(t).B.   Bachelor of Literature *or* of Letters
Lit(t).D.   Doctor of Literature *or* of Letters
LL.B.   Bachelor of Laws
LL.D.   Doctor of Laws
LL.M.   Master of Laws

M

M.A.   Master of Arts
M.Agr.   Master of Agriculture
M.B.   Bachelor of Medicine
M.B.A.   Master in, *or* of, Business Administration
M.C.L.   Master of Civil Law

M.D.   Doctor of Medicine
M.D.S.   Master of Dental Surgery
M.Ed.   Master of Education
M.L.S.   Master of Library Science
M.Pd.   Master of Pedagogy
M.P.E.   Master of Physical Education
M.S. *or* M.Sc.   Master of Science
Mus.B. *or* Mus.Bac.   Bachelor of Music
Mus.D.   Doctor of Music

P

Pd.B.   Bachelor of Pedagogy
Pd.D.   Doctor of Pedagogy
Pd.M.   Master of Pedagogy
Phar.B.   Bachelor of Pharmacy
Phar.D. *or* Pharm.D.   Doctor of Pharmacy
Phar.M.   Master of Pharmacy
Ph.B.   Bachelor of Philosophy
Ph.D.   Doctor of Philosophy
Pod.D.   Doctor of Podiatry

S

S.B. *or* Sc.B.   Bachelor of Science
Sc.D. *or* S.D.   Doctor of Science
Sc.M.   Master of Science
S.J.D.   Doctor of Juridical Science
S.M. *or* Sc.M.   Master of Science
S.T.B.   Bachelor of Sacred Theology
S.T.D.   Doctor of Sacred Theology
S.T.M.   Master of Sacred Theology

T

Th.D.   Doctor of Theology

V

V.M.D.   Doctor of Veterinary Medicine

Abbreviations of Organizations

A

ABA   American Bankers Association; American Bar Association;
  American Booksellers Association
AEC   Atomic Energy Commission
AFL-CIO   American Federation of Labor and Congress of Industrial
  Organizations
AIB   American Institute of Banking
AID   Agency for International Development
AMA   American Medical Association
AP   Associated Press
ARC   American (National) Red Cross
ARS   Agricultural Research Service
ASA   American Standards Association; American Statistical
  Association
ASTA   American Society of Travel Agents

B

BLS   Bureau of Labor Statistics
BTA   Board of Tax Appeals

C

CAP   Civil Air Patrol
CAB   Civil Aeronautics Board
CCC   Commodity Credit Corporation
CEA   Commodity Exchange Administration
CEC   Commodity Exchange Commission
CED   Committee for Economic Development
CIA   Central Intelligence Agency
CID   Criminal Investigation Department
CORE   Congress of Racial Equality
CPSC   Consumer Product Safety Commission
CSC   Civil Service Commission

E

EEC   European Economic Community
EEOC   Equal Employment Opportunity Commission
EPA   Environmental Protection Agency

F

FAA   Federal Aviation Agency
FBI   Federal Bureau of Investigation
FCA   Farm Credit Administration
FCC   Federal Communications Commission
FDA   Food and Drug Administration
FDIC   Federal Deposit Insurance Corporation
FHA   Federal Housing Administration
FMC   Federal Maritime Commission
FPC   Federal Power Commission
FRB   Federal Reserve Board (or Bank)
FRS   Federal Reserve System
FSA   Federal Security Agency
FTC   Federal Trade Commission

G

GAO   General Accounting Office
GHQ   General Headquarters (Army)
GPO   Government Printing Office
GSA   General Services Administration

H

HHFA   Housing and Home Finance Agency
HUD   Housing and Urban Development (Department of)

I

ICC   Interstate Commerce Commission
IFC   International Finance Corporation
IFTU   International Federation of Trade Unions
ILO   International Labor Organization
ILP   Independent Labour Party (Brit.)
IMF   International Monetary Fund
INP   International News Photos
INS   International News Service
IRO   International Refugee Organization
IRS   Internal Revenue Service
ITO   International Trade Organization
IWW   Industrial Workers of the World

K

KC   Knights of Columbus
KKK   Ku Klux Klan

N

NAACP   National Association for the Advancement of Colored
 People
NALS   National Association of Legal Secretaries
NAM   National Association of Manufacturers
NAS   National Academy of Sciences
NASA   National Aeronautics and Space Administration
NATO   North Atlantic Treaty Organization
NBS   National Broadcasting Service
NEA   National Education Association; National Editorial Association
NIH   National Institutes of Health
NLRB   National Labor Relations Board
NMB   National Mediation Board
NOW   National Organization for Women
NPS   National Park Service
NRC   Nuclear Regulatory Commission
NSC   National Security Council
NSF   National Science Foundation

O

OAS   Organization of American States
OECD   Organization for Economic Cooperation and Development
OEO   Office of Economic Opportunity

P

PHA   Public Housing Administration
PHS   Public Health Service
PSI   Professional Secretaries International

R

REA   Rural Electrification Administration
ROTC   Reserve Officers' Training Corps.
RRB   Railroad Retirement Board

S

SBA   Small Business Administration
SEATO   Southeast Asia Treaty Organization
SEC   Securities and Exchange Commission
SSA   Social Security Administration
SSS   Selective Service System

T

TC   Tax Court of the United States
TVA   Tennessee Valley Authority

U

UN   United Nations
UNESCO   United Nations Educational, Social, and Cultural
  Organization
USIA   United States Information Agency
UNICEF   United Nations Children's Fund
UNRRA   United National Relief and Rehabilitation Administration
UPI   United Press International
UPS   United Parcel Service
USDA   United States Department of Agriculture
USIA   United States Information Agency

V

VA   Veterans Administration
VFW   Veterans of Foreign Wars
VISTA   Volunteers in Service to America

W

WHO   World Health Organization

U.S. Postal Service Abbreviations

Traditional and Two-Letter
State and Territory Abbreviations

	Traditional Abbreviation	Postal Abbreviation
Alabama, State of	Ala.	AL
Alaska, State of	Alas.	AK
American Samoa	Amer. Samoa	AS

	Traditional Abbreviation	Postal Abbreviation
Arizona, State of	Ariz.	AZ
Arkansas, State of	Ark.	AR
California, State of	Calif.	CA
Canal Zone	C.Z.	CZ
Colorado, State of	Colo.	CO
Connecticut, State of	Conn.	CT
Delaware, State of	Del.	DE
District of Columbia	D.C.	DC
Florida, State of	Fla.	FL
Georgia, State of	Ga.	GA
Guam	Guam	GU
Hawaii, State of	Hawaii	HI
Idaho, State of	Ida.	ID
Illinois, State of	Ill.	IL
Indiana, State of	Ind.	IN
Iowa, State of	Iowa	IA
Kansas, State of	Kans.	KS
Kentucky, Commonwealth of	Ky.	KY
Louisiana, State of	La.	LA
Maine, State of	Maine	ME
Maryland, State of	Md.	MD
Massachusetts, Commonwealth of	Mass.	MA
Michigan, State of	Mich.	MI
Minnesota, State of	Minn.	MN
Mississippi, State of	Miss.	MS
Missouri, State of	Mo.	MO
Montana, State of	Mont.	MT
Nebraska, State of	Nebr.	NE
Nevada, State of	Nev.	NV
New Hampshire, State of	N.H.	NH
New Jersey, State of	N.J.	NJ
New Mexico, State of	N.M.	NM
New York, State of	N.Y.	NY
North Carolina, State of	N.C.	NC
North Dakota, State of	N.D.	ND
Northern Mariana Islands	No. Mariana Is.	CM
Ohio, State of	Ohio	OH
Oklahoma, State of	Okla.	OK
Oregon, State of	Oreg.	OR
Pennsylvania, Commonwealth of	Pa.	PA
Puerto Rico	P.R.	PR
Rhode Island and Providence Plantations, State of	R.I.	RI
South Carolina, State of	S.C.	SC
South Dakota, State of	S.D.	SD
Tennessee, State of	Tenn.	TN

	Traditional Abbreviation	Postal Abbreviation
Texas, State of	Tex.	TX
Trust Territory	Trust Terr.	TT
Utah, State of	Utah	UT
Vermont, State of	Vt.	VT
Virgin Islands	V.I.	VI
Virginia, Commonwealth of	Va.	VA
Washington, State of	Wash.	WA
West Virginia, State of	W.Va.	WV
Wisconsin, State of	Wis.	WI
Wyoming, State of	Wyo.	WY

Street and Place-Name Abbreviations

Word	Abbreviation	Word	Abbreviation
Academy	ACAD	Clear	CLR
Air Force Base	AFB	Cliffs	CLFS
Agency	AGNCY	Club	CLB
Airport	ARPRT	College	CLG
Alley	ALY	Common	CMM
Annex	ANX	Corner	COR
Arcade	ARC	Corners	CORS
Arsenal	ARSL	Course	CRSE
Avenue	AVE	Court	CT
Bayou	BYU	Courts	CTS
Beach	BCH	Cove	CV
Bend	BND	Creek	CRK
Big	BG	Crescent	CRES
Black	BLK	Crossing	XING
Boulevard	BLVD	Dale	DL
Bluff	BLF	Dam	DM
Bottom	BTM	Depot	DPO
Branch	BR	Divide	DV
Bridge	BRG	Drive	DR
Brook	BRK	East	E
Burg	BG	Estates	EST
Bypass	BYP	Expressway	EXPY
Camp	CP	Extended	EXT
Canyon	CYN	Extension	EXT
Cape	CPE	Fall	FL
Causeway	CSWY	Falls	FLS
Center	CTR	Farms	FRMS
Central	CTL	Ferry	FRY
Church	CHR	Field	FLD
Churches	CHRS	Fields	FLDS
Circle	CIR	Flats	FLT
City	CY	Ford	FRD

Word	Abbreviation	Word	Abbreviation
Forest	FRST	Meeting	MTG
Forge	FRG	Memorial	MEM
Fork	FRK	Middle	MDL
Forks	FRKS	Mile	MLE
Fort	FT	Mill	ML
Fountain	FTN	Mills	MLS
Freeway	FWY	Mines	MNS
Furnace	FURN	Mission	MSN
		Mound	MND
Gardens	GDNS	Mount	MT
Gateway	GTWY	Mountain	MTN
Glen	GLN		
Grand	GRND	National	NAT
Great	GR	Naval Air Station	NAS
Green	GRN	Neck	NCK
Ground	GRD	New	NW
Grove	GRV	North	N
Harbor	HBR	Orchard	ORCH
Haven	HVN	Oval	OVAL
Heights	HTS	Palms	PLMS
High	HI	Park	PARK
Highlands	HGLDS	Parkway	PKY
Highway	HWY	Pass	PASS
Hill	HL	Path	PATH
Hills	HLS	Pike	PIKE
Hollow	HOLW	Pillar	PLR
Hospital	HOSP	Pines	PNES
Hot	H	Place	PL
House	HSE	Plain	PLN
		Plains	PLNS
Inlet	INLT	Plaza	PLZ
Institute	INST	Port	PRT
Island	IS	Point	PT
Islands	IS	Prairie	PR
Isle	IS		
		Radial	RADL
Junction	JCT	Ranch	RNCH
		Ranches	RNCHS
Key	KY	Rapids	RPDS
Knolls	KNLS	Resort	RESRT
		Rest	RST
Landing	LNDG	Ridge	RDG
Lake	LK	River	RIV
Lakes	LKS	Road	RD
Lane	LN	Rock	RK
Light	LGT	Row	ROW
Little	LTL	Run	RUN
Loaf	LF	Rural	R
Locks	LCKS		
Lodge	LDG	Saint	ST
Loop	LOOP	Sainte	ST
Lower	LWR	San	SN
		Santa	SN
Mall	MALL	Santo	SN
Manor	MNR		
Meadows	MDWS		

Word	Abbreviation	Word	Abbreviation
School	SCH	Tower	TWR
Seminary	SMNRY	Town	TWN
Shoal	SHL	Trace	TRCE
Shoals	SHLS	Track	TRAK
Shode	SDHD	Trail	TRL
Shore	SHR	Trailer	TRLR
Shores	SHRS	Tunnel	TUNL
Siding	SDG	Turnpike	TPKE
South	S	Upper	UPR
Space Flight Center	SFC	Union	UN
Speedway	SPDWY	University	UNIV
Spring	SPG		
Springs	SPGS	Valley	VLY
Spur	SPUR	Viaduct	VIA
Square	SQ	View	VW
State	ST	Village	VLG
Station	STA	Ville	VL
Street	ST	Vista	VIS
Stream	STRM	Walk	WALK
Sulphur	SLPHR	Water	WTR
Summit	SMT	Way	WAY
Switch	SWCH	Wells	WLS
Tannery	TNRY	West	W
Tavern	TVRN	White	WHT
Terminal	TERM	Works	WKS
Terrace	TER	Yards	YDS
Ton	TN		

Computer Abbreviations and Acronyms

A

ABM	automated batch mixing
abort	abandon activity
ABP	actual block processor
abs	absolute
AC	automatic/analog computer
ACC	accumulator
ACF	advanced communication function
ACL	Audit Command Language
ACM	area composition machine
ADAPS	automatic displayed plotting system
ADC	analog-to-digital converter
ADIS	automatic data interchange system
ADP	automatic/advanced data processing
ADR	address; adder; analog-to-digital recorder

ADV	advance
AFR	automatic field/format recognition
ALCOM	algebraic computer/compiler
ALGOL	Algorithmic Language
ALP	automated language processing
ALU	arithmetic and logic unit
ANACOM	analog computer
AOC	automatic output control
AP	attached processor
APL	A Programming Language
APT	Automatic Programmed Tools (language)
AQL	acceptable quality level
ARQ	automatic repeat request; automatic request for correction
ARU	audio response unit
ASC	automatic sequence control
ASCII	American Standard Code for Information Interchange
ASDI	automated selective dissemination of information
ASM	auxiliary storage management
ASP	attached support processor
ASR	answer, send, and receive
ATLAS	Automatic Tabulating, Listing, and Sorting System
AUTODIN	automated digital network

B

B	bit; magnetic flux density
BA	binary add
BAM	basic access method
BASIC	Beginner's All-Purpose Symbolic Instruction
BC	binary code
BCD	binary-coded decimal
BDU	basic device/display unit
BIM	beginning of information marker
bit	binary digit
BIU	basic information unit
BN	binary number system
BOF	beginning of file
BOS	basic operating system
BOT	beginning of tape
bpi	bits per inch
bps	bits per second
BPS	basic programming support

BS   backspace character
BTU   basic transmission unit

C

C   computer; compute; control
CA   channel adapter
CAD   computer-aided design
CAD/CAM   computer-aided design/computer-aided
                manufacturing
CAI   computer-aided instruction
CAI/OP   computer analog input/output
CAL   computer-aided learning
CAM   computer-aided manufacturing
CAN   cancel character
CAR   computer-assisted retrieval
CAT   computer-assisted training/teaching
CDC   call directing code
CHAR   character
CIM   computer-input microfilm
CIOCS   communications input/output control system
CIU   computer interface unit
CLAT   communication line adapter
CLK   clock
CLT   communication line terminal
CMC   code for magnetic characters
CMND   command; instruction
CMS   conversation monitor system
CNC   computer numerical control
COBOL   Common Business-Oriented Language
COL   Computer-Oriented Language
COM   computer-output microfilm
CP   central processor
cph   characters per hour
cpm   characters per minute; cards per minute; critical path
                method
CP/M   controlled program monitor; control
                program/microcomputers
CPS   conversational programming system; central
                processing system
CPU   central processing unit
cr   carriage return
CR   call request; control relay
CRAM   card random access method

CROM	control read-only memory
CRT	cathode ray tube
CSL	Computer-Sensitive Language
CST	channel status table
CTR	computer tape reader
CTU	central terminal unit
CU	control unit
CWP	communicating word processor

D

DAA	direct-access arrangement
DAC	data acquisition and control; digital/analog converter
DASD	direct-access storage device
DBAM	database access method
DBMS	database management system
DD	digital data
DDL	Data-Description Language
DDS	digital-display scope
DE	display element
DIP	dual in-line package
DLC	data-link control
DMA	direct memory access
DNC	direct numerical control
DOS	disk operating system
DOV	data over voice
DP	data processing
DRL	Data-Retrieval Language
DRO	destructive readout
DTR	data terminal ready
DUV	data under voice

E

EDP	electronic data processing
EOF	end of file
EOJ	end of job
EOP	end of paragraph
EOR	end of record/run
ESI	externally specified index
ETB	end of transmission block

F

F	feedback

FACT	Fully Automatic Compiling Technique
FDOS	floppy-disk operating system
FF	flip-flop
FIRST	fast interactive retrieval system
FORTRAN	Formula Translation (language)

G

GDT	graphic display terminal
GP	general program
GPC	general-purpose computer
GPR	general-purpose register

H

HSM	high-speed memory
HSP	high-speed printer
HSR	high-speed reader

I

IC	integrated circuit; input circuit
ID	identification
I/O	input/output
IOB	input-output buffer
IOC	input-output controller
ipm	impulses per minute
IR	infrared
ISR	information storage and retrieval

K

k	about a thousand (in storage capacity)
KB	keyboard
kb	kilobytes
KSR	keyboard send and receive

L

LCD	liquid crystal display
LIFO	last in, first out
LILO	last in, last out
LP	linear programming
lpm	lines per minute
lsc	least significant character
lsd	least significant digit

M

M	mega
mag	magnetic
Mb	megabyte
MC	master control
MCP	master control program
MIS	management information system
MPS	microprocessor system
msc	most significant character
msd	most significant digit
MSU	modem-sharing unit
MT	machine translation
MUX	multiplexer

N

n	nano-
NAM	network access machine
NAU	network addressable unit
NC	numerical control
NCP	network control program
NL	new-line character
NO-OP	no-operation instruction
ns	nanosecond

O

OCR	optical character recognition
ODB	output to display buffer
OEM	original equipment manufacturer
OLRT	on-line real time
OP	operations
opm	operations per minute
OR	operations research
OS	operating system
OSI	open-system interconnection

P

P	pico-
PA	paper advance
PC	program counter
PCI	process control interface
PCM	punch-card machine

PCS	punched-card system
PDN	public data network
PERT	program evaluation and review technique
PIO chip	programmable input/output chip
PIU	path information unit
PRT	production-run tape

R

RAM	random-access memory
RAX	remote access
READ	real-time electronic access and display
REM	recognition memory
ROM	read-only memory
RT	real time
RTU	remote terminal unit
R/W	read/write
RWM	read-write memory
RZ	return to zero

S

SAM	sequential-access method; serial-access memory
S/F	store and forward
SLT	solid-logic technology
SOP	standard operating procedure
STX	start of text

T

TLU	table lookup
TOS	tape operating system

U

UCS	user control storage
USASCII	USA Standard Code for Information Interchange

V

VDI	video display input
VDT	video display terminal

W

WC	write and compute
WFL	work-flow language
WIP	work in progress
WO	write out
wp, WP	work processor
WS	working storage/space

X

XMT	transmit

CORRECT FORMS OF ADDRESS

United States Government Officials

Personage	Envelope and Inside Address (Add City, State, Zip)	Formal Salutation	Informal Salutation	Formal Close	Informal Close	1. Spoken Address 2. Informal Introduction or Reference
The President	The President The White House	Mr. President	Dear Mr. President:	Respectfully yours,	Very respectfully yours, *or* Sincerely yours,	1. Mr. President 2. Not introduced (The President)
Former President of the United States[1]	The Honorable William R. Blank (local address)	Sir:	Dear Mr. Blank:	Respectfully yours,	Sincerely yours,	1. Mr. Blank 2. Former President Blank *or* Mr. Blank
The Vice-President of the United States	The Vice-President of the United States The White House	Mr. Vice-President:	Dear Mr. Vice-President:	Very truly yours,	Sincerely yours,	1. Mr. Vice-President *or* Mr. Blank The Vice-President
The Chief Justice of the United States Supreme Court	The Chief Justice of the United States The Supreme Court of the United States	Sir:	Dear Mr. Chief Justice:	Very truly yours,	Sincerely yours,	1. Mr. Chief Justice 2. The Chief Justice
Associate Justice of the United States Supreme Court	Mr. Justice Blank The Supreme Court of the United States	Sir:	Dear Mr. Justice: *or* Dear Justice Blank:	Very truly yours,	SIncerely yours,	1. Mr. Justice Blank *or* Justice Blank 2. Mr. Justice Blank

Note: In this chart the form of address for a man is used throughout except where not applicable. To use the form of address for a woman in any of these positions, use the substitution *Madam* for *Sir* and *Mrs., Miss,* or *Ms.* for *Mr.* Thus *Dear Madam; Mrs. Blank, Respresentative from New York; The Lieutenant Governor of Iowa, Miss Blank; The American Minister, Ms. Blank.* The *Mr.* preceding a title becomes *Madam.* Thus *Madam Secretary; Madam Ambassador.* Use *Esquire* or *Esq.* in addressing a man or woman where appropriate. (For additional information see Chapter 11, page 327.)

1. If a former president has a title, such as *General of the Army,* address him by it.

United States Government Officials *continued*

Personage	Envelope and Inside Address (Add City, State, Zip)	Formal Salutation	Informal Salutation	Formal Close	Informal Close	1. Spoken Address 2. Informal Introduction or Reference
Retired Justice of the United States Supreme Court	The Honorable William R. Blank (local address)	Sir:	Dear Justice Blank:	Very truly yours,	Sincerely yours,	1. Mr. Justice Blank *or* Justice Blank 2. Mr. Justice Blank
The Speaker of the House of Representatives	The Honorable William R. Blank Speaker of the House of Representatives	Sir:	Dear Mr. Speaker: *or* Dear Mr. Blank:	Very truly yours,	Sincerely yours,	1. Mr. Speaker *or* Mr. Blank 2. The Speaker, Mr. Blank (The Speaker *or* Mr. Blank)
Former Speaker of the House of Respresentatives	The Honorable William R. Blank (local address)	Sir:	Dear Mr. Blank:	Very truly yours,	Sincerely yours,	1. Mr. Blank 2. Mr. Blank
Cabinet Officers addressed as "Secretary"[2]	The Honorable William R. Blank Secretary of State The Honorable William R. Blank Secretary of State of the United States of America (if written from abroad)	Sir:	Dear Mr. Secretary:	Very truly yours,	Sincerely yours,	1. Mr. Secretary *or* Secretary Blank *or* Mr. Blank 2. The Secretary of State Mr. Blank (Mr. Blank or The Secretary)
Former Cabinet Officer	The Honorable William R. Blank (local address)	Dear Sir:	Dear Mr. Blank:	Very truly yours,	Sincerely yours,	1. Mr. Blank 2. Mr. Blank

2. Titles for cabinet secretaries are Secretary of State; Secretary of the Treasury; Secretary of Defense; Secretary of Education; Secretary of Energy; Secretary of the Interior; Secretary of Agriculture; Secretary of Commerce; Secretary of Labor; Secretary of Health and Human Services; Secretary of Housing and Urban Development; Secretary of Transportation.

United States Government Officials *continued*

Personage	Envelope and Inside Address (Add City, State, Zip)	Formal Salutation	Informal Salutation	Formal Close	Informal Close	1. Spoken Address 2. Informal Introduction or Reference
Postmaster General	The Honorable William R. Blank Postmaster General,	Sir:	Dear Mr. Postmaster General:	Very truly yours,	Sincerely yours,	1. Mr. Postmaster General *or* Postmaster General Blank or Mr. Blank 2. The Postmaster General, Mr. Blank (Mr. Blank or The Postmaster General)
The Attorney General	The Honorable William R. Blank Attorney General of the United States	Sir:	Dear Mr. Attorney General:	Very truly yours,	Sincerely yours,	1. Mr. Attorney General *or* Attorney General Blank 2. The Attorney General, Mr. Blank (Mr. Blank or The Attorney General)
Under Secretary of a Department	The Honorable William R. Blank Under Secretary of Labor	Sir:	Dear Mr. Under Secretary: *or* Dear Mr. Blank:	Very truly yours,	Sincerely yours,	1. Mr. Blank 2. Mr. Blank
United States Senator	The Honorable William R. Blank United States Senate	Sir:	Dear Senator Blank:	Very truly yours,	Sincerely yours,	1. Senator Blank *or* Senator 2. Senator Blank
Former Senator	The Honorable William R. Blank (local address)	Dear Sir:	Dear Mr. Blank:	Very truly yours,	Sincerely yours,	1. Mr. Blank 2. Mr. Blank

United States Government Officials *continued*

Personage	Envelope and Inside Address (Add City, State, Zip)	Formal Salutation	Informal Salutation	Formal Close	Informal Close	1. Spoken Address 2. Informal Introduction or Reference
Senator-elect	The Honorable William R. Blank Senator-elect United States Senate	Dear Sir:	Dear Mr. Blank:	Very truly yours,	Sincerely yours,	1. Mr. Blank 2. Senator-elect Blank *or* Mr. Blank
Committee Chairman— United States Senate	The Honorable William R. Blank, Chairman Committee on Foreign Affairs United States Senate	Dear Mr. Chairman:	Dear Mr. Chairman: *or* Dear Senator Blank:	Very truly yours,	Sincerely yours,	1. Mr. Chairman *or* Senator Blank *or* Senator 2. The Chairman *or* Senator Blank
Subcommittee Chairman— United States Senate	The Honorable William R. Blank, Chairman, Subcommittee on Forgeign Affairs United States Senate	Dear Senator Blank:	Dear Senator Blank:	Very truly yours,	Sincerely yours,	1. Senator Blank *or* Senator 2. Senator Blank
United States Representative or Congressman[3]	The Honorable William R. Blank House of Representatives The Honorable William R. Blank Representative in Congress (local address) (when away from Washington, DC)	Sir:	Dear Mr. Blank:	Very truly yours,	Sincerely yours,	1. Mr. Blank 2. Mr. Blank, Representative (Congressman) from New York *or* Mr. Blank

3. The official title of a "congressman" or "congresswoman" is *Representative*. Senators are also congressmen or congresswomen.

United States Government Officials *continued*

Personage	Envelope and Inside Address (Add City, State, Zip)	Formal Salutation	Informal Salutation	Formal Close	Informal Close	1. Spoken Address 2. Informal Introduction or Reference
Former Representative	The Honorable William R. Blank (local address)	Dear Sir: *or* Dear Mr. Blank:	Dear Mr. Blank:	Very truly yours,	Sincerely yours,	1. Mr. Blank 2. Mr. Blank
Territorial Delegate	The Honorable William R. Blank Delegate of Puerto Rico House of Representatives	Dear Sir: *or* Dear Mr. Blank:	Dear Mr. Blank:	Very truly yours,	Sincerely yours,	1. Mr. Blank 2. Mr. Blank
Resident Commissioner	The Honorable William R. Blank Resident Commissioner of (Territory) House of Representatives	Dear Sir: *or* Dear Mr. Blank:	Dear Mr. Blank:	Very truly yours,	Sincerely yours,	1. Mr. Blank 2. Mr. Blank
Directors or Heads of Independent Federal Offices, Agencies, Commissions, Organizations, etc.	The Honorable William R. Blank Director Mutual Security Agency	Dear Mr. Director (Commissioner, etc.):	Dear Mr. Blank:	Very truly yours,	Sincerely yours,	1. Mr. Blank 2. Mr. Blank
Other High Officials of the United States, in general: Public Printer, Comptroller General	The Honorable William R. Blank Public Printer The Honorable William R. Blank Comptroller General of the United States	Dear Sir: *or* Dear Mr. Blank:	Dear Mr. Blank:	Very truly yours,	Sincerely yours,	1. Mr. Blank 2. Mr. Blank

United States Government Officials *continued*

Personage	Envelope and Inside Address (Add City, State, Zip)	Formal Salutation	Informal Salutation	Formal Close	Informal Close	1. Spoken Address 2. Informal Introduction or Reference
Secretary to the President	The Honorable William R. Blank Secretary to the President The White House	Dear Sir: *or* Dear Mr. Blank:	Dear Mr. Blank:	Very truly yours,	Sincerely yours,	1. Mr. Blank 2. Mr. Blank
Assistant Secretary to the President	The Honorable William R. Blank Assistant Secretary to the President The White House	Dear Sir: *or* Dear Mr. Blank:	Dear Mr. Blank:	Very truly yours,	Sincerely yours,	1. Mr. Blank 2. Mr. Blank
Press Secretary to the President	Mr. William R. Blank Press Secretary to the President The White House	Dear Sir: *or* Dear Mr. Blank:	Dear Mr. Blank:	Very truly yours,	SIncerely yours,	1. Mr. Blank 2. Mr. Blank

State and Local Government Officials

Governor of a State or Territory[1]	The Honorable William R. Blank Governor of New York	Sir:	Dear Governor Blank:	Very truly yours,	Sincerely yours,	1. Governor Blank *or* Governor 2. a) Governor Blank b) The Governor c) The Governor of New York (used only outside his or her own state)

1. The form of addressing governors varies in the different states. The form given here is the one used in most states. In Massachusetts by law and in some other states by courtesy, the form is *His (Her) Excellency, the Governor of Massachusetts.*

State and Local Government Officials *continued*

Personage	Envelope and Inside Address (Add City, State, Zip)	Formal Salutation	Informal Salutation	Formal Close	Informal Close	1. Spoken Address 2. Informal Introduction or Reference
Acting Governor of a State or Territory	The Honorable William R. Blank Acting Governor of Connecticut	Sir:	Dear Mr. Blank:	Very truly yours,	Sincerely yours,	1. Mr. Blank 2. Mr. Blank
Lieutenant Governor	The Honorable William R. Blank Lieutenant Governor of Iowa	Sir:	Dear Mr. Blank:	Very truly yours,	Sincerely yours,	1. Mr. Blank 2. The Lieutenant Governor of Iowa, Mr. Blank *or* The Lieutenant Governor
Secretary of State	The Honorable William R. Blank Secretary of State of New York	Sir:	Dear Mr. Secretary:	Very truly yours,	Sincerely yours,	1. Mr. Blank 2. Mr. Blank
Attorney General	The Honorable William R. Blank Attorney General of Massachusetts	Sir:	Dear Mr. Attorney General:	Very truly yours,	Sincerely yours,	1. Mr. Blank 2. Mr. Blank
President of the Senate of a State	The Honorable William R. Blank President of the Senate of the State of Virginia	Sir:	Dear Mr. Blank:	Very truly yours,	Sincerely yours,	1. Mr. Blank 2. Mr. Blank
Speaker of the Assembly or The House of Representatives.[2]	The Honorable William R. Blank Speaker of the Assembly of the State of New York	Sir:	Dear Mr. Blank:	Very truly yours,	Sincerely yours,	1. Mr. Blank 2. Mr. Blank

2. In most states the lower branch of the legislature is the House of Representatives. The exceptions to this are: New York, California, Wisconsin, and Nevada, where it is known as the Assembly; Maryland, Virginia, and West Virginia—the House of Delegates; New Jersey—the House of General Assembly.

State and Local Government Officials *continued*

Personage	Envelope and Inside Address (Add City, State, Zip)	Formal Salutation	Informal Salutation	Formal Close	Informal Close	1. Spoken Address 2. Informal Introduction or Reference
Treasurer, Auditor, or Comptroller of a State	The Honorable William R. Blank Treasurer of the State of Tennessee	Dear Sir:	Dear Mr. Blank:	Very truly yours,	Sincerely yours,	1. Mr. Blank 2. Mr. Blank
State Senator	The Honorable William R. Blank The State Senate	Dear Sir:	Dear Senator Blank:	Very truly yours,	Sincerely yours,	1. Senator Blank *or* Senator 2. Senator Blank
State Representative, Assemblyman, or Delegate	The Honorable William R. Blank House of Delegates	Dear Sir:	Dear Mr. Blank:	Very truly yours,	Sincerely yours,	1. Mr. Blank 2. Mr. Blank *or* Delegate Blank
District Attorney	The Honorable William R. Blank District Attorney, Albany county Country Courthouse	Dear Sir:	Dear Mr. Blank:	Very truly yours,	Sincerely yours,	1. Mr. Blank 2. Mr. Blank
Mayor of a city	The Honorable William R. Blank Mayor of Detroit	Dear Sir:	Dear Mr. Mayor: *or* Dear Mayor Blank:	Very truly yours,	Sincerely yours,	1. Mayor Blank *or* Mr. Mayor 2. Mayor Blank
President of a Board of Commissioners	The Honorable William R. Blank, President Board of commissioners of the City of Buffalo	Dear Sir:	Dear Mr. Blank:	Very truly yours,	Sincerely yours,	1. Mr. Blank 2. Mr. Blank

State and Local Government Officials *continued*

Personage	Envelope and Inside Address (Add City, State, Zip)	Formal Salutation	Informal Salutation	Formal Close	Informal Close	1. Spoken Address 2. Informal Introduction or Reference
City Attorney, City Counsel, Corporation Counsel	The Honorable William R. Blank, City Attorney (City Counsel, Corporation Counsel)	Dear Sir:	Dear Mr. Blank:	Very truly yours,	Sincerely yours,	1. Mr. Blank 2. Mr. Blank
Alderman	Alderman William R. Blank City Hall	Dear Sir:	Dear Mr. Blank:	Very truly yours,	Sincerely yours,	1. Mr. Blank 2. Mr. Blank

Court Officials

Personage	Envelope and Inside Address (Add City, State, Zip)	Formal Salutation	Informal Salutation	Formal Close	Informal Close	1. Spoken Address 2. Informal Introduction or Reference
Chief Justice[1] of a State Supreme Court	The Honorable William R. Blank Chief Justice of the Supreme Court of Minnesota[2]	Sir:	Dear Mr. Chief Justice:	Very truly yours,	Sincerely yours,	1. Mr. Chief Justice *or* Judge Blank 2. Mr. Chief Justice Blank *or* Judge Blank
Associate Justice of a Supreme Court of a State	The Honorable William R. Blank Associate Justice of the Supreme Court of Minnesota	Sir:	Dear Justice: *or* Dear Justice Blank:	Very truly yours,	Sincerely yours,	1. Mr. Justice Blank 2. Mr. Justice Blank
Presiding Justice	The Honorable William R. Blank Presiding Justice, Appellate Division Supreme Court of New York	Sir:	Dear Justice: *or* Dear Justice Blank:	Very truly yours,	Sincerely yours,	1. Mr. Justice (*or* Judge) Blank 2. Mr. Justice (*or* Judge) Blank

1. If his or her official title is *Chief Justice* substitute *Chief Judge* for *Chief Justice*, but never use *Mr., Mrs., Miss,* or *Ms.* with *Chief Judge* or *Judge.*
2. Substitute here the appropriate name of the court. For example, the highest court in New York State is called the Court of Appeals.

Court Officials continued

Personage	Envelope and Inside Address (Add City, State, Zip)	Formal Salutation	Informal Salutation	Formal Close	Informal Close	1. Spoken Address 2. Informal Introduction or Reference
Judge of a Court[3]	The Honorable William R. Blank Judge of the United States District Court for the Southern District of California	Sir:	Dear Judge Blank:	Very truly yours,	Sincerely yours,	1. Judge Blank 2. Judge Blank
Clerk of a Court	William R. Blank, Esq. Clerk of the Superior Court of Massachusetts	Dear Sir:	Dear Mr. Blank:	Very truly yours,	Sincerely yours,	1. Mr. Blank 2. Mr. Blank

3. Not applicable to judges of the United States Supreme Court.

United States Diplomatic Representatives

Personage	Envelope and Inside Address (Add City, State, Zip)	Formal Salutation	Informal Salutation	Formal Close	Informal Close	1. Spoken Address 2. Informal Introduction or Reference
American Ambassador	The Honorable William R. Blank American Ambassador[1]	Sir:	Dear Mr. Ambassador: or Dear Ambassador Blank:	Very truly yours,	Sincerely yours,	1. Mr. Ambassador or Mr. Blank 2. The American Ambassador[2] (The Ambassador or Mr. Blank)
American Minister	The Honorable William R. Blank American Minister to Rumania	Sir:	Dear Mr. Minister: or Dear Minister Blank:	Very truly yours,	Sincerely yours,	1. Mr. Minister or Mr. Blank 2. The American Minister, Mr. Blank (The Minister or Mr. Blank)

1. When an ambassador or minister is not at his or her post, the name of the country to which he or she is accredited must be added to the address. For example: *The American Ambassador to Great Britain.* If he or she holds military rank, the diplomatic complimentary title *The Honorable* should be omitted, thus *General William R. Blank, American Ambassador (or Minister).*
2. With reference to ambassadors and ministers to Central or South American countries, substitute *The Ambassador of the United States* for *American Ambassador* or *American Minister.*

United States Diplomatic Representatives *continued*

Personage	Envelope and Inside Address (Add City, State, Zip)	Formal Salutation	Informal Salutation	Formal Close	Informal Close	1. Spoken Address 2. Informal Introduction or Reference
American Chargé d'Affaires, Consul General, Consul, or Vice Consul	William R. Blank, Esq. American Chargé d'Affaires ad interim (Consul General, Consul, Vice Consul)	Sir:	Dear Mr. Blank:	Very truly yours,	Sincerely yours,	1. Mr. Blank 2. Mr. Blank
High Commissioner	The Honorable William R. Blank United States High Commissioner to Argentina	Sir:	Dear Mr. Blank:	Very truly yours,	Sincerely yours,	1. Commissioner Blank *or* Mr. Blank 2. Commissioner Blank *or* Mr. Blank

Foreign Officials and Representatives

Personage	Envelope and Inside Address (Add City, State, Zip)	Formal Salutation	Informal Salutation	Formal Close	Informal Close	1. Spoken Address 2. Informal Introduction or Reference
Foreign Ambassador[1] in the United States	His Excellency,[2] Erik Rolf Blankson Ambassador of Norway	Excellency:	Dear Mr. Ambassador:	Very truly yours,	Sincerely yours,	1. Mr. Ambassador *or* Mr. Blankson 2. The Ambassador of Norway (The Ambassador or Mr. Blankson)

1. The correct title of all ambassadors and ministers of foreign countries is Ambassador (Minister of ——— (name of country), with the exception of Great Britain. The adjective form is used with reference to representatives from Great Britain—*British Ambassador, British Minister.*
2. When the representative is British or a member of the British Commonwealth, it is customary to use *The Right Honorable* and *The Honorable* in addition to *His (Her) Excellency,* whenever appropriate.

Foreign Officials and Representatives *continued*

Personage	Envelope and Inside Address (Add City, State, Zip)	Formal Salutation	Informal Salutation	Formal Close	Informal Close	1. Spoken Address 2. Informal Introduction or Reference
Foreign Minister[3] *in the United States*	The Honorable George Macovescu Minister of Rumania	Sir:	Dear Mr. Minister:	Very truly yours,	Sincerely yours,	1. Mr. Minister *or* Mr. Macovescu 2. The Minister of Rumania (The Minister or Mr. Macovescu)
Foreign Diplomatic Representative with a Personal Title[4]	His Excellency,[5] Count Allesandro de Bianco Ambassador of Italy	Excellency:	Dear Mr. Ambassador:	Very truly yours,	Sincerely yours,	1. Mr. Ambassador *or* Count Bianco 2. The Ambassador of Italy (The Ambassador or Count Bianco)
Prime Minister	His Excellency, Christian Jawaharal Blank Prime Minister of India	Excellency:	Dear Mr. Prime Minister:	Respectfully yours,	Sincerely yours,	1. Mr. Blank 2. Mr. Blank *or* The Prime Minister
British Prime Minister	The Right Honorable Godfrey Blanc, K.G., M.C., M.P. Prime Minister	Sir:	Dear Mr. Prime Minister: *or* Dear Mr. Blanc:	Respectfully yours,	Sincerely yours,	1. Mr. Blanc 2. Mr. Blanc *or* The Prime Minister
Canadian Prime Minister	The Right Honorable Claude Louis St. Blanc, C.M.G. Prime Minister of Canda	Sir:	Dear Mr. Prime Minister: *or* Dear Mr. St. Blanc:	Respectfully yours,	Sincerely yours,	1. Mr. St. Blanc 2. Mr. St. Blanc *or* The Prime Minister

3. The correct title of all ambassadors and ministers of foreign countries is Ambassador (Minister) of _____ (name of country), with the exception of Great Britain. The adjective form is used with reference to representatives from Great Britain—British Ambassador, British Minister.
4. If the personal title is a royal title, such as His (Her) Highness or Prince, the diplomatic title His (Her) Excellency or The Honorable is omitted.
5. Dr., Señor, Don, and other titles of special courtesy in Spanish-speaking countries may be used with the diplomatic title His (Her) Excellency or The Honorable.

Foreign Officials and Representatives *continued*

Personage	Envelope and Inside Address (Add City, State, Zip)	Formal Salutation	Informal Salutation	Formal Close	Informal Close	1. Spoken Address 2. Informal Introduction or Reference
President of a Republic	His Excellency, Juan Cuidad Blanco President of the Dominican Republic	Excellency:	Dear Mr. President:	Respectfully yours,	Sincerely yours,	1. Your Excellency 2. Not introduced (President Blanco or the President)
Premier	His Excellency, Charles Yves de Blanc Premier of the French Republic	Excellency:	Dear Mr. Premier:	Respectfully yours,	Sincerely yours,	1. Mr. de Blanc 2. Mr. de Blanc *or* The Premier
Foreign Chargé d'Affaires (de missi)[6] *in the United States*	Mr. Jan Gustaf Blanc Chargé d'Affaires of Sweden	Sir:	Dear Mr. Blanc:	Very truly yours,	Sincerely yours,	1. Mr. Blanc 2. Mr. Blanc
Foreign Chargé d'Affaires ad interim in the United States	Mr. Edmund Blank Chargé d'Affaires ad interim[7] of Ireland	Sir:	Dear Mr. Blank:	Very truly yours,	Sincerely yours,	1. Mr. Blank 2. Mr. Blank

6. The full title is usually shortened to *Chargé d'Affaires.*
7. The words *ad interim* should not be omitted in the address.

The Armed Forces/Army

Personage	Envelope and Inside Address (Add City, State, Zip)	Formal Salutation	Informal Salutation	Formal Close	Informal Close	1. Spoken Address 2. Informal Introduction or Reference
General of the Army	General of the Army William R. Blank, USA Department of the Army	Sir:	Dear General Blank:	Very truly yours,	Sincerely yours,	1. General Blank 2. General Blank
General, Lieutenant General, Major General, Brigadier General[2]	General (Lieutenant General, Major General, or Brigadier General) William R. Blank, USA[1]	Sir:	Dear General (Lieutenant General, Major General, Brigadier General) Blank:	Very truly yours,	Sincerely yours,	1. General Blank 2. General Blank
Colonel, Lieutenant Colonel	Colonel (Lieutenant Colonel) William R. Blank, USA	Dear Colonel (Lieutenant Colonel) Blank:	Dear Colonel (Lieutenant Colonel) Blank:	Very truly yours,	Sincerely yours,	1. Colonel Blank 2. Colonel Blank
Major	Major William R. Blank, USA	Dear Major Blank:	Dear Major Blank:	Very truly yours,	Sincerely yours,	1. Major Blank 2. Major Blank
Captain	Captain William R. Blank, USA	Dear Captain Blank:	Dear Captain Blank:	Very truly yours,	Sincerely yours,	1. Captain Blank 2. Captain Blank
First Lieutenant, Second Lieutenant[2]	Lieutenant William R. Blank, USA	Dear Lieutenant Blank:	Dear Lieutenant Blank:	Very truly yours,	Sincerely yours,	1. Lieutenant Blank 2. Lieutenant Blank
Chief Warrant Officer, Warrant Officer	Chief Warrant Officer (Warrant Officer) William R. Blank, USA	Dear Mr. Blank:	Dear Mr. Blank:	Very truly yours,	Sincerely yours,	1. Mr. Blank 2. Mr. Blank
Chaplain in the U.S. Army[3]	Chaplain William R. Blank, Captain, USA	Dear Chaplain Blank:	Dear Chaplain Blank:	Very truly yours,	Sincerely yours,	1. Chaplain Blank 2. Chaplain Blank (Chaplain Blank)

Note: Although civilian writers traditionally spell out the rank for all branches of the service, military writers use abbreviations such as *CPT* for *Captain* and *1LT* for *First Lieutenant.*

1. *USA* indicates regular service, *USAR* signifies the reserve.
2. In all *official* correspondence, the full rank should be included in both the envelope and the inside address, but not in the salutation.
3. Roman Catholic chaplains and certain Anglican priests are introduced as *Chaplain Blank* but are spoken to and referred to as *Father Blank.*

The Armed Forces/Navy

Personage	Envelope and Inside Address (Add City, State, Zip)	Formal Salutation	Informal Salutation	Formal Close	Informal Close	1. Spoken Address 2. Informal Introduction or Reference
Fleet Admiral	Admiral William R. Blank, USN Chief of Naval Operations, Department of the Navy	Sir:	Dear Admiral Blank:	Very truly yours,	Sincerely yours,	1. Admiral Blank 2. Admiral Blank
Admiral, Vice Admiral, Rear Admiral	Admiral (Vice Admiral or Rear Admiral) William R. Blank, USN United States Naval Academy[1]	Sir:	Dear Admiral (Vice Admiral, Rear Admiral) Blank:	Very truly yours,	Sincerely yours,	1. Admiral Blank 2. Admiral Blank
Commodore, Captain, Commander, Lieutenant Commander	Commodore (Captain, Commander, Lieutenant Commander) William R. Blank, USN USS Mississippi	Dear Commodore (Captain, Commander) Blank:	Dear Commodore (Captain, Commander, Lieutenant Commander) Blank:	Very truly yours,	Sincerely yours,	1. Commodore (etc.) Blank 2. Commodore (etc.) Blank
Junior Officers: Lieutenant, Lieutenant Junior Grade, Ensign	Lieutenant (Lieutenant Junior Grade, Ensign) William R. Blank, USN USS Wyoming	Dear Mr. Blank:	Dear Mr. Blank:	Very truly yours,	Sincerely yours,	1. Mr. Blank[2] 2. Lieutenant (etc.) Blank (Mr. Blank)

1. *USN* signifies regular service; *USNR* indicates the reserve.
2. Junior officers in the medical or dental corps are spoken to and referred to as *Dr.* but are introduced by their rank.

The Armed Forces/Navy continued

Personage	Envelope and Inside Address (Add City, State, Zip)	Formal Salutation	Informal Salutation	Formal Close	Informal Close	1. Spoken Address 2. Informal Introduction or Reference
Chief Warrant Officer, Warrant Officer	Chief Warrant Officer (Warrant Officer) William R. Blank, USN USS Texas	Dear Mr. Blank:	Dear Mr. Blank:	Very truly yours,	Sincerely yours,	1. Mr. Blank 2. Mr. Blank
Chaplain	Chaplain William R. Blank, Captain, USN Department of the Navy	Dear Chaplain Blank:	Dear Chaplain Blank:	Very truly yours,	Sincerely yours,	1. Chaplain Blank 2. Captain Blank (Chaplain Blank)

The Armed Forces—Air Force

Air force titles are the same as those in the army *USAF* is used instead of *USA*, and *USAFR* is used to indicate the reserve.

The Armed Forces—Marine Corps

Marine Corps titles are the same as those in the army, except that the top rank is *Commandant of the Marine Corps*. *USMC* indicates regular service, *USMCR* indicates the reserve.

The Armed Forces—Coast Guard

Coast Guard titles are the same as those in the navy, except that the top rank is *Admiral*, *USCG* indicates regular service; *USCGR* indicates the reserve.

Church Dignitaries/Catholic Faith

Personage	Envelope and Inside Address (Add City, State, Zip)	Formal Salutation	Informal Salutation	Formal Close	Informal Close	1. Spoken Address 2. Informal Introduction or Reference
The Pope	His Holiness, The Pope *or* His Holiness, Pope _____ Vatican City	Your Holiness: Most Holy Father:	*Always Formal*	Respectfully yours,	*Always Formal*	1. Your Holiness 2. Not introduced (His Holiness or The Pope)
Apostolic Pro-Nuncio	His Excellency, The Most Reverend William R. Blank Titular Archbishop of ____ The Apostolic Pro-Nuncio	Your Excellency:	Dear Archbishop Blank:	Respectfully yours,	Sincerely yours,	1. Your Excellency 2. Not introduced (The Apostolic Delegate)
Cardinal in the United States	His Eminence, William Cardinal Blank Archbishop of New York	Your Eminence:	Dear Cardinal Blank:	Respectfully yours,	SIncerely yours,	1. Your Eminence or less formally Cardinal Blank 2. Not introduced (His Eminence or Cardinal Blank)
Bishop and Archbishop in the United States	The Most Reverend William R. Blank, D.D. Bishop (Archbishop) of Baltimore	Your Excellency:	Dear Bishop (Archbishop) Blank:	Respectfully yours,	Sincerely yours,	1. Bishop (Archbishop) Blank 2. Bishop (Archbishop) Blank
Bishop in England	The Right Reverend William R. Blank Bishop of Sussex (local address)	Right Reverend Sir:	Dear Bishop:	Respectfully yours,	SIncerely yours,	1. Bishop Blank 2. Bishop Blank
Abbot	The Right Reverend William R. Blank Abbot of Westmoreland Abbey	Dear Father Abbot:	Dear Father Blank:	Respectfully yours,	Sincerely yours,	1. Father Abbot 2. Father Blank

Church Dignitaries/Catholic Faith *continued*

Personage	Envelope and Inside Address (Add City, State, Zip)	Formal Salutation	Informal Salutation	Formal Close	Informal Close	1. Spoken Address 2. Informal Introduction or Reference
Monsignor	Reverend Msgr. William R. Blank	Reverend Monsignor:	Dear Monsignor Blank:	Respectfully yours,	Sincerely yours,	1. Monsignor Blank 2. Monsignor Blank
Superior of a Brotherhood and Priest[1]	The Very Reverend William R. Blank, M.M. Director	Dear Father Superior:	Dear Father Superior:	Respectfully yours,	Sincerely yours,	1. Father Blank 2. Father Blank
Priest	*With scholastic degree:* The Reverend William R. Blank, Ph.D. Georgetown University *Without scholastic degree (but member of religious order)* The Reverend William R. Blank, S.J.[2] St. Vincent's Church	Dear Dr. Blank: Dear Father Blank:	Dear Dr. Blank: Dear Father Blank:	Very truly yours, Very truly yours,	Sincerely yours, Sincerely yours,	1. Doctor (Father) Blank 2. Doctor (Father) Blank 1. Father Blank 2. Father Blank
Brother	Brother John Blank 932 Maple Avenue	Dear Brother:	Dear Brother John:	Very truly yours,	Sincerely yours,	1. Brother John 2. Brother John

1. The address for the superior of a Brotherhood depends on whether or not he is a priest or has a title other than superior. Consult the *Official Catholic Directory*.
2. When the order is known, the initials immediately follow the person's name, preceded by a comma.

Church Dignitaries/Catholic Faith *continued*

Personage	Envelope and Inside Address (Add City, State, Zip)	Formal Salutation	Informal Salutation	Formal Close	Informal Close	1. Spoken Address 2. Informal Introduction or Reference
Mother Superior of a Sisterhood (Catholic or protestant)[3]	The Reverend Mother Superior, O.C.A. Convent of the Sacred Heart	Dear Reverend Mother: or Dear Mother Superior:	Dear Reverend Mother: or Dear Mother Superior:	Respectfully yours,	Sincerely yours,	1. Reverend Mother 2. Reverend Mother
Sister Superior	The Reverend Sister Superior *(order, if used)[4]* Convent of the Sacred Heart	Dear Sister Superior:	Dear Sister Superior:	Respectfully yours,	Sincerely yours,	1. Sister Blank or Sister St. Teresa 2. The Sister Superior or Sister Blank (Sister St. Teresa)
Sister[5]	Sister Mary Blank St. John's High School	Dear Sister: or Dear Sister Blank:	Dear Sister Mary:	Very truly yours,	Sincerely yours,	1. Sister Mary 2. Sister Mary

3. Many religious congregations no longer use the title *Superior.* The head of a congregation is known instead by another title such as *President.*
4. The address of the superior of a Sisterhood depends on the order to which she belongs. The abbreviation of the order is not always used. Consult the *Official Catholic Directory.*
5. Use the form of address preferred by the person if you know it. Some women religious prefer to be addressed as "Sister Blank" rather than "Sister Mary" in business situations, but others object to the use of the last name.

Church Dignitaries/Jewish Faith

Personage	Envelope and Inside Address (Add City, State, Zip)	Formal Salutation	Informal Salutation	Formal Close	Informal Close	1. Spoken Address / 2. Informal Introduction or Reference
Rabbi	*With scholastic degree:* Rabbi William R. Blank, Ph.D.	Sir:	Dear Dr. Blank: *or* Dear Rabbi Blank:	Very truly yours,	Sincerely yours,	1. Rabbi Blank *or* Dr. Blank *or* Dr. Blank 2. Rabbi Blank
	Without scholastic degree: Rabbi William R. Blank	Sir:	Dear Rabbi Blank:	Very truly yours,	Sincerely yours,	1. Rabbi Blank 2. Rabbi Blank

Church Dignitaries/Protestant Faith

Personage	Envelope and Inside Address (Add City, State, Zip)	Formal Salutation	Informal Salutation	Formal Close	Informal Close	1. Spoken Address / 2. Informal Introduction or Reference
Archbishop (Anglican)	The Most Reverend Archbishop of Canterbury *or* The Most Reverend John Blank Archbishop of Canterbury	Your Grace:	Dear Archbishop Blank:	Respectfully yours,	Sincerely yours,	1. Your Grace 2. Not introduced (His Grace or The Archbishop)
Presiding Bishop of the Protestant Episcopal Church in America	The Right Reverend William R. Blank, D.D., L.L.D. Presiding Bishop of the Protestant Episcopal Church in America Northwick House	Right Reverend Sir:	Dear Bishop Blank:	Respectfully yours,	Sincerely yours,	1. Bishop Blank 2. Bishop Blank

Church Dignitaries/Protestant Faith *continued*

Personage	Envelope and Inside Address (Add City, State, Zip)	Formal Salutation	Informal Salutation	Formal Close	Informal Close	1. Spoken Address 2. Informal Introduction or Reference
Anglican Bishop	The Right Reverend The Lord Bishop of London	Right Reverend Sir:	Dear Bishop Blank:	Respectfully yours,	Sincerely yours,	1. Bishop Blank 2. Bishop Blank
Methodist Bishop	The Reverend William R. Blank Methodist Bishop	Reverend Sir:	Dear Bishop Blank:	Respectfully yours,	Sincerely yours,	1. Bishop Blank 2. Bishop Blank
Protestant Episcopal Bishop	The Right Reverend William R. Blank, D.D., L.L.D. Bishop of Denver	Right Reverend Sir:	Dear Bishop Blank:	Respectfully yours,	Sincerely yours,	1. Bishop Blank 2. Bishop Blank
Archdeacon	The Venerable William R. Blank Archdeacon of Baltimore	Venerable Sir:	Dear Archdeacon Blank:	Respectfully yours,	Sincerely yours,	1. Archdeacon Blank 2. Archdeacon Blank
Dean[1]	The Very Reverend William R. Blank, D.D. Dean of St. John's	Very Reverend Sir:	Dear Dean Blank:	Respectfully yours,	Sincerely yours,	1. Dean Blank or Dr. Blank 2. Dean Blank or Dr. Blank
Canon	The Reverend William R. Blank, D.D. Canon of St. Andrew's Cathedral	Reverend Sir:	Dear Canon Blank:	Respectfully yours,	Sincerely yours,	1. Canon Blank 2. Canon Blank
Protestant Minister	*With scholastic degree:* The Reverend William R. Blank, D.D., Litt.D. *or* The Reverend Dr. William R. Blank	Dear Dr. Blank:	Dear Dr. Blank:	Very truly yours,	Sincerely yours,	1. Dr. Blank 2. Dr. Blank
	Without scholastic degree: The Reverend William R. Blank	Dear Mr. Blank:	Dear Mr. Blank:	Very truly yours,	Sincerely yours,	1. Mr. Blank 2. Mr. Blank

1. Applies only to the head of a cathedral or of a theological seminary.

Church Dignitaries/Protestant Faith *continued*

Personage	Envelope and Inside Address (Add City, State, Zip)	Formal Salutation	Informal Salutation	Formal Close	Informal Close	1. Spoken Address 2. Informal Introduction or Reference
Episcopal Priest (High Church)	*With scholastic degree:* The Reverend William R. Blank, D.D., Litt.D. All Saint's Cathedral *or* The Reverend Dr. William R. Blank	Dear Dr. Blank:	Dear Dr. Blank:	Very truly yours,	Sincerely yours,	1. Dr. Blank 2. Dr. Blank
	Without scholastic degree: The Reverend William R. Blank St. Paul's Church	Dear Father Blank: *or* Dear Mr. Blank	Dear Father Blank: *or* Dear Mr. Blank:	Very truly yours,	Sincerely yours,	1. Father Blank *or* Mr. Blank 2. Father Blank *or* Mr. Blank

College and University Officials

Personage	Envelope and Inside Address (Add City, State, Zip)	Formal Salutation	Informal Salutation	Formal Close	Informal Close	1. Spoken Address 2. Informal Introduction or Reference
President of a College or University	*With a doctorate:* Dr. William R. Blank *or* William R. Blank, L.L.D., Ph.D. President Amherst College	Sir:	Dear Dr. Blank:	Very truly yours,	Sincerely yours,	1. Dr. Blank 2. Dr. Blank

College and University Officials *continued*

Personage	Envelope and Inside Address (Add City, State, Zip)	Formal Salutation	Informal Salutation	Formal Close	Informal Close	1. Spoken Address 2. Informal Introduction or Reference
President of a College or University	*Without a doctorate:* Mr. William R. Blank President Columbia University	Sir:	Dear President Blank:	Very truly yours,	Sincerely yours,	1. Mr. Blank 2. Mr. Blank *or* Mr. Blank, President of the College
	Catholic priest: The Reverend William R. Blank, S.J., D.D., Ph.D. President Fordham University	Sir:	Dear Dr. Blank:	Very truly yours,	Sincerely yours,	1. Doctor (Father) Blank 2. Doctor (Father) Blank
University Chancellor	Dr. William R. Blank Chancellor University of Alabama	Sir:	Dear Dr. Blank:	Very truly yours,	Sincerely yours,	1. Dr. Blank 2. Dr. Blank
Dean or Assistant Dean of a College or Graduate School	Dean (Assistant Dean) William R. Blank School of Law	Dear Sir: *or* Dear Dean Blank:	Dear Dean Blank:	Very truly yours,	Sincerely yours,	1. Dean (Assistant Dean) Blank 2. Dean (Assistant Dean)
	(If he holds a doctorate) Dr. William R. Blank Dean (Assistant Dean), School of Law University of Virginia	Dear Sir: *or* Dear Dean Blank:	Dear Dean Blank:			*or* Dr. Blank, the Dean (Assistant Dean) of the School of Law
Professor	Professor William R. Blank	Dear Sir: *or* Dear Professor Blank:	Dear Professor Blank:	Very truly yours,	Sincerely yours,	1. Professor (Dr.) Blank
	(If he holds a doctorate) Dr. William R. Blank *or* William R. Blank, Ph.D. Yale University	Dear Sir: *or* Dear Dr. (or Professor) Blank:	Dear Dr. (or Professor) Blank:			2. Professor (Dr.) Blank

College and University Officials *continued*

Personage	Envelope and Inside Address (Add City, State, Zip)	Formal Salutation	Informal Salutation	Formal Close	Informal Close	1. Spoken Address 2. Informal Introduction or Reference
Associate or Assistant Professor	Mr. William R. Blank *or* *(If he holds a doctorate)* Dr. William R. Blank *or* William R. Blank, Ph.D. Associate (Assistant) Professor Department of Romance Languages Williams College	Dear Sir: *or* Dear Professor Blank: Dear Sir: *or* Dear Dr. (or Professor) Blank:	Dear Professor Blank: Dear Dr. (or Professor) Blank:	Very truly yours,	Sincerely yours,	1. Professor (Dr.) Blank 2. Professor (Dr.) Blank
Instructor	Mr. William R. Blank *or* *(If he holds a doctorate)* Dr. William R. Blank *or* William R. Blank, Ph.D. Department of Economics University of California	Dear Sir: Dear Sir: *or* Dear Dr. Blank:	Dear Mr. Blank: Dear Dr. Blank:	Very truly yours,	Sincerely yours,	1. Mr. (Dr.) Blank 2. Mr. (Dr.) Blank

College and University Officials *continued*

Personage	Envelope and Inside Address (Add City, State, Zip)	Formal Salutation	Informal Salutation	Formal Close	Informal Close	1. Spoken Address 2. Informal Introduction or Reference
Chaplain of a College or University	Chaplain William R. Blank Trinity College *(If he holds a doctorate)* The Reverend William R. Blank, D.D. Chaplain Trinity College	Dear Chaplain Blank: *or* Dear Dr. Blank:	Dear Chaplain (Dr.) Blank:	Very truly yours,	Sincerely yours,	1. Chaplain Blank 2. Chaplain Blank *or* Dr. Blank

United Nations Officials[1]

Personage	Envelope and Inside Address (Add City, State, Zip)	Formal Salutation	Informal Salutation	Formal Close	Informal Close	1. Spoken Address 2. Informal Introduction or Reference
Secretary General	His Excellency, William R. Blank Secretary General of the United Nations	Excellency:[2]	Dear Mr. Secretary General:	Very truly yours,	Sincerely yours,	1. Mr. Blank *or* Sir 2. The Secretary General of the United Nations *or* Mr. Blank
Under Secretary	The Honorable William R. Blank Under Secretary of the United Nations The Secretariat United Nations	Sir:	Dear Mr. Under Secretary: *or* Dear Mr. Blank:	Very truly yours,	Sincerely yours,	1. Mr. Blank 2. Mr. Blank

1. The six principal branches through which the United Nations functions are The General Assembly, The Security Council, The Economic and Social Council, The Trusteeship Council, The International Court of Justice, and The Secretariat.
2. An American citizen should never be addressed as "Excellency."

United Nations Officials *continued*

Personage	Envelope and Inside Address (Add City, State, Zip)	Formal Salutation	Informal Salutation	Formal Close	Informal Close	1. Spoken Address 2. Informal Introduction or Reference
Foreign Representative (with ambassadorial rank)	His Excellency, William R. Blank Representative of Spain to the United Nations	Excellency:	Dear Mr. Ambassador:	Very truly yours,	Sincerely yours,	1. Mr. Ambassador *or* Mr. Blank 2. Mr. Ambassador *or* The Representative of Spain to the United Nations (The Ambassador or Mr. Blank)
United States Representative (with ambassadorial rank)	The Honorable William R. Blank United States Representative to the United Nations	Sir: *or* Dear Mr. Ambassador:	Dear Mr. Ambassador:	Very truly yours,	Sincerely yours,	1. Mr. Ambassador *or* Mr. Blank 2. Mr. Ambassador *or* The United States Representative to the United Nations (The Ambassador or Mr. Blank)

STANDARD PROOFREADING MARKS

∧	Make correction indicated in margin.
Stet	Retain crossed-out word or letter; let it stand.
Stet (dotted)	Retain words under which dots appear; write "Stet" in margin.
X	Appears battered; examine.
=	Straighten lines.
✓✓✓	Unevenly spaced; correct spacing.
‖	Line up; i.e., make lines even with other matter.
run in	Make no break in the reading; no paragraph.
no ¶	No paragraph; sometimes written "run in."
out-see copy	Here is an omission; see copy.
¶	Make a paragraph here.
tr	Transpose words or letters as indicated.
d	Take out matter indicated; delete.
delete	Take out character indicated and close up.
ℓ	Line drawn through a cap means lower case.
⊘	Upside down; reverse.
⌣	Close up; no space.
#	Insert a space here.
⊥	Push down this space.
☐	Indent line one em.
⸣	Move this to the left.
⸤	Move this to the right.
⌐	Raise to proper position.
⌣	Lower to proper position.

////	Hair space letters.
wf.	Wrong font; change to proper font.
Qu?	Is this right?
lc.	Set in lower case (small letters).
s.c.	Set in small capitals.
Caps	Set in capitals.
c&sc	Set in caps and small caps.
rom.	Change to roman.
ital.	Change to italic.
☰	Under letter or word means caps.
═	Under letter or word means small caps.
—	Under letter or word means italic.
∼∼∼	Under letter or word means boldface.
⋏	Insert comma.
⋎	Insert semicolon.
⋮	Insert colon.
⊙	Insert period.
/?/	Insert interrogation mark.
/!/	Insert exclamation mark.
-/	Insert hyphen.
∨	Insert apostrophe.
∨∨	Insert quotation marks.
⌄	Insert superior letter or figure.
∧	Insert inferior letter or figure.
[/]	Insert brackets.
(/)	Insert parentheses.
⟶	One-em dash.
⟶	Two-em parallel dash.
Ⓢ	Spell out.

CORRECTED GALLEY PROOFS

HOW TO CORRECT PROOF

s.c. It does not appear that the earliest printers had any method of correcting errors before the form was on the press. The learned learned correctors of the first two centuries of printing were not proof readers in our sense, they were rather what we should term office editors. Their labors were chiefly to see that the proof corresponded to the copy, but that the printed page was correct in its latinity, that the words were there, and that the sense was right. They cared but little about orthography, bad letters, or purely printers' errors, and when the text seemed to them wrong, they consulted fresh authorities or altered it on their own responsibility. Good proofs, in the modern sense, were impossible until professional readers were employed, men who had first a printer's education and then spent many years in the correction of proof. The orthography of English, which for the past century has undergone little change, was very fluctuating until after the publication of Johnson's Dictionary, and capitals, which have been used with considerable regularity for the past 80 years, were previously used on the miss or hit plan. The approach to regularity, so far as we have, may be attributed to the growth of a class of professional proof readers, and it is to them that we owe the correctness of modern printing. More errors have been found in the Bible than in any other one work. For many generations it was frequently the case that Bibles were brought out stealthily, from fear of governmental interference. They were frequently printed from imperfect texts and were often modified to meet the views of those who publised them. The story is related that a certain woman in Germany, who was the wife of a printer, and had become disgusted with the continual assertion of the superiority of man over woman which she had heard, hurried into the composing room while her husband was at supper and altered a sentence in the Bible, which he was printing, so that it read Narr instead of Herr, thus making the verse read "And he shall be thy fool" instead of "And he shall be thy lord." The word not was omitted by Barker, the King's printer in England in 1632, in printing the seventh commandment. He was fined £3,000 on this account.

TABLES OF WEIGHTS, MEASURES, AND VALUES

Long Measure

12 inches = 1 foot
3 feet = 1 yard
$5\frac{1}{2}$ yards or $16\frac{1}{2}$ feet = 1 rod
320 rods or 5,280 feet = 1 mile
1,760 yards = 1 mile
40 rods = 1 furlong
8 furlongs = 1 statute mile
3 miles = 1 league

Common Metric Equivalents

1 inch = 2.540 centimeters
1 foot = 30.480 centimeters
1 yard = 0.914 meters
1 rod = 5.029 meters
1 mile = 1.609 kilometers

Square Measure

144 square inches = 1 square foot
9 square feet = 1 square yard
$30\frac{1}{4}$ square yards = 1 square rod
$272\frac{1}{4}$ square feet = 1 square rod
40 square rods = 1 British rood
4 roods = 1 acre
160 square rods = 1 acre
640 acres = 1 square mile
43,560 square feet = 1 acre
4,840 square yards = 1 acre

Common Metric Equivalents

1 square inch = 6.451 square centimeters
1 square foot = 0.093 square meters
1 square yard = 0.836 square meters
1 square rod = 25.293 square meters
1 square mile = 2.590 square kilometers

Solid or Cubic Measure (Volume)

1,728 cubic inches = 1 cubic foot
27 cubic feet = 1 cubic yard
128 cubic feet = 1 cord of wood
24.75 cubic feet = 1 perch of stone
2,150.42 cubic inches = 1 standard bushel
231 cubic inches = 1 standard gallon
40 cubic feet = 1 ton (shipping)

Common Metric Equivalents

1 cubic inch = 16.387 cubic centimeters
1 cubic foot = 0.028 cubic meters
1 cubic yard = 0.765 cubic meters

Surveyors' Long Measure

7.92 inches = 1 link
25 links = 1 rod
4 rods or 100 links = 1 chain
80 chains = 1 mile

Surveyors' Square Measure

625 square links = 1 square rod
16 square rods = 1 square chain
10 square chains = 1 acre
640 acres = 1 square mile
36 square miles = 1 township

Circular or Angular Measure

60 seconds (60″) = 1 minute (′)
60 minutes (60′) = 1 degree (1°)
30 degrees = 1 sign
90 degrees = 1 right angle or quadrant
360 degrees = 1 circumference

Note: 1 degree at the equator = about 60 nautical miles.

Dry Measure

2 pints = 1 quart
8 quarts = 1 peck
4 pecks = 1 bushel
2,150.42 cubic inches = 1 bushel
1.2445 cubic feet = 1 bushel

Common Metric Equivalents

1 pint = 0.550 liters
1 quart = 1.101 liters
1 peck = 8.809 liters
1 bushel = 35.238 liters

Liquid Measure (Capacity)

4 gills = 1 pint
2 pints = 1 quart
4 quarts = 1 gallon
31.5 gallons = 1 barrel
2 barrels = 1 hogshead
1 gallon = 231 cubic inches
7.4805 gallons = 1 cubic foot
16 fluid ounces = 1 pint
1 fluid ounce = 1.805 cubic inches

Common Metric Equivalents

1 fluid ounce = 29.573 milliliters
1 gill = 118.291 milliliters
1 pint = 0.473 liters
1 quart = 0.946 liters
1 gallon = 3.785 liters

Mariners' Measure

6 feet = 1 fathom
100 fathoms = 1 cable's length as applied to distances or
intervals between ships

120 fathoms = 1 cable's length as applied to
                      marine wire cable
7.50 cable lengths = 1 mile
5,280 feet = 1 statute mile
6,080 feet = 1 nautical mile
1.15266 statute miles = 1 nautical or geographical mile
3 geographical miles = 1 league
60 geographical miles   = 1 degree of longitude on the
    or 69.16 statute miles   equator or 1 degree of meridian
360 degrees = 1 circumference

Note: A *knot* is not a measure of distance but a measure of speed, about 1 nautical mile per hour.

U.S.-British Weights and Measures

1 British bushel = 1.0320 U.S. (Winchester) bushels
1 U.S. bushel = 0.96894 British Imperial bushel
1 British quart = 1.03206 U.S. dry quarts
1 U.S. dry quart = 0.96894 British quart
1 British quart (or gallon) = 1.20095 U.S. liquid quarts (or gallons)
1 U.S. liquid quart (or gallon) = 0.83267 British quart (or gallon)

Avoirdupois Measure (Weight)

27.343 grains = 1 dram
16 drams = 1 ounce
16 ounces = 1 pound
25 pounds = 1 quarter
4 quarts = 1 hundredweight
100 pounds = 1 hundredweight
20 hundredweight = 1 ton
2,000 pounds = 1 short ton
2,240 pounds = 1 long ton

Common Metric Equivalents

1 grain = 0.0648 grams
1 dram = 1.772 grams
1 ounce = 28.350 grams
1 pound = 0.454 kilograms
1 hundredweight (short) = 45.359 kilograms
1 hundredweight (long) = 50.802 kilograms

Note: The avoirdupois measure is used for weighing all ordinary substances except precious metals, jewels, and drugs.

1 ton (short) = 0.907 metric ton
1 ton (long) = 1.016 metric tons

Troy Measure (Weight)

24 grains = 1 pennyweight
20 pennyweights = 1 ounce
12 ounces = 1 pound

Common Metric Equivalents

1 grain = 0.0648 grams
1 pennyweight = 1.555 grams
1 ounce = 31.103 grams
1 pound = 0.373 kilograms

Avoirdupois-Troy Measure

1 pound troy = 5,760 grains
1 pound avoirdupois = 7,000 grains
1 ounce troy = 480 grains
1 ounce avoirdupois = 437.5 grains
1 carat or karat = 3.2 troy grains
24 carat gold = pure gold

Apothecaries' Fluid Measure (Capacity)

60 minims = 1 fluid dram
8 fluid drams = 1 fluid ounce
16 fluid ounces = 1 pint
8 pints = 1 gallon

Apothecaries' Measure (Weight)

20 grains = 1 scruple
3 scruples = 1 dram
8 drams = 1 ounce
12 ounces = 1 pound

Common Metric Equivalents

1 grain = 0.0648 gram
1 scruple = 1.295 grams
1 dram = 3.887 grams

1 ounce = 31.103 grams
1 pound = 0.373 kilogram

Paper Measure

24 sheets = 1 quire
20 quires = 1 ream
2 reams = 1 bundle
5 bundles = 1 bale

Counting

12 units or things = 1 dozen
12 dozen or 144 units = 1 gross
12 gross = 1 great gross
20 units = 1 score

United States Money

10 mills = 1 cent
10 cents = 1 dime
10 dimes = 1 dollar
10 dollars = 1 eagle

Comparison of Centigrade and Fahrenheit Temperatures

0° C = Freezing Point = 32° F
10° C = 50° F
20° C = 68° F
30° C = 86° F
40° C = 104° F
50° C = 122° F
60° C = 140° F
70° C = 158° F
80° C = 176° F
90° C = 194° F
100° C = Boiling Point 212° F

Note: To convert from °F to °C, subtract 32 from °F and multiply by 0.555. To convert from °C to °F, multiply °C by 1.8 and add 32.

Land Measurements

1 rod = $16\frac{1}{2}$ feet
1 chain = 66 feet or 4 rods
1 mile = 320 rods, 80 chains, or 5,280 feet
1 square mile = $272\frac{1}{4}$ square feet
1 acre = 160 square rods
1 acre = $208\frac{3}{4}$ square feet
1 acre = 8 rods × 20 rods or any two numbers (of rods)
      whose product is 160
25 × 125 feet = 0.0717 acre
1 section = 640 acres

TABLES OF METRIC WEIGHTS, MEASURES, AND VALUES

Metric Prefixes and Multiplication Factors

Weight

1 *kilo*gram = 1,000 grams   1 *deci*gram = 0.1 gram
1 *hecto*gram = 100 grams   1 *centi*gram = 0.01 gram
1 *deka*gram = 10 grams   1 *milli*gram = 0.001 gram
1 gram = 1 gram

Length

1 *kilo*meter = 1,000 meters   1 *deci*meter = 0.1 meter
1 *hecto*meter = 100 meters   1 *centi*meter = 0.01 meter
1 *deka*meter = 10 meters   1 *milli*meter = 0.001 meter
1 meter = 1 meter

Volume

1 *hecto*liter = 100 liters   1 *centi*liter = 0.01 liter
1 *deka*liter = 10 liters   1 *milli*liter = 0.001 liter
1 liter = 1 liter

Metric Measurement Conversions

When You Know	Multiply By	To Find

Length

When You Know	Multiply By	To Find
inches (in.)	2.54	centimeters (cm)
feet (ft.)	30.00	centimeters (cm)
yards (yd.)	0.90	meters (m)

When You Know	Multiply By	To Find
miles (mi.)	1.60	kilometers (km)
millimeters(mm)	0.04	inches (in.)
centimeters (cm)	0.40	inches
meters (m)	3.30	feet (ft.)
meters (m)	1.10	yards (yd.)
kilometers (km)	0.60	miles (mi.)

Area

When You Know	Multiply By	To Find
square inches (in.²)	6.50	square centimeters (cm²)
square feet (ft.²)	0.09	square meters (m²)
square yards (yd.²)	0.80	square meters (m²)
square miles (mi.²)	2.60	square kilometers (km²)
acres	0.40	hectares (ha)
square centimeter (cm²)	0.16	square inches (in.²)
square meters (m²)	1.20	square yards (yd.²)
square kilometers (km.²)	0.40	square miles (mi.²)
hectares (ha (10,000 m²)	2.50	acres

Weight

When You Know	Multiply By	To Find
ounces (oz.)	28.00	grams (g)
pounds (lb.)	0.45	kilograms (kg)
short tons (2,000 lbs.)	0.90	tonnes (t)
long tons (2,240 lbs.)	1.01	tonnes (t)
grams (g)	0.035	ounces (oz.)
kilograms (kg)	2.20	pounds (lb.)
tonnes (1,000 kg)	1.10	short tons
tonnes (1,000 kg)	0.98	long tons

Volume

When You Know	Multiply By	To Find
teaspoons (tsp.)	5.00	milliliters (ml)
tablespoons (tbsp.)	15.00	milliliters (ml)
fluid ounces (fl. oz.)	30.00	milliliters (ml)
cups (c)	0.24	liters (l)
pints (pt.)	0.47	liters (l)
quarts (qt.)	0.95	liters (l)
gallons, U.S. (gal.)	3.80	liters (l)
gallons, Imp. (gal.)	4.50	liters (l)
cubic feet (ft.³)	0.028	cubic meters (m³)
cubic yards (yd.³)	0.76	cubic meters (m³)
milliliters (ml)	0.03	fluid ounces (fl. oz.)
liters (l)	2.10	pints (pt.)
liters (l)	1.06	quarts (qt.)
liters (l)	0.26	gallons, U.S. (gal.)
liters (l)	0.22	gallons, Imp. (gal.)
cubic meters (m³)	35.00	cubic feet (ft.³)
cubic meters (m³)	1.30	cubic yards (yd.³)

Metric Equivalents

Linear Measure

1 centimeter = 0.3937 inch
1 inch = 2.54 centimeters
1 decimeter = 3.937 inches = 0.328 foot
1 foot = 3.048 decimeters
1 meter = 39.37 inches = 1.0936 yards

1 yard = 0.9144 meter
1 dekameter = 1.9884 rods
1 rod = 0.5029 dekameter
1 kilometer = 0.62137 mile
1 mile = 1.6093 kilometers

Square Measure

1 square centimeter = 0.1550 square inch
1 square inch = 6.452 square centimeters
1 square decimeter = 0.1076 square foot
1 square foot = 9.2903 square decimeter
1 square meter = 1.196 square yards
1 square yard = 0.8361 square meter
1 acre = 160 square rods

1 square rod = 0.00625 acres
1 hectare = 2.47 acres
1 acre = 0.4047 hectare
1 square kilometer = 0.386 square mile
1 square mile = 2.59 square kilometers

Volume

1 cubic centimeter = 0.061 cubic inch
1 cubic inch = 16.39 cubic centimeters
1 cubic decimeter = 0.0353 cubic foot
1 cubic foot = 28.317 cubic yards
1 cubic yard = 0.7646 cubic meter
1 stere = 0.2759 cord
1 cord = 3.624 steres
1 liter = 0.908 quart dry = 1.0567 quarts liquid

1 quart dry = 1.101 liters
1 quart liquid = 0.9463 liter
1 dekaliter = 2.6417 gallons = 1.135 pecks
1 gallon = 0.3785 dekaliter
1 peck = 0.881 dekaliter
1 hectoliter = 2.8375 bushels
1 bushel = 0.3524 hectoliter

Weights

1 gram = 0.03527 ounce
1 ounce = 28.35 grams
1 kilogram = 2.2046 pounds

1 pound = 0.4536 kilogram
1 metric ton = 0.98421 English ton
1 English ton = 1.016 metric ton

Approximate Metric Equivalents

1 decimeter = 4 inches
1 liter = 1.06 quarts liquid = 0.9 quarts dry
1 meter = 1.1 yards
1 kilometer = 0.625 mile

1 hectoliter = 2.625 bushels
1 hectare = 2.5 acres
1 kilogram = 2.20 pounds
1 stere or cubic meter = 0.25 cord
1 metric ton = 2,200 pounds

MATHEMATICAL TABLES

Mathematical Signs and Symbols

— vinculum (above letters)

÷ geometrical proportion

−: difference, excess

‖ parallel

∦s parallels

≠ not parallels

| | absolute value

· multiplied by

: is to; ratio

÷ divided by

∴ therefore; hence

∵ because

:: proportion; as

≪ is dominated by

> greater than

⊏ greater than

≥ greater than or equal to

≧ greater than or equal to

≷ greater than or less than

≯ is not greater than

< less than

⊐ less than

≶ less than or greater than

≮ is not less than

≪ smaller than

≤ less than or equal to

≦ less than or equal to

≧ or ≥ greater than or equal to

≲ equal to or less than

≦ equal to or less than

≹ is not greater than equal to or less than

≳ equal to or greater than

≸ is not less than equal to or greater than

⊥ equilateral

⊥ perpendicular to

⊢ assertion sign

≐ approaches

≑ approaches a limit

≜ equal angles

≠ not equal to

≡ identical with

≢ not identical with

𝆏𝆏 score

≈ or ≒ nearly equal to

= equal to

∼ difference

≃ perspective to

≅ congruent to approximately equal

≏ difference between

⋄ equivalent to

(included in

) excluded from

⊆ is contained in

∪ logical sum or union

∩ logical product or intersection

√ radical

√ root

√ square root

∛ cube root

∜ fourth root

/ virgule; solidus; separatrix; shilling

± plus or minus

∓ minus or plus

√ fifth root

√ sixth root

π pi

ε base (2.718) of natural system of logarithms; epsilon

ε is a member of; dielectric constant; mean error; epsilon

+ plus

+ bold plus

− minus

− bold minus

× multiplied by

= bold equal

number

℀ per

% percent

∫ integral

| single bond

\ single bond

/ single bond

‖ double bond

\\ double bond

∕∕ double bond

⬡ benzene ring

∂ or δ differential; variation

∂ Italian differential

→ approaches limit of

∼ cycle sine

↰ horizontal integral

∮ contour integral

∝ variation; varies as

∏ product

Σ summation of; sum; sigma

! or ⌞ factorial product

Source: United States Government Printing Office Style Manual (Washington, D.C.: U.S. Government Printing Office, 1984).

Shortcuts in Multiplication

To multiply by					
1-1/4	add		and	divide by	8
1-2/3	"	0	"	"	6
2-1/2	"	0	"	"	4
3-1/3	"	0	"	"	3
5	"	0	"	"	2
6-1/4	"	00	"	"	16
6-2/3	"	00	"	"	15
8-1/3	"	00	"	"	12
12-1/2	"	00	"	"	8
14-2/7	"	00	"	"	7
16-2/3	"	00	"	"	6
25	"	00	"	"	4
31-1/4	"	000	"	"	32
33-1/3	"	00	"	"	3
50	"	00	"	"	2
66-2/3	"	000	"	"	15
83-1/3	"	000	"	"	12
125	"	000	"	"	8
166-2/3	"	000	"	"	6
250	"	000	"	"	4
333-1/3	"	000	"	"	3

For example, to multiply 5 times 2: add 0 to 2 (20) and divide by 2 (20 ÷ 2 = 10). Thus, $5 \times 2 = 10$.

Shortcuts in Division

To divide by					
1-1/4	multiply by	8	and	divide by	10
1-2/3	"	6	"	"	10
2-1/2	"	4	"	"	10
3-1/3	"	3	"	"	10
3-3/4	"	8	"	"	30
6-1/4	"	16	"	"	100
7-1/2	"	4	"	"	30
8-1/3	"	12	"	"	100
9-1/11	"	11	"	"	100
11-1/9	"	9	"	"	100
12-1/2		8			100
14-2/7	"	7	"	"	100
16-2/3	"	6	"	"	100
25	"	4	"	"	100
31-1/4	"	16	"	"	500
33-1/3	"	3	"	"	100
75	"	4	"	"	300
125	"	8	"	"	1,000
175	"	4	"	"	700
275	"	4	"	"	1,100

To divide by

375	multiply by	8	and	divide by	3,000
625	"	8	"	"	5,000
875	"	8	"	"	7,000

For example, to divide 5 by 6-1/4, multiply 5 times 16 (80) and divide by 100 (80 ÷ 100 = 0.80). Thus, 5 ÷ 6-1/4 = 0.80.

GREEK LETTER SYMBOLS

Name of Letter	Greek Alphabet	Name of Letter	Greek Alphabet	Name of Letter	Greek Alphabet
Alpha	A a α^1	Kappa	K κ	Tau	T τ
Beta	B β	Lambda	Λ λ	Upsilon	Υ υ
Gamma	Γ γ	Mu	M μ	Phi	Φ ϕ φ^1
Delta	Δ δ ∂^1	Nu	N ν	Chi	X χ
Episilon	E ϵ	Xi	Ξ ξ	Psi	Ψ ψ
Zeta	Z ζ	Omicron	O o	Omega	Ω ω
Eta	H η	Pi	Π π		
Theta	Θ θ ϑ^1	Rho	P ρ	1. Old style character.	
Iota	I ι	Sigma	Σ σ s^2	2. Final letter.	

INTEREST TABLES

Rate of Savings under Various Discount Terms

½%	10	days net 30 days	=	9%	per annum
1%	"	" " "	"	= 18%	" "
1½%	"	" " "	"	= 27%	" "
2%	"	" " "	"	= 36%	" "
2%	"	" " 60	"	= 14%	" "
2%	30	" " "	"	= 24%	" "
2%	"	" " 4 mos.	=	8%	" "
2%	40	" " 60 days	= 36%	" "
2%	70	" " 90 "	= 36%	" "
3%	10	" " 30 "	= 54%	" "
3%	"	" " 4 mos.	= 10%	" "
3%	30	" " 60 days	= 36%	" "
4%	10	" " " "	= 29%	" "
4%	"	" " 4 mos.	= 13%	" "
5%	"	" " 30 days	= 90%	" "
5%	"	" " 60 "	= 36%	" "
5%	"	" " 4 mos.	= 16%	" "
6%	"	" " 60 days	= 43%	" "
6%	"	" " 4 mos.	= 20%	" "
7%	"	" " " "	= 23%	" "
8%	"	" " " "	= 26%	" "
9%	"	" " 60 days	= 65%	" "
10%	"	" " 90 days	= 45%	" "

Time in Which Money Doubles Itself at Interest

Rate percent	Simple Interest		Compound Interest		
2	50 years		35 years	1 day	
2½	40 ″		28 ″	26 days	
3	33 ″	4 months	23 ″	164 ″	
3½	28 ″	208 days	20 ″	54 ″	
4	25 ″		17 ″	246 ″	
4½	22 ″	81 days	15 ″	273 ″	
5	20 ″		14 ″	75 ″	
6	16 ″	8 months	11 ″	327 ″	
7	14 ″	104 days	10 ″	89 ″	
8	12 ″	6 months	9 ″	2 ″	
9	11 ″	40 days	8 ″	16 ″	
10	10 ″		7 ″	100 ″	

Exact Number of Days between Dates

From Any Day Of	Jan.	Feb.	Mar.	Apr.	May	June	July	Aug.	Sept.	Oct.	Nov.	Dec.
					To the Same Day of the Next							
January	365	31	59	90	120	151	181	212	243	273	304	334
February	334	365	28	59	89	120	150	181	212	242	273	303
March	306	337	365	31	61	92	122	153	184	214	245	275
April	275	306	334	365	30	61	91	122	153	183	214	244
May	245	276	304	335	365	31	61	92	123	153	184	214
June	214	245	273	304	334	365	30	61	92	122	153	183
July	184	215	243	274	304	335	365	31	62	92	123	153
August	153	184	212	243	273	304	334	365	31	61	92	122
September	122	153	181	212	242	273	303	334	365	30	61	91
October	92	123	151	182	212	243	273	304	335	365	31	61
November	61	92	120	151	181	212	242	273	304	334	365	30
December	31	62	90	121	151	182	212	243	274	304	335	365

Simple Interest Tables

Interest on $100 at Various Rates for Various Periods

Days	5%	6%	7%	8%	9%	10%	11%	12%
1	0.0139	0.0167	0.0194	0.0222	0.0250	0.0278	0.0306	0.0333
2	.0278	.0333	.0389	.0444	.0500	.0556	.0611	.0667
3	.0417	.0500	.0583	.0667	.0750	.0833	.0917	.1000
4	.0556	.0667	.0778	.0889	.1000	.1111	.1222	.1333
5	.0694	.0833	.0972	.1111	.1250	.1389	.1528	.1667
6	.0833	.1000	.1167	.1333	.1500	.1667	.1833	.2000
7	.0972	.1167	.1361	.1556	.1750	.1945	.2139	.2333
8	.1111	.1333	.1556	.1778	.2000	.2222	.2445	.2667
9	.1250	.1500	.1750	.2000	.2250	.2500	.2750	.3000
10	.1389	.1667	.1944	.2222	.2500	.2778	.3056	.3333
20	.2778	.3333	.3889	.4444	.5000	.5556	.6111	.6667
30	.4167	.5000	.5833	.6667	.7500	.8333	.9167	1.0000
40	.5556	.6667	.7778	.8889	1.0000	1.1111	1.2222	1.3333
50	.6945	.8334	.9722	1.1111	1.2500	1.3889	1.5278	1.6667
60	.8333	1.0000	1.1667	1.3333	1.5000	1.6667	1.8334	2.0000
70	.9722	1.1667	1.3611	1.5555	1.7500	1.9445	2.1389	2.3333
80	1.111	1.3334	1.5555	1.7778	2.0000	2.2222	2.4445	2.6666
90	1.2500	1.5000	1.7500	2.0000	2.2500	2.5000	2.7500	3.0000
100	1.3889	1.6667	1.9444	2.2222	2.5000	2.7778	3.0556	3.3333

Interest on $100 at Various Rates for Various Periods

Days	13%	14%	15%	16%	17%	18%	19%	20%
1	0.0361	0.0388	0.0417	0.0444	0.0472	0.0501	0.0528	0.0556
2	.0722	.0778	.0834	.0888	.0944	.0999	.1056	.1112
3	.1083	.1166	.1251	.1332	.1417	.1500	.1583	.1668
4	.1445	.1556	.1668	.1776	.1889	.2001	.2111	.2224
5	.1805	.1944	.2082	.2224	.2361	.2499	.2639	.2776
6	.2167	.2334	.2499	.2668	.2833	.3000	.3167	.3332
7	.2528	.2722	.2916	.3112	.3306	.3501	.3695	.3888
8	.2889	.3112	.3333	.3556	.3778	.3999	.4222	.4444
9	.3250	.3500	.3750	.4000	.4250	.4500	.4750	.5000
10	.3611	.3888	.4167	.4444	.4722	.5001	.5278	.5556
20	.7222	.7778	.8334	.8888	.9444	.9999	1.0556	1.1112
30	1.0833	1.1666	1.2501	1.3334	1.4167	1.5000	1.5833	1.6668
40	1.4445	1.5556	1.6668	1.7778	1.8889	2.0001	2.1111	2.2224
50	1.8056	1.9444	2.0835	2.2222	2.3611	2.5002	2.6389	2.7780
60	2.1667	2.3334	2.4999	2.6666	2.8333	3.0000	3.1667	3.3332
70	2.5278	2.7222	2.9166	3.1110	3.3055	3.5001	3.6945	3.8888
80	2.8889	3.1110	3.3333	3.5556	3.7778	4.0002	4.2222	4.4444
90	3.2500	3.5000	3.7500	4.0000	4.2500	4.5000	4.7500	5.0000
100	3.6111	3.8888	4.1667	4.4444	4.7222	5.0001	5.2778	5.5556

FLOWCHART SYMBOLS

Program Flowcharting Symbols

Processing. Group of program instructions that perform a processing function within a program

Input/output. Any function of an input/output device that makes information available for processing, recording, processing information, tape positioning, and so on

Decision. Used to document points in a program where a branch to alternate paths is possible based on variable conditions

Program modification. Instruction(s) that change the sequence of a program

Predefined process. Process, or groups of operations, not specified elsewhere

Terminal. Beginning, end, or point of interruption in a program

Connector. Entry from or exit to another part of the program flowchart

Off-page connector. Used to designate entry to or exit from a page

Flow direction. Direction of processing or data flow

Annotation. Addition of descriptive comments or explanatory notes.

Source: Mary A. DeVries, *Secretary's Almanac and Fact Book* (Englewood Cliffs, N.J.: Prentice-Hall, Inc., 1985).
Note: A *program flowchart* is a diagram that describes a computer program in a series of steps.

System Flowcharting Symbols

Punched card. Punched cards including stubs

Perforated (punched) tape. Paper or plastic, chad or chadless

Document. Paper documents and reports

Magnetic tape.

Transmittal tape. Proof or adding machine tape or other batch-control information

Off-line storage. Of either paper, cards, or magnetic or punched tape

On-line storage. For example, drum or disk storage

Display. Information displayed by plotter or video

Manual input. Information supplied to or by a computer using an on-line device, for example a keyboard

Sorting and collating. Operation using sorting or collating equipment

Clerical or manual operation. Off-line operation not requiring mechanical assistance

Auxiliary operation. Machine operation supplementing main processing function

Keying operation. Operation using a key-driven device

Communication link. Automatic transmission of information from one location to another via communications lines

Source: Mary A. DeVries, *Secretary's Almanac and Fact Book* (Englewood Cliffs, N.J.: Prentice-Hall, Inc., 1985).
Note: A *system flowchart* is a diagram that shows the relationship among events in a data-processing system and describes the flow of data throughout the system.

U.S. AREA CODES AND TIME ZONES

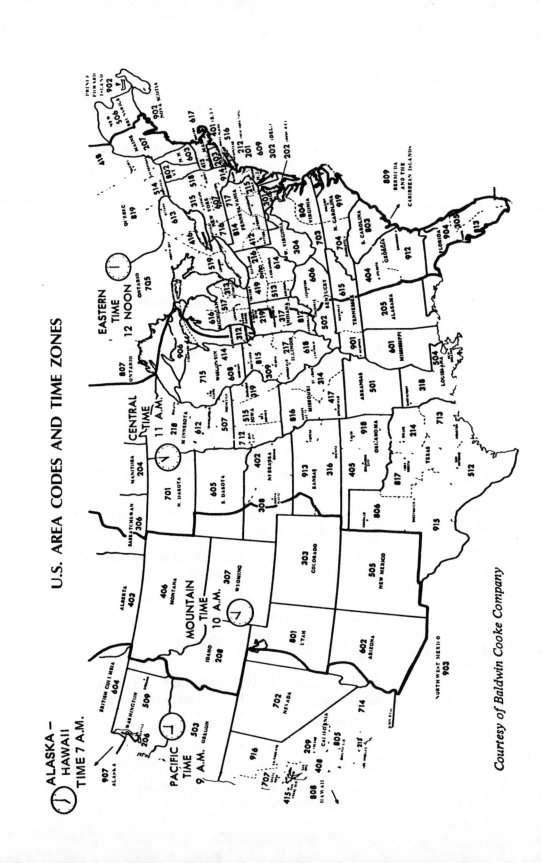

Courtesy of Baldwin Cooke Company

INTERNATIONAL TIME CHART

Aleutian Islands / Tutuila, Samoa	Alaska / Hawaiian Islands	Tahiti	San Francisco & Pacific Coast	Chicago / Central America (except Panama) / Mexico, Winnipeg	Bogota, Havana / Lima, Montreal / Bermuda / New York, Panama	Buenos Aires / Puerto Rico / Santiago / Lapaz, Asuncion	Rio, Santos / Sao Paulo	Iceland	Algiers, Lisbon / London, Paris / Madrid	G.M.T.	Bengasi, Berlin / Oslo, Rome, Tunis / Tripoli, Warsaw / Stockholm	Cairo, Capetown / Istanbul, Moscow	Ethiopia, Iraq / Madagascar	Bombay, Ceylon / New Delhi	Chungking / Chengtu, Kunming	Celobes, Hongkong / Manila, Shanghai	Korea, Japan / Adelaide	Brisbane, Guam / Melbourne, New Guinea, Sydney	Solomon Islands / New Caledonia	Wellington & Auckland
1:00pm	2:00pm	2:00pm	4:00pm	6:00pm	7:00pm	8:00pm	9:00pm	11:00pm	MIDNIGHT	0000	1:00am	2:00am	3:00am	5:30am	7:00am	8:00am	9:00am	10:00am	11:00am	11:30am
2:00pm	3:00pm	3:00pm	5:00pm	7:00pm	8:00pm	9:00pm	10:00pm	MINUIT	1:00am	0100	2:00am	3:00am	4:00am	6:30am	8:00am	9:00am	10:00am	11:00am	MIDI	12:30pm
3:00pm	4:00pm	4:00pm	6:00pm	8:00pm	9:00pm	10:00pm	11:00pm	1:00am	2:00am	0200	3:00am	4:00am	5:00am	7:30am	9:00am	10:00am	11:00am	Mediodia	1:00pm	1:30pm
4:00pm	5:00pm	5:00pm	7:00pm	9:00pm	10:00pm	11:00pm	Medianoche	2:00am	3:00am	0300	4:00am	5:00am	6:00am	8:30am	10:00am	11:00am	NOON	1:00pm	2:00pm	2:30pm
5:00pm	6:00pm	6:00pm	8:00pm	10:00pm	11:00pm	MIDNIGHT	1:00am	3:00am	4:00am	0400	5:00am	6:00am	7:00am	9:30am	11:00am	MIDI	1:00pm	2:00pm	3:00pm	3:30pm
6:00pm	7:00pm	7:00pm	9:00pm	11:00pm	MINUIT	1:00am	2:00am	4:00am	5:00am	0500	6:00am	7:00am	8:00am	10:30am	Mediodia	1:00pm	2:00pm	3:00pm	4:00pm	4:30pm
7:00pm	8:00pm	8:00pm	10:00pm	Medianoche	1:00am	2:00am	3:00am	5:00am	6:00am	0600	7:00am	8:00am	9:00am	11:30am	1:00pm	2:00pm	3:00pm	4:00pm	5:00pm	5:30pm
8:00pm	9:00pm	9:00pm	11:00pm	1:00am	2:00am	3:00am	4:00am	6:00am	7:00am	0700	8:00am	9:00am	10:00am	12:30pm	2:00pm	3:00pm	4:00pm	5:00pm	6:00pm	6:30pm
9:00pm	10:00pm	10:00pm	MIDNIGHT	2:00am	3:00am	4:00am	5:00am	7:00am	8:00am	0800	9:00am	10:00am	11:00am	1:30pm	3:00pm	4:00pm	5:00pm	6:00pm	7:00pm	7:30pm
10:00pm	11:00pm	11:00pm	1:00am	3:00am	4:00am	5:00am	6:00am	8:00am	9:00am	0900	10:00am	11:00am	NOON	2:30pm	4:00pm	5:00pm	6:00pm	7:00pm	8:00pm	8:30pm
11:00pm	Medianoche	MINUIT	2:00am	4:00am	5:00am	6:00am	7:00am	9:00am	10:00am	1000	11:00am	MIDI	1:00pm	3:30pm	5:00pm	6:00pm	7:00pm	8:00pm	9:00pm	9:30pm
MIDNIGHT	1:00am	1:00am	3:00am	5:00am	6:00am	7:00am	8:00am	10:00am	11:00am	1100	Mediodia	1:00pm	2:00pm	4:30pm	6:00pm	7:00pm	8:00pm	9:00pm	10:00pm	10:30pm
1:00am	2:00am	2:00am	4:00am	6:00am	7:00am	8:00am	9:00am	11:00am	NOON	1200	1:00pm	2:00pm	3:00pm	5:30pm	7:00pm	8:00pm	9:00pm	10:00pm	11:00pm	11:30pm
2:00am	3:00am	3:00am	5:00am	7:00am	8:00am	9:00am	10:00am	MIDI	1:00pm	1300	2:00pm	3:00pm	4:00pm	6:30pm	8:00pm	9:00pm	10:00pm	11:00pm	MINUIT	12:30am
3:00am	4:00am	4:00am	6:00am	8:00am	9:00am	10:00am	11:00am	1:00pm	2:00pm	1400	3:00pm	4:00pm	5:00pm	7:30pm	9:00pm	10:00pm	11:00pm	Medianoche	1:00am	1:30am
4:00am	5:00am	5:00am	7:00am	9:00am	10:00am	11:00am	Mediodia	2:00pm	3:00pm	1500	4:00pm	5:00pm	6:00pm	8:30pm	10:00pm	11:00pm	MIDNIGHT	1:00am	2:00am	2:30am
5:00am	6:00am	6:00am	8:00am	10:00am	11:00am	NOON	1:00pm	3:00pm	4:00pm	1600	5:00pm	6:00pm	7:00pm	9:30pm	11:00pm	MINUIT	1:00am	2:00am	3:00am	3:30am
6:00am	7:00am	7:00am	9:00am	11:00am	MIDI	1:00pm	2:00pm	4:00pm	5:00pm	1700	6:00pm	7:00pm	8:00pm	10:30pm	Medianoche	1:00am	2:00am	3:00am	4:00am	4:30am
7:00am	8:00am	8:00am	10:00am	Mediodia	1:00pm	2:00pm	3:00pm	5:00pm	6:00pm	1800	7:00pm	8:00pm	9:00pm	11:30pm	1:00am	2:00am	3:00am	4:00am	5:00am	5:30am
8:00am	9:00am	9:00am	11:00am	1:00pm	2:00pm	3:00pm	4:00pm	6:00pm	7:00pm	1900	8:00pm	9:00pm	10:00pm	12:30am	2:00am	3:00am	4:00am	5:00am	6:00am	6:30am
9:00am	10:00am	10:00am	NOON	2:00pm	3:00pm	4:00pm	5:00pm	7:00pm	8:00pm	2000	9:00pm	10:00pm	11:00pm	1:30am	3:00am	4:00am	5:00am	6:00am	7:00am	7:30am
10:00am	11:00am	11:00am	1:00pm	3:00pm	4:00pm	5:00pm	6:00pm	8:00pm	9:00pm	2100	10:00pm	11:00pm	MIDNIGHT	2:30am	4:00am	5:00am	6:00am	7:00am	8:00am	8:30am
11:00am	Mediodia	MIDI	2:00pm	4:00pm	5:00pm	6:00pm	7:00pm	9:00pm	10:00pm	2200	11:00pm	MINUIT	1:00am	3:30am	5:00am	6:00am	7:00am	8:00am	9:00am	9:30am
NOON	1:00pm	1:00pm	3:00pm	5:00pm	6:00pm	7:00pm	8:00pm	10:00pm	11:00pm	2300	Medianoche	1:00am	2:00am	4:30am	6:00am	7:00am	8:00am	9:00am	10:00am	10:30am
1:00pm	2:00pm	2:00pm	4:00pm	6:00pm	7:00pm	8:00pm	9:00pm	11:00pm	MIDNIGHT	2400	1:00am	2:00am	3:00am	5:30am	7:00am	8:00am	9:00am	10:00am	11:00am	11:30am

INTERNATIONAL TIME DIFFERENTIALS

To determine STANDARD TIME overseas
add (+) to or subtract (-) from
EASTERN STANDARD TIME as indicated:

	E.S.T.		E.S.T.		E.S.T.
Afghanistan	+9½	Finland	+7	Norway	+6
Albania	+6	Formosa	+13	Pakistan	+10 (5)*
Algeria	+6	France	+6	Panama	0
Argentina	+2	Germany	+6	Paraguay	+1
Aruba	+½	Ghana	+5	Peru	0
Australia	+15 (1)*	Great Britain	+5	Philippines	+13
Austria	+6	Greece	+7	Poland	+6 (6)*
Azores	+3	Guatemala	-1	Portugal	+5
Belgian Congo	+6 (2)*	Haiti	0	Puerto Rico	+1
Belgium	+6	Hawaii	-5	Rhodesia	+7
Bermuda	+1	Hungary	+6	Roumania	+7
Bolivia	+1	Iceland	+4	Salvador (El)	-1
Borneo (Br)	+13	India	+10½	Saudi Arabia	+8 (7)*
Brazil	+2 (3)*	Iran	+8½	Singapore	+12½
Bulgaria	+7	Iraq	+8	Spain	+6
Burma	+11½	Irish Republic	+5	Surinam	+1½
Canal Zone	0	Israel	+7	Sweden	+6
Ceylon	+10½	Italy	+6	Switzerland	+6
Chile	+1	Japan	+14	Syria	+7
China	+13 (4)*	Korea	+13½	Thailand	+12
Colombia	0	Lebanon	+7	Tunisia	+6
Costa Rica	-1	Luxembourg	+6	Turkey	+7
Cuba	0	Madagascar	+8	Union of South Africa	+7
Curacao	+½	Malaya	+12½	USSR	+8 (8)*
Czechoslovakia	+6	Morocco	+5	Uruguay	+2
Denmark	+6	Netherlands	+6	Venezuela	+½
Dominican Republic	0	Netherlands Antilles	+½	Vietnam	+12
Ecuador	0	Newfoundland	+1½	Virgin Islands	+1
Egypt	+7	New Zealand	+17	Yugoslavia	+6
Ethiopia	+8	Nicaragua	-1		

Note: (1)* Brisbane, Canberra, Melbourne,
New South Wales, Sydney, Queensland.
(2)* Leopoldville.
(3)* Rio de Janeiro, Sao Paulo, Santos.
(4)* Hong Kong, Peiping, Shanghai, Tientsin.
(5)* Karachi   (6)* Warsaw   (7)* Djeddah   (8)* Moscow

Chapter 19

Glossary of Important Business Terms

BUSINESS LAW

Abrogation. Annulling or repealing a law by an authoritative act.

Acceleration clause. A section of or statement in a contract that makes an entire debt become due and payable immediately when some condition of the contract is breached.

Acknowledgment. Signing a legal instrument and declaring before an authorized official such as a notary public that you executed the instrument.

Affidavit. A written statement sworn to, by the person making it, before someone officially authorized to administer an oath.

Allegation. A statement made by someone who claims it can be proved as a fact.

Allonge. A piece of paper attached to a negotiable instrument that provides space to write endorsements when there is no room on the instrument itself.

Answer. A defendant's formal written response, signed by his or her attorney, to charges and demands made in a plantiff's formal written complaint.

Antitrust laws. Laws to protect trade from monopolies and to prohibit conspiracies and trusts that restrain interstate commerce.

Assignment. The transfer of property or rights to property from one party to another.

Attachment. Taking or seizing a debtor's property to place it under control of a court.

Attestation. Witnessing the signing of a written instrument and signing it yourself to signify that you so witnessed that act.

Bailment. Delivery of property by the owner to another person for temporary care.

Bill of sale. A formal document given by a seller to a buyer as evidence of the transfer of property the bill describes.

Binder. A temporary agreement or insurance contract providing coverage until the actual policy is written.

Blue-sky laws. Laws regulating and supervising stock sales and similar transactions to protect the public from fraudulent deals.

Breach of contract. Failure to perform some act a contract calls for.

Breach of warranty. Failure of a vendor to provide what a warranty promises.

Caveat emptor (Latin). "Let the buyer beware"; a common law doctrine that imposes on buyers the duty of examining goods before buying them.

Certiorari (Latin). "To make sure or to be made certain about something"; a writ issued by a superior court directing an inferior court to send the record of a particular case.

Chattel. Any property other than land and its improvements.

Chose in action (French). A right to recover a debt or receive damages that can be enforced in court.

Civil law. Law handed down from Roman laws under Justinian.

Common law. Law derived from the decision of judges based on accepted custom and tradition.

Complaint. The formal written statement of a plaintiff in a civil lawsuit.

Constructive. That which legally amounts to an act or is implied, even if the act itself has not actually been performed.

Deed. A formal written instrument by which one person transfers title to real property to another person.

Del credere (Italian). An agent who sells goods for someone and guarantees that the buyer will pay for the goods.

Disaffirmance. The repudiation of prior consent.

Earnest money. A buyer's deposit to show good faith and to bind a sale.

Eminent domain. The right of government to take private property for public use or the public welfare.

Endorsement. Writing your name, with or without additional words or a negotiable instrument or allonge.

Equity. In the legal sense, that which constitutes fairness or fair dealing in a particular situation.

Escrow. Money, property, or documents held by someone, possibly a third party, until an act is performed by another person.

Estoppel. A barrier that stops someone from taking a certain position that is inconsistent with previous acts or statements.

Ex parte (Latin). Done by or for one party.

Fee simple. Absolute ownership of real property.

Garnishment. A legal proceeding taken by a creditor, following judgment against a debtor, to compel a third party to pay money to the creditor instead of the debtor.

Guaranty. A contract that guarantees that one party will be responsible to another for payment of a debt or performance of a duty by a third party.

Holder in due course. The legal holder of a negotiable instrument who acquired it in good faith, believing it to be valid.

Indemnity. An express or implied contract to compensate another party for possible or actual loss or damage.

Indenture. A formal written instrument, such as a lease, that defines reciprocal rights and duties.

Interstate/intrastate commerce. *Interstate* commerce is any business transaction conducted directly or indirectly across state boundaries; *intrastate* commerce is any business transaction conducted entirely within a state.

Joint and several. Both together and individually; for example, two parties might be held liable for something either individually or together, depending on the option of a third party.

Libel and slander. *Libel* is written or published defamation or injury to the reputation of another person. *Slander* is oral defamation of another person in the presence of a third party.

Lien. A charge or claim against property that makes the property serve as security until some obligation is discharged.

Liquidated damages. An amount that parties to a contract agree on to satisfy the loss resulting from a breach of contract.

Mechanic's lien. A workman's legal claim to property until monies due to him are paid by the owner.

Option. An agreement whereby one person pays a certain amount of money for the right to buy or sell something within a specified time.

Patent. A right granted by the federal government to make, use, and sell an invention during a specified period.

Personal property. A legal right or interest in something movable, not land or anything permanently attached to land.

Pledge. Placing personal property with a lender as security for a debt until the debt is paid.

Power of attorney. A written instrument giving someone authorization to act for the person signing the document.

Privity. Close, mutual, or successive relationship to the same right of property or the power to enforce a promise or warranty.

Protest. A formal certificate attesting someone's refusal to pay a negotiable instrument you presented for payment.

Quasi (Latin). "Sort of" or "analagous to," as a quasi-corporation.

Quiet title, action to. Proceedings to establish clear title to land.

Quo warranto (Latin). "With what authority"; a proceeding that questions a person's right to do something.

Real property. Land and anything that is attached to it.

Rescission. An action whereby a court annuls or cancels a contract.

Restrictive covenant. A clause in an agreement that limits the action of one of the parties to the agreement.

Slander. See **Libel and slander.**

Statute of frauds. State laws that require certain contracts to be signed and in writing to be valid.

Statute of limitations. State laws that set a time limit within which legal action may be brought.

Statutory law. Rules brought into law by legislative action.

Substantive law. Law that concerns rights and duties, such as contract law, as opposed to procedural law, such as law of pleading.

Summary proceeding. A short form of legal proceeding in which established procedure is disregarded.

Summons. A written notice that informs a defendant that a lawsuit is being brought against him or her.

Supplementary proceeding. The legal procedure by which a judgment creditor conducts an in-court examination of the debtor and others to determine if any assets are available to pay the debt.

Tenancy in common. An estate held by two or more persons by separate and distinct titles but with unity of possession.

Tenancy by the entirety. An estate held by husband and wife by title acquired jointly after marriage.

Tort. A civil wrong done to another person that does not involve a contract, for example, libel.

Trust. Holding property and applying it and its income for the benefit of someone named by the person who created the trust.

Ultra vires (Latin). "Without power"; outside the scope of or in excess of something.

Uniform laws. Similar laws adopted by various states.

Waiver. Voluntarily giving up a right.

Warranty. A promise or affirmation made by a seller to induce a buyer to purchase something.

Without recourse. A phrase used by an endorser of a negotiable instrument meaning that he or she will not be liable if the other party refuses to accept payment.

Workmens compensation. Laws giving protection against injury and death occurring on the job.

Writ. A court order or judge's order authorizing or compelling someone to do something.

"Yellow-dog" contract. An illegal employment contract in which the employee agrees not to join a union.

BUSINESS MANAGEMENT

Affiliated companies. Companies that are related by a community of interest or by way of a parent corporation's ownership of their stock.

Agency. A relationship in which one person authorizes another to act in his or her behalf.

Alien corporation. A business organization incorporated outside the United States and its territories.

Annual report. A report prepared by a corporation at the close of its fiscal year containing audited financial statements and other information.

Arbitration. The submission of a dispute to a third party whose decision is binding.

Articles of incorporation. The document, also known as *certificate of* *incorporation* or *charter,* that creates a private corporation and states what the organization is authorized to do.

Bankruptcy. The procedure by which the property of a debtor is taken over by a receiver or trustee for the benefit of the creditors, thereby relieving the debtor of all debts.

Batching. Processing a group of documents at one time together as a unit.

Bill of lading. A document giving evidence of a contract between a shipper and carrier for the transport and delivery of goods.

Business corporation. A corporation organized to conduct business for profit.

Bylaws. The rules adopted by an organization to establish and regulate its conduct and that of its stockholders, directors, and officers.

Cartel. A close association of companies engaged in similar business.

Certificate of incorporation. See **Articles of incorporation.**

Charitable corporation. A corporation, also known as an *eleemosynary corporation,* that is organized and operated for charitable or nonprofit purposes.

Charter. See **Articles of incorporation.**

Close corporation. A corporation whose capital stock is held by a limited group and not sold to the general public.

Conditional sale. An installment sale in which a buyer gives the seller a promissory note, and title to the goods remains with the seller until all payments have been made.

Consignment. Transferring goods to another party for shipment or sale but retaining ownership and title to the consigned goods.

Consolidation. Combining individual corporations into a new corporation.

Corporation. A legally established organization created to carry out some specified purpose.

Corporation service company. A company that provides services for corporations that they are unable to provide or do not wish to provide for themselves.

Cumulative voting. A system of voting for directors in which each share of stock, or each person, has as many votes as there are directors to be selected.

Domestic corporation. A corporation doing business in the state in which it was incorporated.

Downtime. A temporary halt in machine production or worker performance resulting from equipment breakdown or some other condition affecting normal operations.

Dummy incorporators. Persons who initially serve as incorporators to set up a corporation in a particular state and then drop out.

Eleemosynary corporation. See **Charitable corporation.**

Ergonomics. Human engineering, or the science of effective human-machine interaction.

Featherbedding. The illegal practice of paying for services not performed or not to be performed.

Feedback. Using output from a machine, process, or system as input for another machine, process, or system.

First-in—first out (FIFO). A method of valuing goods that assumes those first acquired are those to be sold first.

Foreign corporation. A corporation doing business in a state other than the one in which it was incorporated.

Holding company. A company organized to control other companies by owning and holding their stock.

Incorporated partnership. See **Close corporation.**

Individual proprietorship. See **Proprietorship, sole.**

Interested director. A director who has a personal interest, which may cause a biased vote, in some matter potentially profitable for the corporation.

Interlocking directorates. Boards of directors of two or more organizations that have one or more directors in common.

Investment company. A company that invests in other companies' securities and sells its own shares to the public.

Joint adventure (venture). An association of two or more persons in a joint business endeavor without the usual requirements of a formal partnership.

Joint stock company. A company created by an agreement of the parties and similar to a corporation except that all owners are liable for company debts.

Last-in—first out (LIFO). A method of valuing goods that assumes those last acquired are those to be sold first.

Limited partnership. A partnership in which a partner's liability for the firm's debts is limited to the amount of his or her investment.

Liquidation. Distributing assets of a dissolved corporation to the stockholders after payment of all corporate debts.

Local-area network (LAN). A system in which interoffice electronic equipment is connected (usually by direct wiring) to form a local network.

Markdown. Reducing the price of goods below the original retail price.

Markup. The amount of the selling price of goods above cost or in addition to the original retail price.

Massachusetts trust. A business association set up in the form of a trust, with permanent trustees similar to directors and beneficiaries similar to stockholders.

Merchandising, retail. Buying merchandise, controlling it, and selling it to consumers.

Merger. Uniting one or more corporations with another one that retains its identity, so that the others become part of the existing corporation.

Merit rating. The change in state unemployment insurance tax according to a company's stabilization of employment, with higher rates imposed on employers with heavy labor turnovers.

Micrographics. The process of reducing information to a microform medium (e.g., film) for storage and retrieval.

Moneyed corporation. A corporation that deals in money or lending of money.

Nonprofit corporation. A corporation organized for some purpose other than making money for its members.

Nonstock corporation. Any corporation other than a corporation that has capital stock, such as an educational institution.

On-line. Generally, the input of data into a terminal that is directly connected to the central processor of a computer.

Palletization. Shipping goods on lightweight wooden platforms to enable the shipment of several units as one large unit.

Parent corporation. A corporation that owns the majority of the stock of another corporation and fully controls it.

Partnership. An agreement between two or more persons to conduct business together for profit as co-owners, with each owner fully liable for all partnership debts.

Preemptive right. The right of existing stockholders to purchase their relative share of new stock to retain their interest in the corporation.

Promoters. Persons who form a new corporation and occupy a position of trust until the stockholders elect an independent board of directors.

Proprietorship, sole. A form of business organization in which ownership is held by one person.

Public corporation. A corporation organized by the federal or a state government to serve as a governmental agency.

Public service corporation. A corporation, also known as a *public utility company,* that supplies public services such as power and is regulated by a public service commission.

Public utility corporation. See **Public service corporation.**

Pyramiding. The process by which a few persons who control a top holding company gain control over vast properties by investing relatively small amounts in a number of interrelated companies.

Quasi-public corporation. See **Public service corporation.**

Registered office. An office set up by a corporation in a state in which it does business or where it is only nominally incorporated to meet that state's statutory requirements.

Reprographics. The facsimile reproduction of documents.

Resident agent. An employee or agent who resides in a state where a corporation is incorporated but only nominally in residence in order to perform the services required by the state's statutes.

Retailing. See **Merchandising, retail.**

Rights. An existing stockholder's right to purchase additional shares of stock at a stipulated price before a certain date.

Silent partner. A partner who has no voice in the partnership management but is fully responsible for the debts of the business.

Stock. Identical units called *shares* that represent ownership in a corporation.

Stock certificate. The written evidence of shares of ownership in a corporation.

Stock corporation. A corporation that has its ownership divided into shares of stock and is authorized to distribute to the holders of this stock proportional amounts of profits in the form of dividends.

Stock insurance company. An insurance company organized like a business corporation, with net earnings distributed to stockholders.

Stock ledger. A permanent record of each stockholder's interest in the corporation and all transfers of the stockholder's interest.

Subsidiary. A company controlled by a holding company or parent corporation that owns all or a majority of its stock.

Telecommunication. Communication of information over a distance between individuals or terminals.

Telecommuting. The process of working at home and transmitting information to the office by computer and telecommunications channel (e.g., telephone line).

Telematics. Derived from the French Term, *télématique,* for information technology.

Time sharing. Use of a device for two or more purposes or by two or more customers.

Trademark. A mark, symbol, or design that legally identifies a company or its products.

Transfer agent. A person, bank, or trust company that maintains a corporation's stock ledger, records all stock transfers, and ensures that the transfer is properly executed.

Vetoing stock. A class of stock that has no right to elect directors but carries the power to vote on certain other matters.

Voting trust. A method of concentrating a company's control in the hands of a few people through an agreement whereby stockholders transfer their stock and voting rights for a specified period.

Voting trust certificate. A certificate of interest given to stockholders in a voting trust who have agreed to transfer their stock and voting rights to the trustees for a specified period.

ACCOUNTING AND FINANCE

Accounts payable. The amount an individual or a business owes to creditors for merchandise and services purchased on open account.

Accounts receivable. The amount due to an individual or a business from customers that purchased merchandise or services on open account.

Accrual accounting. A method of accounting that allocates income and expenses to the period to which they apply regardless of whether the income was actually received or the expenses actually paid.

Ajustment entries. Journal entries made at the end of an accounting period to correct errors and assign income and expenses to the correct period.

Amortization. The gradual reduction of a debt until it is extinguished by a series of periodic payments to a creditor.

Annuity. A series of periodic payments made to a named person(s) for a certain number of years or for life.

Assets. Anything of value that is owned by a business or an individual.

Audit. An examination of accounting records to verify the assets, liabilities, and capital of a business as of a certain date and to verify its financial transactions during the fiscal period just ended.

Balance sheet. A detailed statement of the assets, liabilities, and capital (net worth) of a business organization on a given date.

Bank draft. A check drawn by one bank against funds deposited to its account in another bank.

Bill of exchange. A written document issued and signed by one party that requires another party (the addressee) to pay a specified amount to a third party.

Book value. The price of assets as reported on a financial statement.

Books of original entry. An accounting book such as a journal in which each transaction is first recorded.

Capital. In accounting, the excess of assets over liabilities; in a corporation, capital is the organization's net worth.

Capital stock. In accounting, an account that shows the amount received from stock sales regarded as legal capital; in a corporation, capital stock is evidence of ownership in the form of certificates.

Capitalization. In accounting, the total accounting value of capital stock, paid-in capital in excess of par value, and borrrowed capital in a corporation; the total amount of its securities outstanding in the form of capital stock and long-term bonds.

Cash accounting. A method of accounting that records income at the time it is actually received and expenses at the time they are actually paid.

Cash disbursements journal. An accounting book in which each payment is initially recorded.

Cash journal. An accounting book in which all transactions are initially recorded.

Cash receipts journal. An accounting book in which each receipt of cash (e.g., bank deposits) is recorded.

Certificates of deposit. Written evidence that a specified sum of money is deposited on interest for a certain period.

Circulating capital. See **Working capital.**

Closing entries. Entries in a journal at the end of an accounting period to transfer income and expense account balances to the balance sheet accounts.

Collateral. Something of value pledged to a lender to secure the repayment of a loan.

Common stock. Evidence of unlimited interest in a corporation's profits and assets.

Control account. A general ledger account that summarizes the information of a subsidiary ledger.

Credit. In accounting, the entry in double-entry bookkeeping that records increases in the capital, income, and liability accounts and decreases in the asset accounts.

Cross-footing. Totaling the columns in books of accounts.

Current assets. Assets that will be realized or converted within an accounting period.

Current capital. See **Working capital.**

Current liabilities. Debts and obligations that are met within the accounting period by using current assets or incurring additional liabilities.

Debit. The entry in double-entry bookkeeping that increases asset and expense accounts and decreases capital and liability accounts.

Demand deposits. Deposits payable to the depositor at any time desired.

Depreciation. Periodic loss of value of limited-life assets due to wear and tear, obsolescence, and so on.

Double-entry bookkeeping. A system of recording each transaction twice, as a debit and as a credit.

Draft. See **Bill of exchange.**

Expense account. A record of someone's expenses during a specified period for a specified purpose.

Financial statement. A summary of financial data, such as a balance sheet, prepared from the accounting records.

Fiscal year. The one-year accounting period (any twelve successive months) of business operations.

Fixed assets. Permanent assets such as land and buildings.

Footing. See **Cross-footing.**

General ledger. The accounting book in which all financial transactions are finally summarized in separate accounts (except those kept in a subsidiary or private ledger).

Gross income. The total income an individual or business enterprise receives before any deductions are taken.

Gross profit. The excess of income over the cost of merchandise sold and the expense of doing business.

Imprest fund. See **Petty cash.**

Income statement. A summary of the income and expenses of a business that shows the net profit or loss in a specified accounting period.

Individual retirement program (IRA). A long-term savings program allowing tax-deductible contributions to a personal interest-bearing account, until money is withdrawn and taxed after retirement.

Installment sale. A contract establishing equal payments, or installments, at regular intervals until a debt is fully paid.

Intangible assets. Items of value other than tangible property or the direct right to tangible property, such as patents and franchises.

Journal. Any accounting book in which each financial transaction is initially recorded.

Ledger. A book of final entry in which financial transactions are summarized in separate accounts.

Liabilities. The debts and obligations of a business.

Negotiable instrument. A written instrument signed by the person who draws it that contains an unconditional promise or order to pay a certain sum of money.

Net assets. The excess of the book value of assets (the price as reported on a financial statement) over liabilities.

Net income. Gross, or total, income derived from performing services minus all expenses involved in performing those services.

Net profit. Gross, or total, income derived from the sale of merchandise minus all expenses involved in doing business and minus income taxes.

Net worth. Book value of the assets of a business minus liabilities.

No-par stock. Stock that has no face value on the stock certificate.

Notes payable. A general ledger account showing the amount of promissory notes, or the liability of notes, given by the business.

Notes receivable. A general ledger account showing the amount of negotiable promissory notes a business received from its customers and other debtors.

Overhead. General and administrative expenses of a business such as rent and insurance.

Over-the-counter. A method of trading securities without using any recognized exchange service.

Paid-in capital in excess of par value. Contributions of capital by stockholders that are not credited to capital stock.

Par value stock. Stock that has been given a face value on the stock certificate.

Payroll. The record of all employees wages, salaries, deductions, and net pay for a specified period.

Payroll journal. A book where all payroll information is systematically recorded.

Petty cash. A limited amount of cash kept on hand for disbursements too small to justify the use of checks.

Portfolio. An individual's or organization's holdings of stocks and bonds.

Posting. The process of transferring entries from journals to ledger accounts.

Preferred stock. Stock that is entitled to earnings before common stock payments.

Profit and loss statement. See **Income statement.**

Puts and calls. Options to buy or sell a certain number of securities at a specified price within a specified time.

Sight draft. A commercial draft that is payable on presentation.

Single-entry bookkeeping. A method of accounting that records transactions with debtors and creditors as a single entry rather than two equal debit and credit entries.

Straight loan. A loan for a specific number of years, at a specific interest rate, payable in full at maturity without advance payments of principal.

Subsidiary journal. A specialized accounting book such as a Petty Cash Journal used to record similar transactions that occur regularly and frequently.

Subsidiary ledger. A specialized accounting ledger such as a Plant and Equipment Ledger used to summarize similar journal entries.

Time deposits. Deposited funds that a customer may withdraw at a specified date, for example, thirty days from the date of deposit.

Trial balance. Listing debit and credit balances taken from ledger accounts and totaling them to prove that total debits equal total credits.

Usury. Lending or receiving money at more than the legal rate of interest allowed by law.

Variable annuity. An annuity contract that provides for payments in units of income that vary from time to time.

Working capital. In accounting, the excess of current assets over current liabilities; in a business sense, the capital an organization or individual keeps to pay for daily working needs.

Yield. The annual rate of return on an investment in securities, computed as a percentage of the amount invested.

Index

Abbreviations
  alphabetizing, 16
  apostrophes and, 507
  capitalization of, 512–13
    common abbreviations, 513
    degrees/titles, 512
    initials, 512
    one-letter, 512
    time/years, 512–13
  plural spellings, 478
  state/territory abbreviations
    traditional, 566–68
    two-letter, 566–68
  table of, 540–77
    academic degrees, 560–62
    computer terms/acronyms, 570–77
    general abbreviations, 540–58
    months/days, 559
    organizations, 563–66
    U.S. Postal Service, 566–70
Abstract, reports, 94
Academic degrees, abbreviations, 560–62
Acceptance letters
  accepting invitation, 395–96
    speaking invitation, 396
    accepting membership in professional/
      civic organization, 396–97
Accessories, typewriters, 52
Accommodations, employer's preferences,
    209, 210–11
Acknowledgment, of legal document, 238
Acknowledgments
  of expressions of sympathy, 293–95
    files to keep, 294
    types of, 294–95
Acknowledgment letters
  that also answer, 364–65
  without answer, 363–64
Acting official, correct form of address, 331
Action requested slips, 120
Acts/bills/codes/laws
  capitalization rules, 512–14
    Constitution, 514
      amendments to, 514
    federal/state/municipal codes, 513
    general descriptive terms, 513
    official title, 513
Address
  envelopes, 325–26
  forms of, *See* Forms of address.
Addressing equipment, 127

Adjectives
  capitalization rules, 526, 526–27
  compound terms, 417
Adjustment letters
  travel accounts, 366–67
    incorrect amount, 366–67
    uncredited ticket cancellation, 367
Adverbs, 418
Advertisements/circulars, handing of, 123
Aerogrammes, 157
Agenda, 181
Air Force personnel, forms of address, 593
Airline codes, 206–7
Air mail, international service, 160
Air-travel arrangements, 208–10
  airline clubs, 209
  airline information, 208–9
  employer's accommodation preferences,
    209
  group travel, 209
  making reservations, 209–10
Alphabetical filing, 3–8
  name file, 4
  subject files, 4–8
Alphabetical list, subject files, 7
Alphabetic index guides, 24
  See also Index tabs/labels.
Alphabetizing
  rules for, 14–20
    abbreviations, 16
    articles/prepositions/conjunctions, 17–
      18
      in foreign languages, 18
    basic rules, 14–15
    compound firm names, 16–17
    designations, 17
    government offices, 19
    hyphenated names, 15–16
    married women, 20
    names containing numbers, 18–19
    names of unequal length, 15
    precedence of letters, 15
    s endings, 18
    surnames with prefixes, 17
    titles, 19–20
Alternate subjects, 414–15
Angular measure, 607
Answering calls, 167–68
Answering machines/services, 176
Antagonistic words, 345–46
Antecedents, 415

Apology
  letter of, 368–69
    explanation of oversight, 368–69
Apostrophes
  abbreviations, 507
  contractions, 506–7
  letters/symbols, 507
  possessives, 506
  words, 507
Apothecaries' measure, 610
  fluid measure, 610
  metric equivalents, 610–11
Appendixes, reports, 94, 99
Appointments
  appointment calls, 173
  letters arranging, 369–72
    at employer's request, 369–70
    response to request, 370–82
  reminders of, 47
Appositives, 415
  comma and, 492
Appreciation
  letters of, 372–75
    for assistance, 373
    for favorable mention in speech, 375
    for hospitality, 373–74
    for message of congratulations, 374–75
    for message of sympathy, 374
    for personal favor/service, 373
Area, metric measurement conversions, 613
Area codes, U.S., 622
Army personnel, forms of address, 591
Article citations
  bibliographies, 102–3
  footnotes, 101
Articles, 415
  alphabetizing of, 17–18
    in foreign languages, 18
Assistants
  interviewing, 277–78
  recruitment sources, 277
  training/supervising, 278–79
Atlases, as reference source, 85
Attention line
  envelopes, 326
  letters, 311–12
Attestation clause, legal documents, 238
Automated information/storage/retrieval, 36
Automatic deposits, 228
Automatic dialers, 176
Automatic formatting, electronic typewriters, 52
Auto-travel arrangements, 211–13
  automobile travel information, 211–12
  car rentals, 212
  making reservations, 212–13
Auxiliary verbs, 415
Avoirdupois measure, 609
  avoirdupois-troy measure, 610
  metric equivalents, 609–10

Balance form of account, 246
Balance sheet, 249
Bank statement, reconciliation of, 229–31
Bible references, colon and, 501
Bible terms, capitalization of, 532–33
Bibliographies
  reports, 94
  styles, 102–3
    article citations, 102–3
    book citations, 102
    unpublished material citations, 103
Billings/collections
  calculating charges, 252–54
  collection efforts, pros/cons of, 258
  computers and, 255
  invoices, preparation of, 254–55
  ledger system, 256
  manual billing methods, 256
  multiple-invoice system, 256
  overdue accounts, following up on, 255–58
  standard collection statements, 257–58
  tickler card system, 256
Bills/statements, handing of, 123
Birthdays
  birthday greetings, model letter, 397
  keeping records of, 289
Blank endorsements, 229
Blind-copy notations, 322
Block style, letters, 303
Body
  letters, 314–15
    dates, 315
    enumerated material, setup of, 315
    typing of, 314
  memos, 323–24
  reports, 94
Book citations
  bibliographies, 102
  footnotes, 101
Bookkeeping
  computer-assisted bookkeeping, 251–52
    IRS requirements, 251–52
  debt/credit entries, 242
  double-entry bookkeeping, basic rules of, 242
  system of, 241–42
  versus accounting, 241
Bottom-of-page footnotes, versus notes section, 100
Bottom of page
  corrections/revisions, 72
  footnotes, 100
Bound pages, corrections/revisions, 72
Brackets, use of, 508
Broken quotations, capitalization of, 531–32
Bulk mailings, 128–29
Bulky materials, storage of, 26
Business cards
  reordering of, 298
  use of, 296–98

with gifts, 297–98
size, 296
style, 296–97
women's, 297
Business matters, file-retention program, 32
Business publications, as reference source, 88–89
Business-reply mail, domestic service, 152–53
Business services
  CBX, 175
  direct inward dialing (DID), 176
  electronic mail, 176
  foreign-exchange line, 176
  least-cost routing (LCR), 176
  PABX, 175
  PBX, 175
  PMBX, 275
  tie lines, 176
  WATS line, 175, 176
Business terms
  accounting/finance, 634–39
  business law, 625–29
  business management, 625–29
Business trips
  company, travel departments, 196–97
  preparation for, 194–204
  special secretarial duties, 199–203
  travel agents, use of, 194–96
  travel information, 197–99
  traveling with your employer, 203–4

Cabinets/containers, 12
  adding metal frames to cabinets, 28
Cables
  classes of, 136–37
    full-rate message (FR), 136
    letter telegram (LT), 136
    radiograms, 136
    radio photo service, 136-37
    special services, 137
  counting charges for, 137–38
    addresses, 137
    paid-service indicator (PSI), 137
    signature, 137
    word count, 137–38
  economizing on, 138–39
    time differentials, 138
    urgency of message, 138
    wording, 138–39
  registered code addresses, 137
  sending methods, 135–36
Calendars
  as checklist of recurring items, 45
  as communications tool, 44–45
  daily checking of, 46
  desk, 43
  monthly engagement calendars, 48
  pocket, 43
  preparation of, 44

tickler card file and, 45–47, 48
  wall, 43
  your employer's, 44
    pocket calendar, 44
  your own, 43–44
Calling-card calls, 171
Call sequencers, 176
Canceling reservations, 206
Capitalization
  rules of, 512–34
    abbreviations, 512–13
    acts/bills/codes/laws, 513–14
    courts/judges/cases, 514–15
    drama, 525–26
    education, 515–16
    enumerations, 516–17
    film, 525–26
    foreign names, 517
    geographical terms, 517–18
    government/political terms, 518–21
    headings/titles, 521
    historical terms, 522–23
    hyphenated compounds, 523
    leagues/treaties/pacts/plans, 524
    lists/outlines, 524
    military terms, 524–25
    money, 525
    music, 525–26
    nouns/adjectives, 526–27
    organizations/institutions, 527
    paintings, 525–26
    people/races/tribes, 527
    personal titles, 528–30
    personification, 530
    planets, 530–31
    poetry, 525–26
    political parties/factions/alliances, 531
    quotations, 531–32
    radio, 525–26
    religious terms, 532–33
    resolutions, 533–34
    trade names, 534
Carbon copies, corrections/revisions, 71–72
Carbon-copy notations, 322
Carbon papers
  selection of, 67–68
  shortcuts in using, 68
  typing on, 69–70
Card index, subject files, 7–8
Card lists, holidays, 289
Car rentals, 212
  See also Auto-travel arrangements.
Cases, 415
Cash journal, 243–45
  cash payments journal, 243, 245
    posting to general ledger from, 248
  cash receipts journal, 243, 244
    posting to general ledger from, 247
  general journal, 243
CBX, 175

Centering heads, 61
Centigrade/Fahrenheit temperatures, 611–12
Central processing unit (CPU), stand-alone word processing system, 53–54
Central recording, 76
Central systems, 77
Certificates of mailing, international service, 159
Certified mail
  domestic service, 153
  international service, 159
Ch, sh, ss, x endings, plural spellings, 478
Chain feeding, 64
Change of address service, international service, 159
Charge-out tickler cards, 46
Checks
  endorsements, 228–29
    blank endorsement, 229
    restrictive endorsement, 228–29
    specific endorsement, 229
  filling in stubs, 226–28
  making deposits, 228–29
  reconciliations, 229–31
  supporting documents, 231
  writing of, 226–28
Chronological filing, 10
Church dignitaries
  capitalization of, 532
  forms of address
    Catholic faith, 594–96
    Jewish faith, 597
    Protestant faith, 597–99
Circular/angular measure, 607
Circular files, 21
Cities/states, comma and, 492
Clippings/photos, removal of backings, 30–31
Closing parentheses, 509
Closings
  letters, 353–55
    dated action, 354
    positive words, 354–55
    stilted/formal closings, 353
    suggesting only one action, 353–54
Coast Guard personnel, forms of address, 593
Coded-number file system, 9
Coined phrases, 418
Cold type, definition of, 114
Collect on delivery (COD)
  domestic service, 153
  international service, 159
Collection letters
  casual reminder, 375–76
  firm reminder, 376
  form appeal, 376–77
Collective nouns, 416
College/university officials, forms of address, 599–602

Colon
  Bible references, 501
  dash, 501
  footnotes, 501
  in lists/tabulations, 500
  pauses, 501
  salutations, 501
  time and ratios, 501
Color coding
  color-coded files, 21
  filing systems/techniques, 33–34
Combination files, 13
Comma
  appositives, 492
  cities/states, 492
  common element, phrases with, 496
  compound predicates, 492–93
  compound sentences, 493
  dash, 493
  dates, 493
  ellipsis and, 493
  essential/nonessential phrases and clauses, 493–94
  inseparables, 494
  introductory words, 494
  names, 495
  numbers, 495
  with "oh," 495
  parentheses, 495
  parenthetical words/phrases, 495–96
  participle phrases, 496
  quotation marks, 496–97
  quotations, 496–97
  series comma, 497
Company travel departments
  working with, 196–97
  See also Foreign travel; Travel.
Comparative degree, 416
  See also Adjective; Adverb.
Compass points, capitalization rules, 517
Complaint letters
  error in account, 377–79
    incorrect amount, 377–78
    item not purchased, 378
    returned merchandise not credited, 379
Complement, 416
  See also Direct object; Predicate adjective; Predicate nominative.
Complimentary close
  correct forms of, 315
  letters, 315
  typing of, 315
Compound personal pronouns, 416
Compound predicates, 416
  comma and, 492–93
Compound sentences
  comma and, 493
  semicolon and, 499
Compound subjects, 416–17

Compound terms, 417–18
  adjectives, 417
  adverbs, 418
  coined phrases, 418
  consistency, 417
  fractions, 418
  hyphens, 507
  meaning, 417
  nationalities, 418
  plurals, 417
  plural spellings, 479–80
  titles, 418
  usage, 417
Computers
  abbreviations, 570–77
  automated information storage/retrieval, 36
  computer-assisted bookkeeping, 251–52
    IRS requirements, 251–52
  computer-assisted research, 83–84
    computer-search services, 83
    databases, 83–84
  computerized remote postage meter resetting (CMRS) system, 127
  corrections/revisions, 73–75
  diskettes, filing of, 37–38
  documents
    editing of, 73–74
    printing of, 75
  electronic data-processing files, 13
  high-speed follow-up, 42–43
  information processing, 37
  micrographics, 38–39
  printouts, filing of, 38
  saving text, 75
  time/cost analysis, 39
Condolences
  letters of, 293, 397–99
    to business associate, 398
    to someone with personal injury/illness/property damage, 399
    to widow of employee, 398
Conferences, interruptions, handling of, 271
Confidentiality, 279–80
  away from office, 280
  confidential correspondence, 308–9
  safeguarding office material, 280
Congratulations
  letters of, 399–402
    on business anniversary, 401
    on outstanding community service, 400
    for professional/civic honor, 399–400
    on retirement, 400–401
    on service to company, 401–2
Conjunctions
  alphabetizing of, 17–18
  in foreign languages, 18
Conjunctive adverb, semicolon and, 499–500
Consecutive-number file system, 9

Contact reminder file, 50
  preparation of, 50
Continuation pages, heading on, 323, 325
Continuation sheets, selection and ordering of, 333
Contractions, apostrophes and, 506–7
Contracts/legal documents, 235–38
  filing of, 238
  typing of, 237–38
Contributions
  as expressions of sympathy, 293
  solicitors of, 269–70
Coordinate conjunctions, *See* Conjunctions.
Copy-distribution notation
  letters, 322
  memos, 324
Copyright
  reports
    copyright law, 115–16
    copyright-registration procedure, 117
      copyright notice, 117
      information/forms, 117
    fair-use guidelines, 116
Copyright Handbook (Johnson), 117
Corrections/revisions
  at bottom of page, 72
  on bound pages, 72
  breaking poor typing habits, 70
  on carbon copies, 71–72
  with computers, 73–75
  erasures, 70–71
  on paper masters, 72
  on stencils, 72
  with word processors, 73–75
Correction tape, 52
Cost-consciousness, 276–77
Cotton-content papers, 75–76
Courts/judges/cases
  capitalization rules, 514–15
    bar, bench, 515
    cases, 515
    full title, 514
  court officials, forms of address, 586–87
  judges
    justices, 514
    references to, 515
CPS exam, study outline for, 537–38
Credit
  letters of, 203, 379–80
    providing credit information, 379–80
    requesting credit, 380
Credit acknowledgments, footnotes, 101
Credit entries, bookkeeping, 242
Cross-references, 112
  cross-reference sheet, 25
  permanent cross-references, 25–26
  for storing bulky materials, 26
  when not to use, 26
  when to use, 24–25

Cubic measure (volume), 607
Customs information, 218

Daily appointment schedule, 47
Daily breaks, 263
Daily mail record, 121–22
Dangling modifiers, 418
Dash
  colon and, 501
  comma and, 493
  and other punctuation marks, 502
  principal use, 502
  within series, 502
Databases, 55
  computer-assisted research, 83–84
  modems, 55, 83
  as reference source, 89–90
Dateline, letters, 318
Dates
  comma and, 493
  days between specific dates, 620
Debit entries, bookkeeping, 242
Decimal filing, record classification, 10
Declination
  letters of, 402–6
    for banquet/luncheon/entertainment in-
      vitation, 402–3
    for request to support charitable or other
      organization, 404–5
    for service on civic professional com-
      mittee/board, 403–4
    for speaking invitation, 403
    to attend social event, 405
    to give address/informal talk, 405–6
Deities, capitalization of, 532
Delivery services (private)
  air/ground services
    Federal Express, 155–56
    types of, 155–56
    United Parcel Service, 156
  use of, 156
Departments/boards/committees, capitaliza-
    tion rules, 520
Dependent clauses, 418
Deposits, 228–29
  automatic deposits, 228
  See also Endorsements.
Designations, alphabetizing, 17
Desk calendars, 43
Desk telephone book, 177–78
  employer's personal numbers, 178
Dictation
  equipment, 76–77
  how to take, 77–78
  shortcuts, 79–80
  transcription, 78–79
Dictionaries, as reference source, 85–86
Diplomatic representatives, forms of address,
    587–88

Direct inward dialing (DID), 176
Direct objects, 418
Directories, as reference source, 86–87
Direct quotation, capitalization of, 531
Discrete media, 76
Diskettes
  filing of, 37–38
  storage of, 51
Display screen
  electronic typewriters, 51–52
  stand-alone word processing system, 53
Dividers, 22
Division, 616–17
Divorcees, correct form of address, 329–30
Document memory, 51
Documents
  capitalization rules, 522
  editing of, 73–74
  printing of, 75
Domestic mail service, 149–52
  Domestic Mail Manual, 146
  Express Mail, 149
  first-class mail, 149–51
  fourth-class mail, 152
  second-class mail, 151
  third-class mail, 151
Domestic money orders, domestic service, 154
Donations, keeping records of, 291–93
Double-entry bookkeeping, basic rules of, 242
Double negatives, 418–19
  See also Word usage, troublesome words/
    phrases.
Double spacing, reports, 98, 111
Drama, capitalization rules, 525–26
Dry measure, 608
  metric equivalents, 608
Duplication, elimination of, 30

Editing features, electronic typewriters, 52
Education terms
  capitalization rules, 515–16
    chairmanships, 516
    classes, 515
    courses/subjects, 516
    degrees, 516
    schools, names of, 515
Electric Wastebasket Corporation, 32
Electronic data-processing (EDP) files, 13
Electronic mail, 176
  bulletin board system, 143
  local area network (LAN), 144
  node-to-node stand-alone electronic mail
    system, 143–44
  public data networks, 144
  systems, 143–44
  transmission of, 143–44
  use of, 144
  voice-mail systems, 144
Ellipsis

comma and, 493
ellipsis points, 510
Emotional callers, 270–71
Emphasis, exclamation point and, 503
Employee communications
model letters/memos
follow-ups, 383–84
letters that say no, 381–82
staff appointment, announcement of, 381
transmittal message, 382
Employee compensation record, 224
Employer
first name, use of, 261
greetings friends of, 268
traveling with, 203–4
conduct, 203–4
travel arrangements, 203
Employer's Annual Federal Unemployment Tax Return (Form 940), 226
Employer's Tax Guide (Circular E), 226
Enclosures
enclosure notation
letters, 321
memos, 324
handling of, 125–26
inserting of, 125
size of, 125–26
Encyclopedias, as reference source, 84–85
Endless-loop media, 76
Endorsements
blank endorsements, 229
restrictive endorsements, 228–29
specific endorsements, 229
Enumerated material, setup of, 315
Enumerations
capitalization rules, 516–17
not preceded by colon, 516–17
preceded by colon, 516
parentheses and, 509
Envelopes
addressing of, 63–64
chainfeeding, 64
OCR addressing, 325–27
account numbers, 327
address, 325–26
attention line, 326
mail instructions, 327
personal notation, 326
selection and ordering of, 333–34
Equipment
computers, 73–75
dictation, 76–77
filing, 11–13, 20–22
follow-up filing, 40
mailing, 126–28
mail room, 129
photocopy equipment, 66
typewriters, 51–52
word-processing systems, 53–55, 73–75
Eras, capitalization rules, 522

Erasures, 70–71
Essential/nonessential phrases and clauses, comma and, 493–94
Etiquette
first names, use of, 261
greetings to coworkers, 261
new employees, 261–63
in office lines, 264
office refreshments, 263–64
in parking lots, 264
professional image, 259–61
Exchanges, 175
function of, 175
Executive stationery, 333
Expense report, travel/entertainment, 232
Expletives, 419
Expository notes, 102
Express Mail, 149
international service, 160

F, fe endings, plural spellings, 478
Facsimiles
facsimile machines, types of, 139–40
services, 140
transmission of, 139–40
Fact books, as reference source, 84–85
Fair-use guidelines, 116
Fast telegram, 132–33
Federal Express, 155–56
Federal Tax Deposit Coupon (Form 8109), 226
Figures/letters, plural spellings, 478–79
File guides, 24
File-retention program
development of, 32–33
business matters, 32
personal matters, 32–33
storage-control schedule, 33
Files/records, seminars/conferences, 192–93
File transferral, 31–32
Filing equipment
cabinets/containers, 12
circular files, 21
color-coded files, 21
combination files, 13
dividers, 22
electronic data-processing (EDP) files, 13
lateral files, 11
open files, 11
portable files, 11–12
rotary files, 12
rubber fingers, 21
safety files, 12
sorting trays, 21
specialized files, 13
standard office files, 11
tray files, 12
vertical files, 11

Filing systems/techniques
  aids to fast filing/finding, 20–34
    controlling material taken from files,
      27–28
    cross-references, 24–26
    equipment and techniques, 20–22
    file guides, 21–22, 24
    index tabs/labels, 22–24
    material preparation, 26–27
    misfiles, retrieving of, 28
    streamlining files, 28–34
  alphabetical filing, 3–8
    name file, 4
    subject files, 4–8
  chronological filing, 10
  color coding, 33–34
  computers/automated procedures, 36–39
  decimal filing, 10
  file transferral, 31–32
  follow-up techniques, 39–43
  geographical filing, 9–10
  misfiles, retrieving, 28
  numerical filing, 8–9
  outfolders/guides, 27–28
  preparing material for filing, 26–27
  reminder systems, 43–50
  safeguarding files/documents, 33
  streamlining files, 28–34
    clippings/photos, removal of backings,
      30–31
    determining necessity of files, 34
    duplication, elimination of, 30
    file-retention program, development of,
      32–33
    follow blocks, removal of, 29
    hanging folders/pockets, 28–29
    little-used/odd-sized material, transferral
      of, 31
    magazines/brochures, removal of, 30
    portable draw dividing units, 29–30
    special-purpose folders, 29
  supplies, ordering/storing of, 34–36
  See also Computers.
Film, capitalization rules, 525–26
Financial publications, as reference source,
  88–89
Financing records, 234–35
  Uniform Commercial Code (UCC), 235
Financing statements, 234–35
First-class mail, 149–51
First-day cover mail service, 155
  domestic service, 155
First names, use of, 261
Flowchart symbols
  program flowcharting symbols, 620
  system flowcharting symbols, 621
Flowers, as expressions of sympathy, 293
Folders
  follow-up filing, 40

labels, 22
miscellaneous
  name file, 4
  size of, 21
  subject file, 6–7
subject files, 6–7
Follow blocks, removal of, 29
Follow-up collection systems, 255–56
Follow-up filing
  equipment, 40
  folder arrangement, 40
  follow-up material, 39
  high-speed follow-up, 42–43
    computers/high-speed equipment, 42–43
  methods, 39–40
  system operation, 40–42
  tickler card files, 42
Follow-ups, memo format, 383–84
Footnotes
  colon and, 501
  reports, 100–104
  tables, 109
  types of, 100–101
    article citations, 101
    book citations, 101
    credit acknowledgments, 101
    ibid., 101
    short references, 101
    unpublished material citations, 101
  typing of, 111–12
Foreign-exchange line, 176
Foreign names
  capitalization, 517
  capitalization rules, 517
Foreign officials/representatives, forms of address, 588–90
Foreign travel
  customs information, 218
  letters of introduction for, 215–17
  passport, securing of, 213–14
  special secretarial duties, 214–17
  travel agents, use of, 213
  travel information, 218–19
  travel security, 217–18
  visa, securing of, 214
Formal invitations, preparation of, 289–90
Formal reply, preparation of, 290, 291
Formal reports, 90–93
Former official, correct form of address, 331
Form letters
  file for, 355
  form-letter effectiveness checklist, 356–57
  memo forms, 358–59
  model form letters/paragraphs, 355–56
  personalized processed form letters, 358
  processed form letters, 356
Forms of address
  church dignitaries
    Catholic faith, 594–96

Jewish faith, 597
Protestant faith, 597–99
college/university officials, 599–602
companies, rules for, 328
court officials, 586–87
degrees, 327
esquire, 327–28
foreign officials/representatives, 588–90
men, rules for, 328–29
prominent persons, 331–32
titles, 327
United Nations officials, 602–3
U.S. government
    Air Force personnel, 593
    Army personnel, 591
    Coast Guard personnel, 593
    diplomatic representatives, 587–88
    Marine Corps personnel, 593
    national government officials, 578–83
    navy personnel, 592–93
    state/municipal government officials,
        583–86
women, rules for, 329–31
Fourth-class mail, 152
Fractions, compound terms, 418
Full-block style, letters, 302
Full-rate message (FR), 136
Future-perfect tense, *See* Tense, 419
Future tense, *See* Tense, 419

Galley proofs, sample of corrected proofs, 605
General inquiries, 385
General journal, 243
General ledger, 246
    posting from cash payments journal to, 248
    posting from cash receipts journal to, 247
Geographical filing
    setup of, 9
    system use, 9–10
Geographical terms
    capitalization rules, 517–18
        coast, 518
        compass points, 517
        divisions of world/country, 518
        popular names, 517
        regional terms, 518
Gerunds, 419
    See also Participles.
Gifts
    business cards used with, 297–98
    holiday gift list, 287–88
    money gifts, 288–89
    wedding anniversaries, selecting gifts for,
        289
    wrapping/mailing, 288
Glossary, reports, 94
Goodwill letters, 384–85
Gossip, 280–81

Government offices, alphabetizing, 19
Government officials, forms of address, 578–
    83
Government/political terms
    capitalization rules, 518–20, 518–21
        administration, 518–19
        city, 519
        commonwealth, 519
        county, 519
        departments/boards/committees, 520
        district, 520
        federal, 519
        government, 518–19
        legislative bodies, 520
        legislature, 521
        national, 519
        state, 519
        ward, precinct, 520
Grammar
    complements, 416
    compound personal pronouns, 416
    compound predicates, 416
    compound subjects, 416–17
    compound terms, 417–18
    dangling modifiers, 418
    dependent clauses, 418
    direct objects, 418
    double negatives, 418–19
    expletives, 419
    gerunds, 419
    indirect objects, 419
    infinitives, 419–20
    intervening noun/phrase, 420
    misplaced modifiers, 421
    mood, 421
    nonrestrictive clauses, 421
    omission of words, 421–22
    participles, 422
    person, 423
    predicate nominative, 423
    predicates, 423
    restrictive clauses, 424
    rules of, 414–26
        agreement of verb with subject, 414
        alternate subjects, 414–15
        antecedents, 415
        appositives, 415
        articles, 415
        auxiliary verbs, 415
        cases, 415
        collective nouns, 416
        comparative degrees, 416
    subject, 424
    tense, 424–25
    voice, 426
Greek letter symbols, 617
Greetings
    to callers, 265
    to coworkers, 261

Guides, subject files, 6
Guide words, memos, 323

Handicap bias, 348
Hanging folders/pockets, 28–29
Headings, tables, 107–9
Headings/titles
  capitalization rules, 521
    break in title, 521
    hyphenated compounds, 523
    infinitives, 521
    prepositions, 521
Heads/subheads
  reports, 104–5
    emphasis, 104
    patterns of, 104–5
    typing of, 111
    wording of, 105
Help command, 74
High-speed follow-up
  equipment, 42–43
  types of, 42–43
  See also Computers; Word processing systems.
High-speed messaging
  electronic mail, 143–44
  facsimiles, 139–40
  private services, 143
  satellite transmission, 144–45
  Teletex, 142–43
  telex, 140–42
Historical terms
  capitalization rules, 522
    documents, 522
    eras, 522
    important events, 522
Holidays/seasons/feast days
  capitalization rules, 522–23
    religious holidays, 522
    seasons, 523
    secular holidays, 522–23
  card lists, 289
  extra holiday duties, 287
  gifts
    money gifts, 288–89
    wrapping/mailing, 288
  holiday gift list, 287–88
Hotel reservations, 207–8
  confirmations, 207
  directories, 206–7
  exchange services, 207
  for large meeting rooms, 207
  model letters for, 394
  reservation services, 207
Hot type, definition of, 114
Human relations/personal skills
  assistants
    interviewing, 277–79

    training/supervising, 278–79
  confidentiality, 279–80
  human relations problems, 280–86
    borrowing money, 281
    gossip, 280–81
    injuries/illnesses, 282–83
    lending money, 281
    office politics, 281–82
    personnel problems, 283–86
  money, managing of, 276
  projects
    coordinating, 274
    initiating of, 274
    managing of, 274–75
  time, managing of, 275–76
  working for/with others, 272–74
    more than one person, 273
    one person, 272–73
    other departments, 273–74
Hyphens
  capitalization rules, 523
    compound numerals, 523
    headings/titles, 523
    hyphenated words, 523
  compound terms, 507
  hyphenated words, series, 507–8
  hyphenation of names, 15–16
  time, 508
  word division, 507
Ibid., footnotes, 101
Identification line, letters, 321
Illustrations
  reports, 106–11
    line drawings, 110
    marking instructions, 110–11
    photographs, 110
    working with an artist, 111
Imperative mood, *See* Mood.
Income taxes, 225
Incoming mail
  action requested slips, 120
  advertisements/circulars, 123
  bills/statements, 123
  daily mail record, 121–22
  employer's absence, procedure during, 123–24
  newspapers/periodicals, 122
  opening mail, 119
  personal/confidential letters, 118–119
  requiring employer's attention, 119–20
  requiring others' attention, 120–21
  requiring your attention, 122
  routing slips, 120–21
  sorting mail, 118, 119
Indentation, within reports, 99–100
Indentification line, memos, 324
Indexes
  of minute book, 188
  reports, 95

Indexing
  rules for, 13–14
    business concerns, 14
    individual names, 13–14
    organizations/institutions, 14
  See also Alphabetizing.
Index tabs/labels
  color coded guides, 24
  typing of
    basic rules, 22
    file-drawer labels, 23–24
    folder labels, 22
    guide labels, 23
Indicative mood, *See* Mood.
Indirect objects, 419
Indirect quotation, capitalization of, 531
Infinitives, 419–20
  capitalization rules, 521
  series of, 420
  split infinitives, 420
  tense, 420
Informal invitation, preparation of, 290–91
Informal reply, preparation of, 291
Informal reports, 93
Informals, 296
Information processing, 37
Injuries/illnesses, 282–83
INMARSAT, 145
Inquiry letters, 385–86
  general inquiries, 385
  reply to inquiries, 385–86
Inseparables, comma and, 494
Inside address
  letters, 309–11
    contents of, 309
    typing of, 309–11
Integrated voice-data terminals, 55
INTELPOST, international service, 160
INTELSAT, 144–45
Interest tables, 617–19
Interfaces, 55
International air mail, 160
International Direct-Distance Dialing (IDDD),
  170–71
International Mail Manual, 156
International money orders, international
  service, 160
International postal service
  information sources, 157
  parcel post, 159
  postal union mail, 157–58
    aerogrammes, 157
    letters/letter packages, 1
    matter for the blind, 158
    post cards/postal cards, 1
    printed matter, 158
    small packets, 158
  special mail services, 159–60
    certified mail, 159

    change of address service, 159
    collect on delivery (COD), 159
    Express Mail, 160
    INTELPOST, 160
    international money orders, 160
    mail insurance, 159
    mail reply coupons, 160
    recall services, 159
    registered mail, 159
    restricted delivery, 159
    special delivery, 159–60
    special handling, 159
  special services
    international air mail, 160
International telegrams, 135–36
International time chart, 623
  time differentials, 624
Interrogative sentences, question marks and,
  503
Intransitive verb, *See* Verbs.
Introduction letters
  for business/professional associate, 387–88
  for foreign travel, 215–17
  for personal friend, 386–87
Introductory words, comma and, 494
Inventory control, 35
  supplies, 35
  See also Supplies.
Invitations
  acceptance letters, 395–96
  declination letters, 402–6
  preparation of, 289–91
    formal invitations, 289–90
    formal reply, 290, 291
    informal invitation, 290–91
    informal reply, 291
Irregular nouns, plural spellings, 478
Irregular verbs, *See* Verbs.
IRS regulations
  computer-assisted bookkeeping, 251–52
  travel/entertainment records, 233–34
Itineraries, 199

Keyboard, stand-alone word processing system, 53
KO-REC-COPY, 52

Laid paper, 333
Language
  appropriate use of, 95–96
    sentences, 95–96
    words, 95
Lateral files, 11
Leaders, as punctuation, 510
Leagues, capitalization rules, 524
Leased-channel service, high-speed messag-
  ing, 143

Least-cost routing (LCR), 176
Ledger system, billings, 256
Legal documents, *See* Contracts/legal documents.
Legislative bodies, capitalization rules, 520
Length
  metric measurement conversions, 612–13
  metric prefixes/multiplication factors, 612
Letterhead design, 332–33
  executive stationery, 333
  general characteristics, 332–33
Letterpress, definition of, 115
Letters
  blind-copy notations, 322
  carbon-copy notations, 322
  categories of, 360–61
    personal business letters, 362
    signed by employer, 361–62
    signed by secretary, 360–61
    written in employer's absence, 362–63
  office paper, type and size of, 332
  photocopy notations, 322
  principal parts of, 308–23
    attention line, 311–12
    body, 314–15
    complimentary close, 315
    continuation pages, heading on, 323
    copy-distribution notation, 322
    dateline, 318
    enclosure notation, 321
    identification line, 321
    inside address, 309–11
    mailing notation, 322
    personal notation, 308–9
    postscript, 322
    reference line, 308
    salutation, 312–14
    signature line, 315–20
    subject line, 314
  punctuation style, 307
  reprographic-copy notations, 322
  styles, 301–7
    block style, 303
    full-block style, 302
    official style, 305
    semiblock style, 305
    simplified style, 306
  See also Model letters.
Letters/symbols, apostrophes and, 507
Letter telegram (LT), 136
Letter writing
  appropriate language, 336–49
    antagonistic words, 345–46
    clear/straightforward language, 337
    favorite words/expressions, 344
    meaning, shades of, 345
    nondiscriminatory language, 346–48
    positive approach, 348–49
    sentence length, 344–45
    stilted/verbose language, 336–37
    trite terms, 337–43
    unnecessary words/phrases, 343–44
    word length, 344
  planning for, 336
Line drawings, reports, 110
Lines, etiquette in, 264
Linking verbs, *See* Verbs.
Liquid measure, 608
  metric equivalents, 608
Liquid Paper, 52
List of illustrations, reports, 94
Lists/outlines, capitalization rules, 524
Little-used/odd-sized material, transferral of, 31
Local-area network (LAN), 144
Long-distance telephone service, 170
Long measure, 606
  metric equivalents, 606
  surveyors' long measure, 607

Magazines/brochures, removal of, 30
Mailable items, 146–48
  minimum-size standards, 148–49
  nonstandard mail, 149
Mailgrams, 133, 154
  domestic service, 154
Mailing guidelines
  optical character reader (OCR) addressing requirements, 161
  postage costs, reduction of, 161–63
  zip codes, use of, 160–61
Mailing lists
  large lists, 128
  maintenance of, 128
  small lists, 128
Mailing notation, letters, 322
Mail instructions, envelopes, 327
Mail insurance
  domestic service, 153
  international service, 159
Mail processing
  bulk mailings, 128–29
  equipment, 126–28
  incoming mail, 118–24
  mailing lists, maintenance of, 128
  mailroom efficiency, 129–32
  outgoing mail, 124–26
Mail reply coupons, international service, 160
Mail room
  cutting costs, 130–32
  planning/record keeping, 129
  security, 131–32
  speeding post office processing, 129–30
  supplies/equipment, 129
Manuscript

reports
  checking of, 112–13
  preparation of, 111–12
  typesetting of, 113–14
Margins
  reports, 98
  tables, 109
Marine Corps personnel, forms of address, 593
Mariner's measure, 608–9
Married women, correct form of address, 329
Mass cards, as expressions of sympathy, 293
Mathematical tables
  days between specific dates, 618
  division, shortcuts in, 616–17
  Greek letter symbols, 617
  interest tables, 617–19
  multiplication, shortcuts in, 616
Meaning, shades of, 345
Meetings
  with assistants/coworkers, 189–90
    conducting of, 189–90
    notes preparation, 190
    preparation for, 189
  making arrangements for, 179–83
    agenda, preparation of, 181
    meeting materials, organization of, 181–82
    meeting room
      preparation of, 182–83
      securing of, 182
    notifying meeting participants, 179–80
    visitors, making accommodations for, 183
  meeting minutes
    reading of, 184
    taking of, 185–87
  meeting proxy, sample of, 180
  messages, relaying of, 183–84
  motions, form for recording of, 186
  parliamentary procedure, 184–85
  reserving hotel meeting rooms, 207
  seminars/conferences, 190–93
    files/records, 192–93
    programs/announcements, preparation of, 190–91
    registration procedures, 191–2
  telephone calls during, handling of, 271
Memos
  categories of, 360–63
    signed by employer, 361–62
    signed by secretary, 360–61
    written in employer's absence, 362–63
  format, 301, 307
  memo forms, 358–59
  office paper, type and size of, 332
  principal parts of, 323–25
    body, 323–24
      continuation pages, heading on, 325

copy-distribution notation, 324
enclosure notation, 324
guide words, 323
indentification line, 324
postscript, 325
signature initials, 324
routing of, 359
typing of, 64–65
Memo to Mailers, 146
Merge command, 74
Messages, 183–84
Messenger calls, 173
Metric weights/measures
  metric equivalents
    apothecaries' measure, 610–11
    approximate, 615
    avoirdupois measure, 609–10
    dry measure, 608
    linear measure, 614
    liquid measure, 608
    long measure, 606
    solid/cubic measure, 607
    square measure, 606, 614
    troy measure, 610
    volume, 614
    weights, 615
  metric measurement conversions, 612–13
    area, 613
    length, 612–13
    volume, 613
    weight, 613
  metric prefixes/multiplication factors, 612
    length, 612
    volume, 612
    weight, 612
Micrographics, 38–39
  microfiche, 38
  microfilming, 38
Military terms
  capitalization rules, 524–25
    branches/divisions, 524–25
    names, 524
    titles, 525
Minute book
  corrections to, 188
  indexing of, 188
  reading of, 184
  taking minutes, 185–87
  typing minutes, 187–88
    final copy, 187–88
    rough draft, 187
Misfiles
  retrieving, 28
Misplaced modifiers, 421
  See also Dangling modifier.
Mixed punctuation, 307
Mnemonics, 485–86
Mobile calls, 174–75

Model letters
  business letters, 363–95
    acknowledgments, 363–65
    adjustments, 366–67
    apologies, 368–69
    appointments, 369–72
    appreciation, 372–75
    collection, 375–77
    complaints, 377–79
    credit, 379–80
    employee communications, 381–84
    goodwill, 384
    inquiries, 385–86
    introductions, 386–88
    orders, 388–89
    recommendations, 389–90
    reminders, 390
    requests, 390–93
    reservations, 393–94
    sales promotion, 394–95
  social-business, 395–407
    condolences, 397–99
    congratulations, 399–402
    declination, 402–5
    invitations, 405–6
    seasonal good wishes, 406–7
    thank yous, 407
  social-business letters, 395–407
    acceptance, 395–97
    birthday greetings, 397
Modems, 55, 83
Money
  borrowing, 281
  lending, 281
  managing of, 276
  money gifts, 288–89
Money orders, 133
  postal, 154
Monthly engagement calendars, 48
Months/days, abbreviations, 559
Mood, 421
Motions, form for recording of, 186
Multiple-invoice system, billings, 256
Multiple-line memory, 51
Multiplication, 616
Music, capitalization rules, 525–26

Name file, 4
  combined name/subject file, 8
Names
  comma and, 495
  quotation marks and, 505–6
Narrow labels, typing of, 65
National Five-Digit Zip Code and Post Office Directory, 146
Nationalities, compound terms, 418
Navy personnel, forms of address, 592–93
New employees

extending lunch invitations to, 262
  introductions to coworkers, 262
  providing assistance to, 261–62
  rules to observe as new employees, 262–63
  scheduling periodic conferences, 262
Newspapers/periodicals, handing of, 122
Night letters, 133
Node-to-node stand-alone electronic mail system, 143–44
Nominative case, *See* Case.
Nondiscriminatory language, 346–48
  handicap bias, 348
  racial/ethnic bias, 347–48
  sexism, 346
Nonrestrictive clauses, 421
Nonstandard mail, 149
Notes, reports, 94
Notes section
  bibliography entries, 102
  expository notes, 102
  source notes, 102
  versus bottom-of-page footnotes, 100
Nouns
  capitalization rules, 526–27
    common nouns used in names, 526
    epithets, 526
    names, 526
    with numbers/letters, 526–27
    proper nouns, words derived from, 526
Numbering
  reports, 98–99
    appendixes, 99
    page numbering, 98–99
    within reports, 99–100
Numbers
  comma and, 495
  numbers/fractions, typing of, 56–57
Numerical filing
  advantages/disadvantages, 9
  types of, 9

Objective case, *See* Case.
O endings, plural spellings, 477–78
Office/company books and records
  balance sheet, 249
  billings/collection, 252–58
  bookkeeping, system of, 241–42
  cash journal, 243–45
  checkbook and bank statement, 226–31
  contracts/legal documents, 235–38
  financing statements, 234–35
  general ledger, 246
  payroll accounts, 223–26
  petty cash fund, 220–23
  profit and loss (income) statement, 250
  real estate records, 241
  securities records, 238–41
  subsidiary ledger, 246

travel/entertainment records, 231–34
Office paper
  cotton-content papers, 75–76
  reports, selecting paper for, 97–98
  sulfite-bond papers, 76
Office politics, 281–82
  definition of, 281
  unethical coworker, 281–82
  unethical practices, 281
Official Railway Guide, 210
Official style, letters, 305
Omission of words, 421–22
Open files, 11
Opening mail, 119
Openings
  letters, 349–53
    length of, 349, 350
    phrasing, 352
    previous contract, reference to, 352
    reader's name, inclusion of, 351
    restatement, use of, 349–51
    stilted openings, 351
    techniques, 352–53
    "who, what, when, and why," use of, 352
Open punctuation, 307
Optical character reader (OCR), 125, 130
  addressing requirements, 161
Orders, placing of, memo format, 388–87
Organizations/institutions
  abbreviations, 563–66
  capitalization rules, 527
    official names/titles, 527
    terms not part of name/title, 527
Outfolders/guides, 27–28
Outgoing mail
  assembling mail, 124–25
  enclosures
    handling of, 125–26
    inserting of, 125
    size of, 125–26
  folding letters for, 125
  getting signatures on, 124
Out-of-town telephone calls, 171–72
Overdue accounts
  collection efforts, pros/cons of, 258
  follow-up collection systems, 255–56
  standard collection statements, 257–58

PABX, 175
Pacts, capitalization rules, 524
Page length, determination of, 59–60
Page numbering, reports, 98–100, 98–99
Paging devices, 177
Paid-service indicator (PSI), 137
Paintings, capitalization rules, 525–26
Paper
  feeding numerous sheets of, 62–63
  See also Office paper.

Paper masters
  corrections/revisions, 72
  typing of, 66
Paper measure, 611
Parcel post, 159
Parentheses/brackets
  comma and, 495
  enumerations, 509
  explanatory expressions, 508
  figures, 508–9
  period and, 498
  punctuation within, 509
  questions/answers, 509
  semicolon and, 500
  single parentheses, 509
Parenthetical words/phrases, comma and, 495– 96
Parking lots, etiquette/safety in, 264
Parliamentary procedure, 184–85
Participle phrases, comma and, 496
Participles, 422
  See also Gerund; Dangling modifiers.
Passive voice, *See* Voice.
Passport, securing of, 213–14
Past-perfect tense, *See* Tense.
Past tense, *See* Tense.
Payroll accounts
  employee compensation record, 224
  payroll taxes
    paying taxes to government, 226
    processing of, 225–26
  setting up of, 223
PBX, 175
People/races/tribes, capitalization rules, 527
Period
  initials/abbreviations, 497
  omissions, 498
  outlines, 498
  parentheses, 498
  quotation marks, 498
  sentences, 497
Permanent cross-references, 25–26
Persistent callers, 270
Person, 423
Personal business letters, 362
Personal/confidential letters, 118–19
Personalized processed form letters, 358
Personal matters, file-retention program, 32–33
Personal notation
  envelopes, 326
  letters, 308–9
Personal skills, *See* Human relations/personal skills.
Personal titles
  capitalization rules, 528–30
    acting, under, assistant, 529
    business/professional titles, 529
    compound titles, 530

Personal titles *(cont.)*
general rule, 528
honor/nobility, 529
names, lists of, 530
national government officials, 528
president, 528
state/municipal government officials, 528–29
words in apposition, 529–30
Personification, capitalization rules, 530
Personnel problems
employee grievances, 283
performance problems, 285–86
problems with others, 284
serious conflicts, 283
sexual harassment, 285
Person-to-person calls, 170
Petty cash fund
establishment of, 220
making payments from, 220–21
petty cash voucher, sample of, 221
record of transactions, 221
replenishing fund, 221–23
secretary's responsibilities, 223
Philatelic mail order service, 154–55
domestic service, 154–55
Photocopies
multiuses for, 66–67
photocopy equipment, 66
photocopy log, 67
Photocopy notations, 322
Photographs, reports, 110
Photo-offset lithography, 115
Phrase memory, 51
Placing calls, 166–67
Planets, capitalization rules, 530–31
Plans, capitalization rules, 524
Plurals
of compound words, 417
spelling rules, 477–80
abbreviations, 478
ch, sh, ss, x endings, 478
compound terms, 479–80
f, fe endings, 478
figures/letters, 478–79
irregular nouns, 478
o endings, 477–78
singular nouns, 477
y endings, 478
See also Spelling, rules of.
PMBX, 175
Pocket calendars, 43
Poetry, capitalization rules, 525–26
Political parties/factions/alliances
capitalization rules, 531
names, 531
words derived from names, 531
Portable draw dividing units, 29–30
Portable files, 11–12
Possessive case, *See* Case.

Possessives, apostrophes and, 506
Postage costs, 161–63
Postal equipment
addressing equipment, 127
computerized remote postage meter resetting (CMRS) system, 127
mail room needs study, 127–28
postage meter, 127
postage scale, 126
Postal union mail, 157–58
aerogrammes, 157
letters/letter packages, 157
matter for the blind, 158
post cards/postal cards, 157
printed matter, 158
small packets, 158
Postcards/postal cards, postal union mail, 157
Post office lockbox and caller service, domestic service, 154
Postscript
letters, 322
memos, 325
Precedence of letters, alphabetizing, 15
Predicate adjectives, *See* Adjectives.
Predicate nominatives, 423
Predicates, 423
Preface, reports, 93
Preliminary draft, reports, 97
Prepositions
alphabetizing of, 17–18
in foreign languages, 18
capitalization rules, 521
Present-perfect tense, *See* Tense.
Present tense, *See* Tense.
Printed forms, typing on, 59
Printer, stand-alone word processing systems, 54
Printing/binding
reports, 114–15
arrangements for, 114–15
press proof, checking of, 115
printer
choosing of, 115
locating of, 113–14
Printouts, filing of, 38
Processed form letters, 356
Professional image, 259–61
attributes to develop, 259–61
importance of, 259
Professional women, correct form of address, 330
Profit and loss (income) statement, 250
Program flowcharting symbols, 618
Programs/announcements, seminars/conferences, 190–91
Projects
coordinating, 274
initiating of, 274
managing of, 274–75
Prominent persons

correct form of address, 331–32
  acting official, 331
  former official, 331
  name unknown, 331
  scholastic degrees, people with, 331
  spouses, 331–32
  women, 332
Proofreading marks, 604
Proxy, meeting, 180
Punctuated clauses, semicolon and, 499
Punctuation
  principal marks of, 492–511
    apostrophe, 506–7
    colon, 500–501
    comma, 492–97
    dash, 502
    exclamation point, 503
    hyphen, 507–8
    interrogation point, 503–4
    leaders/ellipsis points, 510
    parentheses/brackets, 508–9
    period, 497–98
    quotation marks, 504–6
    semicolon, 499–500
    virgule, 511
  punctuation and mechanics marks, 539
  style, letters, 307

Question marks
  interrogative sentences, 503
  queries, 503–4
  requests, 503
  series of questions, 504
Quotation marks, 504–7
  comma and, 497
  definitions, 505
  direct quotations, 504
  names, 505–6
  paragraphs, 504–5
  period and, 498
  placement of, 506
  semicolon and, 500
  single quotation marks, 506
  titles, 505–6
  trade terms, 505
  unique words, 505
Quotations
  capitalization rules, 531–32
    broken quotations, 531–32
    direct quotations, 531
    indirect quotations, 531
  quotation sources, as reference source, 85–
    86

Racial/ethnic bias, 347–48
Radio, capitalization rules, 525–26
Radiograms, 136
Radio photo service, 136–37

Real estate records, 240, 241
Recall services, international service, 159
Recommendation letters, 389–90
Reconciliations, 229–31
Record classification, decimal filing, 10
Recruitment sources, assistants, 277
Reference line, letters, 308
References
  short references, 101
  style of, 103–4
Reference sources, 84–90
  atlases, 85
  business publications, 88–89
  databases, 89–90
  dictionaries, 85–86
  directories, 86–87
  encyclopedias, 84–85
  fact books, 84–85
  financial publications, 88–89
  indexes, 87–88
  quotation sources, 85–86
  securities, 89
  style books, 86
  taxes, 89
  word books, 85–86
Refreshments
  daily breaks, 263
  visitors, providing refreshments to, 263–64
Regional terms, capitalization rules, 518
Registered code addresses, 137
Registered mail
  domestic service, 153
  international service, 159
Registration procedures, seminars/confer-
    ences, 191–2
Relative pronoun, *See* Pronoun.
Religious denominations, capitalization of,
    533
Religious holidays, capitalization rules, 522
Religious terms
  capitalization rules, 532–33
    Bible terms, 532–33
    church, 532
    church dignitaries, 532
    deities, 532
    religious denominations, 533
Reminders
  collection letters, 375–77
    casual reminder, 375–76
    firm reminder, 376
  memo format for, 47, 390
Reminder systems
  calendars to keep, 43–44
    desk calendars, 43
    pocket calendars, 43
    preparation of, 44–45
    tickler card file and, 45–46
    wall calendars, 43
  contact reminder file, 50
    preparation of, 50

Reminder systems *(cont.)*
  daily appointment schedule, 47
  monthly engagement calendars, 48
  reminder memos, 47
  reminders, types of, 46–50
  special reminders, 48
Remote-call forwarding, 176–77
Repaginate command, 74
Reports
  appropriate language, 95–96
    sentences, 95–96
    words, 95
  checklist, 96–97
  copyrighting of, 115–17
  indentation, 99–100
  page numbering, 98–99
  parts of, 93–95
    abstract, 94
    appendix, 94
    bibliography, 94
    body, 94
    glossary, 94
    index, 95
    letter of transmittal, 93
    list of illustrations, 94
    notes, 94
    preface, 93
    table of contents, 93–94
    title page, 93
  preparation of, 97–113
    footnotes, 100–104
    heads/subheads, 104–5
    illustrations, 106–11
    margins, 98
    page numbering, 98–100
    paper, selection of, 97–98
    preliminary draft, 97
    printing/binding, 114–15
    spacing, 98
    table of contents, 106
    tables, 106–11
    title page, 106
    typesetting, 113–14
  report binders, 96
  research for, 81–90
    computer-assisted research, 83–84
    inside sources, 82
    outside sources, 81–82
    reference sources, 84–90
  types of, 90–93
    formal reports, 90–93
    informal reports, 93
Reprographic-copy notations, 322
Request
  letters of, 390–91
    explaining delayed action, 392–93
    for favor, 391–92
    granting requests, 392
    for missing enclosure, 390
  question marks and, 503

Reservations, 204–13
  air travel, 209–10
  air-travel arrangements, 208–10
  auto-travel, 213–14
  auto-travel arrangements, 211–13
  checklist, 204
  delays in obtaining, 205
  hotel reservations, 207–8
  letters, 393–94
    hotel reservations, 394
    travel reservations, 393–94
  securing tickets, 205–7
  time/route data preparation, 205
  train travel, 211
  train-travel arrangements, 210–11
Resolutions, capitalization rules, 533, 533–34
Restricted delivery, international service, 159
Restrictive clauses, 424
Restrictive endorsements, 228–29
Robert's Rules of Order, 184
Roman numerals, 539
  general rules for, 539–40
Rotary files, 12
Routing slips, 120–21
RSVPs, 290, 291
Rubber fingers, 21
Ruled lines, typing on, 59

Safeguarding files/documents, 33
Safety files, 12
Sales promotion letters, 394–95
Salutation
  colon and, 501
  correct forms of, 312–14
    women, rules for, 313–14
  letters, 312–14
  typing of, 312
    how to type, 312
    where to type, 312
Satellite transmission, 144–45
Screening calls, 168
Seasonal good wishes, letters of, 406–7
Second-class mail, 151
Secular holidays, capitalization rules, 522–23
Securities records, 238–41
  record of securities transactions, sample of, 239
Security, mail room, 131–32
Security agreement, 234
Self-service postal centers, 154
  domestic service, 154
Semiblock style, letters, 305
Semicolon
  compound sentences, 499
  conjunctive adverb, 499–500
  longer clauses, 499
  parentheses, 500
  punctuated clauses, 499

quotation marks, 500
  in series, 499
Seminars/conferences, 190–93
  files/records, 192–93
  with new employees, 262
  programs/announcements, 190–91
  registration procedures, 191–2
Sentence length, 344–45
Series comma, 497
Sexism, 346
Shared recording, 76
Ships in port, 133
Short references, footnotes, 101
Side margins, tables, 109–10
Signature initials, memos, 324
Signature line
  letters, 315–20
    contents of, 315–16
    typing of, 316–20
      how to type, 316–17
      secretary's signature, 320
      where to type, 316
      women's signatures, 317–20
Signatures, 316
  how to type, 316–17
  secretary's, 320
  where to type, 316
  women's, 317–20
Simplified style, letters, 306
Single parentheses, 509
Single spacing, reports, 98
Singular nouns, plural spellings, 477
Small cards, typing of, 65
Social-business letters, 395–407
Social/business responsibilities
  donations, keeping records of, 291–93
  invitations, preparation of, 289–91
  presents/holiday cards, 287–89
  sympathy, sending expressions of, 293–95
  theater tickets, making arrangements for, 286–87
Social security taxes, 225
Social visiting cards, use of, 295–96
Software, 73
Solid/cubic measure (volume), 607
  metric equivalents, 607
Solidus, 511
Sorting mail, 118, 119
Sorting trays, 21
Source notes, 102
Spacing
  reports, 98
  rules for, 56
Special business telephone services
  answering machines/services, 176
  automatic dialers, 176
  call sequencers, 176
  exchanges
    function of, 175
    types of, 175

leased lines, 176
  office telephone system, special features of, 175–76
  paging devices, 177
  plug-in headset, 177
  remote-call forwarding, 176–77
  switching systems, 175
Special characters, creation of, 57–58
Special delivery
  domestic service, 153–54
  international service, 159–60
Specialized files, 13
Special mail services, 152–55, 159–60
  domestic money orders, 154
  first-day cover mail service, 155
  mailgrams, 154
  philatelic mail order service, 154–55
  post office lockbox and caller service, 154
  self-service postal centers, 154
  special handling, 154
    domestic service, 154
    international service, 159
Special-purpose folders, 29
Special reminders, 48
Special secretarial duties, travel, 199–203
Specific endorsements, 229
Speech
  parts of, 411–14
    adjectives, 412
    adverbs, 412
    conjunctions, 413–14
    interjections, 414
    nouns, 411
    prepositions, 413
    pronouns, 411–12
    verbs, 412–13
Spell-checker, electronic typewriters, 52
Spelling
  commonly misspelled words, 486–88
  improving your spelling, 485–88
    mnemonics, 485–86
  prefixes, *dis-/mis-*, 484–85
  rules of, 477–91
    c endings, 484
    combinations of *i* and *e*, 480
    doubling final consonant, 480–81
    plurals, 477–80
    silent *e* endings, 481
    words ending in *-able, -ible*, 482–83
    words ending in *-ie*, 481
    words ending in *-sede/-ceed/-cede*, 483
    y endings, 484
  suffixes
    -able, -ous, 482
    -ance/-ence, 483
    -ise/-ize, 483
    -sede/-ceed/-cede, 483
  word division, rules of, 488–91
Split infinitives, 420
  See also Infinitives.

Sports/games
  capitalization rules, 533–34
  college colors, 533
  cups, 534
  playing fields, 533
  stakes, 534
  trophy, 534
Spouses, correct form of address, 331–32
Square measure, 606
  metric equivalents, 606
  surveyors' square measure, 607
Staff appointment, 381
Stand-alone word processing system
  central processing unit (CPU), 53–54
  display screen, 53
  keyboard, 53
  printer, 54
  storage, 54
Standard office files, 11
State/municipal government officials, forms
      of address, 583–86
State/territory abbreviations
  traditional, 566–68
  two-letter, 566–68
Stationery
  executive stationery, 333
  selection and ordering of, 332–35
    continuation sheets, 333
    determining weight, 334, 335
    envelopes, 333–34
    judging quality, 334
    letterhead design, 332–33
    office paper, type and size of, 332
    placing orders, 334–35
  See also Office papers.
Station-to-station calls, 170
Stencils
  corrections/revisions, 72
  typing of, 65–66
Storage
  stand-alone word processing systems, 54
  supplies, 36
Storage-control schedule, 33
Street/place-name abbreviations, 568–70
Style books, as reference source, 86
Subject, 424
Subject files, 4–8
  arrangement of, 6
    guides, 6
  combined name/subject file, 8
  folders, 6–7
  index to, 7–8
    alphabetical list, 7
    card index, 7–8
  subject-duplex file, 8
Subject line, letters, 314
Subjunctive mood, *See* Mood.
Subordinate conjunction, *See* Conjunction.
Subsidiary ledger, 246

Sulfite-bond papers, 76
Superlative degree, *See* Adjectives.
Supplies
  business cards, 296–97
  distribution of, 35
  inventory control, 35
  outside purchasing of, 35
  packing for travel, 201
  requisitioning of, 35
  storage, 36
Switching systems, 175
Sympathy
  expressions of, 293–95
    acknowledging expressions of sympathy,
        293–95
    contributions, 293
    flowers, 293
    letters of appreciation, 372–75
    letters of condolence, 293
    mass cards, 293
System flowcharting symbols, 619
Systems software, 73

Table of contents
  reports, 93–94
    typing of, 106
Tables
  preparation of, 106–110
    determining vertical space, 107
    footnotes, 109
    headings, 107–9
    margins, 109
    planning table arrangement, 107
    setup/measurements, 107
    side margins, 109–10
    tab settings, 110
  reports, 106–11
Tab settings, tables, 110
Tabulator, use of, 61–62
Telecommunications interfaces, 55
Teleconferencing, 173–74
Telegrams
  counting charges for, 134–35
    abbreviations, 135
    addresses, 134
    cities/states/countries, 135
    compound words, 135
    initials, 135
    letter/figures, mixed groups of, 135
    personal names, 135
    punctuation marks, 135
    signature/address of sender, 134–35
  domestic service
    classes of, 132–33
    mailgrams, 133
    money orders, 133
    night letters, 133
    ships in port, 133

economizing on, 138–39
    time differentials, 138
    urgency of message, 138
    wording, 138–39
  international telegrams, 135–36
  sending same message to multiple addresses, 134
  typing of, 64–65, 133–34
Telegraphs
  domestic service
    classes of, 132–33
    fast telegram, 132–33
  territory covered by domestic service, 132
Telephone abuse, 172
Telephone reference books
  desk telephone book, 177–78
    employer's personal numbers, 178
  telephone directory, 177
Telephone services
  appointment calls, 173
  International Direct-Distance Dialing (IDDD), 170–71
  long-distance telephone service, 170
  messenger calls, 173
  mobile calls, 174–75
  operating companies, 169–70
  out-of-town telephone calls, 171–72
    calling-card calls, 171
    charges on, 172
    out-of-town information, 171
    telephone abuse, 172
  person-to-person calls, 170
  special business services, 175–77
  station-to-station calls, 170
  teleconferencing, 173–74
  videoconferencing, 174
  Wide-Area Telephone Service (WATS), 172
Telephone use
  answering calls, 167–68
  effectiveness, 165–66
  placing calls, 166–67
    for your employer, 166
    your own, 166–67
  screening calls, 168
  telephone courtesy, rules of, 164–65
  transferring calls, 168–69
  wrong numbers, 169
    incoming wrong numbers, 169
    your own, 169
Telexes, 142–43
  services, 141–42
  Telex I/II, 141
  transmission of, 140–41
Tense, 424–25
Terminal-digit file system, 9
Thank you letters, 407
Theater tickets
  box office purchases, 286–87
  sent through mail, 287

telephone service, use of, 287
  ticket agents, use of, 286
  typing information for your employer, 287
Third-class mail, 151
Threatening callers, 270
Tickets
  agents, use of, 286
  travel, 205–6
    airline codes, 206–7
    canceling reservations, 206
    company accounts/credit cards, 205
    how to check, 206
    payment by check, 206
Tickler card file, 42
  billings, 256
  calendars, 45–47, 48
  charge-out tickler cards, 46
  daily checking of, 46
  tickler card, filling out of, 45
Tie-line service, 176
  high-speed messaging, 143
Time
  hyphens, 508
  managing of, 275–76
Time/cost analysis, computers, 39
Time differentials, 624
Time sharing, word processing systems, 54–55
Time zone, U.S., 622
Title page
  reports, 93
    typing of, 106
Titles, 418
  alphabetizing, 19–20
  quotation marks and, 505–6
Trade names, capitalization rules, 534
Trade terms, quotation marks and, 505
Train-travel arrangements, 210–11
  employer's accommodation preferences, 210–11
  making reservations, 211
  Official Railway Guide, 210
  train information, 210
Transcription, 78–79
Transferring calls, 168–69
Transitive verbs, *See* Verbs.
Transmittal message, 382
  letter of transmittal, reports, 93
Travel
  business trips
    company travel departments, 196–97
    preparation for, 194–204
    special secretarial duties, 199–203
    travel agents, use of, 194–96
    travel information, 197–99
    traveling with your employer, 203–4
  checklist for handling preparations, 197–99
  letters of credit, 203

Travel *(cont.)*
  personal checks, 201
  reservations, 204–13
    air-travel arrangements, 208–10
    auto-travel arrangements, 211–13
    checklist, 204
    delays in obtaining, 205
    hotel reservations, 207–8
    securing tickets, 205–7
    time/route data preparation, 205
    train-travel arrangements, 210–11
  special secretarial duties
    appointment schedule, 199–200
    business appointments, assembling data for, 201
    handling baggage, 201
    itinerary/hotel information, 199
    supplies, packing of, 201
    travel funds, arranging for, 201–3
    travel/hotel information library, building of, 201
  travel advances, 201
  travel accounts
    adjustment letters, 366–67
      incorrect amount, 366–67
      uncredited ticket cancellation, 367
    travel agents, 286
    domestic travel, 194–96
    international travel, 213
    use of, 194–96
      agent selection, 196
      conveying information to, 195
      fees, 196
      indefinite itinerary, 195–96
      services, 194–95
  traveler's checks, 201–3
  travel/entertainment records
    expense report, 232
    IRS regulations, 233–34
    recording data, 231–33
  Travel, Entertainment, and Gift Expenses (IRS publication 263), 233
  travel information, 218–19
  travel security, 217–18
  See also Employer, traveling with; Foreign travel; Tickets.
Tray files, 12
Treaties, capitalization rules, 524
Trite terms, 337–43
Troy measure, 610
  metric equivalents, 610
Typesetting
  reports, 113–14
    checking proofs, 114
    design/typemarking arrangements, 113
    typesetter, locating of, 113–14
Typewriters
  accessories, 52
  features, 51–52

Typing
  attention line, 312
  body of letter, 314
  complimentary close, 315
  continuation heading, 323
  copy-distribution notation, 322
  correcting errors, 70–75
  dateline, 308
  enclosure notation, 321
  identification line, 321
  index tabs/labels, 22–24
  inside address, 309
  mailing notation, 322
  meeting minutes, 187–88
    final copy, 187–88
    rough draft, 187
  personal notation, 309
  postscript, 322
  procedures, 58–66
    addressing envelopes, 63–64
    centering heads, 61
    memos, 64–65
    narrow labels, 65
    organizing work, 58
    page length, determination of, 59–60
    paper, feeding numerous sheets of, 62–63
    paper masters, 66
    planning ahead, 58–59
    printed forms, typing on, 59
    ruled lines, typing on, 59
    small cards, 65
    stencils, 65–66
    tabulator, use of, 61–62
    telegrams, 64–65
    typing above/below line of type, 60–61
    vertical lines, typing of, 60
  reference line, 308
  rules
    numbers/fractions, 56–57
    spacing, 56
    special characters, creation of, 57–58
  salutation, 312
  signatures, 316
    how to type, 316–17
    secretary's, 320
    where to type, 316
    women's, 317–20
  subject line, 314

Unemployment taxes, 225–26
Unethical practices, 281
Uniform Commercial Code (UCC), 235
United Nations officials, forms of address, 602–3
United Parcel service, 156
Unmarried women, correct form of address, 329

Unpublished material citations
　bibliographies, 103
　footnotes, 101
U.S.-British weights/measures, 609
U.S. Directory for Telecommunications Subscribers,
　142
U.S. money, 611
U.S. Postal Service
　abbreviations, 566–70
　　street/place-name abbreviations, 568–70
　　traditional state/territory abbreviations,
　　　566–68
　　two-letter state/territory abbreviations,
　　　566–68
　domestic mail service
　　classes of, 149–52
　　Express Mail, 149
　　first-class mail, 149–51
　　fourth-class mail, 152
　　second-class mail, 151
　　third-class mail, 151
　information sources, 146
　mailable items
　　dispatching of, 146–48
　　minimum-size standards, 148–49
　　nonstandard mail, 149
　special mail services, 152–55
　　business-reply mail, 152–53
　　certified mail, 153
　　collect on delivery (COD), 153
　　domestic money orders, 154
　　first-day cover mail service, 155
　　mailgrams, 154
　　mail insurance, 153
　　philatelic mail order service, 154–55
　　post office lockbox and caller service, 154
　　registered mail, 153
　　self-service postal centers, 154
　　special delivery, 153–54
　　special handling, 154

Vertical files, 11
Vertical lines, typing of, 60
Videoconferencing, 174
Virgule, 511
Visa, securing of, 214
Visitors, 183
　announcing callers, 267–68
　　callers with appointments, 267–68
　　callers without appointment, 268
　callers you refer elsewhere, 270
　contribution solicitors, 269–70
　discovering purpose of call, 265–66
　　caller refuses to state business, 266
　　caller states business, 265–66
　greeting callers, 265
　　friends of employer, 268

　making caller comfortable, 266
　problem callers, 270–71
　　emotional callers, 270–71
　　persistent callers, 270
　　threatening callers, 270
　providing refreshments to, 263–64
　receiving callers, 264
　seeing caller out, 272
　telephone calls for, handling of, 271
Voice, 426
Voice-data integration, 55
Voice-mail systems, 144
Volume
　metric measurement conversions, 613
　metric prefixes/multiplication factors, 612

Wall calendars, 43
WATS line, 175, 176
Wedding anniversaries, selecting gifts for, 289
Weights/measures
　apothecaries' fluid measure, 610
　apothecaries' measure, 610
　　metric equivalents, 610–11
　avoirdupois measure, 609
　　metric equivalents, 609–10
　avoirdupois-troy measure, 610
　centigrade/Fahrenheit temperatures, com-
　　parison of, 611–12
　circular/angular measure, 607
　counting, 611
　dry measure, 608
　　metric equivalents, 608
　liquid measure, 608
　　metric equivalents, 608
　long measure, 606
　　metric equivalents, 606
　　surveyors' long measure, 607
　mariner's measure, 608–9
　metric measurement conversions, 613
　metric prefixes/multiplication factors, 612
　paper weight/measure, 334, 335, 611
　solid/cubic measure (volume), 607
　　metric equivalents, 607
　square measure, 606
　　metric equivalents, 606
　　surveyors' square measure, 607
　troy measure, 610
　　metric equivalents, 610
　U.S.-British weights/measures, 609
　U.S. money, 611
　See also Metric weights/measures.
Western Union, 132–34, 136, 140, 141
　See also Telegrams.
Wide-Area Telephone Service (WATS), 172
Widows
　correct form of address, 329
　definition of, 114

Women
  correct form of address, 329–31, 332
    divorcees, 329–30
    firm composed of women, 329
    man and woman, 330–31
    married women, 329
    professional women, 330
    prominent persons, 332
    unmarried women, 329
    widows, 329
    wife of titled man, 330
  signature line, 317–20
Word books, as reference source, 85–86
Word division, 488–91
  at end of line, 488–89
  hyphens, 507
  rules of, 489–91
    abbreviations, 491
    consonants within word, 490
    dashes, 491
    four-letter words, 489
    hyphenated compounds, 491
    names, 491
    numbers, 491
    one-letter syllables, 489–90
    one-syllable words, 489
    prefixes/suffixes, 490
    two-letter syllables, 490
  syllabication/pronunciation, 489
Word length, 344
Word processing systems
  corrections/revisions, 73–75, 74–75
  documents
    editing of, 73–74
    printing of, 75

open punctuation and, 307
  saving text, 75
  shared systems, 54
  software, 73
  stand-alone system, 53–54
  time sharing, 54–55
Words, apostrophes and, 507
Word usage
  antagonistic words, 345–46
  clear/straightforward language, 337
  favorite words/phrases, 344
  grammar, rules of, 414–26
  meaning, shades of, 345
  sentence length, 344–45
  speech, parts of, 411–14
  stilted/verbose language, 336–37
  trite terms, 337–43
  troublesome words/phrases, 426–76
  unnecessary words/phrases, 343–44
  word length, 344
Work-group systems, 76
World/country divisions, capitalization rules,
  518
Woven paper, 333
Wrong numbers, 169
  incoming wrong numbers, 169
  your own, 169

Y endings, plural spellings, 478

Zapmail, 156
Zip codes, 160–61